War, Foreign Affairs
and Constitutional
Power: The Origins

War, Foreign Affairs

and

Constitutional Power

The Origins

Abraham D. Sofaer

Ballinger Publishing Company • Cambridge, Massachusetts
A Subsidiary of J.B. Lippincott Company

This book is printed on recycled paper.

International Standard Book Number: 0-88410-222-X

Library of Congress Catalog Card Number: 76-15392

Printed in the United States of America

Library of Congress Cataloging in Publication Data

Sofaer, Abraham D
    War, foreign affairs, and constitutional power.

    Includes bibliographical references.
    1. War and emergency powers—United States—History. 2. United States—Foreign relations—Law and legislation—History. 3. Separation of powers—United States—History. I. Title.
KF5060.S.6   342'.73'04   76-15392
ISBN 0-88410-222-X

To
Lyman M. Tondel, Jr.
with affection and high regard;
and to
Shoshanna

Contents

List of Figures

CHARTS

MAPS

Preface

This study of war is a product of war. The war in Indochina led to an enormous outpouring of legal activity,
just as it caused social and political protest. Demonstrators,
lobbyists, litigators, and scholars all used legal argument in pressing
their positions.

On July 7, 1971, the Assembly and House of Delegates of the
American Bar Association, the nation's largest organization of lawyers,
adopted a resolution calling for a study "on the respective powers
under the Constitution of the President and of Congress to enter into
and conduct war."* A committee was formed to organize the project.
Lyman M. Tondel, Jr. became Chairman, and George Wade, Secretary. They secured the necessary funding, primarily from the A.B.A.'s

---

*The resolution, introduced by a group chaired by Marc T. Luxemburg, reads
in full:

Whereas, the War in Indochina has raised serious questions as to the respective
powers under the Constitution of the President and of Congress to enter into
and conduct war, and

Whereas, in order for members of the Bar to uphold and defend the Constitution, as we are pledged to do, it is necessary to have a clear understanding
of said respective powers,

Now, therefore, We call upon the House of Delegates of the American Bar
Association to request the Section of International and Comparative Law
and the Standing Committee on World Order Under Law to study and report
on the respective powers under the Constitution of the President and of
Congress to enter into and conduct war.

A resolution simultaneously introduced to urge immediate withdrawal of all
U.S. military personnel from Indochina was defeated after heated debate.

Fund for Public Education, and launched the study under contract with Columbia University, with the author as director.

This work is more a history of certain events, than an analysis of the constitutional problems to which those events relate. Considerable analysis was necessary to organize the material, and to point out the possible significance of actions and debates. But I have made no effort at this point to reach conclusions on all the issues discussed. This approach was dictated, in my judgment, by the aim of this project—to deepen the ongoing debate over powers relating to war by providing the facts relevant to that debate. The volume also contains a great deal of evidence on constitutional controversies only indirectly related to the power to initiate war, such as disputes over information or the treaty power. These complex questions were included because they continue to arise when the legislative and executive branches are in conflict over some actual or potential military undertaking. Readers most interested in the actual military incidents of each administration—or in any other specific matters—will be able to move directly to them through the table of contents or the index.

The material in this volume demonstrates the relevance of early American history to contemporary constitutional controversies. But it also shows that relying on the statements and actions made during that formative period is as complicated as it is necessary.

Virtually every conceivable constitutional argument was advanced repeatedly, at times one feels almost ritualistically. Even the statements of the most important and influential leaders provide little definitive guidance. Most are offset by equally significant statements of opposing spokesmen. Other statements must be discounted as the product as much of party politics as of principle, or because the spokesman acted inconsistently with his pronouncement. The actions of early leaders reflect their positions on issues more reliably than their constitutional rhetoric. But legislative or executive actions and inactions can seldom be treated as "precedents," in the way we are accustomed to treating judicial decisions. Actions may speak "louder" than words, but not necessarily as clearly or as authoritatively. And the acts of this nation's early leaders were at times as inconsistent and as politically motivated as their words.

Carefully scrutinized, the first forty years of experience under the Constitution presents a complex pattern of practices. Anyone seeking precedents that establish areas of exclusive responsibility for either the legislative or executive branch is likely to be sorely disappointed. Very few such areas existed despite assertions by various leaders that any branch of the government must not intrude on the area of power assigned to any other branch. The legislative and executive branches

functioned as separate entities, but with powers over the same matters. Each was jealous of its authority, and at times sought to increase
its power. But, as Hamilton, Madison and others intended, neither
branch prevailed consistently enough to subordinate the other.

My debts are substantial. Numerous people at the Columbia Law
School have provided the facilities and administrative assistance
necessary to complete this volume. Several law students in my seminar
on the war powers produced useful memoranda, and kept my enthusiasm from flagging. I am grateful to Ann Gill, my student assistant
for the last two years, for her speedy, thorough support, and for her
marvelous disposition. In addition, Susan Rothschild worked on the
study for several months, and provided several helpful memoranda.
Professor Milton Henry worked for two years as project historian,
adding his prodigious energy and extraordinary bibliographic and
research knowledge. His comments and suggestions at early stages
helped shape the final product. Others contributed constructive suggestions, especially Professor Richard Baxter, Judge Henry J. Friendly,
Robert H. Montgomery, Jr., Professor Arthur M. Schlesinger, Jr.,
Lyman M. Tondel, Jr., and George Wade. The two persons to whom I
am most indebted are Enid Sterling, my principal assistant since this
study began, and my colleague Professor Louis Henkin. Enid helped
in every way possible, and most notably by patiently tracking down
the answers to what by now must amount to hundreds of specific
questions. Lou encouraged me throughout. His detailed and insightful
comments led to numerous, material improvements in the manuscript,
for which I am most grateful.

A.D.S.

Introduction

The war in Indochina set off, among other things, an impassioned constitutional debate in the United States. American combat involvement in Vietnam posed momentous questions in Washington: where the decision to go to war lay under the Constitution; what right the executive had to commit armed force to hostilities without congressional authorization; what control of the war-making power remained to Congress. These questions had arisen before in American history and had never been settled. John Quincy Adams doubted in the early republic that they ever would be.* But the Indochina War raised them with new urgency. The spreading public concern led the American Bar Association in 1971 to direct Professor Abraham D. Sofaer of the Columbia University Law School to conduct a study of "the respective powers under the Constitution of the President and of Congress to enter into and conduct war."

Justice Horace Gray observed of a constitutional issue before the Supreme Court in 1895 that it was, "like all questions of constitutional construction, . . . largely a historical question."† Whether or not Gray's aphorism is strictly correct, both sides freely invoked history in the Indochina debate, ransacking the past to find incidents that would vindicate or refute doctrines of inherent presidential power. Those intent on making more than debating points quickly

*"The respective powers of the President and Congress of the United States, in the case of war with foreign powers are yet undetermined. Perhaps they can never be defined." John Quincy Adams, *Eulogy on Madison* 47 (1836).

†*Sparf v United States*, 156 U.S. 51, 169 (1895); *cf.* C. Miller, *The Supreme Court and the Uses of History* 20 (1972).

discovered how sketchy and imprecise knowledge was of the relevant historical episodes. Some new research was performed; but, while the results usefully extended the common fund of information, the researchers were generally on the run toward destinations already chosen, and this could subtly affect even the best work.

After a review of the literature, Professor Sofaer accordingly concluded that the first need was to establish the basic historical facts. He thereupon organized an inquiry into the way the powers relating to war had actually been exercised by the various branches of the American government in the past. Historians and political scientists should have done this long since, of course, and not left so weighty a task to lawyers. But to our shame we failed to do so in any systematic fashion. Though Professor Sofaer found a certain sustenance in the great 19th century historians—Henry Adams especially, but also Hildreth and Bancroft—his essential commitment was necessarily and rightly to the primary sources, executive, legislative and personal.

In confronting these sources, he has admirably eschewed 'lawyer's history'—history shaped to sustain points in a brief. He has avoided the fallacy identified by Professor McIlwain long ago: "No single fault has been the source of so much bad history as the reading back of later and sharper distinctions into earlier periods where they have no place."* He has understood that his primary subject—the initiation of hostilities—did not exist in a vacuum but was inextricably mixed up with a web of related issues bearing on peace and war: control of information, of negotiation, of naval and ground force deployment, of covert action; the treaty power; neutrality; powers of appointment and removal; legislative delegation; and so on. And he has pursued this tangle of questions into the specific contexts where harried Presidents and Congresses reached difficult and unsatisfying decisions under peremptory political and diplomatic pressures.† The result is a masterful, meticulous and impartial work of research and analysis. The illumination this fascinating volume (and its successors) will cast on the workings of the American government and the processes of public decision will be of inestimable benefit to historical scholarship as well as to public debate.

Professor Sofaer, I take it, will offer his own conclusions in due course. But several points emerge from a reading of this first volume. His approach to the Constitution and to the vexing question of the

*C. McIlwain, *The American Revolution: A Constitutional Interpretation* 64 (1958).

†"I have no expectation that any man will read history aright who thinks that what was done in a remote age, by men whose names have resounded far, has any deeper sense than what he is doing to-day." R.W. Emerson, "History."

separation of powers is of high interest. His discussion supports the impression that the ambiguities of the Constitution, especially the mixing and overlapping of powers, were the result not of confusion or fatigue on the part of the Convention but of an intentional design to insure balance among the branches by enabling them to act on the same questions.

The account of the establishment of the new government under the Constitution strengthens our appreciation of what must be acknowledged as, if not the genius of Washington, at least his most unusual tact and wisdom. It also shows how quickly both the executive and legislative branches fell into the roles they have retained more or less ever since, with Congress holding the reserve power to set objectives and limits but the President in direct charge of government operations and especially of foreign and military affairs.

As for the allocation of powers relating to war, Professor Sofaer has uncovered much material on incidents of executive initiative throughout the period. Indeed, one is more than ever impressed, not by the novelty of the Indochina issues, but by the extent to which the Indochina debate reproduced controversies of the early republic. Thus Professor Sofaer shows how Congress under Adams debated competing executive and legislative claims to control the deployment of naval vessels and how Jefferson, withholding information from Congress and the courts, pushed the "private" papers theory of Washington to unprincipled extremes. He shows how, before the War of 1812, legislative delegations of discretion over foreign policy placed in executive hands the power to bring the nation closer to war and how secrecy was used for the same end. Those who believe that the Central Intelligence Agency introduced something new into American life will be edified by Professor Sofaer's account of Jefferson's secret attempt to overthrow the government of Tripoli by covert means from within, of Joel R. Poinsett's covert revolutionary adventures in Argentina and Chile during the Madison administration, and of the clandestine operations mounted by the Madison and Monroe administrations to facilitate the acquisition of West and East Florida. In this last connection, Professor Sofaer argues persuasively that Monroe almost certainly knew of and approved Jackson's plan to attack the Spanish posts during the Seminole War.

Whether the pattern thus revealed of secret presidential warmaking legalizes similar actions by subsequent Presidents is, of course, quite another question. Professor Sofaer's own surmise is that some of the early Presidents deliberately issued excessively vague instructions to venturesome agents, deliberately failed either to approve or disapprove when these agents submitted questionable plans, and thereafter deliberately denied Congress and the public the information necessary to determine whether aggressive acts were authorized—all precisely because they wanted the men in the field to do things that they knew lay beyond the constitutional right of Presidents to order.

Herein lies the vital difference between the early republic and our own. It is less in what Presidents did than in what they believed they had the right to do. Professor Sofaer found no instance of any President in the classical period making the claim so common in our own day that Presidents have *inherent* power to initiate military actions. And in general he shows that the early Presidents, even while they circumvented the Constitution, had a cautious and vigilant concern for consent in a practical if not in a procedural sense. They had legislative majorities; Congress approved their objectives and chose to let them take the lead; they obtained broad delegations of authority; they acted in secret only when they had some assurance of support and sympathy if they were found out; and along the way, even when they occasionally withheld vital information from Congress, they willingly shared much more than did their 20th century successors, including such choice items as the instructions given to envoys despatched on overseas negotiations. In the late 20th century, Presidents, infatuated with latter-day ideas of inherent presidential power, neglected the collection of consent, removed significant executive decisions from the political process and departed considerably from the principles, if somewhat less from the practice, of the early republic.

Still enough had happened, even in the first generation of independence, for Senator Hillhouse, a Connecticut Federalist, to charge thirty years after the drafting of the Constitution that Presidents had acquired "the power, not of declaring war in form, but of adopting a course of measures which will necessarily and inevitably lead to war."* The question remained whether the President could be decisively deprived of this power without making it virtually impossible for him to direct a foreign policy at all.

These questions are still unsolved and are very likely, as J.Q. Adams suggested one hundred and forty years ago, insoluble, at least in the realm of principle. In practice they are best accommodated within the political process, which is no doubt why the Constitution was drawn with considerable looseness in the joints. But we will not even understand the questions until we know what we are talking about. Herein lies the immense public value of Professor Sofaer's work. The American Bar Association has done a great public service by undertaking and suggesting this project.

Arthur Schlesinger, Jr.

*Ch. iv, p. 208.

Constitutional Charts

EXECUTIVE OFFICERS
(1789-1829)

President/ (Vice-President)	Secretary of State*	Secretary of Treasury	Secretary of War	Secretary of Navy	Attorney General
George Washington (John Adams) 1789-1797	John Jay** (Sept. 1789-March 1790) Thomas Jefferson (March 1790-Jan. 1794) Edmund Randolph (Jan. 1794-Dec. 1795) Timothy Pickering (Dec. 1795-May 1800)	Alexander Hamilton (Sept. 1789-Feb. 1795) Oliver Wolcott (Feb. 1795-Dec. 1800)	Henry Knox (Sept. 1789-Jan. 1795) James McHenry (Feb. 1796-May 1800)		Edmund Randolph (Sept. 1789-Jan. 1794) William Bradford (Jan. 1794-Dec. 1795) Charles Lee (Dec. 1795-March 1801)
John Adams (Thomas Jefferson) 1797-1801	John Marshall (June 1800-March 1801)†	Samuel Dexter (Jan. 1801-May 1801)	Samuel Dexter (June 1800-March 1801)	Benjamin Stoddert (June 1798-July 1801)	
Thomas Jefferson 1801-1809 (Aaron Burr 1801-1805) (George Clinton 1805-1809)	James Madison (May 1801-March 1809)	Albert Gallatin (May 1801-April 1813)	Henry Dearborn (March 1801-Feb. 1809)	Robert Smith (July 1801-March 1809)	Levi Lincoln (March 1801-Dec. 1804) John Breckinridge (Aug. 1805-Dec. 1806) Caesar Rodney (Jan. 1807-Dec. 1811)

James Madison 1809–1817 (George Clinton March 1809– April 1812) (Elbridge Gerry March 1813– Nov. 1814)	Robert Smith (March 1809– April 1811) James Monroe (April 1811– March 1817)	William Jones (April 1813– Feb. 1814) George Campbell (Feb. 1814– Oct. 1814) Alexander Dallas (Oct. 1814– Oct. 1816) William Crawford (Oct. 1816– March 1825)	William Eustis (April 1809– Dec. 1812) John Armstrong (Jan. 1813– Aug. 1814) James Monroe (Sept. 1814– March 1815) Alexander Dallas† (March 1815– Aug. 1815) William Crawford (Aug. 1815– Oct. 1816) George Graham, clerk† (Oct. 1816– Oct. 1817)	Paul Hamilton (May 1809– Dec. 1812) William Jones (Jan. 1813– Dec. 1814) Benjamin Crowninshield (Jan. 1815– Sept. 1818)	William Pinkney (Jan. 1812– Feb. 1814) Richard Rush (Feb. 1814– Oct. 1817)
James Monroe (Daniel Tompkins) 1817–1825	John Q. Adams (Sept. 1817– March 1825)		John C. Calhoun (Oct. 1817– March 1825)	Smith Thompson (Nov. 1819– Sept. 1823) Samuel Southard (Sept. 1823– March 1829)	William Wirt (Nov. 1817– March 1829)
John Quincy Adams (John C. Calhoun) 1825–1829	Henry Clay (March 1825– March 1829)	Samuel Southard (March 1825– July 1825) Richard Rush (Aug. 1825– March 1829)	James Barbour (March 1825– May 1828) Samuel Southard (May 1828– June 1828) Peter Porter (June 1828– March 1829)		

*Called Secretary for the Department of Foreign Affairs from July to September 1789.

**Continued service, which commenced during the Confederation, until Thomas Jefferson returned from France.

†ad interim; never formally appointed. Other interim appointees for short periods not included.

DISTRIBUTION OF LEGISLATIVE POWER, 1789-1829

Congress (Duration)	Party*				Legislative Leaders and Affiliations**	
	Senate		House		Senate	House
	Majority Party	Minority Party	Majority Party	Minority Party		
First Congress (Mar. 4, 1789-Mar. 3, 1791)	Ad. 17	Op. 9	Ad. 38	Op. 26	Pierce Butler [DR] (1-4; 7-8) Oliver Ellsworth [F] (1-4) Rufus King [F] (1-4) James Monroe [DR] (1-3)	Fisher Ames [F] (1-4) Abraham Baldwin [F] (1-5) Elias Boudinot [F] (1-3) Thomas Fitzsimons [F] (1-3) Elbridge Gerry [DR] (1-2) William B. Giles [DR] (1-5, 7) Thomas Hartley [F] (1-6) John Laurance [F] (1-2) Josiah Parker [DR] (1-6) Theodore Sedgwick [F] (1-4; 6) Roger Sherman [ ] (1) William L. Smith [F] (1-5)
Second Congress (Mar. 4, 1791-Mar. 3, 1793)	F. 16	D.R. 13	F. 37	D.R. 33	Aaron Burr (DR) (2-4) Roger Sherman [ ] (2-3)	Jonathan Dayton [F] (2-5) William Findley [DR] (2-5; 8-14) William Pinkney [ ] (2; 14) Abraham B. Venable [ ] (2-5)
Third Congress (Mar. 4, 1793-Mar. 3, 1795)	F. 17	D.R. 13	D. R. 57	F. 48	Joseph Anderson [DR] (4-13) William Bradford [ ] (3-5) Albert Gallatin [DR] (3)	Thomas Blount [DR] (3-5; 9-10; 12) Robert Goodloe Harper [F] (4-6) Samuel Smith [DR] (3-7; 14-17)
Fourth Congress (Mar. 4, 1795-Mar. 3, 1797)	F. 19	D.R. 13	F. 54	D.R. 52	James Hillhouse [F] (4-11) John Laurance [F] (4-6) Theodore Sedgwick [F] (4-5)	Theophilus Bradbury [F] (4-5) Samuel W. Dana [F] (4-11) Albert Gallatin [DR] (4-6) Roger Griswold [F] (4-8) James Holland [DR] (4; 7-11) Andrew Jackson [DR] (4-5) Edward Livingston [DR] (4-6; 18-20) Samuel Sewall [ ] (4-6) Samuel Sitgreaves [F] (4-5) Richard Sprigg, Jr. [ ] (4-5; 7) Joseph Varnum [DR] (4-12)
Fifth Congress (Mar. 4, 1797-Mar. 3, 1799)	F. 20	D.R. 12	F. 58	D.R. 48	Andrew Jackson [DR] (5; 18-19) Charles Pinckney [DR] (5-7)	James Bayard [F] (5-7) Matthew Clay [DR] (5-12; 14) Levi Lincoln [DR] (5-7) Harrison Gray Otis [F] (5-6) Richard Stanford [DR] (5-14)
Sixth Congress (Mar. 4, 1799-Mar. 3, 1801)	F. 19	D.R. 13	F. 64	D.R. 42	Abraham Baldwin [F] (6-10) Jonathan Dayton [F] (6-8) Gouverneur Morris [F] (6-7) Wilson Cary Nicholas [DR] (6-8)	Willis Alston [DR] (6-13) Joseph H. Nicholson [DR] (6-9) John Randolph [DR] (6-12; 14; 16-20) Littleton Tazewell [DR] (6)
Seventh Congress (Mar. 4, 1801-Mar. 3, 1803)	D.R. 18	F. 14	D.R. 69	F. 36	John Breckenridge [DR] (7-9)	William Eustis [DR] (7-8; 16-17)
Eighth Congress (Mar. 4, 1803-Mar. 3, 1805)	D.R. 25	F. 9	D.R. 102	F. 39	John Quincy Adams [F] (8-10) James Bayard [F] (8-12) William B. Giles [DR] (8-13) Timothy Pickering [F] (8-11) Samuel Smith [DR] (8-13; 17-22) Abraham B. Venable [ ] (8)	George W. Campbell [DR] (8-10) James Elliott [F] (8-10) John Eppes [DR] (8-11; 13) John Rhea [DR] (8-13; 15-17)

Congress	Senate		House		Senators	Representatives
Ninth Congress (Mar. 4, 1805– Mar. 3, 1807)	D.R. 27	F. 7	D.R. 116	F. 25	Henry Clay [ ] (9–11)	William Burwell [DR] (9–16); Josiah Quincy [F] (9–12)
Tenth Congress (Mar. 4, 1807– Mar. 3, 1809)	D.R. 28	F. 6	D.R. 118	F. 24	James Lloyd [F] (10–13, 17–19)	Ezekiel Bacon [DR] (10–12); Philip B Key [F] (10–12); Edward Livermore [F] (10–11); Wilson Cary Nicholas [DR] (10–11); Jabez Upham [F] (10–11); Nicholas Van Dyke [F] (10–11); Archibald Van Horne [ ] (10–11)
Eleventh Congress (Mar. 4, 1809– Mar. 3, 1811)	D.R. 28	F. 6	D.R. 94	F. 48	Samuel W. Dana [F] (11–16); Outerbridge Horsey [F] (11–16)	Samuel McKee [DR] (11–14); Alexander McKim [DR] (11–13); Daniel Sheffey [F] (11–14)
Twelfth Congress (Mar. 4, 1811– Mar. 3, 1813)	D.R. 30	F. 6	D.R. 108	F. 36	George Bibb [ ] (12–13; 20–23); George W. Campbell [DR] (12–15); Joseph Varnum [DR] (12–14)	John C. Calhoun [DR] (12–15); Henry Clay [ ] (12–16; 18–19); Thomas Grosvenor [F] (12–14); William Lowndes [DR] (12–17)
Thirteenth Congress (Mar. 4, 1813– Mar. 3, 1815)	D.R. 27	F. 9	D.R. 112	F. 68	James Barbour [DR] (13–19); Christopher Gore [DR] (13–14); Jeremiah Mason [F] (13–15)	Philip P. Barbour [DR] (13–18; 20–21); John Forsyth [DR] (13–15; 18–20); Alexander Hanson [F] (13–14); Daniel Webster [F] (13–14; 18–20)
Fourteenth Congress (Mar. 4, 1815– Mar. 3, 1817)	D.R. 25	F. 11	D.R. 117	F. 65	Alexander Hanson [F] (14–16); Robert Goodloe Harper [F] (14)	John Tyler [DR] (14–16)
Fifteenth Congress (Mar. 4, 1817– Mar. 3, 1819)	D.R. 34	F. 10	D.R. 141	F. 42	John Eppes [DR] (15–16); John Forsyth [DR] (15); Harrison Gray Otis [F] (15–17); Nicholas Van Dyke [F] (15–19)	John Floyd [DR] (15–20); Alexander Smyth [ ] (15–18; 20–21); Henry R. Storrs [F] (15–16; 18–21)
Sixteenth Congress (Mar. 4, 1819– Mar. 3, 1821)	D.R. 35	F. 7	D.R. 156	F. 27	William Pinkney [ ] (16–17); Samuel L. Southard [DR] (16–17)	William S. Archer [ ] (16–20); Charles Pinckney [DR] (16); Albert Tracy [DR] (16–18)
Seventeenth Congress (Mar. 4, 1821– Mar. 3, 1823)	D.R. 44	F. 4	D.R. 158	F. 25	Martin Van Buren [DR] (17–20)	Jonathan Russell [DR] (17)
Eighteenth Congress (Mar. 4, 1823– Mar. 3, 1825)	D.R. 44	F. 4	D.R. 187	F. 26	John Branch [DR] (18–21); Littleton Tazewell [DR] (18–22)	Benjamin Crowninshield [DR] (18–21); William C. Rives [DR] (18–21)
Nineteenth Congress (Mar. 4, 1825– Mar. 3, 1827)	Ad. 26	J. 20	Ad. 105	J. 97	John Randolph [DR] (19)	James K. Polk [DR] (19–25)
Twentieth Congress (Mar. 4, 1827– Mar. 3, 1829)	J. 28	Ad. 20	J. 119	Ad. 94	James Iredell [DR] (20–21); John Tyler [DR] (20–24); Daniel Webster [F] (20–26)	

*Data on party affiliation are derived from R. Morris, *Encyclopedia of American History* 560–61 (1976). They are at best rough estimates. Affiliations of Representatives and Senators were first officially reported in the *Congressional Globe* in 1841 and 1843 respectively. *Cong. Globe*, 27th Cong., 1st Sess. 1 (1841), 28th Cong., 1st Sess. 1 (1843). Many members of early congresses, however, had no official party allegiance, and texts that purport to catalogue party strength during that period are unreliable. *See* J. Young, *The Washington Community, 1774–1961* (1961). Party identification of many congressmen is provided in *Notable Names in American History* 50–75 (1973), and *Biographical Directory of the American Congress, 1774–1927*, at 271 n. 4 (1966).

The most accurate method would be to catalogue individual congressmen by their voting record. R. Hofstadter, *The Idea of a Party System* 114 n. 41 (1969). But efforts to proceed in this manner have resulted in breakdowns that place a majority or near majority of many early congresses in neither major party. *See* N. Cunningham, Jr., *The Jeffersonian Republicans: The Formation of Party Organization, 1789–1801*, at 72 n. 17 (1957). Professor Morris's rough breakdown, based on long experience, is therefore the most useful available.

**Representatives and Senators are arranged by the first Congress in which they served, with the numbers of the Congresses in which they served indicated in parentheses; such service was not always continuous.

LEGEND: Ad.—Administration; D.R.—Democratic-Republican; F—Federalist; J.—Jacksonian; Op.—Opposition

The party designations "Administration" and "Jacksonian" are used by Professor Richard Morris to denote affiliations in the nineteenth and twentieth Congresses. Other sources (such as the *Bio-graphical Directory of the American Congress*, from which the party identifications of congressional leaders were taken, continue to use the designations "Federalist" and "Democratic-Republican" through the twentieth Congress. The designation "Democratic-Republican" is used to include Representatives and Senators who were known as "Democrats," "States Rights Democrats," "Anti-Federalists," "Jeffersonian Republicans," "Jacksonian Democrats," etc. *See Notable Names in American History* 50 (1973).

✳

The Constitution of the
United States of America

We the People of the United States, in Order to form a more perfect Union, establish Justice, insure domestic Tranquility, provide for the common defence, promote the general Welfare, and secure the Blessings of Liberty to ourselves and our Posterity, do ordain and establish this Constitution for the United States of America.

ARTICLE I

SECTION 1. All legislative Powers herein granted shall be vested in a Congress of the United States, which shall consist of a Senate and House of Representatives.

SECTION 2. The House of Representatives shall be composed of Members chosen every second Year by the People of the several States, and the Electors in each State shall have the Qualifications requisite for Electors of the most numerous Branch of the State Legislature. . . .

The House of Representatives shall chuse their Speaker and other Officers; and shall have the sole Power of Impeachment.

SECTION 3. The Senate of the United States shall be composed of two Senators from each State, chosen by the Legislature thereof, for six Years; and each Senator shall have one Vote. . . .

The Vice President of the United States shall be President of the Senate, but shall have no Vote, unless they be equally divided. . . .

The Senate shall have the sole Power to try all Impeachments. When sitting for that Purpose, they shall be on Oath or Affirmation. When the President of the United States is tried the Chief Justice shall preside: And no Person shall be convicted without the Concurrence of two thirds of the Members present.

Judgment in Cases of Impeachment shall not extend further than to removal from Office, and disqualification to hold and enjoy any Office of honor, Trust or Profit under the United States: but the Party convicted shall nevertheless be liable and subject to Indictment, Trial, Judgment and Punishment, according to Law.

SECTION 4. The Times, Places and Manner of holding Elections for Senators and Representatives, shall be prescribed in each State by the Legislature thereof; but the Congress may at any time by Law make or alter such Regulations, except as to the Places of chusing Senators.

The Congress shall assemble at least once in every Year, and such Meeting shall be on the first Monday in December, unless they shall by Law appoint a different Day.

SECTION 5. . . . Each House shall keep a Journal of its Proceedings, and from time to time publish the same, excepting such Parts as may in their Judgment require Secrecy; and the Yeas and Nays of the Members of either House on any question shall, at the Desire of one fifth of those Present, be entered on the Journal.

SECTION 6. The Senators and Representatives shall receive a Compensation for their Services, to be ascertained by Law, and paid out of the Treasury of the United States. They shall in all Cases, except Treason, Felony and Breach of the Peace, be privileged from Arrest during their Attendance at the Session of their respective Houses, and in going to and returning from the same; and for any Speech or Debate in either House, they shall not be questioned in any other Place.

No Senator or Representative shall, during the Time for which he was elected, be appointed to any civil Office under the Authority of the United States, which shall have been created, or the Emoluments whereof shall have been encreased during such time; and no Person holding any Office under the United States, shall be a Member of either House during his Continuance in Office.

SECTION 7. All Bills for raising Revenue shall originate in the House of Representatives; but the Senate may propose or concur with amendments as on other Bills.

Every Bill which shall have passed the House of Representatives and the Senate, shall, before it become a Law, be presented to the President of the United States; If he approve he shall sign it, but if not he shall return it, with his Objections to that House in which it shall have originated, who shall enter the Objections at large on their

Journal, and proceed to reconsider it. If after such Reconsideration two thirds of that House shall agree to pass the Bill, it shall be sent, together with the Objections, to the other House, by which it shall likewise be reconsidered, and if approved by two thirds of that House, it shall become a Law. But in all such Cases the Votes of both Houses shall be determined by Yeas and Nays, and the Names of the Persons voting for and against the Bill shall be entered on the Journal of each House respectively. If any Bill shall not be returned by the President within ten Days (Sunday excepted) after it shall have been presented to him, the Same shall be a Law, in like Manner as if he had signed it, unless the Congress by their Adjournment prevent its Return, in which Case it shall not be a Law.

Every Order, Resolution, or Vote to which the Concurrence of the Senate and House of Representatives may be necessary (except on a question of Adjournment) shall be presented to the President of the United States; and before the Same shall take Effect, shall be approved by him, or being disapproved by him, shall be repassed by two thirds of the Senate and House of Representatives, according to the Rules and Limitations prescribed in the Case of a Bill.

SECTION 8. The Congress shall have Power To lay and collect Taxes, Duties, Imposts and Excises, to pay the Debts and provide for the common Defence and general Welfare of the United States; but all Duties, Imposts and Excises shall be uniform throughout the United States;

To borrow Money on the credit of the United States;

To regulate Commerce with foreign Nations, and among the several States, and with the Indian Tribes; . . .

To constitute Tribunals inferior to the supreme Court;

To define and punish Piracies and Felonies committed on the high Seas, and Offences against the Law of Nations;

To declare War, grant Letters of Marque and Reprisal, and make Rules concerning Captures on Land and Water;

To raise and support Armies, but no Appropriation of Money to that Use shall be for a longer Term than two Years;

To provide and maintain a Navy;

To make Rules for the Government and Regulation of the land and naval Forces;

To provide for calling forth the Militia to execute the Laws of the Union, suppress Insurrections and repel Invasions;

To provide for organizing, arming, and disciplining, the Militia, and for governing such Part of them as may be employed in the Service of the United States, reserving to the States respectively, the Appointment of the Officers, and the Authority of training the Militia according to the discipline prescribed by Congress; . . .

To make all Laws which shall be necessary and proper for carrying into Execution the foregoing Powers, and all other Powers vested by this Constitution in the Government of the United States, or in any Department or Officer thereof.

SECTION 9. . . . The Privilege of the Writ of Habeas Corpus shall not be suspended, unless when in Cases of Rebellion or Invasion the public Safety may require it. . . .

No Money shall be drawn from the Treasury, but in Consequence of Appropriations made by Law; and a regular Statement and Account of the Receipts and Expenditures of all public Money shall be published from time to time.

No Title of Nobility shall be granted by the United States: And no Person holding any Office of Profit or Trust under them, shall, without the Consent of the Congress, accept of any present, Emolument, Office, or Title, of any kind whatever, from any King, Prince or foreign State.

SECTION 10. No State shall enter into any Treaty, Alliance, or Confederation; grant Letters of Marque and Reprisal; coin Money; emit Bills of Credit; make any Thing but gold and silver Coin a Tender in Payment of Debts; pass any Bill of Attainder, ex post facto Law, or Law impairing the Obligation of Contracts, or grant any Title of Nobility. . . .

No State shall, without the Consent of Congress, lay any Duty of Tonnage, keep Troops, or Ships of War in time of Peace, enter into any Agreement or Compact with another State, or with a foreign Power, or engage in War, unless actually invaded, or in such imminent Danger as will not admit of delay.

ARTICLE II

SECTION 1. The executive Power shall be vested in a President of the United States of America. He shall hold his Office during the Term of four Years, and, together with the Vice President, chosen for the same Term, be elected, as follows

Each State shall appoint, in such Manner as the Legislature thereof may direct, a Number of Electors, equal to the whole Number of Senators and Representatives to which the State may be entitled in the Congress: but no Senator or Representative, or Person holding an Office of Trust or Profit under the United States, shall be appointed an Elector.

The Electors shall meet in their respective States, and vote by Ballot for two Persons, of whom one at least shall not be an Inhabitant of the same State with themselves. And they shall make a List of all the Persons voted for, and of the Number of Votes for each; which List they shall sign and certify, and transmit sealed to the Seat of the Government of the United States, directed to the President of the Senate. The President of the Senate shall, in the Presence of the Senate and House of Representatives, open all the Certificates, and the Votes shall then be counted. The Person having the greatest Number of Votes shall be the President, if such Number be a Majority of the whole Number of Electors appointed; and if there be more than one who have such Majority, and have an equal Number of Votes, then the House of Representatives shall immediately chuse by Ballot one of them for President; and if no Person have a Majority, then from the five highest on the List the said House shall in like Manner chuse the President. But in chusing the President, the Votes shall be taken by States, the Representation from each State having one Vote; a quorum for this Purpose shall consist of a Member or Members from two thirds of the States, and a Majority of all the States shall be necessary to a Choice. In every Case, after the Choice of the President, the Person having the greatest Number of Votes of the Electors shall be the Vice President. But if there should remain two or more who have equal Votes, the Senate shall chuse from them by Ballot the Vice President. . . .

The President shall, at stated Times, receive for his Services, a Compensation, which shall neither be encreased nor diminished during the Period for which he shall have been elected, and he shall not receive within that Period any other Emolument from the United States, or any of them.

Before he enter on the Execution of his Office, he shall take the following Oath or Affirmation:—"I do solemnly swear (or affirm) that I will faithfully execute the Office of President of the United States, and will to the best of my Ability, preserve, protect and defend the Constitution of the United States."

SECTION 2. The President shall be Commander in Chief of the Army and Navy of the United States, and of the Militia of the several States, when called into the actual Service of the United States; he may require the Opinion, in writing, of the principal Officer in each of the executive Departments, upon any Subject relating to the Duties of their respective Offices, and he shall have Power to grant Reprieves and Pardons for Offences against the United States, except in Cases of Impeachment.

He shall have Power, by and with the Advice and Consent of the Senate, to make Treaties, provided two thirds of the Senators present concur; and he shall nominate, and by and with the Advice and Consent of the Senate, shall appoint Ambassadors, other public Ministers and Consuls, Judges of the supreme Court, and all other Officers of the United States, whose Appointments are not herein otherwise provided for, and which shall be established by Law: but the Congress may by Law vest the Appointment of such inferior Officers, as they think proper, in the President alone, in the Courts of Law, or in the Heads of Departments.

The President shall have Power to fill up all Vacancies that may happen during the Recess of the Senate, by granting Commissions which shall expire at the End of their next Session.

SECTION 3. He shall from time to time give to the Congress Information of the State of the Union, and recommend to their Consideration such Measures as he shall judge necessary and expedient; he may, on extraordinary Occasions, convene both Houses, or either of them, and in Case of Disagreement between them, with Respect to the Time of Adjournment, he may adjourn them to such Time as he shall think proper; he shall receive Ambassadors and other public Ministers; he shall take Care that the Laws be faithfully executed, and shall Commission all the Officers of the United States.

SECTION 4. The President, Vice President and all Civil Officers of the United States, shall be removed from Office on Impeachment for, and Conviction of, Treason, Bribery, or other high Crimes and Misdemeanors.

ARTICLE III

SECTION 1. The judicial Power of the United States, shall be vested in one supreme Court, and in such inferior Courts as the Congress may from time to time ordain and establish. The Judges, both of the supreme and inferior Courts, shall hold their Offices during good Behaviour, and shall, at stated Times, receive for their Services, a Compensation, which shall not be diminished during their Continuance in Office.

SECTION 2. The judicial Power shall extend to all Cases, in Law and Equity, arising under this Constitution, the Laws of the United States, and Treaties made, or which shall be made, under their Authority;—to all Cases affecting Ambassadors, other public Ministers and Consuls;—to all Cases of admiralty and maritime Jurisdiction;—to Controversies to which the United States shall be a Party;—to Controversies between two or more States;—between a State and Citizens of another State;—between Citizens of different States;—between Citizens of the same State claiming Lands under Grants of different States, and between a State, or the Citizens thereof, and foreign States, Citizens or Subjects.

In all Cases affecting Ambassadors, other public Ministers and Consuls, and those in which a State shall be Party, the supreme Court shall have original Jurisdiction. In all the other Cases before mentioned, the supreme Court shall have appellate Jurisdiction, both as to Law and Fact, with such Exceptions, and under such Regulations as the Congress shall make. . . .

ARTICLE IV

* * *

SECTION 3. New States may be admitted by the Congress into this Union; but no new State shall be formed or erected within the Jurisdiction of any other State; nor any State be formed by the Junction of two or more States, or Parts of States, without the Consent of the Legislatures of the States concerned as well as of the Congress.

The Congress shall have Power to dispose of and make all needful Rules and Regulations respecting the Territory or other Property belonging to the United States; and nothing in this Constitution shall be so construed as to Prejudice any Claims of the United States, or of any particular State.

SECTION 4. The United States shall guarantee to every State in this Union a Republican Form of Government, and shall protect each of them against Invasion; and on Application of the Legislature, or of the Executive (when the Legislature cannot be convened) against domestic Violence.

ARTICLE V

The Congress, whenever two thirds of both Houses shall deem it necessary, shall propose Amendments to this Constitution, or, on the Application of the Legislatures of two thirds of the several States, shall call a Convention for proposing Amendments, which, in either Case, shall be valid to all Intents and Purposes, as Part of this Constitution, when ratified by the Legislatures of three fourths of the several States, or by Conventions in three fourths thereof, as the one or the other Mode of Ratification may be proposed by the Congress; . . .

ARTICLE VI

All Debts contracted and Engagements entered into, before the Adoption of this Constitution, shall be as valid against the United States under this Constitution, as under the Confederation.

This Constitution, and the Laws of the United States which shall be made in Pursuance thereof; and all Treaties made, or which shall be made, under the Authority of the United States, shall be the supreme Law of the Land; and the Judges in every State shall be bound thereby, any Thing in the Constitution or Laws of any State to the Contrary notwithstanding.

The Senators and Representatives before mentioned, and the Members of the several State Legislatures, and all executive and judicial Officers, both of the United States and of the several States, shall be bound by Oath or Affirmation, to support this Constitution; but no religious Test shall ever be required as a Qualification to any Office or public Trust under the United States.

ARTICLE VII

The Ratification of the Conventions of nine States, shall be sufficient for the Establishment of this Constitution between the States so ratifying the Same.

* * *

ARTICLES IN ADDITION TO, AND AMENDMENT OF, THE CON-
STITUTION OF THE UNITED STATES OF AMERICA, PRO-
POSED BY CONGRESS, AND RATIFIED BY THE SEVERAL
STATES, PURSUANT TO THE FIFTH ARTICLE OF THE ORIG-
INAL CONSTITUTION.

AMENDMENT I[1791]

Congress shall make no law respecting an establishment of religion, or prohibiting the free exercise thereof; or abridging the freedom of speech, or of the press; or the right of the people peaceably to assemble, and to petition the Government for a redress of grievances.

AMENDMENT II[1791]

A well regulated Militia, being necessary to the security of a free State, the right of the people to keep and bear Arms, shall not be infringed.

AMENDMENT III[1791]

No Soldier shall, in time of peace be quartered in any house, without the consent of the Owner, nor in time of war, but in a manner to be prescribed by law.

AMENDMENT IV[1791]

The right of the people to be secure in their persons, houses, papers, and effects, against unreasonable searches and seizures, shall not be violated, and no Warrants shall issue, but upon probable cause, supported by Oath or affirmation, and particularly describing the place to be searched, and the persons or things to be seized.

AMENDMENT V[1791]

No person shall be held to answer for a capital, or otherwise infamous crime, unless on a presentment or indictment of a Grand Jury, except in cases arising in the land or naval forces, or in the Militia, when in actual service in time of War or public danger; nor shall any person be subject for the same offence to be twice put in jeopardy of life or limb; nor shall be compelled in any criminal case to be a witness against himself, nor be deprived of life, liberty, or property, without due process of law; nor shall private property be taken for public use, without just compensation.

* * *

AMENDMENT XII[1804]

The Electors shall meet in their respective states and vote by ballot for President and Vice-President, one of whom, at least, shall not be an inhabitant of the same state with themselves; they shall name in their ballots the person voted for as President, and in distinct ballots the person voted for as Vice-President, and they shall make distinct lists of all persons voted for as President, and of all persons voted for as Vice-President, and of the number of votes for each, which lists they shall sign and certify, and transmit sealed to the seat of the government of the United States, directed to the President of the Senate;—The President of the Senate shall, in the presence of the Senate and House of Representatives, open all the certificates and the votes shall then be counted;—The person having the greatest number of votes for President, shall be the President, if such number be a majority of the whole number of Electors appointed; and if no person have such majority, then from the persons having the highest numbers not exceeding three on the list of those voted for as President, the House of Representatives shall choose immediately, by ballot, the President. But in choosing the President, the votes shall be taken by states, the representation from each state having one vote; a quorum for this purpose shall consist of a member or members from two-thirds of the states, and a majority of all the states shall be necessary to a choice. And if the House of Representatives shall not choose a President whenever the right of choice shall devolve upon them, before the fourth day of March next following, then the Vice-President shall act as President, as in the case of the death or other constitutional disability of the President—The person having the greatest number of votes as Vice-President, shall be the Vice-President, if such number be a majority of the whole number of Electors appointed, and if no person have a majority, then from the two highest numbers on the list, the Senate shall choose the Vice-President; a quorum for the purpose shall consist of two-thirds of the whole number of Senators, and a majority of the whole number shall be necessary to a choice. But no person constitutionally ineligible to the office of President shall be eligible to that of Vice-President of the United States.

* * *

Chapter 1

The Constitution and Its Background

Any study of the legality of conduct under a written constitution should begin with the document itself. Where the
United States Constitution is unclear, its meaning must be
sought in all the available sources: the ratification debates; the minutes of the Convention; the views of those who drafted or voted on
the relevant provisions; and the background—intellectual, social,
economic, and political—of the participants, of the ratifiers, of the
society in which it all took place, and indeed of the British system
from which the United States had only recently separated. Finally,
this research in constitutional history should, as in any other area
of history or law, be guided by specific questions framed to test the
relevance and importance of the material discovered.

Contemporary events have made several questions concerning
military and foreign affairs especially important.[1] For example, is a
formal declaration of war necessary before the President may undertake any significant military action against a foreign nation? If other
forms of legislative approval may suffice, how explicit must the
authorization be? Is a resolution such as that passed after the Gulf of
Tonkin incident sufficient? Is it enough if Congress knowingly provides the funds for a military undertaking? May the President act
pursuant to a treaty commitment, even though treaties take effect
without the concurrence of the House of Representatives? What
actions may the President undertake without any form of prior
legislative authorization? Does the power to defend the nation extend to preemptive strikes? May the executive engage in actions
"short of war" to protect citizens, property, or interests of the

United States? May the President engage in covert operations to subvert foreign governments or political parties? May Congress control executive branch "undercover" operations of all varieties, or do some fall within the President's exclusive authority? To what extent may Congress reverse executive actions, even if constitutionally undertaken? To what extent may Congress control the conduct of lawful military actions?

These questions far from exhaust the constitutional issues related to war-making. War is an aspect of foreign affairs, and the allocation of powers over foreign affairs depends in significant part upon the general authority and functions of the branches. We must therefore ask: To what extent Congress may control foreign policy, and by what means? May funds be denied, or offices abolished, or resolutions adopted? Under what circumstances, if any, may the President enter into arrangements with foreign nations without submitting them to the Senate for approval as treaties? May the President or other executive officers refuse Congress information it requests, and if so, what steps may Congress take to obtain the relevant information? Are there limits on the President's power to influence legislation, including the budget, or to spend appropriated moneys? Finally, what role if any is the Supreme Court assigned on these issues?

THE CONSTITUTION'S LANGUAGE

The Constitution begins with Congress, vesting "all the legislative powers herein granted" in a Congress consisting of two houses.[2] The House of Representatives is given "the sole power of impeachment," and the Senate "the sole power to try all impeachments,"[3] thus suggesting ultimate control of the presidency. At the same time, Congress is protected from executive control by provisions requiring a meeting "at least once in every year"; assigning each house of Congress control of its own membership; and making legislators immune from arrest during its sessions as well as from questioning in any other place about any speech or debate.[4]

Numerous grants to Congress explicitly confer important powers over fiscal, foreign, and military affairs. Congress is to raise funds, to be spent pursuant to its directions.[5] Congress is empowered to regulate commerce among nations. Congress is to declare war. Even military actions short of war—such as marque and reprisal, captures on land and sea, the definition and punishment of piracy, and "offences against the law of nations"—are placed in Congress's control.[6] Congress is also to decide on the extent and nature of the army and navy, to make rules governing the armed forces authorized, and to provide for the militia and for calling it forth "to execute the laws of the Union, suppress insurrections, and repel invasions. . . ."[7] Finally, Congress is empowered "to make all laws which shall be necessary and proper for carrying into execution the foregoing powers, and all other powers vested by this Constitution in the Government of the United States, or in any department or officer thereof."[8]

The grants to the President are, by contrast, few and vague. The "executive power" conferred in Article II could reasonably be said to mean no more than the power to fulfill the President's duty to see that the laws are faithfully executed.[9] The phrase can, of course, be construed much more broadly, as conferring all powers by their nature "executive" not explicitly withheld. Yet even this construction arguably yields only limited powers, in light of the numerous grants of foreign-affairs and military authority to Congress. The commander-in-chief clause is also consistent on its face with the notion of the President as agent of the legislature.[10] It reads most readily as a grant to manage military engagements and other objectives authorized by Congress.

The foreign-affairs powers explicitly assigned the President appear humble enough: to appoint ambassadors and ministers; to make treaties, with the "advice and consent" of the Senate (and financed to the extent necessary by legislation originating in the House); and to receive ambassadors and other public ministers.[11] The only provisions concerning information merely impose duties on the President. The Constitution says he "shall from time to time" give Congress information on the nation's condition, and specifically that "a regular statement and account of the receipts and the expenditures [by the Treasury] of all public money shall be published from time to time."[12] In retrospect, one can easily see that these powers in combination, together with the President's authority to appoint and direct the foreign affairs and military establishments,[13] potentially placed in his hands the reins of government. But the Constitution's language by no means required this development.

Although the Constitution therefore appears to favor Congress in its grants of power, it lays the foundation for executive claims by assigning the President powers and functions that overlap most of the powers and functions given the legislature. The President, for example, is given legislative responsibilities and authority. He is called upon to recommend to Congress "such measures as he shall judge necessary and expedient. . . ."[14] He is empowered to veto bills and resolutions, which require two-thirds of each House to override.[15] Nothing allows him unilateral authority to raise funds, or to spend them in any way other than Congress directs, but the President's most crucial responsibilities, such as to defend the nation from attack, might justify his borrowing funds for that purpose, or using funds already in the Treasury even though raised and earmarked for other purposes.

The requirement that the President give Congress information from time to time implies that he was expected, in the course of his duties, to acquire material that Congress would need. No provision mandates that he voluntarily give Congress all the information in his possession, however, thereby suggesting that Congress would be required to request information deemed desirable or necessary. Whether the President must comply with every legislative request is left unclear, though Congress is entrusted with powers that it presumably could use to compel compliance.

What of the President's power to use the military under his control in the absence of a declaration of war? The Constitution says Congress shall "declare" war, and it seems unreasonable to contend that the President was given the power to "make" undeclared war, especially since the Constitution gives Congress control of those types of military actions short of formal war commonly resorted to during that time.[16] Yet the clause by no means precludes a construction that would allow the President to use the armed forces to defend the United States against attack. Article I, section 10 provides, in fact, that no state may, without consent of Congress, "engage in war, unless actually invaded, or in such imminent danger as will not admit of delay." One can reasonably contend that at least this much power must be vested in the President to protect the United States as a whole.[17]

The areas of greatest potential executive power, however, are those involving no direct confrontation with legislative powers. Showdowns between the branches have been rare, and most issues of current controversy result from situations in which Congress has delegated power to the President, or in which the President has acted in a legislative vacuum.[18] The Constitution contains little to suggest that Congress is limited in delegating its authority.[19] Broad delegations may be viewed as determinations by Congress of the manner in which the President should exercise his power to execute the law. But Congressmen would probably violate their oath to uphold the Constitution if they delegated, in advance and without limitation, whole powers explicitly assigned to the legislature, such as the power to declare war or to raise revenues. No provision, however, would seem to prevent the legislature from allowing the executive to plan and draft legislation, prepare the budget, control funds and information, conduct foreign relations, or even engage in military actions upon findings largely within the President's discretion to make. Nor does the Constitution prevent Congress from delegating authority in any form, or by any act, from which approval might reasonably be inferred. Congress is in fact assigned power over some military actions that could be resorted to without a declaration of war; and nothing suggests that Congress may not give approval by paying for, or otherwise making possible, an executive action, where the particular facts would justify an inference of approval.

When Congress says and does nothing on a subject, even one over which the Constitution appears to give it ultimate authority, does the President have sufficient power to act until Congress moves to restrain or direct him? In this context, the vagueness in the Constitution's grants to the President operates in his favor. The implicit grant of authority to defend the nation from attack, the role of commander-in-chief, the power to execute the laws, the grants amounting to effective control of the foreign-affairs bureaucracy and dealings with other nations, all combine to provide at least a respectable basis upon which to legitimate executive initiatives. The President could even assert that, absent legislative direction to the contrary, he is a sufficient embodiment of the national sovereignty to exercise its rights under the law of nations. No written provision would directly support his claim, but the degree of trust placed in his office by the Constitution, and the need to fashion a response when Congress has failed to or been unable to act, operate in favor of legitimating such conduct.

Article III, section 1, vests the judicial power in a Supreme Court and in such inferior courts as Congress might establish. The judges are given tenure during good behavior, and a salary not subject to diminution while they serve. Section 2 describes the judicial power as extending to cases in several categories, many of which suggest that issues relating to military and foreign affairs were expected to reach the Court: all cases "arising under this Constitution, the laws of the United States, and Treaties made . . . ; to all Cases affecting Ambassadors, other public Ministers and Consuls; [and to controversies] between a State, or the Citizens thereof, and foreign States, Citizens or Subjects." The Supreme Court is in fact given original jurisdiction over "all Cases affecting Ambassadors, other public Ministers and Consuls, and those in which a State shall be Party. . . ." In all other categories of cases the Supreme Court is granted appellate jurisdiction "with such Exceptions, and under such Regulations as the Congress shall make." The text therefore strongly suggests a role for an independent judiciary in settling at least some forms of disputes over the meaning of laws, treaties, and the Constitution itself, but one over which Congress could exercise control through its power to create courts and to regulate the Supreme Court's appellate jurisdiction.

In sum, then, the Constitution appears to give Congress powers adequate to assure it the final say in foreign and military affairs. Yet it appears not to preclude Congress from delegating most of its functions to the President, or from effectively (though not irrevocably) surrendering them by allowing the President to assume the initiative on the basis of his vague but potentially expandable powers. Was the Constitution actually intended to allocate power in this manner? Or did the Framers intend clearer lines of separation between the branches? Was the President to be Congress's agent, or more?

THE BRITISH EXPERIENCE

The Americans who drafted and adopted the Constitution were overwhelmingly British by origin and were exposed continuously to British institutions and government.[20] They persistently referred back to the British experience in forming the Constitution, and subsequent generations have looked to this experience to enrich their understanding of specific provisions and to test the legitimacy of practices developed with the passage of time.

The hazards of interpolating from British history are formidable. Did the Framers (or at least some of them), for example, form meaningfully detailed conceptions of the British experience? Were those conceptions accurate? Which British practices or events affected the Framers, and in what way? The unwritten English Constitution, Professor J.I. Clark Hare said in 1885, "is not a constant quantity. Like the glacier, which, though seeming fixed and rigid, is yet plastic and suffers a continual change, it has varied in each century, and sometimes in each successive generation."[21]

During the three centuries prior to 1787, the allocation of power among the branches of British government fluctuated drastically and sometimes violently.[22] When Henry VII became the first Tudor King in 1485, the nation desperately needed strong executive leadership. The Tudors provided it. The King and his Council developed into a powerful executive system, which possessed legislative and judicial powers as well, including the infamous Star Chamber. All these functions were merged into the Council, the King's chief instrument for governing. Under Henry VIII and Elizabeth I, the state took over the church. Parliament meanwhile became increasingly active when in session, and occasionally refused to cooperate with the Crown. But the Tudors ruled for long periods without Parliament, and controlled or influenced its membership and actions. The King's "prerogative"* appears generally to have been viewed as beyond the power of either Parliament or the common-law courts to limit, though this principle remained largely untested under monarchs with broad legislative support and great governing skill.

James I became the first Stuart King in 1603. The constitutional claims of King and Parliament began to be advanced with increasing rigidity. Parliament showed new strength, and the King responded by trying to live without it. Between 1603 and 1640, Parliament was kept in session only four and a half years. The demands of war forced James and his successor, Charles I, however, to begin the "marketing of prerogative powers [in exchange for fiscal support] which characterized the rest of the Stuart period."[23] Parliament asserted itself by denying or conditioning funds, impeaching ministers, and petitioning for its rights. By 1640 Charles could no longer rule without Parliament, but was equally unable to retain his powers with Parliament in session. Civil war erupted in 1642, and the intransigent Charles was beheaded in 1649.

Parliament became supreme. It ruled with no King, and without even a House of Lords. Then the army it created to overthrow monarchy led to its own temporary downfall. Britain was ruled by a military junta until 1660. At that point dissatisfaction caused the pendulum to swing once more. The monarchy was restored. Charles II regained much of the power earlier Kings had exercised over appointments, the armed forces, peace and war, treaties and diplomacy, and over Parliament itself. But the old order was gone forever. Parliament had governed alone, and now sought at various points to control national policies through its power over funds and by impeachments. The King's effectiveness stemmed from his use of "influence," and later because of his alliance with Tories who demanded and obtained an Anglican government, unattached to France.

James II's Catholicism destroyed the bonds that bound King and Tory. In 1688 he was unceremoniously displaced by a convention that became a Parliament by designation of the new King it selected, William of Orange. William's powers were preserved in theory, but the extraordinary manner of his ascension substituted a "practical and largely secular notion of monarchy" for the notion of divine right.[24] War once again forced the King to seek Parliament's aid,

---

*The King's prerogative, Blackstone later wrote, enabled him to make treaties or appointments unilaterally, and among other things to declare war, issue letters of marque and reprisal, and raise armies and navies. 1 W. Blackstone, *Commentaries on the Laws of England* 256–58 (17th ed. 1830) [hereinafter Blackstone, *Commentaries*].

and the prerogative was steadily attacked in both military and foreign affairs. The monarchy persevered, however, as ministers influential in Parliament began increasingly and effectively to utilize the Crown's patronage in behalf of the Kings who appointed them.

George of Hanover became King in 1714, and ushered in a period of relative stability in government. Both he and George II cooperated with their Whig ministers in governing, and this combined executive of King and early Cabinet acquired great influence and authority. The British system operated during this period in the manner that writers such as Montesquieu, Voltaire, and Locke praised as the best yet devised by man. Neither branch pressed its theoretical powers to extremes, and neither allowed the other to do so.

But the delicate balance was upset again when George III became King in 1760. He was determined to break the partnership that had developed between King and ministers by subordinating the latter more completely to his will. He succeeded, ironically, to the extent his leading minister, Lord North, prevailed in Parliament. But Parliament forced North from power in 1782. The King regained influence and authority once again when James Pitt became his principal advocate. The prerogative was preserved at least in theory, but the King's authority in fact depended on his willingness to share authority with ministers able to command Parliament's support.*

Given these drastic fluctuations in power, it is hardly surprising that British constitutional practice fails to provide one-sided answers to the questions left unresolved by the language of the U.S. Constitution. The fact is that both Parliament and the Crown asserted them-

*The following exchange between George II and Lord Chancellor Hardwicke, recorded by the Chancellor, dramatically illustrates the power of ministers:

K. I have done all you ask'd of me. I have put all power into your hands and I suppose you will make the most of it.

Ch. The disposition of places is not enough, if your Majesty takes pains to shew the world that you disapprove of your own work.

K. *My work!* I was forc'd—I was threatened.

Ch. I am sorry to hear your Majesty use those expressions. I know of no force—I know of no threats. No means were used, but what have been used in all times, the humble advice of your servants, supported by such reasons as convinc'd them that the measure was necessary for your service.

K. Yes, I was told that I should be opposed.

Ch. Never by me, Sir, nor by any of my friends. . . . Your Ministers, Sir, are only your instruments of Government.

K. (Smiles.) Ministers are the Kings in this country.

When the King continued to deal with his favorites, forty-five of his "servants" resigned. He was forced to recall them two days later when it became obvious that a Cabinet could not be formed. The returning Cabinet now took the opportunity to tell George II that those who were "only his instruments of government" were to be his only instruments. L. Namier, *England in the Age of the American Revolution* 46–47 (1966).

selves successfully at different times on most important issues relating to foreign and military affairs.

Parliament's power over foreign and military affairs was reflected, first, in its control of the purse. By the early seventeenth century the legislature's support had become indispensable for any long-term policy requiring military power.[25] To exercise judgment in foreign affairs, Parliament needed information, and the Crown supplied information voluntarily in several ways.* Both houses of Parliament, and their committees, called upon the executive for information, and often succeeded in obtaining some or all the material sought.† Members frequently asserted that Parliament had an indisputable right to ask for papers.[26]

Parliament often sought to affect directly foreign-affairs decisions. Answers to Royal addresses were heatedly debated because they could signify approval of government policy.[27] Funds were denied, granted, or granted conditionally as a means of permitting or preventing executive plans.[28] Legislation was passed, or agreements made, against the desires of the Crown, to attempt to compel the executive to abide by the legislature's will.[29] When the executive proceeded without legislative approval to exercise part of the royal prerogative—such as to make a treaty—he ran the risk that Parlia-

---

*It became customary for ministers to submit themselves to questioning in Parliament, and during debate on any proposed policy a minister might be compelled to defend the government in detail. Papers, treaties, and written statements were submitted, especially when fiscal support was being sought. The Royal speeches at the opening and closing of Parliament also served as a source of information, in that they reviewed foreign-affairs developments. See F. Flournoy, *Parliament and War* 14-15 (1927); G. Gibbs, "Parliament and Foreign Policy in the Age of Stanhope and Walpole," 77 *Eng. Hist. Rev.* 18, 26, 29-30, 34 (1962) [hereinafter Gibbs, "Parliament and Foreign Policy"]; E. Turner, "Parliament and Foreign Affairs, 1603-1760," 34 *Eng. Hist. Rev.* 172, 184, 190 (1919) [hereinafter Turner, "Parliament and Foreign Affairs"].

†*See generally*, Turner, "Parliament and Foreign Affairs" 172. The House sometimes resorted to a special type of select committee to inquire into matters "of great importance." R. Sedgwick, *The House of Commons, 1715-1754*, at 8 (1970). A particularly striking example is the inquiry into the Treaty of Utrecht, which began in 1715 with a successful motion for all papers relating to the negotiation. 18 *Commons Journal* 22, 40, 49. The next Commons impeached the Earl of Oxford for withholding information from Council and Parliament. *Id.* 209, 215-16. At times the right to receive information was assured in an agreement, such as in the Act of Settlement (1700), which required the consent of Parliament before the crown engaged in war to defend Hanover. Gibbs, "Parliament and Foreign Policy" 21. When the Alliance of Hanover was made in 1727, the House requested and speedily obtained copies of memorials and letters between emissaries of France and Spain. 23 *Lords Journal* 11; 20 *Commons Journal* 714; Gibbs, *supra*, at 31. During his term as Secretary of State, George Canning made the laying of information before Parliament an instrument of foreign policy. R. Pares, *King George III and the Politicians* 201 (1953) [hereinafter Pares, *George III*].

ment might subsequently disapprove, and that the ministers involved might be impeached, dismissed, or even executed.[30] The King himself was not immune, as Charles I and James II so painfully learned.

Despite Parliament's enormous power, the executive managed to assert itself successfully on most foreign-affairs matters. Obtaining funds was the Crown's most substantial obstacle, but Charles I managed to obtain fiscal support without Parliament's approval by calling on local governments to provide ships for the nation's defense, and then accepting monetary payments if the ships were not provided.[31] The King often borrowed money to finance military spending, and could also dismiss Parliament for refusing to provide funds or for any other reason.[32] Whatever Parliament's powers in theory, they could not be exercised during the frequent and extensive periods when it was kept from meeting.

The executive exercised control of information and of foreign affairs during most of the two centuries preceding 1787.[33] Information was frequently withheld from voluntary transmittals to Parliament, and even from transmittals in response to legislative requests.* Just as Parliament claimed the right to ask for information, the Crown, through its ministers, claimed the right to withhold material in its discretion.† Requests for information as to what had occurred in

---

*For example, in 1729 Parliament asked for extensive documents so it could examine closely the state of Anglo-Spanish trade. The documents were carefully screened and edited before their release to Parliament, apparently to withhold statements which threw doubt on the government's assertion that France was a firm ally. Gibbs, "Parliament and Foreign Policy" 32–33. In 1739, during a debate in Commons on motions for papers relating to the convention with Spain, Horatio Walpole said that His Majesty might well be offended at an address which, should he comply with it, could lay open the most private transactions of his Cabinet and discover secrets that ought to be concealed for the good of the kingdom. 103 *Parl. Hist.* 965. When Carteret asked if there were papers other than those which had been delivered to the House, the Earl of Cholmondeley thought the question extremely improper: "His Lordship cannot be properly informed but by one who has the honour to be of his Majesty's council; and we cannot suppose that such a person will divulge, even to this House, a secret which perhaps he is sworn to conceal." Any such inquiry would have to be addressed to the King directly. *Id.* 1016. The King did occasionally permit ministers to inform Parliament of what occurred at Cabinet proceedings. See 2 Turner, *supra* note 22 at 45–46. George Grenville refused to comply with a motion for correspondence relating to the cession of Corsica on the ground that negotiations still continued, an argument frequently made. Pares, *George III* at 202; Turner, "Parliament and Foreign Affairs" 193.

†To Gibbs, an expert in this field, the government's power to withhold material was clear: "The crown, of course, through its ministers had an equally indisputable right to refuse such [legislative] requests, and frequently exercised that right." Gibbs, "Parliament and Foreign Policy" 30. Turner likewise states that executive discretion was frequently exercised, and that calls for information were usually the product of executive management: "Documents were often called for by the houses, and usually communicated as a matter of course, the

Council or "Cabinet" discussions were rejected as improper.[34] To prevent sensitive material from leaking to the legislature, the more powerful Council members often kept such material even from most of the Council;[35] a system was devised, and often used, whereby diplomatic correspondence that the writer wished kept out of official files was denominated "private."*

Foreign-affairs initiatives were taken by both the King and his ministers at various times without consulting Parliament. Many matters were kept secret, so that not even after-the-fact authority was sought. Ministers consciously used their power to present Parliament with situations in which the legislature was virtually forced to go along with executive initiatives.[36] Parliament sometimes punished ministers and even Kings, but the general pattern, due in part to the executive's "influence," was for the legislature to allow the King and his ministers to operate with secrecy and independence, frequently committing the nation to foreign and military engagements without prior legislative approval.

There are, to be sure, identifiable events and institutions in the British experience that explain many aspects of the United States

---

state papers containing many references to 'the Papers to be laid before the Parliament.' But it is plain that much discretion was used. Sometimes ministers considered in private meetings whether information should be communicated; and sometimes arranged that particular papers should be called for." Turner, "Parliament and Foreign Affairs" 190.

*In 1711, for example, Henry St. John (Bolingbroke) wrote to the Earl of Strafford, representing Britain in negotiations at Utrecht: "The public letters which I receive from your Excellency are never read except in Cabinet, the private never even there, unless now and then a passage may be necessary for the information of the Lords." Letter of Jan. 1, 1711, in 2 *Letters and Correspondence, Public and Private, of the Right Honorable Henry St. John Bolingbroke* 131 (1798). Bolingbroke acknowledged that "letters which contain the general thread of business, which are read in Cabinet and have orders given publicly upon them" must be placed by the Secretary of State in his office. But these consequences could be avoided through the use of a dual system of correspondence. Letters dealing with private matters, wrote St. John, "and those which are of a nature not to be communicated even to the Cabinet till her majesty shall think fit" could be kept out of the secretary's office. Letter to Lord Raby, May 8, 1711, in 1 *id.* 196; 1 Turner, *supra* note 22 at 432. See also Bolingbroke's letter to the Earl of Oxford on July 27, 1743, in which he wrote: "Separate, in the name of God, the chaff from the wheat and consider who you have left to employ; assign them their parts; trust them as far as it is necessary for the execution each of his part; let the forms of business be regularly carried on in Cabinet, and the secret of it in your own closet." 2 Turner *supra* at 306.

The system of having both public and private correspondence continued in the Hanoverian period. Townshend, who was with the King in Hanover, wrote to Walpole: "I earnestly recommend to you that my private letters, and particularly what I wrote in my last, may be imparted to no one living but the Duke of Newcastle. . . . [T]he Freedom we use in writing to one another might be of the last ill consequence, if it were even suspected." *Id.* at 275.

Constitution, including: a two-chamber legislature, with sole authority to pass laws,[37] and given numerous privileges and limitations;* and a chief executive, in charge of administering military and foreign affairs. Furthermore, the American Constitution and Bill of Rights rejected the principle that rights and privileges could be overriden by legislation, and sought to place certain rights beyond government's power to change without constitutional amendment.[38] And however much the President may have resembled the British King, the Constitution refused to grant the President the full "prerogative" of the Crown, withholding in particular the power to make binding treaties, to raise armies, and to declare war.[39]

These similarities and differences, however, illustrate those areas in which the United States Constitution is relatively unambiguous. British history is far less authoritative in disputes pertaining to matters left uncertain by the Constitution. In such a dispute the proper question becomes that put by Representative William Findley of Pennsylvania in 1810, when another member relied on Parliament's past actions in claiming that Congress had unlimited power to investigate:

> It is well known that the powers of the House of Commons have been very different at different times. . . . At which of these periods does the gentleman apply the proceedings of the House of Commons as a model for this House?[40]

The general trend in Britain during the seventeenth and eighteenth centuries was for Parliament to gain power at the King's expense. But the pertinent question is how much of this trend was incorporated by the American Constitution.

A partial answer may be found in that the British experience provided the Framers with more than simply two sets of inconsistent precedents in areas of constitutional controversy. It also provided an intellectual framework for constitutional government that was consistently hailed as its greatest achievement.

The most widely recognized component of eighteenth-century British constitutionalism was the doctrine of separation of powers. British institutions evolved so that governmental power was divided along functional lines (legislative, executive, and judicial), with each type of

---

*For example: the right of Commons to originate all money bills; impeachment by the lower house and trial in the upper; immunity of legislators from arrest during legislative sessions and from trial for statements made in debate; an executive power to pardon in all cases but impeachment; the right of each house to decide whether to seat its members, or to debate in secret; the right of Parliament to convene, the executive's desires notwithstanding; and limitation of executive-branch officeholding by legislators.

power primarily assigned to different persons. There can be no liberty, wrote Montesquieu, Locke, and Blackstone, among others, when the right to make and enforce laws is united in the same person or group of persons.[41] Parliament deprived the Crown of much of the lawmaking and judicial functions it exercised under the Tudors. On the other hand, Parliament ruled without a King for only a short time before the Restoration proved the nation's need and desire for a separate executive branch.

The doctrine of separation fails to explain, however, the overlapping authority and continuing conflict that characterized the British system even when it was working best. Both the executive and legislative branches often claimed authority over the same functions, as we have seen, and each managed to sustain its claims at different times. Interconnections abounded.[42]

A second doctrine, also widely extolled during the seventeenth and eighteenth centuries, does much to explain the apparent inconsistencies in British practice.[43] By 1642, as Bernard Bailyn notes, British political thought had absorbed the notion that "liberty had been preserved and could be preserved . . . by maintaining the balance in government of the basic socio-constitutional elements of society: King, lords, and commons." Pure forms—monarchy, aristocracy, or democracy—would degenerate, whereas a "mixing" of these forms within a single system could create "counterpoised pressures" that "might keep the system stable and healthy." This notion assumed separate branches, but with a true "mixing" in each branch of aspects of all the forms of power—legislative, executive, and judicial. "The supposed preserves of each power were in fact thoroughly infiltrated by the others. . . ."[44]

The value of mixing powers to create a constitutional balance was widely accepted as proper political doctrine by the early eighteenth century.* It was espoused in the protest literature against executive

---

*The doctrine was accepted by such leading political opponents as Bolingbroke and James Pitt. After arguing the need for a separation of powers ("independency"), Bolingbroke added the need for checks and balances ("dependency"), which he saw as two aspects of the same constitutional arrangement—balanced government:

> The constitutional Dependency, as I have call'd it for Distinction's Sake, consists in this; that the Proceedings of each Part of the Government, when they come forth into Action and affect the whole, are liable to be examin'd and controul'd by the other Parts. The Independency pleaded for consists in This; that the Resolutions of each Part, which direct these Proceedings, be taken Independently and without any Influence, direct or indirect, on the others. Without the first, each Part would be at Liberty to attempt destroying the Ballance, by usurping, or abusing Power; but without the last, there can be no Ballance at all.

7 *The Craftsman* 87 (1731-37), Special Collection, Butler Library, Columbia

domination, and constituted the very essence of Blackstone's exposition of the British Constitution as a planned mixing of powers, designed to assure balance and therefore liberty. The branches of government—King, Lords, Commons, courts—were conceived as representing different power groups within society. Consequently it made sense to devise a system in which each important group would possess powers that enabled it to check even those powers recognized as having been assigned to the other groups.

This notion is most importantly illustrated in connection with the royal prerogative. The mere fact that a power fell within the ambit of the prerogative did not assure that the King or his ministers could exercise that power with impunity. Blackstone noted that the executive could be (and had been) criticized, even impeached, for the consequences of an exercise of prerogative. Parliament had its own powers which it could use to express its will. On the other hand, implicit in this point was the notion that the executive could take any action falling within the prerogative on its own responsibility, without consulting Parliament in advance. That Parliament's legislative powers included authority to undo what the executive had done, or to punish the executive for such actions, did not necessarily mean that the executive lacked power to act in the first place. The powers involved were, in this manner, "mixed," or more precisely stated, granted to both branches, with ultimate but not necessarily operational authority in Parliament.[45]

Locke made the point explicit in his famous description of "Prerogative":

> Where the legislative and executive power are in distinct hands, as they are in all moderated monarchies and well-framed governments, there the good of the society requires that several things should be left to the discretion of him that has the executive power. For the legislators not being able to foresee and provide by laws for all that may be useful to the community, the executor of the laws, having the power in his hands, has by

---

University. Pitt's analysis was essentially the same, though he emphasized that " 'tis not possible in the nature of things, that the Legislative Power should be independent of the executive." He continued:

> Our Constitution consists indeed of Three Powers absolutely distinct; but if they were also as absolutely independent, no Business would ever be done: There would be everlasting Contention and Dispute till one had got the better of the other. 'Tis necessary, therefore, in Order to the due Exercise of Government, that these Powers which are distinct, and have a Negative on each other, should also have a mutual Dependence, and mutual Expectations.

London Journal, April 4, 1730; cited in W. Gwyn, "The Meaning of the Separation of Powers," 9 *Tul. Stud. Poli. Sci.* 3, 98 (1965). *See* Gwyn's discussion of the journalistic battle between these two men, *id.* 96–98.

the common law of Nature a right to make use of it for the good of the society, in many cases where the municipal law has given no direction, till the legislative can conveniently be assembled to provide for it; nay, many things there are which the law can by no means provide for, and those must necessarily be left to the discretion of him that has the executive power in his hands, to be ordered by him as the public good and advantage shall require; nay, it is fit that the laws themselves should in some cases give way to the executive power, or rather to this fundamental law of Nature and government—vis., that as much as may be all the members of the society are to be preserved.

Yet at the same time Locke made clear his view that the "legislative is not only the supreme power," but "sacred and unalterable in the hands where the community have once placed it."[46] As Corwin explained, "What Locke gives us in the final analysis is *not* legislative supremacy really, but—as his Whig commentators pointed out—'a balanced constitution.' "[47]

The British constitutional experience may well, therefore, provide an answer to the questions left unresolved by the language of the U.S. Constitution. The British allocation of overlapping powers in foreign and military affairs was conscious, and it may be that the ambiguities of the American Constitution were likewise deliberate. We must ask whether, in the manner of the British notion of "mixing," the separate branches of U.S. government were intentionally given powers exercisable over the same subjects, at least within the limits implicit in the specific grants of a written constitution.

COLONIAL, STATE AND NATIONAL GOVERNMENT PRIOR TO 1789

The British experience was far more distant from the Constitution's Framers than their own experiences with colonial and state governments, and under the Continental Congress and Articles of Confederation. A massive literature discusses the American experience prior to 1789, and has produced a variety of explanations for the Revolution and Constitution.* Whatever the differences among these explanations may be, little dispute exists concerning certain major trends

---

*Scholars for several generations have commented upon the period between the Revolution and Constitution, advancing numerous theories, most of which are perfectly consistent with each other but stress one of several important factors. Among the outstanding compilations are R. Morris, *The American Revolution Reconsidered* (1967); E. Latham, ed., *The Declaration of Independence and the Constitution* (1956); G. Wood, ed., *The Confederation and the Constitution* (1973); G. Wood, *The Creation of the American Republic, 1776-1787* (1969); B. Wright, *Consensus and Continuity 1776-1787* (1958).

and attitudes. The prerevolutionary period, to begin with, resulted in a decidedly antiexecutive feeling among colonists. This feeling was translated into state governments that in general were dominated by the legislative branch. A broad spectrum of leaders believed that the performance of state legislatures was so inadequate as to constitute, in itself, a reason for establishing a strong national government. The national government initially established was deemed inadequate, chiefly because of its inability to raise funds, protect commerce, and preserve order, but also because it lacked the leadership and effectiveness that a genuine executive could provide. The period 1776 to 1789 witnessed the gradual development, by necessity, of an executive branch run by persons other than legislators and exercising increasingly broad discretion, especially over foreign and military affairs.

Colonial governments varied. Some were royal colonies (New York and Massachusetts during the reign of King James II); others were survivals of proprietary government (Maryland and Pennsylvania); others of chartered government (Connecticut and Rhode Island). All had governors, appointed or approved by the King of England, except in the substantially independent chartered colonies, where governors were locally elected.[48]

The governors had great powers in theory, including a veto on legislation, "suspending clauses" that prevented enforcement of legislation until approved in England, command of the military, power to dismiss and dissolve the representative legislative bodies, and often authority to raise funds by issuing warrants and to spend on projects such as markets and harbors. Matters concerning foreign relations, commerce, and war were ultimately under the power of the British government, though authority to use military force, especially for defense, was frequently delegated in charters and grants. Dissatisfaction among colonists related as much to actions of Parliament as to those of the King and his governors. But the colonial executive was the mother country's agent, and hence became a prime focus of colonial ire.[49]

Most of the colonies also had legislatures, which came increasingly to mirror the structural division that existed in Britain—two houses, one relatively representative of the people, the other a body analogous to the House of Lords, composed of established, conservative forces. Despite the appearance on paper of overwhelming executive supremacy, the colonial legislatures were remarkably successful in checking and undermining their executives.* The royal

*They used their power over funds to control the conduct of military affairs, sometimes even dictating the disposition of troops. They investigated the military, and sought to discipline individual officers. They appointed committees to

governors, ever subject to dismissal by the crown, hamstrung by rigid and detailed instructions on virtually all important issues, and deprived of patronage and the support of established upper classes— factors that assured the British executive so much of its stability and power during that period—were hard pressed and forced to surrender authority, especially to the lower houses, whose members were selected by a much broader franchise than existed in Britain.[50]

Opposition to British laws and policies was expressed in many ways prior to 1776. Among the most fundamental arguments was the notion that Americans had the rights of Englishmen, one of which was to live under a "fixed" constitution that denied absolute power to any branch of government. Locke, Montesquieu, and Blackstone, among others, were warmly received and ardently quoted, especially their doctrines of separation and mixing of powers.[51] Colonists embraced rather than rejected these English constitutional traditions; their complaint was that Britain failed to abide by the principles in dealing with the colonies.

But these complaints led at first to little tangible recognition of the concepts of separation of powers and mixed government. The Revolution provided colonists an opportunity to subordinate the unpopular executive branch,[52] and they seized the occasion. Of the eight states adopting constitutions between 1776 and 1778, all but New York's "included almost every conceivable provision for reducing the executive to a position of complete subordination."[53] The executive, in general, was a single individual, but his decisions were subject to the vote of an executive council.[54] He generally owed his position to the legislative majority, and served a short term with strict limits on reeligibility. Important powers were sometimes assigned to the executive, but their exercise was usually made subject to the consent of a council or the legislature.[55]

The outstanding exception to this general pattern was New York. That state's constitution of 1777 vested "the supreme executive power and authority of the State" in a governor, chosen by the electorate for a three-year term with unlimited eligibility. He was made "general and commander in chief of all the militia, and admiral of the navy," with qualified but significant powers to appoint, to veto legislation, to dismiss the legislature, and to grant pardons. Even his duties to the legislature signified that he was to play an important role.[56]

---

participate with the executive in planning and supervising military operations. And they persistently interfered with the exercise of other executive powers, including the power of appointment. *See* E. Greene, *The Provincial Governor in the English Colonies of North America* 189-92 (1966); 1 G. Chalmers, *An Introduction to History of the Revolt of the American Colonies* 49, 361-62 (1845); G. Dargo, *Roots of the Republic* 42-43 (1974).

Most state legislatures repeatedly interfered with functions apparently or even explicitly assigned to the executive. Most, also, were sensitive to democratic causes, willing to ease the burdens of debtors through laws and paper money. To encourage intrastate commerce, the legislatures passed laws restricting interstate commerce. Other states retaliated, establishing a pattern destructive of the nation's economic well-being.[57] Shays's Rebellion in Massachusetts was the most dramatic evidence of a general lack of stability and order associated by many with overwhelming legislative supremacy.* George Washington, for example, saw "combustibles in every State."[58]

Leading figures of the time, some of whom later attended the Constitutional Convention, advocated changes in state constitutions to strengthen the executive. The Pennsylvania Constitution of 1776, granting sweeping power to a unicameral legislature, was condemned because it had "no *'distribution* of power into *different* hands, that *one may check another.'* On the contrary, the *executive* and *judicial* powers are made unduly dependent on a *single legislative* body, the Assembly. . . ."[59]

Madison complained in 1784 that the executive in Virginia was too weak. The legislature controlled the governor's salary, and was immune from judicial review. This scheme of things, he noted, gave too much power to one branch, rendering the Constitution "defective in a Union of powers which is tyranny.—Montesq."[60] Jefferson

---

*Debtors banded together, forming a small army, and made demands to be freed from their debts and for a redistribution of property. Massachusetts Governor Bowdoin and the state senate were anxious to put down the insurrection. The lower house, however, refused at first to vote the necessary authority and means, and tried to pacify the rebels. Authority to use the militia was granted to Bowdoin only after the rebels prevented the courts of general session from convening. Bowdoin still lacked adequate forces to put down the revolt. After the legislature adjourned, he raised the force he needed with contributions from private individuals. His actions were approved after the fact, but were so unpopular that he lost office in the next election. *See* V. Hall, *Politics without Parties: Massachusetts, 1780-1791* (1972); R. Morris, "Insurrection in Massachusetts," in *America in Crisis* (D. Aaron, ed. 1952); G. Minot, *The History of the Insurrections in Massachusetts in the Year 1786* (1970 reprint).

The Pennamite Wars, fought between Connecticut settlers, and Pennsylvania citizens and their government over land in western Pennsylvania, is another example of disorder and unfairness caused by legislative control. The Governor (President of the Supreme Executive Council) and Council of Revision (Supreme Executive Council) of Pennsylvania tried to accomplish peaceful and reasonable solutions to this continuing crisis, but the Assembly overrode their efforts. *See generally* O. Harvey and E. Smith, 3 *History of Wilkes-Barré* 1293-1345 (1927). The Pennsylvania Council of Censors at one point demanded papers pertaining to the disturbances, but the Assembly ignored the Council's order. The Council censured the Assembly for secretly raising and arming troops, and reprimanded them for withholding evidence, but the Council lacked power to do more. *Id.* 1430.

concurred. "[T]he powers of government," he wrote, "should be so divided and balanced among several bodies of magistracy, as that no one could transcend their legal limits, without being effectually checked and restrained by the others." He condemned as too powerful the Virginia legislature, despite the fact that its legislators were chosen by the people. "An *elective despotism* was not the government we fought for."[61] Thus, both the need for separation and for mixing were keenly felt, though what had been a device "to involve in the government all the social orders of the body politic" now became largely a means for maintaining balance among the three functional powers, each of which served the people generally and each of which was to be prevented from accumulating too much power.[62]

Experience under the New York Constitution between 1777 and 1787 differed sharply from the experience in most other states. George Clinton was governor for the entire period (and eight years thereafter), and exercised vigorous and independent leadership. He initiated legislative measures, unilaterally moved militia to defend the state and to put down internal disturbances, and as a member of the Council of Revision joined in vetoing some fifty-eight bills in ten years. The legislature attempted to vest virtually absolute power in a Council of Safety, to govern during legislative recess, but Clinton and the Council of Revision ultimately defeated this effort.[63] New York's experience was highly regarded by those who sought devices to check legislative excesses.[64] It helped guide reformers in Massachusetts and New Hampshire, which along with other states revised their constitutions to provide for stronger and more independent executive departments.*

Meanwhile, Americans also demonstrated their distaste for executive power in the national government they initially created. The

*The so-called *Essex Result* in Massachusetts proposed a veto power for the executive as "a check upon the legislative, to prevent the latter from encroaching on the former and stripping it of all its rights. The legislative in all states hath attempted it where this check was wanting, and have prevailed. . . . This attempt has resulted from the lust for domination, which in some degree influences all men, and all bodies of men." By giving the executive a veto, "the encroachments of the legislative will be repelled, and the powers of both properly balanced." The executive should be as small as possible, the New Hampshire literature urged. The "characteristic requisites" of executive power are "secrecy, vigour, and despatch. The fewer persons, therefore, this supreme power is trusted with, the greater probability there is that these requisites will be found." In addition, Delaware (1792) and Pennsylvania (1790) shifted from legislative to direct election of their governors; Georgia (1789) increased its governor's term to two years, and abolished tenure limitation; and Pennsylvania (1790) increased its governor's term from one to three years, with a limit of nine years in any twelve. Georgia did away with its Council in 1789, followed by Pennsylvania in 1790 and Delaware in 1792. C. Thach, *Creation of the Presidency, 1775-1789* at 45-49 (1923); Thorpe, *supra* note 49.

First Continental Congress was formed in 1774, when representatives of several colonies met to discuss mutual problems.[65] Acting without any formal plan of government,[66] the Congress took some foreign-affairs initiatives by sending a list of demands to the King and adopting a declaration of rights.[67] The states retained all legislative power, however, using the Congress as a form of national executive to conduct the Revolutionary War and foreign relations.[68]

The Congress gradually increased its activities, involving itself directly in fiscal, military, and foreign affairs.[69] When Congress needed to act through agents, it initially used ad hoc committees.[70] During 1776 it provided for continuity and on-going supervision by appointing delegates to three standing committees—Treasury, War and Ordinance, and Marine. In December 1776 an ad hoc committee was chosen "to prepare a plan for the better conducting of the executive business of Congress, by boards composed of persons, not members of Congress," and on April 17, 1777, Congress created a fourth permanent committee, Foreign Affairs.[71]

Congress supervised all its affairs in considerable detail during the next four years. The Committee on the Treasury was engaged in extensive and detailed fiscal planning by 1789, reporting to Congress on means for dealing with persistent fiscal crises.[72] Foreign affairs were managed almost entirely by Congress.[73] The Foreign Affairs Committee played a supporting role, providing reports on various issues, and drafts of proposed instructions to ministers abroad.[74] When some American ministers abroad began to send information in "private" letters to individual members of Congress, rather than in official letters,* Congress adopted a motion on March 27, 1779, insisting that the practice be stopped.[75] At the same time Congress recognized the need for secrecy in several ways, sometimes providing its administrators with funds for undisclosed activities.†

*General George Washington resorted to the technique on at least one occasion. He had been asked his advice on a proposed invasion of Canada in alliance with France, and responded in two letters written to Henry Laurens, President of Congress. The first, dated November 11, 1778, gave Washington's logistical and tactical reasons for opposing the enterprise. The second, dated November 14, was written privately, and described the political dangers of allowing France to play an important role in conquering Canada. 13 *The Writings of George Washington* 223, 239-59 (J. Fitzpatrick, ed. 1936); Letter of Nov. 14, 1778, *The Papers of George Washington* L.C. microfilm, series 4, reel 54. The first letter was referred to a committee on the subject, which concurred in Washington's judgment. The second was not referred to in any congressional source, though Washington's point could not have failed to reach Congress. *See* J. Logan, Jr., *No Transfer: An American Security Principle* 21 (1961).

†Congress kept its own deliberations secret. Foreign correspondence was treated with special sensitivity by the progenitor of the Committee on Foreign

Congress would have preferred to control military affairs as closely as foreign affairs, and tried to do so through special committees and detailed instructions.[76] From the start, however, as early instructions to George Washington reflect, Congress delegated discretion to respond to unanticipated situations.[77] Furthermore, emergencies led Congress to delegate sweeping powers to the Board of War and to General Washington, as when Philadelphia was threatened in 1776. Even when Congress issued detailed instructions, they invariably left Washington with at least a veto on all important tactical proposals.[78]

Washington was cautious in exercising authority delegated to him, often referring matters back to Congress for decision; when he did act, he promptly notified Congress and asked for their advice or contrary instructions.[79] He spoke up emphatically, however, when Congress seemed intent on military decisions with which he disagreed, and made important recommendations, many of which were eventually adopted.[80] On one occasion General Washington acted without the authority of Congress when, after the victory at Trenton in December 1776, he unilaterally offered a bounty of $10 to encourage reenlistment. This act violated one of the fundamental tenets of Washington's official conduct—to refrain from any irrevocable pledge of public credit without legislative authority—but he justified the action to Congress as a matter of pay or perish. Congress approved the expenditure and continued to place confidence in him.[81]

Many influential Americans quickly became dissatisfied with the lack of power in Congress, especially its inability to raise funds. Simultaneously, they objected to its lack of effective executive machinery. As early as May 1780, for example, after Charleston fell to the British, Washington complained in a private letter to a member of Congress about "the present state of our Finances . . . [and] the total emptiness of our magazines. . . ." A plan was necessary "to bring out the resources of the Country with vigor and decision. . . ."

Affairs, called the Committee on Secret Correspondence. Any member of Congress could request to see foreign correspondence, though in theory disclosure seems to have depended ultimately on a majority vote. 7 *Journals of the Continental Congress 1774–1789* at 274 (L.C. 1904-37) [hereinafter *JCC*]. *See also* W. Rogers, "Memorandum of the Attorney General," S. Comm. on the Judiciary, 85th Cong., 2d Sess. 140-41 (1958); R. Berger *Executive Privilege: A Constitutional Myth* 197-98 (1974). Congress provided Washington with funds for secret service activities in 1779. 14 *JCC* 526. In 1780, the Board of War requested $50,000 without describing why the funds were needed, offering only its guarantee that the purpose was important. Congress, without debate, ordered the Treasurer to pay to the board the full amount, for which they were to be accountable. 17 *JCC* 558. On February 20, 1783, Congress ordered the Secretary of Foreign Affairs confidentially to communicate the state of the peace negotiations to Washington. 24 *JCC* 142.

Congress lacked power "competent to the great purposes of War," he wrote, powers which should be conferred on Congress or "assumed by them as a matter of right. . . ." He also criticized Congress's failure to speak "in a more decisive tone. . . ." An adequate plan "cannot be effected if the measures to be taken should depend on the slow deliberations" of so large a body. He recommended the "absolute necessity that a *small* Committee should be immediately appointed to reside near head Quarters vested with all the powers which Congress have so far as respects the purpose of a full cooperation with the French fleet and Army on the *Continent*." Such a committee could act with dispatch and energy and provide for exigencies. Plans could be opened to committee members "with more freedom and confidence than to a numerous body. Where secrecy is impossible, where the indiscretion of a single member by disclosing may defeat the project."[82]

On September 3, 1780, Alexander Hamilton added his young but effective voice to the quest for reform in a letter to James Duane, one of New York's representatives in Congress, describing what he thought were the government's deficiencies. Foremost among the problems was Congress's lack of power to raise funds and to enforce decisions. But, he said, "another defect in our system is want of energy in the administration." This partly resulted from the weakness of Congress, he recognized, "but in a great degree from prejudice and the want of a proper executive. Congress have kept the power too much in their own hands and have meddled too much with details of every sort." Congress should deliberate, he said, "and it forgets itself when it attempts to play executive. It is impossible such a body, numerous as it is, and constantly fluctuating, can ever act with sufficient decision or with system." He urged in particular that departments should be placed under single heads instead of boards, whose "decisions are slower[,] their energy less[,] their responsibility more diffused." Since individual department heads would remain, "of course, at all times under the direction of Congress, we shall blend the advantages of a monarchy and republic in our constitution." Rather than weakening Congress, the reform would leave Congress with "precisely the same rights and powers as heretofore, happily disencumbered of the detail." The very reason for the change, however, contemplated more active and comprehensive administration by the departments, and Congress would be expected "to consult their ministers, and get all the information and advice they could from them, before they entered into any new measures or made a change in the old." The impending adoption of the Articles of Confederation was not enough to insure the necessary energy in either the legislative or administrative processes. Hamilton called for a "convention of all the States, with full authority to conclude finally upon a general confederation."[83]

Washington was a ready example of what a good department head could be, and other examples were readily at hand.[84] He wrote Duane on December 26, 1780:

> There are two things (as I have often declared) which in my opinion, are indispensably necessary to the wellbeing and good Government of our public Affairs; these are, greater powers to Congress, and more responsibility and permanency in the executive bodies. . . . [I]f Congress suppose, that Boards composed of their own body, and always fluctuating, are competent to the great business of War (which requires not only close application, but a constant and uniform train of thinking and acting) they will most assuredly deceive themselves.

These recommendations apparently received wide circulation.[85]

Congress sought to improve efficiency by placing some permanent committees and boards under individual secretaries. It could do little to increase its own powers, however, other than to urge adoption of the Articles of Confederation, which took effect on March 1, 1781. The Articles created a "United States of America," in which each "state retains its sovereignty, freedom and independence, and every Power, Jurisdiction and right," not expressly delegated to "the united states, in congress assembled." Congress was delegated important powers, including "the sole and exclusive right and power of determining on peace and war . . . of sending and receiving ambassadors . . . of establishing rules" concerning captures and prizes and "of granting letters of marque and reprisal in times of peace. . . ."[86] But the national government was left without power to enforce its policies and requisitions upon the states, and without an independent executive. A committee consisting of Duane, Madison and James M. Varnum of Rhode Island reported, soon after the Articles were adopted, that Congress needed authority to use the army and navy to compel delinquent states to fulfill their obligations.[87]

Government under the Articles continued to develop much as it had under the Continental Congress. The delegation of power and responsibility to executive officers over foreign[88] and military[89] affairs accelerated as Congress's activities and responsibilities expanded. Washington, in particular, was given broad tactical and even diplomatic powers.[90] As in prior years, he acted cautiously under these delegations, but the increase in his influence caused Pierce Butler, later a delegate to the Philadelphia Convention from South Carolina, to complain that Washington's plans were not even revealed to Congress. "So greatly altered is this *once august body*, that *as little as possible* is intrusted to them."[91]

Washington meanwhile continued to campaign for a new, more powerful national government.[92] The idea gathered momentum.[93] In 1782 New York's legislature became the first to call upon Congress to convene a General Convention. Evidence of the need for change was found, not only in the difficulty of conducting the war against Britain, but in maintaining order after the war ended. During June 1783, for example, soldiers who had not been paid marched to Philadelphia and demonstrated before Independence Hall. State authorities were unwilling or unable to take control, so Congress, helpless before the mutineers, adjourned to Princeton.[94] The states refused to comply with requisitions, so the national debt reached a level that made further borrowing impossible.[95] The states also exacerbated a weakened economy by hampering commerce and issuing paper money; by 1786 the nation was in the throes of a serious depression.[96] Even though the Articles granted Congress "the sole and exclusive right and power of . . . entering into treaties and alliances," some states persisted in interfering with this authority.[97] Talk of disunion spread.[98]

Congress had authority to order military action against Indians, and did so on one occasion.* But when confronted during 1787 with requests for help from the governor of Massachusetts to contain Shays's Rebellion, and from the governor of Pennsylvania in 1788 in connection with the Pennamite Wars, Congress lacked authority to help.[99] The first of these situations caused such serious alarm, however, that federal troops were raised and moved to Massachusetts under the pretense of protecting against the Indians and British.†

---

*After many complaints and a committee recommendation, Congress ordered the executives of Virginia and Pennsylvania to provide militia, with which to fight the Creek Indians of Ohio, when requested by the governor of the Western Territory. The commanding officer was to direct the militia "in conjunction with the said federal troops in protecting and defending the frontiers against any hostilities commenced or meditated by the Indians and in making such expeditions should they continue hostile as the said governor shall direct for repelling such hostilities. . . ." 34 *JCC* 412. *See id.* 369.

†Federal troops authorized to deal with Indians were diverted by Secretary of War Knox to Massachusetts to back up Governor Bowdoin if that step became necessary. 32 *JCC* 39–40. Those opposed to federal intervention sought to prevent further enlistments of troops, supposed to be used against Indians. Supporters frankly recognized that the real object in voting troops was to "countenance the exertions of the Govt. of Mass.," and "that the silent cooperation of these military preparations under the orders of Cong.ˢ had had a great and double effect, in animating the Gov.ᵗ and awing the insurgents. . . ." Charles Pinckney thought the measures adopted "impolitic and not to be reconciled with the genius of free Govts. and if fresh commotions should spring from them, that the State of

Many influential, union-minded, and propertied Americans needed no further proof to support strengthening the national government.[100] This time they turned to the task with the dangers and inefficiencies of unbalanced, legislative government very much in mind.

THE CONSTITUTIONAL CONVENTION

The shortcomings of the state and national governments, their inability to raise funds, maintain order, and govern efficiently, finally led the Continental Congress to respond to a growing demand for reform. On February 21, 1787, the Congress adopted a resolution calling on the states to send delegates to a convention authorized to prepare a plan to "render the federal constitution adequate to the exigencies of Government & the preservation of the Union."[101] The Convention got under way on May 25, 1787, and concluded on September 17, less than four months later.[102] No complete or entirely reliable record of the Convention's deliberations was preserved, but the general pattern of developments can be related with confidence.* Insofar as the executive department is concerned, the

---

Mass.ts alone should be at the charge, and abide by the consequences of their own misconduct." 33 *JCC* 720. Enlistments were continued, however, after Madison responded, virtually conceding that they exceeded Congress's authority, but rationalizing their continuance on the general need to prevent unrest because Great Britain might transform the local danger into a federal concern (33 *JCC* 720-21):

> Mr. Madison would not examine whether the original view of Cong.s in the enlargem.t of their military forces were proper or not, nor whether it were so to mask these views with an ostensible preparation ag.st the Indians. He admitted indeed that it appeared rather difficult to reconcile an interference of Cong.s in the internal controversies of a State with the tenor of the Confederation which does not authorize it expressly, and leaves to the States all powers not expressly delegated; or with the principles of Republican Gov.ts which as they rest on the sense of the majority, necessarily suppose power and right always to be on the same side. He observed however that in one point of view military precautions on the part of Cong.s might have a different aspect. Whenever danger was apprehended from any foreign quarter which of necessity extended itself to the federal concerns, Cong.s were bound to guard ag.st it and altho' there might be no particular evidence in this case of such a meditated interference, yet there was sufficient ground for a general suspicion of readiness in G.B. to take advantage of events in this country, to warrant precautions ag.st her.

*The delegates met in secret, and resolved to communicate nothing to nondelegates. 1 *Records of the Federal Convention of 1787* at 10 n.4, xi (M. Farrand, ed. 1911) (4 vols.) [hereinafter "*Records*"]. The Convention's Journal merely recorded formal motions and votes. Notes taken by several members are invaluable, but incomplete. Madison's notes, which are the most extensive, are known to have been revised thirty years after the Convention. Other members recorded parts of the proceedings in varying degrees of detail, including Rufus King, James McHenry, William Pierce, William Paterson, Alexander Hamilton, and George Mason. *Id.* vii, xi-xii.

delegates moved steadily from an office with little power or independence to an independent, potentially powerful presidency.

The Convention began by considering the so-called Virginia Plan, presented on May 29 by Edmund Randolph and based on a draft by Madison. This plan was designed to vest in a national government powers sufficient to control foreign relations, especially matters relating to war, and to support war or other activities with its own authority. The basic provision for achieving these changes was to confirm in "the National Legislature . . . the Legislative Rights vested in Congress by the Confederation," and to add the power "to call forth the force of the Union agst. any member of the Union failing to fulfill its duty under the articles thereof."[103]

The Virginia Plan provided for an executive branch with two categories of powers: "a general authority to execute the National Laws" and "to enjoy the Executive rights vested in Congress by the Confederation." Executive salaries were to be fixed, assuring at least some independence. In other respects, however, the executive contemplated was unlikely to exercise effective, independent leadership. The number of persons who would constitute the executive was undetermined, leaving open the possibility that a council of some sort would be created. Furthermore, the executive was to be elected by the legislature and would be ineligible for reelection. A power to veto national or state laws was provided, but it was to be exercised by a council of revision of the sort functioning in New York.[104]

On the same day Charles Pinckney* presented a more detailed constitutional scheme. He would have vested in a Congress powers to raise and support the military, and in a Senate the authority over war, treaties, and diplomatic appointments. This plan provided for a single executive, called a President, in whom would be vested "the Executive Power," as well as command of the armed forces. It was referred to Committee of the Whole† but not discussed. Some of its proposals were soon advanced, however, as substitutes for parts of the Virginia Plan.[105]

The first debate concerning the Virginia Plan's provisions took place on June 1. No delegate objected to the language proposing to vest the executive with "general authority to execute the laws." This

---

*Both Charles Pinckney and his cousin General Charles Cotesworth Pinckney were delegates from South Carolina. To avoid confusion, the latter is referred to as General Pinckney.

†The Convention, and later both houses of Congress, used the device of discussing matters in a committee composed of the whole legislative body, to enable everyone to participate, with many of the formal rules governing debate suspended.

is significant, in that executing the laws of an effective national government implied sufficient power to compel obedience to taxes, requisitions, treaties, and other directives. But many delegates protested the plan's proposal to grant its executive "the Executive rights vested in Congress by the Confederation." Charles Pinckney, for example, "was for a vigorous Executive but was afraid the Executive powers of Congress might extend to peace & war . . . which would render the Executive a Monarchy, of the worst kind, to wit an elective one." James Wilson of Pennsylvania attempted to ease Pinckney's fears, reasoning that the British monarchy was not a good guide for defining executive powers, since some of the Crown's prerogatives, particularly those of war and peace, were legislative in nature.[106]

Madison agreed with Wilson, but proposed a substitute resolution clarifying somewhat the powers to be assigned the executive. The executive, he said, "ought to be instituted with power to carry into effect the national laws," a noncontroversial item, and "to appoint to offices in cases not otherwise provided for. . . ." A second part of his resolution suggested authority in the executive "to execute such other powers as may from time to time be delegated by the national Legislature," language which would have enabled the legislature to define the content of "executive power" beyond the power to execute laws. Even this was not enough to satisfy General Charles Cotesworth Pinckney. At his suggestion, the last clause was amended to read "such other powers not Legislative nor Judiciary in their nature as may from time to time be delegated . . . ; " otherwise, he said, "improper powers might be delegated." As amended, the resolution would have limited even the legislature's power to expand executive authority. But this limitation was swept aside when General Pinckney's kinsman, Charles Pinckney, successfully moved to reject the entire second part of Madison's resolution.[108]

Other aspects of the Virginia Plan's executive were challenged by James Wilson. If a national government were to be established, "in theory he was for an election [of the executive] by the people," though willing to accept election by an electoral college, supposing "that this mode would produce more confidence among the people in the first magistrate than an election by the national Legislature." He also contended that the executive should be one man, "as giving most energy, dispatch and responsibility. . . ." He opposed even a council, "which oftener serves to cover, than prevent malpractices." The executive, he proposed, should also have an absolute veto and serve a relatively short term with unlimited eligibility for reelection. Finally, he would have broadened the executive's power of appointment to include judges; "a principal reason for unity in the Executive was that officers might be appointed by a single, responsible person."[109]

The Convention accepted in principle a single executive, many members speaking in favor.[110] Election remained in the legislature, however, for a seven-year term with no further eligibility to serve. An impeachment provision was added—for "malpractice or neglect of duty." The office was granted a veto power, which could be overruled only by two-thirds of each house. Madison's language concerning executive powers was adopted in slightly revised form, limiting the office to executing laws and to making appointments not otherwise vested by the Constitution.[111] Even at this early point, therefore, the Convention implicitly rejected the view advanced by Roger Sherman of "the Executive magistracy as nothing more than an institution for carrying the will of the Legislature into effect. . . ."[112]

On June 15, William Paterson presented the New Jersey Plan. It represented the position of the smaller states, and would have vested all the powers of the Confederation in the legislative branch. A multiple executive, chosen by the legislature, removable on application of a majority of state executives, and ineligible for reelection, would have been given a "general authority to execute the federal acts . . . to appoint all federal officers not otherwise provided for" in the Constitution, and "to direct all military operations" without the power of personal command.[113] Possibly as an antidote for this plan, and equally unacceptable, Alexander Hamilton advanced—without formally proposing—a radically different executive. His "Governour" was to be a single executive, chosen by an electoral college, to serve during good behavior, and to possess an absolute veto. The Senate, chosen indirectly and also for life, was given "the sole power of declaring war," with the "Governour" serving as commander-in-chief of wars "authorized or begun" and as manager of foreign affairs. "Let one executive be appointed who dares execute his powers," he said, who could then serve to check tyranny by either the "few" or the "many."[114]

The Convention turned to the task of choosing between the Virginia and New Jersey plans. It chose the former on June 19.[115] A debate followed on the Virginia Plan's prohibition of executive officeholding by legislators. The provision was supported by several members as necessary to avoid the "corruption" and influence wielded in Great Britain by the executive through its power over such offices. Nathaniel Gorham and Alexander Hamilton cautioned against assuming that such political largesse was entirely improper. "It was impossible to say what wd. be effect in G[reat] B[ritain] of such a reform as had been urged," said Hamilton. "[One] of the ablest politicians [Mr. Hume] had pronounced all that influence on the side of the crown, which went under the name of corruption, an essential part of the weight which maintained the equilibrium of the Constitution." But the clause prohibiting executive officeholding by legislators was sustained by a divided vote.[116]

James Wilson continued to press for election of the executive by the people or by an electoral college. One proposal for an electoral college that was especially favorable to the small states succeeded, but the decision was reversed after the distribution of electors was changed.[117] The notion of independent election, "mediately or immediately by the people," was gaining important adherents, however, which Wilson "perceived with pleasure. . . ." Madison had now made up his mind to support the idea, declaring: "It is essential . . . that the appointment of the Executive should either be drawn from some source, or held by some tenure, that will give him a free agency with regard to the Legislature." Gouverneur Morris warmly supported Wilson: "One great object of the Executive is to controul the Legislature," and election by the legislature would result in schemes within that branch to replace the President.[118]

James McClurg of Virginia made one more effort to define further the executive's powers before the Convention adjourned to allow the Committee on Detail to prepare a draft. He suggested that the committee be guided on whether the executive would have a military force to execute the laws, or command of the militia. Wilson supported this effort, but Rufus King's view that the matter should be left to the committee's "discretionary power" prevailed.[119] The Convention therefore presented the Committee on Detail with only a few resolutions, providing among other things for a single executive who would have a qualified veto, a general authority to execute the laws, and power to appoint officers, other than judges, whose appointments had not been provided for in the Constitution. The executive was to be elected by the legislature, however, for a seven-year term, with no eligibility for reelection and subject to impeachment.[120] Beyond these decisions, the committee had a reasonably clear mandate to avoid an executive that was a mere agent of the legislature, and some strong and influential statements in favor of executive control of the military, election by an electoral college with the possibility of reelection, and the general need for a check on the potential tyranny of the legislative branch.

The Committee on Detail worked for ten days, and presented the delegates a draft Constitution on August 6. The draft vested "The Executive Power of the United States . . . in a single Person," designated "President."[121] The same type of language was used in introducing the other two departments, suggesting that the committee, and Wilson—who proposed the wording—had no specific pro-executive plan in mind. On the other hand, the phrase derived from the New York Constitution, where it served to prevent legislative inroads,[122] so the committee may have wanted to make clear that the President's authority derived from the Constitution, and not from the legislature. The draft also made the President "Commander in Chief of the Army and Navy of the United States, and of the Militia of the several States," and empowered him to recommend legislation and to pardon except in cases of impeachment. At the same time the committee included in the legislature's powers authority to make foreign-relations decisions of importance, to "make war," to provide the means for war, and even "to call forth the aid of the militia, in order to execute the laws of the Union, enforce treaties, suppress insurrections, and repel invasions." The Senate was to send ambassadors, make treaties, and to possess with the House a concurrent veto over the President's election.[123]

The Convention took up the committee's draft, clause by clause. Discussion and decisions of arguable significance were scattered throughout the six weeks during which the Convention deliberated. An early debate on legislative secrecy suggests, for example, that at least Madison and Rutledge felt the Senate was to have an executive role.[124] James Wilson led an attack against granting the House sole authority to initiate revenue measures, using arguments that showed his awareness of the potential power in controlling revenues: "War, Commerce, & Revenue were the great objects of the Genl. Government. All of them are connected with money. The restriction in favor of the H. of Represts. would exclude the Senate from originating any important bills whatever." Randolph's response—that "the means of war" ought to remain in the less corruptible House—is equally instructive, reflecting an understanding that appropriations would be used to control military policy.[125]

Also debated were the issues of executive influence in connection with granting offices to legislators, and the veto power. A vote on the former question was deferred, though not without some forceful assertions on the President's need for influence;* as for the veto, Madison and Wilson lost their effort to join the Supreme Court to the executive in exercising the power, but the debate led to raising

---

*John Francis Mercer of Maryland said: "Governmts can only be maintained by *force* or *influence*," and inasmuch as the executive lacked force, to "deprive him of influence by rendering the members of the [legislature] ineligible to Executive offices" would reduce him to "a mere phantom of authority." 2 *Records* 284.

the proportion of votes required for overriding from two-thirds to three-fourths.[126] On August 15, Mercer suggested for the first time that treaties be made by the executive rather than the Senate, with congressional ratification a prerequisite before a treaty became law.[127]

The draft Constitution assigned Congress the power to "make" war. Charles Pinckney sought on August 17 to vest the power in the Senate alone; the Senate would be familiar with foreign affairs, it already had the power to make treaties of peace, and action by both houses would take too long. Pierce Butler responded that, if informed judgment and efficiency were the relevant criteria, he was "for vesting the power in the President, who will have all the requisite qualities, and will not make war but when the Nation will support it." Madison then "moved to insert '*declare*,' striking out '*make*' war; leaving to the Executive the power to repel sudden attacks." Sherman apparently assumed the President already had power to repel attacks. He thought the clause "stood very well. The Executive shd. be able to repel and not to commence war. 'Make' better than 'declare' the latter narrowing the power too much."[128]

Elbridge Gerry from Massachusetts, who seconded Madison's motion to substitute "declare" for "make," attacked Butler's suggestion: he "never expected to hear in a republic a motion to empower the Executive alone to declare war." Ellsworth then spoke against Pinckney's motion to give the power of war to the Senate. "[T]here is a material difference," he said, "between the cases of making *war*, and making *peace*. It shd. be more easy to get out of war, then into it. War also is a simple and overt declaration. Peace attended with intricate & secret negociations." George Mason of Virginia also was for clogging war and facilitating peace, and therefore "was agst giving the power of war to the Executive, because not (safely) to be trusted with it; or to the Senate, because not so constructed as to be entitled to it." He added that "he preferred '*declare*' to '*make*,'" and Rufus King concurred because "'*make*' war might be understood to 'conduct' it which was an Executive function."[129]

Pinckney's suggestion that the Senate be given the power to make war was rejected overwhelmingly, but Madison's motion to change "make" for "declare" was approved.[130] The change was intended by Madison and Gerry to enable the President to respond to "sudden attacks" without a declaration of war, and by King and others to leave the conduct of war in executive hands. They therefore appear to have intended the clause to authorize the President to defend the United States from attack without consulting the legislature, at least where the attack is so "sudden" that consulta-

tion might jeopardize the nation. But nothing in the change sig-
nifies an intent to allow the President a general authority to "make"
war in the absence of a declaration; indeed, granting the exceptional
power suggests that the general power over war was left in the
legislative branch.[131]

The status of military actions short of war was touched on the
next day, August 18. The Committee on Detail had failed to include
in its list of legislative powers authority to issue letters of marque
and reprisal, which the Articles of Confederation had vested in the
old Congress. Pinckney included the item on a list of "legislative"
powers to submit to the Convention's consideration. Gerry wanted
something "inserted concerning letters of marque, which he thought
not included in the power of war." Pinckney's proposal was agreed
to without further discussion.[132]

The early Convention debates cast virtually no light on the Framers'
understanding of what functions—as opposed to abstract powers—
would be vested in the executive. Were the secretaries, boards and
agencies set up by the Continental Congress to continue under the
control of Congress or become agents of the President? Gouverneur
Morris said early in the proceedings, on July 19, that "there must be
certain great officers of State; a minister of finance, of war, of foreign affairs &c. These he presumes will exercise their functions in
subordination to the executive, and will be amenable by impeachment to the public Justice. Without these ministers the executive
can do nothing of consequence."[133] On August 14, Mercer suggested
a council composed of "members of both Houses." Ellsworth proposed on August 18 a council with members from all three branches,
who "should advise but not conclude the President." Charles Pinckney
wished to have the President free "to call for advice or not as he
might chuse," and warned of the danger that an able council would
thwart the President, while a weak one would enable him to shelter
himself under their sanction.[134]

These comments indicate that Morris, Ellsworth, and Pinckney
contemplated a council with no power to prevent the executive from
any action. Mercer's view was less clear, and may explain Gerry's assertion that he "was agst. letting the heads of the departments . . . have
anything to do in business connected with legislation," presumably
referring to the power to veto laws. John Dickinson, on the other
hand, wanted truly independent advisors, and urged that their
appointment be made by the legislature. The subject was then deferred.[135]

On August 20 Morris formally proposed a "Council of State," consisting of the Chief Justice and the secretaries of Domestic Affairs,
Foreign Affairs, War, Marine, and Commerce and Finance. This

council was not a Cabinet with whom the President was to share power. Rather, the secretaries were to be appointed by the President and to "hold office during pleasure," unless impeached. The functions contemplated for the secretaries of Foreign Affairs and War were essentially those performed under the Confederation in 1787. The President would be able to submit any matter to the Council, and to require written opinions of its members. "But he shall in all cases exercise his own judgment. . . ." This motion, therefore, would have had the Convention recognize as executive functions the day-to-day management of fiscal, foreign, and military affairs, and anticipated a substantial role for the executive in drafting and proposing legislation.[136]

Though highly favorable to executive authority, the proposal did contain elements that might have been construed as potentially conflict-producing. The secretaries had constitutional status, and each was specifically made "responsible for his opinion on the affairs relating to his particular Department."[137] This structure might have enabled the President to evade responsibility himself, even though he would not be bound by their advice. Furthermore, it set up a detailed scheme of government in advance, instead of allowing the legislature to decide from time to time what officers or agencies were desirable, and what functions to delegate to them.

The Convention referred Morris's proposal to the Committee on Detail, which offered a revision on August 22. The committee proposed that the President "shall have a Privy-Council" consisting of the officers described in Morris's proposal, plus the President of the Senate and the Speaker of the House. Their duty would be "to advise him in matters respecting the execution of his office, which he shall think proper to lay before them: But their advice shall not conclude him, nor affect his responsibility for the measures which he shall adopt."[138] This language clearly contemplated executive departments, whose heads would be subordinate to the President. But it gave them no constitutional status, left Congress able to control their functions, and sought to place responsibility for all decisions squarely on the President.

The Convention put off action once again. Members unsuccessfully sought at various points to create an executive council that would have far more power than suggested by Morris and the Committee on Detail.[139] The matter was finally referred to the Brearley Committee,* which reported back a brief provision authorizing the

*This committee, also known as the Committee of Eleven, consisted of Chairman David Brearley of New York, Nicholas Gilman of New Hampshire, Rufus King of Massachusetts, Roger Sherman of Connecticut, Gouverneur

President to "require the opinion in writing of the principal officer in each of the executive departments, upon any subject relating to the duties of their respective offices." Morris, a committee member, explained its decision to omit a council of any sort: "It was judged that the Presidt. by persuading his Council—to concur in his wrong measures would acquire their protection for them." The committee's language, suggesting that executive departments would be created, but leaving their number, form, and functions to legislation, became Article II, section 2 of the Constitution.[140]

Meanwhile, the Convention turned to the treaty power. The Committee on Detail had assigned this power exclusively to the Senate, which could adopt treaties by majority vote.[141] This allocation operated in favor of the small states, and was inconsistent with practice under the Confederation, where nine of thirteen states had to approve treaties and where the Secretary of Foreign Affairs and other agents were used to handle negotiations. Dissatisfied rumblings were heard at various points against Senate control of treaties.[142] Debate began in earnest on August 23, with an effort to allocate parts of the treaty power to branches other than the Senate. Madison observed "that the Senate represented the States alone, and that for this as well as other obvious reasons it was proper that the President should be an agent in treaties." His suggestion evoked no comment, apparently because of general agreement that a national spokesman and negotiator was necessary. Madison seems to have had more in mind for the President than simply to serve the Senate's will, as Congress's agents were expected to do under the Confederation. The President could represent the national interest—as opposed to the interests of individual states—and therefore would become an agent of the nation in treaty formulation, rather than of the Senate. Morris followed with a far more controversial effort to provide that, before any treaty would be "binding," it would have to be ratified by a law, passed by both houses of Congress. He received some distinguished support, but his motion failed.[143]

The treaty clause was eventually submitted to the Brearley Committee, which dealt with the matter along with other unfinished business, most notably the power of appointment. It recommended three important changes in the preexisting allocation: that the President be empowered to make treaties, with the "advice and consent" of the Senate; that the President make most important appointments, also subject to the "advice and consent" of the Senate; and

---

Morris of Pennsylvania, John Dickinson of Delaware, Daniel Carroll of Maryland, James Madison of Virginia, Hugh Williamson of North Carolina, Pierce Butler of South Carolina, and Abraham Baldwin of Georgia. 2 *Records* 473 (Journal).

that Senate approval in these matters be based on a two-thirds vote of the members present.[144] The President would thereby be given the role of negotiating treaties, and also substantial capacity to control the executive departments and to distribute largesse. His treaties and nominations would be subject to Senate approval, however, by an extraordinary majority so as to enable a substantial minority of the states to block decisions felt to be detrimental to their interests.

When the Brearley Committee's recommendation was reported to the Convention, James Wilson renewed the effort to require House concurrence to all treaties. Wilson argued that as treaties "are to have the operation of laws, they ought to have the sanction of laws also. The circumstance of secrecy in the business of treaties formed the only objection," he said, but this was outweighed by the necessity of the legislative sanction. John Sherman replied that "the necessity of secrecy in the case of treaties forbade a reference of them to the whole Legislature." Wilson's amendment was defeated, one state to ten.[145]

The Brearley Committee's proposal to require a two-thirds vote for treaty approval received intensive attention. Efforts were made: to except from the two-thirds requirement "treaties of peace," in order to facilitate an end to any conflict; to enable the Senate to adopt treaties of peace by a two-thirds vote even without the President's concurrence; and to eliminate entirely the two-thirds rule, requiring only majority approval.[146] All these attempts ultimately failed, and the provision was included in the Constitution in virtually the committee's language.

The proposal to enable two-thirds of the Senate to make a treaty of peace against the President's will met objections that reflected an understanding that Congress could control war-making through its exercise of other powers. Thus Gorham "thought the precaution unnecessary as the means of carrying on the war would not be in the hands of the President, but of the Legislature." Gouverneur Morris "thought the power of the President in this case harmless. . . ." He added that "no peace ought to be made without the concurrence of the President, who was the general Guardian of the National interests." Others noted the danger that important interests might be surrendered in treaties of peace, as in any other form of treaty.[147] The Convention's action, therefore, implies that no treaty of any sort could be made without executive approval, but it also reflects a recognition that the President could not realistically pursue a war (or any other diplomatic policy requiring "means") that even one branch of Congress was resolved against.

When the Convention discussed the two-thirds rule in general, those seeking its change were concerned with the possibility that the Senate, rather than the President, would abuse its projected power by refusing to accede to majority will. They noted that the minority had less to fear under the new Constitution than under the Articles of Confederation; "as the Executive was here joined in the business," said Rufus King, "there was a check which did not exist in [the Confederation] Congress where only the concurrence of 2/3 was required."[148] No one questioned these assertions, but the Convention majority voted to retain the two-thirds requirement. The members therefore appear to have assumed that the Senate (and Congress) would indeed be able, and were expected to attempt, to make foreign policy; the two-thirds requirement was retained to check the Senate majority in such efforts.

Little debate arose on the committee's grant to the President of the power to nominate most important officers, including ambassadors. This proposal marked a sharp break with all prior positions advanced except Hamilton's.[149] The President would choose the nation's representatives in foreign affairs, subject to Senate approval, whereas the old Congress—and until September 1787 the proposed Senate—had exclusive control over who represented the nation. Ambassadors remained agents of the nation, in the sense they could be criticized or even impeached for their acts. But they were given office through the President's nomination, and were meant to function under his direction.

Several other changes, some of great significance, were made with little or no discussion in the Convention's final days. The powers to grant letters of marque and reprisal and to regulate captures were assigned to Congress. Power over trade and tariffs was also assigned to the legislature, with one delegate recognizing that an embargo could be the equivalent of war.[150] The commander-in-chief clause was approved as recommended by the Committee on Detail, except that the President's control of the militia was limited to times "when called into actual service of the U—S—."[151] Totally missing was any debate that would have accompanied an understanding of the commander-in-chief clause as creating an undefined reservoir of power to use the military in situations unauthorized by Congress.

Two other actions did, however, further increase the executive's potential power—the shift from legislative election of the President to the electoral college, and a change in the vesting clause of Article I. The Committee on Detail had retained the provision vesting election of the President in the legislature. But when the Convention changed the formula by which the President's election was to take place from a ballot of the Senate to a joint ballot of both houses, the small states were deprived of the advantage that legislative election could provide them. Morris moved swiftly to capitalize on the situation by renewing his proposal to select the President on the votes of electors chosen by the people. After some inconclusive votes, the issue was sent to the Brearley Committee, which proposed that the President be elected by majority vote of an electoral college composed of electors selected by each state in such manner as the state legislature should determine. The committee also recommended that he serve a four-year term, without restriction on reelection, and be subject to impeachment on conviction of treason or bribery by a two-thirds vote of the Senate. With little further debate, and some relatively minor changes, this scheme was adopted.[152] The President thereby acquired a political base independent of the Congress, making the office unmistakably more than an arm of the legislature. On the other hand, the Convention broadened the grounds for impeachment, perhaps reflecting an awareness of the President's independent powers, and the corresponding need for legislative check.

Toward the end of the Convention, on September 8, 1787, a committee was selected to revise the style, and rearrange the content, of the provisions adopted at that point. The drafting was entrusted to Morris, who later admitted to making changes designed to attain objectives that he favored without appearing to violate any of the Convention's agreements.[153] Among other things, he changed the vesting clause of Article I of the draft Constitution to indicate that the legislature's authority was limited to the powers enumerated in that article.* At the same time, he left unchanged the vesting clause of Article II that simply granted "the executive power" to a President. This language of Article II could not be given great significance when originally adopted by the Committee on Detail, because similar language was simultaneously adopted concerning the legislative power. But when Morris eliminated the possibility of any implied, unenumerated grants in Article I, he created the basis for a reasonable argument that the vesting clause of Article II was in fact meant to vest all "executive power" not otherwise withheld. The argument is logical enough. It needs qualification, however, because what Morris may have secretly intended can hardly be attributed to the Convention as a whole, or to anyone for that matter but Morris.[154] And under no circumstances does the argument allow any strong basis for claiming an implied grant of powers inconsistent with specific grants to other branches.

In conclusion, the Framers may have been primarily concerned

---

*Article I begins, "All legislative Powers herein granted. . . ."

with increasing the national government's powers, but in the process they gave considerable attention to how those new powers would be allocated among the branches. The early plans anticipated a weak executive, but Wilson, Morris, Hamilton and others convinced the Convention by degrees to create a unitary and independent executive, with considerable powers. Only a strong executive, they contended, could assure a balanced government.[155]

Nothing in the Convention proceedings is inconsistent with the Constitution's apparent grants to Congress of overwhelming authority to control all military decisions other than tactical. But the President was left with important war-related powers. The change of "make" to "declare" was designed to allow the President to defend the United States and to control the conduct of authorized actions, both responsibilities having the potential for growth. Furthermore, the Convention rejected an effort to enable the legislature to define the content of "executive power," and to limit the legislature's authority to delegate "legislative" or "judicial" power to the executive. This left the President a strong basis for claiming in future controversies that Congress had overstepped its authority by interfering with his constitutional powers. It also left the Constitution void of explicit restraints on Congress's power to delegate broad authority to the President, or to acquiesce in his assumption of greater authority than Convention members may have contemplated.

THE RATIFICATION PROCESS

The Convention adjourned on September 17, 1787. Thirty-nine delegates signed the proposed Constitution of the United States, and submitted it to Congress with what could only be their "opinion" that the new government should begin to function when nine states had ratified. The proposed Constitution's great innovation was a national government with authority to regulate commerce, raise revenues, and handle foreign relations. This new government would be able to recruit and supply armies or call forth the militia, to put down insurrections such as Shays's Rebellion or the mutiny of Confederation soldiers, and to defend against Indians and foreign nations. The proposed government, then, was a radical innovation, albeit designed in part to serve the ends of the dominant economic classes. Three delegates refused to sign, protesting what they regarded as a gross departure from the Convention's delegated authority to revise the Articles of Confederation.[156]

Ratification by nine states was far from a foregone conclusion. One of the thirteen states—Rhode Island—had refused even to be represented at the Convention, and only ratified the Constitution in 1790. Of the remaining twelve states, at least four seem to have been leaning against ratification when the Constitution was circulated for consideration, including the indispensable states of Massachusetts, New York, and Virginia.[157] A monumental political battle ensued. The Constitution's supporters—the Federalists—closed ranks. Men as diverse in their views as Hamilton, Madison and Jay worked together on the *Federalist Papers*, their differences subordinated to the need to secure adoption. Convention delegates returned to their states to become advocates for a document that almost inevitably contained provisions they had strenuously opposed. In the process, they (and the Constitution's opponents) built a record of their understandings invaluable for interpreting the Constitution,* but necessarily colored by their desire to sway the state conventions.

The record of the ratification period is, considering all the debate that took place, sketchy. Several extensive examinations of the proposed government were presented, but of these only one—*The Federalist Papers*—could be termed both comprehensive and analytical.[158] Most other evidence of the period consists of speeches or pamphlets made and issued in the heat of convention debate. It is the *Federalist*, as Jefferson said in 1825, "to which appeal is habitually made by all, and rarely declined or denied by any as evidence of the general opinion of those who framed and of those who accepted the Constitution. . . ."[159] Though its influence on the ratification process can never fully be known, and is probably exaggerated, it played a substantial role in the victories in New York and Virginia.[160] Whatever its specific impact, these papers are widely regarded by historians of all subsequent generations as having captured with a high degree of accuracy the spirit and intent of a broad spectrum of the Constitution's draftsmen and advocates.[161]

Hamilton wrote the early numbers of the *Federalist* to demonstrate the inadequacies of the Articles of Confederation, and to establish

---

*Madison urged in 1796: "If we were to look . . . for the [Constitution's] meaning beyond the face of the instrument, we must look for it, not in the General Convention which proposed, but in the State Conventions which accepted and ratified the Constitution." 5 *Annals of Congress* 776 (April 6, 1796). Albert Gallatin of Pennsylvania said during the same debate (*id.* 734):

The gentlemen who formed the general Convention, however respectable, entitled as they were to the thanks and gratitude of their country for their services in general, and especially on that important occasion, were not of those who made, who passed the instrument; they only drew it and proposed it. The people and the State Conventions who ratified who adopted the instrument, are alone parties to it, and their intentions alone might, with any degree of propriety, be resorted to.

the need for a national government with power to declare war, to raise armies, and to enforce its commands upon individual citizens.[162] These became the most persistently debated questions during the ratification period; the distribution of power among the branches of the proposed federal government was a secondary matter, as it had been during the Convention itself.[163]

Opponents argued that the power to make war should be shared with the states,[164] and that the new government would be led to maintain a large standing army, against the dangers of which the Constitution had failed to provide.* Hamilton questioned the assumption that greater forces would be needed under the new government, but essentially accepted the wisdom of having whatever force necessary to prevent disturbances such as had occurred in Massachusetts and Pennsylvania under the Confederation. Indeed, he anticipated that the nation would someday have far-flung commercial operations, and that a strong navy, as well as an army for border protection, would be essential and desirable.† He argued that the two-year limit on military appropriations would prevent the legislature from vesting "in the executive department permanent funds for the support of an army, if they were ever incautious enough to be willing to repose in it so improper a confidence,"** and he ridiculed

---

*Several states proposed amendments extending state control over creation of a standing army and further defining the circumstances determining its establishment. 1 *Elliot's Debates supra* note 20 at 325-28, 336-37; 2 *id.* 406, 545; 3 *id.* 660; 4 *id.* 245. Patrick Henry and Elbridge Gerry predicted dire consequences—a government of force. 3 *id.* 410-11; "Observations of Elbridge Gerry," in P. Ford, ed., *Pamphlets on the Constitution of the United States* 10 (1968 reprint). Hamilton noted that the British tradition against standing armies involved troops raised without legislative approval; the President had no such power. *Federalist* Nos. 24 and 26. Others noted that such a prohibition would make it extremely difficult to defend the nation effectively. P. Ford, *supra* at 235 (Alexander C. Hanson); J. McMaster & F. Stone, *Pennsylvania and the Federal Constitution 1787-1788*, at 373 (1888) (Thomas McKean). Noah Webster wrote: "There is as little necessity to guard against them [standing armies] by positive constitution, as to prohibit the establishment of the Mahometan religion." P. Ford, *supra* at 52.

†See *Federalist* No. 24 (Hamilton). In *Federalist* No. 4 at 47, John Jay stressed the need for a strong military deterrent to back up negotiations on commercial matters and boundary problems:

> Wisely, therefore, do the . . . [people of America] consider union and a good national government as necessary to put and keep them in *such a situation* as, instead of *inviting* war, will tend to repress and discourage it. That situation consists in the best possible state of defense, and necessarily depends on the government, the arms, and the resources of the country.

**Federalist* No. 26 at 171 (Hamilton). Richard Henry Lee, in "Letters from the Federal Farmer," wrote that the two-year limitation on appropriations would be ineffective: "[I]f a subsequent congress do not within the two years renew the appropriation, or further appropriate monies for the use of the army, the

the notion that the Constitution was defective because it failed to prohibit the President from assuming command in the field. Madison covered much the same ground, beginning in *Federalist* No. 37, defending the entire quantum of authority proposed for the federal government, including the "indefinite power" to raise troops and to control foreign relations.[165] He minimized the allocation, arguing that the Constitution was merely seeking to invigorate powers conferred by the Articles of Confederation rather than to create new ones.[166]

"Publius" (the pseudonym used by the three authors of the *Federalist Papers*) turned to the second category of questions confronting Constitutionalists—the division of federal authority. Madison dealt first with the general objection that the plan failed to separate properly the powers involved.[167] The proposed plan, Madison assured his readers, did not violate the principle of separation as properly understood. Montesquieu had modeled his theory on the British system, Madison observed, in which a strict separation by type of power was not attempted. The genius of the British system, in fact, consisted of its "mixing" of powers, in order to prevent tyranny, which exists when one branch exercises the whole power of another branch, not just a part of that power. "Mixing" therefore was not merely desirable but indispensable to maintain a sufficient degree of separation in practice. "Parchment barriers"—presumably even the device of enumerating powers Madison had earlier noted[168]—would not suffice to control the conduct of politicians. Furthermore, appeals to the people had proved impractical and unreliable in themselves to prevent a tyranny of one branch or the other.[169] The legislature would, unless effectively restrained, assume control of all governmental power, as in Virginia and Pennsylvania, resulting, as Hamilton described it, in an "execrable" form of government.[170] By contrast, executive usurpations were far less fearful, since experience indicated they were usually produced by necessity and that the actions taken generally represented what the legislature would itself have done or authorized. The legislature possessed the power of the purse, which under the proposed plan would be even more overwhelming than in Britain, where the King at least in theory had offsetting prerogatives.[171]

Paper protections—"exterior provisions"—therefore were inadequate to assure proper balance among the branches. The Convention was consequently led, Madison said, to attempt to create an "interior

---

army will be left to take care of itself. When an army shall be once raised for a number of years, it is not probable that it will find much difficulty in getting congress to pass laws for applying monies to its support." C. Kenyon, ed., *The Antifederalists* 227 (1966).

structure" with constituent parts that would keep each other in their proper places.* This could be achieved, first by assuring that each department had a will of its own, which in turn required independent elections wherever possible; and second by making each branch as independent as possible of the others for the emoluments of office. The "great security," however, was to give each branch the constitutional means and the personal motives to resist encroachments on its functions by the others. "Ambition must be made to counteract ambition. The interest of the man must be connected with the constitutional rights of the place."[172]

Madison recognized that his approach suggested at best an unflattering view of human nature, and the *Federalist Papers* are permeated with great skepticism of the human capacity to act responsibly and to resist temptations to seek greater power.† But he unabashedly

---

*The same theme was struck by Roger Sherman, writing in the *New Haven Gazette* on December 25, 1788, in *Essays, supra* note 158 at 240:

> It is by some objected, that the executive is blended with the legislature, and that those powers ought to be entirely distinct and unconnected, but is not this a gross error in politics? The united wisdom and various interests of a nation should be combined in framing the laws. But the execution of them should not be in the whole legislature; that would be too troublesome and expensive; but it will not thence follow that the Executive should have no voice or influence in legislation. The executive in Great Britain is one branch of the legislature, and has a negative on all laws; perhaps that is an extreme not to be imitated by a republic, but the partial negative vested in the President by the new constitution on the acts of Congress and the subsequent revision, may be very useful to prevent laws being passed without mature deliberation.

Noah Webster wrote to the same effect (P. Ford, *Pamphlets, supra* at 42):

> The separation of the legislature divides the power—checks—restrains—amends the proceedings—at the same time, it creates no division of interest, that can tempt either branch to encroach upon the other, or upon the people. In turbulent times, such restraint is our greatest safety—in calm times, and in measures calculated for the general good, both branches must always be unanimous.

†Thus Hamilton commented on his own criticism of anti-Federalists: "We are not always sure that those who advocate the truth are influenced by purer principles than their antagonists. Ambition, avarice, personal animosity, party opposition, and many other motives not more laudable than these, are apt to operate" equally on both sides. *Federalist* No. 1, at 34. In *Federalist* No. 4, Jay wrote of the tendency in man to make war:

> It is too true, however disgraceful it may be to human nature, that nations in general will make war whenever they have a prospect of getting anything by it; nay, that absolute monarchs will often make war when their nations are to get nothing by it, but for purposes and objects merely personal, such as a thirst for military glory, revenge for personal affronts, ambition, or private compacts to aggrandize or support their particular families or partisans. These and a variety of other motives, which affect only the mind of the sovereign, often lead him to engage in wars not sanctified by justice or the voice and interests of his people.

accepted the implications of "this policy of supplying, by opposite and rival interests, the defect of better motives." He continued:

> But what is government itself but the greatest of all reflections on human nature? If men were angels, no government would be necessary. If angels were to govern men, neither external nor internal controls of government would be necessary. In framing a government which is to be administered by men over men, the great difficulty lies in this: you must first enable the government to control the governed; and in the next place oblige it to control itself. A dependence on the people is, no doubt, the primary control on the government; but experience has taught mankind the necessity of auxiliary precautions.

This mixing of powers could not, however, achieve an absolute balance, in Madison's view. "In republican government, the legislative authority necessarily predominates." Two steps in particular were therefore necessary: to divide the legislature into two very different branches, and to fortify the executive through such devices as a power to veto laws.[173]

A theoretical framework established, Madison turned to a discussion of the three branches, and the powers assigned to each. The House of Representatives, Madison noted, had been reserved a role in foreign affairs, even regarding treaties, where legislative sanction was necessary, though he did not specify the situations he had in mind.[174] The principal power of the House, however, was its authority to originate money bills and to pass on all appropriations. This "most complete and effectual weapon" would enable the House to defend even against attempts of the Senate to shift the constitutional balance.[175] Similar discussion of the Senate identified that body as representing, to other nations, the "national character," and as possessing powers essential to avoid corruption in treaties or appointments by assuring a "joint agency" in those functions.[176]

In *Federalist* No. 67, Hamilton opened a systematic examination of the executive, though earlier papers, especially those concerning

---

Madison was no less skeptical, as evidenced by his classic analysis of faction, "the latent causes" of which he found were "sown in the nature of man." He thought it "vain to say that enlightened statement will be able to adjust these clashing interests and render them all subservient to the public good." The only solution was to control the "effects" of faction, which could be accomplished through a representative government of divided powers, rather than a democracy. *Federalist* No. 10, at 79–81. Cecelia M. Kenyon has shown that this outlook was fully shared by the anti-Federalists. "Men of Little Faith: The Anti-Federalists on the Nature of Representative Government," in G. Wood, *supra* note 52 at 64–65. "No theory was more representative of the time than the theory of faction." V. Parrington, "The Great Debate," in E. Latham, ed., *supra* note 58 at 66.

the treaty power, had also commented on the President's authority. Hamilton's first objective was to deal with the contentions of many anti-Federalists that the President would be a monarch.* He summed up the claimed differences in No. 69:

> The President of the United States would be an officer elected by the people for four years; the king of Great Britain is a perpetual and *hereditary* prince. The one would be amenable to personal punishment and disgrace; the person of the other is sacred and inviolable. The one would have a *qualified* negative upon the acts of the legislative body; the other has an *absolute* negative. The one would have a right to command the military and naval forces of the nation; the other, in addition to this right, possesses that of *declaring* war, and of *raising* and *regulating* fleets and armies by his own authority. The one would have a concurrent power with a branch of the legislature in the formation of treaties; the other is the *sole possession* of the power of making treaties. The one would have a like concurrent authority in appointing offices; the other is the sole author of all appointments. The one can confer no privileges whatever; the other can make denizens of aliens, noblemen of commoners; can erect corporations with all the rights incident to corporate bodies. The one can prescribe no rules concerning the commerce or currency of the nation; the other is in several respects the arbiter of commerce, and in this capacity can establish markets and fairs, can regulate weights and measures, can lay embargoes for a limited time, can coin money, can authorize or prohibit the circulation of foreign coin. The one has no particle of spiritual jurisdiction; the

---

*For example, a New York anti-Federalist writing under the sobriquet of "Old Whig" wrote:

> [T]he office of president of the United States appears to me to be clothed with such powers as are dangerous. To be the fountain of all honors in the United States—commander in chief of the army, navy, and militia; with the power of making treaties and of granting pardons . . . is in reality to be a king, as much a king as the king of Great Britain.

The Antifederalist Papers 204 (M. Borden, ed. 1965).
Pennsylvania anti-Federalist Benjamin Workman, writing as "Philadelphiensis," cried (*id.* 212-13):

> Who can deny but the *president general* will be a king to all intents and purposes, and one of the most dangerous kind too—a king elected to command a standing army. . . . The thoughts of a military officer possessing such powers, as the proposed constitution vests in the president general, are sufficient to excite in the mind of a freeman the most alarming apprehensions. . . . This tyrant . . . can at any time he thinks proper, order him out the militia to exercise, and to march when and where he pleases.

Jefferson wrote to John Adams that the executive was powerful and responsible to virtually no one—"a bad edition of a Polish King." Letter of Nov. 13, 1787, in 1 *Adams-Jefferson Letters* 211-12 (L. Cappon, ed. 1959). In addition, a strong antimonarchical feeling was generally felt. *See* L. Dunbar, *A Study of "Monarchical Tendencies" in the United States from 1776 to 1801* (1922); Main, *supra* note 157 at 141.

other is the supreme head and governor of the national church! What answer shall we give to those who would persuade us that things so unlike resemble each other?[177]

Impressive as this catalog appears, Hamilton's comparison was between a President whose powers had yet to be ascertained in practice, and a King whom history had shown to lack the very powers claimed as his prerogative. No King since Charles II had sought to veto a law, to raise armies or to declare war without Parliament's approval, as Governor George Clinton noted in his "Letters of Cato."* Hamilton responded that "The disuse of that power [the veto] for a considerable time past does not affect the reality of its existence and is to be ascribed wholly to the crown's having found the means of substituting influence for authority. . . ."[178] George III was undoubtedly perceived by many Americans as attempting to reinvigorate the monarchy. But his substitution of influence for authority was not a voluntary, purely tactical move. Influence had become by 1787 the only means possessed by a King for accomplishing his objectives; ultimate authority lay in Parliament, largely in the hands of the majority party in Commons. The British legislature had demonstrated that their hereditary, unimpeachable monarch could be removed and replaced with far less ceremony than Congress would have to invoke before impeaching their independently elected President.

Having cataloged the differences between President and King, designed to show the President as the far less powerful, Hamilton immediately turned to the task of showing that the President would be "vigorous." "Energy in the executive is a leading character in the definition of good government. It is essential to the protection of the community against foreign attacks; . . . to the steady administration of the laws; to the protection of property . . . ; to the security of liberty against the enterprises and assaults of ambition, of faction, and of anarchy." A vigorous executive was not at all inconsistent with "the genius of republican government."[179]

How was such an executive to be assured? In the same way Madison had suggested: by giving him a will of his own, adequate financial

*He said in Letter No. IV (*Essays supra* note 158 at 263-64): "[T]hough it may be asserted that the king of Great Britain has the express power of making peace or war, yet he never thinks it prudent to do so without the advice of his Parliament, from whom he is to derive his support, and therefore these powers in both president and king are substantially the same: he is the generalissimo of the nation, and of course has the command and control of the army, navy and militia; he is the general conservator of the peace of the union—he may pardon all offences, except in cases of impeachment, and is the principal foundation of all offices and employments. Will not the exercise of these powers therefore tend either to the establishment of a vile and arbitrary aristocracy or monarchy?"

security, and powers competent to his tasks. An independent will was secured by the Convention's rejecting proposals for a multiple executive, or for a council whose approval the President would have to seek on important matters. As for the danger in having a single executive, Hamilton contended that "the executive power is more easily confined when it is one"—a "single object for the jealousy and watchfulness of the people"—and that a multiple executive might, because of their "united credit and influence" be "more formidable to liberty. . . ."[180]

Duration was an issue intensely debated by the Convention. Hamilton explained the Constitution's provisions as having been designed to secure "personal firmness of the executive magistrate in the employment of his constitutional powers, and . . . stability of the system of administration which may have been adopted under his auspices." A President who served a short term and stood no chance of being reelected would be too little inclined to protect and use his powers. Such a President might be "too little interested in . . . [the office] to hazard any material censure or perplexity from the independent exertion of his powers, or from encountering the ill-humors, however transient, . . . either in a considerable part of the society itself, or even in a predominant faction in the legislative body."[181]

"There are some," Hamilton noted, who are inclined to regard the "servile pliancy" of an executive "to a prevailing current, either in the community or in the legislature, as its best recommendation. But such men entertain crude notions, as well of the purposes for which government was instituted, as of the true means by which the public happiness may be promoted." Though the republican principle demands that the "deliberate sense" of the community govern elected officials, "it does not require an unqualified complaisance to every sudden breeze of passion, or to every transient impulse which the people may receive from the arts of men, who flatter their prejudices to betray their interests." In situations where "the interests of the people are at variance with their inclinations, it is the duty of the persons whom they have appointed to be the guardian of those interests to withstand the temporary delusion in order to give them time and opportunity for more cool and sedate reflection."[182]

These comments, reflecting the need for independence of the executive from the will of the people, were guarded and restrained compared to Hamilton's view of the need for independence from the legislative will. "[H]owever inclined we might be to insist upon an unbounded complaisance in the executive to the inclinations of the people, we can with no propriety contend for a like complaisance to the humors of the legislature." When the people either disagreed with the legislature, or were entirely neutral, "it is certainly desirable that the executive should be in a situation to dare to act his own opinion with vigor and decision." The partition between the branches must be more than nominal; it must be contrived "to render the one independent of the other. . . . It is one thing to be subordinate to the laws, and another to be dependent on the legislative body. The first comports with, the last violates, the fundamental principles of good government; and whatever may be the forms of the Constitution, unites all power in the same hands." A reasonable duration in office—four years—and the possibility of reelection would help in assuring an executive capable of combating "the tendency of the legislative authority to absorb every other. . . .* Certainly there was nothing to fear from a four-year term, said Hamilton, since if Commons could have "reduced the prerogatives of the crown, . . . abolish both the royalty and aristocracy, . . . [and] make the monarch tremble," then the great fear concerning "an elective magistrate of four years' duration with the confined authorities of a President . . . [was] that he might be unequal to the task which the Constitution assigns him. . . ."[183]

Hamilton's arguments supporting the President's eligibility for reelection are equally interesting. The administration of government, he said, is largely executive:

> The actual conduct of foreign negotiations, the preparatory plans of finance, the application and disbursement of the public moneys in conformity to the general appropriations of the legislature, the arrangement of the army and navy, the direction of the operations of war—these, and other matters of a like nature, constitute what seems to be most properly understood by the administration of government.

A prompt turnover in the presidency would tend to cause changes in the men who manage the nation's affairs, thereby occasioning "a

---

*His comments on legislative power were particularly caustic (*Federalist* No. 75 at 433):

> In governments purely republican, this tendency is almost irresistible. The representatives of the people, in a popular assembly, seem sometimes to fancy that they are the people themselves, and betray strong symptoms of impatience and disgust at the least sign of opposition from any other quarter; as if the exercise of its rights, by either the executive or judiciary, were a breach of their privilege and an outrage to their dignity. They often appear disposed to exert an imperious control over the other departments; and as they commonly have the people on their side, they always act with such momentum as to make it very difficult for the other members of the government to maintain the balance of the Constitution.

disgraceful and ruinous mutability in the administration of government." A positive duration of considerable extent, and reeligibility, would each help preserve stability and experience. Nor would reeligibility necessarily lead to less independence or greater ambition in the President. The ineligible executive might be less responsible and all the more dangerous because he could not lawfully prolong himself in power.[184]

Adequate means for the President's support were assured in the plan by making his salary unchangeable while in office. The "great security" against legislative tyranny, though, was to grant the President powers competent to enable him to defend his constitutionally assigned place. The discussions of these powers in the *Federalist* convey important impressions of the Framers' expectations. First, the veto was necessary, since a "mere parchment delineation" would be insufficient to check the legislature's "propensity" to extend their power. That it could be used to negate good as well as bad laws was recognized, but its excessive use seemed unlikely because of the "superior weight and influence of the legislative body, . . . and the hazard to the executive in a trial of strength."[185] The President's power to require opinions of his officers was implicit in his control of administration.[186] The power to nominate was necessary, since a single executive was more likely to propose able people than a multimember legislature, and in any case was always subject to Senate check.[187] The power to remove, though arguably necessary to assure responsibility of officers to the President, was apparently seen as subject to Senate confirmation as well.[188] The clause concerning "giving information to Congress" was treated perfunctorily, but as an executive power rather than a duty.[189] The power to receive ambassadors, "though it has been a rich theme of declamation, is more a matter of dignity than authority."[190] In defending the pardon power Hamilton justified its inclusion in the Constitution partly on the ground that it was "questionable, whether, in a limited Constitution, that power could be delegated by law. . . ."[191]

The commander-in-chief power received extraordinarily short treatment, considering its subsequent importance. What was said contained no hint of any authority based on this provision to use the armed forces without legislative approval. Thus Hamilton pronounced the propriety of the provision "so evident in itself," and so consonant with state practice, "that little need be said to explain or enforce it. . . . The direction of war ('which implies the direction of the common strength') most peculiarly demands those qualities which distinguish the exercise of power by a single hand."* Yet this was no mean prerogative, and had Hamilton anticipated situations other than outright war, in which an executive might tenably have rested on this power, it seems likely that he would have avoided discussing them in a work designed to reassure. Furthermore, no limits were suggested on the legislature's power to authorize military actions by statute or even treaty.

John Jay, who had years of experience as Secretary of Foreign Affairs during the Confederation, took his turn as "Publius" to discuss the treaty power. He recognized the Senate's power to accept or reject any negotiated agreement, but the President in his view would control negotiations and have considerable discretion in managing information:

> It seldom happens in the negotiations of treaties, of whatever nature, but that perfect *secrecy* and immediate *dispatch* are sometimes requisite. There are cases where the most useful intelligence may be obtained, if the persons possessing it can be relieved from apprehensions of discovery. Those apprehensions will operate on those persons whether they are actuated by mercenary or friendly motives; and there doubtless are many of both descriptions who would rely on the secrecy of the President, but who could not confide in that of the Senate, and still less on that of a large popular assembly. The convention have done well, therefore, in so disposing of the power of making treaties that although the President must, in forming them, act by the advice and consent of the Senate, yet he will be able to manage the business of intelligence in such manner as prudence may suggest.

By giving the President authority to negotiate, the nation would be able to profit from sudden developments. "As in the field, so in the

*Federalist No. 74, at 447. James Iredell expanded on the point in the North Carolina Convention, but similarly saw limits on the President's powers (4 *Elliot's Debates, supra* note 20 at 107–108):

> I believe most of the governors of the different states have powers similar to those of the President. In almost every country, the executive has the command of the military forces. From the nature of the thing, the command of armies ought to be delegated to one person only. The secrecy, despatch, and decision, which are necessary in military operations, can only be expected from one person. The President, therefore, is to command the military forces of the United States, and this power I think a proper one; at the same time it will be found to be sufficiently guarded. A very material difference may be observed between this power, and the authority of the king of Great Britain under similar circumstances. The king of Great Britain is not only the commander-in-chief of the land and naval forces, but has power, in time of war, to raise fleets and armies. He had also the authority to declare war.

cabinet, there are moments to be seized as they pass, and they who preside in either should be left in capacity to improve them." Too often, he complained, had the nation "heretofore suffered from the want of secrecy and dispatch. . . ." The Constitution would enable the President to act effectively, since the "matters which in negotiations usually require the most secrecy and the most dispatch are those preparatory and auxiliary measures which are not otherwise important in a national view. . . ." At the same time, the President could take advantage of the Senate's "talents, information, integrity, and deliberate investigations" in the approval process.[192]

Hamilton hammered again at the legitimacy of intermixing the treaty power, in "the true sense of the [separation of powers] rule," and at the need for executive management of negotiations—"the most fit agent in those transactions." To have given the Senate the full power to make treaties "would have been to relinquish the benefits of the constitutional agency of the President in the conduct of foreign negotiations." True, the Senate could have been left with the option of employing the President as negotiator; but the Constitution assured his role because "pique or cabal" might have induced the Senate not to employ him. Furthermore, the President's participation "would materially add to the safety of the society."[193]

At the same time, Hamilton explained, "the vast importance of the trust and the operation of treaties as laws plead strongly for the participation of the whole or a portion of the legislative body in the office of making them." It would, he said, "be utterly unsafe and improper to intrust [the entire power of making treaties] to an elective magistrate of four years' duration." Such an allocation was simply inconsistent with the Federalist view of human nature:

> The history of human conduct does not warrant that exalted opinion of human virtue which would make it wise in a nation to commit interests of so delicate and momentous a kind, as those which concern its intercourse with the rest of the world, to the sole disposal of a magistrate created and circumstanced as would be a President of the United States.[194]

Many anti-Federalists argued that the House should share in making treaties. Hamilton responded that its membership would be too fluctuating, multitudinous, ill-informed and inconsistent for such a role; "decision, *secrecy*, and dispatch, are incompatible with the genius of a body so variable and so numerous." His comments on this point reinforced his earlier suggestion that Senate involvement would sometimes be necessary before a treaty was ready for approval, for he argued that it would be far too inconvenient and expensive to convene the House "to obtain their sanction in the progressive stages of a treaty. . . ."[195]

The theoretical framework established in the *Federalist* enabled the authors to approach the office of President with a perspective very different from that of any likely twentieth-century defense. No such office had existed. No extension, abuse, or controversial exercise of power had occurred. Eighteenth-century fears led primarily to the claim that the President would be an elected monarch. Hamilton disposed of this argument with great style and force, but largely on the basis of unreal comparisons. From that point on, the writers of the *Federalist* justified the presidency with arguments designed to show that the office would be able to prevent legislative tyranny. The President had to be independent, with a will of his own, self-sufficient in salary, and above all in control of powers competent to maintain his constitutional place. Only after extensively demonstrating the adequacy of the President's powers—that the office "combines, as far as republican principles will admit, all the requisites to energy"—did Hamilton turn to comment specifically on whether "it also combines the requisites to safety, in the requisite sense—a due responsibility"? The question is narrow, suggesting as it does that safety could be assured only through devices that called the President to account for his actions, rather than through legislative or judicial powers designed to prevent improper initiatives. But even this limited question received short shrift: a due responsibility "is satisfactorily deducible" from the President's election every four years by electors chosen for the purpose by the people, and from his being subject to impeachment and subsequent prosecution. Perhaps sensing that these devices might not be regarded as adequate, Hamilton disposed of the problem in one cryptic but important sentence:

> In the only instances in which the abuse of the executive authority was materially to be feared, the Chief Magistrate of the United States would, by that plan, be subjected to the control of a branch of the legislative body. What more can an enlightened and reasonable people desire?[196]

Was it sufficient that either the Senate or House could control the executive in the exercise of any authority "materially to be feared"? Hamilton had company in assuming that it was. Richard D. Spaight of North Carolina, for example, said "that it was true that the command of the army and navy was given to the President; but that Congress, who had the power of raising armies, could certainly prevent any abuse of that authority in the President—that they alone had the means of supporting armies, and that the President was impeachable if he in any manner abused his trust."[197] Wilson, too, emphasized the ultimate power of Congress over war-making:

> This system will not hurry us into war; it is calculated to guard against it. It will not be in the power of a single man, or a single body of men, to involve us in such distress; for the important power of declaring war is vested in the legislature at large; and this declaration must be made with the concurrence of the House of Representatives: from this circumstance we may draw a certain conclusion that nothing but our national interest can draw us into a war.[198]

Others noted, however, that Congress would be compelled in times of war, and free in times of peace, to raise armies, which "then the President is to command without any control."[199] He may thus "give us law at the bayonet's point," one opponent warned.[200] The Federalists had no answer to allay these fears. The idea of restraining the legislature in its power to defend the nation in order to avert possible executive usurpation, said Hamilton, "is one of those refinements which owe their origin to a zeal for liberty more ardent than enlightened."[201] Apparently this was more than "an enlightened and reasonable people" could desire.

Few other specific executive powers were discussed in any detail during the ratification process. The judiciary was to play an important role in the system by insuring that Congress passed only constitutional laws, and by adjudicating cases involving foreign persons or nations so that the states created no causes of war.[202] Nothing specific was said, even in Hamilton's masterful analysis, of the judiciary's role in checking executive usurpation. Such a role could only be inferred from the general observation that under a "limited Constitution" the courts are duty-bound "to declare all acts contrary to the manifest tenor of the Constitution void. Without this, all the reservations of particular rights or privileges would amount to nothing."[203] In addition, it must have been generally understood that the federal courts would interpret legislative delegations under their power to pass on all cases arising under the laws, treaties, and Constitution of the United States.[204] But no detailed discussion of this authority was recorded.

What, then, does the ratification period add to our understanding of those features of the Constitution that relate to the power to initiate military actions? The Federalists wanted an executive capable of vigorous administration, independence of will, and powers adequate to assure independence. At least some planning and legislative drafting by the executive was probably expected, and no mention is made of any general limitation on Congress's authority to delegate the exercise of its powers. Congress most definitely was to have the power to raise funds, and to specify their use. Nothing suggests an executive authority to depart from these limitations. On the other hand, no discussion occurred on the extent to which departures from legislative directives might be proper to effectuate some other legislatively approved objective, or to deal with an emergency.

Information issues received considerable attention. Anti-Federalists attacked the provision allowing Congress to withhold from publication such parts of their journals "as may in their judgment require secrecy."[205] Patrick Henry told the Virginia Convention that Congress "may carry on the most wicked and pernicious of schemes under the dark veil of secrecy. The liberties of a people never were, nor ever will be, secure, when the transactions of their rulers may be concealed from them." Nevertheless, he said:

> I am not an advocate for divulging indiscriminately all the operations of government, though the practice of our ancestors, in some degree, justifies it. Such transactions as relate to military operations or affairs of great consequence, the immediate promulgation of which might defeat the interests of the community, I would not wish to be published, till the end which required their secrecy should have been effected.[206]

Henry's ally, George Mason, disapproved of the provision's wording rather than its intent. He suggested that, instead of requiring Congress "from time to time" to publish its proceedings except for the secret parts, the Constitution should adopt the wording of the Articles of Confederation, which provided that Congress "shall publish the Journal of their proceedings monthly, except such parts thereof relating to treaties, alliances or military operations as in their judgment require secrecy." He, too, admitted that "in matters relative to military operations and foreign negotiations, secrecy was necessary sometimes."[207]

The Federalists responded to these attacks by stressing the need for secrecy in foreign and military affairs, implicitly suggesting that they were in favor of trusting Congress's discretion on what to withhold. Said Madison, for example: "The policy of not divulging the most important transactions, and negotiations of nations, such as those which relate to warlike arrangements and treaties, is universally admitted."[208] John Marshall told his fellow Virginians: "In this plan, secrecy is only used when it would be fatal and pernicious to publish the schemes of government."[209] In the North Carolina Convention, James Iredell argued:

> In time of war it was absolutely necessary to conceal the operations of government; otherwise no attack on an enemy could be premeditated with success, for the enemy would discover our plans soon enough to defeat them—that it was no less imprudent to divulge our negotiation with foreign powers, and the most salutory schemes might be prevented by imprudently promulgating all the transactions of the government indiscriminatingly.[210]

These comments were directed at the power of Congress to withhold information from the public. They stress as the policy basis for secrecy, however, the exercise of functions primarily executive—treaty negotiation and military operations. Could the executive withhold information of this sort from Congress when secrecy was deemed essential? Nothing in the Constitution expressly gives the President such power. Furthermore, nothing explicitly establishes any limit on the congressional power to investigate matters relating to their functions. The ratifiers saw Congress as an "inquest,"* and specifically assigned the House and Senate, respectively, the power to impeach and convict all executive officers, including the President.† Finally, Article II, section 3, as we have seen, required the President "from time to time" to "give to Congress information on the State of the Union." At one point James Iredell connected the notion of a duty to provide information, at least to the Senate, with the power to impeach:

> The President must certainly be punishable for giving false information to the Senate. He is to regulate all intercourse with foreign powers, and it is

*In the Massachusetts Convention, Fisher Ames referred to the House of Representatives as "the grand inquisition of the Union," 2 *Elliot's Debates, supra* note 20 at 11; in the North Carolina Convention, Archibald Maclaine termed the House "the grand inquest of the Union at large," 4 *id.* at 44. James Wilson stated in his 1791 Lectures that "the House of Representatives . . . form the grand inquest of the state. They will diligently inquire into grievances." 1 J. Wilson, *The Works of James Wilson* 415 (R. McCloskey ed. 1967).

†Hamilton supported assignment of the power to try impeachments to the Senate in the following manner:

> Is it [impeachment] not designed as a method of *NATIONAL INQUEST* into the conduct of public men? If this be the design of it, who can so properly be the inquisitors for the nation as the representatives of the nation themselves? . . . Great Britain . . . [and] the State constitutions . . . seem to have regarded the practice of impeachments as a bridle in the hands of the legislative body upon the executive servants of the government.

Federalist No. 65 at 397.

his duty to impart to the Senate every material intelligence he receives. If it should appear that he has not given them full information, but has concealed important intelligence which he ought to have communicated, and by that means induced them to enter into measures injurious to their country, and which they would not have consented to had the true state of things been disclosed to them,—in this case, I ask whether, upon an impeachment for a misdemeanor upon such an account, the Senate would probably favor him.[211]

That Congress was intended to possess a sweeping power to inquire, as well as the power to impeach, is not necessarily inconsistent with an executive power to withhold information from the legislature. The *Federalist* unambiguously attributed exclusion of the House from the treaty process, for example, to the need for "decision, *secrecy*, and dispatch."[212] Pierce Butler said that "negotiations always required the greatest secrecy, which would not be expected in a large body" such as the House.[213] John Jay went even further, noting that some informants, though willing to trust the President's word to keep their identities secret, "would not confide in that of the Senate, and still less in that of a large popular assembly." The Convention did well, therefore, in his view, by forcing the President to act with the Senate's advice and consent but at the same time leaving him "able to manage the business of intelligence in such manner as prudence may suggest."[214]

The vague duty to provide Congress with information "from time to time" could arguably have been expected to be governed by the same executive "prudence" suggested by Jay. The power to impeach, meant to be exercised only in the most serious circumstances, could be read consistently with both John Jay's perception of executive management of information and Iredell's insistence on full and accurate disclosure to the Senate: the Congress would be able to remove a President who managed information imprudently to the point of deceiving Congress in the exercise of legislative functions.

Even these indications of intent fail to resolve the questions most frequently at issue in contemporary disputes over information. What could the President do, for example, if Congress sought to negate any executive discretion by requesting information without qualifying the request to permit withholding? Was it expected that the President would surrender the identity of an informant who communicated material on the express understanding that his anonymity would be protected? What of a letter received from an American official in a foreign court, describing that nation in unflattering terms and communicated for the President's sole attention? If the President refused to comply with such requests, could Congress lawfully take any action in their power to compel compliance? What of a request by the House of Representatives for material relating to a treaty? Would the request itself be improper? If not, could a refusal to comply be met with a refusal to cooperate in enforcing the treaty or with other pressure? The ratifiers said nothing that could reasonably be characterized as specifically resolving these questions.

The allocation of powers relating to foreign and military affairs ends up in much the same posture as the allocation of power over information. The ratification debates confirm what the Constitution suggests—that Congress was to have the final say in foreign and military affairs. The President was to manage diplomatic intercourse and negotiations, and to conduct all authorized military operations. But Congress, and especially the Senate, would be able to approve or reject foreign policy in exercising their powers over treaties, appointments, and appropriations. Even Hamilton recognized that the legislature must have ultimate authority. The power to "declare" war could not tenably be read, after examining both the Convention and ratification processes, as limiting Congress's control to formal war-making.[215] Congress was seen by all who commented on the issue as possessing exclusive control of the means of war. No ratifier suggested that the President would be able unilaterally to utilize forces provided for one purpose in some unauthorized military venture. Undeclared wars were far too important a part of the international scene for one safely to assume that the Framers and ratifiers meant to leave that area of power to the President.*

Only the most inflated claims of executive power are settled by these observations, however. The attitude expressed in the *Federalist* was that a vigorous and independent executive was essential to preserve constitutional balance. Consequently it seems understandable that no general argument was advanced against legislative delegations of power to conduct foreign and military affairs. No suggestion was made, for example, that the Constitution prevented Congress from authorizing the President the use of military force under conditions largely within his discretion to determine. Nor was there the slightest indication that Congress was prevented from authorizing actions without declaring war; the constitutional text suggests the contrary by enabling Congress to authorize hostile acts short of war, such as the seizure of prizes. The ratifiers furthermore failed to consider whether a treaty provision might be deemed in

---

*A survey of the 100 years preceding 1787 shows that wars were frequent, but very seldom declared. *See generally* J. Maurice, *Hostilities Without Declaration of War* (1883); C. Ver Steeg, *The Formative Years* 288–300 (1964); R. Ward, *An Enquiry into the Manner in Which the Different Wars in Europe Have Commenced* (1805).

itself to authorize use of the military where necessary or reasonable to accomplish an agreed objective, even though the House had not voted on the agreement. The ratifiers did, however, convey a strong impression that a military appropriation, passed for a specific purpose, could constitute legislative approval for the use of the force authorized to accomplish the purpose contemplated. This seems implicit in the frequent references to the power over appropriations as a legitimate and overwhelmingly effective legislative device for preventing any action or policy attempted by the executive.

The ratifiers gave no attention to the extent of the President's authority to defend the United States. The change from "make" to "declare" was accomplished in part to grant the executive power to defend the nation from "sudden attack," as Madison described it. No discussion occurred on whether the President could act without legislative approval if an attack seemed imminent. Nor was there any writing or debate on what constituted an attack. Was it sufficient to trigger the President's power if a public vessel were fired upon or captured on the high seas?[216] What of a blockade that threatened the nation's welfare and constituted an act of war in international law?[217] The relatively isolated position of the nation at the time, its essentially domestic aspirations, and its lack of any significant naval force all help account for the fact that international crises of the sort described were, if considered at all, pushed aside for more pressing concerns.

The President was surely expected to be able to conduct foreign negotiations and discussions without any specific legislative sanction beyond compensating the necessary officers. The same seems true of military affairs; once troops were raised, the President would be expected to command them. There were limits on how far the President could go in the exercise of these functions, but not very clear limits. Many ratifiers feared an improper use of troops, to suppress liberties and distort the constitutional system. The President's power to command certainly did not extend to such clearly unconstitutional conduct. But could the President exercise his powers in the absence of legislative orders in such a manner as to cause war, or to make hostilities more likely? Did his control of negotiations extend to representing the nation's position in such a manner as to make resort to military solutions more likely? Could he simply refuse to negotiate an agreement where the consequence of his refusal might be war? Could he exercise his military command in a similar fashion, for example by moving troops to a disputed area where armed resistance to the move was likely? Very little evidence is available on these matters.

Jay, Hamilton, Wilson, and perhaps others treated the President's power to negotiate treaties as exclusive; the Senate could approve only those treaties actually submitted.[218] On the other hand they recognized that the Senate would be instructing the President from time to time, and that Congress as a whole could bring great pressure on the executive to implement one policy or another. Several statements also indicate that the President was to act independently in conducting military operations, to insure effectiveness. But Congress could withdraw the means for any such operation, and could at least pronounce its own view of the ownership of disputed territory or of any other potentially explosive issue. The anticipated allocation of powers was the possibility that Congress might allow the executive trigger crises that could lead to military conflict, while at the same time enabling Congress to exert enormous pressure to prevent such crises, even to the point of totally depriving the President of the means for exercising his functions. Implicit in this allocation of powers was the possibility that Congress might allow the executive to act without specific approval, so as to enhance effectiveness and minimize legislative responsibility, and thereby at times compel Congress as a practical matter to support a course of conduct made necessary by the President's independent initiatives.

The ratifiers seemed to anticipate conflict between the executive and legislative branches, and they did not desire the latter automatically to prevail. Hamilton in the *Federalist* specifically espoused a President who would be able and willing to risk both popular and legislative displeasure by resisting policies that he considered contrary to the nation's interests. He must have anticipated that executive resistance in this form would be—indeed, would have to be—placed on some claim of authority independent of legislative command, though not necessarily beyond the legislature's power to control in the final analysis. The most compelling evidence of this is Madison's explanation of how the Constitution intentionally "mixed" powers, so as to create a separation of the branches designed primarily to insure their independence of will rather than a separation along functional lines. The "mixing" theory required an overlapping assignment of powers in order to enable each of the branches to advocate an independent course of action with constitutional propriety. The "lacunae" thereby created in the Constitution are only uncertainties in the sense that the outcome of struggles between the branches in such areas is not preordained; their existence should probably be regarded as intentional, an integral part of the constitutional plan.[219]

The potential for conflicting assertions of power in the Constitution as viewed in the *Federalist* is made even greater by the general approach to constitutional interpretation suggested by both Madison and Hamilton. Madison set the theme in defending the Convention against charges that they had overstepped their authority by proposing so radical a "revision" of the Articles of Confederation. He contended that the delegates had proceeded properly, but then went on to argue that necessity justified their conduct in any event, and that the test of whether to adopt the Constitution should be solely its desirability:

> If they had exceeded their powers, they were not only warranted, but required as the confidential servants of their country, by the circumstances in which they were placed to exercise the liberty which they assumed; and that finally, if they had violated both their powers and their obligations in proposing a Constitution, this ought nevertheless to be embraced, if it be calculated to accomplish the views and happiness of the people of America. . . .[220]

A similar approach is found in the discussion of parts of the Constitution as well. Hamilton explained that no limit was placed on the raising of a peacetime army because necessity might require one.* Madison argued that such a restriction would inevitably be breached, thereby undermining the Constitution's otherwise viable proscriptions; he said, essentially, that the means must be sufficient to the end of security.† In defending the broad powers assigned Congress, Hamilton said that "every government ought to contain in itself the means of its own preservation."[221] And in defending the clause granting Congress all powers necessary and proper to exercise their assigned responsibilities, Hamilton contended the clause was superfluous; a necessary and proper clause is implied in *every* grant.[222] Both Madison and Hamilton, therefore, not only incorporated the doctrines of separation and mixing in their analysis, but arguably also that part of Locke's description of prerogative that recognized an executive power to do what was necessary, though at the risk of being overruled or punished.

*Hamilton wrote: "Cases are likely to occur under our government . . . which will sometimes render a military force in time of peace essential to the security of the society, and that it is therefore improper in this respect to control the legislative discretion." *Federalist* No. 25 at 167.

†Madison asked (*Federalist* No. 41 at 257): "How could a readiness for war in time of peace be safely prohibited, unless we could prohibit in like manner the preparations and establishments of every hostile nation? The means of security can only be regulated by the means and the danger of attack. They will, in fact, be ever determined by these rules and by no others. It is in vain to oppose constitutional barriers to the impulse of self-preservation. It is worse than in vain; because it plants in the Constitution itself necessary usurpations of power, every precedent of which is a germ of unnecessary and multiplied repetitions."

CONCLUSION

The overall picture of the Constitution that emerges from analysis of its text, background, drafting, and ratification is one in which the need for a national government was primary. Having determined to assign great new powers upon a central authority, however, the draftsmen were faced with how to divide that power among its branches. British constitutional history as well as the colonists' experience under George III made totally unacceptable the creation of a monarchy in form or in substance. The legislature, everyone assumed, should hold ultimate power. Experience during the Confederation period, combined with an awareness of the advantages of unitary leadership, on the other hand, turned the nation's leaders against overpowerful legislative government. The goal, therefore, was to design a system both effective and safe. Effectiveness was sought by creating an independently elected executive, assigned responsibility for the administration of government, including foreign affairs and the military. Safety was to come from the fact that the people's representatives would hold ultimate power over all policy, subject to executive and judicial checks designed to offset the effects of "passing delusions" and unconstitutional actions. The President would also be controlled by the electoral system, his relatively short term of four years, and his need to obtain at least legislative, and sometimes judicial, concurrence for virtually all important initiatives.

So the Framers opted neither for the King of Blackstone's defunct description nor for the Parliament that had established its supremacy. The President received less power than the theoretical Crown of Britain, but more than any contemporary British monarch had actually possessed. Congress received less power than Parliament exercised during the constitutional crises of the seventeenth century, but more than Parliament exercised after the system of ministerial government had evolved.

But the Constitution adopted an even more fundamental aspect of the British system. The Framers expected the branches to battle each other to acquire and to defend power. To prevent the supremacy of one branch over any other in these battles, powers were mixed; each branch was granted important powers over the same area of activity. The British and Confederation experiences had led the Framers to avoid regarding controversy between the branches as a conflict between good and evil or right and wrong, requiring definitive, institutionally permanent resolution. Rather they viewed such conflict as an expression of the aggressive and perverse part of human nature that demanded outlet but had to be kept from finding lasting resolution so that liberty could be preserved.

 *Chapter 2*

Establishing a Pattern of Government:
The Administration of
George Washington

Twelve states had ratified the Constitution by September 13, 1788, when Congress chose New York as the site of the new government. On February 4, 1789, presidential electors (chosen directly by state legislators) cast their ballots for first President of the United States. They predictably and unanimously chose George Washington, commander-in-chief of the Revolutionary forces, and presiding officer at the Constitutional Convention. "Our first President," said John Randolph in 1812, "was made for the office, and the office for him. . . ."[1] He was sworn into office at the corner of Wall and Broad Streets in Manhattan on April 30, 1789. A man of little formal education, Washington had earned the respect and devotion of his colleagues and of the people because of his great personal strength and integrity, some brilliant military achievements, and sound judgment.

The First Congress was elected during February, and organized for business in early April. The Senate had 22 members, the House 59. Of these 81 Congressmen, 54 had been members of the Constitutional Convention or of state ratifying conventions; only 7 had opposed ratification. Their acts and understandings of the Constitution are entitled to special weight.* They soon legislated into existence the

---

*This is not to say they always agreed on the Constitution's meaning. At one point during the House debate on the Jay Treaty, William Vans Murray of Maryland bemoaned their lack of agreement (5 *Annals of Congress* 701-702) [hereinafter "*Annals*"]:

We have all seen the Constitution from its cradle, we know it from its infancy, and have the most perfect knowledge of it, and more light than ever a body

executive branch, and fulfilled the promise made by the Constitution's supporters during the ratification debates by sending the states a set of twelve amendments, ten of which were adopted and became the Bill of Rights. Congress also organized the federal courts in the Judiciary Act of September 24, 1789, and John Jay was immediately appointed Chief Justice.

The President sought in his appointments to bring potentially rival factions together, and to profit from the advice of diverse leadership. Thomas Jefferson was appointed to head the Department of State, Henry Knox was made Secretary of War, Alexander Hamilton became Secretary of the Treasury, and Edmund Randolph the first Attorney General. Washington began early to call his major officers together for their advice; he often had them vote on matters and usually accepted the majority view. But the Cabinet was soon divided. Hamilton and other members of the "Federalist" party, who dominated Congress during the first term, favored a strong and active national government, and within that government they advocated vigorous executive leadership. Jefferson and his supporters—who forged the Democratic-Republican party by 1792—favored state over federal power, opposed central fiscal control and a standing army, and preferred legislative to executive leadership on the national level. These preferences, of course, coincided with the fact that Federalist Presidents governed for the first twelve years, whereas the Republicans made dramatic gains in the House under Washington, and eventually controlled Congress during the John Adams administration. The French Revolution evoked disgust and scorn from most Federalists; Republicans generally admired the birth of French democracy, especially during its earlier stages.

The years between 1789 and 1797 were filled with dangers and opportunities. Washington and Congress maintained neutrality in the conflict among the European powers. Hamilton's policies strengthened the nation fiscally, and Washington enforced federal law upon rebellious individuals in the Whiskey Rebellion. A major victory was eventually won against the Wabash Indians, and important treaties were signed with Spain (granting Americans the right to navigate the Mississippi and to deposit goods), and with Britain (obtaining surrender of certain western posts). In making and implementing these decisions, the legislative and executive branches took form. Powers

---

of men in any country have ever had of ascertaining any other Constitution. If, however, a refining spirit can at this day, so full of light shining upon every part of it, excite and establish doubts upon some of its plainest passages, what is the prospect of that posterity which is to be deprived of those lights which its very framers now find incompetent to lead them?

were exercised, assumed, delegated and surrendered in a process that remains familiar and highly relevant to many of the unresolved questions left by the Constitution and its background.

THE EMERGING FRAMEWORK OF EXECUTIVE-CONGRESSIONAL RELATIONS

The modern presidency derives much of its power over foreign and military affairs from the prestige and influence associated with the more general roles it performs. The President's control of the machinery of government enables him to enforce his own policies, and to distribute considerable largesse. The White House and executive departments propose legislative policies, draft legislation, prepare a budget. Once money is appropriated, the executive controls its expenditure. Congress has delegated to recent Presidents broad discretionary powers over a variety of areas. Finally, recent Presidents have claimed the power to withhold information from Congress; to the extent they have succeeded, the executive has retained greater control than might otherwise have been possible over the subjects to which the information relates.

Washington's administration demonstrates how early in the nation's history these issues arose and were at least initially settled. As Richard Hildreth wrote years ago, this was "a period of the greatest importance, as having fixed upon the federal government that character and those methods of administration which it has ever since retained."[2] The congressional debates and private papers of the period are replete with material of great contemporary relevance and significance on the extent to which the executive was assumed to possess or was delegated power over the machinery of government (reflected in the removal debates), legislative planning, expenditures, and information.

Power to Remove

One of the nation's first legislative programs was to continue the executive departments established during the Confederation, and to create new ones.[3] In considering the form of the first department, Foreign Affairs, the question was squarely posed whether the department's chief officer should be subject to removal by the President without cause. The Constitution provided only for a method of appointment, whereby the President nominated and the Senate confirmed. No provision dealt with removal, and evidence of the Framers' understanding was contradictory.[4]

Extensive debate occurred in both houses of Congress on this question.* Those who supported presidential power to remove had a significantly different conception of the executive from those who advocated limits on the President's power to dismiss the heads of departments. The former view, espoused by Fisher Ames of Massachusetts and James Madison, among others, was premised on expansive interpretations of the "executive power," of the power to appoint, and of the duty to take care that the laws be faithfully executed.[5] The latter view was premised on a narrow reading of presidential power; its proponents rejected the notion that the "executive power" could be relied on for authority apart from the President's specifically enumerated powers. Instead they advocated three different models of removal: (1) by impeachment;[6] (2) by the President, but with the Senate's consent, as in the case of appointments;[7] or (3) on terms prescribed by Congress, pursuant to its power to create the offices involved and under the necessary and proper clause.[8]

Madison saw grave dangers of insubordination and faction in restricting removal, since executive officers could ally with groups of Senators against the President. He favored executive authority over removal to help preserve an equilibrium against "the Legislative power [which] is of such a nature that it scarcely can be restrained. . . ." He later said the position that had "prevailed" was "that the Executive power being in general terms vested in the President, all power of an Executive nature not particularly taken away must belong to that department," but he noted that this doctrine was subject to modification.[9] Others who felt that Congress could lawfully control the removal of executive officers thought it expedient nevertheless to empower the President to remove at his pleasure officers of cabinet rank.[10] Consequently the theory on which the majority voted is not entirely clear. In any event, the result was close. The House voted 29 to 22 to authorize the President to remove at his pleasure the head of Foreign Affairs;[11] the Senate divided evenly, and Vice President John Adams cast the deciding vote in favor of executive removal.† Sub-

---

*Most early debates in Congress are from the House. The Senate met behind closed doors until February 20, 1794, when a new method was adopted. See 1 *Annals* 15. The record of House debates, though invaluable, is not always entirely reliable. For example, the reporter at one point noted that he could not hear a member's speech "on account of a high wind" (5 *Annals* 588), and at other times saw fit to summarize arguments.

†Washington's biographer, James Thomas Flexner, comments that "since the matter was so closely contested even with the prestigious Washington in the executive chair, it is hard to doubt that if anyone else had been President, the vote would have gone the other way. This would have resulted in a very different form of government." 3 J. Flexner, *George Washington: Anguish and Farewell, 1793-1799* at 215 (1972).

sequent legislation creating high executive offices also provided for presidential removal,[12] and Washington exercised his power to remove when, in 1796, he recalled James Monroe from the post of Minister to France and appointed Charles Pinckney as Envoy Extraordinary.*

Planning Legislation

Legislators very early perceived dangers in allowing the executive branch to prepare plans and bills. In creating the Treasury Department during May 1789, some Representatives objected to the proposal that the Secretary of Treasury "digest and report plans," arguing that he should only prepare estimates; otherwise, they said, the secretary rather than the House would be originating revenue measures.[13] Others responded that legislative planning of finances had proven inadequate and that even if plans were reported as "bills," they became bills only if the House approved.[14] As passed in 1789, the act establishing the Treasury Department required the secretary "to digest and prepare plans for the improvement and management of the revenue, and for the support of public credit" and "to prepare and report estimates of the public revenue, and the public expenditures. . . ."[15] Soon thereafter the House instructed the secretary to report a plan to support the public credit, and received Alexander Hamilton's "dazzling" (and influential) proposal.[16]

Washington needed no prodding to recommend measures to Congress; the Constitution contemplated that he would. After the Department of War was established, for example, he told Congress that "to be prepared for war, is one of the most effectual means of preserving peace,"[17] and ordered Secretary of War Knox to prepare a plan for organizing the militia.[18]

This early pattern of executive planning was forcefully challenged when Republicans increased their numbers in the House. On January 27, 1792, John F. Mercer of Maryland attacked a bill submitted by the Secretary of Treasury tying revenue-producing measures to an increase in pay for military personnel:

---

*Washington sought advice as to his appointment power on June 24, 1796. 35 *The Writings of George Washington* 96 (J. Fitzpatrick, ed. 1931–44) (39 vols.) [hereinafter "*Washington Writings* (Fitzpatrick)"]. His Cabinet concluded that an additional appointment to Paris could not be made, but that removal would be appropriate and lawful for (1) lack of capacity or qualifications; (2) neglect of duty; (3) ineffectiveness; (4) another, better able minister; or (5) entering into domestic or foreign factions. *The George Washington Papers*, L.C. microfilm, series 2, reel 8 [hereinafter "*Washington Papers*"]. Monroe was regarded by Federalists in Washington's administration as biased toward France and untrustworthy. W. Cresson, *James Monroe* 151–54 (1946).

> I have long remarked in this House that the Executive, or rather the Treasury Department, was really *the efficient Legislature of the country*, so far as relates to the revenue, which is the vital principle of Government. The clause of the Constitution confining to the immediate Representatives of the people, in this House, the origination of money bills, is converted into a Committee of Sanction, that never withholds its assent; a convenient cloak to divert the blame of odious measures from the real authors. . . . [19]

His objections to tying revenue proposals to war plans were vain, however; both the acts to increase the army and to authorize the necessary taxes passed by sizable majorities.[20] Particularly interesting is the response of William Vans Murray of Maryland to arguments against referring such matters to Treasury for planning. The issue, he said, should not be whether to rely on executive-department recommendations, "but the best mode of raising the sum wanted"; he chided the bill's opponents for suggesting no alternative mode.[21]

The issue was raised again on March 7, 1792, when a resolution was introduced to direct the Secretary of Treasury "to report to this House his opinion of the best mode for raising the additional supplies requisite for the ensuing year."[22] Theodore Sedgwick of Massachusetts delivered a comprehensive statement on the need for planning by executive officers. The act establishing the Treasury Department, he said, which made it the Treasury Secretary's duty to digest and prepare plans for the management and improvement of the revenue, led him to hope that the government had adopted the great principle of administration whereby a high officer, adequately paid, would "be responsible to the community to produce to the consideration of the National Legislature, such systematic arrangments in the intricate business of finance, as should give the highest assurance of the support of public credit. . . ." The value of such an arrangement had been demonstrated by experience in other nations and under the Confederation: "It was not long since, that all America had attempted to provide for the public exigencies, by the undigested schemes of legislative financiers. The effects are remembered by all; the revenue was incomparably less productive, and yet the people infinitely more burdened than at present. . . ." By these observations, he did not mean, he said, "to derogate from the responsibility of the character of the House collectively, or of any individual member of it." Though some members may be capable of planning a revenue scheme, their other responsibilities and interests while Congress was in and out of session left too little time to develop the necessary expertise. He could accept the superior knowledge of executive officers in their respective fields, without surrendering confidence in his ability to judge "the expediency of adopting such measures as those officers should recommend."[23]

Opponents to the resolution argued that executive recommendations would be too influential, thereby depriving Congress of its legislative function. Madison suggested a scheme to enable legislators to express their opinions before an executive plan was formulated: a department secretary should be called upon only for facts; the House should then, as a committee, form opinions; and these opinions should be referred to the department secretary, who would report a systematic arrangement based upon them.[24] Sedgwick rejected the notion that when Congressmen "were to consider the reports of the Secretary, they became at once transformed into resistless dupes, incapable of manly investigation, and quietly sailing down the stream of Ministerial influence." To Sedgwick, and many others,[25] Madison's suggestion was impractical, and would destroy the benefits intended by Congress in creating executive offices.[26]

Others who opposed requesting executive assistance noted that the act forming the Treasury obliged the secretary to reply to congressional inquiries, but did not require the House to make such inquiries; that "it was the peculiar duty of this House to originate money bills, and to devise ways and means," therefore making requests for executive opinions "a dereliction of our duty, and an abandonment of the trust reposed in us. . . .";[27] that information should be obtained, but not opinions;[28] that prior practice was improper and should not be repeated; that the practice would lead to a centralization of authority, because officers preparing such plans were appointed and subject to removal by the President; that the present practice demands much time by forcing the House to "see through" executive recommendations; that if the practice is efficient and sound, the House should surrender its role of sanctioning executive recommendations, since "it is much better to have a Minister responsible to the people for the revenue systems they introduce, than to have this responsibility lost in the legislature"; and that if the argument for "greater facility" has merit, it "proves the influence [of Ministers] to be dangerous in a high degree."[29]

The vote was close, 31–27, but the request for an executive plan was made. William Findley of Pennsylvania suggested that some members might have approved because "the session is drawing to a close. . . ." He expressed confidence that, "when a more equal and more numerous representation occupies this floor, this unwarrantable practice of transferring so influential a part of the legislative trust will be changed."[30]

As Findley predicted, the issue arose again; but the practice was reaffirmed. Thomas Fitzsimons of Pennsylvania offered a resolution on November 19, 1792, to direct the Secretary of Treasury to report a plan for reducing the public debt. John F. Mercer of Maryland attacked the resolution, and was joined by several others, including Madison, who attempted to distinguish between "deliberative" functions, to be exercised by Congress, and "ministerial" functions, properly delegated to executive officers.[31] William Vans Murray of Maryland sought to show Madison's distinction was untenable, and argued that an executive report could no further influence the House "than by the weight of the wisdom it contained." Madison conceded "some difficulty in drawing the exact line between subjects of legislative and ministerial deliberations," but persisted in opposing the resolution as transferring the power to determine the form of a tax. He was joined at length by Abraham Baldwin of Georgia who stressed the need to keep the branches of government as separate as possible.[32] But Elbridge Gerry of Massachusetts, who had opposed requesting plans from the secretary at the time the bill establishing the Treasury Department was discussed, announced that he had changed his mind: "He saw an impossibility, if taken up in Committee of the Whole [House], in rendering the intended measure a uniform part of the great financial whole. The clashing of various opinions would prevent it."[33] The vote in Committee of the Whole was 25 to 31 against striking the request.[34] When the matter was referred back to the House, Fisher Ames of Massachusetts, William Findley, and Madison (among others) added full-dress arguments against and for the resolution.* The final vote was 32 to 25 in favor.[35]

The next controversy over executive planning occurred when Representative Fitzsimons moved, on January 20, 1795, to request the President to submit a plan for protecting the frontier, including the number of troops necessary. Madison seemed surprised by this motion "of great novelty and magnitude . . . probably not agreeable to the Constitution." Abraham B. Venable of Virginia "thought that so many motions of this kind would abridge the business of the House. One day the Secretary of War sends us directions," he said, "the second day, the Secretary of Treasury sends us directions; a third day, we are to have directions from another Department, and so on. He hoped that the House would do their own business themselves." Only Josiah Parker of Virginia is recorded in favor of the

---

*Ames was especially brilliant, arguing dispassionately that, while any of several ways of planning finances could be adopted, a reference to the secretary was the most efficient, constitutional, established practice, and could result in no undue influence. 3 *Annals* 715-22. The worthy contributions of Findley and Madison against the reference appear in *id.* 712-15, 722.

motion.* When Elias Boudinot of New Jersey moved to refer the matter to a committee for a report, instead of to the President, Fitzsimons withdrew his motion, noting that a committee already existed to consider the matter. So the matter went to a Committee of the Whole, seemingly on the premise that it, rather than the executive, would formulate a plan to protect the frontiers.[36]

On the next day the House began considering how to defend the frontier. It did not get far. Henry Dearborn of Massachusetts opened (and essentially closed) the effort by moving that the House consider only the establishment of a "defensive" system. "This motion," the reporter recorded, "produced a very long conversation." Jonathan Dayton of New Jersey and Thomas Hartley of Pennsylvania objected, noting the presence of British troops in American posts, and the need to stop Indian depredations. The discussion led Sedgwick to move "that the Committee rise, for the purpose of his making a motion [to the House] for applying to the President to get information on this point." One more speech againt reducing the army, and one Mr. Smith (not further identified by the reporter) had heard enough; he would "vote for the rising of the Committee for the purpose of obtaining information." Jeremiah Wadsworth of Connecticut also joined Sedgwick, arguing that it was entirely appropriate to ask Washington for advice, since he was "not only a President, but a soldier," born and raised on the frontier, and well acquainted with Indians. All this led Dearborn to withdraw his motion. The Committee then rose, and Sedgwick moved to have the President "direct the proper officer to lay before the House a statement of the number of troops that will be necessary to maintain such a line of military posts as it will be expedient to establish, effectually to protect the frontiers of the United States." John Page of Virginia objected to this motion, since "he saw no material difference between it and that which the good humor and candor of the member from Pennsylvania [Fitzsimons] yesterday withdrew"; the motion was otherwise without precedent, he said, and the information was already in the hands of a committee. But the motion narrowly prevailed, 40–37, thus adding military affairs to the list of functions concerning which the executive was called upon to plan.[37]

One formidable obstacle to legislative planning was that many legislators preferred to discuss matters in Committee of the Whole.

---

*4 *Annals* 1121. Jonathan Dayton of New Jersey, a strong advocate of executive power, viewed the resolution as encroaching on the President by calling for information that he could not prudently or practically give. By forcing the President to spell out a plan, it forced him to pledge himself to a course of action, and thereby improperly caused him to reveal how he would exercise the discretion vested in him by the Constitution. *Id.* 1120–21.

Some early attempts to establish smaller committees to work out the ways and means for accomplishing legislative objectives led to the appointment of select committees. But the device was disfavored. When Albert Gallatin of Pennsylvania became a Representative in December 1795, he managed to secure the appointment of a Standing Committee on Ways and Means "to superintend the general operations of finance." This achievement, made possible by the enormously influential Hamilton's resignation and Gallatin's rapid rise to Republican leadership, failed to have significant effect until about 1819, because members continued to prefer operating in Committee of the Whole.[38] One can accurately say, therefore, that while Congress did considerable planning of its own between 1789 and 1797, it consciously turned to the executive branch for plans on particularly important matters, including foreign affairs, military posture, and the early counterpart of the national budget.

Control of Expenditures

Article I, section 9 of the Constitution provides that "no money shall be drawn from the treasury, but in consequence of appropriations made by law. . . ." Congress was expected to ascertain the needs of the nation and to prescribe the means for satisfying those needs. Though the executive may have a legal or constitutional mandate to accomplish certain objectives, the Constitution seems to require that no funds be paid out of the Treasury toward accomplishing any objective unless Congress has appropriated funds for that purpose. These principles have never been disputed. But experience during Washington's administration demonstrates that, even if these principles are acknowledged, important questions about the expenditure of public funds remain unanswered.

The House very early developed the practice of requesting the Secretary of Treasury to submit estimates of the sums that would be needed in the forthcoming year. This task had initially been given to a Committee on Ways and Means in 1789, but the committee was discharged after Hamilton took office because only he had sufficient command of the information required to make a meaningful estimate.[39] The reports submitted by the secretary were quite detailed during Hamilton's tenure; Congress relied heavily on his estimates, and appropriated lump sums for various activities. Thus the Appropriation Act for 1789 granted lump sums for the civil list, War Department, outstanding warrants issued under the previous government, and veterans' pensions. The acts for 1790 and 1791 were similar, except for adding a reference to the estimates in the Secretary of Treasury's report.[40] Only occasionally, beginning in 1791, did Congress appropriate money for more specific purposes.[41]

Republicans began to take an interest in protecting the House's power over the public purse in 1792, when Josiah Parker of Virginia asserted that before making appropriations more than double those of 1791 the House should examine the actual expenditure of funds previously appropriated. Federalists argued that such an inquiry was irrelevant to determining appropriations for the next year, though William L. Smith of South Carolina did suggest some likely causes of the increased need. William Giles of Virginia was "against allowing an unnecessary latitude in appropriations [since it] would generally be found that the expenditures would come up very near to the sum appropriated." The House agreed to have the law express the several purposes for which the moneys were appropriated rather than grant sums in gross with only a reference to estimates of the Secretary of Treasury.[42]

The House passed an appropriations bill for 1793 that "specified all the items of each sum granted to the support of the War Department. . . ." The Senate passed an amended version condensing "the whole into one aggregate sum." This set off a lengthy debate, in which opponents of the Senate version noted the dangers of keeping expenditures out of view, and of thereby conferring discretion on executive officers to adjust their spending on any authorized item without adequate limitation. Proponents stressed the need for flexibility. The Senate's version was rejected 30–31, however, and the bill as adopted specified expenditures in considerable detail, leaving some flexibility in certain items.[43]

The degree of flexibility to be allowed the Secretary of Treasury in handling funds under his control came under direct scrutiny in the House's consideration of several resolutions offered by Giles in February 1793. Giles claimed that Hamilton had violated the law in using a portion of the domestic fund to pay an installment on the foreign debt (instead of paying it out of the money in the government's account in Holland, as the law directed) and paying the interest on that debt out of the foreign fund (instead of paying it out of the domestic fund). Actually, Hamilton had taken advantage of an opportunity to eliminate the risk of loss involved in the transfer of funds across the ocean by agreeing with the French to pay the installment in American goods delivered at Santo Domingo. The goods were paid for with funds held in America. One of Giles's resolutions declared that "it is essential to the due administration of the Government of the United States, that laws making specific appropriations of money should be strictly observed by the administrator of the finances thereof." William L. Smith admitted the proposition as a general rule, but insisted there would be circumstances calling for departures in order to uphold the public credit or assure the public safety; it would then be necessary to examine the circumstances to determine whether the deviation was warranted. Another resolution was proposed to reprimand Hamilton for the particular transaction in question. Republicans saw Hamilton's action as an outright diversion of appropriated money;* but Smith declared that if the secretary had remitted money abroad to pay the interest and drawn bills to bring the foreign fund here, thereby taking an unnecessary loss on interest and other expenses, he would have subjected himself to severe censure. The House vindicated Hamilton by a large majority.[44]

In January 1794, the House appointed a committee, headed by Abraham Baldwin, to examine the state of the Treasury Department.[45] On May 22, 1794, the Baldwin Committee presented a lengthy report, detailing the rules and procedures observed, with regard to collecting, keeping, and disbursing public moneys. The report expressed no opinion on the legality or desirability of the procedures found, and recommended no changes, although one of the practices described—anticipating appropriations—later became an object of dispute.[46] The appropriation acts for 1794 and 1795 followed closely the established form. The only significant exception was that the military appropriations law of December 31, 1794, specifically granted funds to defray the expense of the expedition against the Whiskey Rebellion the previous summer. This appropriation, passed without controversy, indicated at least Congress's acquiescence in Washington's decision to use general military appropriations when acting under the statute empowering him to call out the militia to suppress insurrections.[47] No funds had been appropriated for such an undertaking when the insurrection occurred.†

The first attempt to undercut a law by reducing or eliminating appropriations came in 1796. A group of Representatives, who had unsuccessfully opposed the law establishing a mint, moved to strike

---

*William Findley, a strong supporter of the resolutions, admitted, however, that "an Executive officer, pressed by some urgent and unexpected necessity, may be induced to depart from the authorized path of duty, and have great merit in so doing." But on such an occasion the officer must obtain subsequent ratification of his act by Congress. 3 *Annals* 920-22.

†Gallatin later argued, however, that "even the principle by which the specific appropriations for the several objects of the military establishment have been considered as a general grant for the whole could not authorize the application of a part of that grant to the expenses of that expedition. No farther discretion has been claimed by virtue of that principle than that of indistinctly applying the whole sum appropriated by law to any of the objects enumerated and specified under distinct head in the law itself." He would have had Congress reconvened to appropriate the money before it was spent. 3 *The Writings of Albert Gallatin* 117-18 (H. Adams, ed. 1960), from *A Sketch of the Finances of the United States*, published by Gallatin, November 12, 1796.

from the appropriations bill the funds provided for the mint. Opponents argued that if the House desired to abolish the mint it should act directly and not attempt to accomplish the same thing by refusing to appropriate. But Gallatin said the House had discretion to appropriate or not as it wished, and John Nicholas of Virginia conceived the House duty-bound to weigh the merits of every law in passing an appropriation to carry it into effect. The motion was defeated,[48] however, as was a similar maneuver the next year to block the addition of $172,000 to the naval appropriations bill to enable the President to complete the previously authorized construction of three frigates. Gallatin, for example, said he would vote against the appropriation "because he did not wish to see the frigates at sea, and because he conceived a Navy to be prejudicial to the true interests of this country." Navy supporters argued that the House was obliged to complete the frigates, and claimed there was no danger whatever that the vessels would be manned because the funds to be appropriated were insufficient to accomplish that objective. Gallatin was unconvinced, contending that "they need not be surprised if the vessels were sent to sea, though no appropriation was made for the purpose, should the President suppose there was any plea for doing so." Others added that the President had built ships large enough for 62 guns, even though only 44-gun frigates were authorized. Proponents successfully persisted in their arguments, however, with Parker defending the President because "in relation to foreign nations, he had great power; but, if he went beyond his power with respect to internal regulations, he would be liable to impeachment. . . ."[49]

Gallatin continued to urge greater legislative control of spending, and scored seemingly important victories. First he successfully moved to change the language of the appropriations acts of 1797 to indicate that the executive was expected to spend only up to the amounts listed in each category of expense.* He also sought to add to the military appropriations bill the proposition that "sums shall be solely applied to the objects for which they are respectively appropriated."[50] William L. Smith and others argued that some discretion should be left in the President to avoid embarrassing the Treasury when unforeseen circumstances might deplete the funds appropriated to a particular category of expense. But Gallatin saw danger in the position expressed by the then Secretary of Treasury, Oliver Wolcott, "that it was well known to have been a rule since the establishment of the Government, that the appropriations for the Military Estab-

---

*"Be it enacted . . . [t]hat for the support of the military and naval establishment, for [1797], the following sums be *respectively appropriated*; that is to say. . . ." Act of Mar. 3, 1797, 1 Stat. 508. (Emphasis added.)

lishment were considered as general grants of money, liable to be issued to any of the objects included under that Department." His motion carried, and the language he advocated was included in the final bill, after further debate and an attempt by the Senate to delete it.[51]

Gallatin's successes had little effect. The military appropriation act of 1797 "was no more successful than any other in confining the War Department to the sums specifically appropriated for each head [category] of expenditure." When Secretary McHenry submitted information on the deficiencies he had incurred, Gallatin and others reacted angrily, but the expenses were paid, and no action was taken against McHenry.[52] The very next year the Senate amended the military appropriations act for 1798 to consolidate all appropriations ($1,411,798) under one head, and to strike out the words "which sums shall be solely applied to the objects for which they are respectively appropriated." The House retreated from its earlier position and agreed to the Senate version.[53] Wolcott later admitted having regarded himself free throughout this period to allow transfers of appropriations, because the practice was both necessary and customary.*

Several significant fiscal practices thus became settled during Washington's administration. Appropriations were generally made in lump sums. Even when appropriations were broken down into some detail, administrators felt free to shift funds from one category to another. When funds were available for shifting into categories for which appropriations had been expended, deficiencies were frequently incurred. Deficiencies were also incurred, in some instance, on authorized purposes for which Congress had made no appropriations, such as the military expedition in Western Pennsylvania. Congress acquiesced in these practices, despite articulate but ineffective opposition from Albert Gallatin and the Republican minority.

Delegation of Discretionary Power

Scholars have commonly assumed that Congress has conferred far broader discretion upon Presidents in recent than in earlier periods of the nation's history.[54] This assumption is far from accurate. Congress made many very broad delegations during the first eight years under

*O. Wolcott, *Address to the People of the United States* 14 (1802). In fact, Wolcott had been greatly disturbed by the change in the 1797 acts. He told Hamilton, in a letter dated April 5, 1798, that "the management of the Treasury becomes more and more difficult. The Legislature will not pass laws in gross. Their appropriations are minute. Gallatin to whom they all yield, is evidently intending to break down this Department, by charging it with an impracticable detail." 21 H. Syrett & J. Cooke, eds., *The Papers of Alexander Hamilton* 396-98 (1974).

the Constitution. Several occurred without debate as to their propriety, and many involved subjects unrelated or only tangentially related to the war powers.[55] But broad delegations also were made, after revealing debate, on foreign affairs[56] and military[57] issues calling for highly sensitive judgments,* including whether to use the armed forces against Indians or foreign nations.†

The first delegation dispute took place on September 5, 1789 when Representative Thomas Tudor Tucker of South Carolina objected to allowing the President to designate the permanent seat of the government on any part of a geographic line five to six hundred miles long. He called it a betrayal of public trust for Congress to allow the President to determine a matter of so great a consequence. He claimed to "have no want of confidence in the judgment and discretion of the President, or those whom he may employ," but felt this a business for the legislature alone. His motion to have the commissioners report to Congress rather than to the President lost, 21-29.[58]

A more successful effort to control discretion occurred on April 13, 1790, when a motion was made to strike a clause of a bill that empowered the President to establish post offices and post roads as appeared necessary. The motion was supported with the argument that, since the power to establish roads was expressly vested in Congress by the Constitution, it could not be delegated; "the objects which are connected with this power are of great weight in themselves and are properly cognizable by the legislature. . . ." The clause, after some debate, was struck out.[59] Whether delegations to establish post roads should be made arose several more times during the First Congress, and elicited able argument on both sides; the House refused, however, to confer such authority.[60]

*On June 5, 1794, Washington was authorized to use land and naval forces to keep foreign cruisers fitted out in the United States from carrying on hostile action against a state with which the United States was at peace, and to make foreign vessels depart when by the law of nations or U.S. treaties they ought not to remain. 1 Stat. 384. In the Act of March 26, 1794, 1 Stat. 400, Congress authorized the President to administer and enforce an embargo in the manner best adapted to give it "full effect." Most significantly, in the Act of June 4, 1794, 1 Stat. 372, the President was given virtually complete discretion, during the recess of Congress plus 15 days, as to whether and when to lay an embargo, the vessels to be covered, and the regulations to be adopted in its implementation.

†For example, the Act of Sept. 29, 1789, 1 Stat. 95, 96, granted the President authority "to call into service from time to time, such part of the militia . . . as he may judge necessary" to protect the inhabitants of the frontiers from hostile incursions by Indians. Section 1 of the Act of May 9, 1794, 1 Stat. 367, authorized the President to require the states to have 80,000 effective militia held "in readiness to march at a moment's warning." Discretion as to whether to build up to a certain number of naval vessels was delegated in Act of March 27, 1794, 1 Stat. 350, and Act of June 5, 1794, 1 Stat. 376.

In contrast to the House's stand against broad discretion to establish post roads was its willingness to grant discretion over foreign-affairs expenditures. The President was authorized to spend a lump sum, subject only to maximum limits on salaries for various grades of diplomatic officers, and to a requirement that he "account specifically for all such expenditures . . . as in his judgment may be made public," and state "the amount of such expenditures as he may think it advisable not to specify. . . ."[61] In another instance, the House initially succeeded in deleting from the unpopular excise tax bill a grant of power to the President to set the salaries of revenue officers, partly on the ground that Congress should "retain the power of disposing of their own money." A Senate amendment was eventually added and passed, however, that authorized the President to make such allowances to supervisors and collectors as he deemed proper, but not exceeding an aggregate maximum.[62]

During the remaining years of Washington's administration, discussions concerning discretion revolved largely around military affairs. Some dealt with whether certain powers should be delegated to the President, or whether they should be left with the states.[63] Several, however, concerned the distribution of power between Congress and the President. One of the most significant debates took place in April 1792, when objections were raised to the Senate's proposed addition to the militia bill of a provision authorizing the President, until the end of the next session of Congress, "to call out the Militia, or such part thereof, as the exigence may, in his opinion require, to execute the laws of the Union, suppress insurrections, and repel invasions." Gerry argued that the power sought to be vested was both dangerous and unnecessary. Murray claimed it was the duty of Congress "to define, with as much accuracy as possible, those situations" which justify the use of force, and he delivered a cogent analysis of the ways in which careful drafting could narrow the proposed power:

> It was surely the duty of Congress to define, with as much accuracy as possible, those situations which are to justify the execution in its interposition of a military force. The bill he had in view, he hoped, would attempt to mark with precision the objects the Constitution looked towards, under the words "execute the laws of the Union, and suppress insurrections." What was the occasion to warrant force of that species, was the first object: Who was to judge of its existence, was another: The space or district to which the draft should be or not be confined, was another. And the duration of the service, another. Among these considerations, it could not be forgotten that the civil arm was ever to be united, if not commanding; and how far the Marshals and Judges of the Courts of the Union

ought not to have a power on this subject, deserved more time than the House seemed inclined at present to give this bill. He would take the occasion to declare he had no jealousy as to abuses of power; but this Government is to be administered according to written law, applying to defined objects and situations. It was a Government of definition, and not of trust and discretion.

The Senate's amendment was defeated, and a committee was appointed to prepare a substitute bill, consisting of White, Gerry, and Murray, all of whom had voted against the broad Senate provision.[64]

On April 17, White presented the proposed substitute. It still gave the President power to call the militia in broad terms—"whenever the laws of the United States shall be opposed, or the execution thereof obstructed. . . ." The power was further qualified to apply only where the obstruction could not be suppressed by the judicial process or United States marshals; and the President was required to rely on militia of the state in which the obstruction occurred, unless they were insufficient or uncooperative. Several Representatives objected that the language was still too indefinite, and a motion was made to strike the relevant section. White responded that these objections "were considered by the Committee, and attempts were made to render the clause more express and definite, but it was found they only rendered it more obscure." The motion to strike the clause was defeated, and the bill finally passed on April 26.[65]

In sum, while Congress retained considerable control over establishing post roads, and attempted for a brief time to control military expenditures, Congress conferred broad discretion over important decisions respecting use of the military and the conduct of foreign affairs.

Control of Information

The extent to which the President can control the flow of information to Congress is naturally an issue of great importance in determining the roles played by each branch in foreign relations and war-making.[66] Washington obtained information in the course of his duties and often sent material to Congress on a variety of subjects. One would expect him to have sent information in connection with requests for congressional action.[67] But he did far more. He sent material to keep Congress informed of important developments, including matters that could have led to military actions.[68] Sometimes the material he sent was sensitive enough to cause him to ask

Congress to treat it confidentially. In late 1793, for example, Hamilton urged Washington to withhold from Congress, at least temporarily, papers reflecting Great Britain's depredations on American commerce; Washington refused, and sent the material when Congress reconvened.[69]

On the other hand, Washington withheld considerable information from voluntary transmittals, particularly diplomatic correspondence.[70] For example, Washington carried on an extensive "private" correspondence with Gouverneur Morris during the latter's service in France, first as special agent (1790–92) and then as Minister (1792–94). Morris sent official descriptions of events and activities to the Secretary of State, which were regularly transmitted to Congress. To Washington, he sent more detailed, subjective descriptions of the French Revolution, along with much purely personal material; these letters were invariably withheld from transmittals to Congress.* Congressmen occasionally noticed "gaps" in the material transmitted; more often such withholdings went unnoticed.[71]

Members of Congress seem to have accepted executive withholding of material from voluntary transmittals. No Congressman suggested that the President was required to submit all information as a matter of course. But Congress began almost immediately to call for information not voluntarily submitted. On July 21, 1789, during the First Session of the First Congress, the Senate ordered the Secretary of Foreign Affairs to bring "tomorrow . . . such papers as are requisite to give full information relative to the consular convention between France and the United States." The secretary attended the next day, "agreeably to order, and made the necessary explanations."[72] Congress built into the Act of September 2, 1789, establishing the Department of Treasury, a "duty of the Secretary of the Treasury . . . to make report, and give information to either branch of the legislature in person or in writing (as he may be required), respecting all matters referred to him by the Senate or House of Representatives, or which shall appertain to his office. . . ."[73] Many such requests were made.[74] Both houses seemed particularly confident of their power to demand information about expenditures,[75] and while the precise

---

*See 1 J. Sparks, *Life of Gouverneur Morris* 295 (1832). Numerous letters indicate the understanding between Washington and Morris. *E.g.*, Washington to Morris, Dec. 17, 1790, *Washington Papers* ser. 2, reel 7. On April 6, 1792, after receiving his credentials as Minister to France, Morris asked Washington whether their correspondence should continue as it had: "It is I presume expected that the public Servants will correspond fully and *freely* with the office of foreign affairs. It might therefore be improper not to say *all* in my letters to that office." *Gouverneur Morris Papers*, L.C. microfilm, vol. 17, reel 3. No response could be found, but the "private" correspondence continued as it had. See letters later collected in A.S.P., 1 *Foreign Relations* 379, 393–410.

significance of these requests is open to argument,[76] they clearly establish that Congress felt itself entitled to seek information.*

Congress also sought information through investigations conducted by committees. The first such effort was triggered when, on March 19, 1790, a House committee reported on Robert Morris's request for an investigation into his conduct and accounts as Superintendent of Finance under the Articles of Confederation to rescue his reputation from "aspersions."[77] Roger Sherman of Connecticut moved that a committee be appointed to audit Morris's administration of public moneys, and to report back to the House. Elbridge Gerry opposed a legislative investigation. The President, he said, is the only competent authority to review the conduct of officers of the executive branch. If the House preempts this authority by appointing commissioners, it would destroy the responsibility of executive officers and divest itself of the "great and essential privilege" of impeaching those officers for maladministration. His argument failed, however, and a committee was appointed.[78]

The most important early investigation resulted from the devastating defeat of General Arthur St. Clair by the Wabash Indians in November 1791. Two-thirds of St. Clair's army was either killed or wounded; all had fled ignominiously from the field of battle, many discarding their arms.[79] A motion was made in the House on March 27, 1792 to request the President "to institute an inquiry into the causes of the late defeat of the army under the command of Major General St. Clair...." Several Representatives argued against the motion, some because it improperly interfered with the President, others because they favored investigation by the House. The motion lost, 21-35.

The House thereupon decided, 44-10, to conduct its own inquiry; it appointed a committee to study the defeat of St. Clair, with power "to call for such persons, papers, and records, as may be necessary to assist their inquiries."[80] President Washington decided to cooperate fully with the inquiry, after receiving the unanimous view of his Cabinet that legislative investigations of this sort were lawful.† Sev-

---

*For example, in debating whether to ask the Secretary of the Treasury for a fiscal plan, William Findley argued that there was no need to call for a plan in order to obtain information. If we need information, he said, "the House, by its own authority, has a right to call for information from any Officer or Department, upon any subject respecting which it may originate laws. This is a power incidental to legislation." 3 *Annals* 448.

†Jefferson, writing of the Cabinet meeting on this subject, relates: "We ... were of one mind. 1. That the house was an inquest, and therefore might institute inquiries. 2. That they might call for papers generally...." The "Anas" in 2 *The Works of Thomas Jefferson* 213-14 (Fed. ed. 1904). *See generally* Landis, "Constitutional Limitations on the Congressional Power to Investigate," 40 *Harv. L. Rev.* 153 (1926).

eral executive officers appeared and testified at the committee's hearings.* An effort to allow Secretary of War Knox to challenge the report before the House failed as improper and potentially disruptive of the committee process.†

Though Congress regarded itself as entitled to require reports and testimony and to request information, both houses recognized a need for confidentiality in executive operations. The Act of July 1, 1790, which allocated a lump sum for foreign-affairs expenditures, required the President to account specifically for all expenditures "as in his judgment may be made public. . . ." The President could therefore hire special agents, or pay for secrets, or support other sensitive activities without revealing his conduct.[81] In asking for papers, moreover, Congressmen frequently authorized the President to withhold information the disclosure of which might harm the interests of the United States. On January 20, 1794, for example, Representative William L. Smith of South Carolina raised the possibility that a letter from the Secretary of State to the British Minister had been left out of the information on Anglo-American relations that the President had earlier sent Congress. Madison thought there was an unexplained gap "which should be filled up, but it might do as well to defer the matter for a day or two, till inquiry should be made of the Secretary of State, why it had been withheld? Upon informing the PRESIDENT, he would either give it up, or mention the reasons why he should not." The House agreed to a resolution that the President be "requested to lay before the House the omitted letter, or such

---

*3 Annals 1106. At a later point, about June 26, 1795, when Secretary of State Edmund Randolph anticipated controversy regarding the Jay Treaty, he raised the issue whether executive officers should attend a legislative inquiry on the subject, if called, and whether the questions should be required in advance. No answers were suggested, and the issue never arose; but his questions show how early this problem was anticipated:

> Suppose the Senate should require the attendance of the Secretary of State, to explain generally what they may require; ought he to attend under any circumstances of this kind; or, if he should attend at all, ought not the inquiries to be made of him, to be previously specified in writing, in order that the President, under whose direction alone the Secretary acts, may understand the whole extent of the business beforehand?

11 Writings of George Washington 478, 479 (J. Sparks, ed. 1848) [hereinafter "Washington Writings (Sparks)"].

†The House debated first a motion to inform Knox of the report, and then a request by Knox to appear. The request was referred to a committee appointed to hear additional arguments and information. See 3 Annals 672, 679-89. In addition to the impracticability of the whole House hearing evidence, Representatives argued that to allow the heads of departments to attend the House would tend to destroy "all freedoms of inquiry by Committees," and that, anyway, department secretaries had been invited to attend select committee hearings but came only once, for a brief period, "and then appeared extremely anxious to get away to attend to their offices."

parts as he may think proper."[82] Numerous requests by both houses contained similar language, in effect authorizing the President to exercise a discretion in determining what to submit.* Some Congressmen expressed the view that, even if a request for information contained no qualification recognizing discretion to withhold, the President had the power and the duty to refuse to submit material if in his opinion disclosure would harm the national interest.†

Washington and his officers almost invariably complied with legislative requests for information. They early determined, however, that the President did have discretion to withhold material that Congress requested. The issue first arose when the House committee appointed to investigate the defeat of General St. Clair requested Secretary Knox to supply all papers and communications relevant to the recent campaign. Knox laid the request before the President, who called together his distinguished Cabinet (Hamilton, Jefferson, Knox and Randolph) on March 31, 1792. Jefferson reported in his diary that "the President had called us to consult, merely because it was the first example, and he wishes so far as it should become a precedent, it should be rightly conducted." Jefferson recorded that the President said "he could readily conceive there might be papers of so secret a nature, as that they ought not to be given up." The Cabinet was unprepared to decide and requested time to think and inquire.[83]

They met again on April 2. As noted above, Jefferson reported that all agreed "that the House was an inquest, and therefore might institute inquiries. . . , [and] that it might call for papers generally."

---

*See especially the form of the requests dealt with in detail *infra*. *See also* the discussion of a motion made on December 26, 1796, 6 *Annals* 1703, and decided on January 2, 1797 (*id.* 1763-67), to request the President to supply information about measures taken to carry into effect the treaty with Algiers. Josiah Parker of Virginia and others noted that the President had mentioned difficulties on this subject in his annual message, but had sent no information. Even though Federalists agreed "there could be no question about their right in calling for the information in question," they opposed the demand as disrespectful. *Id.* After the request was approved, 44-31, Parker reported back to the House "that the President informed them that, before he had heard of the resolution, he had directed the necessary papers to be made out, and, as soon as they were ready, they should be laid before the House." *Id.* 1787.

†For example, during a debate concerning a proposed reference to the Secretary of the Treasury for a plan, John F. Mercer of Maryland—an opponent of the reference—stated that executive officers hold "the documents and information that arise in the administration of Government which this House may require of the Executive Magistrate, and which he will communicate as he sees fit. The House may go too far in asking information. He may constitutionally deny such information of facts there deputed as are [not?] fit to be communicated. . . ." 3 *Annals* 707. Other such statements were made in connection with the Jay Treaty debate, discussed *infra*.

They concluded, however, "that the executive ought to communicate such papers as the public good would permit, and ought to
refuse those, the disclosure of which would injure the public: consequently were [*sic*] to exercise a discretion." They also agreed that
the request should have been directed not to Secretary Knox but to
the President, who controlled all department heads and papers, and
undertook "to speak separately to the members of the committee,
and bring them by persuasion to the right channel." No serious
problem seems to have been anticipated, however, since "it was
agreed in this case, that there was not a paper which might not be
properly produced. . . ."[84]

The Cabinet's belief that requests should be addressed to the President was supported in Jefferson's notes only by reference to the fact
that Parliament had customarily addressed the King.[85] The conclusion that the President could refuse to supply information when he
decided that its surrender to Congress might be detrimental to the
nation's interests was apparently reached after the Cabinet considered the case of Sir Robert Walpole. Jefferson cited portions of a
debate in Parliament that tended to support the exercise by the
executive of discretion to withhold material requested.[86] Other portions of that debate, however, support a more sweeping legislative
power, and the House of Commons chose in that investigation to
act as the "Grand Inquest of the Nation," jailing Nicholas Paxton,
Solicitor of the Treasury, for refusing to testify.[87] Possibly because
he was aware of this, Jefferson claimed to have pointed out at the
Cabinet meeting that Parliament and Congress differed in "that the
former was a legislature, an inquest and a council . . . for the King.
The latter was, by the constitution, a legislature and an inquest, but
not a council,"[88] and therefore presumably did not have as broad a
need or right to share confidential material held by the executive.

The Cabinet's conclusion that Washington could withhold information was not acted upon at the time, since "there was not a paper
which might not be properly produced."[89] But there are indications
that the Cabinet's decisions were communicated to members of the
House. On April 4, following the Cabinet meeting of April 2, the
House addressed a formal request to the President that he "cause
the proper officers to lay before this House such papers of a public
nature, in the Executive Department, as may be necessary to the
investigation of the causes of the failure of the late expedition under
Major General St. Clair."[90] Not only did the House shift to addressing the President directly, as the Cabinet felt it should, but it also
requested only those papers "of a public nature." The latter phrase
is somewhat ambiguous, since it may mean those papers that could

properly or safely be made public, or that the House desired all public documents, no matter how sensitive, but did not want the papers of private persons that happened to be in the government's control. The former construction seems far more reasonable, however, and would be consistent with Congress's frequent practice of authorizing discretionary withholding.

Washington soon thereafter was required to deal with a request for information that contained no express grant of discretion to withhold. On January 17, 1794, a motion was made in the Senate to direct Secretary of State Edmund Randolph "to lay before the Senate the correspondences which have been had between the Minister of the United States at the Republic of France [Gouverneur Morris] and said Republic, and between said Minister and the office of Secretary of State." The motion was amended to address the President, rather than the Secretary, and to "request" rather than "direct" that the information be provided, and passed on January 24, by the narrow vote of 13-11.[91]

Washington regarded the material as sensitive and asked his Cabinet for their advice. Three Cabinet members met on January 28 to consider the Senate's resolution, with the following results:[92]

> General Knox is of opinion, that no part of the correspondences should be sent to the Senate:
>
> Colonel Hamilton, that the correct mode of proceeding is to do what General Knox advises; but the principle is safe, by excepting such parts as the President may choose to withhold:
>
> Mr. Randolph, that all the correspondence proper, from its nature, to be communicated to the Senate, should be sent; but that what the President thinks improper, should not be sent.*

*Besides taking part in the Cabinet opinion, Secretary of State Edmund Randolph wrote a few notes to Washington on this matter. He examined Morris's ministerial correspondence and found

> little of what is exceptionable and so much of what the most violent call patriotic. The parts to be withheld will probably be of these denominations: (1) what related to Mr. G[enê]t; (2) some harsh expressions of the conduct of the rulers of France, which if returned to that country, might expose him [Morris] to danger; (3) the authors of some interesting information, who, if known would be infallibly denounced. He speaks indeed of *his court* a phrase which he might as well have left alone.

Randolph to Washington, Jan. 26, 1794, in 4 *Correspondence of the American Revolution* 446 (J. Sparks, ed. 1853). Another letter told about a private meeting with James Madison and Justice James Wilson, suggested by Washington himself. *See* 7 D. Freeman, *George Washington* 151 (1957) [hereinafter "Freeman, *Washington*"]. Randolph quoted Madison as saying:

> There must be many things which the President cannot communicate with propriety: that if he was to select such as he thought proper and transmit

In a separate opinion William Bradford, the Attorney General, stated that "it is the duty of the Executive to withhold such parts of the said correspondence as in the judgment of the Executive shall be deemed unsafe and improper to be disclosed." He dealt specifically with the fact that the request was unqualified, arguing "that the general terms of the resolve do not exclude, in the construction of it, those just exceptions which the rights of the Executive and the nature of foreign correspondences require. Every call of this nature," he continued, "where the correspondence is secret and no specific object pointed at, must be presumed to proceed upon the idea that the papers requested are proper to be communicated; and it could scarcely be supposed, even if the words were stronger, that the Senate intended to include any letters, the disclosure of which might endanger national honor or individual safety."[93]

Washington accepted the view espoused by his Cabinet that he could withhold information in the public interest. On February 26 he responded to the Senate's request, clearly indicating that he had withheld some material:

> I have caused the correspondence, which is the subject of your resolution of the 24th day of January last, to be laid before me. After an examination of it, I directed copies and translations to be made; except in those particulars which, in my judgment, for public considerations, ought not to be communicated.
>
> These copies and translations are now transmitted to the Senate; but the nature of them manifest the propriety of their being received as confidential.[94]

No completely reliable evidence could be found of what material was actually withheld. The *American State Papers* contain forty dispatches Morris sent to Jefferson during 1792 and 1793, including several accompanying items. All the dispatches are printed in full, the reporter of the *State Papers* noting that "the paragraphs which were omitted, in the papers communicated to the Senate, are now supplied." Markings on the originals of the dispatches, contained in

---

them, and the Senate was to make an opposition, the people would go with the President against the Senate.

Letter of Jan. 29, 1794, in *Washington Papers*, series 4, reel 105. Justice Wilson was quoted as having said: "what they [the Senate] ought not to have, ought not to be sent." *Id.*

In a third letter Randolph differentiated between the executive and legislative powers of the Senate. If the Senate's resolution was considered executive action, then Randolph said the request could be totally denied. But Randolph intimated that the resolution ought to be regarded as "legislative," for the sake of avoiding "unnecessary contests." For even in such a situation, he wrote, "the President interposes his discretion, so as to give them no more, than in his judgment, is fit to be given." Randolph to Washington, after Jan. 24, 1794, *id.*

the National Archives, indicate that the material withheld consisted in general of Morris's appraisal of France's leaders, and its military and political situation, expressed often in colorful and derogatory terms.* In any event, no further Senate action was taken to obtain the material withheld.†

The most controversial debates concerning information took place after John Jay successfully negotiated the treaty with Britain that bears his name. The treaty was disadvantageous to the United States in that Jay agreed, contrary to his original instructions, to various restrictions on American commerce. But its promises of peace and that the British would withdraw from the western posts, were sufficient to cause the President to seek its ratification.

The treaty reached Secretary of State Randolph in March 1795. Anticipating a storm of protest, the President appears to have ordered the treaty kept secret until June 8, when he sent it, and "other documents connected with it," to a special session of the Senate. This three-month suppression of information by the President was, according to his biographers, "a course which he hoped would save the treaty from slander [in the press] until the Senate could deliberate it."[95] The Senate could, however, have been called together with relative ease in March; the Second Session of the Third Congress ended on March 3, and Washington reported that the treaty "was delivered to the Secretary of State" on March 7.[96] Word of the treaty may, in fact, have reached the President in time to keep Congress in session, had that been his wish.[97]

The documents sent to the Senate with the treaty included instructions to Jay, and his dispatches back to the United States. Since Jay had departed from some of his instructions, Randolph asked the President to consider withholding some of these potentially embarrassing papers.** Despite the danger to which the treaty would be exposed by full disclosure, the President decided against withholding

---

*Dispatch Number 34 was withheld in its entirety, apparently because it included nothing significant. It contained a discussion of the fluctuation of the French monetary system, as well as two requests for reimbursement from the government (for money given a naval officer in distress and for the cost of engraving passports). Morris to Jefferson, August 7, 1793, in National Archives Microfilm, *Despatches from United States Ministers to France,* M-34, reel 6.

†Randolph reported to Washington on February 24 that his message "appears to have given general satisfaction." He said that Madison had asked "whether an extract could not have been given from Mr. Morris's letter; upon my answering, that there were some things interwoven with the main subject, which ought not to be promulgated, he admitted, that the discretion of the President was always to be the guide." 33 *Washington Writings* (Fitzpatrick) 282.

**7 Freeman, *Washington* 250 n.61. In an undated note, Randolph asked:

1. Ought any letters, written from the department of state, after it was morally certain that they could not reach Mr. Jay before a treaty should be

any information from the Senate. Furthermore, when on June 19 the Senate requested the President to provide Jay's reports while he was Secretary of the Department of Foreign Affairs under the Confederation, and certain other documents, Washington promptly complied.[98] The Senate approved the treaty on June 24, after deleting one article.[99]

The President officially informed the House of the Jay Treaty when the Fourth Congress convened in December 1795.[100] After the treaty was ratified he asked the House to provide $90,000 needed to pay for the arbitral commissions it established. Unlike the Senate, which was predominantly Federalist, the House was by then controlled by Republicans, who in general were highly critical of the treaty. A Republican Representative, Edward Livingston of New York, proposed on March 2, 1796, that the President be requested to provide the House with a copy of the instructions given Jay and the correspondence and other documents relating to the treaty, all of which had already been supplied in confidence to the Senate. The proposed resolution contained no qualification.[101] On March 7, however, before the resolution had been discussed, Livingston sought to amend it—at the suggestion of "gentlemen for whose opinion he had a high respect"—so as to except "such of said papers as any existing negotiations may render improper to be disclosed."[102]

The President read of Livingston's motion in a newspaper on March 3 and immediately wrote a "private" note to Secretary of the Treasury Oliver Wolcott. He recalled "a request somewhat similar to this" either made or considered some two or three years earlier, but not "the conduct that was observed upon that occasion. . . ." He asked Wolcott to consult Alexander Hamilton, by then practicing law in New York, to "learn what the case and result was; and what he thinks ought to be the conduct of the President if Mr. L's motion reached him."[103]

Hamilton reacted with great concern to the news of Livingston's motion. In a letter on March 7 he advised the President against complying with the resolution if it were to pass because:

---

signed, to be laid before the Senate? Some of these letters criticize some things which are actually found in the treaty.

2. Ought any letters, written by Mr. Jay in answer to any of those objections, to be laid before the Senate?

3. If any of the letters mentioned in the second question should explain a difficulty in the treaty, would it be well to select them only, when the rest are withheld?

4. Suppose the Senate call for these letters, are they to be given up?

11 *Washington Writings* (Sparks) 478. (Emphasis omitted.)

[I]n a matter of such a nature the production of the papers cannot fail to start new and unpleasant game. It will be fatal to the negotiating power of the Government if it is to be a matter of course for a call of either House of Congress to bring forth all the communication, however confidential.

Acting as he had when still a Cabinet member, Hamilton offered a draft answer, based on two points—discretion to withhold sensitive material and the lack of any discernible House function to which the information could relate:

A right in the House of Representatives to demand and have, as a matter of course, and without specification of any object, all communications respecting negotiations with a foreign power, cannot be admitted without danger of much inconvenience. A discretion in the executive department how far and when to comply in such cases is essential to the due conduct of foreign negotiations and is essential to preserve the limits between the legislative and executive departments. The present call is altogether indefinite, and without any declared purpose. The Executive has no basis on which to judge of the propriety of a compliance with it, and cannot, therefore, without forming a very dangerous precedent, comply.

Had the House specifically pronounced the treaty a possible ground for impeachment, he said, "the President would attend with due respect to any application for necessary information." But no such declaration had been made.[104]

Even as Hamilton wrote to Washington, James Madison was taking steps to try to amend further Livingston's motion. Federalist Representatives had attacked the motion, contending that the House lacked discretion to deny an appropriation to implement a treaty that had been lawfully adopted. Madison "was not satisfied whether it was expedient at this time to go into a consideration of this very important question." For those not disposed to press the issue, Madison suggested casting "the resolution into such a form as not to bear even the appearance of encroaching on the Constitutional rights of the Executive." This meant adding a further and more sweeping qualification to Livingston's resolution, authorizing withholding of such "papers as, in his judgment, it may not be consistent with the interest of the United States, at this time, to disclose."

Madison's motion was deferred, and on March 8 was rejected 37–47, without further discussion.[105] This set the stage for an extraordinary and extensive debate on Livingston's resolution, occupying over 300 pages of the *Annals of Congress*, and casting considerable light on the thinking of early Congressmen on the allocation of power over information.

Most participants in the debate shared the view that the House had broad power to seek information. The request, said John Heath, a Republican from Virginia (and a founder of Phi Beta Kappa), "is a Constitutional right of this House to exercise now, and at all times, founded upon principles of publicity essentially necessary in this, our Republic, which has never been opposed. . . ."[106] If the Constitution requires the President to give information, said John Page of Virginia, surely the House could appropriately ask for it.[107] Many of those who opposed the resolution conceded the House's power to make such requests.[108] Those who supported the request went further, asserting that the House was duty-bound to call for anything necessary or useful.[109]

The debate also shows that members widely shared the view that the President had discretion to decline to furnish information requested. The proposed request was itself qualified. Some supporters of the resolution suggested, moreover, that the President could withhold any material, not just material relating to pending negotiations. For example, John Swanwick of Pennsylvania said "he saw no impropriety in calling for the information, which the PRESIDENT could withhold if not proper to be given."[110] James Hillhouse, a Connecticut Federalist, conceded the resolution's constitutionality, but asserted that the President "also had an undoubted Constitutional right, and it would be his duty to exercise his discretion on this subject, and withhold any papers, the disclosure of which would, in his judgment, be injurious to the United States; for it is to be presumed that the House of Representatives never would intentionally ask for such papers."[111] Those who argued that the request amounted to a demand were seeking to demonstrate the resolution's illegality or impropriety.* Supporters saw the resolution's qualified form as reflecting appropriate respect and deference to the President and his functions.† Only one member—a supporter—claimed that the House had an absolute power to obtain information it sought.[112]

The chief argument of those who opposed the resolution was that

---

*Robert Goodloe Harper (S.C.), for example, a vehement opponent of the resolution, said if he thought it proper he would change its "milk-and-water style" to a demand and would "insist on the demand." *Id.* 458. Another opponent said that a request to the President "amounts to a requirement; but there can be no right to acquire where there is no obligation to obey." *Id.* 53.

†John Rutherford of New Jersey, for example, thought it wholly proper that the resolution was "expressed in terms so replete with due respect to that great patriot—submitting all to his caution, his great prudence, and good sence. . . ." *Id.* 555. Samuel Smith, also a supporter, rejected Harper's contention that if proper the resolution should be unqualified: "It has been usual, and he hoped always would be, to approach the Chief Magistrate of the Union with proper respect and decorum." *Id.* 623.

the House lacked any discretionary connection with treaties for which the information could be necessary.[113] Given the highly sensitive nature of the material requested, moreover, and the Constitution's having vested the power to negotiate exclusively in the executive, opponents contended that the resolution should state specifically the reasons why the House needed the information.[114] The request was seen as improper and embarrassing to the President by forcing him to decide whether to do his duty in refusing the material, or to accede to the request because of his desire to cooperate with Congress.[115]

Supporters claimed the House had discretion to consider the merits of treaties, especially where the treaty contained provisions relating to international commerce and called for expenditures, both subjects specifically delegated to Congress by the Constitution.[116] The House also, they contended, could use the information in considering possible action against executive officers, and they claimed to need to see the information before they could be expected to state in a request that impeachment was being considered. Some argued that, even if the House contemplated no specific use of the material, they were entitled to request any information pertaining to the state of the Union.[117]

In addition to the many theoretical arguments made on both sides, one practical, political factor seems of special importance. Federalists regarded the call for information as politically motivated, and they were correct. An early speaker, John Heath of Virginia, indicated the proponents' intention to expose the papers to public view, though he purported to support such publicity "to allay their [the public's] sensibility."[118] Soon after, Robert Goodloe Harper, a Federalist leader from South Carolina, contended in effect that publicity was the motion's sole purpose, since the information had been made available to and seen by a House committee, whose chairman was none other than Livingston, and could be seen by "any member of that House who would request it."[119] Theophilus Bradbury, a Massachusetts Federalist, sarcastically added that "if general information were the object, to allay the public sensibility, he should think the better way would be to request the PRESIDENT to publish the papers in all the newspapers throughout the United States."[120] The resolution's supporters conceded that the information had been made available to the Senate, and to a House committee, but argued that this only proved the material was not secret and therefore could readily be provided and published.[121]

The resolution was adopted on March 24, by a vote of 61–38.[122] Washington immediately sought the advice of his Cabinet as to whether the House had a right to the papers, whether he should comply even if the House had no right, and in what terms a refusal or compliance should be stated.[123] Every Cabinet member advised that the House had no constitutional right to demand and obtain the papers. Each also concluded that the President possessed the discretion to deny the request, even if proper; Attorney General Charles Lee and Secretary of War James McHenry felt compliance would be expedient, while Secretary of State Timothy Pickering and Secretary of Treasury Oliver Wolcott argued against complying.*

Further advice also arrived from Hamilton. In a letter dated March 24, he took a frankly political view of the request. "I am not . . . without fear," he said, "that there are things in the instructions to Mr. Jay—which good policy, considering the matter externally as well as internally, would render it inexpedient to communicate."[124] Four days later he wrote that publication of the instructions—"in general a crude mass"—"will do no credit to the administration."[125] If the President decided to send any papers at all, said Hamilton, "they ought only to be the *commissions*, and Mr. Jay's *correspondence*, saying that these are all that it appears to him for the public interest to send." In a draft reply to the House, which arrived late and was not used by Washington, Hamilton proposed rejecting the request primarily because the House lacked any function related to the demand, but also because of the need for discretion in divulging the details of international negotiations; "It is a rule of mutual convenience and security among nations, that neither shall, without adequate cause and proper reserves, promulge the details of a negotiation between them. . . ."[126]

*According to Lee, "The President has the right to decide whether he will comply with a request for papers on a subject properly under Congress' cognizance and which may with propriety be communicated to them." In the area of foreign relations, Lee believed the President "may withhold from [the House] the confidential communications between foreign ministers and our own on the subject of a Treaty either pending or concluded when . . . He shall think it best," and that the President is "bound by the Considerations of Good Faith" to American and foreign ministers to do so on occasions. Lee to Washington, March 26, 1796, in *Washington Papers*, series 4, reel 109. McHenry concluded that "the President is the sole judge of what or whether any papers ought to be laid before the House at this juncture." McHenry to Washington, March 26, 1796, *id.* Wolcott said that the President should give as one of the reasons for denial: "That in the exercise of the duties committed to the President, secrecy and personal confidence are sometimes essential, and that a regard to the public interests and to the obligations of good faith, will not always permit a full disclosure of all documents connected with foreign negotiations." Wolcott to Washington, March 27, 1796, in 1 *Memoirs of the Administration of Washington and John Adams* (G. Gibbs, ed., 1846). Pickering sent Washington a draft of the message eventually sent to the House. The draft contained a passage, omitted from the final version, asserting a discretion in the executive when and how to comply with demands. Draft of Washington's Speech to the House of Representatives, Mar. 26, 1796, *Washington Papers*, series 4, reel 109.

Washington decided to refuse the House request. "From the first moment," he wrote Hamilton, "and from the fullest conviction in my own mind, I had resolved to *resist the principle* wch. was evidently intended to be established by the call . . . and only deliberated on the manner. . . ."[127] In a message dated March 30, he refused the request because the papers were relevant to no House function "except that of an impeachment; which the resolution had not expressed."[128] His message did not directly rely on a claimed power to withhold material; in fact, the final version omitted a statement in an earlier draft that "a discretion in the Executive Department, when and how to comply with such demands is essential to the due conduct of foreign negotiations."[129] The message does suggest such a power, however, in describing the reasons full disclosure might be dangerous:

> The nature of foreign negotiations requires caution; and their success must often depend on secrecy; and even, when brought to a conclusion, a full disclosure of all the measures, demands, or eventual concessions which may have been proposed or contemplated would be extremely impolitic; for this might have a pernicious influence on future negotiations; or produce immediate inconveniences, perhaps danger and mischief, in relation to other Powers. The necessity of such caution and secrecy was one cogent reason for vesting the power of making Treaties in the President with the advice and consent of the Senate; the principle on which the body was formed confining it to a small number of members. To admit, then, a right in the House of Representatives to demand, and to have, as a matter of course, all the papers respecting a negotiation with a foreign Power, would be to establish a dangerous precedent.[130]

The President's refusal to comply confronted the House with the problem of deciding how to respond. On March 31, several Republicans sought to have the President's message referred to a Committee of the Whole. Some Federalists objected, taking the view that, once the President had refused the House request for papers, nothing remained to be done. "The House have made a demand on the PRESIDENT; the PRESIDENT refused it; this must naturally put an end to the correspondence on this subject."[131] No one in favor of the reference to committee contended that it might lead to a further demand for information. Rather, they suggested that, had the President simply refused to comply, the matter could safely have been dropped. But the President had gone further, they argued, and had given his reasons for refusing which, if allowed to stand without response, might be regarded as an accurate statement of the House's powers. "The *President* had given the reasons of his opinion," said Joseph Varnum of Massachusetts, "it was right, also, that the people should know the sense of the House." The vote to refer the matter to committee was 55 to 37 in favor.[132]

Discussion of the President's message began on April 6. Thomas Blount of North Carolina offered two resolutions. The first affirmed a discretionary role for the House in implementing treaties that regulate subjects assigned by the Constitution to Congress. The second declared it unnecessary in requests by the House for information "which may relate to any Constitutional functions of the House, that the purpose for which such information may be wanted, or to which the same may be applied, should be stated in the application."[133] These resolutions were intended only as declarations of policy. In the only major statement recorded on the subject, Madison said that, although "the House must have a right, in all cases, to ask for information which might assist their deliberations on the subjects submitted to them by the Constitution," he agreed that "the Executive had a right, under a due responsibility, also to withhold information, when of a nature that did not permit a disclosure of it at the time." If the President's refusal "had been founded simply on a representation, that the state of the business within his department, and the contents of the papers asked for, required it, although he might have regretted the refusal, he should have been little disposed to criticize it. But the Message had contested what appeared to him a clear and important right of the House; and stated reasons for refusing the papers, which, with all the respect he could feel for the Executive, he could not regard as satisfactory or proper."* This view was consistent with the fact that the declaration proposed in no way suggested that the President lacked power to withhold information. The resolutions were approved, 57–35.[134]

The House's effort to obtain instructions concerning the Jay Treaty thus failed. A clear majority of the House refused to accept the grounds upon which the President placed his refusal to supply the information, but no one challenged the result. The House did reject Madison's motion to soften Livingston's resolution by allowing the President to withhold material the disclosure of which might injure the nation. But this is not a safe indication that the House regarded the President as lacking discretion, since those who opposed making any request apparently voted against Madison's language

*5 *Annals* 773. In a letter to James Monroe, on April 18, 1796, Madison said:

The prevailing belief [in Congress] was, that he [the President] would send a part, if not the whole, of the papers applied for. If he thought any part improper to be disclosed or if he wished to assert his prerogative without coming to a rupture with the House, it was seen to be easy for him to avoid that extremity by that expedient.

2 *Letters and Other Writings of James Madison* 96 (Congress ed. 1867) [herein-

in order to preserve Livingston's motion in the most objectionable form possible.* Had the President chosen to rely on his discretion to withhold material in the public interest, it seems likely that the decision would have been accepted by the House with no further action. And although the President chose to rely primarily on the ground that the House had no discretionary role in reviewing treaties, he almost certainly felt himself empowered to refuse the papers on the ground that disclosure would injure the interests of the nation.†

One final comment on Washington's attitude on information questions is necessary. During 1795 Edmund Randolph resigned as Secretary of State after being confronted by the President with a letter from the French envoy, Joseph Fauchet, to the French foreign office, suggesting that Randolph had asked for a bribe in return for influence and secrets. Randolph engaged in a campaign to clear his name, and sought information from Washington for that purpose. He also asked for confidential and potentially embarrassing material relating to the Jay Treaty, and for permission to publish it. The President gave him access to all the material sought, and to publish any "private and confidential" letter he ever wrote to Randolph. Washington was determined, in the face of Randolph's challenge to his personal integrity, to prove "that he as President had nothing to hide. . . ."[135]

THE CONDUCT OF FOREIGN AFFAIRS

The modern presidency possesses substantial power to cause military confrontations because of foreign-relations decisions. The President

after *"Madison Letters"*]. On April 11, 1796, Madison had written to Jefferson "that the call for papers was refused, and reasons assigned more extraordinary than the refusal." *Id.* 94.

*Madison gave the following description to James Monroe in a letter of April 18, 1796, soon after the events in question:

> In order to render the motion [by Livingston] perfectly unobjectionable, and the more justifiable to the public in case of a refusal of the papers, I moved to enlarge the exception to all such papers as the President might deem it inconsistent with the interest of the United States at this time to disclose. This accommodating amendment was opposed by the whole Treaty party [Federalists], who, being joined by the warmer men on the other side, succeeded in rejecting it.

2 *Madison Letters* 96.

†In a letter to Hamilton, written March 31, immediately after his message to the House was sent, Washington apologized for not having used Hamilton's latest draft. He said that he "understood," however, "that if the Papers were refused a fresh demand with strictures might be expected. . . ." Hamilton's draft was being preserved, he said, "as a source for reasoning if my information proves true." 35 *Washington Writings* (Fitzpatrick) 7-8. Had the House confronted the President, he might have stressed more strongly the claim of discretionary withholding fully developed in Hamilton's draft.

can very materially influence the nation's decision to use force by the manner in which he manages aspects of foreign relations, such as recognition of foreign governments, negotiation, treaty formation, direction of the foreign-affairs bureaucracy, and enforcement of international law. This section examines in some detail foreign-affairs practices during Washington's administration to determine the manner in which the respective foreign-affairs powers of Congress and the President were exercised, and particularly the extent to which the President even then could influence the question of war or peace.

Power over the General Conduct of Foreign Affairs

President Washington quickly assumed the role of communicating with foreign powers. On October 9, 1789 he responded to a letter from the King of France "addressed to the President and Members of the General Congress of the United States" stating that, by the change in the national government, the honor of receiving and answering such letters "has devolved upon me."[136] The Senate twice rejected motions to request the President to communicate messages on behalf of the United States;[137] Oliver Ellsworth of Connecticut said that "neither branch [of Congress] had a right to dictate to the President what he should answer [foreign nations]. The Constitution left the whole business in his breast."[138]

The President also assumed the power of passing upon the credentials and behavior of foreign representatives. This became an extremely sensitive issue after war broke out between France and England in 1793. One question that arose was whether the French Minister Genêt should be received, and the type of reception that he should be given. The President seems to have assumed that he could refuse to receive Genêt, or to qualify his reception, but decided against doing so in order to avoid offending France. Washington also requested Genêt's recall, when Genêt's conduct exceeded his tolerance.[139] In another instance, Washington revoked the *exequatur* of a British consul, after he had caused a small privateer to be fitted out in Boston, which proceeded to harass ships within and around that harbor.[140]

Control of the foreign-affairs bureaucracy early became an issue. A lengthy debate occurred in Congress during 1790 on who was to set the ranks of diplomatic agents. Washington succeeded in obtaining authority from Congress to set the ranks himself, subject to Senate approval, but had "to intimate" that he planned to send ministers to both France and Great Britain.[141] He subsequently adjusted the rank of ministers without prior consultation, though he sought Senate approval after the changes were made.[142] The issue arose again in May 1796, when Washington requested extra funds to finance the upgrading of ministers at Lisbon and Madrid. No one questioned the President's authority to adjust ranks, but several Representatives assumed they had the power to deny the funds necessary to carry the appointments into effect. Others claimed the President should be the final judge of such matters, subject only to a check if he grossly abused his authority.[143] The appropriation was approved.[144]

The first formal negotiation was authorized in 1789, when the Senate approved Washington's request that commissioners be appointed to negotiate with the Creek Indians. When the commissioners failed to obtain an agreement, the President continued the negotiation through his own officers. He later explained to the Senate that, after the failure of the commissioners, "it appeared to me most prudent, that all subsequent measures for disposing them [the Creeks] to a treaty should in the first instance be informal."[145] He began the practice of asking private citizens to make diplomatic contacts as early as October 13, 1789, when he enlisted the help of Gouverneur Morris to determine whether Great Britain was agreeable to observing its treaty of peace with the United States, and whether it had any interest in concluding a treaty of commerce.[146] The President regarded himself unable, however, to appoint an Envoy Extraordinary to France, when the Senate was out of session, and when a Minister was already serving there. He resorted, on the unanimous advice of his Cabinet, to removing the Minister to France (James Monroe), in order to create the vacancy that the Constitution specifically allows the President to fill.[147]

Several other important incidents occurred in connection with treaty negotiation. Washington attempted at first to obtain the Senate's "advice" on treaty terms before negotiations, and not merely its "consent" afterwards.[148] On August 22, 1789, he consulted the Senate in person concerning the terms of a treaty yet to be negotiated with the Creek Indians. With less than one-day's notice the President arrived at the Senate with Secretary of War Henry Knox, and a paper was read describing the situation and posing specific questions to the Senators. Apparently the President had expected to obtain "advice" on the spot. He was sorely disappointed. Senators requested further information and delays to permit discussion and committee consideration. One Senator, unsympathetic to the President, regarded the procedure as an effort to "have these advices and consents ravished, in a degree, from us."[149] Most of the questions were postponed for the weekend, to Washington's chagrin.

On the next Monday, Washington appeared again and obtained satisfactory answers to all his questions. But he never again sought prior consultation in person.[150]

Instead of consulting in person, without adequate notice, Washington began to consult in writing.[151] He apparently assumed "that the Senate was his advisory council of foreign policy generally because its consent was necessary to the making of treaties in which foreign policy at major points crystallizes."[152] He did, however, communicate to foreign ministers his own view of the nation's position on important issues.[153] Furthermore, he consciously began a negotiation with the western Indians in early 1793, by unanimous vote of the Cabinet, without previously consulting the Senate. "We all thought," wrote Jefferson, that "if the Senate should be consulted and consequently apprized of our line, it would become known to [the British Minister George] Hammond, and we should lose all chance of saving anything more at the treaty than our ultimatum."[154]

This pattern was followed again in 1794, when the President authorized John Jay, as special agent, to conduct a secret negotiation with Great Britain. Secretary of State Randolph objected to allowing Jay to sign a treaty without prior Senate discussion, but Washington accepted Hamilton's advice to take the treaty to the Senate after it was made.[155] On the other hand, Washington's assumption of the power to negotiate unilaterally with other nations left unchanged the Senate's power to advise and consent after negotiation. The President consciously accepted the Senate's power to approve treaties conditionally, and thereby in effect to advance "advice" in the form of proposed amendments.[156]

One factor that may have affected Washington's decision to conduct some negotiations unilaterally was his belief in the need for secrecy. He frequently communicated material to both houses in confidence. Yet he soon must have realized that his desire for secrecy would not always be respected. During the time the Federalists controlled the House, they enforced a rule that excluded the public during any debate concerning material sent to the House by the President "in confidence." After the Republicans gained control, they changed this rule to allow the majority to vote for public debate on confidential communications on an *ad hoc* basis.[157] Soon thereafter, the House voted to lift an injunction of secrecy they had placed on some letters sent by the President "in confidence."[158] A similar rebellion of sorts took place in the Senate after the Jay Treaty was conditionally ratified. The President wanted the treaty kept secret until all negotiations were complete. The Senate voted, however, to rescind its injunction of secrecy, although it continued to enjoin "Senators not to authorize or allow any copy [to be made] of the said communication. . . ." Both Senators Pierce Butler of South Carolina and Stevens T. Mason of Virginia smuggled copies out of the Senate chamber, apparently before the secrecy injunction was lifted, and "on the same day that the government planned to make the treaty public, the Republican *Aurora* beat it to the punch by printing an abstract of the terms."[159]

Whether the President has authority to make international agreements without Senate consent is an issue that arose only indirectly. In early 1793 Washington sought the Cabinet's advice as to whether "the Executive, or the Executive and Senate together [have] authority to relinquish to the Indians . . . [land] validly obtained by former treaties?" All but Jefferson were of the opinion "that the Executive and Senate have such authority"; Jefferson felt that the branches lacked such power, even when acting together. Implicitly, the Cabinet seems to have unanimously assumed that the Senate's concurrence would be necessary.[160] An instance in which Washington considered adopting a measure without any Senate consultation occurred in July 1795, just after the Senate approved the Jay Treaty with one article deleted. Washington asked his Cabinet if Senate approval would be required to include a revised version of the article. All its members advised that the article could be revised and included in the treaty without Senate approval. Hamilton disagreed. He felt Senate approval was required. No revision was attempted, however, since Britain agreed to accept the treaty as amended.[161] Washington did seem willing to enter into informal understandings with other nations, for which Senate approval was not sought; and he made an arrangement with Canada concerning postal matters that has been regarded the first "executive" agreement.*

The role of the House in connection with treaties and other foreign-affairs matters first became an issue on August 7, 1789, when the President informed Congress of disputes between the United States and several powerful tribes of Indians, and recommended a temporary commission of three persons to negotiate a treaty. Representative George Clymer, a Pennsylvania Federalist, presented a bill on August 10, before the proposed terms were known, providing for the appointment of commissioners and for the expenses that might be incurred in the anticipated negotiation. Some Representatives objected to the provision purporting to appoint commissioners,

---

*See the discussion *infra*, p. 111. The postal agreement was probably based on §26, Act of Feb. 20, 1792, 1 Stat. 232, 239, which authorized the Postmaster General to make reciprocal arrangements with foreign nations for exchanging mail. *See* W. McClure, *International Executive Agreements* 38–39 (1941).

arguing that the House had no role in treaty-making. Others disagreed, arguing that the House had concurrent jurisdiction in forming treaties "by the exercise of their constitutional powers, necessary to give them efficiency." The reference to commissioners was deleted, at least partly because several members regarded the issue as unimportant.[162]

A far more controversial issue was presented in the Third Congress, when the House considered whether to adopt a resolution calling for the nonimportation of British goods as reprisal for British depredations and impressment. An opponent of the proposed resolution, Samuel Dexter of Massachusetts, noted that the executive had appointed an envoy to negotiate a commercial treaty with Britain. This was the President's responsibility, he said, an incident of the right to make treaties. "But we are now commencing a negotiation ourselves, and prescribing terms of a treaty. . . . This looks to me very much like usurpation, by whatever name we may choose to call it." The proper form of action, he suggested, was a resolution that called upon the President "to pursue with energy a demand for recompense, according to the custom of nations, and pledging ourselves to support him, if the event should prove unsuccessful. . . . I can see nothing further which is Legislative in its nature, or committed to our care by the Constitution, until it shall appear that the negotiation has failed of success."[163] The nonimportation resolution passed, however, after supporters answered that Congress could express its view because it alone was empowered to regulate commerce, and that an expression would aid the negotiation.[164]

The most notorious conflict over the House's role in connection with treaties took place when Washington requested $90,000 to implement the Jay Treaty.[165] After Livingston proposed to request information on the treaty, many members opposed the request on the ground that the House had no role with ratified treaties except the duty to provide the funds necessary for their implementation.[166] House Republicans countered that the House was required to consider the merits of each bill for appropriations, and that no treaty could settle, without House approval, a matter over which the House was given some power by the Constitution—in this case the regulation of commerce.[167] The request passed, but Washington refused to comply on the ground that the papers could relate to no legitimate function of the House "except that of an impeachment; which the resolution has not expressed," as discussed earlier in this Chapter. The Constitutional Convention, he noted, had explicitly rejected the proposition "that no Treaty should be binding on the United States which was not ratified by a law."[168]

The House responded to Washington's challenge by passing a resolution conceding that the House has no "agency in making Treaties," but maintaining

> that when a Treaty stipulates regulations on any of the subjects submitted by the Constitution to the power of Congress, it must depend, for its execution, as to such stipulations, on a law or laws to be passed by Congress. And it is the Constitutional right and duty of the House of Representatives, in all such cases, to deliberate on the expediency or inexpediency of carrying such treaty into effect, and to determine and act thereon, as, in their judgment, may be most conducive to the public good.[169]

But the House did no more than announce its views. The Republican majority came apart on votes to declare the treaty "highly objectionable" or simply "objectionable"; both motions were defeated by the Speaker's deciding vote. The appropriation passed, 51-48, apparently as a result of "petitions, oratory, senatorial threats, and personal pressure. . . ."[170] However, Washington's view of the House's limited role in connection with treaties did not prevent him from frequently informing the House of foreign-affairs matters. He undoubtedly was aware that its cooperation would be necessary and that some issues might pertain to powers specifically assigned to Congress, such as the power to declare war.*

Finally, both the House and the Senate adopted foreign-policy pronouncements in several important instances. For example, on May 15, 1794, the Senate adopted a report that expressed the view that the United States would insist upon the right to navigate the Mississippi. The report noted that negotiations with Spain were underway, and that "it would be improper for Congress to interfere," but the Senate's adamant stand in favor of free navigation must have been obvious to the President.[171] During January of the same year the House debated whether commercial reprisals ought to be taken against Britain. Many Representatives were, like Madison, willing to exercise their judgment and to conclude that negotiation "has failed"; accordingly, a resolution for nonintercourse was adopted over the argument that it would interfere with pending negotiations.[172] The House also adopted a committee report recommending the creation of offices for two or more agents, to be appointed by the President with the consent of the Senate, whose duty would be

---

*For example, on November 7, 1792, the President sent both houses of Congress documents pertaining to Spanish interference with the Creek Indians, apparently designed to undermine the treaty between America and the Creeks. 3 *Annals* 673. On May 20, 1794, he sent both houses information pertaining to "hostile movements" against Spain, seemingly by Americans, and requested their help. 4 *Annals* 102.

to find and aid in obtaining the release of American citizens impressed into foreign service. A provision to this effect passed, over objections that it unconstitutionally interfered with the executive.[173] The Senate, for its part, seemed willing (apparently at the President's suggestion) to extend its foreign-affairs activities to the interpretation of existing treaties. On February 26, 1791, the Senate considered and rejected the French interpretation of a treaty, and "advised" the President that the Senate's construction should be pressed upon France "in the most friendly manner."[174]

Power to Involve the Nation in War

International events during Washington's administration frequently confronted him with situations in which his exercise of foreign-affairs powers could have involved the nation in war. In handling these situations the President was intent on keeping the nation at peace and exceptionally skilled at doing so. He consulted Congress or the Senate before acting on many sensitive matters. But in some important instances he demonstrated that he regarded himself as empowered unilaterally to express and enforce the foreign policy of the United States, even where military consequences could result, subject to congressional correction.

First, some instances of the President's caution. When Washington considered threatening to use force against the Creek Indians in connection with a negotiation in 1789, he sought the Senate's approval before doing so; and the Senate in fact granted only limited authority.* When he wanted to warn the Spanish Minister Gardoqui that the United States would never surrender its claim to navigation of the Mississippi, he determined to express that adamant position

---

*This occurred on August 22, 1789, during Washington's famous trip to the Senate to obtain its "advice and consent" to the terms contemplated in a negotiation with the Creeks. The dispute between Georgia and the Creeks primarily concerned whether certain lands had been ceded by the Creeks to Georgia in prior treaties. One question Washington raised was whether, if the commissioners concluded that the treaties between Georgia and the Creeks were valid and "just and equitable," they "be instructed to insist on a formal renewal and confirmation thereof, and, in case of a refusal, . . . to inform the Creeks that the arms of the Union shall be employed to compel them to acknowledge the justice of the said cessions?" To this the Senate answered affirmatively. 1 *Annals* 71. The Senate was also asked whether, if the treaties were found invalid and the Indians refused to make a deal for the land in question, the commissioners should make the cession to Georgia "an ultimatum." *Id.* 72. Authority to make such a threat was refused. The commissioners were therefore empowered to threaten military action only if they concluded that the prior treaties were valid and equitable. Contemporaneous efforts made in the Senate and House to include in the treaty-appropriation legislation an explicit authorization for military action against the Creeks failed. *Id.* 64–65, 723–25.

"delicately and tenderly," apparently out of concern that a stronger statement, without at least the Senate's consent, would infringe upon Congress's power to declare war.[175] On December 16, 1793, Washington confidentially sent Congress a message that included the following warning received from Spain concerning the Creek Indians: "The continuance of the peace, good harmony, and perfect friendship of the two nations was very problematical for the future unless the United States should take more convenient measures and of greater energy than those adopted for a long time past." Said Washington, "This last declaration left no room to evade ... the appearance of a desire to urge on a disagreement," which apparently was enough to cause him to convey the news to Congress.[176] At one point he refused to make treaties with Denmark and Sweden because, among other reasons, he feared the action might cause war with Britain.* This was undoubtedly in part the result of his determined policy of avoiding war, but it also reflected his respect for, if not complete agreement with, the view that Congress should be consulted before any action is taken that could cause war.†

The Nootka Sound Controversy, 1790. In 1789, Spanish vessels seized the port of Nootka Sound, an inlet on the western shore of Vancouver Islands, and some British vessels. Britain suspended diplomatic relations in February 1790, and war seemed likely.[177] Britain sought an alliance with the United States, but Washington as well as others in his Cabinet suspected the British had designs on Spanish-owned Louisiana and the Floridas.

Washington asked his Cabinet what the United States should do if

---

*Attorney General Bradford wrote to Washington that the Constitution may limit the President's power to commit the United States to an agreement to take part in a war between Britain and Sweden or Denmark. If war took place between those powers, the question of whether to sign a treaty, he said, "would perhaps come more properly before that body in whom the right of declaring war is vested." Letter of July 5, 1794, *Washington Papers*, series 4, reel 105. Randolph felt the objection was avoidable by giving Jay proper instructions. Letter of July 9, 1794, in *id.* Bradford, Knox, and Hamilton all felt the treaties should be avoided because Denmark and Sweden were too weak, and cooperation with them was possible without a treaty. *See id.*, and Knox to Washington, July 2, 1794; Hamilton to Randolph, July 8, 1794, in *id.*

†An example of this theory is a statement by John Page of Virginia, made during the House debate on the resolution to obtain information about the Jay Treaty. The Senate and President can make treaties, he said, but they cannot "instead of securing the rights of neutrality with all the belligerent Powers, sacrifice those rights in favor of one of those Powers, and provoke another to make war on the United States. There are powers which they cannot possess, and, indeed which the Constitution neither gives nor can give, because it would be destructive of itself and of its original intention." 5 *Annals* 560-61. The classic exposition is in the Pacificus-Helvidius debates, discussed *infra* 111-16.

war began between Britain and Spain. Jefferson advised telling the British that the United States would remain neutral, but he suggested joining Spain in guaranteeing the independence of Louisiana and the Floridas.[178] Adams was so apprehensive of British control of New Orleans that he advised siding with Spain against England. Gouverneur Morris, writing on May 29 from England, advocated the policy that Washington adopted—using neutrality as a way of obtaining a favorable treaty of commerce from Britain as well as favorable treatment from Spain regarding the right to use the Mississippi. Instructions prepared by Jefferson to American officials in Britain and Spain, to be sent in secret via Colonel David Humphreys, explicitly warned that the United States would abandon neutrality if Britain sought "conquests adjoining us," or if Spain "does not yield our right to the common use of the Missisipi [sic] and the means of using and securing it."[179]

Washington anticipated that, if war erupted, the British would attempt to capture New Orleans and the Spanish post above it on the Mississippi. He asked advice on how to respond if Britain applied for permission to march troops through United States territory from Detroit to the Mississippi, and on what to do if they took such action without permission. Jefferson recommended that no answer be given the British, if possible, to maintain maximum flexibility. If an answer were required, he suggested granting permission, and if British troops went through without permission, he suggested protesting to keep the issue alive "till events should decide whether it is most expedient to accept their apologies, or profit of the aggression as a cause of war."

Knox agreed with Jay and Adams that neutrality required that British troops be refused passage. If they marched through regardless of a denial, or without making a request, he suggested,

> it might be proper for the President . . . to convene immediately the legis-
> lature if the occasion should be so urgent as to require their meeting at an
> earlier day than the adjournment, and to lay the whole affair before
> them, with his opinion of the measures proper to be pursued.

The reason for this was that "Congress are vested with the right of providing for the common defence, and of declaring war, and of consequence they should possess the information of all facts and circumstances thereunto appertaining." Hamilton contended that passage could be allowed consistent with neutrality, but he agreed with Knox that if the British entered the United States without permission, violently or peacefully,

it would appear advisable immediately to convene the Legislature; to make
the most vigorous measures for war; to make a formal demand of satisfaction; to commence negotiations for alliances; and if satisfaction should be
refused, to endeavor to punish the aggressor by the sword.[180]

The British neither asked permission nor intruded without permission. We cannot know, therefore, what Washington would have said
and done. Clearly, however, he and the Cabinet felt free to choose a
policy of neutrality without convening Congress, and neutrality
implied no clear or safe course. It was a policy that suggested significantly different courses of action to each Cabinet member, all
dangerous. They also felt free to use neutrality, or the threat of an
alliance, as a weapon, to obtain concessions beneficial to the United
States. At the point of confrontation, however, if the British were
to cross American territory without permission, Knox and Hamilton
strongly suggested Congress be called, partly because Congress was
needed to provide the military support, and partly because Congress
was supposed to be consulted under the Constitution. Jefferson undoubtedly would have concurred in this position.

The Proclamation of Neutrality. By far the most important
foreign-affairs decision of Washington's administration, replete with
significant precedents, was the proclamation and implementation of
neutrality. France declared war against England on February 1, 1793.
Congress adjourned on March 2, 1793, ignorant of this news, which
did not reach Philadelphia until early April. The President, informed
at his home in Mt. Vernon, feared that American citizens might
involve the nation in war by siding with one nation or the other, and
immediately resolved on the policy that "the Government of this
country . . . [must] use every means in its power to prevent" involvement.[181] He cut short his visit and proceeded to Philadelphia.[182]
     On April 18, the day after reaching Philadelphia, Washington sub-
mitted a list of thirteen questions to each member of his Cabinet.
The first asked whether "a proclamation [should] issue for the
purpose of preventing interferences of the citizens of the United
States in the war between France and Great Britain, etc.? Shall it
contain a declaration of neutrality or not?" Other questions dealt
with how America should treat the new Republic of France, and
the meaning and applicability of existing French-American treaties.
The thirteenth question asked: "Is it necessary or advisable to call
together the two Houses of Congress, with a view to the present
posture of European affairs. If it is, what should be the particular
object of such a call?"[183]

The first question involved the President's power to decide and enforce, when Congress was not in session, the nation's policy toward belligerents. The entire Cabinet wished to avoid involvement in the European war. Just as in the Nootka Sound controversy, however, neutrality was a policy replete with danger, even if it was the least dangerous course available. The existing treaties with France, and the pro-French feeling within the United States, made neutrality a policy that risked conflict with France. Yet to take any but a firmly neutral position would risk trouble with England.[184] Jefferson asserted that no declaration of "neutrality" should be made, and the word "neutrality" was avoided. But the Cabinet unanimously adopted a statement authorizing a proclamation that "contained a warning or an announcement on every point that was necessary for the preservation of a neutral position. . . ."[185] Even Jefferson referred to the American position as one of "neutrality."[186] The proclamation was issued on April 22, 1793.

On April 28, 1793, Jefferson reported to Washington that the thirteenth question of Washington's circular—whether to convene Congress—'has been decided negatively."[187] Hamilton and the other Federalists understandably might have wanted to defer calling Congress for as long as possible, since the heavily Republican House would be certain to express strongly pro-French sentiment.

But Jefferson's failure to dissent from this decision cannot so easily be explained. During March 1793 he had noted in a letter to Madison the possibility that "the naval powers combined against the French will prohibit supplies even of provision to that country. Should this be formally notified I should suppose Congress would be called," he said, "because it is a justifiable cause of war, as the Executive cannot decide the question of war on the affirmative side, neither ought it to do so on the negative side, by preventing the competent body from deliberating on the question."[188] Possibly Jefferson voted against calling back Congress because he wanted to save his influence to defeat Hamilton's move to have the French Minister Genêt's reception qualified.[189] He also feared, however, that the newly elected Congress might side too vigorously with France, a possibility he mentioned to Madison when suggesting that Congress should be called if war between Britain and France occurred. In any event, by June 2, 1793, Jefferson was writing to Madison that, while he thought it likely that Congress would be convened early, he wished "to keep their meeting off to the beginning of October, if affairs will permit it." Two months later, on August 4, 1793, Jefferson did argue that Congress should be convened earlier than scheduled. But he sought only a starting day in early November, instead of the scheduled opening in December, "because while it would gain a month in making provisions to prevent or prepare for war, it leaves such a space of time for their assembling, as will avoid alarm either at home or abroad."[190] By that time the President's policies had been formulated and largely implemented.

Implementing Neutrality: The Little Democrat. After proclaiming neutrality, President Washington was confronted with many difficult questions. For example, he had to decide how to regard existing treaties, and whether to make the new French minister's reception qualified or absolute. Merchant vessels were soon taken as prizes of war by French ships off the East Coast, requiring Washington to respond to England's demands that the ships be returned, and in the process to determine the extent of America's maritime jurisdiction. Most difficult of all were questions related to the fitting out of privateers in United States ports. Prosecuting Americans for violating neutrality in the absence of any federal statute on the subject created grave constitutional and practical difficulties.

The treaties between the United States and France posed delicate problems. The Treaty of Alliance contained a provision by which the United States "guaranteed forever against all other powers . . . the present possessions of the Crown of France in America." The Treaty of Amity and Commerce contained provisions by which the two countries agreed to allow the reciprocal use of their ports to carry in prizes taken from the enemy, and that no such privilege be accorded to the enemy of either of the parties. Another provision contained an agreement to disallow the use, by an enemy of either party, of the ports of the other party for fitting out privateers, selling prizes, or purchasing food except in extreme circumstances.[191] If these provisions were to be interpreted to give France the special privileges they appeared to confer, the United States would have found it impossible to maintain a neutral position.

Hamilton suggested that Genêt should be received with a warning to the effect that the treaties might be "temporarily and provisionally suspended." He argued in a subsequent memorandum that the guaranty concerning France's possessions in America should be regarded as inapplicable, because France was engaged in an "offensive" war while the guaranty was contained in a "Traite d'Alliance *eventuelle* et *defensive*." To recognize the treaties where there was an option to consider them as not binding would, Hamilton felt, give the parties opposed to France grounds "to treat us as enemies. . . ." While conceding that France's opponents might very well deem it in their interest to disregard American recognition of the treaty commitments—"so long as we, in fact, take no active part in favor of

France"—he thought it wise to avoid "so great an additional risk and embarrassment. . . ." To receive Genêt without reservation, he said, might imply that America regarded itself an ally of France; a reservation would negate the implication and leave the status of the two nations "for future consideration."[192]

Jefferson argued strenuously and effectively against a qualified reception of Genêt, and against renunciation or suspension of the treaties. The guaranty, he pointed out, might never be invoked by France, and even if it were invoked several possible grounds were available to avoid its applicability. Only the reality of danger, he contended, not the mere possibility, could give a nation grounds for renouncing or suspending the obligation, and the guaranty posed no present danger. The provisions relating to prizes were common among nations, he said, and provided no ground for the enemies of France to complain. And the danger apprehended in the promise to prohibit the enemies of France from fitting out privateers in American ports could readily be avoided by refusing "the same thing to France, there being no stipulation to the contrary, and we ought to refuse it on principles of fair neutrality." Genêt could readily be received without qualification, since such a reception had nothing to do with the treaties but only signified recognition of his government. To withhold compliance with the treaties without just cause or compensation would "give to France a cause of war, and so become associated in it on the other side."[193]

The President accepted Jefferson's position. Genêt was received without qualification.[194] Issues concerning the treaties were deferred until their resolution became necessary or desirable. Only when France began to seize prizes in waters near the United States did the government decide that prizes seized within the nation's territorial waters would have to be returned.[195] Even when this and other similar questions had to be decided, answers were given cautiously so as to minimize the risks of offending any of the warring parties; for example, Washington decided to assert a tentative nautical jurisdiction of only three miles (1 sea league), the smallest distance then generally asserted by nations.[196] An unsuccessful effort was made to have many of the difficult questions decided by the Justices of the Supreme Court.[197] The government also adopted Jefferson's interpretation of the treaty provisions relating to the fitting out of privateers in American ports, and made clear to both Britain and France that such conduct by or in behalf of either party would be prohibited.[198]

Possibly the most difficult and dangerous problem posed during the post-proclamation period concerned a French privateer, the

Little Democrat. Originally a British merchant vessel called *Little Sarah*, the *Little Democrat* was re-named after its capture by the French in early May 1793. The ship was brought to Philadelphia to be fitted out as a privateer, and became the subject of several important controversies.

The first problem was created by Britain's demand that *Little Sarah* be returned. Though captured beyond the territorial limits of the United States, the British claimed the ship because it was captured by a privateer that had been outfitted at Charleston, in contravention of American neutrality.[199] Hamilton argued for restitution of the ship; that remedy was available, he said, since it had been seized in violation of American neutrality. Jefferson agreed that France should be prevented from fitting out privateers in American ports, but he felt that restitution should not be ordered in this first case of its kind; an apology to Britain would be adequate.[200] If the commission of the commander of the privateer (given by Genêt) was illegal, the courts would order restitution. If not, then France had the vessel by legal right, and to take it away would be an act of force. "[I]f the case were important enough to require reprisal, ripe for that step, Congress must be called on to take it; the right of reprisal being expressly lodged with them by the constitution, not with the executive."[201]

Washington agreed with Jefferson that restitution should not be demanded. On the other hand, he ordered that all illegally equipped privateers "should depart from the ports of the United States."[202] Genêt ignored this demand, however, and privateers continued to be equipped. In particular, *Little Sarah* was transformed into the fourteen-gun warship, *Little Democrat.* When the Cabinet discovered this, Jefferson went to see Genêt and asked him to hold the vessel for at least four days, until President Washington's return to Philadelphia. Genêt "refused to give any explicit assurance that the brigantine would continue until the arrival of the President and his decision in the case, but made declarations respecting her not being ready to sail within the time of the expected return of the President. . . ." The Cabinet was informed, moreover, that at least two of the brigantine's guns had been purchased in Philadelphia, and that part of its crew were citizens of the United States.[203]

At a Cabinet meeting on July 8, Hamilton and Knox voted to establish a battery on Mud Island, which commanded passage to the sea from Philadelphia, "with direction [to a party of militia] that if the brig Sarah should attempt to depart before the pleasure of the President shall be known concerning her, military coercion be employed to arrest and prevent her progress." Jefferson dissented, arguing that the matter should at least await Washington's return: the act suggested was "of too serious consequence to our countrymen to be brought on their heads by subordinate officers, not chosen by them," especially when the President was due within 48 hours. On the other hand, Jefferson agreed that the United States Attorney for Philadelphia should be informed that Americans might be serving on the ship, so that he could "take measures for apprehending and bringing them to trial."[204]

Hamilton and Knox argued that to allow or suffer the fitting out of privateers in American ports would be "an unequivocal breach of neutrality." They noted that the President and a unanimous Cabinet had already voted to prohibit such conduct and had assured Great Britain that "effectual measures would be taken to prevent a repetition of the practice." Consequently, any failure to act decisively against the contemptuous conduct of the French minister would give Britain grounds for war. They stressed Genêt's conduct, including his most recent letter which refused to accept the President's decision on privateers and implied "an appeal from him to Congress, if not to the people. . . ." Firmness, they suggested, would tend to preserve peace with both Britain and France, but "if war is to be hazarded, 'tis certainly our duty to hazard it with that power which by injury and insult forces us to choose between opposite hazards. . . ."[205]

Washington arrived in Philadelphia, read the papers submitted, and asked Jefferson whether the French minister was to be allowed "to set the acts of this government at defiance *with impunity*? And then threaten the executive with an appeal to the people?"[206] Jefferson responded that he had "received assurance from M. Genêt today" that the ship "will not be gone before the President's decision." He qualified his earlier position somewhat, however, stating that "whatever is aboard of her of arms, ammunition, or men, contrary to the rules heretofore laid down by the President, ought to be withdrawn."[207] Actually, the ship had by then been moved to Chester, "beyond possible effective detention. . . ."[208]

The Cabinet met on July 12, and voted to submit the issues concerning privateers "to persons learned in the laws," and in the meantime to request the minister of France to detain several ships, including *Little Democrat*, "till the further order of the President." No plan was made to detain the vessel by force, the Cabinet apparently proceeding on the assumption that Genêt's representation to Jefferson would be honored or that nothing could be done; in another determination, however, the Cabinet indicated its readiness to authorize the forceful detention of an illegally equipped ship.[209] Jefferson recorded his impression that Washington seemed to wish that the Cabinet had ordered *Little Democrat* stopped by military coercion, but was reluctant to order it himself. He also noted the President's reaction when Knox agreed at Governor Mifflin's request to load four cannon to mount at Mud Island in the event the President approved the project: "The President declared . . . that when the orders were given to the governors to stop vessels arming and coming in our ports, even by military force, he took for granted the government would use such diligence as to detect those projects in embryo and stop them when no force was requisite, or a very small party of militia would suffice. . . . He did not think the executive had a power to establish permanent guards," but had contemplated "only an occasional call on small parties of militia in the moments requiring it."[210]

On July 18, a list of 29 questions was presented to the Justices of the Supreme Court. The questions dealt with interpretations of the French-American treaties, and the rights and duties of nations with respect to prizes, arming of privateers and other matters. None of the questions raised any issue as to the limits, if any, of the executive's authority unilaterally to enforce any of the rights or duties involved.[211] The Justices declined to answer. Meantime, the *Little Democrat* had sailed out to sea, and ultimately became one of Genêt's most successful privateers. The British minister, Hammond, took the matter far less seriously than he might have, and the matter ceased to be a cause for immediate concern.[212]

The Cabinet met on July 29 and set about answering their own questions, since they apparently knew by then that the Justices would decline.[213] These answers were issued as "Rules Governing Belligerents" on August 3, and consisted of a series of prohibitions relating to the arming of vessels and other similar matters.[214] "An administrative law of neutrality had been forged."[215] And in adopting these rules, the Cabinet consciously addressed themselves to whether the prohibitions made were "within the competence of the President to prohibit?"[216] On August 1, after carefully examining Genêt's conduct and correspondence, the Cabinet unanimously voted to request his recall.[217]

The President specifically raised, on August 3, the question whether Congress should be called before December 1, when it was scheduled to meet. Only Jefferson voted for an early call, because of the danger of war with the Creeks and the difficulties of maintaining neutrality. He suggested the first Monday in November as the proper time.[218] Hamilton disagreed. He found that no "circumstance now exists which did not exist months ago, of sufficient force to constitute an extraordinary occasion" that warranted specially convening Congress.[219] Jefferson claimed in his diary that "Knox said we should have had fine work, if Congress had been sitting these last two months." He felt that the Cabinet "do not wish to lengthen the session of the *next Congress*," which was to be controlled by the Republicans in the House.[220] He wrote Madison that the President "should have been for calling Congress himself," but agreed to the majority view.[221]

One factor that was operating in favor of calling back Congress was the executive's difficulty in enforcing the proclamation. Gideon Henfield, American commander of a French privateer, was tried for violating the nation's neutrality, an action deemed by John Jay and others as an indictable common-law offense. The jury acquitted Henfield, however, leading the government ultimately to drop the prosecution of other alleged offenders. After concluding that Congress should not be called back earlier than scheduled, the President issued more detailed regulations prohibiting American cooperation with the belligerents. When Congress reconvened, he called on them "to extend the legal code and the jurisdiction of the Courts of the United States to many cases which, though dependent on principles already recognised, demand some further provisions."[222]

One other matter is worthy of comment. The Cabinet decided, at Jefferson's suggestion, that it would be better to compensate Britain for prizes seized by illegally equipped privateers than to attempt to seize armed French vessels.[223] Washington apparently insisted that the decision to pay compensation be stated to Genêt and Hammond in a manner "so guarded as to convey nothing more than an opinion of the executive."[224] Later, Hamilton became concerned that, if the matter were submitted to the entire Congress, compensation would not be paid. Between nation and nation, he felt, the President's opinion "is equivalent to a virtual engagement. . . ." He therefore suggested, in a confidential letter to the President, that Jay be instructed to insert a provision in the treaty he was then negotiating with Britain that compensation would be paid. If this were done, "the Senate only will have to concur. If provision is to be made by law, *both houses must* concur. The difference is easily seen." Washington was undoubtedly aware that the newly elected House would be controlled by Republicans. But he refused to make any "more pointed declaration to Mr. Hammond on this head at this time." He thought Congress should accept his opinion, but intended to leave the matter for Congress to determine: "[A]lthough the usage of other nations may be opposed to this practice, the difference may result from the difference between their constitutions and ours, and from the prerogative of their Executives." On the other hand, it cannot simply be said that Washington refused "to consent to such a plan."[225] Washington's refusal to detail this matter further with Hammond rested in part on his belief that the matter was not "urgent"; and he specifically noted that it was "one of the subjects committed to Mr. Jay's negotiation, or at least within his powers," and that he had "no objection . . . that he [Hammond] might be informed informally, and verbally, that the negotiation of this, as well as other matters, was transmitted to his own court."[226]

The Pacificus-Helvidius Debate. Popular feeling was initially for France. When the new French Minister Genêt arrived in the United States he was greeted enthusiastically wherever he went, and blatantly violated the principles of neutrality established by President Washington.[227] The proclamation was widely attacked, and these attacks seemed to Jefferson at least to affect the President greatly.[228]

Madison was among the critics. He wrote to Jefferson on June 13, 1793 that he was surprised that the executive would even declare "the *Disposition* of the U.S. on the subject of war & peace," and that such a "prerogative" should have been exercised:

> Perhaps I may have not attended to some parts of the Constitution with sufficient care, or may have misapprehended its meaning. But, as I have always supposed & still conceive a proclamation on the subject could not properly go beyond a declaration of the fact that the U.S. were at war or peace, and an injunction of a suitable conduct on the Citizens. The right to decide the question whether the duty & interest of the U.S. require war or peace under any given circumstances, and whether their disposition be toward the one or the other seems to be essentially & exclusively involved in the right vested in the Legislature, of declaring war in time of peace; and in the P. & S. of making peace in time of war. Did no such view of the subject present itself in the discussions of the Cabinet? I am extremely afraid that the P. may not be sufficiently aware of the snares that may be laid for his good intentions by men whose politics at bottom are very different from his own.[229]

Jefferson had voted to proclaim a state of neutrality, and he became the nation's chief instrument for enforcing that policy;[230] but he sought to disassociate himself from the proclamation in his correspondence with fellow Republicans. On June 23 he answered Madison to the effect that he succeeded in having the word "neutrality" removed from the proclamation because such a declaration would be beyond the executive's competence. Since everyone had agreed to a proclamation, he explained, "it was not expedient to oppose it altogether, lest it should prejudice what was the next question," namely whether a minister from the French Republic should be received.[231]

Hamilton came to the President's defense on June 29, 1793, with the first of a series of articles under the pseudonym "Pacificus." In it he advanced two bases in support of the proclamation. A proclamation of neutrality, he wrote, is a usual and proper manner for making known to the powers at war and to the citizens of the proclaiming nation that the latter is at peace. Furthermore, he claimed, the executive department is the proper one to make such a proclamation. The executive is "the *organ* of intercourse between the nation and foreign nations"; the "*interpreter* of the national treaties . . . between government and government"; the branch charged with executing the law, including treaties; and in "command and disposition of the public force." He broadly construed Article II, section 1 of the Constitution, claiming that "the executive power," vested in the President, subsumes all the power normally considered executive, including the power to proclaim neutrality, except those specifically withheld. Of the powers specifically withheld, Hamilton was willing to assume that the power to declare war "includes the right of judging, whether the nation is or is not under obligations to make war." But this did not preclude unilateral presidential action, in his view, because the branches had concurrent authority: the executive, too, has the power to judge the nation's obligations in execution of his functions, "though it may, in its consequences, affect the exercise of the power of the legislature to declare war." Indeed, he saw an executive duty to preserve peace—as a corollary to the legislature's power to declare war—which necessarily required the executive to determine the nation's obligations under treaties. He did not contend, however, that the executive could "control" the exercise of the war power. "The legislature is still free to perform its duties, according to its own sense of them . . . ."[232]

In addition to vindicating "the authority of the executive on this broad and comprehensive ground," Hamilton advanced a more limited basis for the proclamation—the President's duty to "take care that the laws be faithfully executed." Treaties are laws, said Hamilton, and to enforce the treaties between France and the United States the President had first to determine their meaning. Since those treaties required nothing incompatible with neutrality, the President had the right, and perhaps the duty, "as executor of the laws, to proclaim the neutrality of the nation, to exhort all persons to observe it, and to warn them of the penalties which would attend its non-observance." Such a proclamation did not, in his view, create "new law," but only proclaimed "a *fact*, with regard to the existing state of the nation. . . ."[233]

Jefferson sent the first Pacificus article to Madison on June 30, identifying the author as Hamilton. He maintained that the "declaration of the disposition of the U.S. can hardly be called illegal,"[234] but bemoaned the fact that Hamilton's "heresies" were not being adequately answered. Insofar as it is possible to discern from his letter, the "heresies" were the claims that the President: (1) could proclaim "neutrality"; (2) could "declare that we are *not bound to execute the guarantee*" in the treaty with France that we would protect its possessions; and (3) could declare the treaties suspended. On July 7 Jefferson sent Madison two later articles by Pacificus, and urged him to "take up your pen, select the most striking heresies, and cut him to pieces in face of the public. There is nobody else who can & will enter the lists with him."[235]

Madison was initially reluctant to take on the task. He finally did so, under the name Helvidius, in articles appearing between August 24 and September 14. He attacked, first, Hamilton's broad conception of executive powers, arguing that the powers to make treaties and to declare war are more properly viewed as legislative powers, rather than exceptions out of the executive power. Hamilton's argument was not necessarily inconsistent with this position; he had said that the executive could only *affect* the power to declare war when exercising some other appropriate executive function.[236] But seizing upon Hamilton's concession that the power to declare war includes the power to judge whether the legislature is under an obligation to make war, Madison argued that, under such an assumption, all judgments concerning war were necessarily part of the legislative function:

> Whenever, then, a question occurs, whether war shall be declared, or whether public stipulations require it, the question necessarily belongs to the department to which those functions belong—and no other department can be *in the execution of* its proper functions, if it should undertake to decide such a question.[237]

Hamilton had avoided this difficulty by claiming that the branches have concurrent powers. Madison rejected this position, stressing its logical extremes, and the domestic and international uncertainties that would be generated in its operation. If the executive has a concurrent right to judge whether the nation is obliged to go to war, Madison reasoned, "and the right to judge be essentially included in the right to declare [war], it must have the same concurrent right to declare as it has to judge. . . ." And if both these departments have the right to judge or declare, may they not reach opposite conclusions on the same issue, both of which are constitutional? He noted Hamilton's contention that the executive has a duty "to preserve peace till war is declared," and asked what would happen if the executive concluded that treaty obligations were inconsistent with neutrality. "Is it or is it not the province and duty of the executive to enforce the same laws?" He accepted the notion that the executive is bound to execute the laws of neutrality "whilst those laws continue unaltered by the competent authority," but not, as Hamilton had put it, "to avoid giving cause of war to foreign powers." Rather, he said, the executive is bound to enforce neutrality because it is his absolute duty to preserve peace in all cases, until war is declared, "even if turbulent citizens should consider its so doing as a cause of war at home, or unfriendly nations should consider its so doing as a cause of war abroad."[238]

Madison's argument was therefore more against Hamilton's rationale and language than with the proclamation itself. He insisted on the need "of a rigid adherence to the simple, the received, and the fundamental doctrine of the constitution, that the power to declare war, including the power of judging of the causes of war, is *fully* and *exclusively* vested in the legislature," contending that the only right the executive possessed when a question arose as to whether there was cause for war is to convene and inform Congress. Yet he conceded the legality of the proclamation as a declaration to nations and citizens of the course which the President's duty required him to pursue, so long as the proclamation was not construed "to embrace and prejudge the legislative question, whether there was, or was not, under the circumstances of the case, a cause of war in the article of guaranty." Under this view the President was authorized and required to execute treaties or conduct foreign affairs up until the point that these functions posed questions relating to war or peace. At that point he must—as a matter of duty, not judgment—maintain a position of peace until ordered to do differently by the legislature.[239]

Professor Corwin wrote early in this century that "the great shortcoming of Madison's argument, with all its logical acuteness, is its negative character, its failure to suggest either a logical or practicable construction of the Constitution to take the place of the one it combats."[240] Madison's arguments as Helvidius in fact seem inconsistent with the notion of "mixing" he espoused in the *Federalist* and with his position on the meaning of "executive power" during the removal debates.[241] Nor did Madison's scheme necessarily prevent the executive's actions from causing war. As he recognized, refusing (as part of a neutral policy) to enforce a treaty term to avoid war with one nation might lead to war with its adversary.[242]

Furthermore, while Madison's scheme would allow the executive to negotiate and handle other foreign-policy matters, the executive would presumably have to refrain from any agreement or judgment that involved war or peace. Such restraint could, in some circumstances, cause or increase the likelihood of military conflict. Madison's response to this possibility was that the executive must call the legislature, but otherwise was not responsible for the consequences:

> The executive has no other discretion than to convene and give information to the legislature on occasions that demand it; and whilst this discretion is duly exercised, the trust of the executive is satisfied, and that department is not responsible for the consequences. It could not be made responsible for them without vesting it with the legislative as well as with the executive trust.[243]

The theory advocated by Madison in 1793 as to the appropriate roles of President and Congress had been rejected in practice even before his Helvidius papers saw the light of day. Neutrality had, in effect, been proclaimed. Detailed regulations were developed and eventually implemented by the President. Force was authorized in seizing illegally equipped privateers. The French-American treaties were authoritatively interpreted only to the extent necessary to implement the executive's unilaterally determined policy. Several of the decisions made and avoided—some of treaty construction, others of policy implementation—could have led to military conflict with either France or England. Yet the President and his Cabinet unanimously voted against recalling Congress, thereby determining unilaterally to direct and administer the implementation of neutrality for about a seven-month period.

On the other hand, in many ways the President's actions were in keeping with the spirit of Madison's papers. This is reflected not only in matters of form, such as in the conscious decision not to call the proclamation one of "neutrality," but also in the consistently cautious and even-handed manner in which the President implemented the policy. In general, everything possible was done to preserve the status quo without antagonizing either combatant, and without unnecessarily deciding sensitive questions. The President undoubtedly found this course politically agreeable, since he favored keeping America out of "the policital intrigues or the squabbles of European nations. . . ."[244]

The President explained his actions to Congress on December 3, 1793, when it reconvened. The war in Europe created dangers for the United States, he said, and it became "my duty to admonish our citizens against hostile acts," and to obtain, "by a declaration of the existing legal state of things, an easier admission of our right to the immunities belonging to our situation."[245] Jefferson failed to get the President to disclaim in his address any intention to issue a declaration of neutrality.[246] Yet Hamilton and Randolph failed to convince the President to include in his speech any comments on the undesirability of enforcing treaty provisions,[247] and the President confirmed, according to Jefferson, that "he never had an idea that he could bind Congress against declaring war, or that anything contained in his proclamation could look beyond the first day of their meeting."[248] "It rests with the wisdom of Congress," Washington said, "to correct, improve, or enforce" the plan of procedure he had implemented to preserve neutrality, noting especially the need to involve the judiciary in deciding and enforcing certain questions.[249]

Both houses of Congress praised the President for issuing the proclamation.[250] Their resolutions of approbation were more than mere formalities, since they were felt necessary to offset claims that the proclamation had been unlawful.[251] Congress also passed an "act for the punishment of certain crimes against the United States," on June 5, 1794, which largely adopted the President's plan. No criticism is recorded of the President's conduct. Madison and others spoke against the Act of June 5, 1794, but their purpose was to delay or to amend it in favor of France. Proponents of the legislation, on the other hand, stressed the need to support the President and to maintain as perfect a neutrality as possible.[252] Significantly, the act contained provisions that conferred broad discretion upon the President to use the armed forces in its implementation.[253]

MILITARY AUTHORIZATIONS
AND ACTIONS

When Washington assumed the presidency, the United States had a regular military force of less than 840 men,[254] and he had received no delegation of authority to use either it or the state militias. He was therefore required, regardless of his views on the Constitution's allocation of war-making powers, to ask Congress to support virtually every military effort he wanted to undertake. He asked repeatedly for military support during his administration, and with great conviction reiterated the theme that the best way to preserve peace was to be prepared for war. Without adequate military strength, he warned, the United States would lose its proper place among the nations of the world.*

Congress generally provided the means requested, and often delegated broad discretion to the President to use, regulate and discharge troops. Considerable controversy raged over whether to expand the regular army as opposed to the militia, and whether to build ships that could become the beginning of a navy. The fear of a "standing army" was often expressed.[255] But several important political leaders strongly favored a standing army,[256] and regarded a navy as both inevitable and desirable.[257] Others who would have preferred to have neither army nor navy voted to expand the former and in effect to begin the latter because they perceived the measures as necessary.[258] The construction of public vessels was authorized in order to defend against Mediterranean pirates, despite the warning that the vessels would be attacked and war would result.[259] By the time Washington's administration ended, the United States had a regular force of 7,108, and three large frigates nearing completion.[260]

The President's power as commander-in-chief received some haphazard constructions, hardly definitive but worth mentioning. On August 18, 1789, Representative Thomas Tudor Tucker of South Carolina proposed several constitutional amendments, including one that would have changed Article II, section 2 from a grant of power to the President to "be commander-in-chief" of the armed forces, to a grant of "power to direct (agreeable to law) the operations" of the armed forces. This amendment sought definitively to limit the President's military power to conducting operations ordered by Congress, in the manner specified by Congress. The proposal failed to muster even enough support for a reference to committee for further consideration.[261] An interesting early exchange occurred when Representative James Jackson of Georgia urged an amendment to a treaty appropriation bill that would have authorized the President (subject to unspecified limits) to raise the troops and build the posts he deemed necessary to protect the citizens of Georgia, in the event the Creek Indians refused to agree to terms the commissioners might deem "necessary and just." At Madison's suggestion, this proposed

---

*For example, in his annual message of December 3, 1793, Washington said: "There is a rank due to the United States among Nations, which will be withheld, if not absolutely lost, by the reputation of weakness. If we desire to avoid insult we must be able to repel it; if we desire to secure peace, one of the most powerful instruments of our rising prosperity, it must be known, that we are at all times ready for War." 33 *Washington Writings* (Fitzpatrick) 166. To the same effect, *see, e.g.,* 1 *Annals* 969; 6 *Annals* 1592, 1593-94.

amendment was withdrawn, to be considered along with the President's message of August 10, 1789 "relative to the troops already raised to protect the frontiers from the depredations of the hostile Indians." "By the constitution," Madison argued, "the President has the power of employing these troops in the protection of those parts which he thinks require them most."* Neither the rejection of Tucker's proposed amendment, nor Madison's statement, suggests any consensus for the proposition that Congress could not constitutionally order the President to undertake or to refrain from undertaking military operations. Nothing significant was done or said, however, to create any evidence to support a limited view of the President's authority as commander-in-chief.

Another issue on which several interesting statements were made, though no action taken, is the power to make peace. Here the evidence is clear that early legislators regarded the President and Senate, acting together, as empowered to make peace. During the Jay Treaty debate, to prove that the House lacked discretion to consider the merits of the treaty beyond its constitutionality, Roger Griswold of Connecticut argued that treaties can override laws, using the example that a treaty of peace can lawfully end what both houses of Congress began.[262] Even those who argued that the House could consider the merits of treaties accepted Griswold's assumption concerning the effect of treaties of peace.†

Several important military incidents were clearly authorized by legislation, and need only be mentioned. The most notorious is the action taken to suppress the rebellion in western Pennsylvania against the excise tax. This was treated by Washington as authorized under the Act of May 2, 1792, which empowered the President, if a

---

*1 *Annals* 723-24. In his argument as "Pacificus," Hamilton listed several reasons why the President should be regarded as possessing the power to proclaim neutrality. One of these reasons was that the President was in command and disposition of the public force. 15 Syrett, textual note, *supra* p. 74 at 33, 37-43.

†Thus James Holland of North Carolina said that he believed

the Executive had absolute power to make peace, as by the Constitution he is declared Commander-in-Chief of all the Armies, his situation enabled him to be the best judge of the forces and of the force he had to contend with, and as secrecy was necessary to effecting a Treaty of Peace, that power was properly vested in him, guarded by two-thirds of the Senate. But a Treaty of Commerce presupposes an existing peace, and in those Treaties secrecy is not essential. . . .

5 *Annals* 546-47. John Page of Virginia thought "it an excellence in our Constitution that the PRESIDENT and Senate, though not allowed to declare war, have authority to put a stop to its horrors." *Id.* 560. He argued, however, that the House could not reasonably be required to pass laws to effectuate all the Senate's powers, and that the Senate and President could not prevent future Congresses from expressing their will. *Id.*

judge found the federal laws were being obstructed by combinations too powerful to be suppressed by the courts or the marshal of the district, to call for and use the militia to suppress "unlawful combinations."[263] Another instance was when Washington authorized the Governor of Rhode Island in September 1795 to use that state's militia to restrain intercourse with the British ship *Africa* and thus indirectly compel its departure from American waters. The order was based on the Act of June 5, 1794, which made it lawful for the President "to employ . . . the militia . . . to compel any foreign ship or vessel to depart the United States, in all cases in which, by the laws of nations or the treaties of the United States, they ought not to remain within the United States."[264] Although the *Africa* had searched American ships and impressed several seamen, Pickering wrote the Governor that "the President cannot by means of any military force at his command *directly* compel the *Africa* 'to depart the united States,'" and authorized only indirect pressure, such as preventing the purchase of supplies.[265]

The important military actions under Washington mainly concerned Indian tribes, and were authorized without a declaration of war. The value of these actions as precedents is questionable, since Indians were frequently described as "savages," as compared to the "civilized" nations. The incidents are worth examining, nevertheless. The Constitution makes no distinction between Indians and other nations, and Washington made a point of dealing with the Indians as nations for purposes of treaty-making.[266] Furthermore, the incidents are valuable as evidence of the restraints by which the President regarded himself bound; we can reasonably infer that he would have regarded as applicable to "civilized" nations any constitutional restraint he thought applicable in connection with military actions against Indians.

Military Actions Against the Wabash Indians

Persistent hostilities took place between some tribes of Indians living near the Wabash River and residents of Kentucky and the Western Territory. Citizens were so incensed by Indian raids that they attacked and killed peaceful Indians in retaliation.[267] Governor Arthur St. Clair of the Western Territory described the situation to President Washington on September 14, 1789, and asked that he be given power "to call upon Virginia and Pennsylvania for a number of men to act in conjunction with the Continental troops, and carry war into the Indian settlement. . . ." The few troops St. Clair had at his disposal were scattered, and "though they may afford protection to some settlements, cannot positively act offensively by themselves."[268]

The President (through General Knox) had provided Congress with "a statement of the troops in the service of the United States," which were raised under the Confederation "in order to protect the frontiers from the depredations of the hostile Indians," and for other purposes. "As these important objects continue to require the aid of the troops," he asked Congress that their existence and use be "conformed by law to the constitution of the United States."[269] He later sent St. Clair's request to Congress, urging it to restore authority to defend the frontiers given the Governor of the Western Territory by the Confederation in 1787, by "making some temporary provision for calling forth the militia of the United States for the purposes stated in the Constitution, which would embrace the cases apprehended by the Governor of the Western Territory."[270]

On September 29, 1789, Congress adopted a "bill to recognize and adapt to the constitution of the United States the establishment of the troops raised under the 'resolves' of the previous government." The bill recognized the military force established by the prior Congress on October 3, 1787, with exceptions not here pertinent. Section 5 authorized "the President . . . to call into service, from time to time, such part of the militia of the States, respectively, as he may judge necessary for the purpose . . . of protecting the inhabitants of the frontiers . . . from the hostile incursions of the Indians. . . ."[271] The act did not expressly authorize offensive actions, even though Congress had received St. Clair's letter complaining that he lacked sufficient troops to act offensively.

On October 6, 1789, Washington wrote to St. Clair authorizing him, if the Wabash and Illinois Indians were inclined to war, to call on Virginia and Pennsylvania for up to 1,500 militiamen: "The said militia to act in conjunction with the federal troops, in such operations, offensive or defensive, as you, and the commanding officer of the troops, conjointly, shall judge necessary for the public service, and the protection of the inhabitants and the posts."[272] No copy of this authorization was sent to Congress until over a year later.[273]

Though authorized to act, St. Clair still lacked the means to do so. The President pressed Congress to supply the means. He noted on January 8, 1790 that efforts peacefully to resolve disputes with Indians had failed, and called for "a uniform and well digested plan" for the common defense.[274] A bill was introduced to increase the military establishment. After a debate in which several Congressman objected to what they regarded as the creation of a standing army, the bill passed. In addition to increasing the regular army to 1,216 "noncommissioned officers, privates, and musicians," it renewed the President's authority to call up "such part of the militia of the

States respectively as he may judge necessary" to aid the federal troops "in protecting the inhabitants of the frontiers of the United States. . . ."[275]

Toward the end of 1790, a body of St. Clair's troops, under the command of General Harmar, undertook an offensive expedition against the Indians. Harmar destroyed an unoccupied village, but in other engagements many more Americans were killed than Indians (180 to about 120, by Harmar's estimate).[276]

On December 8, 1790, Washington informed Congress that an offensive expedition had been authorized pursuant to the Act of 1789, and sent them his earlier letter to St. Clair.[277] Both houses responded to this information with general expressions of approbation;[278] no opposition was expressed on the ground that the offensive expedition was legislatively unauthorized.[279] On December 14, Washington informed Congress of Harmar's expedition, without comment.

The House discussed the President's speech the next day. Thomas Hartley of Pennsylvania felt "the prospect that further hostilities would take place between the inhabitants of the frontiers and the Indians, rendered it highly necessary that something should be done immediately." A resolution was introduced calling upon the legislature to give "serious attention" to "Indian affairs." John Laurance of New York noted, however, that "nothing more was necessary . . . in this business than providing the means of defraying the expense. . . . The expedition has been approved of by the House in their answer to the President's speech." He therefore moved a resolution as the sense of the committee "that immediate provision ought to be made to defray the expenses of the expedition against the Indians Northwest of the Ohio," which was accepted without recorded debate.[280]

The frontier states and General Knox feared that Harmar's defeat would further embolden the Indian tribes. He recommended "another expedition against the Wabash Indians, with such a decided force as to impress them strongly with the power of the United States." This time he suggested an army of 3,000 "well arranged troops, in order to be superior to all opposition, and to prevent the trouble and expense of being repeated."[281] Congress authorized a larger regular army,[282] and offensive expeditions were conducted with some success in June and August 1791, pursuant to Knox's explicit authorization.[283] But in November 1791, St. Clair led a major expedition that ended in stunning defeat at the hands of the Indians. About one-half of the new army was destroyed.[284]

Knox sought another escalation. Noting that defensive measures were entirely inadequate, and the need for "a strong coercive force," he recommended to Congress an increase in the regular army to

5,168 non-officers, as well as authority to use the militia, expert woodsmen, patrols, and scouts.[285] This time a heated debate occurred in the House, concerning the relative merits of the militia and the regular army, the dangers of a standing army, and the morality and wisdom of fighting the Indians for their lands.* The House voted to approve the bill, and it became law on March 5, 1792, authorizing three new regiments to be "discharged as soon as the United States shall be at peace with the Indian tribes." In addition, the President was authorized to call up "such number of cavalry as, in his judgment, may be necessary for the protection of the frontiers," and to employ Indians as he thought proper.[286] With the force raised pursuant to this legislation, carefully drilled and seasoned, together with militiamen, General Anthony Wayne defeated the Wabash Indians at the Battle of Fallen Timbers, August 1794.[287]

The offensive actions taken against the Wabash were not expressly authorized by a declaration of war or by legislation. Congress con-

---

See generally 3 *Annals* 337-55. The following are representative excerpts from speeches by members seeking to block further escalation:

> It was urged in favor of the motion, that the Indian war, in which the United States are at present involved was, in its origin, as unjustly undertaken as it has since been unwisely and unsuccessfully conducted; that depredations had been committed by the whites as well as by the Indians; and the whites were most probably the aggressors, as they frequently made encroachments on the Indian lands, whereas the Indians showed no inclination to obtain possession of our territory, or even to make temporary invasions until urged to it by a sense of their wrongs.

Id. 337.

> The expense of such an army as the bill contemplates is an object well worthy of serious consideration, especially at the present moment, when there is scarcely a dollar in the Treasury. Gentlemen would also do well to advert to the progress of this business, and consider where they were likely to stop, if they went on at the present rate. At first, only a single regiment had been raised, and the expense was about $100,000; a second was afterwards added, which swelled the expense to about $300,000; and now a standing force of 5,168 men is contemplated, at an annual expense of above a million and a quarter of dollars. Can this be justified in the present state of our finances, when it is well known that the Secretary of the Treasury, having been requested by the members from a particular State to build a lighthouse on a part of their coast, declined the undertaking, and alleged the want of funds as the reason?

Id. 341.

> We are preparing to squander away money by millions; and no one, except those who are in the secrets of the Cabinet, knows for what reason the war has been thus carried on for three years.

Id. 342. The prevailing argument was that "it is now too late to inquire whether the war was originally undertaken on the principles of justice or not. We are actually involved in it, and cannot recede, without exposing numbers of innocent persons to be butchered by the enemy. . . ." *Id.* 345.

firmed the military force established by the Continental Congress and allowed the President in addition to use such militia as he deemed necessary "for the purpose . . . of protecting the inhabitants of the frontiers . . . from the hostile incursions of the Indians. . . ."[288] This language could be interpreted to allow only defensive actions, since its emphasis is on "protecting" inhabitants from hostile "incursions." Further, the resolution of the Continental Congress that was "confirmed" by the Act of September 29, 1789 is as ambiguous as the Act itself. It called for a corps of 700 troops "stationed on the frontiers to protect the settlers on the public lands from the depredations of Indians," to facilitate the sale of land, and "to prevent all unwarrantable intrusions thereon."[289] Washington authorized St. Clair to take offensive actions, however, extending into territory claimed by the Indians. And while his letter to St. Clair authorizing offensive action is dated October 6, 1789, he sent it to Congress on December 9, 1790, after General Harmar's expedition into Indian territory had been undertaken.

Substantial arguments can be made, however, for the conclusion that offensive actions were regarded as having been authorized. An authorization to "protect" Americans from "incursions" arguably implies enough power, within reason, to do so effectively. Congress did not suggest that the troops were to protect only to the extent they could through defensive operations, without crossing the borders in pursuit or retaliation. The language can reasonably be construed to allow offensive actions, even in Indian territory, so long as they were undertaken to protect frontier dwellers from incursions that had occurred and seemed likely to continue. Certainly Governor St. Clair would have been surprised at the thought that the additional troops he had requested for the Western Territory could only act defensively. In his letter to Washington requesting the troops St. Clair specifically noted that, though existing forces were perhaps adequate to "afford protection to some settlements, [they] cannot positively act offensively by themselves."[290] Washington sent this letter to Congress along with his initial request for troops and militia "for the purposes stated in the Constitution," which would embrace "the cases apprehended by the Governor of the Western Territory."[291] When Washington informed Congress that he had authorized an offensive action, Congress approved his speech and provided the means for further expeditions.

On other occasions Congress refused to authorize offensive actions against Indians,[292] and the administration warned the Governor of Tennessee against conducting such operations.[293] But these instances fail to undermine the likelihood that all participants regarded the operations against the Wabash as authorized. Further offensive actions may have been regarded as too dangerous in light of the young nation's commitment in the Northwest.[294] Washington was especially averse to allowing state governments to act against Indians because of their tendency to be unfair and brutal. When actually confronted with a motion to make the system of frontier protection exclusively "defensive," Congress refused to consider it. "[W]hy tell our Southern friends," asked Thomas Hartley of Pennsylvania, "who are now bleeding, and call upon us to protect and assist them, and desire more offensive operations against their savage neighbors, that we will not comply with their wishes?"[295]

The Fort Miamis Affair

A potentially important military confrontation between the United States and Great Britain occurred immediately after General Wayne's victory over the Wabash. Within sight of the field of battle was a British fort, located on American soil, called Fort Miamis. This was not the only British fort on American territory at the time. In the Treaty of 1783 Britain ceded to the United States the land along the southern shores of the Great Lakes. Despite this agreement, the British refused to surrender a line of forts they had established along those shores until after the Jay Treaty of 1796. The British occupation was often protested, but no outright demand was made that they withdraw from forts in existence at the time of the 1783 treaty.*

Fort Miamis was, however, different from the posts that were occupied by the British in 1783. It was built in 1793, on the site of a fortification abandoned before 1783, because the British Governor of Canada, John Graves Simcoe, claimed to believe that General Wayne's "real objective was Detroit."[296] Americans may well have regarded this alleged fear as a mere excuse employed by the British to continue their policy of aiding the Indians, a policy almost explicitly avowed by Lord Dorchester, Governor General of British

---

*The British presence was tolerated in part because the American Confederation, and later the new United States, lacked power to dislodge them without great effort. Furthermore, Article VII of the Treaty of 1783 allowed Britain a "convenient" period in which to withdraw its troops. *See generally,* J. Bigelow, *Breaches of Anglo-American Treaties* 4–9 (1917). This excuse lost force with time, so the British pressed the argument that Congress had failed to recommend measures for the protection of British subjects and to guarantee the collection of all bona fide debts contracted prior to the treaty, as required by Articles IV and V. *See 2 Treaties and Other International Acts of the United States of America* 151, 154 (H. Miller, ed., 1931). So blatant were the states' violations of the rights of British subjects that President Washington was led to remark: "What a misfortune it is . . . that the British should have so well-founded a pretext for their infractions. . . ." E. Smith, *England and America After Independence* 9 (1900).

North America, in a speech during February 1794.[297] Moreover, whether or not inciting the Indians against Americans was official British policy, Fort Miamis was almost certainly used to provide aid to the Wabash against General Wayne.[298]

Upon learning of Governor Simcoe's plan to build Fort Miamis, Secretary of State Randolph protested vehemently to the British Minister on May 20, 1794, noting that the American Army would be unable to distinguish between the British and others associated in the war.[299] Congress was informed of this protest the very next day, "in confidence," and of the initial British response, which followed immediately upon its receipt, explaining this conduct to be based on a need to protect British interests in the area. Minister Hammond added that these measures would be subject to "final arrangement" in discussions being conducted between the two countries. President Washington noted "the very serious nature of such an encroachment," and called upon Congress to place "the United States in a posture of effectual preparation for an event, which, notwithstanding the endeavors making [*sic*] to avert it, may, by circumstances beyond our control, be forced upon us."[300] Randolph meanwhile explicitly assured the British "that the American army [under Wayne] has no instruction to straiten or annoy [Detroit]. . . ."[301]

American protests were not merely hortatory. On June 7, 1794, Secretary Knox instructed General Wayne that Fort Miamis was not entitled "to the respect to be observed to the previously established posts of Great Britain. If therefore in the course of your operations against the Indian enemy, it should become necessary to dislodge the party at the rapids of the Miami, you are hereby authorized in the name of the President of the United States to do it, taking care after they shall be in your power to treat them with humanity and politeness and to send them immediately to the nearest British garrison." Wayne was warned to act only if success were assured, and to be civil and careful, since Britain did not seem to want war and Jay might be successful in adjusting "all differences in an amicable and satisfactory manner. . . ."[302]

General Wayne defeated the Indians and some unspecified "Canadian" irregulars on August 20, on the banks of the Miami, near the British post. On the next day he received a letter from Major William Campbell, commander of the offending fort, inquiring why an American army was approaching "almost within the reach of the guns of this fort. . . ." Wayne responded angrily that "were you entitled to an answer, the most full and satisfactory one was announced to you from the muzzles of my small arms, yesterday morning, in the action against the horde of savages in the vicinity of your post, which terminated gloriously to the American arms." Had the battle continued until the Indians "were driven under the influence of the post and guns you mention," he added, "they would not have much impeded the progress of the victorious army under my command, as no such post was established at the commencement of the present war between the Indians and the United States." Campbell claimed that Wayne's letter "fully authorizes me to any act of hostility against the army . . . under your command," but asserted that he wanted to avoid war. He warned, however, that "should you, after this, continue to approach my post in the threatening manner you are at this moment doing, my indispensable duty . . . will oblige me to have recourse to those means, which thousands of either nation may hereafter have cause to regret. . . ."[303]

Wayne continued to reconnoiter the fort "in every direction, at some points possibly within pistol shot," and flatly demanded that the British withdraw "to the nearest post occupied by his Britannic Majesty's troops at the peace of 1783. . . ." Campbell refused to withdraw, noting that his orders prevented him from doing so, and repeating his warning. The Americans proceeded to lay waste to "everything within view of the fort, and even under the muzzles of the guns." Campbell took no action, and the tension dissipated without incident.[304]

Congress did not expressly authorize the executive to attack Fort Miamis. Congress did, however, authorize and finance Wayne's campaign, thereby arguably approving any action reasonably related to accomplishing the defeat of the Indians. Secretary Knox's letter carefully instructed Wayne to attack the fort only if necessary to defeat the Indians. Furthermore, Congress knew the fort had been built and was told by the President that its presence could lead to a military confrontation with the British. Congress took no action that suggested disapproval of the President's attitude toward the British fort.

In addition to the arguments for finding the order legislatively authorized, a case can be made for unilateral executive authority to act against the post. Building the post had infringed upon American territory, arguably authorizing the President to treat it with less deference than previously established posts might be entitled. The informal arrangement with Britain confused the issue. Although the post had not existed in 1783, when the treaty was signed, a British fort had existed at that site, and the British contended that its reestablishment was necessary to preserve the status quo at Detroit. But Washington apparently regarded himself empowered to allow the fort to be taken if necessary to defeat the Indians in an authorized engagement.

Though Washington seems to have had respectable claims of authority to attack Fort Miamis, and probably the support of Congress as well, he failed to send Congress Knox's letter authorizing Wayne to act. Several possible explanations exist. Inadvertent omission seems unlikely; numerous messages of far lesser significance were communicated to Congress. More probably Washington wanted to keep his plan concerning the fort secret from the British. He may have felt that Secretary of State Randolph's effort to convince the British to withdraw would be hampered if the British knew that the Americans had no intention to attack the fort unless it became involved in the Indian-American battle. Or he may not have wanted the British to know that the United States was prepared to attack the fort under any circumstances. He may also have wanted to avoid controversy within Congress on the issue, including the possibility of legislative pressure to eject the British forcibly. He had decided to handle the Jay Treaty negotiation without congressional consultation. Therefore he may have felt that Congress, knowing nothing of the delicacy of those proceedings, might unknowingly have jeopardized their successful conclusion if called upon to deal with the existence of Fort Miamis.

One other aspect of this affair is worth noting. Knox's instructions to Wayne were specific and urged caution. Wayne's behavior with respect to the British was less than exemplary, though consistent with his reputation for recklessness that earned him the nickname "Mad Anthony."[305] He unnecessarily threatened and approached the fort, and without any authority demanded that the British withdraw. Conceivably, Wayne would have been even less cautious but for Knox's detailed injunctions, especially the important qualification that allowed an attack on the fort only if necessary to defeat the Indians.

CONCLUSION

Much that is written on the war and foreign-affairs powers of the President and Congress of the United States either asserts or assumes dramatic changes in the relative power and conduct of these two branches over the course of American history. Dramatic events and important changes have undoubtedly taken place. But a close look at executive-congressional relations during Washington's administration indicates that many practices and doctrines commonly assumed to be of relatively recent origin are rooted in the early precedents.

The framework for executive-congressional relations developed during the first eight years differs more in degree than in kind from the present framework. The President was early given, or recognized to possess, the power to remove and thereby to control high executive officers. Those officers were delegated the task of planning governmental policy in the crucial areas of foreign, military, and economic affairs, by Congressmen acutely aware of the "legislative" power that might thus be acquired by the executive. In legislating, Congress delegated broad discretion to the President and departmental secretaries in the same important areas of activity, once again over objections that expressed the danger and constitutional impropriety of broad delegations. Those areas where delegations were refused—aspects of appropriations and the establishment of post roads—appear to reflect the special concern of legislators for detailing expenditures where possible and for controlling matters in which their local constituencies had a direct interest.

Practices respecting the control of information also were established. President Washington usually supplied information on his own initiative—not just information relating to his legislative requests, but also "confidential" material on sensitive international issues, to enable Congress to reach its own judgment. He did withhold some material, particularly "private" correspondence with agents and ministers, the publication of which would have been embarrassing. Most Congressmen appear to have felt that requests for information on delicate matters should be qualified to enable the President to withhold material when its disclosure might prejudice the nation's interests. Washington and all the members of his Cabinets regarded the President as empowered to withhold material "for public considerations." Requested material was twice withheld, though once primarily on the ground that the House lacked discretion in appropriating for duly adopted treaties. No occasion appears to have arisen when any member of Congress accused Washington of abusing the discretion he claimed.

Washington swiftly assumed responsibility for communicating with foreign nations, and unilaterally formulated the nation's foreign policy. He decided twice to maintain neutrality in the face of foreign upheavals, and to implement his neutrality policy with force if necessary. He and his Cabinet were unanimously opposed to calling Congress back into session in 1794, despite at least a theoretical danger that war could occur. Madison's contentions when writing as Helvidius were rejected in practice.

On the other hand, war with Britain or France was at no point imminent while Congress was out of session; when, during the Nootka Sound controversy between Britain and Spain, Washington asked what should be done if Britain marched its troops across United

States territory without permission, Hamilton and Knox recommended that Congress should be called, although the inconvenience of calling Congress back at that time was far greater than at present. Finally, both Washington and Hamilton explicitly conceded Congress's power to change the neutrality policy adopted by the executive, a power Congress itself seems to have assumed by adopting the neutrality policy in legislation and by expressing its view on other subjects through various resolutions.

Washington authorized a few military actions during his administration, most clearly approved by legislation. The "offensive" actions against the Wabash Indians were never explicitly authorized by Congress, either by law or declaration of war. If authority for those actions is to be found, it must be in the letter of St. Clair submitted to Congress requesting more men for "offensive" actions, in Congress's fiscal and military support for the second and third expeditions after learning of the first, and in Congress's commendatory but very generally worded answer to the President's message concerning the first expedition. The action authorized against the British troops at Fort Miamis can also be justified by a process of implication, or as properly within the President's power as commander-in-chief. Washington told Congress of the dangerous situation created by the fort, and then proceeded to adopt the course of authorizing General Wayne to attack the fort if necessary to defeat the Indians in an expedition that was itself clearly supported by Congress.

In sum, the broad outlines of the presidency as we know it today were drawn during Washington's administration. The form it took is attributable in part to Washington's decision to assume control of government operations and policy-making over a range of activities, including foreign affairs and the conduct of military operations. It was also, however, the result of Congress's decisions to allow or to require the executive to plan policy and to exercise broad policy-making discretion in implementing legislatively unarticulated but shared objectives. Neither Washington nor any of his Cabinet ever suggested that Congress lacked constitutional power to plan and detail its policies, steps that would almost certainly have forced the executive into a form very different from the one it assumed.

❋ *Chapter 3*

John Adams and Undeclared
War as National Policy

The Federalists turned to Vice President John Adams as their candidate for second President of the United States. [1]

Unlike Washington, Adams was well educated, and had established his name as a lawyer and political leader, rather than as a military hero.* His political philosophy stressed a "mixed" legislative "department" with three branches (Executive, Senate, House), each having adequate power to check the others. [2] He shared the first President's view that peace could best be maintained through a policy of neutrality with sufficient strength for defense, [3] and expressed no reservations on Washington's decision to issue the Proclamation of 1793, or on any other important foreign-policy precedents established during the first eight years, including the Jay Treaty. [4]

Adams believed a strong executive was essential to the preservation of order, liberty, and prosperity. In a letter to one of his few friends with Republican leanings, Elbridge Gerry, he said efforts of the House to deny the President the power to remove executive officers would tend to produce anarchy:

*His articles and pamphlets gave credence and structure to early opposition to the Stamp Act. He became a pivotal and articulate force in the Continental Congress, where he participated in drafting and securing passage of the Petition of Rights and Declaration of Independence. He was instrumental in the appointment of Washington as commander-in-chief, served as Chairman of the Board of War and Ordnance, and as Commissioner to France. With Franklin and Jay, he negotiated the peace treaty with Britain in 1783, and served as Minister to Britain between 1785 and 1788. As Vice President he was seldom consulted by Washington, but exercised considerable power in the Senate, where he cast no less than 20 tie-breaking votes.

The Unity, Consistency, Promptitude, Secrecy and Activity of the whole Executive authority are so essential in my republican system, that without them there can be no peace, order, liberty, or Property in Society. A republican government without it is worse than a monarchical.[5]

Adams narrowly won election as President. Jefferson received only three fewer votes, and became Vice President under the then-existing constitutional procedure. Republicans took control of Congress, especially of the House. Adams therefore found it impossible to implement his philosophy of firm executive leadership. He was forced to convince a hostile Congress to accept the policies he felt were in the national interest. At no point did he challenge the legislature over any alleged constitutional prerogative.

EXECUTIVE-CONGRESSIONAL RELATIONS

Executive-congressional relations during the Adams administration continued on much the same bases established in the previous administration. Adams removed two Cabinet members for no stated cause,[6] and the executive departments continued to plan and propose legislation on important subjects, including military affairs.[7] Congress, in turn, delegated broad powers over fiscal affairs and highly sensitive subjects, such as the conduct of aliens, and foreign embargoes.[8] Delegations respecting the military were especially extensive.

Adams often communicated information to Congress,[9] but occasionally withheld material from voluntary transmittals.[10] Congress was less reluctant under Adams to request information and conduct investigations than under Washington. The House, for example, initiated a major investigation into what would now be called a "cost-overrun" on the frigates authorized under Washington.* One Congressman

*Act of March 27, 1794, 1 Stat. 350, and Act of April 20, 1796, 1 Stat. 453. Edward Livingston of New York proposed the resolution that would "inquire into expenditures of moneys. . . ." 7 *Annals of Congress* 820 (Jan. 11, 1798) [hereinafter "*Annals*"]. Livingston stressed that how the moneys were expended "was a secret which ought to be laid open," and that "if it were seen that this money would not be appropriated until the estimate in question was received, the House would not be long without it." *Id.* 824. Gallatin gave the history of increases: "In 1794 . . . they were told that $688,000 would be sufficient to build six frigates. In 1796, they were informed there had been a mistake in the matter, but that with $80,000 more three would be finished. In January 1797, the House was again called upon for $172,000; in July, in the same year, for $200,000 and now for $150,000 more. Such calculations he thought wholly unaccountable." *Id.* 835. (Apparently, the administration's latest request was for $130,785. *Id.* 822.)

claimed that such an inquiry implied a censure of executive officers, and should be undertaken only on adequate grounds to suspect misapplication of funds. But the House decided to inquire, without a division of votes for and against, apparently accepting the position that inquiries were appropriate to investigate both the use of, and the need for, funds.[11]

House and Senate requests for information were sometimes qualified to allow withholding if disclosure might harm the United States. [12] Adams complied with all requests, however, even those that permitted withholding.[13] He did occasionally request that sensitive material be held in confidence or returned, requests which Congress seems to have honored.[14] In only one instance did Adams consider withholding material actually requested by Congress, in connection with dispatches relating to the XYZ Affair. Adams ultimately sent Congress the information, but only after intimating that he regarded himself empowered at least to delay disclosure, and under circumstances that made disclosure highly advantageous to him politically.

The XYZ Dispatches: Information Policy and Politics

The XYZ dispatches were messages written by the ministers Adams had sent to France in an effort to avoid war. The messages arrived on March 4, 1798,[15] and not only confirmed that the mission had failed, but related that the ministers had been poorly treated and subjected to an attempted bribe by agents (designated X, Y and Z in the material ultimately given to Congress) of the French Minister of Foreign Affairs, Charles M. de Talleyrand. All but one of the letters were in code. The one uncoded letter described France's latest anti-American decree, which abrogated the "free ships make free goods" principle, and predicted "no hope" of an official reception or peace agreement.

Adams immediately sent the uncoded letter to Congress,[16] undoubtedly hoping to encourage speedy and positive action on his proposals for defensive measures. On March 13 the House voted to consider the recommended measures, after intense debate on the subject of an additional appropriation for the three frigates. John Nicholas, William B. Giles and Albert Gallatin all insisted that the House could act on defensive measures only after receiving a detailed account of what had happened in France.[17]

On the day that Nicholas and Gallatin called for more information, the President asked his Cabinet if "it be advisable to present immediately to Congress the whole of the communications from our minister in France," under an injunction of secrecy, with the names of Talleyrand's agents deleted.[18] Attorney General Charles Lee recommended that disclosure be delayed. He felt that disclosure to Congress would soon be discovered by the French, thereby endangering the lives of America's envoys as well as destroying any chance of further negotiation. On the other hand, he entertained "no doubt . . . that the President should at some other time lay before Congress in confidence these papers, though some objections of an ordinary kind might be made to such a proceeding."[19] Secretary of War James McHenry doubted that disclosure would endanger the envoys or make the French any less willing to negotiate. "It cannot with propriety be called a premature act," he said, "to lay before Congress the proceedings of our ministers as far as is known in one of the most important transactions which can affect the U.S."[20]

On March 19, Adams informed Congress that after considering the dispatches, he saw no hope for peace "on terms compatible with the safety, honor, or the essential interests of the nation."[21] Nevertheless, Adams withheld the dispatches from Congress, without comment, apparently to avoid endangering the envoys.[22] He did this reluctantly, since he realized release of the dispatches probably would have spurred Congress to accept his military recommendations.

Efforts soon took place in Congress to obtain the dispatches. Senator Joseph Anderson moved on March 20 that the Senate request the President, without any qualifying terms, to supply the instructions to, and letters from, the envoys to France.[23] Consideration of the resolution was deferred, but news of its introduction caused Alexander Hamilton* (under an erroneous impression that it had passed) to write Secretary of State Timothy Pickering that nothing could be more proper than a demand by the Senate for the information, and that as much as possible should be communicated. "Confidence will otherwise be wanting, and criticism will ensue which it will be difficult to repel."[24] Pickering responded on March 25 that, independently of motions to request the letters, he thought it "really desirable that not Congress only, but the people at large, should know the conduct of the French government towards our envoys. . . ." Disclosure, he felt, would "detach so many of the adherents to opposition leaders, as to enable the real friends of their country to take promptly all the requisite measures."[25]

Adams seems to have quickly agreed with Pickering and other leading Federalists that disclosure of the dispatches was essential to support the administration's policy.[26] He was probably reluctant to take the initiative, however, having already decided to delay disclosure. Republican leaders misjudged the situation. They thought

*Hamilton was practicing law in New York, but was frequently consulted by Pickering and McHenry on important matters of policy.

Adams was withholding the dispatches to protect himself, and began to criticize him. William B. Giles of Virginia even suggested that the undisclosed material might reveal that the envoys had inadequate authority to deal with the French, and that Adams was therefore responsible for the breakdown in negotiations.[27]

John Allen of Connecticut, an administration supporter, responded to Giles's charge, and to the charges in "a paper printed in this city which is continually insinuating that there is something in these despatches, which, if they were made known, would show that the conduct of the Executive has been improper." He introduced a resolution requesting the President to provide the dispatches *"or such parts thereof as considerations of public safety and interest, in his opinion, may permit."* Republicans objected to the limitations in Allen's motion. Samuel Smith of Maryland wanted the qualifying language deleted, arguing that sensitive papers could be communicated in secret "as is usual in such cases. . . ." Edward Livingston concurred, because he felt it the responsibility of each member to weigh all information on the issue of war or peace, and because the qualifying language "of the resolution proposed to transfer a right to the President which it [the House] ought itself to exercise, as to judging of what it was proper to publish in consideration of the public safety and interest." Giles wanted the request to extend to the President's instructions.[28]

Both Allen and Federalist James Bayard initially opposed these Republican efforts to broaden the resolution, claiming that some presidential discretion must be afforded, that material sent to the House in confidence would eventually be known to France, and that it was "wholly improper" to ask for executive instructions to the envoys. Staunch Federalist Robert Goodloe Harper of South Carolina managed to have the question postponed to Monday, April 2.[29]

By April 2 Allen had modified his position. He would accept all the proposed amendments, he said, if their proponents agreed to a qualification identical to the one used in requesting the Jay Treaty papers, *i.e.* "excepting such parts of said papers as any existing negotiation may render improper to be disclosed." This concession failed to satisfy John Nicholas. The President had said all hope for further negotiations was at an end, and "called upon to act in this desperate state of things, he [Nicholas] thought it would not be right for any part of the papers which had led to it to be withheld from Congress." He said "the Constitution must have intended" that Congress act on the same information as the President "when it placed the power of declaring war in their hands," and he moved to strike Allen's proposed qualification. His threat to vote against a qualified resolution, however, may well have stemmed from increasing fear that the dispatches contained material beneficial to the administration.[30]

The Federalists continued to be extraordinarily accommodating. Allen modified his position once again. While he protested Nicholas's refusal to accept language earlier accepted by the House, he did not want to "give gentlemen an opportunity of voting against the resolution. He would withdraw his amendment; because he believed the President would be authorized by the Constitution to retain such parts of the papers as he may think it improper to communicate . . . and that, therefore, it was immaterial whether the resolution contained any exception, or not." Some Representatives continued to insist that an exception be retained,* but the Federalist leadership supported Allen's strategy. "Upon reflecting," Robert Goodloe Harper concluded that no constitutional question was involved in the present call for papers. The objections to a call for papers relating to the Jay Treaty did "not apply in the present case, as the papers now called for were wanted to throw light upon a subject confessedly within the Constitutional powers of the House," and "if the House had a Constitutional right to ask for information, they had a right to ask for the whole information, and the President would judge how far he could, with propriety, comply with the call." In this case "the whole ought to be called for; and, if the President should think it proper to retain a part, he would doubtless give sufficient reason to the House for doing so." The motion to qualify the request was thereupon defeated without a division.[31]

These Federalist statements asserting an inherent executive discretion to withhold information were, undoubtedly, part of an overall political strategy. The same cannot be said of Gallatin's argument for disclosure that also assumed the President could exercise some discretion in determining whether to disclose the dispatches:

> But if, after having examined the despatches, he [the President] is convinced it will be highly injurious to the public welfare, or endanger the safety of our Commissioners, or prevent the happy issue of our negotiation, to communicate the information, he will either give it, or state his reasons for withholding it to the House.[32]

An unqualified request for the information was approved overwhelmingly, with many leading Federalists voting in favor. Allen and

---

*Thomas Hartley of Pennsylvania thought a qualification proper, for he doubted whether the House could constitutionally call for instructions given to ministers. 8 *Annals* 1369. Harrison Gray Otis of Massachusetts also preferred inclusion of the exception; he wanted to trust the President and to avoid any possibility of harm to the envoys. *Id.* 1370.

John Hanna of New Jersey were designated to present the resolution to Adams, and Allen reported the same day that the President "informed them that he would take the matter under consideration, and do what the public safety should seem to require." Though suggesting in this last statement that he possessed discretion to withhold the material, Adams chose to transmit to both the House and Senate all the instructions and letters "omitting only some names, and a few expressions descriptive of the persons" who attempted to obtain bribes from the envoys. He suggested the materials be considered in confidence until Congress "shall have had opportunity to deliberate on the consequences of their publication; after which time, I submit them to your wisdom."[33] Republicans in both houses opposed widespread distribution of the letters, purportedly to avoid interfering with the possibility of peace, but more likely because their disclosure seemed certain to garner support for the President. They failed, and the dispatches convinced the nation and a congressional majority to support the President's program.[34]

Control of Foreign Affairs

The President continued to exercise day-to-day control of foreign relations, including the processes of negotiating with France. He unilaterally sent ministers to France soon after taking office, and instructed the ministers to return after learning that an effort to bribe them had been made by French agents. He remained receptive to French efforts to renew negotiations and unilaterally sent ministers to France in October 1799, with authority to negotiate a peace agreement.*

On the other hand, Adams involved Congress at many important points in decisions he had made or contemplated making, sometimes even though Congress's cooperation was unnecessary to implement his plans. He advised Congress of his decision to negotiate with France in 1797, and submitted to the Senate for ratification the names of the ministers he had chosen.[35] He also sent to the Senate for confirmation the names of the ministers he chose to negotiate peace in

*On one occasion he advised a federal court before which a sailor, Jonathan Robbins, was being tried for murder, that the sailor should be delivered up to the British as a deserter, pursuant to a treaty. The sailor claimed American citizenship, and Republican Congressmen objected to Adams's actions. Resolutions requesting information and declaring that the President had interfered with the judiciary were defeated, however, after a full-dress statement by Representative John Marshall, who viewed the President's intervention to state the nation's obligations as proper, and assumed that the sufficiency of the evidence against the sailor had been left with and passed on by the judge. *See generally* 10 *Annals* 511–621. The future Chief Justice said: "The President is the sole organ of the nation in its external relations, and its sole representative with foreign nations." *Id.* 613.

1799.[36] Although one of the commonly assumed advantages of an undeclared war was that no formal treaty would be necessary for its termination, Adams sent the convention negotiated with France to a secret Senate session for "consideration and decision."[37] He complied with the Senate's requests for information and accepted its conditional approval of the treaty's terms.[38]

The Republican-dominated House of Representatives sought aggressively to expand its role in formulating foreign policy. After extensive debate, and over objections of improper interference with the President's control of foreign relations,[39] the House voted to include in its answer to the President's address of May 16, 1797 its "hope" of an accommodation if France were offered terms similar to those offered other nations.[40] This sense-of-the-House resolution in effect suggested that France be offered the advantages given Britain in the Jay Treaty. After the pro-French language was included in the answer, most Federalists put aside principle and voted to include language calling on France to "compensate for any injury done to our neutral rights."[41] The House also voted to retain an explanatory preamble in a bill abrogating the treaties between the United States and France,* over objections that the legislature's business was to pass laws, not issue manifestos.[42]

Members asserted that the House could use its power over appropriations to prevent the executive from negotiating a treaty,[43] and to eliminate unnecessary diplomatic offices.[44] The latter issue was pressed most vigorously in the form of a motion to stop granting an overall appropriation for conducting foreign relations, and instead to specify each office, its rank, and salary.[45] Federalists went to great lengths in arguing against this proposal, contending that the House had no alternative but to supply the funds necessary for the President to conduct foreign affairs, that the President could and should be trusted, and even rejecting the notion that it was proper for the House to use its powers to check or balance executive authority.[46] Republicans claimed for Congress the power to create offices, to check the executive, and to control a matter so closely connected with war.[47] The motion narrowly failed, however, with at least some members agreeing that the House had power to specify expenditures, but voting against the resolution as undesirably restrictive.[48]

---

*Samuel Sewall said it was "a novel doctrine to pass a law declaring a treaty void," and Gallatin said the preamble was necessary to justify the extraordinary action. 8 *Annals* 2120, 2126. No one contended that Congress lacked power to take the step, however; Sewall said, in fact, that only Congress had the power. No Senate debate was recorded. 7 *id.* 586–88.

MILITARY ACTIONS AND AUTHORIZATIONS

The military issues that arose during the Adams presidency almost all concerned the Quasi-War with France. All three branches of the government participated. The executive formulated foreign policy, recommended military measures and implemented the measures adopted. Some executive actions were taken without prior congressional approval; at other times, the President refused to act unilaterally, or without clear authority. Most significantly, Adams, unwilling to risk the political consequences of requesting a formal declaration of war, gradually convinced Congress to authorize hostilities without a declaration. Congress debated and determined what military and fiscal means ought to be placed at the President's disposal, and under what terms. The Supreme Court ruled on some of the legal consequences of undeclared war, including the scope of executive power to take military actions pursuant to specific legislative authorizations.

Undeclared War as Conscious National Policy

Relations with France had deteriorated substantially by the time Adams was sworn in as President on March 4, 1797. France had provided substantial military and financial aid to the United States during the War for Independence, but the treaties adopted by the former allies were ungenerously construed after 1793 to enable America to remain neutral in the war between France and Britain. Tension increased as French decrees were issued between 1793 and 1796 making American trade increasingly difficult. Ratification of the Jay Treaty, which granted substantial concessions to Britain, led France to decree on July 2, 1796, that "the flag of the French republic will treat neutral vessels, either as to confiscation, as to searches, or capture, in the same manner as they [neutrals] shall suffer the English to treat them."[49] Then, only two days before Adams took office as President, a French decree revoked the principle that "free ships make free goods" and condemned as a pirate any American serving in the crew of a private or public ship of an enemy of France. The French also suddenly began enforcing a treaty provision requiring ships to keep lists of their crews, seizing American merchant vessels that lacked such lists.[50] On June 21, 1797, the Secretary of State reported to Congress 316 captures of American ships by the French since July 1796.[51]

Adams probably knew by the time of his inauguration that France planned a decree largely revoking the principle that "free ships make free goods."[52] He nevertheless expressed, in his inaugural address, "a sincere desire to preserve the friendship [with France] which has been so much for the honor and interest of both nations"; at the same time he was determined to maintain neutrality and to seek reparations for the injuries done to Americans "by whatever nation, and, if success cannot be obtained, to lay the facts before the Legislature, that they may consider what further measures the honor and interest of the Government and its constituents demand. . . ."[53] Adams apparently believed that France wanted peace, and appointed a special commission to negotiate an agreement.[54]

A crisis was almost immediately triggered, however, by the news that France had refused to receive, and had expelled, Charles Cotesworth Pinckney, sent as Ambassador to replace Monroe. Hamilton had heard this news by March 22, when he wrote to Pickering suggesting that Congress be convened "at as *short a day* as a majority of both houses can assemble," and that a three-member commission be appointed to negotiate with France. He proposed that various defensive measures be implemented through Congress, including an embargo, the creation of a naval force to serve as convoys, authorization to American merchant vessels and convoys to arm and capture when attacked "but not to cruise," and organization of a provisional army of 25,000 to be ready in case of war.[55] Even before Hamilton's letter reached Pickering, the President—with the apparent concurrence of his entire Cabinet, including those who felt further negotiation with France was pointless—had decided to call Congress into special session. A proclamation to this effect was issued on March 25, calling Congress into session less than two months later, on May 15.[56]

Meanwhile, on March 3, 1797, the Act of June 5, 1794, which prohibited the arming of merchant vessels, expired, creating general uncertainty on the right to arm.[57] Adams caused an order to be issued on April 8, 1797, allowing the arming of vessels engaged in trade to the East Indies, because it was clearly lawful to defend by military force against pirates. But much as Washington had done in 1793, he prohibited entirely the arming of vessels engaged in European or West Indian commerce.[58] Arming vessels in trade with Europe or the West Indies, a letter accompanying the order recited, "raises a presumption, that it is done with hostile intentions against some of the belligerent nations, and may cover collusive practices inconsistent with the Act of Congress of June 1794, unless guarded by provisions more effectual than have been hitherto established."[59] Hamilton communicated his chagrin; he felt that prohibiting the arming of vessels was legally indefensible and unnecessary.[60] But, as

Pickering explained, Adams was determined to avoid congressional criticism for enabling merchantmen to defend themselves against searches that France arguably could conduct under international law or under its treaties with the United States.[61]

When Congress convened, Adams recommended preparing the nation to defend itself and its commerce. He made clear that his order restricting arming was intended "to prevent collisions with the Powers at war, contravening the Act of Congress of June [1794] . . . and not from any doubt . . . of the policy and propriety of permitting our vessels to employ means of defence, while engaged in a lawful foreign commerce." He asked Congress to prescribe regulations to permit arming for defense.[62] But he did not recommend war. The United States was unprepared to fight a war, great sympathy existed among the citizenry for France, and a negotiated settlement was still possible. Some Federalists were convinced that war was inevitable, but other leaders (including Hamilton and Fisher Ames) were for pursuing all avenues to peace short of dishonor.[63]

Congress was unprepared to accept Adams's recommendation to adopt defensive measures.* They refused even to authorize regulating the arming of merchant vessels, despite claims that Adams lacked authority to act unilaterally.[64] The President was authorized to employ three frigates constructed during Washington's tenure, however, after interesting debate (discussed below) on the extent of his discretion to use the vessels.

On November 23, 1797, Adams once again urged Congress to prepare for defense, stressing that a healthy commerce was essential to the nation and that there was no "reasonable ground on which to raise an expectation, that a commerce, without protection or defense, will not be plundered."[65] Congress still refused to act, even after news that a French ship had attacked a British vessel in the Charleston harbor.[66]

The President struggled to arrive at a policy toward France. On January 24, 1798 he asked his Cabinet whether, if the mission to France failed, an immediate declaration of war should be sought

---

*An interesting example of the early prevailing sentiment is the House's reaction to a proposal for an additional corps of artillery. This unnecessary measure, Republicans contended, would be one more step toward a standing army, "the constant attendant upon despotic Governments." "More money and more troops was apt to be an increasing passion," Abraham Baldwin predicted, "always attending large delegations of power. . . ." He hoped "this country would form an exception, and show that some of the miseries of the world were not the inseparable condition of man." Harper tried to add a pragmatic note, saying the U.S. had forts and needed men in them, and "Gentlemen could not be serious in supposing that the liberty of this country would be endangered by 900 additional men." Nevertheless, the proposal was rejected. 7 *Annals* 327-28, 343, 347.

from Congress. Attorney General Charles Lee felt the envoys should be recalled, that merchant ships should be allowed to arm, and that the President should recommend a declaration of war.[67] Secretary of War McHenry replied on February 15, after being tutored by Hamilton.[68] The people were generally averse to war, he said, and a portion of them particularly averse to war with France. He recommended, instead, an undeclared war as the national policy:

> An express declaration of hostility . . . would . . . subject us to all the chances of evil which can accrue from the vengeance of a nation stimulated by . . . extraordinary success. . . . A mitigated hostility will [therefore] be the most likely to fall in with the general feeling, while it leaves a door open for negotiation, and secures some chances to avoid some of the extremities of a formal war.

He suggested that Congress be asked, among other things, to permit merchant vessels to arm for defense, to empower the President to provide for more ships, and to authorize an army of 16,000 men with an auxiliary of 20,000 more.

At this point the President received firm evidence that the mission to France had failed, and that the ministers had been poorly treated and asked to pay bribes. The so-called XYZ dispatches from the American ministers, describing the whole sordid affair, arrived on March 4.[69] Adams asked his Cabinet on March 13 whether he should communicate the dispatches to Congress and whether "to recommend . . . an immediate declaration of war."[70] The dispatches, as we have seen, were disclosed pursuant to request, in part to garner legislative support for actions against France. As to the measures he should recommend to Congress, Lee suggested defensive preparation and, "whenever we shall hear of our envoys having left France . . . a formal declaration of war."[71] But McHenry persisted in his view that a "qualified hostility" was preferable to a formal declaration of war, since France had qualified her hostility and had held out "terms of accommodation, tho' humiliating and inadmissable in their present nature and form. . . . Such a procedure as this, while it secures the objects essential and preparatory to a state of open war, involves in it the fewest evils, and the greatest number of possible chances and advantages."[72] He advised that Congress be asked to set aside existing treaties with France, provide ships, an army, and revenue.

Adams accepted McHenry's advice in all respects except his recommendation for an army. The President announced to Congress on March 19, 1798, that he had studied the dispatches and concluded there was no basis to expect peace. He called again for defensive preparations, and unilaterally suspended the order he had issued restricting the arming of merchant vessels.[73] But he did not request a declaration of war.[74]

Republicans in Congress sensed the nation's drift toward war, and began to press for a definitive legislative determination of the question, hoping thereby to avert armed conflict.* The President's announcement of March 19 led Representative Richard Sprigg, Jr. of Maryland to claim it had become "necessary that the House should declare whether this country was to have peace or war." He later suggested three resolutions, one declaring it inexpedient for the United States "to resort to war" with France, another to restrict the arming of merchant vessels, and the third to adopt defensive preparations. [75]

Samuel Sitgreaves of Pennsylvania sought to head off the first resolution, contending that Congress's failure to declare war sufficiently expressed its sentiment that resort to war would be inexpedient. Abraham Baldwin responded that the whole power of war and peace was in the hands of Congress, that Congress was not the instrument merely to give "the sound of war," and that when others were saying that war exists, the House, if it disagrees, ought to say that we are at peace. Particularly interesting is John Nicholas's argument, directed against a proposal by Harrison Gray Otis to amend

*Jefferson termed Adams's message "insane" in a letter to Madison. He suggested that, if the Republicans could muster a majority, they should pass a bill prohibiting arming, and adjourn to consult constituents. 10 *The Writings of Thomas Jefferson* 9–10 (A. Bergh, ed.; Memorial ed. 1907). Madison agreed with the strategy, and added that Congress should at least demand the information upon which the President had acted. He continued:

> The constitution supposes, what the History of all governments demonstrates, that the Executive is the branch of power most interested in war, and most prone to it. It has, accordingly, with studied care, vested the question of war in the Legislature. But the doctrines lately advanced strike at the root of all these provisions, and will deposit the peace of the Country in that Department which the Constitution distrusts as most ready, without cause, to renounce it. . . . Congress ought clearly to prohibit arming, and the President ought to be brought to declare on what ground he undertook to grant an indirect licence to arm. The first instructions were no otherwise legal than as they were in pursuance of the law of nations, and, consequently, in execution of the law of the land. The revocation of the instructions is a virtual change of the law, and consequently a usurpation by the Executive of a legislative power. It will not avail to say that the law of nations leaves this point undecided, and that every nation is free to decide it for itself. If this be the case, the regulation being a Legislative, not an Executive one, belongs to the former, not the latter authority, and comes expressly within the power, "to define the law of nations," given to Congress by the Constitution. I do not expect, however, that the Constitutional party in the H. of Rep[s] is strong enough to do what ought to be done in the present instance.

Madison to Jefferson, April 2, 1798, 2 *The Letters and Other Writings of James Madison* 131–32 (Cong. ed. 1867).

Sprigg's resolution to announce it inexpedient "to declare" war, rather than "to resort" to war. "[I]f gentlemen were ready to say we were not prepared to declare war," said Nicholas, "and at the same time were not ready to say it is not expedient to resort to war, it proved they thought war might be made without being declared." He claimed the President "had taken measures which would lead to war," and that "he had never heard it doubted that Congress had the power over the progress of what led to war, as well as the power of declaring war; but if the President could take the measures which he had taken, with respect to arming merchant vessels, he, and not Congress, had the power of making war."[76]

Republican strategy shifted, however, from pressing Sprigg's resolutions to seeking the XYZ dispatches. Adams's decision to communicate the dispatches shattered any hope of passing the resolutions, so great was the revulsion against France. Indeed, immediately after the dispatches were revealed, John Allen, an administration supporter, sought to have the House take up and decide Sprigg's resolution that war with France was inexpedient. The Republicans no longer wanted to pursue the matter and sought a postponement, which Federalist leaders accepted to avoid discussion.[77]

Congress then began to pass the measures long sought by the administration, conferring broad discretion over a variety of military matters.[78] Congress adopted a general appropriation for fortification, for example, despite efforts to specify the places to be fortified and the amounts to be spent at each place; proponents successfully urged that the President be allowed to decide these matters, even to the point of not spending the funds if that course seemed advisable.[79] By far the most heated delegation debate, however, was over the proposal to authorize the President to raise a substantial army when he deemed it necessary.[80] Republicans claimed this innovation would amount or lead to an unconstitutional transfer of the war power to the President.* Federalists argued that Congress could

---

*Gallatin's constitutional analysis was, as in many other situations, the most telling for the Republican view:

> The Constitution has declared that the raising of an army is placed in Congress, but this bill goes to declare that this power shall be vested by law in the President. That is the principle of the bill; and if Congress were once to admit the principle that they have a right to vest in the President powers placed in their hands by the Constitution, that instrument would become a piece of blank paper. . . . And if they could delegate the power of raising an army to the President, why not do the same with respect to the power of raising taxes? He supposed the House would next hear of provisional taxes, to be raised if the President shall think fit. . . . If the circumstances of the Union required an army, let it be raised; if not, he wishes to give no power to raise it—especially, as the President, if he saw necessity, could call Congress together, if he should find that the circumstances of the country required it.

choose to rely on the President's discretion in order to avoid the cost of raising troops unnecessarily.* The bill was passed, but only after being amended to authorize the President, "till the next meeting of Congress," to raise troops "in the event of a declaration of war against the United States, or of an actual invasion . . . or of imminent danger of such invasion, discovered, in his opinion, to exist."[81]

Adams no longer considered seeking a declaration of war. Within three months of receiving the XYZ dispatches, Congress transformed the national policy from peace to war, without a formal declaration. During July 1798, the House once again considered whether to declare "the state and relation subsisting between the United States and the French Republic."[82] The debate reflects a sophisticated understanding of the advantages in fighting a declared rather than an undeclared war;† yet motions to discuss whether war should be declared were withdrawn or defeated because "no member is ready to make the declaration which had been so often spoken of. . . ."[83]

The constitutionality of fighting an undeclared war was considered

---

8 *Annals* 1526-27 (Apr. 24, 1798); *See also id.* 1655-56 (Gallatin); 1532 (Baldwin); 1638 (Brent); 1649 (R. Williams), all of whom argued that the power to declare war might similarly be delegated.

*Pinckney agreed with Gallatin "that it was the object of those who formed the Constitution, that the powers of Government should be distributed among the different departments, and that they ought not to be assigned or relinquished." But he refused to accept the argument that

> this bill gave away from Congress the power of raising an army to any other department of Government. If this power was generally transferred, to the President, he might at all times raise an army, without the consent of Congress; but it would not be said that this would be the case, if this bill should pass. It is not doubted that the Legislature may order an army to be raised by the President, in case of a declaration of war, or of an invasion; but gentlemen say the contingency ought not to depend upon the opinion of the President. But, Mr. P. said, this must either be done, or you must burden your constituents unnecessarily, by raising the army before it is wanted.

8 *Annals* 1660 (May 10, 1798).

"[A]ll the military force of the country is by the Constitution placed at the disposal of the President," Sitgreaves noted, so objections to according him power were legally baseless and proceeded from distrust. *Id.* 1732. Otis said Congress could, as a practical matter, violate the Constitution in countless ways, but they did not do so; the President, he suggested, should likewise be trusted. *Id.* 1733. We ought to guard against the abuse of power, said Williams, "but to say a power shall not be granted, because it is liable to be abused, goes against placing power anywhere." *Id.* 1741.

†Sitgreaves contended the issue should be considered:

> We are . . . now in a state of war. The House know that, by the distribution of powers under this Government, it is only competent for the Congress to declare the country in war; therefore, until that declaration is made by this department, the Executive and Judiciary cannot act in the same way as if the country was at war. In other countries, the Executive Department can create war; but here it cannot.

8 *Annals* 2117 (July 6, 1798). Samuel Sewall (Mass.) was unimpressed. He was

by the Supreme Court, even as the Quasi-War raged. In *Bas* v. *Tingy*, the commander of an American public vessel claimed he was entitled to an award for salvage amounting to one-half the value of an American merchant ship and cargo he had recaptured from the French. He based his claim on the Act of March 2, 1799, which allowed salvage of one-half the value of any American-owned vessel taken from "the enemy" more than ninety-six hours after its seizure. The merchant vessel's master claimed the Act of March 2, 1799 was inapplicable because, among other reasons, France was not an "enemy," since Congress had not declared war. The relevant act, he argued, was that of June 28, 1798, which authorized salvage to public-owned vessels for recapturing American-owned vessels from the French in the amount of one-eighth the whole value.

The Court held the Act of March 2, 1799 applicable. The word "enemy" did apply to France, the Justices said, for essentially two reasons: it properly described the situation between the two nations; and Congress had intended to describe France when it said "enemy." War did not come in just one variety, wrote Justice Bushrod Washington. "Every contention by force, between two nations, in external matters, under the authority of their respective governments, is not only war, but public war." If war is declared, it is "solemn" or "perfect" because "all the members of the nation declaring war are authorized to commit hostilities against all the members of the other, in every place, and under every circumstance." As compared to this "general authority," hostilities may be "more confined" and "limited as to places, persons, and things; and this is more properly termed imperfect war ... because those who are authorized to commit hostilities, act under special authority, and can go no further than to the extent of their commission." The hostilities with France were limited, but constituted war nonetheless, because they were external and "authorized by the legitimate authority of the two governments," he said, after reviewing the legislation passed to deal with French depredations. "If they were not our enemies, I know not what constitutes an enemy."[85]

Justice Samuel Chase agreed that Congress could declare a general war or wage a war "limited in place, in objects, and in time." A declared war is governed by the laws of war; the "extent and operation" of a limited war "depend on our municipal laws." France was

---

against declaring war at present. "As to the Judicial Courts," he said, "they would find no difficulty in acting according to the situation of things, without troubling themselves with the nice distinctions which gentlemen seemed inclined to make between a state of war, and a state of hostility." *Id.* 2118.

an enemy, albeit "partial" because Congress treated her as such.[86] Instead of perceiving danger in allowing Congress to authorize military action without a formal declaration, Justice Chase praised Congress for proceeding piecemeal, in the face of public opposition:

> The acts of Congress have been analyzed to show, that a war is not openly denounced against France, and that France is nowhere expressly called the enemy of America: but this only proves the circumspection and prudence of the legislature. Considering our national prepossessions in favor of the French republic, Congress had an arduous task to perform, even in preparing for necessary defense and just retaliation. As the temper of the people rose, however, in resentment of accumulated wrongs, the language and the measures of the government became more and more energetic and indignant; though hitherto the popular feeling may not have been ripe for a solemn declaration of war; and an active and powerful opposition in our public councils, has postponed, if not prevented that decisive event, which many thought would have best suited the interest, as well as the honor of the United States.

He even compared "the progress of our contest with France" with "the progress of our revolutionary contest; in which, watching the current of public sentiment, the patriots of that day proceeded, step by step," from supplication to "the bold and noble declaration of national independence."[87]

Control of the Conduct of War

Congress could control the course of the war with France through its power to refuse funds, or to refuse to supply naval vessels, or to supply only certain types of vessels. Early in the conflict, however, it became clear that significant differences of opinion existed over the extent of Congress's authority to control the use of vessels, once supplied.

Legislative Control of Public-Owned Vessels. Congress was first of the three branches to consider the issues. On June 9, 1797, a resolution was proposed that the President be authorized "to provide a further naval force in addition to the three frigates already provided, whenever, in his opinion, the circumstances of the country shall require the same. . . ." Republicans objected, arguing that only the legislature should determine whether vessels were necessary. Federalists noted other instances of such delegations, but accepted limitations allowing the purchase of additional vessels only if the President perceived a danger to the coast when Congress was in recess.[88]

Far more controversial was an amendment proposed by Albert

Gallatin to require any vessel obtained by the President "to be stationed within the United States." Many objections were raised, most notably Harrison Gray Otis's statement that the amendment "appeared repugnant to the power placed in the President by the Constitution. If a naval force was raised," he said, "it would rest with the President how it should be employed, as he was commander-in-chief. The Legislative could say whether the vessels should be employed offensively or defensively, but to say at what precise place they were to be stationed, was interfering with the duty of the commander-in-chief. . . ." Gallatin's amendment lost 49 to 38, and the resolution passed.[89]

Otis's statement suggests an inherent executive power over at least some aspects of the conduct of military operations. Otis also said, however, that Congress could determine whether the vessels should be used offensively or defensively, and added that the President "would have no right to send these vessels to the West Indies or as convoys. . . ." Otis's only claim in the President's behalf was that Congress could not require the vessels to be kept at a precise place, and the President could "defend the seacoast as he pleased." This was actually consistent with Gallatin's resolution, since the limitation Gallatin proposed did not state a "precise place," as Otis's argument assumed, but would have restricted the ships to a nine-mile-wide area along the entire coast.[90]

In any event, the Federalists' success in striking Gallatin's proposed amendment was short-lived. When the resolution was reported to the House the next day by the Committee of the Whole, Giles complained of the power it vested and moved to require that the ships "be employed within the jurisdiction of the United States." Federalists contended that the matter was settled. But Samuel Sewall (a leading Federalist) then proposed an amendment allowing the President to use the vessels "to defend the seacoast of the United States, and to repel any hostility to their vessels and commerce within their jurisdiction." This helped satisfy Gallatin's desire to avoid war by preventing the use of galleys for convoys or to repel attacks on ships outside United States waters. The amendment was accepted without a division, and the resolution passed as amended.[91]

Discussion of these issues began anew when the Senate passed a bill with provisions authorizing the President to "employ" the three frigates provided for in earlier legislation to protect America's commerce, harbors, and seacoast, and authorizing a maximum of nine additional vessels with no more than 20 guns each.[92] When the bill reached the House, the provision authorizing nine new vessels was deleted. William Giles moved, in addition, to limit use of the frigates to the jurisdiction of the United States, an action earlier agreed to by the House in connection with the additional vessels it had voted to provide. Many members objected to so restrictive a use of frigates, commanded by "men of ability and character, well instructed as to their duty with respect to the law of nations." The Speaker, Jonathan Dayton, moved to strike the clause relating to how the frigates should be employed; he wanted to allow the President, "as commander-in-chief," to determine whether the frigates should be used as convoys or outside the nation's jurisdiction. "He was sure that confidence would not be abused; . . . [the President] would have better opportunities than they had, of determining the best manner" to employ the vessels. Parker claimed "it would be highly improper in them to dictate to the President how he should use these vessels," and others asserted that the House had no "right to direct the public force," and that the President should be left the power "to make use of the frigates as he pleased," unilaterally adjusting to changing circumstances. Harper found it safe to leave the use of force to the President "because he could employ it in a manner only applicable to peace; to employ it otherwise would be a breach of his power. . . . [If] he abuses it, upon his own head would lie the responsibility, and not upon them."[93]

The opposing constitutional argument was made by Nicholas, among others. He "denied the right of the President to apply the naval force of the United States to any object he pleased," and said:

> When a force was raised for a particular object, he agreed that it was his [the President's] business to direct the manner in which this force should be used; but to say he had the right to apply it at his discretion, was to make him master of the United States; if that were the case, he said, the powers of that House were gone. When they raised men for the protection of the frontier, would the President, he asked, send them to any other place? He insisted upon it that they had a right to say the vessels should be kept in the river Delaware, if they pleased; the President might afterwards direct their conduct. If a contrary doctrine were to prevail, if they did not give up the right of declaring war, they gave up the power, which would inevitably lead to war.[94]

Several members took intermediate positions on the constitutional question. Gallatin agreed that, in ordinary times, Dayton's position "was a good one," but under present circumstances he wished to give directions. Otis, on the other hand, conceded that Congress had the right to direct the public force, but felt they should demonstrate their confidence in the President under present circumstances, in part "to show the world that we are not a divided people." Samuel W.

Dana of Connecticut, another Federalist, echoed this view, arguing that Congress had the power to control deployment, but this "was no reason why they should insist upon exercising it." Samuel Smith, of Maryland, a Republican, recognized that "if the power of employing the frigates was wholly left with the President," he could *cause* war even if he lacked the power to declare war; at the same time, though, he felt it "a poor employment for these frigates, after all the expense which they had cost, to keep them within the jurisdiction of the United States."[95]

After some strategic maneuvering, a proposed amendment to prevent using the frigates as convoys to any foreign place succeeded by two votes.[96] The Senate reopened the issue, however, by refusing to concur with the House in restricting the use of the frigates and in striking the provision authorizing the President to procure and employ nine additional vessels.[97] At first the House majority in favor of restricting the President's discretion held together. But a motion to "adhere" to the convoying restriction, and thereby to preclude any conference or negotiation with Senate representatives on the issue, lost by a narrow margin. The Senate then retreated from its position with respect to the nine additional ships, but voted to adhere to its position allowing the President to "employ" the frigates without the House restriction. Faced with the possible loss of the entire bill, a handful of Representatives changed their votes, and the House agreed, 51–47, to delete the restriction on employing the frigates.[98]

The final debate on controlling the naval force came soon after release of the XYZ dispatches, when a majority of both Houses of Congress began to line up solidly behind the President's war policy.* On April 9, 1798, the Senate passed a bill to authorize the President to procure up to sixteen vessels of not more than twenty-two guns each to protect the trade of the United States, "to be armed, fitted out, and manned, under his direction."[99] Section 4 empowered the President, in order to secure the commercial and navigational rights

---

*On April 12, 1798, the House considered a resolution to provide additional artillerists. When some members objected because troops were being wasted on the frontier, Dayton labeled their argument "another attempt to usurp the place and duties of the Chief Magistrate, and to wrest from him, or what was equally unconstitutional, to participate with him [in], one of the most important attributes of the office, that of Commander-in-Chief of the Army. . . ." Gallatin responded that "he could not conceive that he had not a right to take into consideration the present disposition of the United States, in order to ascertain how far it was necessary to increase their number." He conceded "that the President of the United States, and the Secretary of War under him, had the disposition of the troops of the United States; but he also knew that if more were asked for, for any particular service, and Congress did not agree to provide so many as were asked," then troops would be moved from where they were needed least to where they were needed most. The resolution carried. 8 *Annals* 1402–403, 1407–12.

of Americans under the law of nations and treaties, "to employ the armed vessels of the United States, as convoys, when he may think proper to afford such protection, or in any other manner which, in his judgment, will best contribute to the general interests of the United States."[100]

In the House, Nicholas moved to strike the fourth section; he opposed allowing convoys because they would certainly cause war. Dayton supported convoying, and felt they could be used consistent with the law of nations. But he and other Federalists agreed with Nicholas, for different reasons, that section 4 should be deleted. Once the force was established, he said, "the President, according to his Constitutional power, as Commander-in-Chief, could employ it as he thought proper." Section 4 "might be of dangerous precedent," since it implied that the President needed Congress's approval to convoy. Members of Congress "were stepping beyond their proper province when they went so far . . . as to declare who shall be authorized and empowered to direct such force, and more especially the manner in which it shall be employed." The Constitution had already done these things "by committing to the President . . . the command of the Army and Navy, to be directed and employed by him as should seem best, consistently with the state in which we might happen to be. . . ."[101]

Dayton anticipated objections that his views would enable the President to make war without legislative approval. His response was that, while Congress alone decided whether or not to declare war, "whether the declaration should be made, or refused to be made, the military and naval force was not the less under the direction of the President, to be used as should appear to be most likely to promote the general welfare, having regard to the existing state of things, whether of peace or war." He saw no "distinction in principle between employing a naval force to protect our merchantmen in the prosecution of a fair and lawful trade . . . and employing the military in enforcing the execution of the municipal law." If an act of Congress is necessary in this instance, he argued, one would also be needed to authorize protection, thus far afforded without legislative authorization, to goods passing through Indian territory or across lakes used by other powers; "in both cases, but especially the latter, hostilities might ensue upon the armed force protecting what was under its charge, and war might be the consequence." Harper adopted essentially the same view:

The President, he knew, could not alter the existing state of things. Admitting that state to be at peace, the President could not induce a state of war. But in what manner the public force, when provided by Congress, should be employed, conformably to the state of peace and the rights and duties resulting from it, was for the President to direct, under his responsibility, not for the House. The business of the House was to fix the state of the country, and provide force; that of the President to employ the force, according to that state.[102]

Gallatin argued that the President's power to employ force was subordinate to Congress's authority to direct how the force it provided ought to be applied. He rejected Dayton's attempt to equate the President's power on the high seas with his power to protect commerce going from one part of the United States to another: "Within our own territory . . . we have exclusive jurisdiction, [and] . . . no interruptions can take place, except from an invading enemy; but, over the sea we have no such jurisdiction." Finally, he pointed out that Dayton's logic in permitting the President to grant convoys assumed a distinction "which is not recognised in the Constitution, viz.: between the power of making war, and the power of committing hostility. Because it necessarily results from the power of granting convoys, that the President has also the power of authorizing the commission of hostilities."[103]

Sewall could not accept Gallatin's suggestion that the President had so much less power to protect citizens engaged in commerce abroad than to protect those engaged in domestic trade, that the former "were to be abandoned to the elements, or to the hostility of mankind, wherever they went." Nicholas did not deny that the President could protect commerce in time of peace, but said that, if "the peace of this country was lost" by a protective measure unauthorized by Congress, "the President would be justly chargeable with having lost it."[104]

Section 4 was stricken without a division. Dayton then moved an amendment to add an introduction to the succeeding sections regulating convoys. Nicholas cogently responded that the regulations were improper "if, according to the gentleman's own opinion the President has the power to employ these vessels as he pleases." Dayton argued there was no inconsistency, but Nicholas quoted the language involved, some of which would clearly have controlled the President's conduct. Even Otis was unconvinced that the regulations were consistent with Dayton's theory of unilateral presidential authority. He preferred the regulations to the theory, advancing instead a theory of concurrent power: "The President is Commander-in-Chief of the Army, and of the Militia when called out," he said, "but Congress might, nevertheless, direct the use of them." Otis "believed, therefore, it would be equally proper to leave the employment of these vessels wholly to the President, or to direct them to be employed as convoys." The question was one of expediency, and he thought the regulations expedient. Harper, who agreed with Dayton's theory, argued against the regulations, and Dayton ("happy to find that very many members concurred with him in opinion") withdrew his motion, and the material concerning regulations was deleted without opposition.[105]

After a motion was passed to reduce the number of vessels provided from sixteen to twelve, Gallatin affirmatively sought to prohibit their use, "in time of peace," as convoys to any foreign port or place. We lack enough vessels to convoy effectively, he argued, and the practice was likely to cause all-out war. The motion lost after long debate. Particularly interesting is Dana's rejection of what he termed Gallatin's assumption that we can defend our property only after a declaration of war. He stated, however, without opposition or qualification by other Federalists, that "it was not contemplated either to authorize reprisals or captures," claiming that convoying could lawfully be used by neutrals under the law of nations.[106]

Had Gallatin's motion not been made, the House's position on executive authority to use vessels would have been completely unclear. Virtually everyone had voted to strike sections 4 through 7, but for entirely different reasons. Gallatin's motion to prohibit convoying was, to the extent ascertainable, opposed only by those who wanted to leave the President free to convoy, and they apparently felt he could so do without express legislative authority. On the other hand, the vote to refuse to prevent convoying does not necessarily support Dayton's view that the House could not constitutionally have prevented convoying had it wished to do so; many Representatives may have agreed with Otis and Samuel Smith that such a restriction might be lawful but was inexpedient. Neither does the vote mean that the House believed the vessels could be used by the President "as he saw fit"; many in the majority may have agreed with Dana and others who noted that the President could take only defensive actions, consistent with international law, and specifically that no authority was conferred to capture or take reprisals. A similar qualification is probably what Harper and Dayton had in mind when they said the President could act as he saw fit, consistent with the "existing state of things." The bill passed on April 24, with all the House amendments.

The qualifications that Federalist leaders attached to their claims of inherent executive power to deploy vessels are important. They reflect no support for any sweeping claim of power to use the Navy unilaterally, in the best interests of the United States. One difficulty with these qualifications, however, is their ambiguity. What does it mean to say that the President may not "change the state of things from peace to war," or that he may act only "defensively"? Several of those early Representatives felt that the law of nations governed the President's conduct in the absence of legislative direction. So whatever would be lawful under international law would by definition be either consistent with peace or "defensive." The law of nations was itself unclear, however, on issues crucial to the time, such as the scope of the right of belligerents to search neutral vessels, and the right of neutrals to use convoys. Consequently, a power to deploy consistent with the law of nations authorized the President to act in a manner that could conceivably lead to war. Congressmen that wanted to have the vessels used with greater flexibility and effectiveness may have been willing to risk giving the President discretion. Others may have delegated power to use the vessels without further instructions in order to avoid responsibility for deciding in advance how far to let the President go; certainly a theme of the debates was that the President would be responsible if his orders changed the nation's state from peace to war.

Executive Instructions to the Naval Fleet. After providing the President with frigates and galleys in April 1798, Congress created a Department of the Navy, which began purchasing ships, pursuant to the authority delegated in the Act of April 27. By early May the frigates so long awaited were approaching readiness, and several purchased vessels were being prepared to handle naval assignments. [107] On May 12, just before the first ships were ready, Secretary of War McHenry wrote Hamilton for advice as to the "instructions that it will be proper to give their Captains." Noting the probability that the ships would meet with French privateers, in possession or control of American merchantmen, or cruising the coast intending to capture American vessels, or while the frigates engaged in convoying, he asked "what instructions ought to be given to meet such cases, or enable them to afford competent protection to our merchantmen, and preserve the Executive from any future accusation of having, by its orders, involved the country in war?"[108] The debates in Congress concerning how the frigates and other authorized vessels should be employed had probably led McHenry to be cautious, and to seek to protect the President from charges of de facto assumption of the power to make war.

Hamilton responded soon after, demonstrating an equal concern to avoid actions of even questionable legality. He had not seen the law providing the naval armament, he said, and so could not tell whether it gave "any new power to the President" in employing the ships. "If not, and he is left at the foot of the Constitution, as I understand the case, I am not ready to say that he has any other power than merely to employ the ships as convoys, with authority to *repel* force with *force* (but not to capture) and to repress hostilities within our waters, including a marine league from our coasts. Anything beyond this must fall under the idea of *reprisals*, and requires the sanction of that department which is to declare or make war." The strategy Hamilton proposed was for Adams to restrict his activity to clearly lawful conduct, and thus force Congress to provide the greater authority needed to protect America's trade effectively:

> [T]hat as different opinions about his power have been expressed in the House of Representatives, and no special power has been given by the law, it will be expedient for him, and his duty, . . . to come forward by a message to the two Houses of Congress declaring that "*so far* and *no farther*" he feels himself *confident* of his authority to go in the employment of the naval force; that as . . . the depredations on our trade demand a more extensive protection, he [brings] . . . the subject under review of Congress by a communication of his opinion of his powers, having no desire to exceed the constitutional limits.[109]

McHenry, in characteristic fashion, adopted Hamilton's plan of action, and proposed it to Adams on May 18. After analyzing existing legislation concerning the naval armament, McHenry concluded that, "the President cannot derive authority [from the laws] to do more than employ the ships as convoys," nor to authorize anything "further than to repel force by force, not including the power of capture, or even the exertion of force a moment longer than it is employed against them." All beyond defending the seacoast and repelling hostility to American vessels or commerce "within their jurisdiction . . . is considered to come within the sphere of reprisals and to require the explicit sanction of that branch of the government which is alone constitutionally authorised to grant letters of marque and reprisal." The situation, he said (in Hamilton's words), was "so delicate and important as that of war," and therefore, "it will not be proper for the President to proceed upon doubtful and undefined authority." Instead, he urged Adams to pressure Congress into delegating more authority by making clear that the frigates and other vessels would otherwise be severely restricted in their activities.[110]

Adams concurred. When the U.S.S. *Ganges*, one of the first purchased vessels, was ready to sail on May 22, its captain, Richard Dale, received instructions that severely restricted his authority. Since "Congress possess exclusively the Power to declare War, grant letters of Marque and Reprisal, and make Rules concerning Captures on Land and Water, and as neither has yet been done, your Operations must accordingly be partial and limited." After defining the jurisdiction of the United States, the instructions ordered Dale, if he found armed vessels "committing Depredation on our Coast or attacking or having taken . . . any vessel . . . , to make every Exertion to prevent the Execution of such unlawful Proceedings, and to defend or liberate or retake the Vessel pursued, attacked or captured, and send in the offending Vessel, to some port of the United States, to be delt [*sic*] with according to Law. . . ." On the high seas, Dale was ordered, if "attacked by any armed Vessel . . . , to defend yourself to the Utmost. If the Assailant strikes, examine her Papers, and if She has not a regular Commission, and then in force, bring her into some Port of the United States, to be tried as a Pirate." Protecting the nation's jurisdictional rights was clearly given priority, since Dale was instructed to cruise between "the Capes of Virginia and Long Island," and to change course from time to time "so as to afford the best Protection in your Power to our jurisdictional Rights, and especially to all Vessels of the United States, in coming or going off the Coast."[111]

Despite McHenry's analysis, a respectable argument could have been made that Congress had authorized more than Dale's instructions allowed. Hamilton explicitly noted in his letter to McHenry that he had not seen the naval armament bill, and his advice assumed that it conferred no authority beyond that possessed by the President "at the foot of the Constitution." McHenry noted in his letter to Adams that the Act of July 1, 1797 authorized the President to cause the three frigates to be "manned and employed," and in another section to employ revenue cutters "to defend the sea coast, and repel any hostility to their vessels and commerce within their jurisdiction." An act passed on April 27, 1798, he wrote, provided for additional vessels to protect the trade of the United States, but "is silent even on the subject of employing the vessels." McHenry found it "singular that the provision of the act of the 1st of July 1797, only extends to direct and authorise the employment of the Revenue Cutters in an explicit manner. viz.: 'To defend the sea coast and repel any hostility to their vessels and commerce, within their jurisdiction.' This," said McHenry, "is the extent to which the instructions can by any construction be carried."[112]

One might easily disagree with McHenry's assertion that no construction of relevant legislation could justify actions other than those specifically authorized for revenue cutters. Hamilton felt the Constitution itself allowed convoying and defending vessels on the high seas, and McHenry espoused this view in his letter to Adams. The House debates prior to passing the Act of July 1, 1797, addressed the issue of whether the President had or should have greater power to use the frigates than he had been delegated in connection with the revenue cutters. Many legislators contended that the President could use the frigates as he saw fit, so long as he did not change the "state of things" or act "offensively"; and it seems to have been uniformly assumed that, unless Congress applied to the frigates the restrictive language governing employment of the revenue cutters, the President would be free to use the frigates to convoy and defend American vessels on the high seas.[113]

In any case, the Act of July 1, 1797—and especially the language governing the revenue cutters—was not the most pertinent source available for determining Congress's intent. The *Ganges* was a vessel purchased pursuant to the Act of April 27, 1798. Congress had refused to place limitations on the President's authority to use the vessels authorized by that act; in particular, as we have seen, the House rejected Gallatin's effort to prohibit use of those vessels for convoying to foreign ports during peace. Dana said that no one intended the vessels to be used for captures and reprisals, and no one contested his statement. But numerous Federalists contended that convoying, even on the high seas, could be done consistently with a state of peace and was therefore within the President's power. Dayton and Harper assumed the President could use force to protect commerce, even if his actions might lead to war.

McHenry's narrow construction of the President's power under then-existing legislation supports the notion that the power to take military actions that significantly increase the risk of war must be clearly delegated. Both Hamilton and McHenry demonstrated considerable concern that the President order only clearly proper actions in so delicate a matter. Yet their concern stemmed at least in part from political considerations peculiar to the existing situation (though not necessarily unique). The President's defensive program had been opposed all along by a very substantial part of Congress, and the nation was similarly divided. While Congress had authorized the President generally to "employ" the frigates, it had done so by very narrow margins, especially in the House, as Hamilton, McHenry and Adams knew. Indeed, they were probably aware that a majority of the House in July 1797 had opposed delegating broader discretion to use the frigates than had been given to use the cutters, and that the bill had passed only after the Senate adhered to its version. Congress's increased willingness by May 1798 to go along with the President's program may have made it all the more desirable that Congress be called upon to delegate more authority and thereby assume equal responsibility for the consequences of the contemplated military actions. McHenry's narrow construction of the President's authority served to place greater pressure on Congress than a broad construction might have placed. Furthermore, no practical sacrifice in war-making capacity was involved by issuing restrictive instructions, since the U.S.S. *Ganges*, or even two or three more ships, could not have been used aggressively or as convoys on the high seas and were much more sensibly utilized in protecting the seacoast and the coastal trade.

If Adams narrowly construed his power to utilize the navy as part of a strategy to force further, more explicit delegations of power from Congress (as Hamilton and McHenry intended), the strategy worked. On May 22, the same day McHenry issued his first set of instructions, Representative John Sitgreaves introduced resolutions to authorize both the public and private armed vessels of the United States to defend against, capture, or destroy attacking French vessels, to recapture American vessels, and, with respect to public armed vessels, to take or destroy armed French vessels found near the American coast. He asked that the resolutions be referred to the Committee for the Protection of Commerce, chaired by Samuel Sewall, to report by bill or otherwise.[114]

Opponents sought delay, or a reference to Committee of the Whole, arguing that the President had ample authority to defend commerce under existing legislation, and that the resolution would allow commanders to breach international law and therefore was a war measure, albeit "partial." Significantly, Gallatin did not object in principle to the making of "partial" war: "It might be proper for us to make a kind of partial war, in preference to a general war, in order to throw the blame of declaring war upon our enemy." Declarations of war had, he noted, been resorted to far less frequently in the present century than in the past. But a partial war was unwise in the present situation, he felt, and would eliminate any chance of further negotiation. Federalists ridiculed the possibility of further negotiations, and argued that the President needed more authority. The House voted on May 24 to refer the resolutions immediately to Sewall's committee.[115]

Meanwhile, on May 23, the Senate passed a bill that authorized the President to order commanders of public vessels to seize and bring into the United States, for adjudication under the law of nations, any French vessel that commits, or is "found hovering on the coasts" for the purposes of committing, depredations on American vessels. Sewall reported to the House on May 25, recommending passage of the Senate's bill. It was forced through the House in one day. As soon as the act became law, on May 28, orders were issued to naval commanders in Adams's name that expanded their power by repeating virtually verbatim the statutory language.[116]

Congress later expanded the President's authority even further, and eventually authorized seizure of any armed French vessel.[117] Adams and his Secretary of Navy continued to issue orders carefully limited to statutory authority explicitly conferred. In one instance, where the orders issued went beyond the statutory language, a Supreme Court case resulted, discussed below, which with one other decision provided significant guidance on the allocation of power to control the course of war.

Adams issued important naval instructions in at least two situations apart from the war against France.* On both occasions he showed less restraint, and less concern that he might cause war, than he had demonstrated during the Quasi-War.

The first instance arose from an incident in November 1798 when the American sloop-of-war *Baltimore*, commanded by Captain Isaac Phillips, was stopped in the Caribbean by a British squadron, commanded by Captain Loring of the H.M.S. *Carnatic*. Loring ordered a search of the *Baltimore* to locate British subjects, and carried off fifty-five men, returning fifty but impressing the other five.[118] This was the first time, says historian Gerald Clarfield, that any nation "claimed the right to impress seamen from on board a United States vessel of war."[119]

When Adams heard of this event, he immediately stripped Phillips of his command and discharged him from the service. He also ordered Secretary of the Navy Benjamin Stoddert to instruct all naval commanders that "on no pretense whatever, you permit the public Vessel of War under your command, to be detained, or searched. . . . If force should be exerted to compel your Submission, you are to resist that force to the utmost of your power—and when overpowered by superior force, you are to Strike your flag and thus yield your Vessel as well as your Men—but never your men without your Vessel."[120] In

*Bernard C. Steiner states in his *The Life and Correspondence of James McHenry* 439 (1907), that McHenry (presumably at the President's request), to defend the United States from a rumored French invasion of the Spanish Southwest, sometime between August 2 and November 6, 1798 ordered General James Wilkinson to "stop any French troops ascending the Mississippi under Spanish flag and to advance into Spanish territory, to defeat an advancing foe, if the danger of mischief be so imminent that it cannot otherwise be certainly prevented." As there was no French invasion through Louisiana, Wilkinson did not carry out this order, even if given. Steiner cites no source, and no copy of the order has been found.

effect, commanders were told to force any foreign vessel to commit an act of war rather than submit to a search.

The second instance concerned the Barbary States (Algiers, Morocco, Tripoli and Tunis), which during the eighteenth century regularly plundered Mediterranean trade and enslaved or ransomed captives.[121] The United States sought at first to deal with this problem by paying tribute and signing treaties. But the young nation lacked funds to pay enough for safety, and the treaties were only sporadically honored. The frigates authorized during Washington's administration were intended to protect "the commerce of the United States" from the "depredations committed by the Algerian corsairs. . . ."[122] By the time the vessels were launched, however, the Quasi-War with France had begun, and the ships were enlisted in protecting commerce in the coastal waters at home.[123]

As the Quasi-War drew to a close, the executive branch moved steadily toward a policy of using armed vessels to defend against the Barbary States. Consuls stationed in those nations increasingly urged a show of force.[124] On January 11, 1800, Secretary of State Pickering wrote to William Eaton, consul at Tunis, that the United States would probably send a naval squadron to the Mediterranean when peace with France was firmly established. He contemplated vessels "sufficient to destroy the corsairs of any one, or of all these regencies together." He noted a recent, successful operation by a lone Portuguese ship against a Tripolitan cruiser, which led to a treaty highly favorable to Portugal, and found this set of events "encouraging" and "a happy demonstration of a mode of treatment of the Barbary Powers which all the maritime Christian nations might successfully adopt."[125]

In about May 1800, John Quincy Adams, Minister at Berlin, informed Secretary of State John Marshall that Sweden and Denmark wanted to take joint action with the United States to protect their Mediterranean shipping from attacks. The President responded to his son's news by insisting in a letter to Marshall dated July 11, 1800, that America faithfully fulfill its treaties with the Barbary Powers, even though he regarded them as unfavorable. "I know not how far we can acceed [*sic*] to the proposition of uniting with Sweden and Denmark" in providing convoys to protect each other's trade, he wrote; but he supposed that "convoys for our own trade . . . we may appoint at any time and in any seas . . . according to our treaties and the law of nations." If any of the Barbary powers "should break their treaties with us and recommence hostilities on our trade, we may then be at liberty to make any reasonable arrangement with Sweden and Denmark."[126]

Soon after, Secretary of Navy Stoddert issued instructions to Captain William Bainbridge, which conformed to the President's conviction that America could convoy its own trade. Stoddert told Bainbridge to proceed with the frigate *George Washington* to Algiers to deliver a cargo of tribute owed to the Dey. He suggested that Bainbridge touch at Gilbraltar, Tangiers, or Cadiz to learn whether any of the Barbary powers was committing hostilities against American vessels. If so, it would become Bainbridge's "duty to give to American vessels and citizens, all the protection in your power, on your passage to Algiers as well as on your return—but your cargo being valuable, . . . you should not go much out of your way." Bainbridge was told, moreover, when at Algiers, to "keep up the strictest discipline, and the most Warlike appearance to make the best impressions of our discipline and power. . . ."[127]

Adams and Marshall were correct in assuming that international law allowed nations to defend their commerce against piratical attacks.[128] They also had reasonably sound bases for concluding that Congress would approve the expedition, in the history of Congress's desire to proceed against the Barbary States as soon as possible, and in the fact that the House ultimately agreed to delete a convoying restriction from the bill authorizing Adams to "employ" the frigates. Furthermore, while strong arguments could be raised against using convoys against France and Britain, who as belligerents possessed a right to search neutral vessels for contraband, no member of Congress suggested any such basis for restraint in dealing with the Barbary powers, whose purpose was to take ships or exact tribute. The situations were similar in one respect, however; in both, "defensive" actions could conceivably lead to war. Adams felt free to proceed despite this danger.*

Judicial Decisions on the Control of Naval Operations. The Supreme Court made clear its view in *Bas* v. *Tingy* that Congress could opt for "partial" or "imperfect" war, and make an "enemy" of a foreign nation without formal declaration.[129] Soon thereafter the Court was presented—in *Talbot* v. *Seeman*—with a case in which an

---

*Bainbridge in fact took no military actions during his voyage. When he reached Algiers, he was ordered by the Dey to sail to Constantinople with an ambassador and some presents to the Sultan. Both Bainbridge and O'Brien, the American consul, refused to comply, but the Dey literally impressed the ship into his service. Bainbridge commented: "There was no alternative [to compliance] but war with that Regency." The incident only added to American resentment, and Secretary of State James Madison wrote to O'Brien in May 1801 that the subject might later be reopened. *See* R. Irwin, *The Diplomatic Relations of the United States with the Barbary Powers, 1776-1816*, at 94-95 (1931).

American commander was denied salvage for rescuing a vessel owned by citizens of a neutral nation. The Court agreed that no salvage could be paid for an unlawful recapture, but concluded that the recapture was lawful because authorized by Congress. "The whole powers of war being, by the constitution of the United States, vested in congress," wrote Chief Justice Marshall, "the acts of that body can alone be resorted to as our guides in this enquiry." No one denied that Congress could authorize general or limited hostilities; the issue was whether the limited hostilities authorized included the recapture of a neutral vessel, and Marshall found that they did.[130]

In *Little* v. *Barreme* the Court faced a more difficult controversy—whether a seizure pursuant to an executive instruction was invalid because the instruction exceeded the power delegated by Congress.[131] A merchant vessel covered by Danish papers, called the *Flying Fish*, was captured during the war by two American naval vessels, the U.S.S. *Boston* and the U.S.S. *General Greene*, on suspicion of violating the act prohibiting commerce with France. Section 1 of the act broadly outlawed Americans from using their own vessels, or employing other vessels, to go from anywhere to any French port, and from being employed in any traffic or commerce with any person within the jurisdiction of France; it authorized seizures of such vessels within the jurisdiction of the United States. Section 5 authorized the President to instruct commanders of public ships to seize any vessel on the high seas bound or sailing *to* any French port.[132] The orders issued to commanders instructed them to pay close attention to Section 5 "and govern yourself accordingly," but also told them to "be vigilant that vessels or cargoes really American, but covered by Danish or other foreign papers, and bound *to* or *from* French ports do not escape you."[133]

When captured, the *Flying Fish* was returning to the Dutch port of St. Thomas *from* the French port of Jeremie. The vessel was undoubtedly trading with the French. The American commanders had probable cause to believe, moreover, that the ship was American-owned, or controlled. But they were unable to prove American ownership or control at trial. The District Court therefore ordered that the vessel be returned to its owners, as neutral property, but refused to grant damages against the American commanders for the capture and detention, because they had acted on the basis of probable cause, and because the captain of the *Flying Fish* had been duplicitous and fraudulent. The Circuit Court reversed, and granted $8,504 damages.

The Supreme Court unanimously affirmed the Circuit Court's decision, in an opinion by Chief Justice Marshall. Section 1 of the nonintercourse act, he found, outlaws all forms of commerce with France, but "obviously contemplates a seizure within the United States. . . ." Section 5 "gives a special authority to seize on the high seas and limits that authority to the seizure of vessels bound, or sailing *to*, a *French* port. . . ." The President, "whose high duty it is to 'take care that the laws be faithfully executed,' and who is commander-in-chief of the armies and navies of the United States, might . . . without any special authority for that purpose, in the then existing state of things, have empowered the officers . . . to seize" American vessels engaged in any commerce with France. Congress had indicated, however, that the law should be "carried into execution" on the high seas by the seizure of American vessels bound *to* French ports, and not *from* such ports. Consequently, however reasonably the American commander may have suspected the *Flying Fish* to be American, the Court "could not excuse the detention of her, since he would not have been authorized to detain her had she been really American."[134]

Marshall had great discomfort in ruling against the American commanders. He noted that the law would often be evaded "if only vessels sailing to a French port could be seized on the high seas," and "that this act of Congress appears to have received a different construction from the executive of the United States; a construction much better calculated to give it effect." He had even greater difficulty accepting the decision to hold the commanders liable in damages and seems to have gone along simply to maintain unanimity.[135]

The decision may reflect the Court's desire to protect the rights of neutral vessels, an understandable concern in light of the nation's persistent assertion of neutral rights. More plausibly, though, the decision rests on the notion, articulated in both *Bas* v. *Tingy* and *Talbot* v. *Seeman*, that declared war involved a delegation to the executive and all citizens of general authority to commit hostilities against the enemy, while the conduct of undeclared or "imperfect" war was limited to those actions authorized by Congress. As Justice Washington expressed it, in an "imperfect" war "those who are authorized to commit hostilities . . . can go no further than to the extent of their commission."[136] *Little* v. *Barreme* did not explicitly discuss the President's inherent authority; the commanders seem not to have raised the issue. Nor did the decision directly pertain to whether Congress could, if it chose, delegate broadly the power to conduct an undeclared war (or control more closely the conduct of a declared war). The Court did clearly hold, however, that government agents could not successfully defend themselves on the basis of executive orders, issued during an undeclared war, that authorized actions outside the scope of a specific legislative delegation. Congress's authorization to seize vessels sailing *to* French ports was read implicitly to deny the power to seize vessels sailing *from* such ports. The decision strongly suggests, therefore, that the Justices assumed Congress could lawfully have directed the executive not to seize such vessels, and thereby control the conduct of an undeclared war at least to that extent.

CONCLUSION

Little new was added under Adams to the pattern of executive-congressional relations set during Washington's administration. Executive planning continued. Congress delegated broad discretion over most areas of activity, and created new executive departments. The President generally shared important information with Congress. His only effort to withhold material was when he delayed revealing the XYZ dispatches to avoid endangering the lives of American ministers. Intense and illuminating debate was generated by the successful effort to request production of the XYZ dispatches, but no new doctrinal developments occurred. Congress continued to use its investigative powers, scrutinizing a "cost-overrun" and production delays connected with the first frigates built in United States history. Most foreign-affairs initiatives were presidential, but Adams consistently consulted Congress on his decisions, especially his appointments. He settled the Quasi-War by treaty, although no treaty was required under international legal practice.

Important new developments took place in connection with military affairs. The President and his party consciously adopted the policy of fighting an undeclared war, in large part to avoid the political complications of securing a formal declaration. While the war's opponents complained about this policy, no serious effort was made in Congress to challenge its legality or to force a vote on a declaration. The Supreme Court unambiguously confirmed the power of Congress to authorize hostilities in any degree without declaring war.

Adams seldom acted without prior congressional approval in military matters. He did, however, unilaterally issue important orders concerning the arming of merchant vessels. Congress debated, but failed to affirm or reject, the President's policy. Though initially reluctant to provide the military means for fighting a war, Congress vigorously pursued a war policy after the breakdown of negotiations with France in 1798. Some important debates occurred on impoundment of funds and the propriety of allowing the President to raise an army on certain contingencies, including an "imminent threat of invasion." By far the most significant debates, however, were those preceding passage of the bills to provide naval forces. They contain enlightening—though hardly definitive—material on the President's power as commander-in-chief and on Congress's power to control the conduct of war. The statements of Representatives Dayton, Harper, Sewall and others are strikingly similar at first reading to more recent assertions that the President can use any military force provided by Congress in any manner he sees fit to protect the interests of the United States, and that Congress lacks power to control him.

But there were explicit or implicit qualifications. For example, Otis emphatically supported the President's right to control the precise location of naval forces, but conceded Congress's power to determine whether vessels should be used offensively or defensively. Dana, another Adams supporter, felt that the President could use the navy to convoy, but not to capture or take reprisals. Even Dayton, Harper and other outspoken advocates of executive power assumed that the President's action must be "defensive," or within the limits allowed by international law, or "consistent with the existing state of affairs, war or peace." If the President's unilateral conduct changed the nation's state from peace to war, he would bear sole responsibility for the consequences.

Important as these qualifications are, the constitutional power attributed to the presidency by Federalist leaders and many other Congressmen is great even in retrospect. The law of nations was unclear on issues crucial to the times, such as the right of belligerents to search neutral vessels. To say that the President had to act consistently with that law therefore left him with broad discretion, analogous to the royal prerogative described by Blackstone. If the rights he asserted were challenged, his actions could lead to war. Under the theory of these leaders, the restraint implicit in after-the-fact review of the President's conduct was the proper way to control that conduct.

Adams and his advisors actually pursued an extremely cautious course in deploying the first naval vessels Congress provided. He authorized those vessels to protect American commerce within the jurisdictional waters of the United States; on the high seas, the vessels were permitted to defend only themselves. These orders resulted in part, however, from Adams's desire to avoid criticism, and because he wanted to force Congress to delegate more power. The President was ready to take vigorous, potentially war-causing actions against other nations when he felt he was on strong legal ground, as in his orders to naval officers after the *Baltimore-Carnatic* affair to resist forcefully any effort to search their vessels, and in undertaking a defensive expedition to the Mediterranean.

The Supreme Court made clear that it regarded Congress as the ultimate source of authority on whether and how the nation would make war. It granted relief against a seizure that exceeded the limits of authority implied by a statute, strongly suggesting that Congress has power to control the conduct of war, even over a subject—the seizure of American merchant vessels trading with an enemy—that Chief Justice Marshall suggested might well have come within the President's authority, in the absence of any legislative regulation. Both branches could act, in other words, but Congress had the final say.

Chapter 4

Jefferson and the "Revolution of 1800"

INTRODUCTION

Thomas Jefferson came to the presidency after having made monumental contributions to the birth and strength of the nation. At 26 years of age, in 1769, he began six years of service in the Virginia House of Burgesses. This spirited man drafted the Declaration of Independence as a delegate to the Continental Congress. He worked to implement a more perfect government in his native Virginia, where he served as Governor. His great breadth and capability enabled him, when back in Congress, to devise a decimal monetary system, draft the plan used for organizing new territories, and later to serve as Minister to France. He was Washington's choice as Secretary of State and, although he complained to Madison and other friends about some of the first President's foreign policies, he almost invariably voted for them in Cabinet. He split with Hamilton, however, on fiscal and other national policies, and resigned his Cabinet post in 1793. In 1797 he polled the second highest number of electoral votes and became Vice President under John Adams. But he was excluded from meaningful participation in that administration, and busily involved himself in marshalling the fledgling Republican party for the presidential election of 1800. In that election he tied with Aaron Burr in electoral votes, and was selected by the House with Hamilton's support.[1]

His first term, from 1801–1805, was sensationally successful. He wielded great power in Congress because his Republican party controlled both houses. Congress passed virtually all his important programs, and prevented what he and his supporters regarded as improper interference with the executive.[2] Naval actions against the Barbary states ended in highly advantageous treaties. Purchasing the Louisiana Territory doubled the nation's size, and helped insure its future greatness, without bloodshed. Commerce thrived. The military establishment, taxes, and the national debt were reduced. And Jefferson won overwhelming victory in his bid for reelection.

Jefferson's second term was, by contrast, extremely frustrating. Repeated efforts to obtain parts of West Florida without force ended in failure. Both Britain and France harrassed American commerce, and the former virtually blockaded the major eastern harbors. British war vessels regularly impressed American seamen, and humiliated an American armed vessel by firing on it, killing several men and impressing others. Though many Republican Congressmen wanted war against Britain, Jefferson opted instead for an embargo. Whatever its merits, the embargo was Jefferson's most unpopular policy. Congress went along with the President's program until very close to the end of his second term, but by then the Republicans were no longer united. Adding to this unhappy picture was the troubling presence of Aaron Burr. His conspiracy gave Jefferson an additional concern, and the successful defense of his indictments undoubtedly embarrassed the President.

The Jefferson presidency is especially important to any study of the distribution of power among the branches of American government. Jefferson hailed his victory over John Adams as the "Revolution of 1800."[3] Of course, this was no bloody revolution, such as Jefferson said men of liberty should be prepared to face each generation.[4] Nor was the phrase used to represent a pro-French attitude, of which Federalists frequently accused Republicans; Jefferson and most of his followers strongly agreed with the Federalist policy of neutrality. Rather, the triumph of Republicans over Federalists was called a revolution because of what it was supposed to mean for the allocation of power between the federal and state governments, and among the branches of the federal government.

Republicans stood for several changes in the way in which the nation had been governed.[5] They wanted to construe narrowly the powers conferred by the Constitution upon the federal government. Most matters other than foreign relations were to be left to the states. They wanted the federal government to spend less, especially on the army and navy, and to reduce the debt at a faster rate. They espoused legislative supremacy, with greater congressional participation in formulating national policies, including policies concerning foreign relations. They had objected, during the period of Federalist control, to legislative planning by executive officers, and to statutes assigning broad powers to the President to conduct military and foreign affairs. They had battled, with little success, for greater control of expenditures by specifying appropriations. They had insisted on Congress's right to information in the President's control. Many of them had claimed that Congress should be consulted as soon as possible on issues relating to its specifically assigned powers, including the power to declare war, and that the House in particular had the power to judge the wisdom of treaties in exercising its authority over public finances. The election of 1800 swept these Republicans into control of the government and therefore signaled a major overhaul in the pattern of executive-congressional relations established under Washington and Adams.

But events during Jefferson's two terms demonstrate that the allocation of power between Congress and the executive changed little if at all from the pattern established in the first two administrations. The Republican-dominated federal government took many steps that apparently violated the doctine of strict construction of federal power, including the purchase and absorption of Louisiana, admission of Ohio, continuing the Bank of the United States, and enforcing the embargo. Many of these actions represented reversals of positions Jefferson had previously adopted;[6] "what is practicable," he once confided to a friend, "must often controul what is pure theory."[7] Though federal spending and the debt were reduced during the first few years, and the navy drastically cut,[8] the framework of executive-congressional relations remained in general as it had been under Washington and Adams. As Leonard White says, "Jefferson fully maintained in practice the Federalist conception of the executive power."[9]

EXECUTIVE-CONGRESSIONAL RELATIONS

The executive branch under Jefferson continued to engage extensively in planning and drafting legislation.[10] Congress by this time expected executive leadership, and on several occasions important legislative initiatives were opposed on the ground that the President had not requested the actions proposed.[11] Several changes streamlined the operations of Congress, including the establishment of floor leaders. But these developments were designed to aid Jefferson in implementing his programs.[12] Only in subsequent administrations did they operate to weaken rather than enhance the President's influence.

Control of Expenditures

Republican legislators had battled during the Washington and Adams administrations against the unwarranted discretion they perceived was delegated to the executive by general appropriations. Their efforts to control executive spending failed, except for some short-lived, ineffective victories in connection with the language of appropriations bills.[13]

When Jefferson became President he made Albert Gallatin—a champion of specific appropriations—his Secretary of Treasury. Gallatin urged Jefferson to declare himself behind the Republican position.[14] Jefferson obliged by calling in his first annual message for specific appropriations wherever practicable:

> In our care, too, of the public contributions intrusted to our direction, it would be prudent to multiply barriers against their dissipation, by appropriating specific sums to every specific purpose susceptible of definition; by disallowing all applications of money, varying from the appropriation in object, or transcending it in amount[;] by reducing the undefined field of contingencies, and thereby circumscribing discretionary powers over money.[15]

The Republican-dominated House seemed ready to respond to Jefferson's suggestion, and formed a committee to investigate whether executive departments were spending moneys for the purposes designated.[16] The committee criticized many expenditures as unauthorized, especially those related to military affairs. Federalists defended these expenditures, accurately contending that it had become common practice to shift funds appropriated for one purpose to another.[17] The Republican majority seemed bent on further action. They refused to recommit the committee report, and voted to call for comprehensive information relating to military spending.[18]

These insubstantial actions marked the high point of the Republican effort to control executive spending. The investigation was allowed to lapse after the information requested had been supplied,[19] and appropriations practice under Jefferson soon became largely indistinguishable from practice during the Federalist period. By 1804 Jefferson wrote Gallatin approvingly of Congress's practice of throwing all items in the estimates supplied by executive agencies into sums "in gross . . . , binding up the Executive discretion only by the sum, and the object generalized to a certain degree."[20] Even the assumption implicit in Jefferson's letter that, where an appropriation was specific in terms, it bound the executive, came to be ignored by department heads other than Gallatin; they "stubbornly construed their appropriations, in whatever form, as 'in gross.' "[21] Further, when funds appropriated for a purpose, general or specific, ran out, the Republican Secretaries of War and Navy continued the practice begun as early as 1794 of incurring deficiencies, and Congress invariably appropriated the necessary funds after the fact.[22] Jefferson himself suggested this course to Gallatin, for expenses incurred in sending an extra vessel to Morocco in 1802.[23] On one other occasion, Madison joined with Jefferson in construing an appropriation more broadly than Gallatin.[24]

An exchange in April 1806 between Representatives David R. Williams of South Carolina and John Randolph of Virginia exemplifies the extent to which Republicans had accepted prior practice by that time. Williams, a vehement opponent of all naval spending, objected to Randolph's motion to provide a single appropriation of $411,950 "for repair of vessels, store rent, pay of armorers, freight, and other contingent expenses." Williams moved to strike "contingent expenses," asking Randolph as Chairman of the Committee of Ways and Means to explain what expenses were meant to be "contingent." Randolph, by this time at odds with Jefferson, said "he was as much in the dark as the gentleman as to the items of contingent expenditure . . . ," and that the Secretary of Navy had asserted "without entering into any explanation" that the sum was not too large. He would not have moved so large a sum, Randolph said, "but from the conviction that whether they provided the money or not, it would be spent, and an additional appropriation made the next session"; an appropriation bill, in these circumstances, was "a mere matter of form."[25]

The Committee of the Whole approved the sum suggested by Randolph, but Williams urged the House to strike the appropriation for "contingent expenses" until the Secretary of Navy supported it with more than a mere opinion. Federalist Samuel Dana, who opposed specific appropriations for the armed services, crowed that the administration's opposition to Williams's amendment proved that the theory espoused in the President's first annual message "could not be carried into effect, as to the military or naval service." Republican Roger Nelson of Maryland in effect agreed. He described himself as having been "very early in favor of specific appropriations," but claimed that Jefferson's policy—"founded in good sense"—had never been intended to apply "to such a case as this," since the unforseeable necessities of naval and military expenditures required flexibility. While "an adherence to specific appropriations was highly desirable in all cases where it was practicable, as in meeting civil expenses, . . . for military purposes, they must necessarily go in the old way." The motion to make the appropriation specific was defeated, and the bill passed without a division.[26]

The most dramatic example of unilateral executive spending took place after the British warship *Leopard* attacked the American frigate *Chesapeake*, on June 22, 1807. The incident made war between Britain and the United States seem imminent, causing the President to issue a proclamation on July 2 interdicting the use of American waters by British warships.[27] In addition, the Cabinet voted on July 28 to concentrate all available funds, appropriated for fortifications, on the fortification of New York, Charleston and New Orleans; to purchase timber for about 100 gunboats on credit, even though Congress had not authorized the gunboats; and to purchase on credit 500 tons of saltpetre and 100 tons of sulphur "on the presumption that Congress will sanction it."[28] The purchases were accordingly made.

After Congress convened on October 26, 1807, the President sent his annual message describing the situation and explaining why he had issued the proclamation and ordered that further arms be purchased. He made no effort to defend the purchases of supplies as being legally authorized. Rather, he claimed his orders were justified by "the emergencies threatening us":

> The moment our peace was threatened, I deemed it indispensable to secure a greater provision of those articles of military stores with which our magazines were not sufficiently furnished. To have awaited a previous and special sanction by law would have lost occasions which might not be retrieved. . . . I trust that the legislature, feeling the same anxiety for the safety of our country, so materially advanced by this precaution, will approve, when done, what they would have seen so important to be done, if then assembled.[29]

On November 9 a bill was introduced in the House to appropriate funds to cover the expenditures. Federalists sought information "as to where the purchase money had been obtained," arguing that the appropriation "was declaratory of their approbation of the conduct of the Executive; [and] they were therefore entitled to information on the subject." They defended Jefferson's actions, however, and said the occasion proved that the "doctrine of 1801" requiring specific appropriations had been found untenable, and that Jefferson had properly recognized and exercised his discretionary power.[30]

The only Representative who spoke against Jefferson's conduct was John Randolph. The President had not merely mingled funds, Randolph noted, or spent unappropriated funds on an authorized object, he had spent unappropriated funds on an unauthorized object. Sounding the same note struck by Madison writing as Helvidius in the debate on the Neutrality Proclamation, Randolph "thought Congress ought to have been immediately convened on the capture of the *Chesapeake*, and our Ministers at London instantly recalled. . . . Congress being convened, the nation should have been put into a posture of defence, waiting a reasonable time to receive redress by an envoy."[31]

Several Representatives came to Jefferson's defense, arguing that his conduct had precedent,[32] that the emergency justified his acts ("the safety of the nation is the supreme law"),[33] that most though not all the expenditures were for objects already authorized by law,[34] and that "it was the duty of the President to adopt such measures as would have been authorized by Congress had they been sitting at the time."[35] Delay in calling back Congress was justified for several reasons, they argued, principally because the President wisely "had postponed the meeting till the fermentation should have subsided. . . ."* Randolph protested that Congress should have been "convened at a time when they would have felt a deep and particular sense of national indignity . . . and not to have suffered this impression to be weakened."[36] But he joined the overwhelming majority (124-2) in voting for the appropriation, comparing his position to that of a husband with a spendthrift wife, or a man "paying a gambling debt to a swindler"; honor forced him to pay, but not to approve.[37]

Delegations of Discretionary Power

During the Federalist period, Republican legislators had protested frequently and vehemently against legislation delegating broad discretion to the President. They felt that broad delegations amounted to an abdication of legislative responsibility. And, they argued, where the discretion concerned sensitive issues of foreign affairs or the power to use the armed forces, Congress was effectively—and unconstitutionally—delegating the power to initiate war.

---

*17 *Annals of Congress* 826 (1853) [hereinafter "*Annals*"]. John Smilie (Pa.) said he was more temperate than Randolph, and alluded to "an ancient nation, who were wont to discuss great national questions twice, once when they were drunk, that they might not want spirit, and once when they were sober, that they might not be deficient in prudence." He suggested that Jefferson's decision had saved them from being "under the immediate influence of passion. . . ." *Id.* 830. Willis Alston (N.C.) concurred, stating that "we were now better prepared to decide. . . . [I]f by this [prudent] course war had been averted, the voice of the nation would approve it." *Id.* 840. See also *id.* 842 (Upham). Gardenier (N.Y.) accused Smilie of suggesting that the nation was drunk; Smilie replied "that the hour of extreme feeling was not the proper time for deliberation." *Id.* 848.

Similar objections were voiced during Jefferson's presidency, and in some instances laws that would have delegated broad powers were defeated. Notable among these was an effort to empower the President to expel British warships from American harbors,[38]* and to issue letters of marque and reprisal against whichever of Britain and France failed to repeal its objectionable edicts.† Neither of these

---

*Introduced by John Quincy Adams soon after the *Chesapeake* affair, the bill required that all British ships depart American waters on pain of attack. 17 *Annals* 34. The Senate passed the bill on December 2, 1807 (*id.* 44), but it made no progress in the House. During its first reading, Representative William Burwell of Virginia moved that discussion be deferred:

> He thought they should deliberate before they gave the President of the United States the power of interdicting our ports and harbors to foreign armed vessels; it was a power exclusively reserved to Congress. This bill would, besides, place the Executive of the country in a very awkward situation, requiring from him services which the existing state of the country would not authorize him to perform. It was well known that it had been doubted whether the United States possessed a force competent to expel foreign armed vessels from our waters. If it was necessary to adopt such a measure, the power should certainly be left with Congress, and no authority given to the Executive to do an act which might involve the country in war.

Id. 1243-44. Discussion of the bill was postponed indefinitely on April 25, 1808. 18 *Annals* 2279-80.

†A bill with this power passed the Senate (19 *Annals* 436), over the following objection of James Hillhouse (Conn.) (*id.* 424-25):

> The Constitution says, "The Congress shall have power to declare war, grant letters of marque and reprisal, and make rules concerning captures on land or water." The exercise of this authority, given by this section to the President, to grant letters of marque and reprisal is to rest on the revocation or modification of the edicts of France or Great Britain, so as not to violate the neutral commerce of the United States. And this complicated question is left to the judgment and unlimited discretion of the President. His individual opinion on the nature of a variety of edicts not specified, and which will admit of various constructions, is to govern. If the condition on which such a power was to be exercised, were some specified event, certain and precise in point of fact, which is not this case, it might be questioned whether the Constitution would, even then, warrant Congress in delegating to the President the power of declaring war, or of granting letters of marque and reprisal.

Representative Thomas Blount (N. Carolina) first introduced the idea in the House on January 5, 1809, and Edward Livermore (Mass.) opposed it as a delegation of the power to declare war. He said he was not surprised, however, "for they seemed to have arrived at a period when they should choose a Dictator, and vest him with the power of life and death." *Id.* 989. The issue was raised again on January 30, when Nicholas proposed a resolution for simultaneously repealing the embargo and authorizing letters of marque and reprisal, provided that the unlawful edicts of France or Britain remained in force. *Id.* 1232. Repeal was set for March 15, but the provision regarding letters was struck. *Id.* 1421, Act of March 1, 1809, §12, 2 Stat. 526, 531. When the Senate bill was taken up by the House, its proposed grant of power to issue letters was opposed by Milnor "on the ground that the Constitution . . . provided that Congress alone should have the power to declare war, and this bill, by giving the President a discretion to judge when that war should commence, transferred the power to him." 19 *Annals* 1504. Livermore added that "the bill did not contemplate a legislative

extreme bills appears to have had Jefferson's support.[39] And while Congress did deny the President some part of the broad powers he sought to enforce the embargo laws,[40] as well as the power to increase the army,* or the "Peace Establishment,"† in general the Republican majority adopted the practice of prior Congresses, and granted broad discretion. Thus, for example, the President was delegated the power both to increase the number of and discharge seamen,** to discharge troops,‡ and either to arm or leave unarmed all but four of the nation's naval vessels.[41] On foreign-affairs matters, Congress authorized the President, among other things, to prohibit the entry of foreign vessels into American waters and to enforce the prohibition; to suspend the embargo selectively;*** to impose and

---

act for issuing letters of marque and reprisal against a particular enemy, but gave the power to the President to choose with which of the belligerents he would take sides and against which he would declare war." *Id. See also id.* 1507-08 (Dana). James Holland (N. Carolina) defended the delegation as conferring no discretion or legislative power. "The event was fixed [when] the President . . . should forthwith issue letters of marque and reprisal." *Id.* 1505. The section was deleted, however, by the comfortable margin of 74-33 (*id.* 1517), and the Senate acquiesced (*id.* 451). Even more sweeping proposals to authorize the President's use of force were likewise defeated. *Id.* 1523-31.

*The bill for an additional army, as originally considered, had a clause giving the President discretion to increase the number of each company of infantry and riflemen to 100 men. On March 20, 1808, Archibald Van Horne (Md.) moved to strike the discretionary clause because, while he had confidence in the President, he was averse to giving this power to any one person; "and he believed the spirit of the Constitution prohibited it." 18 *Annals* 1857. Lyon, Rowan, and Stanford contributed support, saying the bill contradicted the constitutional mandate that Congress shall raise armies; and it also contradicted the old Republican opposition to a construction of the Constitution that would permit such a delegation. A motion to strike the clause carried. *Id.* 1860.

†John Chandler (Mass.) led the constitutional attack, wanting to provide the men, rather than leaving the matter to the President's discretion. *Id.* 1621. Fisk could not perceive the difference between providing the troops and allowing the President to raise them. Taylor suggested that flexibility is needed, since "nowadays, a formal declaration of war is dispensed with, and a *coup de main* is the order of the day." *Id.* 1624. The bill, which would have allowed an increase of up to 2,000 men "in all cases of imminent danger, when, in his [the President's] opinion the defense or safety of the United States shall require it" (*id.* 1620), was postponed indefinitely (*id.* 2280).

**See, Act of January 31, 1809, §2, 2 Stat. 514. Lyon criticized the Republican majority for voting in favor of the seamen bill: just another proof, he said, "that power makes men Tories." 18 *Annals* 1500. But Smilie argued that it made more sense to allow the President to decide the matter while Congress was out of session than to require an early call, or to mandate raising seamen without heed to events that might arise during recess. *Id.*

‡18 *Annals* 2062, Act of April 12, 1808, 2 Stat. 481. Stanford said (18 *Annals* 1950): "It was once a fashion with us to object to . . . giving the President discretion to raise, or not raise, an army. That was urged to be the duty of Congress alone, and was a power not to be transferred. This bill withholds that discretion in appearance, at least, but, it seems, gives the power of disbanding."

***The bill empowered the President to suspend the embargo, in the event of peace between the European nations, "or of such changes in their measures

suspend the nonimportation laws; and to employ land and naval forces to prevent violation of the embargo laws.[42]

The majority's willingness to delegate broad powers led the Republican Representative Richard Stanford of North Carolina to comment: "Let me ask how it will be possible, in a few years, for any political observer or historian to draw a line of distinction between parties. . . ."[43] Senator Chauncey Goodrich of Connecticut made the same point, in effect, when he criticized Gallatin for recommending, and Giles for supporting, a bill to improve enforcement of the embargo that delegated broad powers over commerce to revenue and customs officers.[44] Giles's response is remarkable. He cited precedents, many of which he and other Republicans had previously opposed. Sounding like the Federalists of prior Congresses, he observed that the line between executive and legislative power was impossible to fix and claimed that the bill had gone as far as practicable in defining the President's duties. He described the delegation issue as "an old and abstract question, often heretofore brought into view, and [one that] leads to endless discussion." He was "unwilling to look into retrospection; it could only produce an unpleasant and unprofitable examination. . . . I would rather follow the example of a celebrated Roman conqueror. It was his maxim always to forget the last defeat, and to turn his whole thoughts upon the best means of obtaining victory in the next battle."[45]

Control of Information

In many respects, information practice under Jefferson appears similar to practice under the Federalists. Jefferson frequently provided material without any prior request, sometimes sensitive material that the President thought should be kept confidential.[46] He once delayed disclosure of a proclamation ordering citizens in the Lake Champlain area to stop violently resisting the embargo;[47] but both Washington and Adams had delayed disclosure of even more important material—the Jay Treaty and the "XYZ" papers—to avoid

---

affecting neutral commerce, as may render that of the United States sufficiently safe, in the judgment of the President. . . ." 18 *Annals* 2065. Congress would have to be recalled, said George Campbell of Tennessee, if this power, conditioned as Congress saw fit, were not delegated. *Id.* 2083–86. Other supporters noted several precedents for the bill. Findley in particular made a careful argument for the necessity of such delegations in connection with foreign affairs. *Id.* 2224–29. Opponents urged this was a transfer of legislative power, but one concern seemed especially important: that the bill would enable the President to cause war by lifting the embargo against one nation and retaining it against the other. Federalists like Philip Key (Md.) and John Rowan (Ky.), who favored suspending the embargo, opposed placing it in the President's discretion to do so. *Id.* 2118, 2124–25, 2232–35. After several efforts to particularize the bill were defeated, it passed, 60–36. *Id.* 2237–45.

what they felt might be detrimental consequences. Congress frequently requested information, on a variety of subjects, including military[48] and foreign affairs.[49] But many potentially important efforts to obtain information were blocked by legislative majorities, just as they had been under Washington and Adams.[50] Most requests calling for sensitive material contained language exempting anything the President felt should not be disclosed,* and Jefferson occasionally withheld material from Congress in responding to requests that allowed him to do so.† Jefferson indicated at other times that he regarded himself empowered unilaterally to withhold material to avoid damaging the nation's interests, regardless of whether the legislative request was qualified.** But he never explicitly rejected an unqualified congressional request.

Executive Withholding of "Private" Correspondence. Apparent similarities in practice between Jefferson and his predecessors regarding information obscure developments of great significance. Espe-

---

*E.g., 15 *Annals* 67-68, 70-71 (Senate motion requesting President to supply copy of letter from Monroe to Madison, amended 1/21/06 to specify date and to qualify request for disclosure "if he shall judge the same to be proper. . ."), *id.* 71 (letter provided); 16 *Annals* 336 (House request for information relating to Burr conspiracy "in possession of the Executive, except such as he may deem the public welfare to require not to be disclosed . . ."), *id.* 39-43 (some information provided). That a motion for information was qualified was no guarantee of its adoption, though adding a qualification enabled Jefferson's political opponents to argue more effectively that Congress should request information, since, they asserted, the President could always withhold material the disclosure of which might be harmful. *See, e.g.,* 12 *Annals* 312; 15 *Annals* 85; 18 *Annals* 1640, 1648.

†The clearest example is in Jefferson's response to a House request for material relating to the conspiracy of which Aaron Burr was suspected, except such as the President believed the public interest required him to withhold. Jefferson withheld material "under the reserve" contained in the resolution. See *infra* 190-92.

**In connection with the French vessel *Berceau*, Jefferson wrote to William Giles that he regarded a resolution that would have requested his reasons for refitting the ship as improper, and said if a resolution "is passed on ground not legitimate, our duty will be to resist it." April 6, 1802, 8 *The Writings of Thomas Jefferson* 141, 142 (P. Ford, ed. 1892-99) (10 vols.) [hereinafter "*Jefferson Writings* (Ford)"]. The House on January 11, 1808, passed a request for material relating to whether any officer of the United States had received money from any foreign government, after Josiah Quincy unsuccessfully objected to the lack of a qualification allowing the President to withhold "confidential" correspondence. 18 *Annals* 1460. Jefferson responded on January 15, that "he would give to the House such information not improper to be disclosed." *Id.* 1464. In responding to requests from both houses of Congress for copies of all decrees and acts promulgated since 1791 by the belligerent European powers affecting the commercial rights of the United States, Jefferson sent the decrees that could be obtained "and are supposed to have entered into the views of" each House. 19 *Annals* 299, 908. See also the several claims by Jefferson of power to withhold material from the court in the Burr conspiracy trial, *infra* 193-95.

cially striking is Jefferson's systematic implementation of a dual system of diplomatic correspondence.

Earlier administrations had used codes and "private" correspondence in foreign-affairs matters, and most coded and "private" letters never reached Congress.[51] Jefferson, especially interested in codes and cyphers,[52] continued to use them as President, and consequently much of the important diplomatic correspondence between 1802 and 1809 was conducted in some form of cypher. Few if any of these coded letters were made available to Congress, apparently for the same reasons that much diplomatic correspondence was withheld under Washington and Adams: many contained tentative suggestions, arguments, and delicate proposals concerning other nations;* many were laced with personal gossip or political speculation;† in others the writer was obviously letting off steam, and disclosure would have damaged the nation's effectiveness in negotiating;** and the disclosure of most was unnecessary to communicate a full and fair picture of the policies that the executive was pursuing.

Jefferson added a new dimension to the use of codes and "private" correspondence, however. Soon after taking office, when he was faced with the possibility that France would assume control of New Orleans, he sent the American Minister in France, Robert R. Livingston, a code for deciphering future messages. "Why a cipher between us," asked Jefferson rhetorically, since "official things go naturally to the Secretary of State and things not political need no cipher?" Because, Jefferson explained, information falls into three categories: "1. matters of a public nature, and proper to go on our records, should go to the secretary of state. 2. matters of a public nature not proper to be placed on our records may still go to the secretary of state, headed by the word 'private.' But 3. there may be matters merely personal to ourselves, and which require the cover of a cipher more than those of any other character." This latter category, "and

---

*For example, William Pinkney wrote Madison on July 10, 1808 that Britain's Foreign Secretary Canning had informed him "extra-officially" that there would be no objection to restoring the men taken from the *Chesapeake*. H. Wheaton, *Some Account of the Life, Writings, and Speeches of William Pinkney* 398 (1826). Premature disclosure might have endangered the arrangement.

†On one occasion, for example, Jefferson wrote to Monroe that he was skeptical of the ability of one of Monroe's fellow negotiators (apparently Pinkney) to move swiftly to an acceptable arrangement with Britain. Letter of Oct. 26, 1806, in 10 *The Works of Thomas Jefferson* 296-97 (Fed. ed. 1904-1905) (12 vols.) [hereinafter "*Jefferson Works* (Fed.)"]. Jefferson apparently felt he needed to say this to Monroe, to offset the effect of his fellow negotiator; at the same time, public disclosure would have had traumatic consequences.

**Some striking examples are William Pinkney's letters to Madison during December 1807, in which he expressed outrage and exasperation at Britain's policies. H. Wheaton, *Some Account of the Life, Writings and Speeches of William Pinkney* 71-75 (1826).

others which we cannot foresee may render it convenient and advantageous to have at hand a mask for whatever may need it." This letter of April 18, 1802 was one for which the cipher would normally be used, but "writing by Mr. Dupont [de Nemours] I need no cipher," Jefferson said, having required the trusted Frenchman to place the letter in Livingston's hands after reading it himself.[53]

The categories outlined by Jefferson in his letter to Livingston are susceptible to his labels of "public," "private" and "personal" only if the words are deprived of ordinary meaning. The letter itself states that some matters of a "public nature" should be marked "private" and kept out of "our records." And in calling matter in the third category "merely personal" Jefferson seems clearly to have been referring to the fact that he wanted some information kept strictly between Livingston and himself, rather than attempting to describe the nature of the information in the letters. The April 18 letter assuredly dealt with "public" rather than "personal" matters. It noted that Madison had written fully to Livingston concerning the question of Louisiana, but continued that Jefferson could not "forbear recurring to it personally." He told Livingston that the nation that holds New Orleans is "our natural and habitual enemy," and if France takes possession it might force the United States to ally with Britain.[54] This prediction of war, meant to guide Livingston, was certainly not "personal" in the ordinary sense. It was an official letter, about an important public matter, that Jefferson wanted kept secret.

In a subsequent letter to Livingston, dated October 10, 1802, Jefferson complained of France's unfriendliness, and repeated that "*my* letters to you being merely private, I leave all details of business to their official channel."[55] A year later he sent to Congress what purported to be the official correspondence bearing on the Louisiana Purchase; the letter of April 18, 1802 was not among the materials he sent. He may of course have had good reasons for withholding the letter, as one of his biographers suggests.* But the nondisclosure was clearly deliberate, and part of a scheme for further nondisclosure.

*Professor Dumas Malone offers the following justification:

He was wise in withholding it, for by that time he no longer needed to threaten the French with an Anglo-American alliance, and the revelation of the fact that he had done so might have added to diplomatic complexities and domestic political difficulties. His strongest verbal effort to prevent the carrying out of the agreement between France and Spain was made off the record.

He was providing background material for Livingston and also for Du Pont de Nemours, who bore the letter on a visit to his native France and was permitted to read it. . . .

In a closely guarded private letter the President could use threatening language without issuing an official ultimatum or formal instructions.

4 D. Malone, *Jefferson and His Times* 255 (1948-74) (5 vols.) [hereinafter "Malone, *Jefferson*"].

The full extent to which Jefferson actually used the scheme he devised is difficult to determine. The evidence demonstrates, however, that he and his correspondents and officers engaged to a significant extent in a dual correspondence of sorts, frequently involving the use of codes, and designed in part to withold letters dealing with official matters from Congress and the public. On March 8, 1803, for example, Monroe sailed to France to complete negotiations leading to the Louisiana Purchase. He carried with him instructions, both official and "private." The official instructions, written by Madison, were sober in tone, and authorized an offer for New Orleans and other areas.[56] The private instructions, written by Jefferson, were far more emphatic in stressing the importance of purchasing New Orleans—"We are satisfied nothing else will secure us against a war at no distant period."[57] Jefferson had already told Monroe, moreover, that, if he failed to reach a satisfactory arrangement with France, he might have to cross the channel and negotiate with the British.[58] These dire predictions and strategies were absent from the official instructions, and the "private" instructions were not turned over to Congress along with the papers later represented to be the relevant correspondence.

Another example of a dual correspondence are the letters Jefferson wrote between 1807 and 1809 to Secretary of State Madison and others discussing strategies and alternatives respecting relations with Britain; virtually all were withheld.* Further, many letters actually surrendered to Congress on this subject refer to other letters that were not surrendered.[59] In connection with Aaron Burr's conspiracy, discussed below, Jefferson withheld material from Congress because he had promised confidentiality to his correspondents. During Burr's trials, Jefferson and his lawyers claimed a privilege before Chief Justice Marshall to withhold material "confidentially" given to the President. Other material was simply withheld from the court and from Burr, apparently also because it was supplied by Jefferson's "agent," James Wilkinson.[60]

Congress made it easy for Jefferson to withhold material in his personal possession by requesting on several occasions information "in possession of the Department of State."[61] An attempt to depart from this practice occurred on January 4, 1809, virtually at the end of Jefferson's administration, when Senator James Lloyd of Massa-

---

*See, for example, the letter to Madison of August 27, 1805, speculating on a possible treaty with Britain, whereby the United States would become its ally in exchange for a guarantee of Louisiana and the Floridas, and stating that Monroe would probably propose the arrangement. 10 *Jefferson Works* (Fed.) 172. Other examples include: Jefferson to Madison, Feb. 1, 1807, *id.* 374 n.1; Jefferson to Monroe, March 21, 1807, *id.* 374.

chusetts moved to request the President to submit copies of all "official as well as informal correspondence between Mr. Rose [the British negotiator on the *Chesapeake* affair], and the Secretary of State or any other [American official], not already communicated." Two days later, Senator Timothy Pickering of Massachusetts went even further in suggesting intentional nondisclosure by moving to add a preamble declaring that a Senate member (presumably either Pickering or Lloyd) had stated that, in addition to the "official" papers communicated by Jefferson during the last session, "there had been certain informal overtures . . . which overtures and their result ought . . . to be made known to the people of the United States." Both the preamble and the resolution were soundly defeated, but no one denied the practice.[62]

During the same January, the *Boston Centinel* printed a letter from British Secretary of State Canning to William Pinkney, United States Minister in Britain, that had been withheld by Jefferson from the correspondence previously sent to Congress. In it Canning claimed Pinkney had verbally suggested a settlement different from that contained in a written offer. Jefferson then sent Canning's letter to Congress on January 17, along with Pinkney's reply. Canning's letter had been withheld from the earlier transmittal, he explained, because "the answer of Mr. Pinkney to the letter of Mr. Canning had not been received . . . and a communication of the latter alone would have accorded neither with propriety nor with the wishes of Mr. Pinkney. When that answer afterwards arrived, it was considered that as what had passed in conversation had been superceded by the written and formal correspondence on the subject, the variance in the statement of what had verbally passed was not of sufficient importance to be made the matter of a distinct and special communication. . . ." Since Canning's letter had appeared in print, however, "unaccompanied by that of Mr. Pinkney, in reply, and having a tendency to make impressions not warranted by the statements of Mr. Pinkney, it has become proper that the whole should be brought into public view."[63]

Nicholas vehemently attacked the British for distributing, and the *Centinel* for publishing, Canning's letter. Barent Gardenier of New York defended the paper, faulting the President for having seen the importance of these documents "only when one of the letters was published. . . ." Said Nathaniel Macon of North Carolina: "I should wish to see the Administration of this Government lay aside the practice of giving a little at a time. . . ."[64]

Jefferson's dual system of correspondence was specifically criticized when Senator Hillhouse of Connecticut spoke on February 21,

1809, against the bill interdicting commercial intercourse with France and Britain. The bill, he said, could bring this country to the precipice, from which we might "plunge the nation into war," but we have not "the whole information" regarding Britain and France. "It is withheld from us." And he continued:

> It is manifest, from the documents which have been communicated by the President of the United States, that there has been a double geared correspondence between our foreign Ministers and the Department of State. An official correspondence, and a private correspondence. As regards England, we have very little of the private correspondence. As regards France, we have but a small portion of either the official or private correspondence. Can any one believe that, during such a critical period of our affairs with that nation, for very long intervals there should have been no communications or correspondence between our Government and our Minister at the Court of France? The very letters we have, refer to others which must contain important information. Why this concealment? Such as was not proper to be made public might have been sent confidentially, as is frequently done. It ought to be known before we determine on committing the peace of the nation.[64]

Neither Jefferson nor any member of the Senate contested Hillhouse's claim that a dual correspondence existed.

Legislative Efforts to Obtain Information. Another important difference in information practice under Jefferson as compared to his predecessors pertains to the willingness of Congress to utilize its powers to seek information. Congressional majorities during earlier presidencies had often blocked efforts to secure information. But the Republican-dominated legislature under Jefferson went even further in this regard, preventing Congress from acquiring material essential to review and formulate foreign policy.

First, the power to investigate was sparingly used. The House voted to inquire into the spending practices of officers in the Adams administration, but nothing came of that effort. On more controversial matters, the House flatly refused to investigate, as for example into the attack on the American frigate *Chesapeake* by the British warship *Leopard*.[65] A particularly interesting debate was triggered by John Randolph's motion on December 31, 1807 to request the President to conduct an investigation to determine whether General James Wilkinson had received moneys from Spain while serving as an officer of the United States.[66] Even this attempt to recommend an *executive* inquiry met substantial opposition, many claiming it would improperly interfere with the President's role as commander-in-chief, and concerned a matter on which Congress lacked authority to act.[67] The resolution ultimately passed, with supporters analogizing it to a request for information;* but a motion to authorize a *legislative* inquiry into the subject was soundly defeated,† despite arguments basing the House's duty and power to inquire on its authority to declare and provide for war.**

*17 *Annals* 1264 (Burwell, Johnson, Macon); 18 *Annals* 1450-51 (Bibb). Elliot said, in arguing for the resolution, that among Congress's implied powers was the power "to pass resolutions calling upon the Executive for information...." He then continued (17 *Annals* 1312-13):

> The information which we ask may or may not be given by the Executive. It is true that it is his Constitutional duty to give us information from time to time; but at what time and in what manner is left to his own discretion. Where we have no coercive we have no legislative authority. The information, if it be obtained, may or may not be such as to require or even to induce us to act legislatively. . . . In every instance we may or may not legislate in consequence of what we obtain, and we do not legislate in the act of asking for it. We cannot coerce the communication, we cannot even demand it, we can only request it. We ask the President to do his duty in the one case as well as in the other.

The House later passed an unqualified request for all information in the government's control relating to combinations for dismembering the Union or corruptly receiving funds from foreign nations, ignoring Quincy's protest that the motion failed to give the President "power to withhold confidential correspondence. . . ." 18 *Annals* 1460. Jefferson responded that "he would give to the House such information not improper to be disclosed . . ." (*id.* 1464), and later sent all the material he said he was able to locate (*id.* 1482-84, 1564).

†18 *Annals* 1461. The motion was made by John Rowan, and supported by several members who contended the committee could be delegated the power to subpoena. *E.g.*, 17 *Annals* 1263, 1302-1303 (Gardenier); 1371 (Rowan); 1413 (Eppes). Others claimed no such power could be exercised (except to impeach). *E.g.* 1298-1300 (G.W. Campbell); 1301 (Milnor); 1413-16 (Fisk). Samuel Dana felt "the privilege of this House must be deemed precedent and paramount to the authority of any court martial or court of inquiry," but opposed a House investigation in this case. *Id.* 1315. John Love (Va.), on the other hand, characterized the House as resembling a Star Chamber rather than a grand inquest (*id.* 1337), and claimed the St. Clair inquiry was inapposite, (*id.* 1346). See also the skeptical comments of Findley, a veteran of the St. Clair investigation, in *id.* at 1361.

**Said Rowan (17 *Annals* 1348):

> Who makes war? This House. Who conducts it by appropriations of blood and treasure? This House. Shall it be said that we have power to make war and to support it, and not to inquire into the loyalty of our commander? It was said that the President had confidence in him. Mr. R. said, there might be a case (he did not mean to say that it now existed) in which a President would conspire with the Commander-in-Chief against the Government; and, as the latter officer was accountable to the President only, whatever confidence they might possess in the President would be unavailing. . . . Suppose a battle was impending, by which the fate of the nation was to be decided, and the House had a suspicion that the commanding officer was disaffected, or had a disposition to injure the interest of the country, would they not inquire into the case? Certainly they would; and thus he contended that this power of inquiry was inseparably incident to the great power of making war.

184 War, Foreign Affairs and Constitutional Power

Republicans also became extraordinarily sensitive to executive prerogatives when requests for information were proposed. Though some legislators reiterated the view that any member had the right "to call for any information on any subject," this principle was in fact applied only when the requests could not interfere with or embarrass the executive.[68] For example, when a motion was made early in Jefferson's first term to request him to explain why he had repaired a French vessel seized during the Quasi-War, Republican leaders Giles and Samuel Smith said they would vote for the request,[69] although they regarded it as politically motivated, unnecessary, and improper in that it sought the President's motive.* Jefferson reacted angrily, however; he told Giles the request was malicious and improper, and threatened to refuse compliance unless it was reformed.[70] Giles then moved to delete the offending language, because "he did not wish unconstitutionally to interfere with the Executive Department."[71] The motion succeeded, 49-27, and the House voted unanimously to request all papers relating to the vessel's sale, purchase and repair, without asking the President's purpose.[72]

Outright refusals to request foreign-affairs material began in late 1802, when Congress became concerned about Spain's suspension of the right of Americans to deposit goods in New Orleans, and about

---

Rowan later rested also on the power to provide for the general welfare. *Id.* 1425. A similar argument was made by Marmaduke Williams (N.C.) based on the power to raise and support armies (*id.* 1422):

> By the Constitution, Congress have the right to raise and support armies, and to make rules for the government of the same. Suppose it was necessary now, and we know not how soon it may be, to increase our military force; and suppose we had some proof that our commander was a traitor to his country, or intended to subvert the Government, and this House knew where they could procure the testimony to show this corruption. Would any person, under those circumstances, contend we had no right to use the means to collect the evidence; and would this House pass a law to raise an army before they made the inquiry? Certainly not. . . . In a Government like this the conduct of every person holding a high office should always be subject to investigation. And the conduct of none in the Government is more interesting to the people than the Commander of the Army, whose character should be unsuspected as much as the President himself. . . .

Ezekiel Bacon (Mass.), on the other hand, stated that "to save the Republic," even an interference by the people might be justified; "this would be a case in which all Constitutional power must give way." *Id.* 1351. But no such case was presented, he said, and therefore no legislative inquiry should be initiated.

*The request, proposed by Griswold, was that the Secretary of State be directed to report "whether the sum of $32,839.54, laid out in repairing the corvette *The Berceau* . . . was expended, in order to equip her for the service of the United States, or for the purpose of delivering her to the French Republic, agreeably to the stipulations of the Convention between the United States and France." 11 *Annals* 1133-34. *See id.* 1134, 1139-40, 1141, for Republican reaction.

the apparent cession of Louisiana by Spain to France. An unqualified request, proposed by John Randolph, the Republican majority leader, that the President provide the House "such papers as are in the possession of the Department of State" relating to Spain's violation of the treaty granting Americans the right of deposit, passed unanimously.[73] The administration wished, however, to keep the right-of-deposit issue "entirely separate from the question of the cession of Louisiana to France," apparently because negotiations were in progress.[74] Cooperating with this wish, the House rejected a motion made on January 4, 1803 by the Federalist leader, Roger Griswold, for copies of documents received concerning Spain's cession of Louisiana to France, and a report explaining the terms of the transfer "unless such documents and report will, in the opinion of the President, divulge to the House particular transactions not proper at this time to be communicated."[75] Griswold argued that the information was necessary because the cession might require further efforts to protect the frontier; the resolution would aid rather than hinder the President's negotiations by indicating the House's readiness to support the President, a necessary development since "the powers of the Executive are not competent to ulterior measures. He has only the power of negotiation; he has no other. Though he may prevent an aggression by employing force, he cannot enforce compensation for injuries received."[76] But Randolph treated the motions for information related to the cession as expressing a lack of confidence in the executive, to whom he asserted the Constitution allocated control of the conduct of foreign affairs.[77]

Another important example of the legislature's refusal to pass requests for information took place in October 1803, when Jefferson sought Senate approval of the treaty providing for the Louisiana Purchase. The overwhelmingly Republican majority in the Senate ratified the treaty, after very little debate, and after summarily rejecting a motion for more information, especially for documents showing that France had good title to the area it had agreed to sell.[78] Jefferson then sought the House's agreement to carry the treaty into effect. Griswold moved on October 24 for copies of treaties and other documents relating to whether Spain had effectively ceded the Louisiana Territory to France.[79] Randolph claimed to hold "in the highest veneration the principle established in the case of the British Jay Treaty . . . that, in all matters requiring legislative aid, it was the right and duty of this House to deliberate, and upon such deliberation, to afford, or refuse, that aid, as in their judgments public good might require"; and he conceded that it was "equally the right of the House to demand such information from the Executive, as to them appeared necessary to enable them to form a sound conclusion. . . ." But, he said, this demand for information was made to delay and would interfere with negotiations.[80] Another Republican, Samuel Mitchill of New York, said he firmly believed the President had complied with the constitutional injunction to give Congress information of the state of the Union, and if the President had "anything else needful for the deliberation of the House, he was willing to think the Chief Magistrate of the Union would have spontaneously imparted it."[81] Griswold's resolution then lost, by the narrow margin of 57–59,[82] reflecting how badly the issue shattered the Republican majority of about 102–39.*

The most dramatic demonstration of Congress's refusal to request information concerning foreign affairs was acted out between 1807 and 1809, when Jefferson sought to prevent war with Britain and France by adopting and enforcing an embargo.

Jefferson proposed an embargo in December 1807, citing a French decree aimed at neutral shipping. Representative Gardenier moved to request copies of communications regarding the French decree referred to by the President, but the motion was voted down, and debate virtually precluded.[83] Federalists bemoaned the lack of information. They initially supported the President, however, claiming that without information they had no other choice.[84] As the time to enforce the embargo neared, opposition to the President's program increased, frequently reflecting itself in debates concerning information. On February 2, 1808, for example, Jefferson sent some more British decrees to Congress, "as a further proof" of the need for an embargo.[85] Many members were unconvinced. When the House soon thereafter considered a bill proposing to authorize an increase in the military, Nicholas Van Dyke of Delaware moved a resolution requesting the President to communicate such information on foreign relations "as he may deem consistent with the public interest" to enable the House to judge how much to increase the military establishment. James Elliott of Vermont defended the resolution, noting it was a request which the President was privileged to deny,†

---

*A resolution in the Senate on February 23, 1804, requesting information concerning the measures adopted by the President pursuant to the Act of February 6, 1802, authorizing actions against Tripoli, was defeated on February 27, without recorded debate. 13 *Annals* 260, 262.

†"Every gentleman knows that we have not the power to coerce information; our power is limited to a request. . . . The Constitution has said, that the President shall, from time to time, communicate such information he deems proper; and has thus made him the judge of what is proper for communication; but practice has long established the principle, that the House of Representatives have the right to request information whenever they choose to ask it." 18 *Annals* 1641–44.

and that the material requested pertained to possible war against Britain, France and Spain and was therefore the legislature's business. Republicans countered that the President had promised to provide information to enable Congress to carry out its duties, and that he should and could be trusted to do so when the state of negotiations permitted disclosure. "Does any man doubt," asked Archibald Van Horn of Maryland "that he will give us information, when it is necessary to act?"[86]

Jefferson's policies, and his withholding of information, had begun to have an effect, however, even on those unwilling to vote for information requests. Thus, while opposed to a formal request for information, Van Horn and Bacon said they would vote against any increase in the military unless the President justified his request with information. The President would be responsible if, because he failed to perform his duty to supply information, the House refused to adopt measures required for the public safety. Quincy objected to leaving the entire responsibility on the President; "we ourselves are now called upon to act," he said, adding that the House both needed information, and had a right to information. But the resolution was tabled, perhaps because it was deemed, in the words of Matthew Clay from Virginia, "not improper, but premature."[87]

Though no request for information was made at this point, the House seemed determined to refuse to increase the military; they also voted against Jefferson's request for a new militia system, and sent to committee a law that would have further tightened the embargo.[88] "Darkness and mystery overshadow this House and this whole nation," said Gardenier on February 20, 1808, in opposing the embargo enforcement bill. "We sit here as mere automata; we legislate without knowing, nay, sir, without wishing to know, why or wherefore."[89] On February 26, Jefferson apparently capitulated to this indirect pressure by sending Congress several letters to and from America's ministers in France and Britain concerning the objectionable decrees. He asked Congress to keep the messages confidential, and repeated his request for an increased military force.[90] His request for confidentiality was not honored, and a motion was made in the House to ask the President to provide any letters accompanying the representations of America's minister to Paris. This motion was narrowly defeated,[91] however, and the House soon thereafter passed the bill supplementing the embargo, and began to consider a bill to expand the army.[92]

Hardly a month went by before Quincy once again raised the information issue. He noted the dangers the nation faced because of the European war and claimed "that the official information existing within the country, touching any of our legislative duties, should be in the possession of this House. . . . This is no time for the refinements of Constitutional delicacy," he said; if we have been deprived of information we should request it immediately. He noted that letters provided the House referred to others that had not been provided. But his resolution requesting dispatches concerning France's decrees met the same fate of three prior motions during that session, when the House voted to refuse to consider it.[93]

On March 17 Jefferson sent additional French and Spanish decrees to Congress.[94] Opposition to the embargo continued to grow, however, and took concrete form when Representative Jabez Upham of Massachusetts spoke on March 21 against the bill to raise an additional military force. He effectively ridiculed the administration's shifts in policy regarding a military force, and complained that Congress was yet to be informed of the purposes of an increase. "To call on a deliberative body to act discretionarily, and, at the same time, to refuse to give that body information on the subject-matter on which it is to act, is a contradiction. It is, indeed, an imposition." He conceded that the constitutional provision regarding information contemplated that the President "is, of his own mere motion, to give information from time to time to Congress. . . ." But, he said, there are "cases in the course of legislation, where so far from being improper or indecorous, it becomes the duty of the House to solicit information." This was as much such an occasion, he argued, as if the President had asked for a declaration of war. The President may refuse to supply information, Upham conceded, but the House could refuse to pass the legislation requested; and Upham announced his resolve to vote against the military increase.[95]

Jefferson may have been preparing to supply further information even before Upham spoke. On the day after Upham's speech, the President supplied what he claimed to be "the whole" of the proceedings with Britain regarding the *Chesapeake* affair.[96] Legislative pressure thus apparently succeeded in securing more comprehensive material. Disputes about information became markedly less important after this communication; Jefferson continued to supply more information on his own initiative, and Republicans became increasingly disenchanted with the embargo, irrespective of any executive information on the matter.[97] Most motions for information made during the last session of Jefferson's administration passed, though not always without controversy.[98]

Executive Privilege and the Judiciary.   In at least three instances during Jefferson's administration, litigants sought evidence through the federal courts from executive officers. The arguments and actions of participants in those disputes are pertinent to then-current conceptions of the President's authority to withhold information.

The first controversy was *Marbury* v. *Madison*,[99] in which Charles Lee, acting as counsel for Marbury and others, called as witnesses two State Department clerks and Attorney General Levi Lincoln, who had been Secretary of State during the earliest days of Jefferson's first term. Lee needed to prove that commissions had been executed appointing his clients as justices of the peace to establish his case for requiring Secretary of State James Madison to surrender the commissions. The clerks and Lincoln objected to being sworn and claimed to be free to refuse to reveal any facts relating to department business. Lee conceded that the witnesses need not reveal facts relating to those discretionary functions performed by the Secretary of State under the President's direction.* He argued, however, that duties such as recording or fixing seals to commissions were purely ministerial, and the officers were "bound by the same rules of evidence" applicable to other ministerial officers, and had "no exclusive privileges." The Court accepted Lee's contentions and ordered all three witnesses sworn, allowing them to object to particular questions as seeking confidential facts. Two of the witnesses objected to one question each, and the Court sustained them, since the information sought was deemed immaterial; but Lee obtained the proof necessary to proceed with his famous but losing cause.[100]

A second instance took place during the trial in 1806 of Samuel Ogden and William Smith for participating in an expedition led by one Francisco de Miranda to liberate South America from Spanish control.[101] The defendants, claiming as justification that they had acted with acquiescence of the United States, subpoenaed Henry Dearborn, Secretary of War; James Madison, Secretary of State; Robert Smith, Secretary of the Navy; and three clerks in the Department of State. Madison replied that the officers could not attend: "Sensible of all the attention due to writs of subpoena issued in these cases, it is with regret we have to state to the court that the President of the United States, taking into view the state of our public affairs has specifically signified to us that our official duties cannot, consistent therewith, be at this juncture dispensed with. . . ." In fact, he added, because of pressing duties none of the witnesses would

---

*Lee said that "there are, undoubtedly facts, which may come to their knowledge by means of their connection with the secretary of state, respecting which they cannot be bound to answer. Such are the facts concerning foreign correspondencies, and confidential communications between the head of the department and the president." 5 U.S. (1 Cranch) at 141–42 (1803).

ever be able to attend, and he asked the court if their testimony by deposition would suffice. The court decided that an attachment should not issue for the witnesses, since their evidence was not material. Their testimony could only be used to mitigate, not justify, the offense, and the jury could hear no evidence of mitigation, since it was their duty to find only guilt or innocence.[102]

By far the most important and notorious confrontation between the executive and judicial branches took place in connection with the trials of Aaron Burr for treason and high misdemeanor. Jefferson received a stream of letters concerning Burr's activities in the West from various sources beginning early in 1806,[103] but ordered no actions until after November 25, when the President received further evidence of the conspiracy from General James Wilkinson.* Wilkinson sent Jefferson two letters dated October 21, one of which was marked "confidential," and an unsigned memorandum dated October 20.[104] The unsigned document described a powerful conspiracy. The "confidential" letter suggested that the conspiracy might include a revolt in the western territories, and greatly exaggerated the extent of the enterprise.[105] The Cabinet met, and on November 27, 1806, a proclamation was issued directing civil and military officers to seize all vessels and conspirators aligned with Burr.[106]

Congress went into session on December 1, 1806. Jefferson mentioned the conspiracy only generally in his annual message, and communicated none of the letters or other material he had by then received.[107] On January 16, 1807, John Randolph said he could no longer "rest satisfied in that state of supineness and apathy" into which he claimed the House had lapsed. He moved a resolution that called upon the President: (1) for all information relating to any illegal combination, except that which Jefferson believed the public welfare required him to withhold; and (2) to report what steps he had taken and proposed to take against such a conspiracy.[108] Both parts of the resolution were attacked as reflecting "a want of confidence in the Executive." Congress had authorized the President to put down insurrections, one member argued, and Jefferson apparently felt he had sufficient means to do the job, since he had asked

---

*Wilkinson, commander of American military forces in the new Louisiana Territory, evidently had been initially sympathetic to Burr's plans. He met Burr in Philadelphia (where Burr was taking refuge from indictments for Hamilton's death), and they reportedly discussed the possibility of creating a new nation in the West. They continued to plan in Washington during the final months of Burr's term as Vice President. Wilkinson, who was also being paid by Spain for information that would be useful in protecting Florida and Mexico against the United States, eventually exposed Burr to Jefferson, claiming to have "discovered" the plot. M. Smelser, *The Democratic Republic* 113-17 (1968).

for no further legislative support. "I believe the President will communicate to us all the information that is necessary and proper for us to possess," said James Holland of North Carolina, "and his not having communicated it in this instance is conclusive evidence to my mind of the impropriety of asking it."[109] Others defended the House's right and need for information, and contested the view that the executive should be left unilaterally to suppress a dangerous conspiracy.[110] Said James Lloyd of Massachusetts: "If the doctrine of confidence is to be carried to this length, that you, who are the guardians of the people, shall sit idle spectators of every impending storm, I shall never subscribe to it."[111] The request for information carried overwhelmingly, 109-14. The second part of Randolph's resolution, however, was amended to request only information on the steps the President had taken, not those he intended to take. It then narrowly passed, 67-52.[112]

Jefferson responded on January 22, 1807. He purported to describe, "under the reserve" or qualification contained in the resolution, the information he had received. The material, he said, was "voluminous; but little has been given under the sanction of an oath, so as to constitute formal and legal evidence." It contained "such a mixture of rumors, conjectures, and suspicions, as renders it difficult to sift out the real facts. . . . In this state of the evidence, delivered sometimes too under the restriction of private confidence, neither safety nor justice will permit the exposing of names," except Burr's, "whose guilt is placed beyond question."

Though he had received evidence of Burr's conspiracy in early 1806, Jefferson claimed he began to receive "intimations" of the conspiracy "in the latter part of September" 1806, and that not until October were the outlines of the scheme sufficiently clear to warrant sending a confidential agent to the area. The President said he had received a letter from General Wilkinson, dated October 21, which recounted that an agent of Burr had carried Wilkinson certain important communications, and an invitation to join the conspiracy. "The General," wrote Jefferson, "with the honor of a soldier and fidelity of a good citizen," immediately sent the information and made arrangements to stop the enterprise. Three of Burr's principal conspirators had been arrested, Jefferson noted, two of whom (Erick Bollman and Samuel Swartwout) Wilkinson had sent East, "probably on the consideration that an impartial trial could not be expected, during the present agitation of New Orleans. . . ."[113] Actually, Jefferson knew, or should have known, that Wilkinson sent the conspirators East in defiance of writs of *habeas corpus* that had been issued for their production before the circuit court in New Orleans.[114]

Jefferson sent at least thirteen different documents to Congress between January 22 and February 19, 1807. They included depositions and letters from Wilkinson accusing Burr and his associates of the conspiracy, letters from Burr to Wilkinson concerning Swartwout's role, a letter reporting that Burr had protested his innocence, and a letter from Wilkinson dated December 26, 1806, explaining that he had pretended to be a conspirator. A reasonably thorough examination of available sources indicates, however, that Jefferson withheld over fifty documents.[115] In addition to several orders and instructions to and from his subordinates,[116] the material withheld included letters from a variety of sources accusing several people of conspiring with Burr, particularly Wilkinson. Several of these items were marked confidential, or were obtained on express promises of confidentiality, as Jefferson had told Congress.[117] In particular, Jefferson withheld Wilkinson's "confidential" letter of October 21, 1806, the memorandum Wilkinson had included with it, and a letter from Wilkinson dated November 12. He also kept secret until Burr's trial an important affidavit of Erick Bollman, which had been obtained on the promise it would not be used against Bollman, and which detailed Wilkinson's part in the affair.[118]

Most of the material withheld could readily be categorized as hearsay, dangerous to the reputations of persons against whom the government had no concrete evidence. Some especially important items were withheld, however, apparently because Jefferson regarded himself free to promise confidentiality. Jefferson would have had difficulty in claiming that disclosure of most of these items, especially the first-hand reports of co-conspirators, would have adversely affected the "public welfare." The material might have been given to Congress in confidence, moreover, as Robert Smith suggested.[119]

Whatever Jefferson's motives, withholding these letters concealed the fact that the President had been on notice of the conspiracy since about February 1806, rather than September as he told Congress, and that several people with first-hand knowledge had accused Wilkinson of being a conspirator. Congress had long known from newspaper accounts of Wilkinson's possible involvement in the conspiracy. Revealing the substance of the evidence against him would therefore have caused little unfair injury, and was arguably necessary to present a balanced picture, since Jefferson did send Congress Wilkinson's explanation for his close contacts and connections with Burr. The record permits the inference that Jefferson was consciously protecting Wilkinson, possibly because he believed Wilkinson's story, or because he needed Wilkinson, initially to put down the conspiracy, and later to testify against Burr.

Burr was arrested on February 19, 1807. Grand jury proceedings commenced on May 22. On June 24 and 26 Burr was indicted for treason against the United States, and for planning an expedition against Spanish territory (a misdemeanor). He was ultimately acquitted on both charges, because Chief Justice Marshall, who presided throughout as one of two trial judges sitting for the U.S. Circuit Court at Richmond, Virginia, ruled that a large part of the government's evidence could not be used.[120] A proceeding thereafter was commenced on the government's motion to commit Burr to the U.S. Circuit Court for Ohio on another misdemeanor charge, which was ultimately dismissed.

We are here concerned with Burr's efforts to obtain, through the court, information from Jefferson that Burr claimed was material to his defense. Three separate efforts occurred, the details of which are treated elsewhere.[121] Several important decisions and arguments were made, however, that deserve summary.

The first effort involved Burr's request for a subpoena *duces tecum* to the President (and others) requesting the October 21 letter from Wilkinson, referred to by Jefferson in his message to Congress, "together with the documents accompanying such letter." Justice Marshall granted Burr's request.[122] Jefferson and his lawyers did not oppose a subpoena for papers,* but claimed that secret or "private" material could not be subpoenaed, and that the President "alone is competent to decide" what must be suppressed.[123] Burr's attorney claimed materiality was for the court to decide, not the President or prosecution. Any secret material, not proper to disclose, could be withheld by the court, they claimed, and no privilege existed to withhold merely "confidential" or "private" material.[124] Marshall's opinion upholding Burr's claim took similar positions. He recognized that

---

*Jefferson insisted he could not be compelled to testify in person, and at no time during the Burr proceedings was the President's appearance actually sought. The subpoena issued to Jefferson expressly waived his appearance if the documents listed were provided. Jefferson's attorneys all conceded, however, that the President's personal attendance could be demanded if essential, especially in a treason trial. Compare the concession of counsel for Marbury in Marbury v. Madison, 5 U.S. (1 Cranch) 137, 149 (1803), that the President may not be summoned to court, but only impeached. Marshall explicitly held that the President could be summoned in person. Jefferson rejected the proposition that his duties would ever permit attendance, and prepared to resist any such call by ordering Hay to instruct the local marshal to refuse to cooperate with the court if necessary. He expressed his willingness, however, to submit to deposition. *See* 1 D. Robertson, *Reports of the Trials of Colonel Aaron Burr for Treason* 131, 136, 149, 182, 254–55 (1808); 9 *Jefferson Writings* (Ford) 62n.; 10 *Jefferson Works* (Fed.) 400n. The original subpoena is on file at the Clerk's Office, E.D. Va., Richmond. The author has had access to a copy of the subpoena kindly supplied by Professor Dumas Malone.

some material might have to be suppressed, if its disclosure would "endanger the public safety" or be "imprudent" or against "the wish of the executive," so long as it was "not immediately and essentially applicable to the point. . . ." But no showing of this had yet been made, and "will have its due consideration, on the return of the subpoena." He rejected outright any general claim of privilege based on the "confidential nature" of Wilkinson's letter.[125]

Jefferson claimed he had given the October 21 letter referred to in the subpoena to Attorney General Ceasar Rodney. But Rodney, it developed, had a second letter from Wilkinson dated October 21, which, Jefferson assured United States Attorney George Hay who handled the prosecution, "had no relation to the facts" stated in his message to Congress.[126] He told Hay, therefore, to obtain a copy of the missing October 21 letter from Wilkinson,* and Burr eventually accepted the copy after his need for the letter had been mooted by his acquittal of the treason charge on September 1.[127] Actually the letter held by Rodney contained Wilkinson's defense against charges in the press concerning the conspiracy, and might have been extremely useful in undermining Wilkinson's credibility.[128] The subpoena clearly covered this additional letter of October 21, as well as the memorandum Wilkinson had prepared describing the conspiracy, since they were "documents accompanying" the letter of which Burr was aware. Jefferson therefore effectively precluded Burr from obtaining these potentially exculpatory materials by keeping from the court and even from Hay the fact that they were relevant and were being withheld.

Burr's second effort to obtain information occurred during his trial on the misdemeanor charge. He asked that a subpoena issue to Hay for a letter from Wilkinson to Jefferson dated November 12, 1806.[129] Hay conceded he had the letter, but claimed the right on the President's behalf to withhold parts that he thought improper to communicate.[130] Marshall issued the subpoena, and when Hay withheld some paragraphs, Marshall ruled that, while the President had a

---

*At the same time Jefferson wrote Hay that every effort would be made to uncover Wilkinson's letter, he wrote Wilkinson: "If you have a copy of it [the letter], and chuse to give it in, it will, I think, have a good effect; for it was my intention, if I should receive it from Mr. Rodney, not to communicate it without your consent, after I learned of your arrival." Letter of June 21, 1807, 168 *The Papers of Thomas Jefferson* 29560, reel 62 (LC microfilm). One cannot be certain that Jefferson really meant to obtain Wilkinson's permission before sending the letter to the court, but his statement is consistent with his practice of suppressing "confidential" letters. "It was not TJ's custom to disclose confidential letters." 5 Malone, *Jefferson* 325 n. 35.

right to seek to withhold secrets as well as embarrassing material, Hay could not exercise that qualified privilege in the President's behalf.[131] Jefferson then excised those portions he felt should be kept confidential, claiming they were immaterial to the prosecution.[132] When the trial reconvened on September 9, Burr's attorneys raised no objection to the deletions Jefferson had made. But once again this appears to have been because the letter had become unnecessary. On that same day Marshall ruled that most of the government's evidence on the misdemeanor charge was inadmissible, making Burr's acquittal on September 15 a foregone conclusion.[133]

Here, too, Jefferson's characterization of the information he withheld as "immaterial" was inaccurate. In the deleted portions of the November 12 letter Wilkinson made certain allusions possibly implicating two highly trustworthy officials—Governor Claiborne of Louisiana and his secretary, Cowles Meade—of conspiring with Burr.[134] This unsupportable accusation could have been used to undermine Wilkinson's credibility, and was therefore of potential use in exculpating Burr.

When the government later began proceedings to have Burr committed for trial in Ohio, the November 12 letter became the focus of Burr's third effort to obtain information. During the hearing on the government's motion, Wilkinson admitted having presented the entire letter to the grand jury. John Wickham demanded its production. Hay opposed: "The president had been consulted on the subject; and he has excepted such parts as he thought it would be improper to produce." Marshall seemingly agreed with Hay, since "after the president had been consulted, he could not think of requiring from General Wilkinson the exhibition of those parts of the letter which the president was unwilling to disclose." Burr's attorneys protested that the President should be given no special deference and that the excised paragraphs were in fact material. Marshall persisted in refusing to direct production of the excised portions without further proof of their relevance, but he agreed "to leave the accused all the advantages which he might derive from the parts actually produced; and to allow him all the advantages of *supposing* that the omitted parts related to any particular point." Had the proceeding been a trial rather than a commitment hearing, Marshall added, he would have prevented it from continuing until the excised portions were produced.[135] Marshall therefore recognized a limited privilege, but in the context of a commitment proceeding, and after allowing the defense to make any suppositions they pleased about the withheld information.

Control of Foreign and Military Affairs

Jefferson and the nation were confronted with several major foreign-affairs problems. Spain created one set of difficulties by selling Louisiana to France, and by closing New Orleans to Americans as a place to deposit their goods.[136] After some negotiation, and considerable good fortune, the United States managed to purchase Louisiana from France. Spain, in the meantime, decided to allow American commerce to continue on the Mississippi, but it refused to sell the Floridas. France and Britain created even more serious problems by interfering with American commerce and impressing sailors; war almost erupted when a British ship attacked an American public vessel. Jefferson's favored policy to counteract interference with American trade was to impose an embargo on all foreign commerce, rather than to make war. This policy became increasingly unpopular and was replaced, on the day Madison took office as President, with a policy of non-intercourse aimed particularly at Britain and France. Finally, long-standing difficulties with the so-called Barbary powers led Tripoli to declare war. An interesting conflict resulted, discussed in detail below, leading ultimately to a settlement favorable to the United States.

Executive Initiatives.   Jefferson acted with vigor, ingenuity and independence in dealing with the difficulties he faced. He instructed Livingston and Monroe, for example, to warn France that, if it insisted on holding New Orleans, it would inevitably force the United States to ally with Britain.[137] He expressed the same warning directly to the French chargé, Pichon, in private conversations.[138] He also promised extravagantly on occasion, as when he assured Pichon in July 1801 that "nothing would be easier than to furnish your army and fleet with everything, and to reduce [the black revolutionary in Santo Domingo, General] Toussaint [L'Ouverture] to starvation."[139] He carried on his relatively free-wheeling correspondence in confidence, moreover, designating many of his letters "private" and withholding them from Congress.[140]

Many of Jefferson's most important foreign-affairs initiatives were well within the Federalist view of executive authority. His dismissal of the Spanish Minister, Marquis de Casa Yrujo, for example, could have led to trouble with Spain, but was analogous to Washington's dismissal of Genêt.[141] The several proclamations he issued, in various emergencies, all could reasonably be based on legislative authority.[142] The purchase of Louisiana, though much more extensive than contemplated by Jefferson, was authorized by Congress in principle and subsequently approved and funded.[143] Jefferson silently swallowed his constitutional scruples in allowing Congress to absorb Louisiana without a constitutional amendment, but they were scruples that not even Madison or Gallatin shared.*

Difficulties with Britain led to a negotiated treaty, signed by Monroe in England, but rejected by Jefferson because it failed to include a provision concerning impressment.[144] He withheld the treaty from the Senate, apparently for the reason stated by Madison, that "if he is determined not to accept [it], even should the Senate advise, why call the Senate together?"[145] Those who supported a reference to the Senate did so on practical, political grounds, predicting correctly that Federalists would use the President's action to place on him the responsibility for further deterioration of Anglo-American relations. But even some Federalists recognized that the President acted within his constitutional authority when he refused to submit the treaty.[146]

More significantly, though Jefferson was unwilling to submit the treaty to the Senate, he was willing to use it as an "informal" understanding between Britain and the United States. He instructed Monroe that "[i]f the treaty cannot be put into acceptable form, then the

---

*See 1 *The Writings of Albert Gallatin* 111, 113-14 (H. Adams, ed. 1960) [hereinafter *"Gallatin Writings"*]. During July and August 1803, Jefferson took the position that the Constitution had not given the general government the power "of holding foreign territory, and still less of incorporating it into the Union." Jefferson to John Dickinson, Aug. 9, 1803, in 8 *Jefferson Writings* (Ford) 262. To Senator John Breckenridge he confessed to having gone beyond the Constitution in executing the agreement, trusting that the nation would uphold him. Aug. 12, 1803, *id.* 244n.

He sensed, however, the dangers in revealing his views. "I infer that the less we say about constitutional difficulties respecting Louisiana the better," he wrote to Madison on August 18, "and that what is necessary for surmounting them must be done sub silentio." *Id.* 245n. See the similar statements in letters to Breckenridge and Paine, *id.* 244-45n. On September 3, Senator Wilson Cary Nicholas predicted that, if Jefferson stated publicly that the treaty exceeded constitutional authority, it might be rejected by the Senate, or at least lead to Jefferson's being charged with willful illegality. Letter of Sept. 3, 1803, in 4 Malone, *Jefferson* 318 n.16. Jefferson continued to state his view privately that the treaty was unauthorized, extrapolating to the general position that a contrary construction would render the Constitution indefinite and therefore dangerous: "Our peculiar security is in possession of a written Constitution. Let us not make it a blank paper by construction. I say the same as to the opinion of those who consider the grant of the treaty making power as boundless." Letter of Sept. 7, 1803, in 8 *Jefferson Writings* (Ford) 247-48n. He thought it "important in the present case to set an example against broad construction by appealing for new power to the people"; but not important enough to risk losing the treaty. "If however our friends shall think differently," he concluded, "I shall acquiesce with satisfaction, confiding that the good sense of our country will correct the evil of construction when it shall produce ill effects." Indeed, he wrote Gallatin that he wanted Congress to approve the treaty "without talking," because of the schedule set for ratification. Letter of Aug. 23, 1803, in 1 *Gallatin Writings* 144-45.

next best thing is to back out of the negotiation as well as we can, letting it die away insensibly; but, in the meantime, agreeing informally, that both parties shall act on the principle of the treaty. . . ."[147] The British refused the offer, but had this arrangement been made, it would have resembled a so-called "executive" agreement, albeit tentative, in that the Senate's consent would not have been sought. On the other hand, Jefferson may have contemplated notifying Congress, since the substance of his instruction to Monroe was communicated to the legislature.[148] An informal agreement was in fact entered into with Spain in 1806 to establish neutral territory on both sides of the Red River, to avoid possible conflict between Spanish and American troops. The Senate's consent was not sought, but Congress was promptly informed of the arrangement.[149]

Jefferson did not always inform Congress, however, of informal arrangements he had settled upon. On October 22, 1808, the President met with his Cabinet and agreed to what in retrospect was a "pan-American" policy toward Cuba and Mexico:

> Unanimously agreed in the sentiments which should be unauthoritatively expressed by our agents to influential persons in Cuba and Mexico, to wit, "if you remain under the dominion of the kingdom and family of Spain, we are contented; but we should be extremely unwilling to see you pass under the dominion or ascendency of France or England. In the latter case should you chuse to declare independence we cannot now commit ourselves by saying we would make common cause with you but must reserve ourselves to act according to the then existing circumstances, but in our proceedings we shall be influenced by friendship to you, by a firm belief that our interests are intimately connected, and by the strongest repugnance to see you under subordination to either France or England, either politically or commercially."[150]

Implementation of this policy had to be left to Madison's administration, which began soon after its adoption; meanwhile, Congress was not advised of the Cabinet's resolve.

The incident that caused one of Jefferson's most significant unilateral decisions was the attack by the British armed vessel *Leopard* on the American ship of war, *Chesapeake.* On June 22, 1807, the *Leopard* followed the *Chesapeake* out of Hampton Roads, Virginia, and signalled to deliver a letter. The letter proved to be an order from Admiral Berkeley at Halifax directing that the *Chesapeake* be searched for British deserters, if met at sea. The 36-gun *Chesapeake* at first refused to submit. But the 50-gun *Leopard* opened fire. The *Chesapeake* was disabled, suffered three men killed and eighteen wounded, and its Captain agreed to submit to a search, resulting in the impressment of four of his crew.[151] This unprecedented humiliation of an American public vessel raised a storm of protest through-out the United States.

Jefferson convened his Cabinet as soon as he heard of the attack. They unanimously approved a proclamation,* as well as a call upon all state governors to prepare their quotas of 100,000 militia in case Congress approved an expedition into Canada.[152] They also agreed to purchase certain equipment and ammunition, for at least part of which they lacked legislative authority. Jefferson subsequently explained these purchases as necessitated by the "emergency," and submitted the matter to Congress, which approved them overwhelmingly.[153]

Finally, the President sought to retaliate for the attack, and to defend the nation, by ordering Governor William H. Cabell of Virginia on July 8, 1807 to use regular troops and militia to cut off all supplies to British armed vessels and again on July 24, noting that "the act of Congress for the preservation of peace in our harbors . . . authorizes a qualified war against persons of their demeanor," and that "the captives may certainly be held as prisoners of war."[154] The rules, Jefferson said, which should govern all communications with the British—those "sanctioned by the practice of nations in a state of war"—were implicit in the decision, "taken in conformity with the Act of Congress," to treat "as public enemies British armed vessels in or entering our waters . . . ."[155] Furthermore, Jefferson urged caution in implementing even what he regarded as authorized actions,† telling both Cabell and George Clinton, his Vice President, that Congress and not the executive should decide whether the attack justified war.** Jefferson made similarly deferential statements directly to Congress on other occasions.[156]

---

*Gallatin wrote Joseph H. Nicholson on July 17, 1807, that the Cabinet had only two options—war or the proclamation, the latter of which "was recommended not only by the nature of our Constitution, which does not make the President arbiter of war, but also by the practice of civilized nations . . .," referring to incidents including Nootka Sound. 1 *Gallatin Writings* 338.

†Jefferson insisted, for example, that violators of his order could be treated as prisoners of war; but he told Governor Cabell to release the prisoners seized "as an act of favor. . . ."10 *Jefferson Works* (Fed.) 436. He wrote that Captain Stephen Decatur, in command at the Norfolk Navy Yard, was not to attack blockading vessels "without orders from me"; Decatur could attack the British without prior presidential approval only if "they attack Norfolk or enter Elizabeth river. . . ." 1 *Writings of Thomas Jefferson* 476 (Mem. ed. 1907). Finally, though the British failed to withdraw their vessels from U.S. waters, as ordered, the President took no action against them.

**He wrote to Cabell on June 29, 1807: "Whether the outrage is a proper cause of war, belonging exclusively to Congress, it is our duty not to commit them by doing anything which would have to be retracted. We may, however, exercise the powers entrusted to us for preventing future insults within our harbors, and claim firmly satisfaction for the past." 10 *Jefferson Works* (Fed.) 432-

Jefferson moved and readied troops and vessels at other pivotal times during his presidential tenure. In all these situations he continued, as after the *Chesapeake* affair, to exercise his authority over military forces with considerable caution. After the Senate ratified purchase of the Louisiana Territory, Congress passed an act authorizing Jefferson to occupy, by force if necessary, the area ceded by France.[157] Jefferson had kept alive a claim that the area ceded included West Florida, the territory to the east of the Mississippi River up to the Perdido River.[158] (See Map No. 2, p. 293.) He was willing to leave this claim dormant, however, as Gallatin recommended.[159] He therefore instructed General Wilkinson to take possession of New Orleans, but to move against Baton Rouge—located in West Florida—only if Spain refused to surrender New Orleans.[160]

Congress gave Jefferson another opportunity to seize West Florida by adopting legislation on February 24, 1804 establishing a revenue district centering on the bay and river of Mobile, deep in contested territory.[161] Jefferson once again preserved peace by declining to use the full authority arguably conferred. Madison assured Spain that the relevant statutory provision had been included to enable the executive to accept the area if Spain surrendered it voluntarily, and Gallatin instructed his Collector of Revenue to refrain from occupying the area by force, or from any act that could· "endanger the peace of the United States."[162]

Jefferson's frustration over not being able to acquire West Florida increased gradually after 1804. He attempted through secret negotiations to convince Spain to sell,[163] meanwhile telling Congress that the hope of avoiding a confrontation was diminishing.[164] He specifically disclaimed authority to use "offensive" force,* but he did authorize "defensive" action in an area that Spain claimed as its territory.[165] When fighting almost erupted in the contested area,† he

---

33. On July 6, 1807, he wrote Clinton that "We act on these principles. . . . That the power of declaring war being with the Legislature, the executive should do nothing, necessarily committing them to decide for war in preference of non-intercourse. . . ." *Id.* 448-49.

*He said at one point (15 *Annals* 19):

> Considering that Congress alone is constitutionally invested with the power of changing our condition from peace to war, I have thought it my duty to await their authority for using force in any degree which could be avoided. I have barely instructed the officers stationed in the neighborhood of the aggressions, to protect our citizens from violence, to patrol within the borders actually delivered to us, and not to go out of them, but, when necessary, to repel an inroad, or to rescue a citizen or his property; and the Spanish officers remaining at New Orleans are required to depart without further delay.

†During the period February to October 1806, various incursions had been made by Spanish patrols across the Sabine River into territory claimed by the

advised Congress so that "they may fully understand the state of things" and take such actions as "they shall deem sufficient."[166]

Throughout his remaining term as President, Jefferson sought, sometimes by wild schemes, to gain control of the Floridas.* Enforcement of the embargo gave Commodore David Porter an opportunity to harass Spanish commerce and in other ways to act out his conviction that Baton Rouge should be seized in order to avoid its surrender to Britain.[167] Though Navy Secretary Smith may have "shuddered" on reading Porter's dispatches, as Porter's biographer suggests, Porter ceased harassing the Spanish only after he heard that the embargo had been repealed by the nonintercourse law of March 1, 1809.[168]

The Jefferson administration also sent a military expedition to New Orleans in late 1808, apparently anticipating problems with Britain. General James Wilkinson, placed in command, was specifically instructed to limit his activities to defensive operations.[169] By the time Wilkinson left for the West, however, Jefferson no longer feared

---

United States under the Louisiana cession. *E.g.*, Major Porter to Secretary of War, Feb. 8, 1806; William Claiborne to Governor Herrera, Aug. 26, 1806, 16 *Annals* 914, 917. Major Porter reported that his object was accomplished by requiring the Spanish to withdraw to the other side of the Sabine, which they did. *Id.* 913. General Claiborne restricted himself to writing strong letters of protest, but advised the Spanish Governor that force would be used to protect American rights. *Id.* 919, 921. Both men were under orders "to permit no adverse post to be taken, nor armed men to remain within it." Jefferson to Congress, March 20, 1806, *id.* 913. In addition, General Wilkinson had been ordered to proceed to the Sabine to resist disturbance of "the existing state of things." General Wilkinson to Governor Cordera, Oct. 4, 1806, *id.* 922, 923. He expressed his intention to demand Spanish troop withdrawal, and in case of refusal to be "governed by circumstances." Wilkinson to Secretary of War, Oct. 21, 1806, *id.* 924. The Spanish apparently were tractable, for no incident of force was reported. *See* President's annual message, December 2, 1806, in which he describes peaceful withdrawal of Spanish troops west of the Sabine River. *Id.* 11.

*At one point, he wrote to Minister Bowdoin in France that "we expect from the friendship of the Emperor that he will either compel Spain to do us justice, or abandon her to us. We ask but one month to be in possession of the City of Mexico." Letter of April 2, 1807, 2 *Bowdoin and Temple Papers* 372-73 in 6 Mass. Hist. Soc. Collections, 7th Series (1907). Napoleon is said to have offered the Floridas to America in exchange for an alliance against Britain, but claimed to know nothing of this offer when the United States reported its resolve to remain neutral. See 4 H. Adams, *History of the United States* 293-311 (1889). Jefferson saw an especially tantalizing opportunity in the Spanish uprising against Napoleon during 1803. He wrote to each member of his Cabinet on August 12 of that year (11 *Jefferson Works* [Fed.] 42-43):

> Should England make up with us, while Bonaparte continues at war with Spain, a moment may occur when we may without danger of commitment with either France or England seize to our own limits of Louisiana as of right, and the residue of the Floridas as reprisals for spoliations. It is our duty to have an eye to this in rendezvousing and stationing our new recruits and our armed vessels, so as to be ready, if Congress authorizes it, to strike in a moment.

war with Britain, and wished to avoid decisions that would have to be implemented by Madison.[170] When Wilkinson later indicated some interest in taking West Florida, President Madison's Secretary of War ordered that "no interference of any kind in the affairs of the territories of Spain should take place, or be encouraged or permitted by any person or persons, whether civil or military belonging to or under the authority of the United States."[171] The expedition terminated without military incident soon thereafter.

Jefferson's efforts to protect coastal waters illustrate how actions justifiable under international law could lead to war. Jefferson explained to Congress on December 3, 1805 that merchants in American waters were being plundered, not only by armed vessels without commissions, the seizure of which was authorized by the law of nations and domestic statutes,[172] but also by vessels with "illegal commissions, [and] others with those of legal form, but committing piratical acts beyond the authority of their commissions," the seizure of which could involve significant risk of error. The line between illegal pirate and lawful privateer was often difficult to draw, especially by an American officer exercising on-the-spot judgment. Still, Jefferson announced that orders had issued "to arrest all vessels of these descriptions found hovering on our coasts, within the limits of the Gulf Stream, and to bring the offenders in for trials as pirates."[173] Congress accepted Jefferson's actions, including his unilateral decision to pursue pirates and illegal privateers in all areas up to the Gulf Stream, far beyond the previously claimed three-mile limit.*

During Jefferson's administration the first clear examples began to accumulate of how war could be caused by executive officers, without even the express approval of the President, let alone that of Congress. Commodore Porter demonstrated in two incidents that naval officers could create dangerous confrontations at sea. While commanding the *Enterprise*, docked at Naples in early 1806, Porter received information that two of his seamen had deserted and were on board a British vessel. The British captain assured Porter that the men were not aboard, but Porter later discovered that the British

---

*John Quincy Adams recorded in his diary a visit with Jefferson on November 30, 1805, at which Jefferson suggested the wisdom of claiming up to the Gulf Stream as territorial waters. Jefferson said that the limit set under Washington was the most conservative claim possible, to avoid offending France. In reply to Adams's observation "that it might be well, before we ventured to assume a claim so broad, to wait for a time when we should have a force competent to maintain it," Jefferson replied that, in the meantime, "it was advisable *to squint at it*, and to accustom the nations of Europe to the idea that we should claim it in future." 1 J.Q. Adams, *Memoirs* 376 (C. Adams, ed. 1874).

had deceived him. Porter regarded his treatment by the British as "an indignity . . . to my Flag," and threatened to "take measures to obtain satisfaction." The British managed to mollify Porter, and the dispute subsided.[174]

The incident at Naples probably contributed, however, to Porter's reaction during July 1806 when a British seaman insulted one of Porter's officers in the harbor at British-controlled Malta. The seaman was ordered aboard the *Enterprise*, given twelve lashes and sent away. An investigation was instituted by port officers, who instructed Porter to remain at Malta until the Governor granted him permission to depart. Porter rejected this order, despite a British threat that his vessel would be fired upon if he attempted to leave. He sailed immediately, without incident, stating that to submit an American vessel of war to British orders would establish a dangerous and undesirable precedent.[175] Jefferson and his administration had given no orders covering circumstances such as Porter faced. No evidence could be found that Porter's actions caused displeasure in Washington, and Porter in fact received increasingly important commands thereafter.*

A final set of interesting activities pursued under Jefferson is the series of expeditions sent across the nation's western borders.† The earliest and most famous of these was led by Meriwether Lewis and William Clark into the Louisiana Territory during a tension-filled period, just after its cession by Spain to France, and before its acquisition by the United States.[176] Jefferson sought permission from France and Spain for what he described as a scientific expedition;

---

*Porter did become greatly concerned that he would be punished for his conduct at Malta. He wrote to the Secretary of Navy on Oct. 29, 1807 that "in this instance I may have exceeded the bounds of discretion," but he hoped that he would be punished no worse than the many British officers who had insulted the United States and have "not attoned [sic] for such outrages." Porter claimed that he only punished the man after repeated insults and cited a precedent in which a British Captain had flogged an American who had insulted him in 1799. Letter of Oct. 29, 1807, *Letters Rec'd. by Sec'y Navy from Masters Commandant* National Archives microfilm M-147, reel 1.

†Jefferson's presidency also included a private expedition by Venezuelan patriot Francisco de Miranda to foment revolution in certain South American countries. The expedition was suppressed by the federal government, but not until Miranda was able to equip and man some ships, and get himself captured. At a subsequent trial of some of Miranda's aides, the defendants claimed that Jefferson and Madison knew of, and had approved, their project. Both the President and Secretary of State denied knowledge and approval, but no judicial findings were made on the issue, since the court held that the defendants could be proved guilty of the acts charged even if approval had been obtained. United States v. Smith, 27 F. Cas. 1192, 1231 (No. 16,342) (C.C.D.N.Y. 1806). *See generally* 4 I. Brant, *James Madison: Secretary of State 1800-1809*, ch. 24 (1953).

France granted a passport and Spain refused, though the Spanish Minister did not go so far as to prohibit the project.[177] Jefferson then sought legislative approval and support, explaining in a confidential message that the expedition could advance the nation's commercial interests and future security.[178] He assured Congress that Spain would regard the project as scientific and would not oppose it. Congress approved, and appropriated the necessary support.[179] Instructions then issued to Lewis, predicting that the French passport should suffice. Lewis was permitted, however, to defend against "unauthorized opposition" by individuals or small parties, but told to decline any engagement with a superior force, authorized or unauthorized.[180] These instructions were kept from Congress, but no serious confrontation occurred, for by the time the expedition penetrated the Louisiana Territory in 1804 it had been purchased by the United States.

The House Committee on Commerce and Manufactures reported on March 8, 1804 that exploration of the Red and Arkansas rivers would benefit the United States, especially during times of peace.[181] An expedition led by William Dunbar in October 1804 created no trouble with Spain, since it used a route distant from Spanish posts.[182] A second expedition was dispatched in 1805 for the purpose of making contact with Indian tribes along the Red River, an object Jefferson undoubtedly knew would offend Spain, which claimed the territory was not part of the Louisiana Purchase. On July 28, 1806, the second Red River expedition was turned back by Spanish forces, and Jefferson reported the incident to Congress.[183] Governor Claiborne of the Mississippi Territory and the Spanish commander exchanged harsh words, but the problem was resolved by the so-called Neutral Ground Agreement of November 5, 1806, under which United States forces were to remain behind the Arroyo Hondo east of the Red River, and Spanish forces were to remain behind a point west of the Red River.[184]

Meanwhile, on July 15, 1806, General Wilkinson had dispatched Captain Zebulon M. Pike on another expedition of the Red and Arkansas rivers. Secretary of War Dearborn had suggested secret reconnaissance activities on February 26, 1805, to obtain military intelligence.[185] Wilkinson issued instructions to Pike on July 19 ordering him also to negotiate with Indians, and noting that he would have to "be extremely guarded with respect to the Spaniards—neither alarm nor offend them unnecessarily."[186] Jefferson appears personally to have approved in general the notion of such an expedition, and Secretary of War Dearborn was specifically sent Wilkinson's instructions on August 2.[187] Notice to Dearborn came only after the expedition was underway, but Dearborn took no action to terminate the project or to limit its objectives. On December 2, after Dearborn had received Wilkinson's instructions, Jefferson asked Congress to authorize exploration of the Red and Arkansas rivers, without revealing to Congress the fact that an expedition was already underway.* He may have requested a further expedition, which was inconsistent with the Neutral Ground Agreement, only because he knew one had already been undertaken.

Congress failed to appropriate further funds to explore the Red and Arkansas rivers. Pike, meanwhile, had rough going and eventually surrendered without resistance to Spanish troops near the Rio Grande on February 26, 1807.[188] The administration paid the costs of the expedition out of War Department funds, in addition to some debts claimed by Spain to have been incurred by Pike.[189] Letters were then sent by Dearborn to Congress seeking compensation for Pike, and representing that the President had received Wilkinson's instructions and approved the project.[190] Congress refused to comply. Its action cannot safely be regarded as disapproval of the expedition or of Jefferson's conduct, however; the expedition's costs had already been paid, and some evidence indicates that legislators associated Pike with Wilkinson, whom many regarded as having conspired with Aaron Burr.[191]

Legislative Participation. The principal reason Jefferson was able to conduct foreign and military affairs with as much if not more independence than his predecessors is that Congress let him. The Republican-dominated legislature largely supported his objectives, and granted him broad discretion over such concerns as the protection of harbors and enforcement of the embargo.[192] Requests for information and proposed investigations were frequently blocked, largely on the ground that they might interfere with the President's powers or responsibilities.† Minority legislators protested, but with

---

*16 *Annals* 13. He may have informed congressional leaders of the expedition, however. On Feb. 22, 1808, Representative Willis Alston of North Carolina "said it would be recollected that he was chairman of the committee appointed to inquire what compensation should be made to Captains Lewis and Clarke. On the investigation of this subject, he was told it might be necessary to make a certain appropriation to explore certain waters, and was told that Captain Pike was then engaged in it under the orders of the Government." 18 *Annals* 1659–60. Jefferson had earlier indicated his view that prior legislative authorization was required. See Jefferson to Dunbar, Mar. 13, 1804, 139 *Jefferson Papers* 24018, reel 48.

†In addition to the examples given *supra* 182–88, Randolph said in response to an effort by Griswold and Dana to obtain information relating to the closure of New Orleans (12 *Annals* 361):

By the Constitution of the United States, the Executive is the representative of the United States to foreign nations. It is furnished with organs by which to receive their propositions, and to communicate our own. The Con-

little effect.* Jefferson's system of "dual correspondence" was known to Congress, but left unchallenged.

In many situations the House or Senate refused to express its view on a matter, thereby leaving the President with the responsibility (and the power) to decide. For example, the Senate refused to determine whether France had complied fully with its agreement to sell the Louisiana Territory before appropriating the necessary funds, after argument that the function of construing treaties is executive.[193] The Senate also rejected a bill authorizing and regulating the President's dismissal of foreign ministers for misconduct. John Quincy Adams argued that legislative authority was necessary, because the President might dismiss for national differences, not just for misconduct, thereby committing an act "equivalent to a declaration of war" under the law of nations.† Republicans, however, regarded the legislation unnecessary and an implicit criticism of Jefferson's then-recent refusal to communicate further with the Spanish Minister.[194] Legislators also sought to have Congress autho-

---

stitution, therefore, presumes that to this department may be entirely confided our negotiations with foreign states. To this House is given the sole power to originate money bills, and the Constitution supposes that a perfect reliance may be had upon it for executing this all important trust. . . . The same confidence is reposed in the Executive with respect to exterior relations . . . [W]e have the same right to presume that the constituted authority would take the proper steps in relation to his department, that he has to presume that we will raise the necessary revenue and pass the proper laws.

*In the preceding instance, for example, Griswold and others argued that the information was necessary because the cession might require further efforts to protect the frontier. 12 Annals 312. See supra 185-86.

†15 Annals 152. In European nations, where the general grant of the executive power is deemed to include the power to declare war, said Adams, this distinction would be unimportant. "But our Constitution has expressly made the declaration of war a Legislative act, and by fair inference, whatever is by the customs of nations equivalent to a declaration of war, we are bound to consider as a Legislative act also." He conceded that the President possessed the power to refuse to receive a minister, but this he said "is not ordering him away, much less is it sending him home." The bill was necessary to make clear when the President could send ministers home, thereby removing any doubt on this important question. He strongly supported the view that the President should possess the power to remove ministers for misconduct: "considering the nature of a foreign Minister's privileges, and the danger and urgency of the cases wherein men invested with that character most frequently abuse them, to deny the President the exercise of the only means which can control them, is to deny the nation itself the means of self-defence in the most perilous extremities." He recognized that this argument could be used to justify allowing the President to remove foreign ministers for national differences, presumably because war could also result from a removal for misconduct. But he rejected its application, in language and theory very similar to that used by Madison writing as Helvidius (id. 154-55): "In every possible case when a public Minister could be ordered home on account of national differences Congress must be in session, or must be summoned for that purpose. Such a state of things cannot suddenly arise. It is a measure never to be resorted to, unless with the settled determination of war; and its exercise never can be necessary for the President, to the execution of his Constitutional powers."

rize the President to take New Orleans and the Floridas before their purchase from France,* to grant money for troops to punish Spain for its conduct in West Florida,[195] and after the *Chesapeake* affair to attack any British armed vessel that entered an American port.[196] But all these attempts to have Congress establish policy were defeated as extreme and too restrictive of executive discretion.

Perhaps indicative of Congress's attitude during this period is Representative Richard Johnson's (Ky.) pledge on December 11, 1807 that "he was one who would rally around and support the Executive in every measure which it might pursue in a conflict with a foreign power in vindication of the honor and rights of the people."[197] This kind of support was given, as the Federalist leader Samuel Dana noted, without the benefit of information adequate for Congressmen to form their own judgments of the situation.[198] Even Dana went along with the President at this stage, essentially on the rationale that, since the President was acting unilaterally and Congress was uninformed, the President would bear full responsibility for his actions.†

---

*The policy originally proposed by Alexander Hamilton was "to seize at once on the Floridas and New Orleans, and then negotiate." 10 *Works of Alexander Hamilton* 445-46 (H. Lodge ed. 1885). Negotiation might help, said Senator James Ross of Pennsylvania, but "more than negotiation was absolutely necessary, [and] . . . more power and more means ought to be given to the President, in order to render his negotiations efficacious." 12 *Annals* 83. He introduced resolutions stating that the United States have an indisputable right to navigate the Mississippi and to a place of deposit in New Orleans; that this right has been denied; that it was necessary to obtain "complete security" of the right; and that the President be authorized "to take immediate possession of such place or places, in the said island, or the adjacent territories, as he may deem fit and convenient for the purposes aforesaid," and to raise up to 50,000 militiamen and spend up to $5 million. *Id.* 94-96. The resolutions were defeated after Republicans called them a ploy to embarrass Jefferson, and an attempt unconstitutionally to transfer the war power from Congress to the President (12 *Annals* 215-16) (Mason):

> Gentlemen tell us that they are willing to entrust to the Executive the power of doing war, or not, at his discretion. . . . Why do not gentlemen give away that which they have some authority or right to bestow? Who gave them the power to vest in any other authority than in Congress the right of declaring war? The framers of this Constitution had too much experience to entrust such a power to any individual. . . .

†Dana said (17 *Annals* 1166):

> [T]here was not in the possession of the House a copy of any despatches relative to the affair of the Chesapeake; if they had not in possession any document which could give them precise information on the subject, it was not to be expected that they could be deliberate upon it; if this information was out of their possession and in the possession of the Executive, the whole course of proceeding rested with the Executive. . . . As the Executive magistrate had charge of foreign relations and the command of the whole public force, as this was a time of uncertainty and anxiety and as the House had not the control of public affairs, Mr. D. was disposed to give to the Executive that kind of force which he understood him as strongly recommending, though, not that which he himself preferred.

The legislature's awareness of the President's power to cause war in conducting foreign and military affairs is perhaps most clearly symbolized by a constitutional amendment proposed by Senator James Hillhouse of Connecticut. Hillhouse complained that the President had acquired "the power, not of declaring war in form, but of adopting a course of measures which will necessarily and inevitably lead to war."[199] No one questioned the validity of his analysis. But his suggested solution to the problem—that the President be selected from the Senate, for one-year terms—was ignored.[200]

Even as the President demonstrated his capacity to cause war, and as Congress confirmed and expanded that capacity, Congress showed itself able ultimately to control both foreign and military policy. Discretion over funds and other matters was delegated or allowed, for example, by conscious decision of the Republican majority. When a delegation was felt unnecessary or objectionable it was rejected, as in the numerous proposals to authorize the President to issue letters of marque and reprisal against British or French vessels interfering with American commerce.[201] Jefferson was allowed to conduct the nation's affairs with vigor and in secret because Congress largely supported his objectives and chose to let him lead. When the legislative majority wished to express its favored policy on a subject, even if only to support the President, it did so.[202] For example, in response to the President's report that good relations with Morocco had been restored, the Senate resolved, without recorded opposition, that "it is inexpedient for the United States to pursue further hostilities against the Emperor of Morocco, unless they should be rendered necessary by future aggressions."[203] Jefferson ultimately lost the legislature's support by determinedly pursuing the embargo.[204] Even this enormously powerful and influential President was, in the end, dependent upon the legislative will.

MILITARY ACTIONS AGAINST THE BARBARY POWERS

The only outright military conflicts during Jefferson's administration were with the Barbary powers. The underlying reasons for these conflicts were commercial: Tripoli, Algiers, Tunis and Morocco gained a considerable part of their revenue from piracy and extortion. The United States paid tribute to these powers while it had no navy with which to defend its commerce; even after a navy was built up, its use against the Barbary States was deferred during the Quasi-War with France. After that war ended in September 1800,[205] however, President Adams sent the frigate *George Washington* to the

Mediterranean with instructions to convoy and defend American vessels during the course of its journey.

When Jefferson took office on March 4, 1801, he had hoped to dismantle the navy, which he claimed to detest.[206] But news of the impressment of the *George Washington* by Algiers, and of increased demands by the Pasha of Tripoli, caused the President to order that a naval squadron be prepared for a Mediterranean expedition.[207]

Expedition Under Commodore Dale, 1801

In a letter to Wilson C. Nicholas, dated June 11, 1801, Jefferson said he had information that Tripoli had commenced depredations on American vessels during March, and that Stoddert and Samuel Smith (the former and acting Secretaries of the Navy) had recommended that three cruisers and a tender be sent to the Mediterranean "to protect our commerce against Tripoli. But as this might lead to war," he wrote, "I wished to have the approbation of the new administration. . . . It was the 15th of May before Mr. Gallatin's arrival enabled us to decide definitely."[208] The Cabinet decision of May 15, he reported, was unanimous, and the vessels sailed on June 1.

Discussion at the Cabinet meeting of May 15 focused on what actions the squadron could lawfully take against the Tripolitans if they attacked American vessels or declared war on the United States. Jefferson's notes indicate that Levi Lincoln felt "our men of war may repel an attack on individual vessels, but after the repulse, may not proceed to destroy the enemy's vessels generally." Gallatin disagreed:

> To declare war and to make war is synonymous. The exve cannot put us in a state of war, but if we be put into that state either by the decree of Congress or of the other nation, the command and direction of the public force then belongs to the exve.

Smith agreed with Gallatin. Dearborn and Madison stressed only that the cruise should go forward openly. Jefferson specifically asked: "[May] the Captains . . . be authorized, if war exists, to search for and destroy the enemy's vessels wherever they can find them?" All except Lincoln agreed they should, and three members felt "they may *pursue* into the harbours. . . ."[209]

Orders were issued to Commodore Richard Dale on May 20, 1801. They recited that the Tripolitans would probably attack American commerce unless it was protected, and told Dale to determine, on his arrival at Gibraltar, whether all or any of the Barbary powers had declared war against the United States. "[I]f there should be any cause for apprehension from either of those Powers [Algiers or Tripoli] , you must place your ships in a situation to chastise them, in case of their declaring War or committing hostilities." If all the Barbary powers had declared war against the United States, "you will then distribute your force in such manner . . . so as best to protect our commerce and chastise their insolence—by sinking, burning or destroying their ships and vessels wherever you shall find them." Dale was to control the ports of any of the nations that declared war, and to treat any prisoners taken with humanity "and land them on any part of the Barbary shore most convenient to you."[210] Unknown to Jefferson at the time, Tripoli had declared war on the United States on May 14.[211]

Legislative authority for sending an expedition to the Mediterranean was less than clear. Secretary of Navy Smith told Dale in his instructions that the President had ordered the Mediterranean cruise under the authority of a law passed during the last session of the Adams administration "providing for a Naval Peace Establishment." The act referred to provided only that six of the frigates retained "be kept in constant service in time of peace,"[212] and may have been passed to prevent the new President from putting the entire navy out of commission.[213] Smith's orders construed the law to require the President to employ a part of the navy. He said the President had ordered the expedition because he was "anxious to promote the views of the Constituted authorities," and because "one great object of the present squadron is to instruct our Young officers. . . ."[214] Authority for the expedition seems therefore to have been based on the position that power to utilize the naval forces may be inferred from legislation merely providing such forces.

When Dale reached Gibraltar he found two Tripolitan vessels there, one with Tripoli's naval commander. He still did not definitely know that Tripoli had declared war, so he merely blockaded rather than captured the vessels. "What a pity he did not know of the war," Jefferson wrote Madison on September 12, 1801, so "he might have taken their admiral and his ship."[215] By July 24, 1801, however, when he arrived at Tripoli, Dale had learned of the war. He warned the Pasha that he intended to take Tripolitan vessels and subjects at every opportunity,[216] and issued orders implementing this threat to the captains of vessels in his squadron.[217]

The tender vessel to Dale's squadron was the 12-gun schooner *Enterprise*, commanded by Lt. Andrew Sterrett. Dale ordered Sterrett on July 30, 1801 to sail to Malta to obtain water for the squadron and to return to Dale's station off Tripoli.[218] He anticipated that Sterrett might meet and engage Tripolitan vessels, and instructed

THE BARBARY POWERS

(Map No. 1)

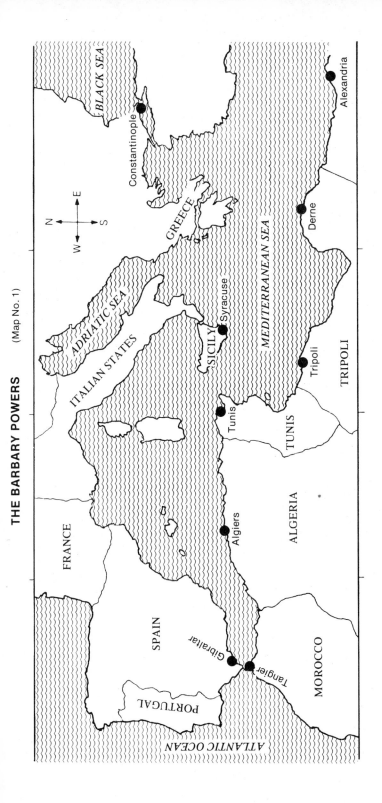

Adapted from "Map of the Mediterranean Region," 1 *Naval Documents Related to the United States Wars with the Barbary Powers* 140 (Office of Naval Records, 1939).

211

him, if an engagement occurred on his way back from Malta, to seize and return with any captured vessels if he could do so safely. On his passage to Malta, however, Sterrett was told to engage any corsair he could manage, but instead of capturing the vessel to "heave all his Guns Over board Cut away his Masts, and leave him In a situation, that he can Just make out to get into some Port." Dale warned Sterrett not to "chace [sic] out of your way particularly in going, as you have not much water on board."[219]

On August 1, just after leaving Gibraltar, Sterrett encountered a 14-gun Tripolitan cruiser. After three hours of intense battle, the *Enterprise* was victorious. Sterrett ordered the cruiser stripped of its guns and masts and set adrift.[220] He then proceeded on his assigned journey to Malta.

Jefferson had received a full report of Sterrett's victory by December 8, 1801, when he delivered his first annual message to Congress. He told Congress he had sent a squadron to the Mediterranean "with orders to protect our commerce against . . . threatened attack," and that its arrival was timely, since Tripoli had meanwhile declared war and blockaded the area. He then reported on Sterrett's encounter, attributing the release of the Tripolitan vessel to constitutional rather than tactical considerations:

> Unauthorized by the Constitution, without the sanction of Congress, to go beyond the line of defense, the vessel, being disabled from committing further hostilities, was liberated with its crew. The Legislature will doubtless consider whether, by authorizing measures of offence also, they will place our force on an equal footing with that of its adversaries. I communicate all material information on this subject, that, in the exercise of this important function confided by the Constitution to the Legislature exclusively, their judgment may form itself on a knowledge and consideration of every circumstance of weight.[221]

Most commentators have accepted this famous statement of deference to Congress as accurate and made in good faith.[222] Actually, as we have seen, the Cabinet had authorized offensive actions, and Dale had been instructed accordingly.* Sterrett released the corsair

---

*The paragraph in Dale's instructions that deals with a possible declaration of war by Tripoli alone commands a blockade and cruising under disguise to "give you a fair chance of punishing" the Tripolitan vessels, and otherwise contains no explicit authority to destroy them. A strained argument could therefore be made that Jefferson had not authorized offensive actions in the event of a war with Tripoli alone, though a more likely reason for the language is that Tripoli was regarded by Jefferson as "the least considerable" of the Barbary states (11 *Annals* 12), and as such might have been expected to disguise its vessels or keep them in harbors. In any event, the contention would have no doctrinal significance. The instructions to Dale clearly authorized offensive actions against Algiers alone, against all the powers together, and probably against Tunis, acting alone or in

for purely tactical reasons, because he was on his way to Malta, rather than on his way back.

This fact would have been clear to Congress, had Jefferson indeed communicated "all material information," as he said he would. On December 8 he sent various letters to Congress providing background, and revealing that Dale's squadron was being dispatched to protect American commerce. On December 22, after the House had already discussed Jefferson's request for authority, he sent documents describing Sterrett's encounter, as well as the instructions given Dale. The instructions made clear that Dale had authority to sink, burn and destroy vessels, but nothing Jefferson sent made clear that Dale had authorized Sterrett to take offensive actions against Tripoli. Sterrett had returned to the United States by November 17, 1801, and presumably had supplied the administration with the instructions issued to him by Dale on July 30, 1801.[223]

These facts undermine the importance widely attributed to Jefferson's statement to Congress regarding Sterrett's conduct. But the orders issued to and by Dale, even as broadly construed, seem constitutionally defensible under even a relatively narrow view of executive power. The grant of authority to Dale to protect American commerce from attack was no broader in principle than the orders issued under Adams to Bainbridge in 1800. All other authority granted was conditioned on any of the Barbary powers declaring or making war. The Framers had not explicitly considered how much power the President possessed to act militarily against a nation that had declared war upon the United States. One might reasonably infer, however, from the power to defend against attacks on the United States—universally held to be granted by the Framers—a power to act offensively against any nation that declared and made war. This was the view adopted by both Gallatin and Hamilton, and probably by Madison as well.* Hamilton, in an attack on Jefferson's first an-

---

concert with Tripoli. 1 *Naval Documents Related to the United States War with the Barbary Powers* 467 (1939). So, even assuming that Jefferson ordered only defensive actions in the event Tripoli alone declared war, he did so for some pragmatic reason and not from any principled belief that Congress had to be consulted before offensive actions could be authorized against a power that had declared war on the United States. Indeed, the orders to Dale seem to permit the squadron to capture and destroy ships that attacked American commerce even if war had not been declared, and the statement in the orders that prisoners be put ashore suggests that the capture and destruction of vessels were contemplated. *Id.*

*Much later, on Nov. 16, 1827, Madison wrote to James Monroe: "The only case in which the Executive can enter on a war, undeclared by Congress, is when a state of war has 'been actually' produced by the conduct of another power, and then it ought to be made known as soon as possible to the Department charged with the war power. Such a case was the war with Tripoli during the administration of Mr. Jefferson." 3 *Letters and Other Writings of James Madison* 600 (Cong. ed. 1867).

nual address, called it "a very extraordinary position" that "between two nations there may exist a state of complete war on the one side and of peace on the other." The sanction of Congress was not needed in such an instance to wage war offensively, he said, for the state of war had been thrust upon us making "nugatory" Congress's exclusive province to change our position into a state of war.[224]

We can only speculate on Jefferson's motivation in suggesting to Congress that he lacked the power to act offensively against a nation that had both declared and made war on the United States. Probably he wanted Congress's explicit approval of military actions against Tripoli. His statement provided a basis for sharing with Congress responsibility for the intensity with which the war was to be conducted. His message to Congress specifically asked for authority for "measures of offense," the granting of which would enable him to dispatch expeditions such as Dale's without basing their legality on the sole fact that vessels of war had been constructed and placed within his power to utilize.

If Jefferson's description of Lt. Sterrett's conduct was intended to cause Congress to authorize offensive actions, he succeeded. Debate on the Mediterranean situation began on December 14, 1801, even before the information Jefferson promised had been provided, when Representative Samuel Smith said that Congress should "immediately . . . come to a decision that would enable the President more efficiently to protect our trade." He proposed "that the President be authorized by law, further and more effectually to protect the commerce of the United States against the Barbary Powers."

Joseph Nicholson of New York disliked the resolution because it expressed approval of the expedition before the House was fully informed. He therefore moved to strike the words "further and more effectually." He renewed this motion the next day, arguing that unless "further and more" were struck, the House would "pledge ourselves to increase the naval force at present at the disposition of the President"; there was no reason to make such a pledge, argued Nicholson, until the President asked for more ships.[225]

Representatives Eustis, Giles, and Samuel Smith disagreed with Nicholson's construction. The resolution concerns, not the quantum of force under executive disposition, said Giles, but "the measures proposed to be taken by the Executive." "The President . . . has informed us that he has hitherto acted on the defensive," said Eustis; the "question now is, whether he shall be empowered to take offensive steps." Smith said that, since we are at war with Tripoli, "the President felt himself at liberty to act efficiently" against that power; but it was necessary to give him authority to act against Algiers and Tunis in case they attacked our trade, especially in the recess of Congress. Nicholson's amendment lost, and Smith's original resolution passed.[226]

The committee appointed to draft a bill pursuant to this resolution reported on January 7, 1802. The recommended legislation would have empowered the President "fully to equip and employ such vessels . . . as he shall deem requisite" to protect American commerce and seamen in the Mediterranean and adjoining seas; "that they be empowered to capture Tripolitan vessels; and that the President be authorized to commission private vessels, with power to capture vessels of Tripoli."[227]

Debate in Committee of the Whole was brief. No one objected to the authority conferred with respect to Tripoli. But Bayard sought to amend the act to extend the President's power to grant letters of marque and reprisal to Algiers and Tunis, as Smith's resolution had implied. Dana objected that the amendment appeared to invite war. Bayard countered that "there was a great difference between the Barbary Powers and civilized nations; it was on account of the perfidiousness of those Powers, that he wished it left to the direction of the President to exercise the power vested in him when he should think proper. . . ." He wanted the President to act by authority of law, moreover, to "prevent those doubts that have been expressed, by some, of the constitutionality of his measures the last Spring and Summer; though . . . he was disposed to approbate the proceedings of the Executive on that occasion." Dana and Giles objected, but Bayard persisted in his motion: "The gentleman from Connecticut [Mr. Dana] says that there are no doubts on his mind but that the President has a Constitutional right, as the Commander-in-Chief of the Army and Navy, to do as he has done; but it should be remembered that many have doubts; and why should the gentleman be opposed to this amendment, which will preclude all doubt on the subject?" Bayard's motion to give Jefferson power to grant letters of marque and reprisal against vessels of Algiers and Tunis was defeated without a division, and the bill passed the House on January 22, 1802.[228]

The Senate passed the bill unamended on February 1, rejecting motions to strike the provisions allowing the President to grant letters of marque and reprisal under certain conditions to private vessels, and to add to the preamble a statement that "a state of war now exists with" Tripoli.[229] In its final form the act gave explicit authority to the President to capture and make prizes of any Tripolitan vessel, and in sweeping terms "to cause to be done all such other acts of precaution or hostility as the state of war will justify, and may, in his opinion, require."[230]

Several aspects of Congress's response are worth noting. First, although Bayard claimed that some had doubts about the constitutionality of Jefferson's orders to Dale, no one actually expressed such doubts. On the other hand, the resolution and law were passed in response to Jefferson's message, suggesting that Congress regarded the President's asserted need for authority as at least tenable.* That the House rejected an effort to authorize the President to grant letters of marque and reprisal with respect to vessels of Algiers and Tunis is too ambiguous an act to suggest an understanding that the President could not move offensively against those powers if they declared war on the United States. It does indicate, however, that the House regarded the grant of such a power as inviting war, and they were unwilling to delegate such authority even with respect to "uncivilized" nations. The law eventually passed delegated broad authority to the President to act so long as a state of war existed, perhaps as much authority as a declaration of war would have delegated. Finally, some Representatives viewed Congress's action as effectively approving what Jefferson had already done, suggesting that they assumed legislative approval for military actions could be given retroactively.

Efforts to Overthrow the Pasha from Within

Congress's broad delegation to the President of power to conduct the war against Tripoli led to several naval encounters, some spec-

---

*Actually, Congress would probably have accepted a claim that expeditions such as Dale's could be undertaken on executive order, once the necessary vessels were provided. This is suggested by numerous factors, including an exchange that occurred after the House Committee of Ways and Means introduced a bill on March 21, 1804, which provided for a tax to finance Mideast operations. 13 Annals 1204. Griswold contended the next day that no adequate showing had been made that additional funds were actually needed. Id. 1212, 1213. Nicholson affirmed his confidence that the President would effectually utilize the vessels provided, claiming his sole object was to give the President "the power of using the means of the United States with energy; leaving the discretion in him, as it necessarily must be, to use it as he should think proper. If we were about to raise an army to commence hostilities against a foreign nation," said Nicholson, "it would not be the province of the House to inquire how it should be directed. Having authorized the raising and equipping it, it would forthwith come solely under the power of the Executive Department—our power being confined to supplying the means by which it may be raised." Id. 1214. Dana, who joined Griswold in opposing the tax, agreed "that, after the force is raised, the President, in virtue of his authority as Commander-in-Chief, is to have its whole direction; but it is perfectly novel to me to learn that we are not previously to be informed of the extent to which it is proposed to carry it." Id. 1218. The bill passed both houses, however (id. 1225, id. 303), and in its final form imposed a tax for the purpose of defraying the expenses of equipping, officering, manning and employing the vessels deemed necessary by the President to protect American commerce and seamen "and for carrying on warlike operations against the Regency of Tripoli, or any other of the Barbary Powers, which may commit hostilities against the United States. . . ." Act of March 26, 1804, 2 Stat. 291.

tacular, but all well within the general understanding of the actions contemplated.* One extraordinary military plan was undertaken, however, that no member of Congress could have anticipated. It was to promote the overthrow of the Pasha of Tripoli by his exiled brother, in exchange for the brother's commitment to grant substantial concessions to the United States. The enterprise is noteworthy because it represents the first intervention by United States forces and agents in the domestic affairs of another nation, establishing a pattern against which subsequent interventions may be compared.

Soon after Jefferson's decision to send a squadron to the Mediterranean under Dale, information reached Washington of a plan to overthrow the Pasha of Tripoli. The Pasha—Joseph Caramanly—was no angel. He had murdered his father and eldest brother to become ruler. Another older brother, Hamet, fled the country to avoid a similar fate. James L. Cathcart, American consul at Tripoli, focused on Hamet as the tool for achieving a stable relationship with Tripoli. He suggested to Madison, in a letter dated July 2, 1801, the possibility of "dethroning the present Bashaw, and effecting a revolution in favor of his brother Hamet, who is at Tunis, and thereby insure the United States the gratitude of him and his successors: for so long as Joseph the Bashaw lives, our commerce will not be secure." He said he had requested William Eaton, consul at Tunis, "to ascertain how far said Hamet would be willing to engage in an expedition of that nature," noting that even Hamet's presence on board an American vessel would panic his brother and promote American interests.[231]

On September 5, 1801, Eaton reported to Madison on what he now described as a project to join with "the rightful" Pasha in an attack by land, "while our operations are going on by sea." The present ruler's subjects were very discontented, he wrote,[232] and "would rise *en masse* to receive" Hamet.[233] Eaton's plan seemed foiled when, in March 1802, Hamet accepted Joseph's offer to return to govern Derne and Benghazi, in part no doubt because Joseph held Hamet's wife and children as hostages. But Eaton, acting without prior authority even from Cathcart, prevailed upon Hamet to change his mind.[234]

By August 22, 1802, Secretary of State Madison had received word of Eaton's actions, designed to make "use of [Hamet] against

---

*For example, on October 31, 1803, the frigate *Philadelphia* was captured while pursuing a Tripolitan vessel near the shore. Commander Stephen Decatur and a small band of followers destroyed the *Philadelphia* in Tripoli's harbor, under heavy fire, on February 16, 1804, so that the vessel could not be used against American forces. Lord Nelson characterized this exploit as "the most bold and daring act of the age." G. Allen, *Our Navy and the Barbary Corsairs* 173 (1905).

the Bashaw." Madison noted in a letter to Cathcart how difficult it would be to judge and manage Eaton's project from so great a distance. He also added that "it does not accord with the general sentiments or views of the United States to intermeddle with the domestic controversies of other countries. . . ." But by then Congress had authorized all "acts of precaution or hostility as the state of war will justify," and Madison could not resist the project, writing that "it cannot be unfair, in the prosecution of a just war, or the accomplishment of a reasonable peace, to take advantage of the hostile cooperation of others." He anticipated the possibility that Hamet's object might be unattainable, and said the honor of the United States and "the expectations he will have naturally formed" would require America "to treat his disappointment with much tenderness; and to restore him, as nearly as may be, to the situation from which he was drawn. . . ."[235] But he authorized cooperating with Hamet only "[a]s far . . . as the views of the brother may contribute to our success"; Secretary of Navy Smith ordered Commodore Richard V. Morris on August 28 that Hamet was not to be an obstacle to achieving an acceptable peace with Tripoli.[236]

The plan to cooperate with Hamet was deferred, in part because the American squadron was temporarily withdrawn from the Mediterranean. On May 26, 1804, however, Jefferson recorded that the Cabinet decided to furnish $20,000 to "the Ex-Bashaw [Hamet] to engage cooperation."[237] On May 30, Eaton was appointed "Navy Agent" for the Barbary powers, apparently as a prelude to a new initiative.[238] On June 6, orders were issued to Commodore Samuel Barron, commander of a new Mediterranean expedition, to use Hamet's cooperation if he found it expedient.[239] At the same time, Tobias Lear was commissioned to negotiate a peace with the ruling Pasha, but informed by Madison that "we are still willing to avail ourselves" of Hamet's cooperation, if Barron deemed it useful.[240]

Hamet, meanwhile, had settled in Egypt. On September 13, 1804, Barron put the plan to cooperate with Hamet into motion. He ordered Captain Isaac Hull in writing to take the *Argus* to Alexandria purportedly for refitting and other innocuous purposes. Actually, as later reported, Hull's true orders were verbal, the written ones being "intended to disguise the real object of your expedition, which is to proceed with Mr. Eaton to Alexandria, in search of Hamet—and to convey him and his suit" to such "place on the coast as may be determined the most proper for cooperating with the naval force under my command. . . ."[241] Hull was authorized to assure Hamet of Barron's "most effectual" cooperation "against the usurper," and in reestablishing Hamet as Pasha.

On Januray 3, 1805, Hamet wrote Eaton, agreeing to cooperate. Eaton wrote Barron and the Secretary of the Navy in February that plans had been made whereby Hamet was to proceed by land to Derne, with naval support at that place, and ultimately to Tripoli. The cost of the expedition, meanwhile, had climbed at least $10,000 beyond the $20,000 authorized, and Eaton requested some field artillery and 100 Marines. Hamet had promised, Eaton reported, that the extra funds would be repaid as soon as he was established in Derne and Benghazi; and he pledged the tribute of certain nations to pay American expenses if he became Pasha. A convention describing the commitments undertaken by both sides, and requiring the United States to aid Hamet "so far as comports with their own honor and interest" was signed by Hamet and Eaton on February 23.[242]

The possibility of facing a joint action between Hamet and Barron led the ruling Pasha to seek peace. In this project he obtained invaluable help from Captain Bainbridge, who as a prisoner of the Pasha warned Barron with considerable urgency that all American prisoners (about 300) would be killed by Joseph if Hamet's expedition succeeded.[243] In addition, the Danish Consul, Nicholas C. Nissen, acted as intermediary between the Pasha and Barron, and managed to get negotiations started.[244]

Apparently responding to the changing circumstances, Barron warned Eaton, in a letter dated March 22, against committing the United States to placing Hamet upon the throne. "The consequences involved in such an engagement cannot but strike you forcibly, and a general view of our situation, in relation to the reigning Bashaw and our unfortunate countrymen in Tripoli, will be sufficient to work its inexpediency." He promised every aid within his authority and means, but told Eaton that "no guarantee or engagement to the exiled prince, whose cause, I must repeat, we are only favoring as an instrument to our advantage . . . must be held to stand in the way of our acquiescence to any honorable and advantageous terms of accommodation which the reigning Bashaw may be induced to propose. . . ." The final outcome, he said, would depend on Hamet's capacity and popularity once he gained possession of Derne; "should he be found deficient . . . he must be held as an unfit subject for further support or cooperation." He denied Eaton's request for 100 Marines. On April 6 Barron sent this letter to the Secretary of the Navy, adding that reports he had received of Hamet's character made him less hopeful of the project, and that the contest was likely to be more arduous than anticipated.[245]

Meanwhile, the army Eaton and Hamet had put together was on the move. It was a motley conglomeration, consisting of a handful of Americans, some Greek mercenaries, and about 2,000 Arabs, all hired for the purpose, with their women and children. Nevertheless, this group managed to conquer Derne. Eaton was forced, however, to seek further fiscal and military support. He had already spent $30,000, but urged Barron to exercise "the unlimited discretion vested in the Commander-in-Chief, in regard to all the exigencies of war," by exceeding the Secretary of the Navy's instructions. While Eaton felt victory was obtainable, and thought it would be morally improper to discard Hamet, he cautioned Barron that Hamet and his men lacked the ability, following, and resources to take Tripoli without substantial American military and fiscal support.[246]

On receiving this news, Barron wrote to Lear that Hamet's "want of energy and military talents, his total deprivation of means and resources, the great expense already incurred, and the large sum which would be required ... far exceeding both the resources placed at my disposal, and the powers vested in me by my instructions, compel me to relinquish the plan."[247] He believed, however, that the seizure of Derne would cause the reigning Pasha to moderate his demands, and urged Lear to accept Joseph's overtures for negotiation. Barron repeated much of this to Eaton, explicitly terminating American support.[248] On June 3, a treaty between Tripoli and the United States was signed, which required the withdrawal of American forces and support, granted many privileges to American trade, and provided for the eventual release of all American prisoners and Hamet's family.[249] Eaton received word of this on June 11, and managed to evacuate Hamet and his retinue, the Greeks and the Americans, leaving their cursing Arab supporters to the mercies of Joseph.*

Eaton returned to America a hero.[250] Hamet applied to Jefferson

---

*This is how Eaton described the evacuation in a letter to Commodore John Rodgers, June 13, 1805, in C. Prentiss, ed., *The Life of the Late General William Eaton* 362-63 (1813):

[A]ll the Constellation's boats were laid along side our wharf. I ordered the Captain of cannoniers to embark his company with the field pieces and a ten inch howitzer which fell into our hands on the 27th of April; and after them the Greek company. This was executed with silence and alacrity; but with astonishment. The marines remained at their posts. When the boats were seen returning I sent a messenger to the Bashaw requesting an interview. Understanding the purport of this message, he immediately repaired to the fort with his retinue; dismounted, and embarked in the boats. The marines followed with the American officers. When all were securely off, I stepped into a small boat which I had retained for the purpose, and had just time to save my distance when the shore, our camp, and the battery, were crowded with the distracted soldiery and populace; some calling on the Bashaw; some on me; some uttering shrieks; some execrations! Finding we were out of reach, they fell upon our tents and horses, which were left standing; carried them off, and prepared themselves for flight.

for financial relief, basing his claim in part on an alleged commitment by the United States to place him upon the throne.[251] Jefferson communicated this request to Congress, along with relevant correspondence.[252] He had earlier recognized that the operation with Hamet "contributed doubtless to the impression which produced peace";[253] but he rejected Hamet's claim, as well as Eaton's support for it, strongly suggesting to Congress that Eaton's zeal led him to exceed his authority.[254] A Senate committee presented, on March 17, 1806, a report highly critical of the government's abandonment of Hamet, and recommended a bill for Hamet's support.[255] After considerable debate, Hamet received a modest payment;[256] Eaton was more handsomely rewarded.[257] No one raised any question, however, concerning the legality or propriety of the joint action with Hamet. Everyone apparently assumed that the sweeping delegation— "to cause to be done all such other acts of precaution or hostility as the state of war will justify, and may, in his opinion, require,"[258]— granted in response to Jefferson's report of Sterrett's encounter, extended to the plan to make Hamet Pasha. The only significant complaint heard in Congress was that the President reneged on his alliance with Hamet, not that he had made one.

Difficulties with Morocco

The scope of the President's unilateral authority to act against attacks upon American vessels, or against a nation that had declared war on the United States, became an issue again in 1802, only a few months after Jefferson reported to Congress on Sterrett's encounter.

Although an American blockade of Tripoli was in effect during early 1802, the Emperor of Morocco granted permission to the Tripolitan ambassador to take wheat to Tripoli, and agreed to assist in securing the release of the crew of a Tripolitan vessel blockaded at Gibraltar. American naval commanders on the scene refused to grant passports to the Emperor's vessels for these ventures. The Emperor thereupon ordered away the American Consul, James Simpson, and declared war on the United States. He allowed Simpson to return soon thereafter, however, and an agreement was reached that restored peace.[259]

Jefferson learned that Consul Simpson had been ordered away from Morocco before hearing that war had been declared. He wrote to Gallatin from Monticello on August 9, 1802, that he intended to leave extra frigates in the Mediterranean to deal with the emergency. "And a very important question is," he said, "what is the nature of the orders which should be given to the commanders of our vessels in the Mediterranean with respect to Morocco? As circumstances look towards war, I have asked the opinions of the heads of Departments on the preceding questions. . . ."²⁶⁰ Gallatin responded on August 16, 1802, urging compromise and gifts, but reiterating his view that the President could fight, capture or destroy vessels of any nation that made war on the United States:

> The executive cannot declare war, but if war is made, whether declared by Congress or by the enemy, the conduct must be the same, to protect our vessels, and to fight, take, and destroy the armed vessels of that enemy. The only case which admits of doubt is whether, in case of such war actually existing, we should confine our hostilities to their armed vessels or extend them by capture or blockage to the trade. The policy of adopting either course must depend on the power we may have to injure that commerce.²⁶¹

Secretary of War Dearborn, like Gallatin, advised Jefferson, on August 15, that he should order American officers to protect United States commerce "by all means in [their] power against any of the Barbary Powers who shall declare war or actually commence war upon the United States."²⁶² Secretary of Navy Smith limited his advice to a situation of declared war, recommending that Jefferson instruct the officers to defend American commerce against Morocco or any other Barbary power that may have declared war, and "in such case to proceed against [them] in the same manner as they have been authorized with respect to Tripoli."²⁶³

By August 20 Jefferson and the Cabinet appear to have been informed of Morocco's declaration of war. On August 23 Jefferson wrote Madison that he had approved Smith's suggestion that another frigate be sent to the Mediterranean in addition to the *New York*.²⁶⁴ About five days later, Secretary Smith issued an order to Commodore Morris, in the Mediterranean, that as Morocco had declared war the President instructed Morris "to protect our Commerce by all the means in your Power against the armed vessels of any Barbary State that may either declare or wage War against us. The *New York* is dispatched to join your Squadron and you will soon receive as a further reenforcement the *John Adams*."²⁶⁵

On August 30, after learning from newspaper accounts that Simpson had been recalled to Morocco, Jefferson wrote Smith that sending the *John Adams* may be "unnecessary" and "an improper use of the confidence reposed in us by Congress. That tho they gave us extensive authority to arm yet they *trusted* we would employ it no further than should be basically necessary."²⁶⁶ Smith, however, evidently believing that a show of force would help keep peace,²⁶⁷ wrote Jefferson on September 14 that he would prefer keeping the

John Adams in readiness.[268] Jefferson yielded and, after conferring with Madison, concluded that the advantages of the voyage outweighed its expense.[269]

The uncertainties caused by Morocco's behavior led Jefferson to include in the draft of his annual message of December 1802 a request for legislative authority "to act offensively in case of war declared or waged by . . . Barbary Powers" other than Tripoli.[270] When Gallatin read the draft he expressed surprise. He felt the President already possessed authority to act offensively against a nation that declared or waged war, and accurately recalled that such a power had been exercised against Tripoli.* "It is true," he said, "that the message of last year adopted a different construction of the Constitution," referring to Jefferson's explanation for why Sterrett had not captured the Tripolitan corsair. "[B]ut how that took place," said Gallatin, "I do not recollect."[271] Jefferson removed the request for authority from his draft address.

A final incident contributes to an understanding of how Jefferson viewed his authority to take offensive measures against a nation that made war on the United States. It took place during July 1803. Captain William Bainbridge, at that time commanding the frigate *Philadelphia*, encountered the Moroccan frigate *Mirboka*, and discovered that she had captured an American brig. He learned that the Captain of the *Mirboka* had been secretly instructed to capture Americans, contrary to a treaty Morocco had made with the United States. Bainbridge held the Moroccans as prisoners of war, and during September several American vessels made a show of force at Tangier Bay. This led the Emperor to recognize the blockade of Tripoli, to release an American brig, and to reestablish friendly relations.[272]

The President informed Congress of Captain Bainbridge's seizure of the Moroccan frigate on November 4, 1803. He reported the capture without intimating in any way that Bainbridge lacked authority to do exactly what Lt. Sterrett had *not* done; indeed, he said it was "fortunate" that Bainbridge had taken the vessel. He noted that in-

---

*Gallatin wrote:

I do not and never did believe that it was necessary to obtain a legislative sanction in the last case: whenever war does exist whether by the declaration of the United States or by the declaration or act of a foreign nation, I think that the Executive has a right, and is in duty bound, to apply the public force which he may have the means legally to employ, in the most effective manner to annoy the enemy. If the instructions given in May or June, 1801, by the Navy Department to the commander of the Mediterranean squadron [Dale] shall be examined, it will be found that they were drawn in conformity to that doctrine; and that was the result of a long Cabinet discussion on that very ground.

Gallatin to Jefferson, Dec. 1802, 1 *Gallatin Writings* 105.

quiries were being made as to the state of affairs between Morocco and America, and said it was "for Congress to consider the provisional authorities which may be necessary to restrain the depredations of this Power, should they be continued."[273] A bill to confer power on the President was promptly considered, and passed the House unanimously on November 17.* William Eustis observed that the bill was "an exact transcript" of the act passed in 1801 concerning Tripoli.[274]

Before the act to confer additional authority for actions against Morocco was passed by the Senate, the President informed both houses that all differences with Morocco had been amicably adjusted. He praised all the officers involved, including Captain Bainbridge, for "the proper decision . . . that a vessel which had committed an open hostility, was of right to be detained for inquiry and consideration. . . ."[275] Once again Jefferson was far from forthright, apparently to avoid taking a position inconsistent with his report on Sterrett's encounter. His suggestion that Bainbridge meant only to detain the Moroccan vessel had no basis in fact. The *Mirboka* was returned to Morocco, but only as part of a negotiated settlement.[276] Furthermore, Jefferson himself treated the seizure as a capture by recommending "a just idemnification for the interest acquired by the captors," a suggestion Congress adopted.[277]

CONCLUSION

The presidency of Thomas Jefferson was, in retrospect, a test of the extent to which the doctrinal differences that separated Republicans from Federalists really mattered. An implementation of Republican principles would have caused a shift from the pattern of executive leadership in foreign and military affairs to greater congressional input and control.

In reality, little changed. Jefferson more probably increased the powers of the President at the expense of Congress. This came about in part through the outright abandonment of Republican principles. Republicans averse to allowing the likes of Washington, Adams, Hamilton, Randolph, Pickering and Knox to plan fiscal, foreign and military policies were willing if not downright eager to have their

---

*Just before the vote was taken, Crowninshield moved an amendment to the first section to deny authority to capture or detain any vessel bearing the flag of a European power, even if it contained goods bound for Morocco, unless the goods were contraband. Dana opposed on the ground that "the nature of the instructions to commanders of American vessels was confided to the President, who would, no doubt, adopt such regulations as should be proper." The amendment was easily defeated. 13 *Annals* 563-64.

own leaders—Jefferson, Gallatin and Madison—do so. Spending discretion was never curbed, and the vehement arguments raised by Republicans against broad delegations of power over foreign and military affairs in prior administrations were recalled only by Federalists and a handful of Republican renegades. After some reductions in the army and navy, Jefferson recommended and obtained increases necessary to implement the embargo and to control and absorb the territory of Louisiana.

Jefferson also broadly construed his authority to conduct foreign and military affairs. He conducted diplomacy with vigor and in secret, making informal threats and promises to obtain concessions. He unilaterally authorized seizures of armed vessels, in waters extending to the Gulf Stream, under circumstances that might have led to conflicts, and otherwise condoned military movements and actions that could have caused serious complications. In sending Dale to the Mediterranean he construed a statute that simply provided naval vessels as sufficient authority to order an expedition to an area where those vessels were likely to become engaged in the forceful defense of American commerce.

Schachner neatly sums up Jefferson's early doctrinal posture: "Stick to the Constitution, he warned; do not attempt to prostitute our laws and system of jurisprudence on the basis of interpretive shadings of convenience."[278] But by 1807 Jefferson had arrived at an interpretation of the executive clause that amounted to a complete justification for adopting any measure necessary to accomplish an authorized end. "[I]f means specified by an act are impracticable," he said, "the constitutional power [to carry laws into execution] remains, and supplies them."[279] Utterly frustrated by the departures from Republican doctrine—and unalterably alienated from Jefferson—John Randolph described this political experience as having taught him there were only "two parties in all States—the *ins* and *outs*; the *ins* desirous so to construe the charter of the Government as to give themselves the greatest possible degree of patronage and wealth; and the *outs* striving to construe it so as to circumscribe . . . their adversaries' power. But let the *outs* get in . . . and you will find their Constitutional scruples and arguments vanish like dew before the morning sun."[280]

Jefferson's abandonment of Republican ideology would be of little concern if judging his achievements were the sole objective. His achievements were substantial, and most would agree far outweighed his failure to adhere to the constitutional philosophy he inflicted upon himself. Furthermore, Jefferson had prior congressional approval for virtually all the broad objectives he sought: acquisition of

New Orleans and West Florida; protection of neutral commerce and jurisdictional waters; suppression of piracy. He was freewheeling in implementing these policies, making promises and "predictions" that could only have been interpreted as threats. But he exercised great care when utilizing the armed forces, successfully avoiding war with the major powers. He acted without consulting Congress in some important situations. But like Washington he acted without recalling Congress in order to avoid legislative pressure to go to war, rather than to prevent Congress from deciding against war at an early stage. Had Jefferson shared Hamilton's more robust view of executive power, or even the moderate, principled views of his brilliant advisor Albert Gallatin, he would have been able to carry out most if not all his plans without constitutional inconsistency and embarrassment.

Jefferson did more, however, than merely abandon Republican doctrine for Federalist principles. He engaged in new practices and offered new justifications in order to escape his doctrinal strait-jacket. Perhaps the most important new practice he implemented affecting the control of foreign relations was to use designations of "private" or "confidential" to keep some public and official diplomatic correspondence and other information from Congress. Any official information would, under Republican doctrine, have been subject to legislative call. Instead of openly assuming and exercising a power to withhold material for public considerations, as Washington had done, Jefferson seems to have preferred to avoid potential doctrinal confrontations and legislative interference by simply keeping Congress— and in the Burr trial, a federal court—ignorant of information within his possession or control.

The most important new doctrine he invoked came after the *Chesapeake* affair, when he ordered purchases of arms and supplies that had not been authorized by Congress. The purchases conflicted with Republican theory, under which the executive could spend only appropriated funds for authorized purposes. Rather than reexamine and reshape Republican theory to allow for conduct he felt essential to the nation's well-being, Jefferson supplemented that theory with a doctrine of emergency power, similar to the King's prerogative as Locke had explained it. Under that doctrine, as applied by Jefferson, a President is permitted to violate the Constitution in an emergency, though he does so at the risk of having his judgment rejected by the legislature or the people. Jefferson's conviction that the executive lacked power to spend for defense during a legislative recess was thereby preserved in theory, but ignored in practice; and the practice was rationalized by a doctrinal assertion that conferred discretion upon the executive to take any form of action deemed necessary to deal with any situation perceived as an emergency. He later invoked the same theory to explain why he had subordinated his constitutional scruples in allowing Louisiana to be absorbed without a constitutional amendment:

> A strict observance of the written laws is doubtless *one* of the high duties of a good citizen, but it is not *the highest*. The laws of necessity, of self preservation, of saving our country when in danger, are of higher obligation. To lose our country by a scrupulous adherence to written law, would be to lose the law itself, with life, liberty, property and all those who are enjoying them with us; thus absurdly sacrificing the end to the means.[281]

A tenable argument can therefore be made that doctrinal differences between Jefferson and the Federalists did indeed matter. The differences did not, as intended, deter Jefferson and most Republicans from doing the very things one might have expected a strong Federalist leader and legislative majority to do. Vigorous, inventive leadership was part of Jefferson's nature, and widely regarded by Congress and the public as essential at that time in the nation's history. But the strictures of Republican doctrine may well account for Jefferson's developing a system of secrecy largely immune from legislative check, and invoking a doctrine of emergency power that relegated the legislature to the exercise of extreme after-the-fact remedies in all national crises. These new developments may have had little real importance in Jefferson's time, since most of his conduct can be rationalized under a more robust but precedented view of executive authority. Nothing, however, prevented future Presidents from using and extending the practices and principles applied by Jefferson to situations far more constitutionally objectionable than those in which he invoked them.

※ *Chapter 5*

The Post-Jeffersonian Republicans:
Expansionism and Executive Power

The major historical events during the twenty years following Jefferson's administration were the War of 1812
against Britain, and the acquisition of West Florida, East
Florida, and Spain's territorial claims in the Pacific Northwest.
The War of 1812 was legislatively approved by a formal declaration. But it followed closely upon President James Madison's exercise
of a broad and legislatively delegated power to prohibit trade with
Britain while continuing it with France, and consequently illustrates
the relationship between the exercise of foreign-affairs discretion
and the initiation of formal war.

The territorial acquisitions under Madison, James Monroe and
John Quincy Adams were caused in large part by unilateral executive conduct in a series of overt and covert operations. In addition,
a policy of minimizing European influence in North and South
America was pursued in numerous ways, until its full-blown emer-
gence in 1823 as the Monroe Doctrine.

The three men under whose leadership these developments occurred differed from each other, of course. Madison was essentially
a thinker, diminutive, apparently nonassertive though capable of
great persistence, and more committed to Republican doctrine than
his predecessor.[1] Monroe, while no intellectual, had "indomitable
perseverance," great administrative skill, and considerable personal
charm.[2] Adams, like his father, was prideful and pugnacious, a difficult man of awesome discipline and powerful intellect.[3]

Yet in many significant ways these men were alike. All were Republicans of the Jeffersonian wing of the party. All made enormous

contributions to the young nation before becoming President. Madison was probably more responsible than any other single individual—except perhaps Hamilton—for the form and adoption of the Constitution.* Monroe opposed the Constitution (at the age of thirty), but rendered invaluable services to his country, most notably in negotiating the Louisiana Purchase.† Adams held the rank of Minister under three of the four Presidents that preceded him, and negotiated the Treaty of Ghent and the cession of Florida.** Each was, in a sense, groomed for the presidency, by serving as Secretary of State in the administration that preceded his election. All shared certain basic foreign-policy objectives that led them toward common goals; indeed, they worked together so extensively that differences among them were compromised or blurred in the exercise of their various powers. Finally, whatever differences existed among the three, the

*He began public service early. At 25 years of age he helped draft the Virginia Constitution of 1776. He served on the Virginia Council of State and then in the Continental Congress and the Virginia House of Delegates. He actively supported a stronger Union, and played an extremely important role at the Federal Convention of 1787. He wrote 29 of the *Federalist Papers*, and was largely responsible for securing ratification of the Constitution in Virginia. In 1789 he became for eight years a member of the new House of Representatives, where he proposed the Bill of Rights. From 1801 to 1809 he served as Jefferson's Secretary of State, and then defeated Charles C. Pinckney to become the fourth President. *See generally* 6² *Dictionary of American Biography* 184-93 (A. Johnson, ed. 1957); *Encyclopedia of American History* 1095 (R. Morris, ed. 1976).

†Monroe studied law under Jefferson, after having fought in the Continental Army. He served in the Virginia House of Delegates and the Continental Congress, and as a United States Senator from 1790-94. He was recalled by Washington from France in 1796 because, as a consequence of "his own decided [French] sympathies," Monroe failed "to defend the Jay Treaty" to the French government. He became Governor of Virginia from 1799-1802, and once again served as Governor in 1811, after having been envoy extraordinary to France and minister to Britain. He was Madison's Secretary of State from 1811-17 (except for 1814-15, when he was Secretary of War), and was then elected President for two terms. *See generally* 7 *Dictionary of American Biography*, *supra* at 87-93; *Encyclopedia of American History*, *supra* at 1105.

**This eldest son of John Adams got his first taste of the diplomatic service at 14 years of age, when he became secretary to Francis Dana in Russia. Washington appointed him Minister to the Netherlands, and urged his father to advance John Quincy despite any charge of nepotism. His father appointed him Minister to Prussia, and the Republicans sought strenuously to embarrass the President for the appointment. He joined the Republicans, however, in supporting Jefferson's embargo policy, which cost him his Senate seat. He then taught at Harvard, was Minister to Russia (1809-14), chairman of the commission that negotiated the Treaty of Ghent (1815-17), and President Monroe's Secretary of State (1817-25), with whom he formulated the Monroe Doctrine. He became President in 1824, despite the fact that he had less electoral votes than Andrew Jackson. Jackson defeated him, however, in 1828, after which he served for 17 years in Congress, where he was prominent for his early anti-slavery position. *See generally* 1 *Dictionary of American Biography*, *supra* at 84-93; *Encyclopedia of American History*, *supra* at 971-72.

radically contrasting style and system of their successor, Andrew Jackson, make them proper subjects for simultaneous treatment.

Madison was the leading and most distinguished spokesman of the Jeffersonian Republicans. During the years of Federalist control, he advocated a federal government of limited powers; supported closer legislative control over spending; frequently sought narrower delegations of power to the President; and opposed executive control of foreign affairs.* Writing as "Helvidius," he advanced the view that Congress must be consulted before the President undertakes any action, even in exercising powers specifically delegated to him, that could lead to war and thereby deprive the legislature of its right to decide between war and peace. He initially opposed the national bank and enlarging the military establishment. He condemned the Alien and Sedition Acts as repugnant to the Bill of Rights he had authored.

Yet Madison's views were not always consistent. He had early recognized the need for a strong federal government, with virtually complete control over foreign affairs. At the Federal Convention it was he and Elbridge Gerry who moved to change the clause granting Congress the power to "make" war to read "declare" war, recognizing the need for the President to "repel sudden attacks" without prior legislative consent. Though Madison may not have intended it, the concept of defensive actions had expanded even before he took office as President. He favored recognizing the President's power to remove executive officers, invoking a theory of the executive power much like Hamilton's. When President Jefferson maintained or increased the broad powers of the executive branch, his faithful Secretary of State and heir apparent raised no objection. As President, Madison's acceptance of essentially Federalist notions of national power is symbolized by his signing a bill chartering the Second Bank of the United States, and his aggressive actions in West and East Florida pushed presidential initiative to new extremes.[4]

*Highly critical of the way in which John Adams was handling relations with France, Madison wrote Jefferson on May 13, 1798:

> The management of foreign relations appears to be the most susceptible of abuse of all the trusts committed to a Government, because they can be concealed or disclosed, or disclosed in such parts and at such times as will best suit particular views; and because the body of the people are less capable of judging, and are more under the influence of prejudices, on that branch of their affairs, than of any other. Perhaps it is a universal truth that the loss of liberty at home is to be charged to provisions against danger, real or pretended, from abroad.

1 *The Writings of James Madison* 140–41 (G. Hunt, ed. 1901–10) (9 vols.) [hereinafter "*Madison Writings* (Hunt)"].

Monroe and Adams were, like Madison, Republicans, though Adams's conversion came relatively late in his political career. They did not, however, share even Madison's theoretical aversion for executive power or preference for legislative control. Among the reasons Monroe had opposed the Constitution was that he disliked its giving the Senate a share in what he felt were executive powers; and unlike other Virginia anti-Federalists he supported the office of President, though he joined them in demanding a Bill of Rights. As negotiator under Jefferson, and as Secretary of State under Madison, Monroe advocated and implemented plans for vigorous executive initiatives, especially to acquire the Floridas. As President he largely left to Congress the control of domestic affairs, but sought to control the nation's foreign policy. Among his most dramatic initiatives were his actions in East Florida, his effort to suppress piracy in the West Indies and at Amelia Island, and his promulgation of the Monroe Doctrine.[5]

Adams frankly believed that the Presidency should be the "center of hopes and expectations" for the nation, and above partisan politics. His "conception of the office . . . was of a superior tribuneship of the whole people, above the vulgarity and vicissitudes of party struggle, a symbol of high principle and rectitude." Adams thought the President "should be elevated to it on the basis of a disinterested insight into principle possessed by the whole people."[6] The irony of Adams's election in 1824 was that he received fewer electoral votes than his opponent, Andrew Jackson, and was elected in the House when Henry Clay, the third candidate, threw his support to Adams. Many believed the election had been a "corrupt bargain" between Adams and Clay, who was soon thereafter nominated Secretary of State.

Despite his narrow hold on the office, Adams continued to see presidential power in broad terms. "The powers of the executive department," he later wrote, "explicitly and emphatically concentrated in one person, are vastly more extensive and complicated than those of the legislature." Furthermore, during his tenure as Secretary of State Adams felt that Congress was constantly and unfortunately encroaching on the "powers and authorities of the President."[7] He saw the conduct of foreign affairs especially as an executive domain.[8] He believed that "the error in our Constitution" had been to grant the power to declare war to Congress, a power "which, according to Montesquieu and Rousseau, is strictly an Executive act."[9] He was certain that "*defensive* acts of hostility may be authorized by the Executive" without prior congressional approval.[10] On the other hand, he was apparently committed to seeking legislative approval for any decision to use force in defending other nations.[11]

EXECUTIVE-CONGRESSIONAL RELATIONS

The deterioration in presidential influence over Congress, which marked the final year of Jefferson's administration, continued under his successors. This occurred, not because Madison, Monroe or Adams "avowed as a guiding principle their subordination to Congress," but because as Presidents they were either weak leaders or were "frustrated by factional opposition beyond their control."[12] Madison and Monroe were harassed by powerful Federalists and leaders of the splintered Republican party, such as Daniel Webster, John Calhoun, Henry Clay and John Randolph. Adams was potentially a strong leader, and aggressively sought to implement his programs, but he lacked adequate political support.

The shift in power from the executive to Congress that took place during these years manifested itself in several ways. Congress increased its activities, and the Republican majority began using its caucus to select presidential nominees.* Executive nominations and other recommendations were defeated on several occasions, and both houses of Congress showed their readiness to confront the President. Growth of congressional influence and activity was, therefore, tangible and in some instances dramatic.

Yet the importance of this increase in legislative power has been overstated. Its institutional impact appears to have been negligible. The executive branch, for example, continued to prepare and submit plans and legislation,[13] and Congress frequently requested executive planning, especially on military matters.[14] Executive departments grew considerably in size during this period, and while Congress succeeded after the War of 1812 in reducing government

---

*The Republican nominating caucus was formed by 1800, but it was not until 1808 that it made an important decision—to nominate Madison instead of Monroe. Ralph Harlow said of this event: "Jefferson had made the Republican party, and as maker he ruled it. The party in its turn made Madison president, and what need was there to bow before the idol it created?" *The History of Legislative Methods in the Period before 1825* at 194 (1917). *Compare* the far more critical and enlightening analysis of James S. Young, *The Washington Community, 1800-1828* at 110-17 (1966). Other important changes that strengthened Congress during this period were the assumption of new powers by Henry Clay as Speaker of the House—which he used to push for war against Britain—and the increased number and influence of standing committees, substituting for the gross inefficiency of discussion in Committee of the Whole. *See generally* L. White, *The Jeffersonians* 54-59 (1951).

expenditures by cutting the army and navy, efforts to reduce the size of department staffs were unsuccessful.[15] Congress, the Presidents and various executive officers did implement reforms in the management of the Departments of War, Navy and State, among others.[16] But these reforms ultimately served to strengthen rather than weaken the executive branch.

Under Madison the Senate refused to confirm a handful of appointments, most notably the recess designation of Albert Gallatin as Minister Plenipotentiary to Russia, while serving as Secretary of Treasury. In addition, members of both the Senate and House increased their power over appointments to certain federal jobs in the states from which they were elected.[17] Especially significant was the Tenure of Office Act of 1820, which vacated most important executive offices every four years. This enabled the Senate periodically to pass on all appointments to these offices, and thereby improved its opportunity to secure appointments congenial to its members.[18]

These developments were, however, more in the nature of increases in legislative patronage than changes in the principles or basic structure that governed the relationship between Congress and the President. While legislators persistently pressed for greater patronage,[19] virtually every legislative effort to get Congress to take stands based on principled limitations on executive power failed. For example, the Senate refused to adopt a resolution declaring improper all recess appointments to positions not previously filled; some members openly advocated inherent executive power to judge whether an office was "created" during recess by exigencies, thereby enabling the President constitutionally to fill the position.[20] And the most notable success scored by Congress in connection with appointments—the Tenure of Office Act—served to increase executive as well as legislative patronage, as Andrew Jackson later demonstrated.

On several occasions during the presidencies of Madison, Monroe and Adams, Congressmen protested against proposed delegations to the executive of broad discretionary powers; sometimes these delegations were narrowed or refused. In general, however, broad delegations were frequent, and usually legislated without any recorded protest. Broad delegations were most common, in fact, in the areas of foreign and military affairs, discussed in greater detail below.

Discretion over expenditures also continued much as it had in prior years.[21] Presidents Madison and Monroe frequently resorted to the power under the Act of March 3, 1809 to transfer appropriations from one category of expenditure to another, reporting at least some of their actions as that Act required.[22] They also periodically incurred "emergency" expenditures, for which no authorization or appropriation had been made.[23] Executive departments mingled appropriations, such as the pay and clothing accounts for the army.[24]

Congress took no steps to curb these and other related practices until December 30, 1816, when Calhoun proposed that the Committee on Ways and Means inquire into the expediency of repealing the provision in the Act of March 3, 1809 empowering the President to transfer appropriations. The Committee corresponded with some of the department heads, only to discover that practices were even more lax than had been suspected. This led, however, only to a minor and ineffective reform, and no further actions were taken until 1820.[25] At that time Congress discovered that the War and Navy Departments were bringing forward unexpended balances from prior years, instead of placing them in the surplus fund as the Act of 1795 seemed to require, and that all the departments were making contracts in anticipation of appropriations. The Act of 1820 attempted several remedies, but all proved ineffectual.[26] Persistent deficiencies in many of the myriad categories of expenditure compelled administrators to transfer funds illegally, and usually these transfers (in the form of "borrowing" from surplus categories of expenditure) were not even reported to Congress.[27] So when Andrew Jackson assumed the presidency, "the balance in fiscal affairs between the executive and legislative branches remained about where the Federalists had left it."[28]

Control of Information

Jefferson had successfully controlled the flow of information to Congress during most of his presidency. Madison and Monroe lacked the legislative support Jefferson had enjoyed, but largely succeeded in determining what information Congress should be given. To an extent this was achieved openly, with Congress's acquiescence. In some important situations, however, even the existence of information was kept secret, under the rationale that it was "private" or "confidential," or without any pretense of explanation. Adams, who had much less influence in Congress than his predecessors, appears to have withheld little material information, and to have responded fully to legislative requests.

Voluntary Transmittals. All three Presidents, and their department heads, voluntarily submitted large quantities of information to Congress, including material on potentially dangerous international situations.[29] Madison, for example, informed Congress of his request that the British Minister, Francis Jackson, be recalled; of the take-over of parts of West Florida; and of threats made by Algiers.[30] Monroe communicated material relating to delicate relations with Spain; the takeover of Amelia Island; and other events.[31] Adams reported on the Panama Congress and the Brazilian blockade.[32]

The voluntary transmittals of these Presidents were far from complete, however. The sheer bulk of diplomatic and military correspondence carried on between 1809 and 1829 made it undesirable if not impossible to communicate a complete record of all activities. Much material was withheld simply because its transmittal was unnecessary to give Congress an accurate picture of the issues involved. Madison, Monroe and Adams all went much further than this, though, in deciding what to withhold from their transmittals. All three Presidents, and some of their officers, continued in some degree the practice of designating some letters "private" or "confidential," and of respecting such designations by their correspondents. These practices were, of course, designed in part to keep material from reaching foreign governments and the general public,* to avoid embarrassing a foreign diplomat or government,† to collect

---

*Madison continued Jefferson's reliance on codes. He had written many coded letters before becoming President; after 1809 he wrote at least two. On August 11, 1812, he wrote in cipher to Joel Barlow, Minister to France, concerning the French decree revoking earlier decrees against neutral shipping, Britain's possible responses to the French action, and mentioning that Barlow might be recalled because of France's behavior. 2 *Letters and Other Writings of James Madison* 540 (Cong. ed. 1865-67) (4 vols.) (partly in cipher) [hereinafter *"Madison Writings* (Cong. ed.)"]. Confidentiality was clearly desirable for such a letter, to avoid trouble with France over Madison's harsh words. But confidentiality also served Madison's decision to keep Congress ignorant of Barlow's earlier letter describing the French decrees as fraudulent. See Barlow to Madison, May 12, 1812, *Madison Presidential Papers*, series 1, reel 14, discussed *infra*, at 283-91. The second coded letter was written on August 2, 1813, to Albert Gallatin, and was a detailed analysis of how and why Gallatin's nomination as envoy to negotiate with Britain in Russia was defeated. 8 *Madison Writings* 252 (Hunt). Nothing injurious to the nation was involved; Madison simply wished to keep secret his personal and highly critical observations of the Senate's conduct, and of his own unsuccessful strategy. No evidence could be found that Monroe used codes after becoming President. Reel 602 of the *Adams Family Papers* contains ciphers and keys, six of which belonged to John Quincy Adams, all dated before he became President. See also J.Q. Adams to Richard Rush, August 15, 1818, in 6 *Writings of J.Q. Adams* 433 (W. Ford, ed. 1913) (7 vols.) [hereinafter *"J.Q. Adams Writings"*].

†For example, Madison withheld from Congress a "private" letter from William Pinkney, Minister to Britain, to Robert Smith, Secretary of State, dated January 4, 1810, in which Pinkney related a conversation with the new Foreign Secretary, Lord Wellesley. Wellesley took positions in that interview, according to Pinkney, that varied from his later positions, at least in part because Wellesley was uninformed, spoke for himself only, and without sufficient care. Pinkney thanked Madison for refusing to send Congress the letter even after it had been specifically requested, as its publication, "which must necessarily have followed,

foreign intelligence effectively,* and for other similar reasons.† But designations of "private" and "confidential" were also used to keep information from reaching Congress, even when the material dealt with "public" issues.

One of the most significant series of withholdings took place after Madison chose to accept an unauthenticated representation from the French government that it had revoked decrees that violated neutral commerce; on that basis he ordered a suspension of trade with Britain, as a statute authorized him to do. He informed Congress of his decision, but withheld information indicating that France was in fact seizing American vessels. When the French finally produced what purported to be the decree revoking its earlier decrees, America's Ministers to France and Britain wrote letters pronouncing it a fraud. These letters arrived only after America had declared war against Britain, but before Congress had begun in earnest to prepare for the conflict. Yet Madison withheld the letters from his voluntary transmittals.**

would have produced serious embarrassment." Pinkney to Madison, August 13, 1810, in W. Pinkney, *Life of William Pinkney* 244, 245 (1969).

*Special agents sent to foreign nations were occasionally instructed to transmit the information they collected in "private" or "confidential" communications. *See* note 160, *infra;* J.Q. Adams to Thomas Randall, April 29, 1823, in 1 W. Manning, *Diplomatic Correspondence of the United States Concerning the Independence of the Latin-American Nations* 185–86 (1925).

†During 1820 a French vessel, the *Appollon*, was seized in Spanish waters off Amelia Island for violating the revenue laws of the United States. *See* discussion *infra* at 349. The French protested vehemently, and its minister even informally threatened war. Adams initially urged President Monroe to communicate the whole correspondence on the affair to Congress, but changed his mind because he feared the letters might provoke undue excitement against France. The matter was mentioned in Monroe's annual message of December 5, 1821, but all the relevant material was withheld, apparently to preserve a climate conducive to negotiations with France on all commercial dealings. A convention with France was signed the next year and Monroe sent some information on the *Appollon* dispute to Congress with his message of December 4, 1822; much material was withheld, however, including all items reflecting that the controversy had been intense and at times angry. *See* 5 J.Q. Adams, *Memoirs* 419–23 (C. Adams, ed. 1874–77) (12 vols.) [hereinafter *"Adams Memoirs"*]; 38 *Annals of Congress* 11–15 (1853) [hereinafter *"Annals"*]; A.S.P., Documents, Legislative and Executive, 5 *Foreign Relations* 149–214. Among the documents withheld were: letters between Albert Gallatin, Minister to France, and Baron Etienne de Pasquier, French Foreign Minister, and between Gallatin and Secretary of State Adams (2 *The Writings of Albert Gallatin* 186–253[H. Adams, ed. 1960]); the Treasury instruction of May 6, 1818, ordering seizure of vessels within Spanish waters, which the French Minister at Washington, Hyde de Neuville, claimed was unconstitutional (2 *id.* 190, 191, 251, 252; 5 *Adams Memoirs* 414–15); and two letters sent by Spanish Consular Agent Clarke to Colonel James Forbes inviting him to establish a port at St. Mary's to evade the revenue laws of the United States (2 Gallatin, *supra* at 196).

**He withheld the letters even from responses to legislative requests. *See infra* at 279–90, for details of the entire affair.

Important material was also withheld in connection with military ventures. Madison and his Secretary of State, Monroe, worked secretly to foment revolution and assume control of Spanish Florida, and all the truly revealing correspondence during these efforts was withheld. When he became President, Monroe failed to transmit important information relating to the Seminole War, particularly Andrew Jackson's offer to attack East Florida on his own responsibility, and other letters revealing that Jackson had very different reasons for occupying parts of Florida from those which Monroe advanced to Congress. Adams, too, initially withheld, in connection with the Panama Congress, documents that suggested more dangerous purposes for that meeting than those claimed by Adams and Secretary of State Henry Clay.*

Very early in Madison's first term an incident took place that involved the removal of a letter from State Department files, and hence from Congress's power to seek to obtain. On June 14, 1809, the French Minister, Louis Turreau, wrote a scalding criticism of American policy to Secretary of State Robert Smith. The letter purported to be "personal," but was in reality an official outburst against the recent, ill-fated agreement Madison had reached with the British Minister David Erskine. Either Madison or Smith prevailed upon Turreau to withdraw the letter, and the original was apparently returned to the French legation. Years later, in 1813, a copy reached the *Federal Republican*, a Georgetown newspaper published by Federalist Representative Alexander Hanson. The paper noted editorially that the letter was far more offensive than the "circular" that caused Madison to request the recall of Francis Jackson, Erskine's successor.[33]

Madison counterattacked through John Graham, the State Department's Chief Clerk, who suggested in a more sympathetic newspaper that Smith (who had been dismissed by Madison for other reasons) must have leaked the copy, noting that Smith had handled the affair, and had allowed Turreau to withdraw the original as an act of disavowal. After some debate the House requested information on when and by whom the letter had been withdrawn; Madison supplied letters from Monroe and Graham essentially attributing the Turreau letter's removal to Smith.[34] Federalists attempted to show that the letter was removed after relations with Britain soured, possibly even in exchange for Francis Jackson's recall. Graham's letter recited, however, that he distinctly remembered the letter's withdrawal before that event.† Beyond this allegation, no effort was made to

---

*These last three examples are discussed in detail *infra*, at 298, 319-20, 358, 364-65, 262-63 respectively.

†When Graham saw the letter in the *Federal Republican*, he contacted Madi-

establish that allowing a letter to be withdrawn was improper as a matter of principle.[35] Several years later, Monroe instructed the State Department to return to Joel Poinsett the letters written by him while serving as an agent in South America.*

Efforts by Congress to Obtain Information. Congress sought in several ways to obtain information not voluntarily submitted. One new development was to require executive departments to file many more regular and special reports.

Reports and Investigations. During the Washington administration annual reports were filed only by the Treasury Department. "By the end of the Jeffersonian era," Leonard White notes, "every department submitted an annual report which was transmitted to Congress with the President's annual message and referred to the appropriate House committee." The number of regular reports required grew dramatically after Jefferson. The subjects of these reports covered a wide range of issues, and special reports were required when Congressmen suspected irregularities, which "fulfilled somewhat the same function as the question hour in the House of Commons."[36]

Legislative investigations also became much more common, and were often conducted by committees delegated the power to issue subpoenas.[37] Considerable opposition developed against some inquiries on the ground that they would improperly intrude into executive affairs. For example, efforts to initiate inquiries into the conduct of the War of 1812 were almost uniformly rejected; instead, Congress asked President Madison for information concerning the defeats suffered during the war.[38] A motion to inquire into the removal from the State Department of French Minister Turreau's letter was rejected on similar grounds, and an information request was passed instead.† Motions to refer to various committees certain

---

son. The President claimed to recollect very little but in fact suggested several facts that strengthened his position, including Smith's control of the affair, and its occurrence before news of the rejection of Erskine's agreement reached Washington. 2 *Madison Writings* 571–73 (Cong. ed.). Graham's recollection thereafter corresponded precisely with Madison's. 26 *Annals* 1060.

*See the discussion at notes 160–62, *infra,* and accompanying text.

†Calhoun argued that the motion failed to meet the three constitutional prerequisites of a legislative inquiry: "a specific object ought to be first stated; secondly, what was expected to grow out of it; and thirdly, that the object was of a character to warrant the investigation." Without these limitations, he said, an inquiry "would violate the spirit of the Constitution. By that instrument, diplomacy was confided wholly to the Executive." The House may have power to require information on diplomatic affairs, but through the executive, not through inquiries. 26 *Annals* 890. Alexander Hanson (Md.) and others rejected this contention, arguing that information given by any member may

aspects of Andrew Jackson's behavior, as appointed Governor of Florida, were also rejected.[39] Other motions to conduct inquiries appear to have been rejected because they seemed designed to embarrass or harass the President.[40]

These votes cannot be construed as authoritative expressions based on principle, however. After extensive and revealing debate, for example, the House authorized an inquiry into the conduct of General Wilkinson.[41] An inquiry was also held by a House committee into the causes of the humiliating invasion and destruction by the British of the national capitol.[42] Refusals to inquire seem to have been based on general considerations of policy and convenience, as opposed to principle, in which the need to avoid undue interference with the executive was an important but by no means constitutionally controlling factor.[43]

Attempt to Interview the President. One extraordinary effort to obtain information took place after Madison submitted to the Senate for confirmation his recess appointments of Gallatin, Adams and Bayard as envoys to negotiate with Britian and Russia, and of James Russell as Minister to Sweden. The Senate asked Madison if Gallatin retained his office as Secretary of Treasury while he was serving as envoy, and Madison replied that Gallatin held both offices. The nomination was then referred to a select committee, and its chairman, Joseph Anderson of Tennessee, attempted to get Madison to meet with the committee to discuss the appointment. Madison refused, noting that the resolution appointing the committee contained no such authority. The Senate promptly authorized both Anderson's committee and the committee formed to consider Russell's nomination " to confer" with the President. Senator William Wells of Delaware, chairman of the committee on Russell's nomination, obtained an appointment with Madison for June 16, but the President became ill and the meeting was postponed.[44]

By July 6 Madison had recovered sufficiently to resume the duties of his office. He dictated a letter noting that he had received a copy of the Senate resolution authorizing the Wells committee to confer with him on Russell's nomination. "Conceiving it to be my duty to decline the proposed conference with the committee," he said, "I think it proper to address the explanation directly to the Senate."

---

be made the subject of the inquiry. Apparently losing his self-control, he argued that concealment of the letter, if proved, constituted a high misdemeanor by the President. *Id.* 891-92. Some who felt an inquiry constitutionally proper, declined to support one so politically motivated. *See id.* 894-98. The request is at *id.* 901. A subsequent motion to inquire into the same subject also failed. *Id.* 1128-30.

The attempt to confer in person violated past practice, he wrote, and threatened the proper balance of power between the branches:

> [T]he Executive and Senate, in the cases of appointments to office and of treaties, are to be considered independent and coordinate with each other. If they agree, the appointments or treaties are made. If the Senate disagree, they fail. If the Senate wish information previous to their final decision, the practice, keeping in view the Constitutional relation of the Senate and Executive, has been, either to request the Executive to furnish it, or refer the subject to a committee of their body to communicate, either formally or informally, with the head of the proper department. The appointment of a committee of the Senate to confer immediately with the Executive himself, appears to lose sight of the co-ordinate relation between the Executive and the Senate, which the Constitution has established, and which ought therefore to be maintained. . . .
> I add only that I am entirely persuaded by the purity of the intentions of the Senate . . . and that they will be cheerfully furnished with all the suitable information in possession of the Executive, in any mode deemed consistent with the principles of the Constitution, and the settled practice under it.[45]

On July 8, the Wells committee submitted a report to the Senate. Only the President's letters were recorded by the Senate secretaries, but the report was probably similar to an unpublished article, written for a newspaper, by Senator Rufus King of New York, one of the committee members. King claimed "that the President intended to receive and confer with the committee," but then changed his mind. "The Senate are a great, the greatest, power in the Constitution," King wrote, "created . . . to impart wisdom, stability, and safety to the laws." To vote on a nomination submitted to it by the President, the Senate needed the same information that the President possessed. The executive was "bound to impart such information to the Senate when requested." Cabinet officers were but creations of the President, and Madison's suggestion that a committee of the Senate should confer formally or informally with the head of the proper department "tends to degrade the Senate." King suggested that it would not degrade "the person or office of President Madison, should he, as President Washington did, receive and confer with a committee of the Senate concerning the exercise of a power in the discharge of which the consent of both President and Senate is required."[46]

Despite Madison's letter of July 6, and although the Senate had already declared incompatible the offices of Secretary of Treasury and Envoy Extraordinary, Anderson was determined to press the issue further. He wrote to Madison on July 12, enclosing the Senate's resolution of June 16 and requesting an interview. On July 14 Madison replied that he would "receive the Committee of the Senate" on July 16, but that "the committee are apprized, by his late message to the Senate, of the grounds on which he will be obliged to decline the proposed conference with the committee upon the matter of that resolution." On July 16 the Anderson committee met with the President and presented him with copies of the Senate resolution. Madison said "that he was sorry the Senate had not taken the same view of the subject which he had done, and that he regretted that the measure [concerning Gallatin] had been taken under circumstances which deprived him of the aid or advice of the Senate." Anderson made no reply and waited for the President to continue. When Madison refused to elaborate, the committee retired.[47] On Monday, July 19, Anderson reported his committee's actions to the Senate. The Senate, which had already deemed it inexpedient to appoint a Minister to Sweden, rejected Gallatin's nomination by a vote of 17 to 18, and then confirmed Bayard (27 to 6) and Adams (30 to 4).*

Requests for Information. Resolutions passed by each house remained the most common technique for obtaining information from the executive. Requests were frequent, and usually uncontroversial. But many motions for information were blocked by the house to which they were presented, for a variety of reasons. Much controversy also occurred over whether requests should be qualified to allow executive withholding, and over the significance of communications in confidence.

Both houses of Congress, at several critical points, refused to pass requests for information. For example, soon after Madison announced he had accepted France's purported revocation of its decrees against neutral shipping, motions were made to ask him the basis on which he had ascertained that the decrees had in fact been revoked.[48] These efforts were blocked by Republican majorities during the Third Session of the Eleventh Congress, and allowed only after the issue had become somewhat stale and Britain had refused

---

*26 *Annals* 89, 90. Irving Brant says of these events:

> The President's illness robbed him of personal contact with wavering senators. . . . The President's position was thus limited to a bald declaration of executive prerogative that produced the appearance, at least, of the curtness and asperity complained of by foreign diplomats. But from his sickbed he halted the most ambitious attempt yet made, under the new Constitution, to make the President subordinate to the Senate in their co-ordinate activities.

6 I. Brant, *James Madison, Secretary of State, 1800–1809* at 194 (1941–61) (6 vols.) [hereinafter "Brant, *Madison*"].

to revoke its Orders in Council.[49] Information requests concerning the basis for the takeover of West Florida met a similar fate, as did requests for material related to the President's recommendation that war be declared against Britain and later Algiers.[50] When Monroe sought authority to enforce the Adams-Onis Treaty if Spain refused to ratify it, a motion was made in the House to request the President to communicate any information in his possession of the extent of territory Onis had been authorized to cede (which was more than the line actually negotiated); the motion was defeated.[51]

Several reasons were given on these and other occasions for opposing motions to request information. The most sweeping rationale was that the executive must be presumed to have communicated all the information on a given question which "he deemed important to the public interest . . . and not inconsistent with that interest at present to communicate."[52] This reasoning was invoked most frequently when the issue concerned foreign affairs, since the executive was said to be solely responsible for conducting such affairs; by allowing the President to decide what information to submit and what to withhold, some reasoned, the whole responsibility for what resulted was left with him rather than Congress.* Others invariably argued, on the other hand, that Congress had a right to call for information at any time, and was responsible for foreign-affairs issues because the Constitution delegated to it many relevant powers, including the power to declare war.[53] Any danger to the public interest from executive communications could be avoided, they contended, by authorizing the President to withhold material the disclosure of which might be prejudicial.

Many other reasons were given for blocking—or attempting to block—information requests. Some were regarded as unnecessary, since adequate information had already been provided.[54] Others were said to be improper, in that negotiations were still in progress;

---

*For example, Representative Alexander McKim (Md.) said in response to a motion to obtain all available information concerning relations with Britain and France: "It was to be presumed, if information was necessary and could be communicated with propriety, that the President would not withhold it." He wanted to place "the whole responsibility" on the President "without burdening the House with any part of it." This particular motion passed, however, after Samuel Dana argued "that the House had a right to call for information at any time." 21 *Annals* 2020–21. An instance in which the side making these arguments prevailed was when a motion was defeated for information of the extent to which Spain had been willing to cede territory in the Adams-Onis Treaty. See 35 *Annals* 948–49 (Jan. 27, 1820). In addition, the House rejected language in a request that would have called for the instructions to be issued to the Ministers sent to the Panama Congress. 2 *Register of Debates in Congress, 1825-1837* at 1241–43, 1246, 1253, 1281, 1301 (including Webster's argument that such a request would improperly interfere with the treaty power) (1825-37)(29 vols.) [hereinafter "*Register*"].

244 War, Foreign Affairs and Constitutional Power

or that they requested "unofficial" material; or that the information sought was not relevant to the subject under discussion, or to any possible legislative action.[55] Some proposed requests were attacked as too general, others as too specific. All these arguments against requesting information generally failed;[56] the only requests consistently rejected were those that explicitly asked for the President's opinion or state of mind.[57]

Though reasons for votes on motions for information were often given—and undoubtedly were important to some Congressmen on certain occasions—one cannot escape the impression that reasoning based on principle played a far less influential role than partisan politics. Many motions for information were made to embarrass or harass the executive.[58] The House, for example, requested Madison to send a copy of the "circular" written by British Minister Francis Jackson that caused Madison to request his recall, even though the circular had been widely published in the press.* Other requests were proposed, apparently by arrangement, to make the executive look good, and predictably evoked partisan opposition.[59] Only partisan considerations, moreover, explain fully the frequent rejection of motions with important informational objectives, but potentially embarrassing or troublesome consequences to the administration involved.[60]

Both houses of Congress continued to qualify requests for information. Where the subject matter concerned foreign affairs, the overwhelming majority of requests authorized the President to withhold information if he thought its disclosure inconsistent with the public interest.[61] Furthermore, requests for sensitive material concerning military matters—presumably because of their foreign-affairs overtones—were often qualified.[62] On several occasions, language authorizing withholding was specifically added to proposed, unqualified requests, sometimes after revealing debate.†

*The request came up when the House was called upon to consider passing a resolution adopted by the Senate pledging the nation's strength in support of Madison's position. Some advocates of the motion (which also requested a widely published dispatch) argued that, when the House acted on a matter that might lead to war, they should have all the information the President had before him. 20 *Annals* 714. Federalists rejected the suggestion that their only purpose was to embarrass the President, arguing that they had a right to the "official" version. The request was narrowly adopted, probably on the votes of Republicans who felt "that any member had a right to ask of the Executive any public document which he deemed necessary for the government of his conduct in Legislative matters." *Id.* 711 (Macon), 714 (Bibb). Madison responded by sending copies of the documents, both cut out of newspapers. *Id.* 742-43.

†Daniel Webster introduced five resolutions concerning the French decree purportedly promulgated to suspend restrictions on neutral trade, the first four of which were qualified. All five passed the House, but only after the fifth was

The most extensive debate during this period on the need and significance of a discretionary clause took place when the House was urged to strike the words "if not incompatible with the public welfare" from a request for information relating to the Panama Congress.[63] Supporters argued that the House needed *all* relevant information to formulate policies and laws, especially on matters that could lead to war, and that the House could be trusted with the same information sent the Senate.[64] Adopting an absolutely uniform practice of inserting a qualifying clause, one member argued, was tantamount to accepting a doctrine of "confidence in public functionairies," which he hoped "will never be carried to such lengths in this Government."[65] John Forsyth of Georgia, chairman of the Committee on Foreign Relations, regarded the discretionary clause a mere "courtesy," used "not because the House have no right to demand information, or that the President has any right to withhold it." The Constitution made the President the organ by which information "is obtained—not for his use only, but for that of the Senate and of the House of Representatives." When, in the exercise of its constitutional authority, the House wanted anything "from the President, we have the right to demand, and the power to compel the production of it . . . : by the ordinary process of its Sergeant-at Arms, to take it, if treacherously withheld. . . ."[66]

Daniel Webster replied to Forsyth, insisting that the discretionary clause conferred real discretion to withhold and was not a mere formality.[67] Henry Storrs of New York noted that "this is a call on a co-ordinate branch . . . charged by the Constitution with the management of the foreign negotiations of the country. . . . Now, that comity which ever characterize our intercourse with the Executive, has settled, long ago, that respectful form which every call for

---

qualified to allow withholding if "the public interest should forbid such a disclosure." 26 *Annals* 310. *See also* 31 *Annals* 406–409 (Forsyth objected to request for information relating to South America as lacking the "usual qualification" excepting information the disclosure of which the President might deem incompatible with the public interest; request modified accordingly and passed) (Dec. 5, 1817); 38 *Annals* 733–34 (Floyd sought to delete qualifying clause in motion for correspondence leading to Treaty of Ghent, since restoration of peace obviated any need for secrecy; Lowndes objected to departure from usual form, arguing President had continuing right to exercise discretion; clause retained and motion adopted) (January 17, 1822); 2 *Register* 806–807, 815–17 (Buchanan accepts a qualification of his motion for information regarding Commodore Porter's court martial after Webster "inquired whether it was not usual, in calling on the President for copies of correspondence, to refer the matter to the exercise of a discretion on the part of the President, as to the propriety of making the communication asked for. To communicate correspondence, without reserve, might, in some cases, and possibly in this, be prejudicial to the public interest").

information from that co-equal Department has usually assumed."
The President had assured Congress that the nation's neutrality
would be preserved, and "if we cannot rely on this declaration, thus
solemnly made to us and the world, will gentlemen profess any
greater faith in any thing which he may send to us, in answer to a
call from the House?"[68] Others went beyond comity, arguing that
the President possesses the discretionary power to withhold information under the Constitution, and that it would be his duty to exercise
this judgment, even if the terms of the request were "wholly unqualified."* The request ultimately passed was qualified to allow
withholding.[69]

Congress frequently did pass unqualified requests for information
concerning military affairs, and occasionally even for information
concerning foreign affairs. Usually the information sought in such
requests could be disclosed without prejudice.[70] But sometimes
requests included no qualification even though Congress could not
have been certain that disclosure would be entirely safe.[71] Members
on occasion moved to request the transmittal of information "in
confidence," arguing that if material could not be publicly disclosed
it should nevertheless be submitted to Congress.[72] These efforts
generally failed, though a notable exception occurred when Adams
called on the Senate to approve sending ministers to the Panama
Congress.[73]

Presidents sometimes submitted information "in confidence," but
the technique had grave weaknesses, obvious even then, if secrecy
was in fact desired. Each house, it was clear, had the power to make
public the material sent to it in confidence. Consequently an executive request for confidentiality was at best a recommendation. Even
where majorities of both houses might respect the recommendation,
at least some observers felt that disclosure of any material sent to
the legislature was virtually inevitable.[74]

The practices governing disclosure in confidence were discussed in
some detail when the Senate censured Senator Timothy Pickering of
Massachusetts for publicly reading a letter sent to it in confidence by
Jefferson.[75] Samuel Dana of Connecticut, who opposed even this

---

*2 *Register* 1262 (Cook), 1274 (Sprague). Alfred H. Powell of Virginia
argued that the President had a right to exercise discretion in sending information to the Congress, a discretion "sanctioned by the example of Washington,
and, in the exercise of that power, he will give or withhold information, whatever shape we may give the resolution, or whatever language we may employ."
Id. 1283. Thomas Mitchell of South Carolina agreed that the President had a
duty to exercise discretion in communicating information, but felt that deletion
of the proviso would "more fully express to the President" the House's wishes.
Id. 1274–75.

relatively mild disciplinary action, argued that the President lacked power "to lock our lips in eternal silence," and suggested that the issue was whether Pickering had disclosed anything damaging. "All the President can properly do," he said, "is to refer to us as men of discernment . . . capable of judging on public concerns, to judge of the propriety of acting confidentially on any subject."[76] Samuel Smith of Maryland appeared to reject this proposition, arguing that when the President communicates material to the Senate "in confidence," he assumes that no man will divulge any part. "If we depart from our usual line of conduct in this respect, it cannot be expected that the President will hereafter place so much reliance on us as to give us confidential communications on any subject."[77] But the Senate did not go so far as to rule out future rejections of executive requests for confidentiality. The resolution of censure, introduced by Henry Clay, declared that the public reading of a paper confidentially communicated, "the injunction of secrecy not having been removed," violated Senate rules.[78] Secrecy was, in other words, up to the Senate (or House) majority at any given time, though not within the discretion of individual members to breach.

President Adams was unwilling even to recommend to Congress a course of action respecting material sent in confidence. On December 19, 1824, David Trimble of Kentucky called for a letter previously sent in confidence to the House by Jefferson. He argued that the call was proper, since the material had been sent in 1803, and the executive having once imposed secrecy could now decide whether it was still warranted. On December 27 President Adams replied, in confidence, transmitting a copy of Jefferson's message of January 18, 1803, and leaving it to the discretion of the House whether to publish the letter.[79] In 1826 the Senate requested Adams's opinion as to whether material he had sent in confidence relating to the Panama Congress could be published without detriment to the public interest. Adams once again left the matter to the Senate's discretion, refusing to accept responsibility for the decision. The Senate resolved both that they could properly ask the executive whether material sent in confidence could be published, and that they could unilaterally lift such restrictions; but they took no further action.[80]

During this period, Congress considered whether confidentiality ought to be removed from the secret journals and papers of the Continental Congress. On March 27, 1818, a resolution passed both houses authorizing publication of the material up to 1783, but authorizing the President to withhold any parts of the foreign correspondence.[81] On February 2, 1820, a resolution was submitted in the House to authorize publication of the Journals for the period

1783-1789. George Strother of Virginia argued it would be heresy to deny the people history "in which might be discovered . . . the secret springs which had impelled to many of the public acts of the Government." Some argued that secrecy was necessary to protect persons still living, and to keep our domestic bickerings from the world's eyes. Henry Baldwin of Pennsylvania urged that, since Congress's earlier predecessors had seen fit not to publish sections of the Journal, this Congress ought not to remove that veil of secrecy in haste. Daniel Cook of Illinois argued that old "wounds which time had cicatrized, should not be opened again." A resolution passed both houses on April 21, 1820, authorizing publication of the material "under the direction of the President."[82]

Executive Response. Presidents Madison, Monroe and Adams responded in various ways to requests for information. Usually the information requested was supplied, even if it had originally been withheld from a voluntary transmittal as "private" or confidential. For example, the House in December 1809 requested, if not "improper to be communicated," a dispatch from Minister to Britain Pinkney to Secretary of State Smith that was referred to in a letter earlier supplied.[83] Madison sent the relevant parts of the dispatch, though Pinkney had designated it "private." He later explained to Pinkney that the letter was too closely related to matters before the House to withhold, and that its disclosure could clarify Pinkney's conduct without damaging the nation's interests.*

On April 19, 1822, the House requested President Monroe to provide, "if not injurious to the public good," any letter written by Representative Jonathan Russell, who had been one of the commissioners who negotiated the Treaty of Ghent with Britain, detailing his position on certain issues.[84] Monroe replied on May 4 that no such letter was in the State Department files, but that he had such a letter marked "private" in his personal papers. He added that Russell had supplied the State Department with what purported to be a "duplicate" of the private letter; that the letter dealt with a difference of opinion between Russell and the other peace negotiators,

---

*The request was probably politically motivated, and Federalists argued that Republicans should crave an opportunity to demonstrate the President had nothing to hide. 20 *Annals* 720. Some Republicans were unwilling to vote for information merely "to stop the cavilings of captious federalists" (*id.* 725), but others wanted to deprive the opposition of the argument that they lacked all the necessary information (*id.* 722). The motion was easily adopted, and Madison sent "extracts." His explanation to Pinkney (Jan. 20, 1810), indicates that his normal practice was to respect requests for confidentiality from American diplomatic officers, even of matters not truly personal. 2 *Madison Writings* (Cong. ed.) 468, 470.

including Secretary of State John Quincy Adams; and that the issue involved had been resolved. After "full consideration," Monroe "thought it would be improper for the Executive to communicate the letter called for, unless the House, on a knowledge of these circumstances, should desire it; in which case" it would be accompanied with a report from Adams containing his own view of the matter.[85] Russell and his supporters by then realized that Monroe and Adams knew that the "duplicate" Russell had prepared was full of self-serving statements and inaccuracies, added to undermine Adams. They therefore opposed a motion by Timothy Fuller of Massachusetts to call for the material. The motion passed,[86] however, and Monroe furnished both the original and Russell's duplicate, "set in deadly parallel columns," together with Adams's comments.[87] A final example occurred when Adams was President. After two unqualified requests, Adams sent the Senate full information in confidence concerning the Panama Congress.[88]

Although Madison, Monroe and Adams generally communicated information specifically requested by Congress, there were times when they did not send everything the legislature sought. Such withholding was accepted without objection when the request involved was qualified to authorize withholding, and where the President announced that he had withheld material falling within the bounds of the request. After some Congressmen got hint of the fact that Madison had withheld another "private" letter from Pinkney,* for example, a motion was made on March 26, 1810 that the House request production of the letter if it did not "require secrecy." Orchard Cook of Massachusetts noted the possibility that "it might be an unofficial without being a confidential letter. Whether it was confidential or not, some answer would be received." Alexander McKim of Maryland said that he had not read the letter but had received a satisfactory account. He now understood the "purport" of it, and it could not be got "except called for, being an unofficial

---

*An "unofficial" letter from Pinkney to Smith had apparently been widely circulated, in which Pinkney suggested that the offending British Minister Jackson would be recalled, and that certain British officials were eager for peace. Representative Edward St. Loe Livermore of Massachusetts, who introduced the request for the letter, contended that such information was important; Nicholas Van Dyke of Delaware agreed, especially since Congress was considering bills to reduce the army and navy. 21 *Annals* 1622-23. *See also id.* 1624 (Mumford and Goldsborough). Some members opposed the call, one arguing that an official message would soon arrive. *Id.* 1623-24 (Burwell). But other administration supporters called for the motion's passage, to avoid Federalist criticisms. *Id.* 1622-24 (Cook). Representative Lyon said "that this private letter, which had been made so public, reminded him of a sign he had seen of 'private entertainment'; so private, that it was advertised by a sign." *Id.* 1624.

letter, because it would be indecorous in the President to submit it to the House without a call." Dana, who had previously indicated his belief in the President's discretion to withhold material, said he "was not disposed to call upon the President to violate private confidence." But "if information from a public Minister as to the manner in which he had done his public duty had been received in a letter at the Department of State, it was an abuse of terms to call it a private letter." The motion passed, 109 to 14. Madison replied two days later that a letter such as the one requested had been received, but that it was "private" and "unofficial" and involved "personal considerations of a delicate nature"; he therefore considered that the letter was not within "the purview of the call of the House," and withheld it. No further effort was made to obtain the letter; Pinkney later concurred in Madison's judgment, noting that disclosure of the letter would have been embarrassing to the British Foreign Secretary.[89]

In another instance the House passed a request on January 4, 1825, asking President Monroe for certain material relating to the prospective court martial of Commodore Charles Stewart,[90] "so far as he may deem compatible with the public interest. . . ."[91] Monroe replied on January 10, noting that the resolution called for documents "if such a communication might now be made, consistently with the public interest, or with justice to the parties concerned." He informed the House that he had relieved Stewart from duty and had instituted a court martial against Stewart and John B. Provost, political agent in Peru. "In this stage," Monroe wrote, "the publication of these documents might tend to excite prejudices which might operate to the injury of both. . . . It is due to their right, and to the character of the Government, that they be not censured without just cause, which cannot be ascertained until, on a view of the charges, they are heard in their own defence, and after a thorough and impartial investigation of their conduct. Under these circumstances, it is thought that a communication, at this time, of these documents, would not comport with the public interest, nor with what is due to the parties concerned." Monroe's message was read and ordered to lie on the table.[92] No debate followed his refusal to comply.*

*On December 24, 1823, soon after Monroe announced the doctrine that bears his name, Representative Rollin C. Mallary of Vermont moved to request information on any European designs to aid Spain in regaining its colonies, noting that his concern was aroused by the strong language in the President's annual message. The motion, requesting only "such information . . . which may be disclosed without injury to the public good," passed without opposition. 41 *Annals* 879. On January 9 the Cabinet unanimously approved a response, made on January 12, that the President had "no information on that subject, not

In some instances, Presidents Madison and Monroe not only withheld information requested in a qualified resolution, but did so without revealing its existence. The Senate and House requested, several months after war was declared on Britain, that Madison provide all information "he may possess," and in the Department of State, concerning "the time and manner of promulgating" the French decree on which Madison had relied in suspending commerce with Britain.[93] Madison sent misleading excerpts, and withheld letters from American ministers flatly characterizing the decree a fraud, without any hint to Congress that any relevant material had been held back.* Another interesting example occurred when the House requested Monroe to lay before them "any information he may possess, and think proper to communicate, relative to the proceedings of certain persons who took possession of Amelia Island" and set up the "establishment" that Monroe had ordered suppressed.[94] The call for information caused a stir in the Cabinet. One of the documents in the President's possession, Secretary of State Adams recorded in his diary, incriminated the British government in the affair. After some discussion with Adams, Monroe "thought proper to omit certain passages of the letter in the communication to the House, but to give a copy of the whole to Mr. Bagot to be communicated to his Government." The British Minister Bagot "expressed himself much gratified with the delicacy of this proceeding, and said he did not believe there was a word of truth in the story told by the British officer, Colonel McDonald," Adams recorded.[95] On December 15, copies of the Amelia Island papers, minus the portion deleted by the President, were turned over to the House. Monroe only vaguely suggested that some material had been withheld,† and no further discussion took place in the House.

---

known to Congress, which can be disclosed without injury to the public good." *Id.* 986; 6 *Adams Memoirs* 230. The House took no further action. Monroe in fact had little evidence of European designs to aid Spain not already widely known. His pronouncement had resulted from a suggestion by Britain to issue a joint statement against any intervention in South America. See J. Logan, Jr., *No Transfer: An American Security Principle* 160–61 (1961).

*The information Madison revealed led opponents to suspect that a decree had been supplied to the American Minister to France, Jonathan Russell, but intentionally withheld, causing Britain to refuse to repeal its own edicts against neutral commerce. Further requests passed both houses, asking when official information of the decree was first received and by whom. 26 *Annals* 92, 302, 310. No additional material was provided, but the Senate blocked Russell's appointment as Minister to Sweden by resolving that creation of the office was "inexpedient." *Id.* 94. See the discussion *infra* at 289.

†In his letter of transmittal, Monroe wrote that he was enclosing a report of the Secretary of State "containing all the information of the Executive, which it is proper to disclose, relative to certain persons who lately took possession of Amelia Island and Galveston." 31 *Annals* 448. Monroe gave the House

No instance was found in which Madison, Monroe or Adams explicitly refused full compliance with an unqualified request. This is not very significant in itself since, as we have seen, Congress often refused to request sensitive material, and almost invariably authorized withholding of sensitive material actually requested. But even where Congress demanded material without qualification, the executive found ways of avoiding compliance without explicitly refusing it. One rationale was to construe the request so as to limit its scope.[96] Another device was simply to ignore the request, or at least to delay responding. On November 9, 1814, for example, the Senate adopted a motion by Jeremiah Mason of New Hampshire to have Madison submit "as far as practicable" the number of military enlistees in each state since the war, the year and terms of enlistment, and the number and distribution of noncommissioned officers. After two months elapsed without any response, Senator Mason proposed a resolution requesting the President to explain his failure to comply.[97] No action was taken on this motion, and Mason appears to have let the matter lapse.[98] In 1826 the House adopted a resolution requesting President Adams to provide information relating to the Panama Congress, even though the Senate had not yet approved the nominations of ministers. Adams considered telling the House he would respond only after the Senate had approved the nominations, and when Adams sought an appropriation. He was persuaded simply to ignore the request until that time, however, to avoid antagonizing House members.[99]

Individual members of Congress complained at various times about the incompleteness of information sent by the executive in response to requests.[100] Representative Joseph Pearson of North Carolina, for example, protested on February 16, 1814 that the information transmitted by the executive was inadequate, consisting of "scraps and extracts."[101] Though no one contested his allegations, neither house could marshal a majority to challenge the executive's practices.

---

some indication of the reasons he might withhold material in his response of January 29, 1822, to a request for material that would be consistent with the public interest to disclose on aspects of Andrew Jackson's conduct as Governor of Florida (38 *Annals* 826–27):

Being always desirous to communicate to Congress, or to either house, all the information in the possession of the Executive respecting any important interest of our Union, which may be communicated without real injury to our constituents, and which can rarely happen, except in negotiations pending with foreign Powers; and deeming it more consistent with the principles of our Government, in cases submitted to my discretion, as in the present instance, to hazard error by the freedom of the communication rather than by withholding any portion of information belonging to the subject, I have thought proper to communicate every document comprised within this call.

The chief reason for this deference to executive discretion appears to have been party politics. Republican majorities dominated Congress, and in general protected the executive from what they regarded as politically motivated interference by the minority in the form of information requests. Constitutional principle does appear, however, to have played a part. A number of legislators—even among the minority—expressed the view that the executive was empowered to withhold material regardless of the form of legislative requests.*

Whether executive officers other than the President did or could withhold material from Congress and its committees was an issue tangentially raised on at least two occasions. In 1814, a House committee appointed to inquire into the destruction of Washington by the British called for information from several executive officers, among them Secretary of Treasury George W. Campbell. In a letter to Campbell, Madison appears to have assumed he could restrain Campbell from testifying about their conversations. But he urged Campbell to testify completely, particularly on certain points of conflict between Madison and General John Armstrong, who, since his dismissal as Secretary of War, was seeking to place blame for the defeat on the President:

> That you may be under no restraint whatever from official or personal confidence, I think it proper to intimate to you that, in relation to myself, I hope that no information you may be able to give will be withheld from either of those considerations. . . . I am anxious that every circumstance may be reached that can throw light on it . . . and the more . . . so because I understand that a statement furnished by the late Secretary of War implicates me in two particulars. . . . Your recollection of my reply to your remarks, and of my communication of what passed between me and Genl. Armstrong, may, in connection with recollections of others, aid in elucidating truth.[102]

The second instance resulted from House efforts to obtain information on liquidation and payment of American claims against France.[103] The Committee on Foreign Relations reported on May 24, 1824, that little progress had been made on the issue, and urged that measures be taken to impress upon France the necessity for an

---

*For example, Representative Daniel Sheffey (Va.) said that "all admit [a President's] discretion whether or not the information asked would injuriously affect the public interest." 26 *Annals* 173. After William Burwell (Va.) introduced a resolution to require the President to use armed vessels to protect certain trade, Dana suggested that "required" be changed to "requested." Burwell had no objection, "but he thought the expression 'request' was confined to calling upon the President for information, a case in which it was at his option to comply or not." 20 *Annals* 1226 (Jan. 19, 1810). See *supra* at 244–46.

early and definite adjustment. The House voted, as the Committee recommended, to request the President to supply all correspondence with France on the subject at the next legislative session.[104] On April 14, 1826, Committee Chairman John Forsyth supplied Secretary of State Clay with another House resolution requesting all correspondence and instructions given to the American Minister in France, James Brown. Clay replied on April 17, agreeing to submit the correspondence, but refusing to supply the instructions:

> In respect to the general Instructions given to Mr. Brown which have not yet been communicated to either Branch of Congress, I do not feel myself authorized to state what they do or do not contain without the direction of the President, and the impropriety of any public disclosure concerning them, during the pendency of negociations will, I presume, appear to the Committee.[105]

Control of Foreign Affairs

The division of power over foreign relations between Congress and the executive continued in most respects to follow the pattern established from 1789 to 1809. The President acted as "sole organ of the nation"[106] and was recognized by Congress to be the nation's spokesman and negotiator with foreign nations.[107] In most instances the President took the lead in both formulating and implementing foreign policy, usually acting pursuant to broad congressional delegations or promptly seeking legislative approval thereafter.

Madison sought and obtained legislative authority for many actions, including the wars against Britain and Algiers.[108] He had done much, however, before the declaration to bring about war with Britain through the exercise of discretion and by withholding information, as discussed below. When Algiers insisted on tribute after being defeated, he announced that the United States would fight rather than pay, and then informed Congress.[109] Not only did Congress agree to most executive requests, it frequently acted without any concrete information. For example, when Madison recommended an embargo on April 1, 1812, Congress promptly complied even though, as Josiah Quincy said, "the President has not communicated to us one document or reason for the measure."[110] Requests for necessary information, even when qualified, were blocked at several crucial points.[111] Most significantly, Madison appears to have conspired with Governor Claiborne and others to take over West Florida from Spain, resting the legitimacy of his conduct on less-than-explicit indications of congressional approval. He used the same technique in an effort to take control of East Florida, where the case for legislative authority was much weaker.[112]

Monroe continued Madison's aggressive policies in East Florida; indeed, he had engineered those efforts as Madison's Secretary of State. He ordered the takeover of Amelia Island without consulting Congress, and also tolerated, if not authorized, General Andrew Jackson's conquering much of the province.[113] Congress was informed of these activities after the fact, and failed either to disapprove them or to prevent their repetition. Congress's reluctance to accept responsibility for military actions was also shown when Monroe requested authority to land on Spanish-held islands in search of pirates. Congress simply provided the President with the necessary vessels, leaving him to interpret and enforce the nation's rights under international law.[114] Congress aggressively pressed Monroe to recognize the South American republics, perhaps speeding that process. But recognition ultimately came at the President's recommendation, after the treaty with Spain was safely ratified. Finally, in his annual message to Congress in 1823, Monroe unilaterally announced the doctrine that bears his name, warning Europe and Russia against colonizing in the Americas or interfering with the new South American republics. The pronouncement was issued after Cabinet consideration of its constitutional propriety, Monroe apparently accepting Adams's argument that it could be published without legislative approval precisely because "the act of the Executive could not, after all, commit the nation to a pledge of war."* Congress appears to have understood the statement as involving no military commitment,† and Monroe applied it in that manner.**

*6 *Adams Memoirs* 207-208. Attorney General William Wirt questioned whether the United States should take "so broadly the ground of resistance to the interposition of the Holy Alliance by force to restore the Spanish dominion in South America." But if we were to be committed to defending the new republics, he suggested that "all documents ought to be communicated to Congress, and they ought to manifest their sentiments in the form of resolutions, and that the Executive ought not to pledge the honor of the nation to war without taking the sense of the country with them." *Id.* 202, 205. Adams agreed that if the doctrine were to operate as a commitment to go to war, "a joint resolution of the two Houses of Congress should be proposed and adopted to the same purport." But he disliked the idea of a joint resolution, for "this would render it necessary to communicate to them [the Congress], at least confidentially, the existing state of things." Instead of waiting for Congress to deliberate and vote, Adams urged the President to "act promptly and decisively." *Id.* 202, 208.

†At Adams's suggestion, Monroe's draft address was amended to delete criticism of the invasion of Spain by France, and recognition of Greece as an independent nation. He felt the message should focus on the Americas, in "general terms" that "pledged nothing." 6 *Adams Memoirs* 196-99. The language of Monroe's statement also contained no pledge; it promised noninterference with existing colonies and neutrality in conflicts between Spain and other nations. Efforts to establish new colonies, and interference with independent governments, would be viewed as "dangerous" and "unfriendly." A change in neutral-

Adams, too, exercised independence and leadership in foreign affairs. He unilaterally accepted an invitation to participate in the Panama Congress, for example, and dispatched vessels to deal with, and negotiated an end to, Brazil's blockade of Buenos Aires.[115] He supported Joel Poinsett, who as Minister to Mexico was seeking to upset the existing regime for one more favorable to the United States.[116] And he took the lead in negotiating with Britain on the boundary question in the Northeast, authorizing Gallatin to propose or agree to anything that Gallatin thought would satisfy the nation and pass the Senate.[117] He was much more cautious than his predecessors, however, in authorizing military projects.

Though executive initiative and control was the general rule during this period,† much evidence accumulated of Congress's power and capacity to make foreign policy, and to refuse to follow policies urged by the executive. Consistent with the general pattern of deference to the executive, the Senate and House refused to adopt several declarations of policy,[118] sometimes after argument on their consti-

---

ity would take place only if warranted "in the judgment of the competent authorities of this Government. . . ." 41 *Annals* 22-23.

Congress requested information on European designs to aid Spain, but accepted Monroe's statement that he had no information that could be disclosed without injury to the public good. *Id.* 986. John Randolph commented that the pronouncement was quixotic, and that he would not commit the United States to defend any South American nation incapable of maintaining its own independence. *Id.* 1188. Floyd of Virginia later claimed that he had denounced the message as "assuming an unwarrantable power; violating the spirit of the Constitution, . . . and indirectly leading to war, which Congress alone had the right to declare." 2 *Register* 2446. But these isolated reactions suggest that most members did not view the pronouncement as binding upon the nation to go to war in the event of any specific European intervention.

**The new government of Colombia sought in July 1824 to determine the scope of Monroe's doctrine by asking whether the United States would join Colombia in a defensive alliance, and whether an expedition by Spain would be regarded as an expedition of the Holy Allies (the alliance between France, Austria, Russia and Prussia), because France controlled Spain. Adams replied on August 6, 1824, that such commitments were not contemplated by Monroe's statement, since "by the Constitution of the United States, the ultimate decision of this question belongs to the Legislative Department of the Government." A similar request by Brazil in 1825 was rejected on similar grounds. *See generally* D. Perkins, *The Monroe Doctrine, 1823-1826* at 187, 190, 194-98 (1927). When Joel R. Poinsett used the word "pledged" in a statement as Minister to Mexico, Secretary of State Clay was forced to explain the term as an expression of executive opinion that the nation would act if allied Europe attempted to subvert the liberties of South American nations. A.S.P., 5 *Foreign Relations* 908.

†On April 2, 1810, John Randolph criticized Madison for failing to recommend measures deemed expedient, and argued that nonintercourse in the meantime should be repealed. In the process, he stated, with typical exaggeration and eloquence, his perception of the allocation of power over foreign affairs (21 *Annals* 1709-10):

tutional propriety.* But they passed at least two important declarations: a resolution of both houses approving Madison's dismissal of the British Minister Francis Jackson, and pledging the nation's military strength in support of the President;† and a House resolve, passed to put pressure on President Monroe, expressing its support "for the success of the Spanish provinces of South America which are struggling to establish their liberty and independence," and pledging "its Constitutional support to the President . . . whenever he may deem it expedient to recognise the sovereignty and indepen-

---

If the President of the United States, who is charged with the execution of the laws, whose knowledge respecting all our foreign relations is perfect as that of finite man can be—if he, on whom (do what you will) the execution of these measures must ultimately rest, has recommended no measures as necessary and expedient, it hardly becomes—I will not say a member of this House, but me, to step in "where angels fear to tread." And until the President of the United States who stands at the helm of our Government, shall disclose his plan of operations to this House—until the efficient Prime Minister of this country, who has an almost omnipotent control over our foreign affairs, and nearly as great over our domestic, shall disclose his sentiments, it is idle and ridiculous for members of this House to be popping up in their seats with shreds and patches and disjointed members of systems which can never make a whole one.

*The most interesting debate was on Randolph's motion to approbate Madison's conduct in responding to British overtures, taken by many as an indirect way of criticizing Jefferson. It was laid on the table after arguments against pronouncements, interference with the executive, and wasting time by commenting on annual messages. 20 *Annals* 93, 95, 114-15, 142-43, 197. Randolph cited precedents (resolutions approving Washington's neutrality proclamation and Jefferson's conduct after Spain closed New Orleans to American trade). *Id.* 142-43. Many seemed confident of House authority, but felt no need existed for an expression of their support. *E.g., id.* 167-74 (Ross). Though opposed to passage, Dana contended that the House had ample power to act, resting on the war power. *Id.* 139.

†Senator William B. Giles of Virginia introduced the resolution arguing that, while the Constitution invests the President with the power to receive Ambassadors—which includes all "the incidental or consequential powers" that flow from this "general expression"—"Congress is invested with the power, without limitation or qualification, 'to declare war.' Now, sir," Giles said, "it must be obvious to every understanding, that these several powers are so intimately connected, and may be so dependent upon each other, that the exercise of the power conceded to the President may consequentially involve the necessity of the exercise of the power conceded to Congress, as in the case now under consideration. The refusal of the executive to receive any further communication from His Brittanic Majesty's Minister [Mr. Jackson] may consequentially involve us in war with Great Britain." To Giles, this meant that "Congress must speak—Congress must act. Congress never can shrink from its Constitutional responsibility." He stressed also the practical significance of making Britain realize "before she decides upon this subject" whether she "will be called upon to act against an united, harmonized Government and people." 20 *Annals* 485-87. The motion passed the same day, December 8, 1809. *Id.* 509. The House concurred on January 3, 1810, after much more extensive debate, in which opponents attacked it as a pronouncement and an interference with the executive. *Id.* 909-10, 940-41, 967-68, 1052, 1151.

dence of any of the said provinces."* Both were adopted despite
claims that they encroached upon executive powers.†

The Senate, in at least two important cases, refused to approve
foreign-affairs appointments.[119] Christopher Gore of Massachusetts
was not satisfied, however, with these concrete demonstrations of
the Senate's unquestioned power. He moved five resolutions on
July 19, 1813, including one that would have had the Senate declare
that the President's constitutional power "to fill up all vacancies"
during recess did not justify appointment to "any office not before
full." The resolutions failed to pass, after arguments that the Senate
should avoid abstract generalizations; that it had no business attempting to define the President's powers; and that it should recognize the need for offices "created by the occasion," a device used by
Presidents in the past, and one which Congress could easily control
through its powers over appropriations and treaties.** Adams appeared to challenge the Senate's power over appointments when he
suggested he could send ministers to the Panama Conference without
Senate confirmation. But the Senate forced Adams to retreat from
his position.‡

*37 Annals 1081, 1091. The resolution was attacked as endangering peace
and tending to produce a collision with the executive by encroaching on its
power. Proponents asserted that the House could lawfully express its opinion,
and that they at least shared the power to recognize foreign states. Id. 1081-85,
1088.

†A relatively uncontroversial declaration of policy took place on April 9,
1818, when the House approved a committee report condemning the imprisonment without cause of an American citizen by Spain, and stating that "this
House will support and maintain such measures as the President shall hereafter
adopt" to obtain his release. At the same time the House voted down an amendment to authorize the President to make reprisals on the Spanish consul if the
American was not released. 32 Annals 1713.

**26 Annals 90, 651-57, 695-707, 759. The law of nations, if not the Consti-
tution, creates any office necessary for the conduct of foreign affairs, Outerbridge Horsey of Delaware contended; if the President is unable to act "with
utmost secrecy and despatch," he might, for example, lose an opportunity to
make peace. Id. 716. Gore called the theory of offices created by necessity a
"queer fancy," based not upon the Constitution but upon a dangerous doctrine
of implied powers, and noted that no necessity existed anyway, since the President clearly had the power as commander-in-chief to negotiate peace agreements. He distinguished the precedents cited as involving "private agents" who
lacked authority to bind the nation, or the acts of Jefferson and therefore not
entitled to respect. In any case, he said:

> No precedents can weigh against the plain sense and meaning of the Consti-
> tution and its express provisions. A contrary position would involve this
> palpable absurdity, viz: to render the Government superior to the Constitu-
> tion; which is contrary to the fundamental principle of all society, that the
> Constitution is superior to and of right ought at all times to direct and con-
> trol all the measures of Government.

Id. 745, 750-54.

‡Adams accepted the invitation to attend and informed Congress on Decem-

The House, too, debated its power to affect appointments. Most notably, Henry Clay attempted several times to have the House vote to appropriate funds for ministers to South American republics, even before the President had recognized them. Despite the arguments that such a vote would interfere improperly with the executive and might lead to war with Spain, the House approved Clay's proposal on one occasion.[120] Clay and his supporters contended that nothing in the Constitution prevented Congress from expressing its opinion to the President on recognition of a foreign regime, and that if war resulted from recognition urged by Congress, it would be constitutionally proper since it would have followed a legislative determination of policy.* This resolution, and other efforts,[121] placed pressure on Monroe to recognize the South American republics, and when Monroe proposed recognizing five regimes, the House adopted resolutions approving the recommendation as well as an appropriation to send ministers.[122] A resolution was then proposed in the Senate that would have amended the appropriation to declare that the President could not appoint the ministers during recess; it was attacked as improper and withdrawn.[123] The appropriation passed, and Congress adjourned, enabling Monroe to attempt recess

---

ber 6, 1825 that ministers "will be commissioned" for the purpose. 2 *Register* 3 (appendix). By December 25 the President had modified his position to the extent that he sent nominations for the Senate's approval; but he claimed the "measure was deemed to be within the constitutional competency of the Executive," and to be seeking the Senate's opinion of the venture's expediency. *Id.* 1209, appendix 43. John Branch of North Carolina offered a resolution declaring that the President lacks power "to appoint ambassadors or public Ministers, but with the advice and consent of the Senate," or to fill vacancies in recess. 2 *Register* 589. Though advised that he could defeat the resolution on the floor, Adams chose "the humiliating experience of sending to the Senate an explanation of my own words," rather than risk its adoption. 7 *Adams Memoirs* 99. The resolution finally came up for interesting debate in March 1826, and was permanently tabled on April 27, by a vote of 23 to 21. 2 *Register* 642.

*32 *Annals* 1500. George Tucker of Virginia also made this point, asking whether, if a contemplated action might lead to war, it was not proper that Congress, "the constitutional organ for declaring war," assume the responsibility for it. "Or, is it consistent with the spirit of our Constitution that the Executive should pursue a course which leads to hostilities without an intimation of the opinion and wishes of the nation. . . ? I think not." *Id.* 1590. Clay later argued that the House had "the right to recognise, in the exercise of the Constitutional power of Congress to regulate foreign commerce." *Id.* 1616. And to those who claimed that the recognition of Buenos Aires would lead to war, he said (*id.* 1618–19):

> If it was cause of war, the Executive ought not to have the right to produce a war upon the country without consulting Congress. . . . There would be very little difference in principle between vesting the Executive with the power of declaring war, or with the power of necessarily leading the country into war without consulting the authority to whom the power of making war is confided.

appointments. But he decided, after consulting his Cabinet, to delay any appointments until Congress reassembled.*

An arrangement was made with Britain during Monroe's first term that has subsequently been called the precursor of executive agreements.[124] During negotiations to end the War of 1812, Britain proposed that the United States maintain no warships on the Great Lakes. American negotiators rejected the proposal because it would have allowed Canada to continue to maintain a naval force on those waters.[125] After the Treaty of Ghent, however, Congress authorized the President to sell or lay up all the armed vessels on the Lakes except those needed to enforce the revenue laws.[126] Over a year later, in April 1817, negotiations resumed, culminating in an exchange of notes between British Minister Charles Bagot and Acting Secretary of State Richard Rush. Each side agreed to reduce the number of armed vessels on the Lakes to a bare minimum.[127] Secretary of Navy Benjamin Crowninshield immediately implemented the agreement, which was a simple matter, since the American force on the Lakes was already within the agreed-upon limits.[128]

In December 1817 Monroe advised Congress of the arrangement, but sent no copy to either the House or Senate.[129] No member of either house questioned this procedure. On January 14, 1818, Bagot asked Secretary of State Adams if the agreement would be sent to Congress, since it was "sort of a treaty"; Monroe "did not think it necessary. . . ."[130] On April 6, 1818, however, Monroe sent the letters to the Senate to consider "whether this is such an arrangement as the Executive is competent to enter into by the powers vested in it by the Constitution, or is such a one as requires the advice and consent of the Senate," and if the latter, "should it be approved"?[131]

The Committee on Foreign Relations proposed a resolution that two-thirds of the Senate approve "the arrangement" and "recommend" that it be carried into effect. The resolution was adopted unanimously on April 16, after a meeting in executive session.[132] Monroe then proclaimed the arrangement in effect on April 28.[133]

---

*Monroe was inclined to agree with Adams that "the *words* of the Constitution were against the exercise of the power" of appointments to previously unfilled offices during recess, but "the *reason* of the words is in its favor." *See also* his letter of May 10, 1822, to Madison, who shared the position that recess appointments to previously unfilled offices were proper. 6 *The Writings of James Monroe* 285-86 (S. Hamilton, ed. 1898-1903) (7 vols.) [hereinafter "*Monroe Writings*"]. The Cabinet members opposed to the appointments were Calhoun and Secretary of Navy Thompson, both of whom warned against adverse Senate reaction. 6 *Adams Memoirs* 24-25. See A. Whitaker, *The United States and the Independence of Latin America, 1800-1830*, 370-92 (1941).

Britain never formally adopted the arrangement in council, and no ratifications were exchanged.[134]

These events demonstrated that formal agreements with foreign nations could be made other than by treaty. This arrangement, though, differed from more recent executive agreements in that it was preceded by legislation giving the President discretionary authority over the subject matter, involved no change in the level of the nation's naval force actually on the Great Lakes, and was ultimately approved by the Senate's adoption of a resolution requiring a two-thirds vote for passage.*

Controversy over foreign-affairs powers also erupted between the branches of Congress. After the Treaty of Ghent was ratified by the Senate, John Forsyth of Georgia, Chairman of the House Committee on Foreign Relations, introduced a bill to repeal certain commercial laws inconsistent with the treaty.[135] After considerable debate the bill passed, and the House rejected a Senate bill that simply declared that all laws inconsistent with the treaty had been repealed.[136] Those opposed to Forsyth's version argued that treaties were self-executing, and that foreign confidence in treaties would be greatly undermined if legislative sanction were required.[137] Supporters contended that, although a treaty was generally higher than a law, this was not true where an appropriation was necessary or, as in this case, where the Constitution specifically assigned to Congress the subject matter the treaty purports to regulate.[138] "If the treaty-making power may regulate commerce without the sanction of Congress," said Philip P. Barbour of Virginia, "then the same Power may declare war without the sanction of Congress."[139] The Senate rejected the House bill,†

---

*Professor Arthur Schlesinger, Jr. notes, however, that "since the Rush-Bagot agreement involved continuing obligations, it clearly fell into the category Vattel had reserved for treaties. Moreover, an arms-control compact with a nation with which the United States had fought two wars in forty years would certainly seem of sufficient consequence to call for formal ratification." *The Imperial Presidency* 87 (1973).

†Opponents of the House position varied in their contentions. Eligius Fromentin of Louisiana made the sweeping argument that "the President and the Senate of the United States are the attorneys, in fact, of the people of the United States, to make, in their name, with a foreign nation, every contract which they conceive to be demanded for the interest of the people of the United States." 29 *Annals* 61. James Barbour of Virginia, on the other hand, distinguished between treaties of commerce and those of war or finance, arguing that in the former area treaties were self-executing. *Id.* 51–55. Those favoring the House bill included Nathaniel Macon of North Carolina (*id.* 75) (convention affects revenue power); George Campbell of Tennessee (*id.* 83–84) (treaty relating to power assigned to Congress is only a pledge to act through legislation); and Jonathan Roberts of Pennsylvania (*id.* 66–68) (treaty cannot become law without approbation of Congress, which has all power to make laws).

and a conference committee was formed to resolve the dispute. It recited generalities in support of both positions in its report, and adopted aspects of each bill in a version that obtained approval from both houses.[140] Other efforts by House members to prevent a renunciation of territory by treaty,[141] to repeal laws inconsistent with a commercial treaty with Denmark,[142] and to eliminate funds for a mission to Russia that had obtained Senate approval,[143] all failed.

The most extensive controversy concerning the allocation of foreign-affairs powers followed Adams's proposal that ministers be sent to the Panama Congress. The information obtained by the Senate and House, already antagonistic toward Adams, created suspicions, or gave credence to feigned suspicions, that sending ministers to Panama might result in binding commitments to defend the South American republics.[144] In passing upon the nomination of ministers, the Senate Foreign Relations Committee reported that "instead of confining their inquiries to the mere fitness of the person nominated . . . it is not only the right, but the duty of the Senate, to determine, previously, as to the necessity and propriety of creating the offices themselves. . . ." An examination of all the circumstances led the committee to conclude that sending the ministers would be "not expedient."[145] The Senate debated this recommendation and approved the nominations, but in a manner that fully accorded with the committee's underlying assumption of the Senate's obligation to pass on the wisdom of attending the Conference.[146]

The House was faced with a similar issue when Adams sought an appropriation to pay the ministers's expenses. The Foreign Affairs Committee recommended the appropriation, after finding the Conference was to be but an assembly of diplomatic agents, clothed only with power to discuss and negotiate, whose "engagements" would have to be ratified in accordance with the constitutional processes of each attending nation.[147] Opposition initially took the form of a proposed amendment declaring that the United States was neutral and that the ministers "ought not be authorized to discuss, consider, or consult, upon any proposition of alliance, offensive, or defensive . . . or any stipulation, compact, or declaration, binding the United States in any way. . . ."[148] The proposal was attacked as an unconstitutional interference with the President's power to conduct foreign negotiations, and with the power of President and Senate to form binding treaties; the mere existence of the "physical" power to block the appropriation, argued Webster, did not establish the propriety of its exercise.[149] James K. Polk of Tennessee (later the eleventh President) and others believed the House was obliged to exercise discretion in voting "the People's money, for any purpose," and thereby to act as a check upon the President and Senate.[150]

William C. Rives of Virginia was among those of the opinion that to condition the appropriation was also proper, because "if we may pronounce *all* [the mission's] . . . objects to be inexpedient, we may surely pronounce some of them to be so." It was a misconception to consider the President and Senate in sole control of foreign affairs, he said, since the entire legislature was assigned the power over war.[151] A majority voted to add the proposed amendment, but the appropriation was then defeated by a combination of its opponents and of its supporters who refused to accept it as amended.[152] The appropriation then passed, without the amendment, and was approved by the Senate after a similar amendment was rejected.[153]

A particularly interesting aspect of the debates concerning the Panama Congress was that several legislators recognized, especially in the Senate, that the President could have ordered special agents or other diplomatic officers to go to Panama and once there, without making any binding commitment, "pursue a course of policy which will justify other nations in making war upon us."* These observations have led one scholar to comment that "both advocates and opponents of the mission" agreed that, if the President could unilaterally settle on a diplomatic policy and pursue it, "it was likewise within his power, and his alone, to determine whether or not its consequences might involve the peace and safety of the country."[154]

---

*2 *Register* 200 (H.L. White, Tenn.) The point was asserted with particular force by a mission supporter, Senator J.S. Johnson of Louisiana (*id.* 223):

> There is nothing peculiar in the present case. The President has, at all times, the power to commit the peace of this country and involve us in hostilities, as far as he has power in this case. To him is confided all intercourse with foreign nations. To his discretion and responsibility is entrusted all our delicate and difficult relations: all negotiations and all treaties are conducted and brought to issue by him. He speaks in the name and with the authority of this Government with all the Powers of Europe. That confidence has never been deceived. The character, talent, and public virtue, which placed them in that high station, is the guarantee of their conduct. Their own fame, their love of country, make it their interest and their duty to cultivate peace, commerce, and honest friendship, with all nations: and all the motives of self-love and ambition conspire to ensure from them, as from us, a faithful discharge of the trust confided to them by the Constitution and the country. But there must be confidence. No Government can exist without it. And this distrust and jealousy of the Executive will destroy all power to do good, and all power to act efficiently.

Van Buren added an extensive comment to the same effect, contending that the President could send ministers even if Congress refused to cooperate, "and the contingent fund will supply the means."*Id.* 235.

Yet the debates make clear that many—probably most—of those legislators would *not* have agreed that the President had exclusive power to decide on the mission involved. Each house was aware of its power to pass on the wisdom of attending the Conference, the Senate through its approval of appointments and both the House and Senate through their power over appropriations. Many agreed that the President might find ways of going ahead regardless of Congress's view, and even the House amendment sought only to convey an "opinion" to influence the President's actions. But no member expressed the notion that the opinions of either house, if given in any form, could have been disregarded. On the contrary, opponents to the House amendment argued that it should not be passed because the President would have no choice but to obey it.* Furthermore, while most if not all members would have agreed that an independent course of conduct by the President would have inevitably influenced the course of events and possibly limited the legislature's options, no member said the President could require Congress to support any pledge to use military force.† And the President and his Secretary of State explicitly disclaimed the power to commit the nation.

The Use of Executive Agents.   The broad agreement among members of Congress that the President could use special agents was supported by practice. Agents were frequently used for intelligence-gathering and in some instances, such as in the case of West Florida, to help bring about American objectives.[155] The most significant mission of this sort occurred when Madison sent Joel R. Poinsett, secretly and without Senate approval, to South America as an agent

*Alexander Thomson of Virginia assumed that if Congress could "command," the President would have to obey. Not only would this upset the system of checks and balances, it would lead to an undue concentration of power in a branch of government unsuited to give diplomatic advice because of its large numbers and inability to act with concert, energy and dispatch. 2 *Register* 2338. William S. Archer, also of Virginia, and also an opponent of the amendment, said: "Can any President act in opposition to the opinion of the House? *A fortiori,* no President can have such pre-option." *Id.* 2379.

†Many, in fact, specifically disclaimed that the Monroe Doctrine was any such pledge. For example, Senator Hayne denied that "Monroe ever pledged this nation to go to war or make treaties to prevent the interference of any European nation in the present contest. I deny that he had a right to make any such pledge. . . . Mr. Monroe's declaration . . . was intended to produce a moral effect abroad." 2 *Register* 161–62. Senator Holmes of Maine said that "The President of these United States has no power whatever to pledge the People of this Union to any nation in anything. And every declaration of his, made to the world, must be understood by other nations, not as a *pledge* of what we *must* do, but as an *opinion* of what we *will* do. Until Congress concur, or assent to a measure affecting our foreign relations, nothing is binding." *Id.* 268.

for seamen and commerce. Poinsett did some commercial work, but he broadly construed instructions from Secretaries of State Smith and Monroe,* and worked intimately with revolutionary leaders in Argentina and Chile, suggesting commercial and military plans, helping them obtain arms, and actually leading a division of the Chilean army against Peruvian loyalists.[156] Nothing in Poinsett's instructions specifically authorized these activities. But he had kept the administration advised of most of his plans and received virtually no directions for long periods of time, and no orders to refrain in any way from aiding the revolutionaries. After the Chilean campaign he wrote to a friend: "I may be blamed by the government and by my fellow citizens but I have acted right; and I have been so long a solitary wanderer that I am accustomed to content myself with my own approval."[157] In fact he was not blamed, but thanked for his services,[158] and given new diplomatic assignments, eventually becoming Minister to Mexico.[159]

The executive department's handling of Poinsett is important because it is consistent with how Madison and Monroe used agents and even military officers in West and East Florida. Poinsett was given broad leeway to advance the republican cause, without any commitment from the administration. He was told to write in code,[160] and all his important communications were withheld from Congress. Manning reports, in fact, that Monroe specifically instructed that Poinsett's letters be removed from State Department files and returned to him.[161] Congress, furthermore, made it easy for the administration to keep Poinsett's activities secret by making virtually no requests for information and by exempting from one request "those communications, which in the opinion of the Executive, it would be improper to disclose."[162] These actions were of course consistent with Congress's decision to allow agents to be

---

*The letter from Smith, dated August 27, 1810, told Poinsett that, in the event any South American country separates from its parent nation, "it will coincide with the sentiments and policy of the United States to promote the most friendly relations and the most liberal intercourse between the inhabitants of this hemisphere." 1 *Joel R. Poinsett Papers* 20 (Pa. Hist. Soc.). Monroe went somewhat further in his letter of April 30, 1811, appointing Poinsett consul-general for Buenos Aires, Chile and Peru (*id.* 67 and 68):

> The disposition shown by most of the Spanish Provinces to separate from Europe, and to erect themselves into independent states excites great interest here. As inhabitants of the same Hemisphere, as neighbors, the United States cannot be unfeeling spectators of so important a movement. The destiny of these provinces must depend on themselves. Should such a revolution however take place, it cannot be doubted that our relations with them will be more intimate, and our friendship stronger than it can be while they are colonies of any European power.

appointed without Senate approval and to be paid out of "secret service" or contingency funds.*

A somewhat different situation confronted the Adams administration in 1827. Condy Raguet, chargé d'affaires to Brazil, protested vehemently against Brazil's blockade of the Argentina coast in 1826, including the seizure of American seamen and vessels violating the blockade. He urged "decisive measures," but received little guidance.[163] The only instructions sent him during an important, eighteen-month period approved his "zealous exertions" to prevent abuse of the law of blockade, and ordered him to remonstrate promptly and firmly in every instance in which the law seemed in danger of violation.[164] When the administration received Raguet's particularly incensed letters concerning the treatment of the officers and crew of an American vessel,[165] Secretary of State Clay wrote Raguet that parts of his dispatches had "occasioned the President the most lively regret" because a relationship seemed to have arisen between Raguet and the Brazilian government "which [might] possibly affect the public interests committed to [his] charge." Clay noted that the President was empowered by the Constitution to determine "the nature of instructions which may be sent to you, and of orders to the commanders of our public vessels. . . . If those instructions or orders do not correspond in all respects with your wishes or expectations, you must recollect that he is enabled, at this distance, to take a calmer view of things than you are; that we have relations with other nations besides those which exist with the Brazils; and that, even if we had not, war or threats of war ought not to be employed as instruments of redress, until after the failure of every peaceful experiment." He added that even the President's authority for "throwing out warlike measures" was limited because "the Constitution having wisely confided to Congress alone the power of declaring war, it cannot be known in all cases, beforehand, that the denunciation will be certainly followed by the commencement of hostilities."[166]

*The formalistic approach taken by Congress toward private agents as opposed to appointed officers is reflected by Monroe's request for funds to pay the "commissioners" he appointed during recess, without Senate approval, to survey the South American political scene. Several Representatives objected "upon the principle that the commissioners ought to have been nominated to the Senate." 4 Adams Memoirs 71-72. Resistance dissolved, however, when the appropriation for these agents was shifted, without opposition, from a specific budget line to the President's "secret service" or contingency fund. 32 Annals 1464-67, 1652. The only functional basis mentioned for distinguishing private from public agents was that the former lacked authority to bind the nation. 26 Annals 753. Actually, regular officers could be disavowed, and private agents could cause dangerous controversy although their acts might be "unofficial."

Clay's warning arrived too late to prevent a rupture. When Brazil seized another American merchant vessel in March 1827, Raguet demanded his papers, closed the mission, and left for home. Adams and Clay concurred that Raguet "could not be sustained," and promptly notified the Brazilian chargé in Washington that no interruption of relations was desired.[167] Adams explained to Congress that Raguet's action, "dictated by honest zeal for the honor and interests of his country; motives which operated exclusively upon the mind of the officer who resorted to it, has not been disapproved by me," but that a new chargé had been appointed.[168] This gentle treatment of Raguet may well have resulted from Adams's desire to avoid controversy, including criticism of his failure to instruct the chargé more frequently and carefully.

Role of the Supreme Court. Some comments on the Supreme Court's activities on foreign-affairs issues is in order. First, where neither Congress nor the executive had indicated its view of a matter, the Court apparently felt free to apply what it felt were the controlling standards of international law.[169] Where the legislative and executive branches had spoken clearly on a matter, such as recognition of a foreign nation, the Court expressly deferred to their collective, political judgment.[170] Finally, the Court recognized that Congress had considerable latitude in conferring upon the executive discretionary power to conduct foreign affairs by refusing to invalidate the delegation under which Madison recognized a nonexistent French decree and suspended commerce with Britain.[171] On the other hand, the Court refused to agree that the declaration of war against Britain by itself authorized the seizure within the United States of timber owned by a British subject; the Court insisted that Congress would have to approve specifically an action so much at variance with the accepted practice of other nations.[172]

MILITARY AFFAIRS AND ACTIONS

The principal military engagements of the period 1809-1828 are discussed in detail below. Some general observations are made here on how the branches functioned, and on numerous significant but relatively minor incidents and practices.

The War of 1812 led to the first serious challenge in the nation's history of the federal government's power to control military affairs. The governors of four states—Massachusetts, Connecticut, Rhode Island and Vermont—refused to comply with federal requisitions for militiamen, and to allow regular army personnel to command their militia.[173] The issue was resolved in favor of federal power in *Martin v. Mott*,[174] where the Supreme Court held that Congress could provide for calling up the militia in case of "imminent danger of invasion," and that the President was sole judge, under the law, of whether the exigency existed.* But the governors's actions did great harm to the nation's war effort.[175]

A frequently heard argument, prior to and during the War of 1812, was that the Constitution permitted only "defensive" wars. When Madison recommended a volunteer corps in 1810, Senator Bayard argued against providing one because he felt offensive actions would more likely be undertaken; the Constitution, he said, "in relation to foreign nations, does not contemplate conquest, but defence only. . . ."[176] Supporters of the proposal offered broad definitions of "defensive" actions,[177] or contended that no such limitation existed in the case of militia organized under federal authority.[178] The volunteer force was denied.[179]

The issue arose again in early 1812, just before war was declared. Many legislators claimed that the war was unconstitutional because the Constitution contemplated that the nation would engage only in "defensive" war, whereas a war that included an invasion of Canada was clearly "offensive."[180] Legislators opposed to this view argued that "defensive" war had to include "offensive" actions necessary to make an effective defense.[181] They said the President had authority to use the militia outside the United States under the commander-in-chief clause, because of his power to execute the laws, since a declaration of war is a law requiring execution.[182] Others refused to accept the premise that only defensive wars were contemplated, arguing that the Constitution allowed the national government to undertake any military action judged expedient.[183] The volunteer force and the war were ultimately authorized.[184] Even

---

*The Court noted the dangers and inconvenience that might result from allowing state officials to challenge the President's determination, including the possible disclosure of "important secrets of state, which the public interest, and even safety, might imperiously demand to be kept in concealment." 25 U.S. (12 Wheat.) 19, 31 (1827). This power to be exclusive judge, the Court said, will seldom be abused (*id.* 32):

> In a free government, the danger must be remote, since in addition to the high qualities which the Executive must be presumed to possess, of public virtue, and honest devotion to the public interests, the frequency of elections, and the watchfulness of the representatives of the nation, carry with them all the checks which can be useful to guard against usurpation or wanton tyranny.

The Court also held that the federal government did not even have to allege that an imminent danger of invasion had actually been found to exist by the President. "When the President exercises an authority confided to him by law, the presumption is, that it is exercised in pursuance of law." *Id.* 32-33.

after war was declared, opponents persisted in pressing the argument that it was unconstitutional and sought to block the appropriations necessary for its prosecution.[185] Members of the majority branded this activity "moral treason,"[186] claimed it untenable to limit the executive to defensive measures,[187] and managed to push through the necessary legislation.

The allocation within the federal government of power over military affairs was a complex mix of sometimes contradictory practices; but patterns do emerge. Congress had the upper hand, in that it controlled the extent and type of the armed force at the executive's disposal. When Madison became President, he had few men or vessels under his command.* Congress demonstrated that it could govern the armed forces by refusing increases in the size of the army and navy;[188] by mandating other increases;[189] by determining how much should be spent on such matters as fortifications;[190] by initiating military experiments;[191] and by authorizing the administrative reorganization of both the army and navy.[192] When new units were voted, Congress almost invariably specified their nature, number, composition, duration of service, and salary;[193] and appropriations for their support were frequently specific.[194] Furthermore, no established force was sacrosanct; Congress often reduced or modified the forces provided, especially the relatively large army recruited for the War of 1812.†

Congress seems to have been more willing to order inquiries and request information from the executive on military affairs than on

---

*The regular army's actual strength by January 1810 was 6,954 men, of which 4,189 were members of new regiments. The navy had only 16 seaworthy vessels of significant size, and some eight gunboats, in readiness. *See generally* D. Cooney, *A Chronology of the United States Navy, 1775-1965* at 15-43 (1965); H. Sprout and M. Sprout, *The Rise of American Naval Power, 1776-1918* at 25-104 (1939).

†Act of Mar. 3, 1815, 3 *Stat.* 224. Madison requested 20,000 men, but Congress approved only up to 10,000. Forsyth in the House said he feared the time had passed when rational recommendations of the executive would be given weight. Sheffey retorted that he was glad the time had come when executive recommendations would be weighed only on their merits. 28 *Annals* 1213-14. Other statements were made concerning the legislature's responsibility to form its own judgments. Senator Giles noted in debating against providing only six instead of ten regiments that Madison's message, while designating "the kinds of force suited to the occasion, leaves the quantum of each to be judged of and decided by Congress, where the responsibility did and ought to rest," and he added that he would not recede from his constitutional duty by foisting it upon the executive. 23 *Annals* 38. *See also* Grundy's statement against delegating power to the President "of speaking armies into existence, and again of speaking them out of existence. . . . He [Grundy] was against throwing the responsibility which ought to remain with Congress upon the President. . . . We are the best judges of the kind of force which it is fitting to employ." *Id.* 612. *Accord, id.* 617 (McKim).

foreign relations.[195] On January 22, 1810, for example, Representative Thomas Newton of Virginia moved that the President be requested to provide detailed information on the condition and distribution of the regular army, especially at New Orleans. The resolution passed "by a great majority," despite objections to its being unqualified and concerned with the disposition of the army, a subject properly for the commander-in-chief and not within the cognizance of the House.* Another unqualified request was for information on what the President was doing about hostile expeditions being prepared in American ports against powers at peace with the United States. It passed, despite the claim that the House should presume "the Executive had done its duty. . . ."[196] Sometimes the President's failure to provide adequate information became a reason for refusing to grant his requests for men or supplies.[197]

Congress authorized several military operations. War was declared to exist with Britain on June 18, 1812. It recognized that war had been commenced by the Bey of Algiers on March 3, 1815.[198] Madison sought authority to retaliate against Britain for violations of the usages of war, and Congress granted his request on March 3, 1813.[199] Congress also authorized the President to use the land and naval forces when war had been neither declared nor recognized: for example, to prevent certain vessels from entering United States waters;[200] to enforce the embargo of April 4, 1812;[201] to occupy or maintain authority in East Florida under certain circumstances;[202] to occupy all of Florida west of the Perdido not already occupied;[203] and to protect American commerce from piracy.[204] Authority to employ the armed forces was delegated by implication when Congress prohibited various activities and provided for their punish-

---

*Representative Dana "suggested the propriety of qualifying the resolution, as it embraced perhaps too minute an inquiry into the state of garrisons, and might require information which it might not be proper to communicate. . . ." He assumed, however, "that the President would have firmness enough to withhold such information as he should deem improper to make." John Dawson (Va.) saw no possible advantage in the resolution, and much possible harm by "exposing the situations on our frontiers. The President of the United States, as Commander-in-Chief, had a right to make such disposition of the Army as he thought proper; and it was a subject which did not properly come within the cognizance of the House." Newton and Benjamin Tallmadge of Connecticut disagreed with these views, arguing that it was Congress's duty to inquire into the state of the armed forces. 20 *Annals* 1256–57. The President responded on February 1, sending a memorandum of the Secretary of War setting forth the information sought. 21 *Annals* 1367. A dispute erupted over whether the information should be printed, some contending this would be unsafe, others noting that details about an army of five or six thousand were inconsequential to an enemy and important to our citizens. *Id.* 1367–68. The motion to print carried, 50–38. *Id.* 1368. Said one member: "No other nation in existence ever officially exposed to the world the precise state and disposition of its military force." *Id.*

ment,[205] and Congress was especially specific in providing for the issuance of letters of marque and reprisal, and in authorizing other programs for permitting private citizens to perform military services.[206] Congress occasionally refused to delegate military power in terms felt to be too vague.*

Congress frequently chose, however, to place the formation and implementation of military policy in executive hands. It sought executive advice and plans concerning the armed forces,[207] some members arguing as a matter of principle against any increase in military spending not requested by the President.[208] In some instances the President was authorized to raise or discharge certain numbers of troops when he deemed it proper;[209] to lay up such ships as the public interest would permit "in the event of a favourable change in our foreign relations";[210] and to build and employ new vessels if circumstances led him to conclude they were necessary.[211] Appropriations became, at times, very general,[212] and executive departments spent funds inconsistently with the purposes specified without any legislative check.† Broad discretion was frequently delegated, in one instance even to customs collectors to control vessels suspected of violating neutrality.[213] Information requests that might embarrass or interfere with the executive were often defeated,** as

---

*On April 30, 1810, an amendment was proposed to the bill concerning commercial intercourse with Britain and France that would have authorized the President "to employ the public armed vessels in protecting the commerce of the United States and to issue instructions . . . conformable to the laws and usages of nations . . . ." 21 *Annals* 2022. J.G. Jackson, an administration supporter, objected on the ground that the "law of nations" was too ill-defined to make for clearly defensible actions by the President and that the nation's naval forces were too scanty to enforce the definition so far advanced. *Id.* 2023-24. The amendments were rejected, and the Senate receded from its earlier approval of the section. *Id.* 2026, 2051-52; 20 *Annals* 679-80.

†See *supra* at 234-35. An example of Congress's willingness to be lax concerning appropriations was the bill to provide for protection of the maritime frontier. A House committee reported it had been unable to get details from the Secretary of War, beyond his assertion that $1 million was necessary. While some members objected to allowing so great a sum to be spent at the secretary's discretion (*e.g.*, Hall and Rhea), others (Cheves, Mitchell, Tallmadge, Potter, Wright, Sheffey and Widgery) spoke for the bill, saying it was impossible to foresee what might be necessary and that the President "who is intrusted with the use of the military force . . . might very well be intrusted with the expenditure of this money . . . on such fortifications as he might deem it necessary to erect or repair." 23 *Annals* 1029-30. The bill passed, 88-25, and ultimately became law, though the appropriation was reduced to $500,000. Act of March 10, 1812, 2 *Stat.* 692.

**For example, the House refused on June 8, 1812, just before war had been declared, to consider a resolution that would have "directed" the Secretary of War to provide comprehensive information on the number of troops enlisted under various laws, the improvements recently made in seacoast fortifications, "and that he state as far as practicable the actual state of such fortifications or works, and the quantum of resistance they are, in his opinion, calculated to

were inquiries into the conduct of military operations.* And attempts to control the conduct of the war against Britain failed,[214] although individual Congressmen expressed the view that the Constitution gave Congress ample power to control the course of war.[215]

Arguments concerning proposed increases in the armed forces reflected remarkable concern for the possible dangers of authorizing armed forces of relatively substantial size. Republican ideology, though in disarray after eight years under Jefferson, disfavored military spending, in large part on the ground that it increased executive branch influence.† Congress provided increases in the army only

---

afford against the attack of any naval Power." 24 *Annals* 1485 (vote of 37–82). During debate on a bill to authorize reenlistments, on January 13, 1814, Representative Morris S. Miller of New York strongly objected to appropriating any more men or money for the war until Congress had more information. "Ignorant, hoodwinked, blinded as we are, it ought not to be claimed or expected of us to pass this bill. I think the Administration ought not to call on us for more men till they have answered the inquiry which we made of them touching the causes of the failure of our arms. And I much doubt whether this House ought to grant another army, before it has made a thorough investigation of the causes of the late disasters and disgrace which have followed our arms." 26 *Annals* 958. Despite Miller's objections, the bill passed, 97 to 58. *Id.* 979.

*Representative Bradley moved on July 9, 1813, to authorize an inquiry into "the causes which have led to the multiplied failures of the arms of the United States on our Western and Northwestern frontier"; the motion was laid on the table, 76–67. 26 *Annals* 415, 421. Those opposed objected principally to the expediency and practicability of such an inquiry during war, and not on the ground that the House lacked power to investigate military defeats. See *id.* 415–16. Another motion, to inquire into the furlough policy on the northwest frontier, was defeated after some constitutional arguments, most notably by George M. Troup of Georgia (*id.* 867):

> To Congress was granted the power of raising armies and granting supplies for them; but to the Executive was confided the exclusive control and direction of the armies when raised. To enable him properly to execute this duty, the President had been vested with the most arbitrary powers—the power of dismissing without assigning a cause, and jointly with the military courts, of cashiering, and inflicting on officers other punishments, even unto death. The power then of controlling military movements, said Mr. T., is not with us, but with the Executive. He may dismiss any officer of the Army and even the Secretary of War, for misconduct; and the power of control, possessed by this House is the power of impeaching the President if he fail in the performance of his duty.

Grosvenor replied that "Congress had the power to make rules and regulations for the government of the Army; and without any invasion on the functions of the Executive, the granting of furloughs might be made a subject of legislation—and he merely wished to inquire whether such legislation was necessary." *Id.* 868. Troup deprecated the tendency to intrude into the management of the army, but he did suggest that Congress could make "a motion to request the Executive to order all the officers now absent to repair to their posts." The motion was laid on the table. *Id.* 871.

†Randolph was the most classical, if eccentric, spokesman of this view. A standing army was "uncongenial" with republican government, he said, because it could be the "life and soul of a military despot." 23 *Annals* 707–708. Though

just before war against Britain was declared. After the war, Congress reduced the army to 10,000 men from 33,000, disregarding Madison's recommendation that 20,000 be retained.[216]

Congress was also initially reluctant to provide a navy and, as late as January 1812, refused to authorize any new frigates. Opponents argued that a small navy would be pointless against Britain's large fleet, and costly.[217] Some predicted a navy would vastly increase executive power, and tend to draw the nation into unwise adventures abroad.* Supporters of a larger navy demonstrated greater strength and ingenuity, however, than those who sought a larger army. They noted that the Constitution specifically empowered Congress "to provide and maintain a navy," and contended that the nation's commercial interests could only be protected by large, armed vessels.[218] The navy was less dangerous to liberty and less expensive than an army, some claimed; others more enthusiastically asserted the navy "should be cherished and supported," and established on a perpetual basis to advance the nation's interests.† Though new vessels were at first denied, Congress approved the repair of three existing frigates, as well as the purchase of timber for the next three

---

in debate members spoke of "marching and countermarching" the troops they contemplated providing, their only control over them will be through the power to withhold supplies: "as to how, or where, or when they shall be employed, this House has no control whatever." *Id.* 708.

*A peacetime navy, said Adam Seybert (Pa.), may "become a powerful engine in the hands of an ambitious Executive. . . ." 23 *Annals* 824-25. To convert the United States into a great naval power, argued Samuel McKee (Ky.), "would prove the destruction of our happy Constitution," creating a class interested in fostering war, and invested with the means for causing it. *Id.* 834, 843-44. McKee quoted from instructions of the Virginia Legislature of 1801 to their Senators in Congress, presumably written by the present "Chief Magistrate of the United States" [Madison] (*id.* 841-42):

> With respect to the Navy, it may be proper to remind you, that, whatever may be the proposed object of its establishment, or whatever may be the prospect of temporary advantages resulting therefrom, it is demonstrated by the experience of all nations who have ventured far into naval policy, that such prospect is ultimately delusive; and that a navy has ever, in practice, been known more as an instrument of power, a source of expense, and an occasion of collisions and wars with other nations, than as an instrument of defence, or economy, or of protection to commerce. Nor is there any nation, in the judgment of the General Assembly, to whose circumstances this remark is more applicable than to the United States.

See also *id.* 880-81 (Johnson) ("would involve us in continual wars with other nations").

†*Id.* 820 (Cheves); 859-75 (Bassett); 895 (Law). Cheves addressed himself to the problem Republicans might have in supporting naval increases. A navy was not inherently anti-republican, he claimed. Republicans had opposed one in 1798 because they "believed it was to be employed for improper objects. . . ." *Id.* 819.

years, the latter decision indicating its willingness to proceed with construction if necessary.[219]

After war was declared, many new vessels were authorized.[220] When the war ended, Congress responded to Madison's recommendation that they provide "for the gradual advancement of the Naval Establishment" by appropriating $1 million for each of the next eight years, and authorizing several capital ships.[221] Squadrons were established in the Mediterranean, the West Indies and the Pacific. The recession of 1819 caused Congress to cut back its naval spending, but by that time a force substantial enough for simultaneous involvements throughout most of the world had been established.[222] Further increases were authorized to meet particular problems, such as West Indian piracy and the Brazilian blockade.[223]

Congress not only provided forces which were necessarily at the executive's disposal, its actions in some instances encouraged, rather than controlled, executive discretion over those forces. For example, instead of granting explicit authority to President Monroe to land on West Indian islands in search of pirates, under specified circumstances, Congress provided vessels, either with no use specified[224] or reciting only that they be used to suppress piracy in the Gulf of Mexico "and the seas and territories adjacent."[225] Another example took place in 1826, when Congress provided operating expenses for armed vessels in a context that made clear they were intended for use against the Brazilian blockade of Buenos Aires and to combat piracy. Efforts to specify those purposes, or to permit the transfer of specific vessels, were rejected because "no law was necessary to authorize the President to transfer a vessel from one station to another," and in order to leave the navy with maximum flexibility.[226]

One limited but significant restraint on executive power to act under broad delegations was imposed by the Supreme Court in *Brown v. United States*.[227] After war against Britain was formally declared, an attorney for the United States seized some British owned timber landed in Massachusetts before the declaration of war. The local United States Attorney relied on the declaration of war as authority for the seizure, and in at least one prior case the Court had suggested that a declaration allowed any and all acts of hostility.[228] But the Court ruled this seizure unauthorized. The Constitution was a document imbued with moderation, concluded the majority, and should be read to require the legislature more specifically to authorize a measure in conflict with the law of nations. The express grant to Congress of power to "make rules concerning captures on land and water" was read to apply to domestic captures as well as those abroad, and required Congress to promulgate the rules more specifically. That Congress had frequently legislated with specificity concerning enemy individuals and property, the majority found, was evidence supporting its decision. Justice Story dissented vigorously, contending that the executive could seize an enemy alien's property when war was generally declared, though not moneys owed him; Story agreed, however, that Congress could have limited and regulated the President's authority in pursuing a general war.[229]

Presidents Madison, Monroe and Adams all recognized, explicitly at times, limits on their authority to wage and even to cause war. Madison did so in seeking authority to retaliate against British depredations, as well as a declaration of war.[230] Monroe did so in explaining why he had agreed to return the Spanish posts occupied by Jackson during the Seminole War.[231] Clay did so in behalf of Adams when the United States chargé d'affaires in Brazil was too freely threatening military action;[232] Adams himself was willing to threaten against a bond requirement imposed by Brazil but indicated that action could be taken only after Congress approved.* When examined in context, however, these and other executive statements and actions deferential to legislative power cannot be taken at face value; on other occasions the same Presidents acted with great independence and aggressiveness.†

Finally, events during the period 1809 to 1829 demonstrated that discretion over military forces rested, not only in Congress and the President, but with executive officers down the chain of command,

*After imposing a blockade on all shipping to Argentina in December 1825, the Brazilian government in April 1828 issued an ordinance requiring American vessels to post bonds in assurance that they would not go to Buenos Aires. A.S.P. 6 *Foreign Relations* 1069. Secretary of State Clay issued instructions to the American chargé d'affaires to remonstrate against the bonds and "if necessary, to state to the Brazilian Government that our naval officers would be instructed to resist it." Adams reminded Clay that "the threat might be held out, but before giving the instruction to naval officers the authority must perhaps be asked from Congress." 7 *Adams Memoirs* 495. A week later, Adams told Secretary of the Navy Southard, when asked what instructions should be sent to Commodore Biddle regarding the Brazilian decree, that the chargé's warning might supersede the necessity of resistance. "The instructions now to be given to Commodore Biddle would be to disregard the decree in everything short of hostile conflict, and, if that should fail, the authority of Congress would be asked for the use of force." *Id.* 500. Adams's threat worked. The bond requirement was dropped with no resort to force.

†The context of each important statement, and other executive operations, are discussed throughout the rest of this chapter. In a circumstance analogous to the Brazilian situation, Secretary Clay authorized Commodore Isaac Hull forcibly to resist a Peruvian decree authorizing seizure and condemnation of vessels transporting Spanish property of any kind, if the decree was applied in international waters. Letter of Dec. 20, 1825, in 4 *The Papers of Henry Clay* 928-29 (J. Hopkins & M. Hargreaves, eds. 1959-73) (5 vols.) [hereinafter "*Clay Papers*"].

particularly field and naval commanders. Efforts were made to prevent unilateral conduct by such officers. Madison asserted his authority over Secretary of War John Armstrong in 1814, establishing rules designed to insure that the War Department remained subordinate to the President.[233] The next year a dispute occurred between the recently established Naval Board, composed of seagoing heroes, and the relatively inauspicious Secretary of Navy, Benjamin W. Crowninshield. Madison resolved it in favor of the latter, insisting that the principle of civilian supremacy, as well as the need to "preserv[e] that unity of action which is essential to the Executive trust," required that the Naval Board be responsible to the secretary, who in turn "is to be understood to speak and to act with the Executive sanction."[234] When General Andrew Jackson asserted in early 1817 that all Department of War orders concerning his own subordinates go through him,[235] Monroe treated the affair as a misunderstanding, but wrote Jackson in August that "[t]he principle is clear, that every order from the dept. of war, to whomever directed, must be obeyed."[236] In December, Secretary of War Calhoun confirmed Jackson's position in principle that orders from the department should be transmitted through the chain of command; but he maintained the department's right to make necessary exceptions.[237]

These principles notwithstanding, the period is filled with incidents in which army or naval officers unilaterally determined whether to utilize forces under their command against Indian and foreign nations. George Mathews used his authority as agent in East Florida to give military aid to the "patriots" who wanted to overthrow Spanish authority in the province.[238] David Rodgers, commanding the *President,* determined it was proper to attack the British warship *Little Belt* in 1810.* Commodore David Porter, in command of the Pacific squadron, unilaterally annexed Nukahiva, one of the Falkland Islands, in November 1813, after siding with one major local tribe and destroying the other.[239] Andrew Jackson occupied Pensacola in 1814, and in 1818 he launched the Seminole

---

*Rodgers was patrolling the eastern seacoast and claimed that he thought he had encountered the 36-gun frigate *Guerrière,* a British man-of-war that had recently impressed a sailor from an American vessel. Rodgers hailed the vessel, which became evasive and then fired on Rodgers. All-out firing ensued, and the British vessel, which turned out to be a sloop, suffered severe damage, including 32 men killed or wounded. See A.S.P., 3 *Foreign Relations* 495–96 (Rodgers's report to court of inquiry). The British captain's account had Rodgers firing first, and Albert Carr says that, "if found, the *Guerrière* was to be required to return the impressed men; and few on board the *President* doubted that this would be their chance to avenge the *Chesapeake.*" A. Carr, *The Coming of War* 290 (1960).

War, capturing several Spanish posts despite orders instructing him not to attack them.[240] Stephen Decatur sailed to the Mediterranean in 1815, with orders to force Algiers to cease its depredations and release all American hostages without ransom; he went further after completing his assignment and forced Tripoli and Tunis to submit to American demands.* When the leaders of Foxardo, Puerto Rico, insulted an American officer in 1824, Commodore Porter landed 300 men from the West Indian squadron and forced an apology by threatening to destroy the town.[241] In 1826, Captain T. D. Elliott and Commodore Biddle risked their public vessels-of-war by refusing to submit to orders of a Brazilian blockading squadron that they not sail to Buenos Aires.†

Porter was the only officer whose conduct was deemed sufficiently improper to warrant punishment. He was ordered back to Washington because of the Foxardo incident; once there, his angry denunciations of the President and Secretary of Navy destroyed any chance of avoiding a court martial. The court convicted him of disobeying orders and insubordination. It was unmoved by the argument that his conduct was justified under international law; by his

---

*Peace with Britain enabled the Madison administration to deal with Algiers, which had enslaved Americans and declared war. Decatur quickly captured two Algerine ships in June, killing 53 and taking 500 others prisoners. He then sailed into the harbor at Algiers, and the Dey submitted. On July 26 he sailed into Tunis Bay. After consulting with Consul General Mordecai Noah, Decatur demanded $46,000 from the Dey of Tunis as damages for two ships taken by Americans as prizes during the war against Britain, but released by the Dey to the British. The Dey agreed to settle. In early August, Decatur landed at Tripoli and there demanded $30,000 in damages for two captured British ships released by the Pasha. The Pasha was inclined to make war, but he too yielded in the face of Decatur's superior force. See G. Allen, *Our Navy and the Barbary Corsairs* 289-91 (1905); A. MacKenzie, *Life of Stephen Decatur* 245 (1846); C. Paullin, *Diplomatic Negotiations of American Naval Officers* 116 (1912).

†Elliott was attempting to sail from Rio de Janeiro to Buenos Aires when intercepted by the Brazilian blockading squadron and ordered to change course. He replied that a blockade did not apply to neutral vessels-of-war; that British and French public vessels were sailing to Buenos Aires daily; "that he [Elliott] would allow him [the officer] 30 minutes to deliberate on his future actions, and at the expiration of that time he would proceed, prepared to resist all consequences; that the flag he wore carried under it the sovereignty of the soil it represented; that violated, the soil became invaded; and that he should defend his ship to the last moment." The Brazilians backed down, offering Elliott supplies and best wishes for a pleasant journey. Extract from Log-Book of the U.S.S. *Cyane*, April 3, 1826, in A.S.P., 6 *Foreign Relations* 284. Biddle had much the same experience, except that he explained to Clay that he would not have tested the principle involved for its own sake, but that, given a real object in view—to pick up stranded American seamen—he remained firm in performing his "public duty." Letter of Dec. 9, 1827, *id.* 1098. See also Elliott's reaction to a French request to search American merchant vessels at Buenos Aires. Letter to Southard, June 11, 1826, *id.* 292.

effort to show that Andrew Jackson had gone much further in Florida without punishment; or by the fact that Puerto Rican authorities applauded his conduct.[242] Porter's principal defense was that a charge of disobeying orders could not rest on a departure from general instructions issued by the central government, but only on departures from specific instructions, given by a superior officer in the field. Broad directives necessarily left the execution of policy largely to the discretion of the field commander, Porter argued, pointing to the extremely vague instructions issued in his case. But Porter's argument was too sweeping in its terms, and his behavior, both before and during the proceedings, had made too many enemies to enable him to succeed.[243]

Porter's conviction was far from a total vindication of the adminstration's position, however. Nor did it necessarily signal a rejection in future, particular cases of the principle for which Porter too sweepingly argued. Despite conviction on such apparently serious charges as disobedience and insubordination, Porter was sentenced to a six-month suspension, without loss of pay or privileges. The panel added that Porter's conduct, though censurable, was caused by "an anxious disposition, on his part, to maintain the honor and advance the interest of the nation and the service."[244]

The reasons given by Porter's court-martial panel against further punishment undoubtedly explain in part why none of the other officers who arguably acted beyond or against his orders was even reprimanded. These were men motivated, not only by ambition and love of adventure, but also by genuine desire to advance the nation's interests. They were frequently required to make on-the-spot judgments, and acted in a tradition in which officers were expected to guide their conduct by such vague concepts as "the usages of nations," the "national interests," and "honor."[245] They often achieved desirable objectives, and became popular heroes, which made disciplining them even more difficult.* Furthermore, to discipline an American officer in some contexts was felt to be undesirable because it might advance the interests of the foreign nations involved.

The facts behind each of these incidents, however, reveal a pattern that may be the most compelling reason why tighter control was not

---

*Decatur, for example, was praised on his return from the Mediterranean by the press and the public. At a public dinner in Norfolk he responded to a toast with his now famous adage: "Our country! In her intercourse with foreign nations may she always be in the right; but our country, right or wrong." M. Smelser, *The Democratic Republic, 1801–1815* at 313 (1968). Madison praised Decatur's "high character" and "gallantry" (29 *Annals* 12), and Congress showed its appreciation by passing the Act of April 27, 1816, providing $100,000 as prize money to be distributed to Decatur and his men. 3 *Stat.* 315.

asserted over military leaders.[246] In virtually every instance the orders issued were vague, conferring broad discretion as to the means open to achieve objectives that were themselves often only suggested.[247] Many of the officers involved communicated their intentions in time to enable the President to prevent the enterprise undertaken; but no orders to desist were issued.[248] In the major incidents considered, involving East and West Florida, the evidence strongly suggests that the administration actually formulated or approved the schemes in which the officers became involved.[249] Finally, in most of the incidents described, the executive failed to provide or actually withheld from Congress and the public the information necessary to determine whether the acts were authorized.[250] In short, the executive, during this period, may have wanted officers in the field to undertake projects that would have been beyond what were then perceived to be the constitutional limits of the President's authority.

Executive Discretion, Secrecy and the War of 1812

The War of 1812 was the first declared war in United States history. Military actions taken against Britain after war was declared were therefore legislatively authorized and pose no constitutional difficulties. The circumstances leading up to the formal declaration, however, show how the President's power to control foreign affairs and information can influence strongly the legislature's decision to declare war.

When Madison became President, Britain and France were at war. Each nation had passed restrictions on the extent to which neutrals, such as the United States, could trade with other combatants.* Congress replaced the embargo with the Act of March 1, 1809, which prohibited commercial intercourse with Britain and France, but empowered the President to suspend the Act's prohibition in the event that either belligerent repealed its edicts restricting American commerce.[251]

Madison negotiated an agreement with British Minister David

---

*The Berlin Decree, announced by France in November 1806, responded to Britain's 1806 blockade of the Continent by declaring illegal all commerce with Britain. All vessels of Britain and its colonies were refused entry in continental ports, and all British goods declared valid prize. Britain then passed its Orders-in-Council of 1807, declaring a blockade of all enemy countries, their colonies and ports excluding the British flag, and prohibiting all trade with, and in the products of, such countries and ports. France retaliated with the Milan Decree declaring that any vessel that permitted an examination by a British warship, or voyaged to Britain, or paid a British duty, would be lawful prize. *See generally* S. Bemis, *A Diplomatic History of the United States* 99, 140, 147-50 (4th ed. 1955).

Erskine soon after becoming President, which included a commitment to repeal the Orders in Council, Britain's edicts against trade with France. This commitment, by a minister far from London, was not the actual repeal contemplated by the Act of March 1, 1809. But Madison decided to accept the commitment and issued a proclamation on April 20, 1809, suspending limits on trade with Britain. When Congress convened, it adopted Madison's decision in the Act of June 28, 1809.[252]

Britain rejected the agreement negotiated by Erskine, and refused to repeal its Orders in Council. Francis Jackson, sent to replace Erskine as British Minister, insulted the United States by alleging in a letter he later published that Madison knew all along that Britain would find the Erskine agreement unacceptable.[253] Madison terminated communications with Jackson. He also issued a second proclamation, on August 9, 1809, revoking his earlier proclamation and reinstituting nonintercourse.[254] Madison anticipated objections to his second proclamation "on the ground that the power given to the Executive [to suspend nonintercourse], being special, was exhausted by the first exercise of it; and that the power having put out of force the laws to which it related, could, under no possible construction, restore their operation." He explained to Jefferson, however, that the second proclamation was necessary because "the indispensable prerequisite [to the proclamation suspending nonintercourse], a repeal of the Orders in Council, did not take place."*

When Congress reconvened in December 1809, both houses adopted a resolution supporting the President's treatment of Jackson, and pledging the nation's strength to protect its honor.[255] On December 19, Representative Nathaniel Macon of North Carolina, former Speaker of the House and Chairman of the Committee on Foreign Affairs, reported a bill which would have continued nonintercourse, but in a modified form. The bill also would have authorized the President, in case either France or Great Britain revoked or modified its edicts violating neutral commerce, to declare

---

*Indeed, Madison noted, his first proclamation did not conform to the power delegated to him by the Act of March 1, 1809, which required "a past and not a future fact to be proclaimed," whereas the proclamation pointed to the future repeal of the Orders in Council. "This difficulty was felt at the time of issuing the first proclamation," he wrote, "but it yielded to the impossibility of otherwise obtaining, without great delay, the coveted trade with Great Britain, and an example that might be followed by France. . . ." The thought was that the eventual repeal of the Orders would "give a constructive validity" to the proclamation, and the intervening session of Congress could cure any defect in the plan. In fact, Congress had been urged to deal with the subject, since the proclamation "was not in a form, nor under the circumstances, contemplated by law," but could not "be brought to attend to the subject. . . ." Letter of Aug. 16, 1809, in 2 *Madison Writings* (Cong. ed.) 451–52.

by proclamation that the act would not apply to the commerce of that nation.[256]

Some members opposed the bill because they claimed it would lead to war.[257] Others opposed it because they favored war with Britain and preferred more forceful action.[258] In the House the section authorizing the President to revoke nonintercourse was amended to include the words "in his opinion," making clear that the President was to judge whether either Britain or France had ceased violating neutral commerce.* It then passed the House, but Senate changes were so extensive that a conference committee was unable to salvage the legislation.[259]

On April 7, 1810, Macon proposed a second bill, taking a radically different approach. It proposed to end nonintercourse with both Britain and France as of May 1, 1810, but provided that, if either nation should, before March 1811, revoke or modify its edicts so as to cease violating the neutral commerce of the United States, the President shall proclaim that fact; and if the other nation failed to revoke or modify its decrees within three months thereafter, the restrictions of the Act of March 1, 1809 would be revived against that nation.[260] Macon's Bill No. 2, as it came to be called, passed the House on April 19.[261]

The Senate added a provision to the bill authorizing the President, when he deemed it "expedient," to employ public armed vessels to protect commerce, pursuant to instructions "conformable to the laws and usages of nations. . . ."[262] The House refused to accept this amendment, after argument that it would be an unconstitutional delegation of power,† and the Senate finally agreed to its deletion.** The bill became law on May 1, 1810.[263]

---

*John Montgomery of Maryland objected: "The United States had once been tricked by a manoeuvre of the British Ministry, and he did not wish them again to be placed in that situation." He wished to strengthen the bill so as to prohibit the President from suspending nonintercourse until hostilities on neutral commerce had "actually" ceased, not just when an end was promised. Macon replied that adding "in his opinion" would not "add much to the discretion of the President; for, as the section already stood, it would be a matter of opinion when the belligerents ceased to violate our rights. There must be some mode of ascertaining when their decrees were so changed as to cease to violate our neutral rights." 20 *Annals* 1195.

†21 *Annals* 2026. Representative John G. Jackson of Virginia, Dolly Madison's brother-in-law, led the opposition. "If it be expedient to protect commerce, let Congress say so," Jackson argued, "and then devolve on the President power to carry their acts into execution. It seems to me with equal constitutionality we might refer to the President the authority of declaring war, levying taxes, or of doing everything which the Constitution points out as the duty of Congress. All legislative power is by the Constitution vested in Congress. They cannot transfer it." Congress must pass specific legislation regarding convoying and the protection of commerce for "the exercise of which we may and most probably shall come in collision with the definitions of other nations, and thus

Congress's termination of nonintercourse was of far greater benefit to Britain than to France. The act offered England trade with the United States, and imports that England badly needed to sustain its war effort. France could not benefit from the bill, because it lacked an effective navy to convoy merchant ships. Francis Jackson boasted to his superiors that Congress "has completed my triumph by repealing, without any consession on our part, the famous Non-Intercourse Law . . . for the repeal of which Erskine last year had agreed to sacrifice our Orders in Council. . . . They have covered themselves with ridicule and disgrace."[264]

Napoleon had a way out of his dilemma, however. As one scholar explains, "if he could induce the American Government to believe that he was prepared to revoke his decrees, and if upon that basis the Nonintercourse Act should be revived against England, there was an excellent chance that a second Anglo-American war would result."[265]

Madison anticipated precisely this reaction. On May 23 he wrote to William Pinkney that the new act may appear "feeble," but "it is possible that one or other of those powers may allow it more effect than was produced by the overtures heretofore tried." The present law could be regarded by Britain or France "not as a coercion or a threat to itself, but a promise of attack on the other." Britain, he realized, "may conceive that she has now a compleat interest in

---

be brought into war." Jackson said he was unwilling to allow any other branch of government but Congress to define the law of nations. "It is a legislative power, which we cannot transfer; and if we could, it would be inexpedient to do so. Why are we assembled here, if, when it becomes our duty to decide on our great relations with foreign nations, we shrink from the task and throw the responsibility of measures on other departments of the Government?" *Id.* 2022.

**"With almost excessive nicety," Arthur Schlesinger, Jr. writes, "Madison objected to this as an unconstitutional delegation by Congress to the Presidency of war-making decisions." *The Imperial Presidency* 28–29 (1973). Schlesinger relies upon a letter from Irving Brant to Senator Jacob Javits, dated April 3, 1972, and inserted in the *Congressional Record* on April 10, 1972 (118 *Cong. Rec.* 11971, 11973–74). Brant's letter in turn relies in part upon a letter from Madison to Jefferson, written April 23, 1810. Madison's letter does not mention the Senate amendment, however, which is understandable since it was written before the amendment was introduced. Madison does refer to the "unhinged state" of Congress, but this seems a comment on Congress's overall performance, as Brant treats it in his biography. 5 Brant, *Madison* 135. Brant's letter to Javits also relies on the fact that Representative Jackson, whose opposition to the Senate amendment appears above, was Madison's brother-in-law: "the whole House knew that although the words were Jackson's, the thoughts came from the President." 118 *Cong. Rec.* 11974. This may have been the case, but it is pure speculation. Madison did go on record against such a provision in a letter to William Pinkney on January 20, 1810, but his argument was based exclusively on the proposition that Congress should adopt military measures rather than threaten force. 8 *Madison Writings* (Hunt) 90–94.

perpetuating the actual state of things, which gives her the full enjoyment of our trade, and enables her to cut it off with every other part of the world. . . . But . . . this very inequality . . . may become a motive with . . . [France] to turn the tables on Great Britain, by compelling her either to revoke her orders, or to lose the commerce of this country."[266]

On August 3, 1810, Napoleon dictated a letter for his Foreign Minister, the Duc de Cadore, informing the American government that, as a consequence of Macon's bill, "the decrees of Berlin and Milan [France's edicts against trade with its combatants] are revoked and that after the 1st of November, they will cease to have effect; it being understood that, in consequence of this declaration, the English shall revoke their Orders in Council . . . or that the United States, conformably to the act you have just communicated, shall cause their rights to be respected by the English."[267] This announcement left uncertain whether the Berlin and Milan decrees were definitely to be revoked on November 1, or whether their revocation was contingent on America's acceptance of the proposal as sufficient to trigger the proclamation authorized by Macon's bill. The letter also failed to mention whether vessels already seized would be released. Secretary of State Smith had informed General John Armstrong, American Minister at Paris, on June 5 and July 5, 1810, that no arrangement on the basis of Macon's bill could be made with France unless the Emperor released American vessels seized under the decrees.[268]

When Armstrong received Foreign Minister Cadore's letter, he forwarded it to Secretary of State Smith without inquiring whether an imperial order existed to support its contents. The letter therefore arrived in the United States with no evidence to confirm the validity of its contingent and noncomprehensive representations.[269] Furthermore, Madison also received letters from Armstrong to Cadore on August 20 that protested seizures of American merchant vessels by private armed ships bearing official commissions originally issued in blank, and from Armstrong to Smith on September 10, stating that "the System of which . . . the decrees of Berlin and Milan make a part, is fast recovering the ground it had lost."

Despite the doubts these facts raised about France's intentions, Madison accepted the French representation as adequate. Smith reportedly felt that the President should accept France's declaration as a substitute for the fact of repeal "in this case, since France might be in earnest and because the threat of nonintercourse might 'bring England to the point.' "[270] On November 2, the day after Napoleon's promise was to become effective, Madison issued a proclamation declaring that France had repealed its decrees, and warning Britain that nonintercourse would be renewed against it unless the Orders in Council were repealed within three months.[271]

Members of Madison's Cabinet, though concurring in his decision,[272] sensed its gravity. Smith told French Minister Turreau: "The Executive thinks that the measures he shall take in case England continues to restrict our communications with Europe will lead necessarily to war"; and Gallatin also viewed war as inevitable after the proclamation, if nonintercourse with Britain were resumed.[273]

The Eleventh Congress reconvened on December 3, 1810. On December 5 Madison informed both houses of France's declaration that the decrees of Berlin and Milan would cease to have effect on November 1, and that, "the revocation of them being such that they ceased at that date to violate our neutral commerce, the fact . . . was announced" by his proclamation of November 2.[274] Madison of course could not have known on November 2 whether France had in fact stopped enforcing its earlier decrees on November 1. He had recognized in a letter to Armstrong on October 29 that "no direct authentication of the repeal of the French decrees has been received by you," but said a proclamation would issue because "it is hoped that France will do what she is understood to be pledged for. . . ."[275]

Congress had two months to determine whether it wished to ratify or reject Madison's decision. Britain had announced its willingness to repeal its Orders in Council, but only if adequate evidence were presented that France had actually revoked its decrees.[276] Pertinent to Congress's decision were letters Madison received from Armstrong indicating that France was continuing as of September to enforce its decrees. Yet Madison withheld from Congress Armstrong's letter to Cadore of August 20, and deleted the paragraph in his September 10 letter to Smith that indicated France continued to enforce its decrees. At the same time, comprehensive information was revealed to Congress and the public indicating Britain's intransigence. The "general process of selection," Irving Brant has noted, "left no doubt that, having determined to stand by his action of November 2, President Madison preferred to disclose nothing that would give a handle to assailants of it."[277]

On January 15, 1811, Representative John Eppes of Virginia, acting for the Foreign Relations Committee, introduced a bill to confirm the policy of nonintercourse with Britain.[278] John Randolph sought to bypass Eppes's bill by moving to instruct the Committee to report legislation repealing Macon's Bill No. 2, thus automatically revoking the President's proclamation.[279] He and others argued that Madison's action needlessly risked war; that French seizures continued; and that France's revocation was inadequate in that it was unofficial, qualified and conditional.[280] James Emott of New York claimed Madison lacked discretion to issue the proclamation, since no "actual and practical revocation" of the decrees had occurred.[281] Matthew Lyon of Kentucky acknowledged discretion had been delegated, but argued "that the national faith had not been constitutionally pledged; that they were never authorized, as a component part of the Legislature, to give such a power to another branch of the Legislature or to the Executive."[282]

Those opposed to Randolph's motion supported the proclamation, but rested their arguments primarily on the need to avoid undermining the nation's credibility, rather than on the genuineness of France's representation.* Robert Wright of Maryland reminded Emott and Lyon that Madison's proclamation concerning France was "formally and substantially a copy" of the proclamation he had issued after concluding an agreement with Erskine. The opposition then had not complained that the proclamation looked to future acts by Britain, but had praised Madison's action.[283] Randolph's motion to repeal was defeated, 45 to 67.[284]

The House thereafter adopted an amendment to Eppes's bill that allowed the President to lift nonintercourse if Britain should cease violating America's neutral commerce.[285] Another amendment—to allow the President to revoke nonintercourse if the British made a "satisfactory" agreement regarding impressment—was rejected.[286] Then, after one of the nation's earliest filibusters, the bill passed at five o'clock on the morning of February 28, 1811. The Senate concurred on March 2.[287] Thus Congress confirmed the President's exercise of discretion under Macon's Bill No. 2, and conferred discretion upon him once more to decide what Britain had to do to avoid nonintercourse, and possibly war.

The British government persisted in its refusal to revoke the Orders in Council, citing the lack of evidence that France had actually revoked its decrees.[288] The so-called "war hawks" of the Twelfth Congress pressed for war, after Madison convened the legislature on November 4, 1811.[289] Opponents cited France's inconsistent behavior, and the "juggling" of its decrees.[290] Madison recommended

---

*Repeal of Macon's Bill No. 2, Eppes argued, would undercut the President's ability to conduct foreign affairs, in that he had relied upon the legislation in issuing the proclamation. 22 Annals 865–67. Robert Wright (Md.) said that repeal would constitute "a direct violation of the plighted faith of our government. . . ."; he viewed our understanding with France as binding as a solemn treaty. Id. 870–72. William Burwell of Virginia agreed the nation had given its word to France, and he could not, therefore, urge repeal of Macon's Bill No. 2. He argued against imposing nonintercourse with Britain, however, until France actually fulfilled its promises. Id. 873.

specific preparations for war. On December 6, 1811, Monroe, by then Secretary of State, wrote to a relative: "The government is resolved, if Great Britain does not revoke her orders in council, in a short time, to act offensively towards her."[291]

Meanwhile, Joel Barlow was dispatched as Minister to France. He reached Paris in September 1811, but was ignored for two months by the Foreign Minister, the Duke of Bassano. When Bassano granted an interview, he held out hopes of further agreement, but was evasive on details.[292] On April 21, 1812, however, Britain formally declared its readiness to revoke the Orders in Council if France absolutely revoked its decrees by some authentic and unconditional act.[293] Barlow called Bassano's attention to the new British order, arguing that France must now publish an authentic act of repeal, effective November 1810.[294]

Bassano surprisingly claimed, after some hesitation, that a Decree of St. Cloud, dated April 28, 1811, had definitively revoked the Berlin and Milan decrees in regard to American vessels. Barlow asked why the decree had not earlier been published or communicated. Bassano said it had in fact been supplied to Barlow's predecessor, Jonathan Russell, as well as to the French Minister in Washington, Serrurier. Barlow asked for a copy, and Bassano soon sent him what purported to be the decree; in his letter of transmittal, Bassano did not repeat his claim that the decree had earlier been shown to Russell or Serrurier.[295]

Barlow was skeptical of the decree's authenticity. He sent it to Russell, by then Minister to Britain,[296] and to Secretary of State Monroe, noting that he had "made no comment on the strange manner in which it had been so long concealed from me, and probably from you."[297] On May 12, 1812, he wrote Madison in candid terms, recounting that Bassano produced the decree after Barlow told him that without it "a war against England was impracticable; but with it might be regarded as infallible."[298] The decree, Barlow suspected, "was created last week . . . in consequence of my note of the 1st of May." "I know not in State-ethics by what name such management is called," Barlow continued, but he regarded the decree as potentially useful to the United States in justifying its policy toward Britain—be it a nonwar policy if Britain were to repeal the Orders in Council on the basis of the St. Cloud decree, or continuation of the present policy of commercial restriction that would surely lead to war.*

*William Lee, United States consul at Bordeaux, wrote a letter to Madison marked "confidential" on May 24, expressing his opinion that the Decree of St. Cloud "was no doubt drawn up for the occasion," since it had not been

Russell sent the back-dated decree to Robert Stewart, Lord Castlereagh, British Foreign Secretary, on May 20, 1812, as soon as he received it from Barlow.[299] He found the decree "embarrassingly transparent," and wrote a "private" letter to that effect to Monroe on June 30.[300] Castlereagh told the House of Commons the decree was "so palpable a juggle" the government intended to ignore it.[301] Pressure against war became too intense to resist,[302] however, and Britain repealed its Orders in Council on June 23, 1812.[303] But by then the United States had declared war.

John Randolph must have known a recommendation of war was imminent when he rose on May 29 to speak against that policy. Among his arguments was an offer to prove by "unequivocal evidence" that the Decrees of Berlin and Milan had not been repealed, and that Madison knew it. No one challenged his assertion, but his arguments were unavailing.[304]

Madison recommended war on June 1, 1812.[305] On that date he could not yet have received Barlow's letter of May 12, but he must have suspected that France had never formally revoked its earlier decrees. Despite this he refused to accept Britain's conditional offer to revoke its Orders, as he arguably could have done under the delegation of discretion in the most recent nonintercourse act. Instead he made repeal of the Orders in Council a subordinate issue, breathing new life into the impressment question, despite the fact that the House had refused to make an agreement on impressment a precondition to suspending nonintercourse. He also paid $50,000 out of the State Department's "contingency" fund to one John Henry, an agent of the Governor-General of Canada, for letters that purported to indicate a scheme among the British and certain Federalists to destroy the Union by forming a confederation between the eastern part of the United States and Britain.[306]

Congress declared war on June 18.[307] The vote in the House was 79 to 49; in the Senate the decision was much closer, 19 to 13.[308] After providing support for war preparations, Congress adjourned on July 6.

During the legislature's recess, Madison received the letters written by his ministers communicating the Decree of St. Cloud, as well as their opinions that it was fraudulent. On August 11 Madison replied to Barlow in cipher that the latest decree "will be an everlasting reproach to . . . [France]." He anticipated that it "may, nevertheless, be used by Great Britain as a pretext for revoking her orders, not-

---

communicated in the usual way and had not been promulgated in the manner required by the Napoleonic Code. *Madison Presidential Papers,* LC microfilm, series 1, reel 14.

288 War, Foreign Affairs and Constitutional Power

withstanding the contrary language of Lord Castlereagh in Parliament." If Britain did so in the hope of avoiding war, "the same dislike to the war may possibly produce advances for terminating it, which, if the terms be admissible, will be readily embraced." If a settlement were achieved with Britain, Madison predicted war with France in retaliation for its continued failure to grant redress for depredations.[309]

Congress reconvened on November 2, 1812. In his annual address on November 5, Madison announced that France had issued a formal decree revoking the Decrees of Berlin and Milan. He was careful not to attribute any date to the decree, and said that the French procedure, "although made the ground of the repeal of the British Orders in Council, is rendered, by the time and manner of it, liable to many objections."[310] He said nothing about the decree's authenticity, however, and communicated none of the letters he had received or written that reflected adversely upon the decree's authenticity.

Information about the decree's promulgation was clearly pertinent to the issue of whether peace should be made with Britain in light of its repeal of the Orders in Council. A motion passed the Senate on January 18, 1813, requesting the President to provide the French decree "together with such information as he may possess, concerning the time and manner of promulgating the same; and, also, any correspondence or information touching the relations of the United States with France, in the office of the Department of State, not heretofore communicated, which, in the opinion of the President . . . is not incompatible with the public interest to communicate."[311] The President purported to comply with this request on January 26, enclosing several extracts of letters between Barlow and Bassano, and between Barlow and the Secretary of State.[312] He withheld other letters, however, including those from Barlow, Russell and Lee describing the decree as having been concocted in response to Britain's declaration. He did not advise the Senate that he was withholding relevant material because it was "private" or "confidential" or because its disclosure might injure the interests of the United States. He merely withheld the material without revealing its existence. A similar resolution passed the House on March 1, 1813, and was treated in the same manner as the Senate's.[313]

Opposition to the war continued in Congress. Some argued France was in bad faith.[314] Others specifically condemned Congress for delegating to Madison the power to accept French representations without concrete proof of their accuracy.* The correspondence withheld by Madison would have made the authenticity of the Decree of St.

*The war was caused, argued Representative Cyrus King of Massachusetts (26 *Annals* 1078):

Cloud another major issue. Instead, war opponents seized upon the statement in one of Barlow's letters that Bassano claimed to have given the decree to Russell and Serrurier soon after its alleged issuance. Several Congressmen argued that, had Britain known earlier of the formal decree, its Orders would have been repealed in time to avoid war. They suggested that Russell or someone else in the government may have intentionally suppressed its publication to prevent Britain from repealing its Orders, thereby preserving that issue as a cause of war.[315]

Suspicions of Russell took concrete form when Madison recommended that Russell be sent as the first Minister to Sweden. During June 1813 a Senate committee was instructed to inquire into the expediency of Russell's appointment, and whether he had sent "any communication . . . admitting or denying the declaration of the Duke of Bassano to Mr. Barlow. . . ."[316] The Committee reported on June 7 that it had met with Secretary Monroe at the Department of State regarding Bassano's statement, and that Monroe had said that Russell had made "no official denial or admission" but that he had sent Monroe a "private letter" in which Monroe "understood that allegation to be unequivocally denied." The committee, apparently unsatisfied by this defense, recommended against sending a Minister Plenipotentiary to Sweden, and its resolution was ultimately adopted.[317]

The controversy over Russell and the Decree of St. Cloud next surfaced in the House when Daniel Webster, newly elected from Massachusetts, used the issue to attack the administration's war policy. "The revocation of the Orders in Council of Great Britain was the main point on which the war turned," he said, "and it had been demanded for the reason that the French decrees had ceased to exist." Yet evidence regarding the French repeal was contradictory, Webster pointed out, and the issue posed by the Duke of Bassano's allegation was whether the decree ordering repeal had been withheld from Congress. Webster offered resolutions calling

---

by conferring upon your President a power which could only be exercised by the three branches of the Legislature (inclusive of the Executive) by vesting him with the arbitrary, the dangerous power, of enforcing or repealing one of your laws at his pleasure. Sir, what right had these three branches to delegate to one of them a power which the people had entrusted to the whole? . . . I allude to the force given by the act of March, 1809, to a proclamation of your President; and which, as was to have been expected, was afterwards so notoriously abused; whereby he was to enforce the provisions of your non-intercourse law against one of the belligerents, if the other by a certain time repealed or modified her edicts. Which power was even enlarged by the act of the 2d of March, 1811, whereby the proclamation of the President was made the only evidence of the fact upon which it ought to issue; whether, as in the first case, that fact had happened or not.

for information on when and by whom the government received its first intelligence of the French decree dated April 28, 1811, repealing the decrees of Berlin and Milan; whether Russell had ever admitted or denied Bassano's allegation, and any correspondence on that subject; whether the French Minister in the United States (Serrurier) had ever informed the government of the decree; and for any information on this subject possessed by the President, including whether Madison had ever acquired from France "any explanation of the reasons of that decree being concealed" or made "any remonstrance, or expressed any dissatisfaction . . . at such concealment."[318] After extensive debate on the propriety of these requests,* they were adopted on June 21 with qualifications authorizing Madison to withhold information which would be inconsistent with the public interest to communicate.[319] Daniel Webster and John Rhea of Tennessee, appointed to carry the resolutions to the President, reported that Madison was too ill to read them.[320]

On July 12, 1813, the President, again purporting to supply the information requested by Webster's resolutions, forwarded a report from Secretary of State Monroe with seventeen other letters and documents.[321] The letters from Barlow, Russell and Lee, describing the French decree as fraudulent, were withheld without comment. Opponents to the war unquestionably used the controversy over the Decree of St. Cloud, as Irving Brant states, "to insinuate that Madison had brought on the war by concealing this decree."[322] Madison had not concealed the decree. He had, however, withheld material that, if revealed, would have proved the decree a sham, and would have given the opposition a powerful argument for reconsidering the declaration of war, at a point when the nation was not yet geared up for the conflict. Madison did not want the war reconsidered merely because the Orders were repealed. He had decided to seek other concessions as well, including an end to impressment. As

---

*Several members asserted a broad right to demand information. *E.g.*, 26 *Annals* 231 (Shipherd: "on subjects which are interesting to our constituents"). Thomas Grosvenor of New York asked: "How can we speak or act upon subjects inseparably connected with our foreign relations, if the Executive, the only organ of communication with other nations, may be suffered at his sovereign will and pleasure to withhold from us all his correspondence? By admitting such a course of practice, the President has had the destinies of this nation in his hands," making it understandable how the nation has been plunged into "an unnecessary and a wanton war." He particularly condemned the practice of communicating only "garbled *extracts* of letters from and to the French Government." Unlike the British system, where the executive runs foreign relations until it loses Parliament's confidence, "the foundation of our whole system of Government is *responsibility*. The President and most of his dependents are by the Constitution obnoxious to the animadversions of this House. And every official man in the Republic is responsible to the people." *Id*. 201. (Emphasis in original.)

Monroe later explained: "Having gone to war, it seemed to be our duty, not to withdraw from it, till the rights of our country [respecting impressment] were placed on a more secure basis."[323]

The legality of Congress's delegation to the President in Macon's Bill No. 2, that enabled Madison to force a confrontation with Britain on the basis of the Cadore letter, was tangentially raised in the Supreme Court in *Cargo of the Brig Aurora* v. *United States.*[324] The *Aurora's* cargo was seized when it arrived in New Orleans during February 1811, over three months after Madison's proclamation of November 2, 1810. Joseph R. Ingersoll argued for the owners that the President's proclamation was not meant by Congress to have the force of law. "Congress could not transfer the legislative power to the President. To make the revival of a law [the Nonintercourse Act] depend upon the President's proclamation, is to give that proclamation the force of law." John Law responded for the government that "the legislature did not transfer any power of legislation to the President. They only prescribed the evidence which should be admitted of a fact, upon which the law should go into effect." Justice William Johnson delivered the Court's decision on this point, stating simply: "We can see no sufficient reason, why the legislature should not exercise its discretion in reviving the act of March 1st, 1809, either expressly or conditionally, as their judgment should direct."[325] During the same term the Court also decided *The Schooner Anne* v. *United States*, in which counsel for the condemned schooner's owner noted that in fact "evidence communicated to Congress . . . show[s] that in March, 1811, the Berlin and Milan decrees were not repealed and that the repeal did not take place till the 28th of April." Justice Johnson replied in oral argument: "That point was considered in the case of the Aurora."[326] The Court was therefore willing to uphold seizures and condemnations pursuant to Madison's proclamation, despite the discretionary nature of his act, and although the proclamation was later proved to have been based upon an erroneous factual premise.

The Seizure of West Florida, 1810

Jefferson had sought to expand the nation's borders to the south and west.* An area west of the Mississippi River was obtained from

---

*Bemis describes the significance of the Floridas with special flair:

> In the hands of any foreign power they were a pistol pointed at the heart of the future Continental Republic. East Florida was the butt of the pistol, Pensacola the trigger-guard, and the "panhandle" of West Florida was the horizontal barrel with its muzzle pressed against the nation's life-artery, the Mississippi River, just above New Orleans.

S. Bemis, *John Quincy Adams and the Foundations of American Foreign Policy* 302 (1956).

France as part of the Louisiana Purchase. Both Jefferson and his then Secretary of State Madison claimed that the Louisiana Purchase also included much of what was then known as West Florida, consisting of the areas between the Mississippi and Perdido Rivers (marked A, B and C on Map 2), including the town of Mobile.[327] In the Act of October 31, 1803, Congress authorized the President "to take possession of, and occupy the territories ceded by France to the United States" by employing "any part of the army or navy of the United States . . . which he may deem necessary. . . ."[328] Rather than risk conflict with Spain, Jefferson accepted the voluntary surrender of New Orleans and left West Florida in Spanish hands without expressly relinquishing America's claim.

Congress gave apparent approval to Jefferson's claim to West Florida by providing in the Act of February 24, 1804 that the President, "whenever he shall deem it expedient," might establish a separate customs district at Mobile, at the very heart of the disputed area.[329] Spain became acutely concerned, but Secretary of State Madison assured the Spanish Minister that the so-called Mobile Customs Act would not be extended "beyond the acknowledged limits of the United States," unless it became possible to do so through an agreement with the Spanish government.[330] The Act was therefore construed, at least for the purpose of calming the Spanish Minister, as authorizing a tax district when and if the area was voluntarily ceded by Spain. In reality Jefferson was determined that West Florida should become part of the United States. He made clear his willingness—even eagerness—to use force if necessary to obtain the area, though only with the consent of Congress. That his resolve was based on political and nationalistic considerations, rather than on the Louisiana Purchase, was clearly reflected by his desire to take East Florida (Areas D and E on Map 2) as well, "probably" Cuba, and apparently even Mexico.[331]

No sooner had Madison assumed the presidency than he received news that West Florida was ripe for takeover by the United States.[332] During March and April 1809, William Claiborne, Governor of the Orleans Territory, wrote "private" letters to Secretary of State Robert Smith reporting that the Spanish Governor of the Floridas, Vizente Folch, shared the view that East and West Florida, "detached as they were from the other Spanish provinces, . . . were unimportant possession and ought and would be ceded to the U. States."[333] Early the next year Samuel Fulton, adjutant-general of the West Florida militia, wrote Madison that, as Spain was likely to fall to Napoleon, he would be glad to help the United States take possession of the area.[334]

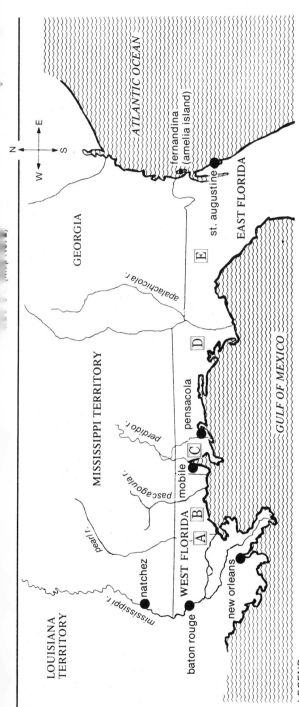

LEGEND

A. Territory claimed by United States 1803-10, as part of Louisiana Purchase; proclaimed independent by the inhabitants, September 1810, and occupied by United States the following December; incorporated with State of Louisiana, 1812 (Act of April 14, 1812).

B. Claimed by United States 1803-10, as part of Louisiana Purchase; brought under military and civil jurisdiction of United States, 1811; incorporated with Mississippi Territory in 1812 (Act of May 14, 1812).

C. Claimed by United States 1803-10, as part of Louisiana Purchase; American jurisdiction proclaimed there by Claiborne in 1811 and Holmes in 1812, except in the town of Mobile; but incorporated with Mississippi Territory in 1812 (Act of May 14, 1812).

D. Invaded by Jackson in 1814 and 1818; ceded by Spain to United States, along with E, by the Adams-Onis Treaty of 1819.

Claiborne, possibly sensing an approaching rebellion against Spain, went to Washington during the summer of 1810, and wrote an extraordinary letter dated June 14 to William Wykoff, Jr., a judge of the parish at West Baton Rouge. Claiborne noted that Spain's fall to Napoleon seemed inevitable, and that the United States claimed eastward to the Perdido. He said he was "persuaded under present circumstances, it would be more pleasing that the taking possession of the Country, be preceded by a Request from the Inhabitants. —Can no means be devised to *obtain such Request?*"[335] He went on to suggest how Wykoff and his friends should proceed:

> The most elligible means of obtaining an expression of the wish of the Inhabitants of Florida, can best be determined by themselves. —But were it done, thro' the medium of a Convention of Delegates, named by the People, it would be more satisfactory. —In the event, that a Convention is called, it is important that every part of the District as far at least as the Perdido be represented, and therefore I feel solicitous, that you should be at some pains to prepare for the occasion the minds of the more influential characters in the vicinity of Mobile. —Whether this can be done, by yourself in person, or by some Citizen of Baton Rouge in *your confidence*, is left to your discretion.

Writing as though his was an official letter, Claiborne instructed Wykoff to "consider this Letter as confidential, and in pursuing the object referred to, you will act with all circumspection which its nature requires"; in "your Dispatches to me," he wrote, "your Signature may be omitted."[336]

Available evidence overwhelmingly proves that Claiborne's letter and plan were authorized by the President, as Claiborne himself reportedly claimed on June 20 in a letter to Governor David Holmes of the Mississippi Territory.[337] Secretary of State Smith wrote to Wykoff, officially selecting him "for the confidential purpose of proceeding without delay into East Florida, and also into West Florida, as far as [P]ensacola for the purpose of diffusing the impression that the United States cherish the sincerest good will towards the people of the Floridas as neighbours . . . , and that in the event of a political separation from the parent Country, their incorporation into our Union would coincide with the sentiments and policy of the United States." Wykoff was expected, Smith continued, to extend his "enquiries as far as opportunities may occur, . . . to the residue of West Florida," apparently meaning Areas B and C on Map 2, east of the Pearl, extending as far as the Perdido but not including Pensacola.[338] On the same day, Smith wrote to Senator William Crawford of Georgia, requesting Crawford to name another agent, and explictly invoking presidential authority.[339] Finally, Madison wrote Smith on July 17 that Governor David Holmes of the Mississippi Territory should be encouraged to report information about West Florida, and "also to be attentive to the means of having his militia in a state for any service that may be called for. In the event either of foreign interference with W.F. or of internal convulsions," he wrote, "more especially if threatening the neighboring tranquility, it will be proper to take care of the rights and interests of the U.S. by every measure within the limits of the Ex. authority." He asked Smith: "Will it not be advisable to apprize Gov. H. confidentially, of the course adopted as to W.F. and to have his co-operation in diffusing the impressions we wish to be made there?"[340]

Smith's response to Madison, if any was made, has not been found. But on July 21 he wrote to Holmes, passing on Madison's instructions regarding the militia. In order that Holmes "be fully apprized of the course adopted as to the Floridas," Smith added, "and therefore the better able to co-operate in diffusing the impression we wish to make there, I deem it proper to send you the enclosed copy of instruction . . . and extracts of a letter from Governor Claiborne to Col. William Wykoff, written under a sanction from the President. . . . The instructions contained in this letter are entirely confidential," he added, "and are to be executed in a manner the least calculated to incite alarm."[341]

Citizens of West Florida meanwhile vented their dissatisfaction with Spanish rule in a series of meetings held in late June and July.[342] On July 24, 1810, Wykoff reported to T.B. Robertson, Secretary of the Orleans Territory, that the "revolution" was underway.[343] A proposed constitution for West Florida reached Washington by August 22, 1810.* On that day Madison pointed out to Albert Gallatin the draft constitution's proposed power in the temporary government "*to grant lands.*" By this time Madison was contemplating intervention. "Should it become necessary for the Executive to exercise authority within these limits before the meeting of Congress, I foresee many legal difficulties," he wrote to Gallatin.[344] Gallatin replied on September 5 that the "law . . . which authorizes the President to take possession of Louisiana will legally cover any . . . measures which policy may dictate in relation to that part of West Florida" claimed by the United States. The difficult issues, said Gallatin, were

*While West Florida residents were still planning their revolution, Madison received word that a group of Mississippi Territory residents were conspiring to attack Mobile and Pensacola, apparently for personal gain or adventure. The plan was abandoned after warnings from federal authorities and Governor Holmes. 6 *Territorial Papers of the United States* 92-93, 98, 99-100, 101-102, 113-14 (C. Carter, ed. 1940).

political and moral, not legal: "What ground ought generally to be taken consistent with justice, the rights and interests of the United States, and the preservation of peace, is the difficult question."[345] Only twelve days later Gallatin conveyed to Madison information concerning Britain's intention to intervene in Cuba and the Floridas; the situation required "some immediate decision," he said.[346]

Neither Madison nor Gallatin suggested calling Congress into early session, to obviate the need for unilateral executive decisions. Madison was clearly aware of the issue, and in his "Helvidius" papers he had criticized Washington for unilaterally issuing the Neutrality Proclamation. On October 19, 1810, most probably before receiving word of the West Florida Convention's formal request for American protection, Madison wrote Jefferson that the crisis in West Florida presented "serious questions, as to the authority of the Executive, and the adequacy of the existing laws of the U.S. for territorial administration." He expressed the fear that acting before Congress had convened would subject an executive order "to the charge of being premature and disrespectful, if not of being illegal."[347] No response from Jefferson has been found; but, whatever Jefferson's view, Madison decided to proceed unilaterally—and vigorously—leaving undisturbed Congress's scheduled meeting date of December 3.

The West Florida revolutionaries met in convention during September and October 1810. On September 26 the Convention President, John Rhea, sent Governor Holmes an official copy of the West Florida Act of Independence for transmittal to Madison, and a request that the United States "take the present Government and people of this State under their immediate and special protection, as an integral and inalienable portion of the United States"; he proffered several reasons for American intervention. Holmes forwarded these documents to Secretary Smith, listing them as enclosures to a covering letter dated October 17.[348]

The Declaration and request for protection provided Madison with precisely the situation Claiborne's letter to Wykoff had suggested. But Madison had failed to anticipate that the Declaration would create one complicating factor: The revolutionaries of West Florida were treating the area as an independent state, not as a territory already belonging to the United States. To agree to the request would therefore constitute an implicit recognition of West Florida as an independent state, and consequently an abandonment of the United States claim under the Louisiana Purchase. An intervention under such circumstances would also provide Spain with just cause for war. The longer Madison delayed, moreover, the more firmly established the revolutionaries might become; they had captured the Spanish fort at Baton Rouge on September 22 and taken the Governor prisoner, were preparing naval attacks on Mobile and possibly Pensacola, and seemed determined to make grants of land.[349]

On October 27, two days after receiving the Declaration and request for protection, Madison issued a proclamation deeming it "right and requisite that possession should be taken" by the United States of the area south of the Mississippi River to the Perdido. The proclamation recited that the United States had always regarded the territory as part of Louisiana, but had acquiesced in leaving it under Spanish authority, because of "confidence in the justice of their cause, and in the success of candid discussion and amicable negotiation with a just and friendly power. . . ." Delay in reaching a satisfactory adjustment with Spain, however, had caused a crisis subversive of Spanish authority, and a threat to the revenue and other laws and security of the United States; a failure by the United States to take possession under these circumstances "might be construed into a dereliction of their title, or an insensibility to the importance of the stake. . . ." A takeover of the area was proper, he concluded, since "in the hands of the United States it will not cease to be a subject of a fair and friendly negotiation and adjustment," and since "the acts of Congress, though contemplating a present possession by a foreign authority, have contemplated also an eventual possession . . . by the United States. . . ."[350]

On the same day, Smith instructed Claiborne to publish and execute the proclamation in the territory involved. Claiborne was to take the area, organize the militia, prescribe bounds of parishes, establish courts, and seek to get the residents represented in the Orleans Legislature. He was told that "[i]f, contrary to expectation, the occupation of this Territory . . . should be opposed by force, the commanding officer of the regular troops on the Mississippi will have orders from the Secretary at War to afford you, upon your application, the requisite aid," and he and Holmes could draw upon their militia. "Should, however, any particular place, however small, remain in possession of a Spanish force, you will not proceed to employ force against it, but you will make immediate report thereof to this Department." Smith cautioned Claiborne to be "temperate and conciliatory," and informed him that the President had authorized him to draw up to $20,000 to defray necessary expenses.[351] Claiborne was able, without any fighting, to occupy Baton Rouge in early December 1810, and in 1811 he extended American control to the Pascagoula River, about forty miles from Mobile.[352]

The West Florida revolutionaries took Madison's proclamation and preemptory takeover as a betrayal. They had contemplated American protection and eventual annexation, but only after reaping the fruits of their victory, apparently by granting land to themselves.[353] Their General Assembly asserted after Claiborne's occupation that the rights of West Florida were being threatened by the "overwhelming power of a neighbouring Nation on whose professions of regard for justice and the laws of Nations, we had relied with implicit confidence." The elected President of the "West Florida Republic," Fulwar Skipwith, expressed his disappointment to his friend and State Department official John Graham in a letter dated December 23, 1810. The most honorable course for the United States, he said, would have been to accept a surrender of West Florida's independence, "as had been solicited," an apparent reference to Claiborne's letter to Wykoff of June 14, 1810, which Skipwith later explicitly cited as the representation on which the revolutionaries had relied.[354]

On December 5, 1810, Madison officially informed Congress of his actions in West Florida and presented Congress with a copy of his proclamation.[355] For many Congressmen this was the first they had heard of Madison's actions. The proclamation and accompanying orders had been kept from public view, except in West Florida itself. News of the action was slow in reaching Washington from what was then the southwestern frontier. Irving Brant notes that keeping the orders secret for as long as possible enabled Claiborne to assume full control of West Florida without any complaints from European ministers. But Madison thereby not only "presented European ministries with a *fait accompli*,"[356] as Brant notes; he presented Congress with one as well.

Madison told Congress that Spanish authority in the area had been subverted; he had acted to assure control to the Perdido "to which the title of the United States extends, and to which the laws provided for the Territory of Orleans are applicable." He was sure, he said, that "the legality and necessity of the course pursued" would find favor with Congress, which would "supply whatever provisions may be due to the essential rights and equitable interests of the people thus brought into the bosom of the American family."[357]

Given Madison's own privately expressed doubts of the legality and propriety of his conduct, it is hardly surprising that many Congressmen—especially New England Federalists—denounced his actions. Even assuming he was authorized to enter the area, no legislation supported his decision to treat West Florida as part of the Orleans

Territory, subject to its laws and government.* Debate, in fact, first arose on a Senate bill to extend the territory and laws of Orleans to the Perdido, and to set up procedures for settling title to those lands.[358] Some Senators argued that title to West Florida was not in the United States, and that the takeover was inexpedient. But motions to refer the bill to a committee for a legal opinion as to America's title, and to request the President to submit "all the documents, papers, or other evidences in his possession, relating to the title of the United States," were defeated.[359]

Senator Outerbridge Horsey of Delaware argued that Madison lacked authority for his proclamation because it was both an act of war and of legislation, powers the Constitution granted exclusively to Congress. "War," explained Horsey, "because it directs the occupation of this territory by a military force. The regular troops . . . are ordered to march, and if they should not be found adequate to the object, the Governors of the Orleans and Mississippi Territories are directed to call out the militia. . . ." Horsey deemed insignificant the President's order that the troops take no action against any place, however small, remaining in possession of a Spanish force. War could still result, since the Americans might be attacked by the Spanish, or even by the "revolutionists, assuming their proceedings are not all a sham. . . ." The proclamation was an act of legislation, he added, because "it annexes the territory in question to the Orleans Territory; it creates a governor; it enacts laws, and appropriates money. . . . This proclamation is substantially the bill under discussion, except that it . . . contains the further and important provision for raising the troops and the money necessary for carrying it into execution." Congress, Horsey claimed, had authorized no such actions. The Act of October 31, 1803, authorizing occupation of the Louisiana Territory, had expired in October 1804, he argued, by order of a bill passed March 20, 1804; the Mobile Customs Act of 1804 contemplated possession "by a friendly negotiation," and not by force, as evidenced by Secretary of State Madison's letter to the Spanish Minister. Consequently Madison's proclamation and the accompanying orders constituted "an unwarrantable assumption of power and a violation of the Constitution."[360]

Henry Clay of Kentucky replied that the President's actions were legislatively authorized. The Act of October 31, 1803 contained two sections, he said, the first of which authorized the President to occu-

---

*Irving Brant says of this action: "Compelled to choose between strict legality and an extension of executive authority, Madison extended it." 5 Brant, *Madison* 186.

py the land ceded by France. This section, Clay contended, was not limited by the Act of March 1804; only the second, which provided for the establishment of a provisional government, expired in 1804. Furthermore, in the Mobile Customs Act the "boundaries [of the Orleans Territory] are so defined as to comprehend West Florida." And other acts authorized the President "to remove by force, under certain circumstances, persons settling or taking possession of lands ceded to the United States." Clay concluded:

> The president has not, therefore, violated the Constitution, and usurped the war-making power, but he would have violated that provision which requires him to see that the laws are faithfully executed, if he had longer forborne to act. . . . The President, by his proclamation, has not made law, but has merely declared to the people of West Florida what the law is.[361]

Whereas Horsey urged that the United States show restraint in West Florida, even "if Europe has become barbarous," Clay regarded the President's action as "propitious"; had the President failed to exercise the discretionary power placed in him, said Clay, "he would have been criminally inattentive to the dearest interests of this country."* Horsey unhappily predicted that, before the close of the session, a bill might be introduced to take possession of East Florida as well.[362] Clay hardly regarded this possibility as unwelcome, declaring his "hope to see, ere long, the *new* United States . . . embracing not only the old thirteen States, but the entire country east of the Mississippi, including East Florida, and some of the territories to the north of us also."[363]

Horsey's prediction was fulfilled even sooner than he suspected. On January 3, 1811, Madison communicated "in confidence" letters from Governor Folch of the Floridas to the Secretary of State, and to Colonel John McKee at Fort Stoddert, indicating Folch's conditional resolve to deliver "this province to the United States

---

*22 *Annals* 55, 62. Senator John Pope of Kentucky traced the argument for American title to the area, and contended that Congress had already asserted title and left to the President's discretion when the claim should be enforced. The President had acted only when the nation's well-being was threatened; had he not done so "[h]e would have been charged with imbecility, and fear of incurring responsibility." The area was necessary to America's security, and the Spanish government from which it was taken would probably soon be out of power. Spain, moreover, had seized much American commerce; "could we not, on the principle of the attachment law, as an act of self-justice, seize on this territory to secure satisfaction?" He urged the Senate not to waste time "in discussion and refining abstract questions of right and wrong. . . . This fondness for lengthy discussions, has even drawn upon Congress the reproaches of the ladies; they begin to say—less talk, more action." *Id.* 37-42.

under an equitable capitulation. . . ." Also sent in confidence was a letter dated December 15, 1810, from the British chargé d'affaires J.P. Morier to Smith expressing "deep regret" at the President's proclamation and message concerning West Florida. The area could as well have been kept "a subject of negotiation and adjustment" in Spanish hands, he contended, and he asked how the President's commitment to negotiate, expressed in the proclamation, could "be made to accord with the declaration in his Message to Congress, (implying permanent possession,) 'of the adoption of that people into the bosom of the American family?'" Because of these communications, together with the "peculiar interest" of the United States in the destiny of East Florida, Madison recommended a declaration of policy to prevent the territory from passing into the hands of any foreign power other than Spain. He also asked Congress to authorize him, under circumstances described below, to take temporary possession of any part of the area.[364]

Madison's message made East rather than West Florida the chief subject of the Senate's further deliberations. Congress took no action concerning West Florida until May 1812, when a bill passed incorporating the area into the Mississippi Territory.[365] Claiborne and others in the meantime pressed the application of the West Florida revolutionaries for payment of debts incurred in overthrowing the Spanish.* Congress passed on April 18, 1814, without recorded debate, an act authorizing the Secretary of State "to liquidate, according to principles of Justice and Equity, all the Claims of the inhabitants of the said late Province of West Florida . . . for advances by them made for the use and benefit of the United States prior to, and since the taking of possession of the said portion of the said late province. . . ."[366] Secretary of State Monroe authorized Reuben Kemper, one of the most radical of the West Florida revolutionaries, to collect the claims. On May 5, 1817, Acting Secretary of State Richard Rush construed the Act to allow reimbursement of the cost of subsistence and accommodation of troops employed by the Convention or the provisional government, probably including am-

---

*6 *Official Letter Books of W.C.C. Claiborne, 1801–1816*, at 24–25 (D. Rowland, ed. 1916) (6 vols.). Thus Claiborne said in a letter on January 1, 1812 to Representative John Dawson of Virginia:

I am well aware of the delicacy of the subject; —But really Considerations of Justice, plead powerfully in favour of the petitioners. —of the proceedings of the Conventionalists the United States have profited; —The Revolution, they effected, was the immediate cause of placing the Country in possession of the United States, & it would seem just, that the expenses of that revolution, should be paid by the party benefited.

munition and arms. Rush also wrote that he had conferred with President Monroe, who felt that salaries and claims for vessels purchased were also covered.[367]

The final chapter of the West Florida story was written in 1829, when litigants attempted to secure Supreme Court review of the validity of the title of the United States to the area.[368] James Foster and Pleasants Elam brought an action in ejectment to recover a tract of land, in what was once West Florida, in the possession of the defendant, Neilson. They based their claim on a land grant made by the Spanish governor on January 2, 1804, and ratified by the King of Spain on May 29, 1804. Neilson answered that the territory within which the claimed land was situated had been ceded—before the grant—to France, and by France to the United States as part of the Louisiana Purchase. The grant, the defendant argued, was thereby void as having been made by persons who lacked title.[369]

A federal district court held for the defendants, and the cause was brought before the Supreme Court on a writ of error. The issue in the case, as framed by Chief Justice Marshall, was: "To whom did the country between the Iberville and the Perdido rightfully belong, when the title now asserted by the plaintiffs was acquired?" Marshall noted all the major arguments for and against the proposition that title had been conveyed to the United States by the Louisiana Purchase. He reviewed the Act of October 21, 1803 authorizing the President to take possession of the territory ceded by France, the Mobile Customs Act, and the Louisiana Organizations Act of March 26, 1804. He noted, too, the failure of Monroe's mission to Madrid and Spain's "infinite repugnance to the surrender of territory."[370]

Marshall refused, however, to pass upon the merits of the plaintiffs' contentions, thereby upholding the lower court's decision to deny ejectment. "In a controversy between two nations concerning national boundary," he wrote, "it is scarcely possible that the Courts of either should refuse to abide by the measures adopted by its own government. There being no common tribunal to decide between them, each determines for itself on its own rights, and if they cannot adjust their differences peaceably, the right remains with the strongest." Congress and the President were the departments to assert the nation's interest against other nations, he said, and "[i]f the course of the nation has been a plain one, its Courts would hesitate to pronounce it erroneous."[371]

Tench Coxe and Daniel Webster, arguing for the plaintiffs, contended that Madison's 1810 proclamation, and the subsequent occupation of West Florida by United States troops, could not "change the relative rights of the parties, or vary the construction" to be given a treaty. Marshall referred to the 1810 proclamation, however, as "an assertion of the title of the United States." Even "had this suit been instituted immediately after the passage of the act for extending the bounds of Louisiana," the courts would have been bound by the judgment of the political branches. A decision "that the Spanish construction of the treaty of St. Ildefonso was right, and the American construction wrong . . . would," he wrote, "have subverted those principles which govern the relations between the legislative and judicial departments, and mark the limits of each."[372]

Intervention in East Florida, 1811–1813

One can fairly state that Madison acted with far more independence and vigor in West Florida than his earlier conception of presidential power would have allowed. He plotted in secret, used agents and troops, threatened force, and eventually proclaimed and effectuated the occupation of an area ruled by Spain. He did these things without calling back Congress, and kept his proclamation secret until it was safely implemented. But while his actions were inconsistent with the principles he had expounded as "Helvidius," they were largely consistent with the view of presidential power advocated by Hamilton and most Federalists. Congress had passed a statute that on its face represented a claim to the area, and Madison could, as Gallatin assured him, rely upon his power to interpret and execute the laws to justify his actions. Congress had also provided troops, and most early Federalists would have agreed that the President had discretion to use the troops in executing any of his constitutional responsibilities. Finally, though Congress had not been called back earlier than scheduled, the proclamation and military takeover were submitted to the legislature for consideration and approval; as Hamilton put it in the Pacificus-Helvidius debate, Congress was accorded the "final say."[373] Viewed in this perspective, Madison might be said to have acted with greater caution in West Florida than the Constitution required, in that he specifically denied authority to the United States forces to attempt to take any Spanish-occupied position by force. Those positions—particularly Mobile —were left in Spanish hands until Congress explicitly authorized their occupation, except for the temporary takeover of Pensacola by Andrew Jackson in 1814.

While Madison's actions in West Florida can arguably be squared with the Hamiltonian view of executive authority, his administration's virtually simultaneous efforts to acquire East Florida are more difficult to justify by that standard.

From the beginning of his presidency Madison planned the same fate for East as for West Florida. When Claiborne reported to Secretary Smith in early 1809 that Spanish Governor Folch was seeking to abandon Spanish-held possessions, he mentioned both West and East Florida.[374] Claiborne's subsequent letter to Judge Wykoff suggesting a plan for securing a request by local citizens for American protection focused primarily on West Florida; but he also wrote more generally of the inevitable union of "Florida" and the United States.[375] And Secretary Smith's letter appointing Wykoff an agent instructed him to communicate the administration's desires in East as well as West Florida, though Wykoff's primary responsibility was the area around Baton Rouge.[376] The chief agent to implement administration policy in East Florida was chosen in a different manner.

On June 20, 1810, the same day as his letter to Wykoff, Smith wrote to Senator William H. Crawford of Georgia, sending information "of the policy of the President, in relation to the Floridas." A respectable gentleman, he noted, had been instructed to convey the President's wishes to the people around Baton Rouge "and thence as far as the Perdido. . . ." The President, he informed Crawford, wishes "to have the advantage of your cooperation so far at least in selecting a gentleman of honor and discretion qualified to execute a trust of such interest and delicacy. . . ."[377] Crawford answered that, in response to Smith's "confidential communication," the "execution of the delicate trust therein created was, by me entrusted to Genl. George Mathews," former Governor of Georgia.[378] Smith replied on October 2, taking "great pleasure" in assuring Crawford that the President was "perfectly satisfied" with Crawford's execution of the "delicate trust." "It was indeed a most fortunate circumstance that threw in your way Genl. Mathews," Smith continued, "who well understanding the views of the executive, cannot but be happy in promoting them."[379]

Smith hoped that Mathews could help bring about a demand by East Florida residents for American protection, and an end to Spanish rule. But Americans were far less numerous in East than in West Florida; the former territory was not ready for revolution. While the West Florida revolutionaries were in convention, drafting a declaration of independence, Crawford was able to report to Smith very meager evidence of organized opposition to Spain in the east.[380] By October 27, when Madison ordered Claiborne to occupy part of West Florida, nothing in East Florida provided any hope for intervention. Yet Madison wrote on October 30, in a letter to William Pinkney justifying the West Florida intervention: "East Florida also is of great importance to the United States, and it is not probable that Congress will let it pass into any new hands."[381]

Madison's hopes for a prompt acquisition of East Florida were considerably enhanced during November and December 1810. Though the local citizens could not soon "deliver" the area, several credible sources reported that Spanish Governor Folch had written for authority to surrender the Floridas to the United States.[382] Most significantly, Folch sent to Secretary Smith, through Col. John McKee, a letter dated December 2 that stated: "I have decided on delivering this province to the United States under an equitable capitulation, provided I do not receive succor from Havanna or Vera Cruz, during the present month."

Madison sent Congress Folch's letter on January 3, 1811, with his confidential message urging that steps be taken to protect the interest of the United States in East Florida. To deal with the potential British threat, and the opportunity offered by Folch, Madison recommended, first, that Congress consider "the seasonableness of a declaration that the United States could not see, without serious inquietude, any part of a neighboring territory, in which they have, in different respects, so deep and so just a concern, pass from the hands of Spain into those of any other foreign Power." He also recommended, in case Folch's promise materialized, that Congress authorize "the Executive to take temporary possession of any part or parts of the said territory, in pursuance of arrangements which may be desired by the Spanish authorities; and for making provision for the government of the same, during such possession." But he went further. "The wisdom of Congress will, at the same time, determine," he wrote, "how far it may be expedient to provide for the event of a subversion of the Spanish authorities within the territory in question, and an apprehended occupancy thereof by any other foreign Power."[384]

Congress, acting in confidence, responded promptly to Madison's request for a declaration. On January 12 a joint resolution was adopted stating that "the United States cannot see, with indifference, any part of the Spanish Provinces adjoining the said States eastward of the river Perdido, pass from the hands of Spain into those of any other foreign Power."[385]

A bill to enable the President to take possession of East Florida was introduced in the Senate by Henry Clay on January 7. The so-called No-Transfer Act (so called because it sought to prevent a transfer from Spain to any other foreign nation) authorized the President to use the armed forces of the United States to take possession of

East Florida in the event that an agreement for that end should be reached with the "local authority," or "in the event of an attempt to occupy the said territory, or any part thereof, by any foreign government. . . ." Any territory gained under the Act was to be held by the United States subject to negotiation. Notably lacking was a grant of authority to take possession of the area in the event of "subversion of the Spanish authorities," one of the bases for intervention suggested in Madison's confidential message. On the other hand, the bill did not expressly require that the voluntary surrender be by the "Spanish authorities," as Madison's message contemplated, but by the "local authority."[387]

On January 10, the Senate passed the bill with minor amendments, and sent it to the House for approval.[388] Administration opponents in the House strongly objected, but amendments to allow use of the armed forces only to repel foreign occupation, and to authorize or require the President eventually to return the area to Spain, were defeated.[389] So while Congress was unwilling explicitly to authorize a takeover in the event of an internal upheaval, they refused to limit the President's authority to cases of foreign intervention or to require, or even authorize, the return of the territory to Spain; they required only that territory taken be held "subject to future negotiations," a phrase that Madison had used in connection with West Florida at the same time that he called for its incorporation "into the bosom" of the United States. A motion to remove the injunction of secrecy was defeated, and on January 12 the House adopted the Senate version.[390]

The Mission of General Mathews.   Madison selected General George Mathews and Colonel John McKee as commissioners to effect the capitulation of West Florida and to carry out the provisions of the No-Transfer Act for East Florida. Mathews was thoroughly familiar with the administration's efforts in East Florida; he had been engaged in the enterprise since Senator Crawford selected him as agent for the federal government. McKee was the man to whom Folch transmitted his original offer to surrender.[391] Senate confirmation was sought for neither appointment.

"Confidential" orders were sent on January 24, 1811, by Secretary of War William Eustis to Brigadier General Wade Hampton and Colonel Thomas P. Cushing, respectively the commanding officers of the Mississippi Territory and Fort Stoddert. The orders recited the provisions of the No-Transfer Act, and said that the President, "for the purpose of taking possession and occupying the territory aforesaid, and in order to maintain therein the authority of the

United States to employ any part of the Army and Navy of the United States which he may deem necessary, has appointed General George Mathews with power to agree to and complete on the part of the United States any arrangement which may be proposed for the purpose aforesaid." In executing his duty, Mathews might "call upon you for such detachment of troops under your command as may be necessary to occupy and maintain certain military posts within the territory aforesaid. He will consult with you and you will be pleased to concert with him such measures, and make such dispositions of the forces under your command as shall be best calculated to attain the objects in view."[392]

On January 26, 1811 the Secretary of State instructed Mathews and McKee to proceed to Florida "with all possible expedition." Their "trust" was to be concealed from general observation, Smith wrote, "with that discretion which the delicacy and importance of the undertaking require." The principal purpose of the Mathews-McKee mission was "the amicable surrender of the possession of the territory by the local ruling authority." In addition, they were to exercise the powers delegated the President to avoid a takeover of East Florida by any foreign power; and were told that naval and military forces would be at their disposal.[393] Further orders were issued to local commanders to cooperate with Mathews and McKee; gunboats, sloops and supplies were sent to the area, and Army Captain T.A. Smith was instructed to move his men to Point Petre, on the Georgia-Florida border, and to "practice your men with musket and rifle."[394]

Mathews arrived at St. Mary's, in Southern Georgia, on February 25. He wrote the Secretary of State, in barely literate fashion, that he had contacted the "Gentelmin" whose names he had given Smith in Washington, and found them "well disposed to sarve our Govrnment." He noted, however, that not one soldier or armed vessel had arrived in the St. Mary's River, which flows between Georgia and Florida, and "from this cause its thought not proper to attempt Enething at present." But he hoped that when he returned from Mobile in April "to have it in my power to carry the President's wishes into afect." Mathews noted that his "commission only goes to West Florida while our Instruction imbrace East Florida." He asked the Secretary of State to enlarge his commission and mail it to him.[395]

The preliminary soundings by Mathews and other activities in East Florida did not go unnoticed. On January 7, 1811, the acting surveyor-general of East Florida, George Clarke, wrote to the Governor of St. Augustine, Henry White, that Mathews had official instructions to assist a revolution in East Florida, which was nearly ready. A few Spanish subjects on the East Florida side of the St. Mary's River had only to call across the river for aid and, under the pretext of answering their call, Mathews would cross the river to support them. Clarke doubted the veracity of his information.[396]

The first official move by Mathews and McKee was to send their aide, Ralph Isaacs, to Pensacola to deliver the American terms of surrender to Governor Folch. But Folch had changed his mind. Issacs reported that "the insurgents were not formidible" to Folch, who "had received from his government the relief he had so long expected." Besides, Isaacs wrote, Folch believed "the proclamation of the President of the U. States, and the capture of Baton Rouge has produced a new order of things. . . ."[397] In early April, Mathews visited Folch at Pensacola. Folch said he had written to Spanish authorities recommending transfer of Florida to the United States, but did "not at this time feel himself justified in surrendering the province." Folch promised Mathews, however, that he would never surrender Florida to any "trans-atlantic power," particularly England or France.[398]

Folch's refusal to surrender East Florida led Mathews and McKee to begin considering the use of force. They showed General Covington in New Orleans the "confidential orders" of the Secretary of War, dated January 24, 1811, and their instructions from Smith, dated January 26, and asked Covington whether he would supply troops on their application. Covington refused, saying that requisitions would have to be approved by the commanding general, except "in the event of an attempt to occupy any part of the Territory in question by the troops of a foreign power. . . ." Mathews and McKee promptly wrote to the new Secretary of State, James Monroe, that "there existed a material difference of opinion between the Commanding General and ourselves on the construction of the order from the Department of War to the Commanding Officer of this Post." They requested Monroe's advice.[399]

On June 29, 1811, Monroe replied to seven letters from Mathews and McKee, some of which were written after the letter describing their dispute with Covington; but he failed to list or mention the letter concerning Covington. Monroe told them that "as it appears that there is no longer any probability that Governor Folch will deliver up the country under his jurisdiction, in the manner he proposed, the President thinks it is useless for you to remain longer where you are." Instead, Governor Claiborne was vested with authority to deal with Folch concerning West Florida. In a private letter to Mathews of the same day, however, Monroe explained that the official letter was "not intended to interfere with the state of things relating to East Florida, especially if you entertain any reasonable hope of success there," and he asked for information on the subject.[400]

During early July the British Minister, Augustus Foster, obtained an interview with Monroe and protested the occupation of West Florida. According to his report to Foreign Secretary Wellesley, Foster went on to ask Monroe if "certain documents" he had seen were genuine, including Madison's message to Congress, the letters from Folch and "what was styled an Act of Congress for the purpose of empowering the President [to occupy East Florida], in case arrangements for that purpose shall take place on the part of the local authorities in East Florida. . . ." Monroe claimed to know nothing of the Act, but Foster reported that when he pressed the issue Monroe "betrayed by his laughter his consciousness of their being genuine." Foster anticipated an American takeover of East Florida, along the "nefarious" pattern followed in the West, and he reported to Wellesley:

I then, My Lord, put the case to him of another Mr. Skipwith being at the head of a party of Insurgents composed of American Refugees; another Governor Folch calling out for protection against those Insurgents; and a fresh impulse of humanity felt by the American Government, and I asked him if in such case the United States would not be disposed to fulfill the provisions of the Act of Congress. The American Minister could not answer me in the affirmative in words, but as far as countenance of manner could betray, he showed what was the intention of his Government.*

On August 3 Mathews provided information, as Monroe had requested, including an explicit statement of his plans. "The quiet possession of E. Florida," he wrote, "could not be obtained by a amicable negotiation with the powers that exist there." But he added:

the inhabitants of the province are ripe for revolt; they are however incompetent to effect a thorough revolution without external aid—if two hundred stand of arms & fifty horsemen swords were in their possession I am confident they would commence the business, and with a fair prospect of success. These could be put into their hands by consigning them to

*Foster to Wellesley, July 5, 1811, British Foreign Office Archives, Ref.: F05-76-X/K2420, at 14-18. He reported the news that negotiations between the United States and Folch had broken down, but said "it is impossible to shut our eyes to the evident disposition which exists here to take advantage of any propositions which may hereafter be made from East Florida." Nothing short of a direct threat of war would restrain the Americans, he said.

the commanding officer at this post, subject to my order. I should use the most discreet management to prevent the U. States being committed and although I cannot vouch for the event, I think there would be but little danger.[401]

The scheme Mathews contemplated was modeled on the success-ful pattern of the West Florida intervention, just as British Minister Foster anticipated. If the insurgents assumed control of any signifi-cant part of East Florida, they would then become the "local au-thority" from whom the United States could arguably accept a ces-sion under the No-Transfer Act. His August 3 letter to Monroe made clear, however, that the local residents could achieve success only with American arms, which he thought could be discreetly provided.

Monroe made no reply to this letter, which greatly concerned Mathews. He journeyed to Georgia to give Senator Crawford full information to communicate to the Secretary of State. In a letter to Monroe dated October 14, 1811, Mathews complained that Mon-roe had not answered his August request for guns and swords. Gov-ernor Folch, Mathews noted, had been relieved of command and shipped to Havana under arrest; removal of the "tyrannical gover-nor" had calmed the inhabitants and lessened the spirit for revolt. He gave little credence to a rumor that he had been relieved of his author-ity, but said "should the information prove well founded I must entreat you to give me the earliest notice, for altho- I ever am ready to devote my best abilities to my country, yet I do not wish to remain in its em-ploy any longer than I can render it useful and acceptable service."[402]

Crawford forwarded this letter to Monroe on November 5, when he arrived in Washington. He promised to call on Monroe after the Senate convened. No record of the planned meeting between Craw-ford and Monroe has been found, but it seems likely that one took place. Professor Pratt notes that on November 18, possibly in re-sponse to these communications, the Secretary of Navy ordered a local officer, Captain Hugh Campbell, to proceed immediately to the St. Mary's River and take command of the vessels there. Monroe also heard of Mathews's activities through protests filed by British Minister Foster; he ignored Foster's complaint, however, just as he had the communications from Mathews.[403]

Mathews, meanwhile, had concluded that if the "patriots" were to succeed the United States would have to help them with more than just arms and supplies. Unlike the situation in West Florida, the East Florida insurgents had only a small population from which to draw recruits. Mathews lured American citizens to the province by offering land bounties for their support, and he sought to enlist "volunteers" from the regular U.S. troops at Point Peter.[404] On February 27 he contacted the naval commander, Captain Hugh Campbell, to arrange for naval assistance to the "patriots"; "circumstances justified the expectation of a speedy change in the political affairs of that country," he said, requesting that a naval force be held ready to act.[405] Campbell wrote immediately to Secretary of Navy Hamilton for instructions,[406] but events were moving too quickly for a timely response.

On March 11 Mathews wrote Campbell that "the business upon which we conversed relative to East Florida was ripe for execution. . . ." He asked for fifty muskets, bayonets, pistols and swords, arranging for "Mr. [John Houston] McIntosh [the "patriot" leader] at this time to select out of the swords and pistols, such and as many as he may deem expedient giving receipts for them. . . . I shall hereafter have occasion to solicit your further cooperation agreeably to my Instructions." Campbell reported Mathews's requests to Navy Secretary Hamilton on March 21, stating that he at first refused to comply "but on his producing Instructions from the President . . . I did consent to go certain lengths. . . ."[407]

On March 12, meanwhile, with United States arms, and with United States gunboats lying in reserve, the "patriot" rebellion began. McIntosh had written to Representative George M. Troup of Georgia, informing him that "before you can receive this, the Province of East Florida will have undergone a Revolution and probably [will be] in the quiet possession of the officers of the government of the States." Their plan was to invade Florida from the north, first capturing Amelia Island, and taking St. Augustine on the night of March 18, by surprise. "The thing has been for some months in a position between General Mathews and myself, but I am afraid never would have been accomplished had not the General been governed by the Spirit of his Instructions and the declared wishes of his Country."[408]

Troup received McIntosh's letter the day the rebellion began and immediately went to visit the Secretary of State. After their meeting Troup wrote Monroe: "Since I left you it has occurred to me a new aspect may be given to the subject of the letter received this morning. JHM [McIntosh], having long resided in the Province & bound himself in the prescribed form of allegiance may be considered a subject of the King of Spain—if his *Party* be made up of Spanish subjects, as is no means improbable at least in great part, to a revolution of the government by Spanish subjects nothing can be objected— But will it be possible," Troup asked, "to keep out of sight the agency of . . . . [Mathews] "?[409]

The "revolution's" first objective was the territory west of the

St. Mary's River, known as Rose's Bluff. The insurgents occupied the territory without resistance on March 14. Mathews notified Major Jacint Laval, who was in command at Point Peter during the absence of Lt. Col. Smith, that "the local authorities of East Florida" wished to surrender Rose's Bluff. In his capacity as Commissioner, Mathews called on Laval "to march a detachment of fifty men to take peaceable possession of Rosse's [sic] Bluff tomorrow morning."[410] Laval refused. "The instructions I have from the Secretary at War of which you have . . . a Copy," Laval replied, "are the only [orders] I can act by. . . . The stile of this instruction is so clear as to leave no ambiguity. The United States are not to be committed in the taking & the possession as will evidently appear by the Caution in my instructions."[411] Mathews demanded to know whether the fifty "volunteers" Laval had earlier promised Mathews and McIntosh in the presence of Captain Campbell would be allowed to leave.[412] Laval refused to let the men go when he found out they were not to be employed as soldiers of the United States but as part of the insurgent force.[413]

Mathews wrote immediately to Monroe, complaining of Laval's conduct, and asking for a new commandant who would cooperate. "Had Major Laval complied with the order contemplated in my letter," he claimed, the independence of the Floridas "would in all probability have been completely established." The situation was now changed, and "the time has arrived when something must be done, & if ever you expect the Floridas, send on immediately the companies of artillery & Infantry I requested in my former letter—recal [sic] Major Laval & if the President has confidence in me leave no discretion in the officer commanding in complying with my requests or orders."[414]

After seizing Rose's Bluff, the patriots turned to Amelia Island and its capital, Fernandina. McIntosh sent a summons to Don Justo Lopez, the Spanish commandant, stating that, because the United States had decided to take the province by "conquest," the patriots had been "caused" to agree to place it under their protection. He informed Lopez that the insurgents "have already secured all the country between the rivers of St. John's and St. Mary's" and demanded the surrender of Amelia Island. One article of the proposed terms of surrender was that the island would be ceded to the United States within twenty-four hours after capitulation.[415] Lopez refused to resign until he learned if the United States supported the invasion. He wrote to Captain Campbell and Major Laval asking them if the "United States had determined to take possession of this province by force of arms."[416] Laval replied that he had "the greatest satisfaction in informing you that the United States are neither principals or [sic] auxiliaries, and that I am not authorized to make any attack upon East Florida."[417] Campbell, however, replied that his naval force was not intended "to act in the name of the United States," but that he would act to support "a large proportion of your inhabitants who have thought proper to declare themselves independent, and are now in the act of supplicating you to unite with them in their cause."[418]

On March 17, eight U.S. gunboats, dispatched by Campbell, sailed into the harbor of Fernandina. Colonel Lodowick Ashley of the patriot force sent Commandant Lopez a letter informing him that he was about to land. "I will not fire a single gun, or commit any disorder," he wrote, "if they do not fire upon me. But, in the event that they do, we will show no quarters. . . ."[419] Lopez offered to discuss surrendering the post to Mathews and the United States,[420] but these offers were refused. Finally, he called the citizens together, and "by a vote of the citizens generally" decided to surrender on March 17.[421] Lopez wrote to his superior that the citizens had surrendered "in consequence of eight United States gun-boats anchoring in front of this station, with two cables fore and aft, their guns turned upon the town, the matches lit, and a perfect order of attacking us," and because the line of communication with St. Augustine had been suspended. On the following day, March 18, General Mathews accepted the island for the United States from the "local authority."[422]

Meanwhile, on March 17, Lt. Colonel Thomas Smith returned to his command. Major Laval was placed under arrest, and Smith reported to the Secretary of War that "in obedience to my instructions of the 26th of Jan'y 1811, I have sent a detachment of fifty men to receive and defend in the name of the United States, the town of St. Fernandina and the island of Amelia." At the same time, Smith and Campbell, unsure of their authority, sought further instructions from their superiors.[423] They proceeded for the next several days, however, to follow the "patriots" across the St. John's River toward St. Augustine, receiving from the 'patriots," as the "local authority," the posts in the intervening area.[424] As Professor Pratt explains: "Thus Smith would keep within his orders, which authorized him to take over and defend such posts as might have been surrendered to the United States by the local authorities."[425] The "patriot" forces, with their American supporters, reached and laid siege to St. Augustine in April.

On March 21 Mathews proudly wrote Monroe of the cession from "the constituted authorities of East Florida" of the territory between the St. Mary's and St. John's Rivers. He predicted that the entire province would soon be "conquered."[426] On April 16, 1812, Mathews wrote President Madison declaring that "the commission with which I am trusted is now I flatter myself approaching to a close, and I fondly hope in such a manner as will be satisfactory to you & honorable & advantageous to our common country." Again he claimed that "the Constituted Authorities of East Florida" had ceded the province through their "commissioner." To raise his army, Mathews revealed that he had given "large bounties . . . to adventurers that came to support the people," but that "there will remain a large and valuable country at the disposal of the States with live oak, cedar and pine sufficient to build all the Navy the nation may ever want."[427]

Mathews apologized for not being able to report the cession of all of East Florida. He blamed the delay on Laval's refusal to cooperate, and mentioned that Laval was under arrest.* Mathews assured the President, however, that Laval's unwillingness to cooperate with Mathews formed no part of the charges against him, "as it would be the only means whereby government could be implicated in all this business." He pledged he had not,

> in any instance committed the honor of Government or my own reputa-
> tion, by any act—nor have I pursued any clandestine means to accomplish
> the objects of my mission with any subject of E. Florida. The applica-
> tions were made to me to know on what terms the government would
> receive them, to which I gave such replys as were justified by my instruc-
> tions, and in every instance I conferred with men whose rank in society
> was respectable.[428]

Full of enthusiasm for his project, Mathews began arranging for a territorial government for Florida with McIntosh at its head. He was reported by Captain Campbell to be anticipating the conquest of Pensacola, Mobile, Mexico and even Peru. Though Campbell had cooperated with requests from Mathews for aid, he informed Hamilton that he had warned Mathews "that the Publick Manner in which the Patriots were to be assisted [at Amelia] by the Gun Boats will be sufficient cause for England as the Ally of Spain to join with that nation and retaliate." Mathews replied, according to Campbell, that to bring on war was a good purpose, and that "he held himself ac-countable for the transaction and felt confident of success." In

---

*Laval was released about one month later. He served throughout the War of 1812 as a major, but was later dropped from the army roll and given a posi-tion as military storekeeper. Smith went on to become a brigadier general. J. Pratt, *Expansionists of 1812* at 203 n. 20 (1957).

Campbell's view, Mathews had become "dangerous beyond conception."[429]

Events were conspiring against Mathews, however. Apprised of Mathews's activities, the British Minister registered vehement protests on Spain's behalf, placing pressure on Madison either to acknowledge or repudiate his commissioner. At roughly the same time the so-called John Henry letters were published, revealing a British plot to commit intrigue with American citizens. This made it highly embarrassing for the administration to acknowledge supporting a similar plot in East Florida.[430] Furthermore, Madison had decided on war with Great Britain and sent a message to Congress on June 1, 1812. He may have been reluctant to have East Florida become an additional matter of controversy until the declaration was secured, and since Spain was England's ally, war would afford Britain an opportunity to occupy the area on grounds of self-defense.[431] Finally, while Monroe made no effort to stop Mathews or the military from conspiring with the patriots, nothing he had ever written to Mathews permitted so open and flagrant a use of the armed forces against a friendly power.[432] It was probably not until early 1812 that Monroe realized the full extent to which American support would be necessary to have a "revolution" succeed.

On April 4, 1812, Monroe broke his long silence by dismissing Mathews. "I am sorry to have to state," Monroe began in his "official" letter, "that the measures which you appear to have adopted for obtaining possession of Amelia island and other parts of East Florida, are not authorized by the law of the United States . . . under which you have acted." It was never, Monroe wrote, "the policy of the law, or purpose of the Executive, to wrest the province forcibly from Spain," but only to hold the province if it were in danger of falling into the hands of a foreign power. Monroe pointed to the government's policy toward West Florida. If the administration "did not think proper to take possession by force of a province to which they thought they were justly entitled, it could not be presumed that they should intend to act differently in respect to one to which they had not such a claim."[433]

In a private letter of the same day, Monroe expressed his pain at dismissing Mathews, "but as the govt. never contemplated taking possession of the country except by friendly arrangement with the Spanish governor, or others, or to prevent possession being taken by a foreign power, it has been impossible to act differently." Monroe pointed to the law of 1794 which prohibited offenses against neutrals under severe penalties. "I have thought it improper to mention this fact in an official letter to you," Monroe added, "but it is one which had its weight in the part which the govt. has taken." Monroe closed by assuring Mathews of "the utmost confidence."[434]

Monroe officially disavowed the actions of Mathews on April 6, in a statement to the British minister for communication to Don Louis de Onis, the unrecognized minister of the Spanish regency.[435] Hamilton ordered Campbell to cease cooperating with Mathews on April 8, and Campbell acknowledged this order on April 25, stating that he had withdrawn the gunboats from Spanish waters.[436] On April 24 Madison wrote Jefferson that "in E. Florida, Mathews has been playing a tragi-comedy in the face of common sense, as well as of his instructions. His extravagancies place us in the most distressing dilemma."[437] The "dilemma" apparently was that Madison wanted East Florida but not in the way Mathews had procured it. The Federalist press carried a barrage of criticism, refusing to accept the administration's disavowal as genuine.[438]

Senator Crawford, who had acted as an intermediary between Monroe and Mathews, wrote to Monroe on April 19 that he was fearful "poor old Mathews . . . will die of mortification & embarrassment when he is made sensible of the utter-most extent of his disappointment."[439]   To assuage Mathews, Monroe sent Mathews' assistant, Colonel Ralph Isaacs, with a personal message. Two years later, in a letter to the Secretary of State, Isaacs claimed that Monroe instructed him to tell Mathews that

> the Executive were hurt in being compelled to do violence to the feelings of Genl. Mathews—that in your [Monroe's] private letter you had expressed the President's as well as your own feelings upon the subject —& that . . . I must find Genl. Mathews & assure him that no reproach be ever cast upon him by government (& that I might give to him an assurance that it was your belief he would be soon reinstated)—that the Executive was persuaded that he acted from the purest motives—that he pursued what he supposed to be the *intent of his instructions*, but with rather too much zeal.[440]

Mathews was crushed by his dismissal. He replied to Monroe in June that he had "no doubt" he could justify his conduct in East Florida to "an impartial public" if he exposed "confidential instructions and communications."[441] Isaacs claimed that he had prevented Mathews from

> giving publicity to much that he supposed would have a tendency to impair the confidence of the public in the Executive. I prevented him publishing a set of Instructions made by your predecessor in 1812 [Robert Smith]—much of what is called "back stairs" instructions & approbation—the letters advising your Depart. of all his proceedings—more, a conver-

sation he had with the President in Jan. 1811 wherein of the Congressional $100,000 appropriation an application of part was to be made to corrupt Govr. Folch if the Province of W. Florida could not be subjugated, or obtained, without, & that the color or pretext for taking & putting into his private coffers the cash should be his want of it to remove the troops &c &c &c.[442]

In July 1812, Mathews headed north, reportedly "to blow them all up at Washington." But his case never reached the public. He died on August 30, 1812, in Augusta, Georgia.[443]

Continued American Occupation, 1812–1813. On April 10, 1812, six days after dismissing General Mathews, Monroe requested David B. Mitchell, Governor of Georgia, to take charge of American affairs in East Florida. He pointed out that this commission would be in the best interests of the nation, "and peculiarly to the State of Georgia." Mitchell's attention was drawn to the Act of January 15, 1811, under which Mathews had been given his instructions. These instructions, Monroe added, "correspond fully with the law." But, Monroe said, Mathews had transgressed by using American troops to "disposses the Spanish authority for force. I forbear to dwell on the details of this transaction, because it is painful to recite them." Mitchell was to negotiate *"directly,"* "in harmony" with the Spanish officer in charge of the province, for "the restoration of that state of things in the province which existed before the late transactions." He was to undertake this action because "[t]he Executive considers it proper to restore back to the Spanish authorities Amelia island and such other parts, if any, of East Florida, as may have thus been taken from them." Enclosed in the letter was an order from the Secretary of War to the commander of the U.S. troops to evacuate the country, when Mitchell instructed them to do so. But Monroe's order had one important qualification. He expressed fear for the safety of those people who had aided General Mathews in occupying parts of East Florida. "It will be improper," he wrote, "to expose these people to the resentment of the Spanish authorities." Accordingly, Mitchell was "to come to a full understanding with the Spanish Governor on this subject," presumably agreeing to withdraw only after an understanding had been reached.[444]

Monroe had reason to expect that Mitchell would construe his orders to avoid withdrawing American troops from East Florida. As Governor of Georgia, Mitchell's avowed policy was to take over East Florida.[445] According to a letter to Monroe from Colonel Ralph Isaacs, who carried Monroe's instructions to Mitchell, Monroe intended Mitchell to keep control of the area. "[A]fter reading the '*sine qua non*' [in Mitchell's instructions] that render'd the restoration of the Province utterly impracticable, you said to me—Gov'r. Mitchell will understand this wont he? to which I replied—he is not dull of comprehension Sir! . . . Nor can you forget," Isaacs added, "that at every interview I was assured that government were concerting . . . measures to keep the Province & save harmless the Patriots. . . . [T]o use your own words," Isaacs reminded Monroe, "not a *hair* of the *head* of any person concerned in the revolution of E.F. should be hurt in consequence of their exertions, in that business, that they should not suffer in person or property for their efforts or encouragements." This letter was written two years after the events in question, by a possibly biased participant.[446] Yet it fits an otherwise consistent picture, and was never refuted by Monroe. The French Minister Serrurier reported in fact that Monroe, soon after sending his instructions to Mitchell, conceded that Mathews had clearly exceeded his instructions, but said that, since "things had reached their present condition, there would be more danger in retreating then advancing; and so, while disavowing the General's too precipitate conduct, they [the troops] would maintain the occupation."[447]

Upon arriving at St. Mary's to assume command, Mitchell wrote Monroe promising to "endeavor to terminate the unpleasant business in which the United States have been made a party by the indiscreet zeal of their Commissioner." He sought clarification of his April 10 instructions. What was he to do if "the Spaniards are reinforced by British Troops of any discription before the United States Troops can be withdrawn?" And what should he do if the "patriots" would not give up their cause?[448]

In a letter dated May 27, 1812, Monroe made the administration's policy more explicit. He reminded Mitchell that under the No-Transfer Act it was "the duty of the President to prevent the occupation of East Florida by any foreign Power." Mitchell was to take appropriate action to prevent the entrance of any foreign force, particularly British troops. "It is not expected," Monroe added, "if you find it proper to withdraw the troops, that you should interfere to compel the patriots to surrender the country, or any part of it, to the Spanish authorities. The United States are responsible for their own conduct only, not for the inhabitants of East Florida." On the other hand, Monroe now specifically ordered Mitchell to protect the "patriots" from harm: "Indeed, in consequence of the compromitment of the United States to the inhabitants, you have been already instructed not to withdraw the troops, unless you find that it may be done consistently with their safety, and to report to the Government the result of your conferences with the Spanish authorities, with your views, holding in the mean time the ground occupied."[449]

Mitchell seems to have understood Monroe's message as Isaacs said it was intended to be understood. He wrote to Spanish Governor Estrada at St. Augustine on May 4, 1812, assuring him that "the transactions which have recently taken place . . . were not authorized by the [U.S.] government." He invited negotiations to preserve harmony between Spain and the United States, but made no suggestion that he was prepared to withdraw. On May 9 the Governor responded, demanding an American withdrawal before any negotiation. At about the same time, Spanish troops attacked some Americans camped outside St. Augustine. Mitchell then sent an aide-de-camp to Estrada to inform him of the assurances required by the United States before withdrawal; "that such assurances will not be given," Mitchell wrote Monroe, "I have reason to believe." On June 11 a new Spanish Governor once again demanded that Mitchell withdraw. Mitchell replied that the attack on American troops had "precluded all further efforts on my part to continue the correspondence," and that no withdrawal would occur until the Governor explained the earlier attack. The Governor tried to explain away the attack as having been directed exclusively against the rebels, but Mitchell rejected the explanation, and sharply criticized the Spanish for using black troops.[450] At that point communication between the two commanders apparently ceased.

Mitchell wrote to Monroe on July 17 that letters he had received from members of Congress induced him "to believe that an act would have passed as soon as war was declared, authorizing the President to take possession of the posts yet occupied by the Spaniards in the two Floridas. . . ." Expressions in Monroe's communications had, Mitchell wrote, "confirmed" Mitchell's expectations. "Under these impressions I have remained here [at St. Mary's] making every preparation for that event."[451] Apparently the administration shared Mitchell's view, for on June 19, the day after war was declared on Britain, Representative Troup, an annexation supporter, moved in secret session that a committee inquire into the expediency of authorizing the President to occupy East and West Florida without delay. The motion passed, and the committee presented a bill on June 22 authorizing occupation of those territories. Still acting behind closed doors, the House passed the Floridas-Occupation bill on June 25, 1812, and sent it to the Senate.[452]

The following day the House, by a narrow vote of 58 to 51, adopted a resolution requesting the President, "if, in his opinion, it be compatible with the public interest," to lay before the House, confidentially or otherwise, "full information of all the proceedings" had by virtue of the No-Transfer Act, "and also copies of all instructions there may have been issued by the Executive branch of the

Government under said act." The President purported to comply on July 1. Among the important materials he sent were the letter of January 26, 1811, in which Secretary of State Smith gave Mathews his instructions; the official letter of April 4, 1812 dismissing Mathews for exceeding his authority; and the letters to Mitchell dated April 10 and May 27, 1812, instructing Mitchell to turn over the area to the Spanish if no foreign force entered it, and only after an agreement was reached insuring the safety of the "patriots."[453] Not included in the transmittal, however, were the Mathews letters reporting his intentions and requesting arms and military support; Troup's letter to Monroe acknowledging American support for the revolution; Monroe's "private" letter to Mathews giving him "assurance"; and instructions issued to Mathews by Smith or through Crawford prior to January 1811. Some of these materials were not technically within the scope of the House resolution, since they were not instructions issued under the No-Transfer Act. But Monroe's silence, after being informed of Mathews's intentions, undoubtedly caused Mathews to assume his plans were unobjectionable. By withholding these letters Madison was able to keep from Congress the full extent of his administration's involvement.[454]

The Floridas-Occupation bill was referred by the Senate to a select committee, which on June 30 reported it without amendment. On July 1 the Senate considered the bill and "instructions of the President . . . on the subject," presumably the letters sent the same day to the House. Senator Crawford of Georgia offered an amendment to authorize the military occupation of Canada if the opportunity arose during the war with Britain. This amendment, Crawford apparently hoped, would win votes from members who favored an invasion of Canada, but would otherwise vote against the takeover of East Florida. On July 2 Crawford's amendment was adopted 20 to 10. But on July 3, when the amended bill came up for a final vote, antiadministration Republicans joined with Federalists to defeat it, 14 to 16.[455]

Administration policy was relatively unaffected by the Senate's refusal to ratify the occupation of East Florida. On July 6, 1812 Monroe wrote to Mitchell, noting that he had delayed sending instructions out of "the expectation, that Congress might, in consequence of the war with England, make some modification of the law under which you acted." Monroe informed Mitchell, however, that the Senate had rejected the proposed bill. This meant only that "the authority of the Executive remains unchanged, being precisely what it was at the commencement of the present session. . . . Since the rejection of the bill in the Senate," wrote Monroe, "the President thinks that it will be most advisable to withdraw the troops from East Florida, provided British troops have not landed in it, and in that event also, provided they be superior to any force which we have in that quarter." In the event of a British invasion, he added, the occupation of East Florida "is not to be considered as abandoned." Monroe took note of reports that "an additional force of five hundred men" had landed at St. Augustine. He presumed them to be Spanish reinforcements ready to oppose the "patriots" and American forces. But "if they be black," Monroe cautioned, Mitchell would be safe in assuming "they are British." In any case, Monroe concluded, "it is also probable, even should that contingency not occur, that the consequences of the war may give a new view of the subject, in the course of the year, and induce Congress, at the next session, to authorize the President to take possession of the country."[456]

Mitchell wrote back to Monroe on July 17, expressing "surprise and mortification" at learning that the Senate had rejected the Floridas-Occupation bill. Not only had he refrained from withdrawing, he had "ordered such reinforcements to the support of Colonel Smith, as I deem necessary to enable him to maintain his ground . . . or to take possession, if ordered." He had taken this step, he informed Monroe, because the Spanish had "armed every able bodied negro within their power, and they have also received from the Havanna a reinforcement of nearly two companies of black troops." Under the circumstances, Mitchell wrote, "I feel that it is a duty I owe the United States, and Georgia in particular, to assure you, that the situation of the garrison of St. Augustine will not admit of the troops being withdrawn." Indeed, he had "carefully avoided making any proposition for withdrawing the troops, under the fullest conviction that such a step was not intended. . . ."[457]

Others also pressed Monroe to continue the occupation. On July 30 the patriot leader McIntosh wrote, as "Director of the Territory of East Florida," that they had been promised American support and "through official and semi-official channels, 'that not a hair of our heads should be touched' "; he therefore protested the proposed withdrawal.[458] Senator Crawford wrote from East Florida on August 6 predicting great "dissatisfaction . . . if the troops are withdrawn, the country given up, & the patriots abandoned." He argued that, since the patriots had now adopted a constitution and formed a government, they could properly be deemed the "local authorities" under the No-Transfer Act, from whom a cession might be accepted.[459]

Monroe initially made no response to these requests. Nor did he take any further steps to obtain a withdrawal. The administration was forced to act, however, when the position of U.S. troops in the area substantially deteriorated. The patriot and U.S. forces suffered setbacks during the summer and fall of 1812, and eventually were forced to retreat from their camp on the outskirts of St. Augustine.[460] Colonel Smith's position there was particularly precarious: most of his troops were volunteers whose terms would end on September 19. Mitchell complained to Monroe that he had received no instructions concerning Smith's position since requesting reinforcements in July; and on October 19 he urged Monroe to order U.S. recruits in Georgia to replace the volunteers in East Florida.[461]

Thus forced to act, the administration decided to strengthen rather than to withdraw American forces. Secretary of War Eustis wrote to General Thomas Pinckney on October 4 that "I am directed by the President to request your attention to the detachment under Lt. Col. Smith, and that you will order him to be reinforced."[462] Then, on October 12, Monroe relieved Mitchell of his assignment in favor of General Pinckney, a more experienced military man. Monroe thanked Mitchell for his service; he had "the entire approbation" of the President, and had given "proof of patriotism." That "more precise instructions were not given you, for the reinforcement of the troops under the command of Colonel Smith, in case the Spanish authorities should refuse to give you the satisfactory assurance desired in favour of the people in East Florida, to whom the publick faith had been pledged, proceeded from a hope and belief," explained Monroe, "that that contingency would not happen, and a confidence if it did, that your judgment, looking distinctly to the nature of your trust, and its duties, would supply the omission."[463]

In a letter formally appointing General Pinckney, Monroe described the authority conferred by the No-Transfer Act, and went on to tell Pinckney that Mathews had been dismissed because "he had erred by excess of zeal only." The dismissal of Mathews, and the qualified order that Mitchell withdraw, were steps taken to prove to Spain the "moderation and friendship" of the United States. This spirit of conciliation was not returned by the Spanish, according to Monroe. They refused to grant amnesty to the rebels, and had attacked U.S. troops while Mitchell was negotiating with Spanish authorities. Furthermore, "the savages have been excited to commit hostilities against us" and "hostilities have likewise been committed by the Spanish troops themselves." In short, wrote Monroe, "East Florida has become essentially a British province." Because of the situation, concluded Monroe, "the President thinks it due to the injured rights and interests of the United States, as well as to their honor, to maintain the ground on which you now stand, and to collect your force at Point Peter, for the purpose of protecting our own country, and chastising the savages who have committed hostilities; of watching the movements of England, and of the Spanish forces acting under English influence, and of taking such ulterior measures, as may be found to be proper and necessary."[464]

American troops were therefore maintained in East Florida while Monroe began negotiations with Don Luis de Onis for the peaceful cession of the territory. Onis responded to Monroe's inquiries in vague terms, but Monroe continued to believe a treaty of cession might be concluded. Onis finally demanded that the United States divest itself of the area it had seized in West Florida, which Congress had by then added to the Mississippi Territory. The administration refused to negotiate on this issue, and talks were broken off in December 1812.[465]

The administration then prepared for a military assault. On December 2, 1812, Secretary of War Eustis wrote General Pinckney to reinforce his position on the St. John's River and to prepare a force "for offensive operations, preparatory to the entire possession of the Province of East Florida." At the same time Eustis ordered two thousand Tennessee militiamen under Andrew Jackson to join General Wilkinson in New Orleans.* On January 13, 1813, Monroe, acting as Secretary of War after William Eustis resigned, informed Pinckney that "it is intended to place under your command an adequate force for the reduction of St. Augustine, should it be decided on by Congress, before whom the subject will be in a few days.[466] By the end of January 1813, substantial numbers of American troops were poised for attack—Wilkinson and Jackson on the west, Pinckney on the east. They were an enthusiastic force; Jackson wrote to the Secretary of War that his volunteers were "the choicest of our citizens, who go at the call of their country to execute the will of the government, who have no constitutional scruples . . . and . . . will rejoice at the opportunity of placing the Americn eagle on the ramparts of MOBILE, PENSACOLA, and FORT ST. AUGUSTINE. . . ."[467]

Administration supporters moved in December 1812 to obtain

---

*Pinckney sought from Mitchell information on the state of negotiations with the Spanish. Mitchell explained that, because of his "expectation of war with England, and, consequently, a determination on the part of our government to take the Floridas, [he was led] to decline in my second reply . . . [to the Spanish Governor] making any proposition for withdrawing the troops. . . ." He added his conviction that the Spanish would not consent to assuring the safety of the former rebels. Mitchell to Pinckney, Dec. 17, 1812, in *Secret Acts, supra* note 450, at 50.

congressional approval to occupy Mobile and East Florida. A committee was appointed to consider the question, and several requests
for information were passed.[468] The information provided disclosed
that the government had no precise knowledge of any British movement toward East Florida, that the desire of the inhabitants of East
Florida was to be under the protection of the United States, and that
Spanish Minister Onis had no power to negotiate a cession.[469]

On January 19 the committee reported a bill to authorize the
President "to occupy and hold" all of West Florida, west of the
Perdido River (including Mobile), which is "not now in possession
of the United States," and by its second section "to occupy and hold
all ... of East Florida, including Amelia Island." Senator Samuel
Smith of Maryland moved to strike the second section, thereby denying the President authority to occupy East Florida. Heated debate
ensued, until on February 2 the Senate voted 19 to 16 in favor of
Smith's motion.[470]

Of the entire debate that preceded this second rejection of administration policy only one speech is preserved. It was delivered
by Senator William Hunter of Rhode Island, and gives some idea of
the issues considered, several of which concern the war-making powers of the legislative and executive branches.

Hunter resented the fact that Madison had not frankly espoused
the legislation under consideration. He felt the Constitution required the President to give Congress information and to recommend
measures he thought necessary and expedient.[471] He conceded that
Congress had both an independent power and duty to act, as others
in the debate had argued; but "in a case involving a change of our
relations from a state of peace with a friendly nation to that of war,
no instance can hardly be imagined, in which our primary interference would be justifiable." For legislative initiative in declaring
war would "be in as little accordance with the spirit of the Constitution as it is contrary to the uniform practice under it." Whether to
declare war, Hunter said, should depend on the executive's reasons
for recommending it, so if it was later discovered that the recommendation had proceeded from "base, corrupt, or traitorous motives," the national honor could be redeemed by impeachment.[472]

Hunter rejected Madison's position that there was no Spanish
government with which to negotiate, and suggested that America
had created a revolution in East Florida rather than found one,
through private if not public instructions to Mathews. He strenuously
attacked the argument, made by others, that an occupation of East
Florida was not formal war, and therefore need not be declared.
"If this is not war," Hunter said, "but something done only in

reference to and for the security of an indemnity; a reducing of a legal *lien* into possession; a process to confirm peace; an instrument of negotiation;—it is a measure the President already has in his power; it is the treaty-making power; he can act without our aid." But this was most certainly war, he contended, by any sensible definition. Congress should therefore declare war and "[l]et the people of this country understand it. . . . Why should we shroud our intention in dastardly ambiguity," he asked. "This evasive course . . . is what our Constitution . . . prohibits, deprecates, and disdains." Indeed, Hunter continued, undeclared, "offensive" war was unconstitutional:

> By our Constitution, there can be no merely constructive declaration of an offensive war; it must be a direct one. As a Legislature, we have the power, not of making war, but of declaring war. Congress shall have power "to declare war." This clause, so worded, must evidently settle the old litigated question raised by many writers on the laws of the nations, viz: whether a declaration should not always precede an offensive war? We are to *declare* it, to announce it in plain terms to our people, and to the enemy. It is intended we should refer them to a plain declaration of the change of our condition—not draw them into it by an act circuitously leading to this result, and involving this as an inevitable consequence. . . . To *declare* war, is a precise, technical, appropriate, unambiguous, undeceiving phrase. It is the peculiar idiom of a just and wise nation. The declaration with us must always precede the act; of course, I refer to offensive war. Defensive war explains and declares itself.[473]

Though the Senate struck section 2 from the proposed bill, the majority did not necessarily support all that Federalist Senator Hunter said. Hunter, for example, was led by his principles to oppose granting authority even to take possession of Mobile, in West Florida. If the United States had title, he said, the President could act unilaterally;[474] if not, to grant authority would have been to authorize an undeclared war, which he argued was unconstitutional. Yet the Senate passed the section of the law that authorized occupation of Mobile, by a vote of 22 to 11, on February 5. Three days later the House, also in secret session, passed the bill.[475] Some Senators may well have distinguished the two situations, viewing the occupation of West Florida as lawful without a declaration because based on a treaty, but seeing the occupation of East Florida as either unconstitutional or inconsistent with the law of nations.

Faced with a second defeat in its effort to secure authority to occupy East Florida, the administration appears finally to have accepted Congress's will. On February 16 John Armstrong, the new Secretary of War, wrote to Andrew Jackson in Natchez informing him that "[t]he causes of embodying and marching to New Orleans the corps under your command having ceased to exist, you will, on the receipt of this letter, consider it as dismissed from public service. . . ." Jackson refused to dismiss his troops until he had marched them back to Tennessee, but at that point they were disbanded. Pinckney's troops were likewise disbanded or ordered elsewhere.[476] In March, Onis approved an act of amnesty for the East Florida rebels "who have been induced to revolt by an agent of the United States, whose proceedings in that respect were unauthorized," and Governor Kindelan of East Florida published the proclamation on March 15, 1813.[477] On April 27, 1813 Colonel Smith's troops left Camp New Hope, setting the camp buildings afire. On May 6, 1813 the Spanish entered Fernandina, and by mid-May all American troops had left East Florida. Mobile was occupied by Wilkinson in mid-April, bringing most of West Florida under American control.

The East Florida "patriots" continued to skirmish with the Spanish. Some of them retreated into the Indian territory of Alachua, and tried to reestablish their relationship with the United States.[478] Monroe refused to have anything to do with them. "The United States being at peace with Spain," he informed them, "no countenance can be given by this government to the proceedings of the revolutionary party in East Florida, if it is composed of Spanish subjects—and still less can it be given them if it consists of American citizens."[479] Monroe still hoped to obtain East Florida in the negotiation process with Britain, and instructed the American peace negotiators to keep in mind "the object" of the No-Transfer Act.[480] But Gallatin, one of the negotiators, was unsympathetic; he "insisted upon and received, for purposes of negotiation, a formal statement of the withdrawal of the American forces from East Florida."[481] The province remained in Spanish hands until Monroe succeeded to the presidency, and Andrew Jackson invaded it in 1818.

Andrew Jackson in the War of 1812

Occupation of Pensacola, 1814.   Andrew Jackson's desire to move against the Spanish posts in Florida was only temporarily foiled.* He had hardly returned to Tennessee when his troops were called up

---

*Jackson's enthusiasm can be seen, not only in his letter to Monroe promising to ignore constitutional restraints, *supra* at 323, but also in an address to his troops, while he waited vainly in 1813 for orders to invade. See 1 J. Bassett, *Life of Andrew Jackson* 79 (1911).

again by the state government to suppress the hostile Creeks. Jackson fought several battles, breaking Creek resistance in Georgia and the Mississippi Territory, and returned to Nashville on May 28, 1814. When General William Henry Harrison resigned, Jackson was appointed general in the regular army, in command of the Seventh Military District. He forced the Creeks to sign the Treaty of Fort Jackson in August 1814, and then attended to the defense of Mobile.[482]

During this period Jackson renewed his effort to convince the administration to authorize attacks across the Florida border. On June 27, 1814, he wrote Secretary of War Armstrong that he had obtained corroboration that 300 British soldiers had landed at the mouth of the Apalachicola, "and are arming and exciting the Indians to acts of hostility against the United States." He asked what action he might take if the British and Spanish were protecting and supplying the hostile Creeks, and inducing them to actions against the United States:

> Will the government say to me to require a few hundred Militia (which can be had for the campaign at one days notice) and with such of my disposable force in regulars proceed to————and reduce it. If so I promise the war in the south has a speedy termination and British influence forever cut off from the Indians in that quarter.[483]

Further information received by Jackson convinced him that the British had landed near Pensacola in three large vessels, with 4,000 men. He wrote Armstrong on July 30, suggesting a prompt attack.[484] "How long will the . . . United States tamely submit to disgrace and open insult from Spain?" he asked on August 5. "I can but regret, that permission had not been given by the government to have seized on Pensacola[;] had this been done the american Eagle would now have soared above the fangs of the British Lyon [sic]."[485] Five days later Jackson sent his private secretary, Charles Cassedy of Tennessee, to the national capitol with a letter for Armstrong, emphasizing the tactical importance of possessing Pensacola.[486] On August 30 he wrote again, describing Pensacola as "the strong point from which G. Britain can and will an[n]oy our military operations."[487] Finally, on September 5, Jackson wrote Monroe, Acting Secretary of War, describing the tactical value of Pensacola and urging its seizure:

> As Spain has become our enemy covertly if not openly, as carrying on in concert with G. Britain from Pensacola hostilities against us by her Indians, for the safety of the U.S. why will not the Government order the British to be expelled and Pensacola Seized. . . ? I beg you to take a glance

at the situation of Pensacola—its fine harbour, now in the possession of our deadly foe, and at once you will see its importance in the hands of the U. States, and Order accordingly.[488]

Jackson's requests for authority to attack Pensacola arrived in Washington during a time of turmoil and disaster. A British force marched into the city on August 24, destroyed numerous buildings, burned papers, and disrupted the operations of government. Before the attack, on July 18, Secretary of War Armstrong appears to have written a letter authorizing Jackson to attack Pensacola if the Spanish were voluntarily cooperating with the British.* Mysteriously, however, this straightforward response to Jackson's request of June 27 reached Jackson about six months later, on January 17, 1815.† By then, Jackson had attacked and withdrawn from Pensacola.

Jackson received no guidance concerning Pensacola during August. On September 5, soon after the British had left Washington, Acting Secretary of War Monroe acknowledged Jackson's letter of August 10, and stated that "vigorous operations will be required in the lower

---

*Armstrong said in his letter: "The case you put is a very strong one and if all the circumstances stated by you unite, the conclusion is inevitable. It becomes our duty to carry our arms where we find our enemies." He noted that the President wanted to maintain peace with Spain, and that Jackson should distinguish between voluntary and involuntary acts of the Spanish authorities. "The result of this enquiry must govern. If they admit, feed, arm, and co-operate with the British and hostile Indians, we must strike on the broad principle of self-preservation. Under other and different circumstances, we must forbear." Letter of July 18, 1814, *Madison Papers*, series 1, reel 16.

†Armstrong later claimed that his letter conditionally authorizing Jackson to attack was carried to the post office for transmittal but intercepted—by Madison or Monroe, he suggested—and mailed only after Jackson had won the battle at New Orleans in January 1815. 2 J. Armstrong, *Notices of the War of 1812* at 175 (1836). Jackson is reputed to have said that, had he received Armstrong's letter before his attack, he would have immediately moved against the Barancas, thereby preventing its destruction, and would have been able in other ways to conduct a more effective assault. "A gentleman of the Baltimore Bar," *Some Account of General Jackson* 157 (1828). Both Armstrong and Jackson were, by the time this controversy erupted, alienated from Madison and Monroe. The latter two exchanged letters, stating that they had no recollection of Armstrong's letter, but Madison's letters indicate that he would have regarded an attack as unjustified or unwise; Madison wrote, in fact, that he had refused, on October 8, 1813, to authorize an attack on Pensacola when certain blockhouses were destroyed on the American side of the Perdido. *See* letters of October 29 and November 16, 1827, 3 *Madison Writings* (Cong. ed.) 596, 600; letters of October 3 and November 2, 1827, 7 *Monroe Writings* 120, 124. Conceivably, Madison did withhold Armstrong's letter because he did not subscribe to the position attributed in it to him. What appears to be the original may be found in Madison's unpublished papers, along with letters written and dispatched in July 1814. *Madison Papers*, series 1, reel 16. *See generally* 6 Brant, *Madison* 335–36; 1 J. Parton, *Life of Andrew Jackson* 593 (1861) (3 vols.); 2 *Correspondence of Andrew Jackson* 13n. 2 (J. Bassett and J. Jameson, eds. 1926–35) (7 vols.) [hereinafter "*Jackson Correspondence*"].

country." Monroe wrote that it was "desirable" that Jackson proceed to New Orleans, but added—"unless circumstances should render another point more eligible."[489] On September 21, Charles Cassedy—Jackson's emmissary to Washington—apparently obtained an interview with Monroe. Two days later, he reported in a letter written at the War Department that Monroe would support Jackson against the Spanish:

> I had a long conversation with the Secretary of War on the day before yesterday, relating to every point of importance. . . . I am also convinced, that you will receive all the support in the power of the government, relating to the Spaniards, if it should be necessary to notice them in a hostile manner. Col. Monroe spoke in *strong* terms on that subject, as well as on subjects relating to extensive national policy.[490]

Monroe seems to have been unwilling explicitly to authorize an attack on Pensacola. But on September 17 he wrote a letter that must have confirmed the impression conveyed by Cassedy. He acknowledged receiving several of Jackson's letters, including that of August 10 "by Mr. Cassida," and recognized that "it seems probable that a considerable British force had been landed at Pensacola, with the connivance of the Spanish authorities there, and at Havanna. . . ." He then went on to review the troops available to Jackson, and added that "taking all circumstances into consideration" the President had ordered 5,000 troops from Tennessee to march to Jackson's aid, and that 2,500 men be held in readiness in Georgia. "Full confidence," he added, "is entertained in your judgment in the discharge of this discretionary power vested in you."[491]

Jackson, meanwhile, was busy defending the Mobile area and recruiting troops. He wrote Monroe on September 8 that the British and Spanish flags were flying together in the forts at Pensacola, and the British were actively enlisting Spaniards and Indians. "This leaves the character of Spain no longer doubtful. I hope shortly to have sufficient force to carry into effect any order I may receive from the Government."[492] The next day Jackson wrote a particularly angry letter to the Spanish governor at Pensacola, which he also sent to Monroe. He openly threatened the commandant and even the lives of some Spanish sailors he held prisoner; and he sarcastically noted that, since Spain was allowing enemies of the United States sanctuary, "your Excellency cannot be surprised, but on the contrary will provide for my soldiers and Indians a Fort in your Town should I take it into my head to pay you a visit."[493]

On September 12, 1814, four British ships appeared off the Fort at Mobile Point. A battle began on September 15. Jackson's defenses held and the British retreated to Pensacola, with one ship lost, another crippled, thirty-one men killed, and forty wounded; only four Americans were killed and five wounded.[494] Governor Claiborne wrote on October 2 that he was "anxious to hear, that you had planted the American Standard on the Forts of Pensacola; the Government must anticipate it, and the Nations will applaud the Act. . . ."[495] But Jackson continued as late as October 10 to seek approval from Monroe: "I beg leave to refer to my former letter as to the necessity of having possession of Pensacola, and confidently hope to receive instructions relative thereto."[496]

Jackson's attitude changed dramatically after he received Monroe's instructions of September 27, and presumably Cassedy's letter of September 23. He acknowledged Monroe's instructions on October 26, and advised the Secretary that the hostile conduct of the governor of Pensacola had induced him to drive the British and Indians from that place, and to take possession of the forts below Pensacola called the Barancas. "This will put an end to the Indian war in the south as it will cut off all foreign influence." Jackson did not claim to have been authorized to attack Pensacola. But he may well have regarded the September 27 letter as conferring discretion to act on his own responsibility. "As I act without the orders of the government," he wrote, "I deem it important to state to you the reasons for the measure I am about to adopt." These he gave as: the threatened safety of that area of the nation; hostility of the Spanish government by allowing the British to use Pensacola as a refuge, and to refit for further expeditions; and an alleged admission by the Governor that he had armed Indians and sent them into American territory. "I feel a confidence that I shall stand Justified to my government for having undertaken the expedition. Should I not I shall have consolation of having done the only thing in my own opinion which could give security to the country by putting down a savage war, . . . an ample reward for the loss of my commission."[497]

On November 6, Jackson and some 6,000 troops faced Pensacola. His demands for its surrender were rejected, so Jackson attacked the next day. Opposition collapsed, but the British destroyed the Barancas on November 8, before abandoning it. Jackson described the action in a letter to Monroe on November 14. "Not having the Sanction of my Government," he wrote, "or the means of repairing the fortifications [at Barancas], I determined not to occupy them, . . . [and to] withdraw my troops . . . for the protection of the frontier. . . . Thus Sir I have broken up the hot bed of the Indian war and Convinced the Spaniards That we will permit no equivocations in a nation professing neuterality, whilst we most scrupulously respect national, neutral, and Individual rights."[498]

On October 21, Monroe answered Jackson's letter of September 9, which had included his threats to the Spanish governor. "I hasten to communicate to you," Monroe wrote, "the directions of the President, that you should at present take no measures, which involve this Government in a contest with Spain." The governor's conduct should be presented to Spain through "ordinary channels," rather than presented by "an attack on Pensacola," though the President approved the "manly tone" of Jackson's correspondence with the governor.[499]

The expedition to Pensacola was over by the time Jackson received Monroe's October 21 letter. He acknowledged it on November 20, noting that his letter of November 14 described his "visit" to Pensacola, and that the governor had actively aided the British. "I flatter myself that I have left such an impression on the mind of the Governor of Pensacola, that he will respect the American Character, and hereafter prevent his neutrality from being infringed." Nor did Jackson indicate any doubt in his own mind of the propriety of his conduct. He said, in fact, should the governor "suffer the British again to occupy his Town, and the Indians to return, This District cannot be protected unless they are (as you have expressed in your letter of 7 September) promptly expelled."[500] He added on December 10 that he had heard that the governor had refused British aid in rebuilding the Barancas, replying that "when they wanted aid, they would apply to their friend General Jackson." His visit, he suggested, had had a "good effect."[501]

News of Jackson's invasion reached Monroe on December 5. Two days later he wrote Jackson that he had hoped his letter of October 21 would have arrived "in time to prevent the attack, which you then contemplated making, on the British at Pensacola." The conduct of Spanish authorities "may justify the measure," but the President had wanted to avoid it because he had undertaken new efforts to obtain justice with amity. "Should you have made the proposed attack, you will, on the receipt of this letter, withdraw your troops from the Spanish Territory, declaring that you had entered it for the sole purpose of freeing it from British violation."[502]

Jackson appears to have responded to this letter on February 13, 1815. During the interval, he had been engaged in defending New Orleans. By February the British had retired after suffering great casualties, so Jackson reviewed his various military operations. Among them was his attack on Pensacola. He wrote that it had been the only effective way of securing the frontier from British and Indian operations. "With the history of that expedition you have been made acquainted; and you will pardon me for observing Sir that whatever our relations with Spain may be, or however desirous we may be to preserve them, it was expecting a little too much of good nature to suppose that when we were seeking to defend our country against invasion, we should sit quietly down, and see her give aid and comfort to our enemies without attempting to prevent it." The attack "may have been an act of rudeness towards our worthy friend and neighbor," he wrote, not warranted by the "civilities" governing intercourse between "polished" nations. "I am but little versed in the etiquette or punctillios of these matters; and I must take the liberty of adding, that whenever I shall be entrusted with the defence of an important section of my country I am quite sure it will not be sacrafised [*sic*] by too strict an attention to them."[503]

No reply by Monroe has been found. Nor is there any evidence to indicate that Madison or Monroe considered punishing Jackson or were even displeased with the Pensacola incident. Jackson's triumph at New Orleans no doubt helped the administration to overlook any impropriety that may have been felt concerning his conduct. But it seems doubtful that either Madison or Monroe would have claimed Jackson's actions were unexpected. Only a few years thereafter, Monroe turned to Jackson to direct the war against the Seminole Indians in East Florida. Furthermore, Monroe specifically wrote Jackson on July 3, 1816 that the attack on Pensacola was "justified." An historian named Major La Tour, Monroe wrote, had asked for government documents on the subject of West Florida and Louisiana for a new edition of his book. Madison had agreed to give La Tour the material, including documents related to

> Pensacola, being of opinion, that the violation of the Spanish neutrality by the British, justified fully, the incursion which you made on them, and that the part which the gov't. took, as evinc'd by my letters to you respecting that mov'ment, one before, & the other after it was made, the first bearing date on the 21 of Octr. the second on the 7th of Dec'r, show a spirit of moderation towards Spain almost without example. It is true, I was not very severe on you, forgiving the blow, nor ought I to have been, for a thousand considerations, which I need not mention.[504]

The administration failed to inform Congress of the Pensacola incident or to send Congress any of the relevant correspondence. Had the material been sent, it would have raised questions of potential concern to the legislature, including whether the attack was justifiable under international law, and even assuming it was, whether the executive could order or allow the attack without prior legislative approval. Furthermore, the administration might have been forced to accept responsibility for the attack, or to attribute it to Jackson's unilateral decision. Apparently Congress was officially apprised of the incident on November 18, 1818, in a memorandum concerning the Seminole War, in which Secretary of State John Quincy Adams admitted to the action but justified it on the ground of British invasion of neutral Spanish territory.[505]

Martial Law in New Orleans. The southern campaign during the War of 1812 involved one other action of relevance to this study. While preparing for the British attack at New Orleans, Jackson declared martial law. His declaration was accepted, though not without resentment. After the British had been defeated in a major encounter, and unofficial reports circulated that a treaty had been signed, resentment grew. Citizens from the local militia wanted to return home. Jackson refused to allow any reduction in his army, and acted to prevent desertions. Creoles began to apply to the French consul for French citizenship, and then for discharges. Jackson countered by issuing a declaration requiring all French citizens to move at least 120 miles out of New Orleans. The French consul protested. Jackson ordered him away from the city for interfering with martial law. Louaillier, a Louisiana legislator, criticized Jackson in an unsigned newspaper article. Jackson found out Louaillier's identity and arrested him. A federal judge, Dominick A. Hall, issued a writ of *habeas corpus* for the legislator. Instead of producing the prisoner, Jackson ordered the judge arrested as well; and when the local United States Attorney sought relief from a state judge, he and the judge swiftly received the same treatment. A court martial acquitted the arrested legislator, but Jackson set aside their verdict. The very next day, however, official news arrived that the treaty of peace was concluded. Jackson revoked martial law and released his prisoners.[506]

Judge Hall was unwilling to accept the matter as concluded. As soon as the celebrations of peace had subsided, he ordered Jackson to show why he should not be held in contempt for defying the court's writ of *habeas corpus*. Jackson contested the court's jurisdiction over acts committed during martial law and sought to introduce a document containing his defense. Jackson's defense was that necessity required his declaration of martial law, and that the measures taken pursuant to that declaration were reasonable and not an abuse of the power assumed. "He thought, in such a moment, constitutional forms must be suspended, for the permanent preservation of constitutional rights. . . ." He agreed that the necessity "must not be doubtful; it must be apparent, from the circumstances of the case, or it forms no justification." This test was met, he claimed, reciting the many emergency steps taken by the Louisiana legislature, executive and judiciary. Furthermore, arresting the Louisiana legislator and Judge Hall was necessary to stem the evasions and desertions that were taking place among Jackson's men. British troops remained in the vicinity when the *habeas corpus* petition had issued, and Jackson had felt it essential to maintain strict order and preparedness until the city was truly safe.[507]

Judge Hall excluded Jackson's defense. He presented the General, instead, with a set of questions asking whether Jackson had arrested the judge and others. Jackson refused to respond, but returned to court to be sentenced. Judge Hall reportedly said: "The only question was whether the Laws should bend to the General, or the General to the Law."[508] Yet he imposed no confinement, a triumph for Jackson. Instead he fined Jackson $1,000, which the General promptly paid. Jackson thereafter addressed a crowd of citizens, reportedly stating that everything necessary to preserve the nation must be done, but "whenever the danger was past, to submit cheerfully to the operation of the laws, even when they punished acts which were done to preserve them." He said, according to his biographer Philo Goodwin, that to prevent "necessity from becoming the pretext for oppression, it was perhaps right that he who resorted to it should undergo the penalty of the law, and find his indemnity in the approbation of his own conscience, and the evidence that his acts were done only to serve his country."[509]

The administration reacted to Jackson's arrest of Judge Hall far more swiftly and emphatically than it did to his attack on Pensacola. On April 12, 1815, Secretary of War Alexander J. Dallas wrote Jackson concerning reports "respecting certain acts of military opposition to the civil magistrate, that require immediate attention, not only in vindication of the just authority of the laws, but to rescue your own conduct from all unmerited reproach." The representations received made it appear "that the Judicial power of the united states has been resisted, the liberty of the press has been suspended, and the Consul and subjects of a friendly Government [France] have been exposed to great inconvenience, by an exercise of Military force and command."[510] Jackson replied on May 23, sending as his explanation a copy of his defense before Judge Hall. "If the peculiar circumstances under which I was compelled to act do not justify the measures which I pursued, I neither deserve confidence nor am ambitious to retain it."[511]

Dallas replied on July 1. The President, he wrote, was convinced of Jackson's patriotic motives and would willingly abstain from further remarks on the subject "were he not apprehensive, that the principle of your example, and the reason of his silence, might be hereafter misunderstood, or misrepresented." President Madison, wrote Dallas, "has seen with satisfaction" that Jackson had based his justification "exclusively upon the ground of 'a necessity, not doubtful, but apparent from the circumstances of the case'; and that when you call them 'measures of necessity,' you mean measures, 'without which the country must have been conquered, and the Constitution lost.' " Madison regarded the position as proper:

> The military power is clearly defined, and carefully limited, by the Constitution and laws of the United States; but the experience of the best regulated Governments teaches us, that exigencies may sometimes arise, when (as you have emphatically observed) "constitutional forms must be suspended, for the permanent preservation of constitutional rights." If, therefore, a crisis of that nature existed at New-Orleans, the President could feel no disposition to condemn the measures, that were adopted as indispensable, to rescue the Country, from impending danger; nor does he even deem it material, at this time, to enter into a critical examination of the evidence, which is adduced to prove the existence of the crisis. Some difference of opinion will naturally occur, on such occasions, as to the extent, or the duration, of the alledged necessity; but where no difference of opinion can occur, as to the purity, or the sincerity, of the motive to action; where the exigency was great, and where the triumph has been compleat; the judgment of a responsible and distinguished officer, merits implicit confidence.

Dallas continued, however, that necessity "which creates its own Law," must not be confused with ordinary rules of military service. "In the United States there exists no authority to declare and impose Martial law, beyond the positive sanction of the Acts of Congress." And while a commander has broad power to ensure discipline and safety in his garrison, his power is compatible with the rights of citizens and an independent judiciary. Therefore, if a commander suspends liberties and supercedes the civil courts, "he may be justified by the law of necessity, while he has the merit of saving his country, but he cannot resort to the established law of the land, for the means of vindication."[512]

Having "stated the President's general view of this interesting subject," Dallas sought to reassure Jackson of Madison's "confidence and esteem." Jackson was far from reassured, however. When he journeyed to Washington later that year, he went to visit Dallas, prepared to give a full explanation of his conduct. Dallas said no further explanation would be required, that the President had fully accepted Jackson's position, and that the matter would be laid to rest.[513] This apparently meant, among other things, that Congress would not be asked to review Jackson's conduct. In fact, no report was made to Congress by the executive of the arrests or of Madison's inquiries and Jackson's position. Many years later, in 1844, and after debate, Congress restored the fine Jackson had paid at Judge Hall's order, with interest.*

Acquisition of the Floridas, 1818: Armed Intervention and Diplomacy

When James Monroe became President in 1817, all of East Florida, and part of West Florida (east of the Perdido), remained in Spanish control. Both Monroe and his Secretary of State, John Quincy Adams, favored prompt acquisition of that vital area. British adventurers encouraged, and Spain tolerated, disturbances by Indians and runaway slaves. That these disturbances were the product of justifiable resentment against white Americans was of little if any concern to the administration. They were determined to pacify the area.

Monroe proposed a plan to Spain, after peace with Britain in 1815, under which the United States would accept the Colorado River as the southwestern boundary of the Louisiana Purchase, and relinquish all claims to Texas and for prior breaches by Spain of treaty commitments, in exchange for the Floridas and a cancellation of Spanish monetary claims. The proposal was rejected. Spain was in no hurry to settle, since any agreement was certain to be unfavorable.

*Act of Feb. 16, 1844, 5 Stat. 651. The debate in Congress revolved primarily around the significance to be accorded resolutions of several state legislatures ordering their delegations to vote for the bill. Some House members did argue against undoing the punishment of an act suspending the Constitution and laws of the United States. And the Senate Judiciary Committee unsuccessfully proposed an amendment to counteract the possible implication, from the repayment with interest, that Judge Hall had acted improperly. But the refund passed, members obviously aware of Jackson's impecunious state, and supporters asserting that the bill suggested nothing critical of Judge Hall but simply refunded the money Jackson paid. Senator Daniel Huger (S.C.), though he disagreed with Judge Hall's decision, said he would not have changed what had happened (Cong Globe, 28th Cong., 1st Sess. 274 (1844)):

> It presented to the public mind one of the best moral pictures recorded in modern history. There was General Jackson, the conqueror of kingdoms, returning to New Orleans, and presenting himself at the feet of justice, and bowing to the supremacy of the law. This was a moral picture more venerable, in his mind, than the victory achieved at New Orleans itself. The moral was much more important; and he trusted that, to the end of time, it would not be forgotten.

Spain was ultimately forced to negotiate, however. The South American movements for independence were then underway, demanding Spain's attention and its dwindling material and military resources. But possibly the greatest pressure on Spain to negotiate resulted from a military action against Amelia Island, and Andrew Jackson's invasion of Florida during the Seminole War. The story of how the Floridas were acquired is therefore one in which diplomacy and force were intimately related.

Occupation of Amelia Island. During the summer of 1817 a group of pirates, vagabonds and adventurers, led by a Scotsman, Sir Gregor McGregor, occupied Amelia Island off the Georgia coast in Spanish East Florida. On June 29, McGregor "annexed" the island, using it as a base for South American revolutionaries to prey on Spanish commerce. Spain failed to suppress the enterprise. The island soon became a center for pirates and illicit privateers, as well as a rather insecure refuge for runaway slaves.[514] Later that year, one Louis Aury arrived at the island with about 150 followers. On October 4, Aury declared the island part of the Republic of Mexico, continuing the types of activities engaged in by McGregor. A similar establishment was set up at Galveston within territory claimed by the United States.[515]

At a meeting of Monroe's newly appointed Cabinet on October 30, 1817, Secretary of State Adams suggested that "the marauding parties at Amelia Island and Galveston ought to be broken up immediately."[516] Later, Adams prepared a letter of instruction to the United States Minister in Spain, explaining the proposed action.[517] Orders drafted by George Graham, acting Secretary of War, for Major James Bankhead, and by Benjamin Crowninshield, Secretary of the Navy, for Captain J.D. Henley, were issued on November 12 and 14. They instructed Henley and Bankhead to sail with six ships and 200 men, and to occupy Amelia Island peacefully if possible, but by force if necessary.[518] Later instructions to Bankhead from newly appointed Secretary of War John C. Calhoun, dated December 16, 1817, emphasized the President's desire that force be avoided if possible, and suggested that Bankhead informally allow Aury sufficient time to evacuate.[519] On December 22, the United States expedition arrived off Amelia Island. The following day, General Aury surrendered the island without bloodshed.[520]

Congress assembled while the Amelia Island expedition was in route. In his annual message of December 2, President Monroe briefly reviewed the history of the "private, unauthorized adventure" at Amelia Island led by McGregor and Aury. The island, he wrote, had become "a channel for the illicit introduction of slaves from Africa into the United States, an asylum for fugitive slaves from the neighboring States, and a port for smuggling of every kind." He then announced that "[a] just regard for the rights and interests of the United States required that they should be suppressed" and that force had been sent to restore order.[521] The references to piracy and slavery suggested that Monroe regarded himself as acting under the Act of April 30, 1790, outlawing piracy, or under the Act of March 2, 1807, prohibiting the importation of slaves.*

Opposition to the expedition arose promptly in the House. Speaker Henry Clay, disappointed that Monroe had not chosen him as Secretary of State, attacked the expedition on December 3. The United States was, in his view, siding with Spain against the "patriots" of South America.[522] Adams recorded on December 6 that Clay had "mounted his South American great horse," seeking to do what John Randolph had failed to accomplish—"overthrow the Executive by swaying the House of Representatives."[523] On December 8, John Rhea of Tennessee introduced a resolution calling for papers relating to Amelia Island and Galveston, and requesting the President's reasons for ordering the offensive. The clause requesting the President's reasons was deleted, but the resolution passed. Monroe responded within a week.[524]

Representative Henry Middleton of South Carolina, Chairman of a select House committee appointed to consider the smuggling of slaves from Amelia Island, asked Secretary of State Adams for his suggestions on a draft of the committee's report.[525] The committee's final report, incorporating Adams's reasoning and language, concluded that the 1807 act prohibiting the importation of slaves authorized

---

*Secs. 8, 9, 1 Stat. 113-14; 2 Stat. 426-28. Madison wrote on December 9 to congratulate Monroe on his first annual message and said in regard to Amelia Island:

> The only questions which occur relate to the proposed suppression of the establishment at Amelia Island; if to be effected by a military force employed out of our territorial claims, and to the latitude of the principle on which the right of a civilized people is asserted over the lands of a savage one. I take for granted that the first point was well considered; and the last may be susceptible of qualifying explanations.

Monroe Presidential Papers, L.C. microfilm, series 1, reel 6. Monroe replied on December 22 (6 *Monroe Writings* 45):

> The documents relating to Galveston and Amelia Island, published in this days paper [*National Intelligencer*] will reach you with this. They shew the reasons which operated with the Executive in taking the measures noted in your letter. They appeared to be conclusive, as being mere piratical establishments, probably unauthorized by any of the Colonies, but forfeiting all claim to consideration by their conduct, if authorised. . . .

the President to use the navy in territorial waters to seize and bring in for condemnation vessels engaged in the slave trade. Also, the report rested on the formerly secret No-Transfer Act and joint resolution of Congress, both of January 15, 1811 (earlier shown to Middleton by Adams), by which the President was empowered to seize any part of Florida in the event of an attempt by a foreign government to occupy the area.* The committee concluded that those who took over Amelia Island proposed to establish an independent government, and thus constituted, in effect, a foreign power attempting to occupy the territory. The report noted that McGregor and Aury had issued commissions to privateers, ostensibly in the name of Venezuela and Mexico, to prey on the commerce of nations with which the United States was at peace; Amelia Island was intended as a refuge for such privateers. As the United States had treaty obligations with various nations to protect their commerce against piratical depredations, it was obligated to take "from this piratical and smuggling combination their place of refuge," in order to avoid claims for indemnities. The report was read and accepted, but not discussed or acted upon.[526]

The President meanwhile received news that Amelia Island had been occupied by American forces. The Cabinet met during January 1818, to decide the island's disposition. "The President had partly drawn up a message to Congress, stating the taking of Amelia Island, and concluding that the troops which took it would be withdrawn," Adams recorded in his diary. "Mr. Crawford, Crowninshield, and Wirt are with the President, for withdrawing the troops." Adams and Calhoun were for retaining possession. To retain the island, they argued, might prove an advantage in later bargaining with Spain. The slave traders and pirates had been dispersed, so the slavery and piracy acts could not justify retention. But Adams pressed the argument that retention was justified by the No-Transfer Act of 1811. Indeed, at the meeting on January 9, Adams "presented for consideration the doubt whether, having taken possession under the act of January, 1811, the Executive had a right to withdraw the troops and

---

*Adams recorded that he had described the secret laws to Middleton as (4 *Adams Memoirs* 32):

> those singular anomalies of our system which have grown out of that error in our Constitution which confers upon the legislative assemblies the power of declaring war, which, in the theory of government, according to Montesquieu and Rousseau, is strictly an Executive Act. But as we have made it legislative, whenever secrecy is necessary for an operation of the Executive, involving the question of peace and war, Congress must pass a secret law to give the President the power.

abandon the island unless authorized thereto by a new act of Congress."[527]

Adams's argument "staggered" Crawford, and opposition to continued occupation crumbled. Monroe decided to retain the island "for the present" only,[528] and announced the successful occupation to Congress on January 14. This time, he based his action primarily on the No-Transfer Act:

> The law of 1811, lately published,* and which it is therefore proper now to mention, was considered applicable to the case, from the moment that the proclamation of the chief of the enterprise [McGregor] was seen, and its obligation was daily increased by other considerations of high importance already mentioned, which were deemed sufficiently strong in themselves to dictate the course which has been pursued.

He also implied his action was justified under a 1795 treaty with Spain. By that treaty Spain pledged to control the inhabitants of its territory; its failure to do so made American intervention permissible. "To a country over which she [Spain] fails to maintain her authority," Monroe said, "and which she permits to be converted to the annoyance of her neighbors, her jurisdiction for the time necessarily ceases to exist."[529]

On January 8, 1818, the Spanish Minister Onis protested the seizure of Amelia Island and demanded its return. Adams devised still another justification for the seizure and continued occupation of the island—the right of self-defense under international law. "We had not . . . committed any hostility against her. We had been obliged, in our own defence, to take the place in defence of our laws, of our commerce, and that of the nations at peace with us, Spain included."[530] This rationale of self-defense was undoubtedly produced by the administration's search for a more tenable justification for retaining the island. Senator James Barbour of Virginia, for example, pro-administration Chairman of the Senate Foreign Relations Committee, informed Monroe on February 26 that many friends of the administration "did not consider the occupation of the island as warranted by the law of 1811."[531] As Professor Eugene

---

*The injunction of secrecy placed on the law of 1811 at its passage had been removed during the next session by the Senate on motion of Senator George Bibb of Kentucky, July 6, 1812. 24 *Annals* 1694. Nevertheless, Adams wrote on December 30, 1817, that it had not yet been published. 4 *Adams Memoirs* 32. However, at least two newspapers had unofficially published the act, the first, a Connecticut paper, having obtained it from an opponent of the Madison administration some weeks after the close of the session in which it passed. The administration journal, the *National Intelligencer*, then republished it on October 17, 1812, at 3, col. 1.

Rostow recently noted, "it is difficult to suppose that McGregor's regime constituted a 'foreign power' or a 'foreign government' within the intendment of Congress."[532] Even the President's original message to Congress referred to it as a "private, unauthorized adventure."

The takeover and retention of Amelia Island pressured Spain to reopen negotiations on the Floridas, just as Adams and Calhoun expected. On hearing of the intervention, Spain's Foreign Minister Pizarro wrote to the Spanish Minister of War that "the difficult negotiation based on the cession of the Floridas will be useless, as we shall not have them to cede."[533] Onis, meanwhile, began to negotiate as earnestly as his instructions allowed. He wrote a series of notes to Adams beginning on December 6, 1817, developing the argument that the United States had no right to any territory near the Mississippi Delta.[534] Adams offered the Colorado River as the southwestern boundary on January 16, 1818. Onis countered with a proposal to make the border a point halfway between the Mermentau and Calcasieu Rivers, about thirty-five miles east of the Sabine, and squarely within Louisiana. That proposal was unacceptable, and Monroe authorized Adams to move east from the Colorado to the Trinity River, halfway to the Mermentau.[535] Onis was not yet free to move further west, but movement had begun; and, most importantly, Spain had been forced to see the untenability of retaining the Floridas. Meanwhile, events began to unfold, under the leadership of Andrew Jackson, that placed even greater pressure on Spain to reach a settlement.

The Seminole War and the Adams-Onis Treaty. Andrew Jackson defeated the Creek Indians in 1814, and imposed upon them the Treaty of Fort Jackson, by which certain of their claimed representatives ceded several millions of acres of land. Dissatisfied Creeks fled into Florida and joined the Seminoles, where they came under the influence of anti-American advisors, primarily British and Spanish. Also in Florida, along the Apalachicola River, were hundreds of fugitive blacks, who at one point seized a fort stocked with arms by British officers.* These groups periodically engaged in battles with whites, sometimes very bloody battles.[536]

*The fort was abandoned by a British officer, Edward Nicholls, in 1815, to the Creeks, but was seized by fugitive blacks who used it for plundering across the border and luring other blacks from slavery. 1 J. Bassett, *Life of Jackson* 234–38 (1911). On March 15, 1816, Secretary of War Crawford instructed Andrew Jackson, in command of the Southern Division, to demand that the Spanish reduce the fort, on the "principle of good neighborhood," adding that, unless Spain acted, the United States would act. 2 *Jackson Correspondence* 236–

In November 1817, as the Monroe Cabinet was considering whether to occupy Amelia Island, Major General Edmund Gaines invited a hostile Seminole chief to a meeting at Fort Scott, Georgia. The Seminole leader refused to attend, so Gaines ordered his men to bring the chief by force. This led to an attack on the Seminole village of Fowltown. In retaliation, the Seminoles on November 30 ambushed an American ship, killing thirty-four soldiers, and several women and children. [537]

Gaines was eager to retaliate. He was ordered by Acting Secretary of War George Graham on November 12, however, to proceed to Point Peter, to back up the assault on Amelia Island.[538] On December 2, Graham repeated this order, advising Gaines that "the temper manifested by the principle [sic] European powers, make it impolitic in the opinion of the President, to move a force at this time into the Spanish possessions, for the mere purpose of chastising the Seminoles. . . ."[539] But when news of the Fowltown incident reached Washington, Graham wrote on December 9, expanding Gaines's authority to attack the Seminoles:

Should the Indians, however, assemble in force on the Spanish side of the line, and persevere in committing hostilities within the limits of the United States, you will, in that event, exercise a sound discretion as to the propriety of crossing the line for the purpose of attacking them, and breaking up their towns.[540]

Within days, word of the Apalachicola massacre reached Washington. Gaines's authority was increased even further. In orders dated December 16, newly appointed Secretary of War John C. Calhoun instructed Gaines to assemble all the regular forces available, and with militiamen from Georgia to reduce the Indians by force. If the Indians failed to make reparations, Calhoun wrote, "consider yourself at liberty to march across the Florida line and to attack them within its limits, should it be found necessary, unless they should shelter themselves under a Spanish post. In the last event, you will immediately notify this Department."[541] Calhoun

---

37. The fort was destroyed on July 27, by a gunboat convoy, specifically instructed by General Edmund Gaines to take that action if the blacks opposed the convoy. The convoy acted after hearing that the fugitives had already attacked and slain a boat crew, and in blowing up the fort, they killed 270 fugitives and wounded about 60. See W. Cresson, *James Monroe* 303 (1946) [hereinafter "Cresson, *Monroe*"], which in some respects is inaccurate. *Compare* Report of Sailing-Master J. Loomis, Aug. 13, 1816, A.S.P., 4 *Foreign Relations* 559-60. For congressional reaction, see 33 *Annals* 786, 797-803, 988-89 (action criticized as unlawful, but information request rejected).

sent a copy of these instructions to Andrew Jackson, then in Tennessee.[542] Congress was in session at the time of these orders, but was neither consulted nor informed.

Gaines, meanwhile, protested his orders from Graham to back up the Amelia Island expedition.[543] He wanted to attack the Seminoles. Administration policy shifted, but on December 26, only ten days after authorizing Gaines to cross into Florida in fighting the Seminoles, Calhoun ordered Jackson to assume command. He authorized Jackson to "call on the Executives of adjacent States for such an additional militia force as you may deem requisite," and to "adopt the necessary measures [against the Indians] to terminate a conflict which it has ever been the desire of the President, from considerations of humanity, to avoid; but which is now made necessary by their settled hostilities." Calhoun did not repeat his December 16 warning to Gaines not to attack any Spanish posts.* On the same day, Calhoun authorized Gaines to cooperate with Jackson in attacking the Seminoles, after Amelia Island had been secured.[544]

Monroe sent Jackson personal encouragement in the same mail with Calhoun's instructions. "This is not a time for you to think of repose," he wrote. "Great interests are at issue, and until our course is carried through triumphantly, [and] every species of danger to which it is exposed is settled on the most solid foundation, you ought not to withdraw your active support from it."[545]

On January 6, 1818, after receiving Calhoun's instructions to Gaines of December 16, but before receiving the December 26 order to assume command, Jackson wrote "confidentially" to Monroe his famous proposal for conquering the Floridas. He suggested the United States should occupy not only Amelia Island, as the President had recently ordered, but should seize and hold all of East Florida "as an indemnity for the outrages of Spain upon the property of our Citizens. . . . [T]his can be done," he assured the President, "without implicating the Government; let it be signified to me through any channel, (say Mr. J. Rhea) that the possession of the Floridas would be desirable to the United States, and in sixty days it will be accomplished."[546]

Five days after writing his confidential note, Jackson received Calhoun's instructions of December 26, ordering him to assume control of the Florida expedition, and Monroe's accompanying letter. He

---

*Many sources assume or state that the December 26 orders incorporated the earlier orders to Gaines by reference. For example, Cresson states that Jackson was given command on December 26, "subject to the restrictions already imposed upon Gaines." Cresson, *Monroe* 304. One might reasonably conclude the restriction was intended, but it was not expressly imposed.

promptly called for volunteers in Tennessee and Kentucky, instead of complying with Calhoun's instruction to ask the Governors for militiamen. He then rode to Fort Scott and marched across the border. With relentless energy, and the help of volunteers and Creek mercenaries, Jackson reached the Spanish fort of St. Marks on April 6. Even before arriving there, Jackson had written to Calhoun on March 25, revealing his intention to seize the fort for use as a depot, if it was in Spanish hands, or to hold it indefinitely for the United States if he found it in Indian hands.* He did as he promised, the helpless Spanish commandant quickly surrendering.[547]

At St. Marks, Jackson found and arrested one Alexander Arbuthnot, an elderly trader and friend of the Indians, whom he held for trial. His men also captured two Indian leaders, the Seminole prophet Francis and Chief Homollimico, whom Jackson summarily ordered hung. Later, while on an expedition to find another Indian leader, Jackson's men arrested Lieutenant Robert C. Ambrister, formerly of the British Royal Colonial Marines. Ambrister and Arbuthnot were tried for their lives by a military commission between April 26 and 28. Arbuthnot, who pleaded not guilty, was convicted of inciting the Indians to war and of spying. Ambrister, who pleaded "guilty with justification" to the charge of aiding and comforting the enemy, was sentenced to be shot. Shortly thereafter the court reconsidered Ambrister's sentence and ordered instead that he be given fifty lashes and one year in prison. But Jackson overruled the court's reconsideration. On April 19, 1818, Arbuthnot was hung and Ambrister shot.[548]

At this point, Jackson apparently considered returning home. He had written his wife on April 20, 1818, that he would disperse "a few red sticks"—a phrase used to describe Seminoles because of their practice of announcing war by circulating such sticks—and return to Tennessee. His letter to Calhoun on the same day repeated this intention, but added that Governor Don Jose Masot, at Pensacola in West Florida, had been supplying Indians. On May 5, Jackson wrote Calhoun of reports that Seminoles were being sheltered and armed at Pensacola, and that, if these reports were true, "Pensacola must be occupied with an American force, The Governor treated according to his deserts or as policy may dictate." He an-

---

*He rested his case on Spain's failure to keep its treaty obligation to control the Indians (A.S.P., 1 *Military Affairs* 698):

> The Spanish Government is bound by treaty to keep her Indians at peace with us. They have acknowledged their incompetency to do this, and are consequently bound, by the law of nations, to yield us all facilities to reduce them.

nounced his intention to leave strong garrisons at occupied Spanish posts, including Pensacola, "should it become necessary to possess it." The continued presence of the American army in Florida was necessary, he said, as long as Spain failed to fulfill her treaty obligation to keep the Indians in Florida at peace. The measures he had adopted were "in pursuance of your instructions," and would, he believed, "meet with the approbation of the President."[549]

Jackson then moved his troops toward Pensacola. On May 23, Masot demanded that he retire. Jackson replied that "Pensacola has, for some months past, been entirely under the control of the Indians." He noted that this was the third time an American army had been forced to visit Pensacola to expel an enemy; "this time," he said, "it must be held until Spain has the power or will to maintain her neutrality."* Masot denied that Pensacola had aided hostile Indians, and said Jackson's actions violated an assurance the President had given Congress two months earlier, on March 25, that no hostilities would be committed against Spanish posts. Masot demanded that Jackson evacuate Pensacola and cease his "partial war against West Florida"; if not, Masot would "repel force by force."

Jackson immediately entered Pensacola, however, encountering little resistance, and on May 26, set up cannon and howitzers directed at Masot's position, the fort at Barancas. On May 28, after some firing, Masot surrendered. Jackson appointed one of his men military governor of Pensacola and proclaimed the revenue laws of the United States to be in force.[550]

On June 2, Jackson wrote both Monroe and Calhoun, describing the capture of Pensacola and urging that the captured posts be retained. "The Immutable principles therefore of self defence justified the occupancy of the Floridas" he wrote to Calhoun, "and the same principles will warrant the American Government in holding it untill such time as spain can guarantee by an adequate military force the maintaining her authority, within the colony."[551] In a "private" letter to Monroe, Jackson went on to say "our disposable force was too small to hazard many excursions through our country in persuit of the enemy." Though "worn down with fatigue," emaciated, in pain and coughing blood, his desire to seize Spanish territory remained awesome. An additional force, he said, "would insure Ft St

---

*Jackson was more blunt in addressing the commanding officer of Pensacola, stating that, if his troops were fired on in the act of entering the city to procure supplies from an American vessel, he would "put to death every man found in arms," and demanding that the Spanish troops there be put under his direction. 2 *Jackson Correspondence* 371.

Augustine and another Regt. and one Frigate and I will insure you Cuba in a few days." In closing, Jackson said:

should my acts meet your approbation it will be a source of great consolation to me, should it be disapproved, I have this consolation, that I exercised by best exertions and Judgt. and that sound national policy will dictate holding Possession as long as we are a republick.[552]

Neither letter mentioned finding any hostile Indians at Pensacola; but Jackson did enclose several depositions attesting to the fact that Masot had aided the Indians.

Following the capture of Pensacola, Jackson returned home to Tennessee. On August 7, he wrote Gaines of reports that Spanish officials at St. Augustine were inciting the Indians to further hostilities and furnishing them with supplies. Gaines was to investigate, and should he find the report accurate and believe his troops to be sufficient, he was to "take and garrison with American Troops Fort St Augustine and hold the garrison prisoners, until you hear from the President of the U States. . . ." On August 10, Jackson wrote Monroe of his order to Gaines, expressing his hope Monroe would approve, and his belief that self-defense "Justified by the laws of nature and of nations will Justify this seizure. . . ." He expressed his "confidence" that the United States would not surrender the captured forts until Spain gave a solemn guarantee to fulfill its treaty obligations, and enclosed a report by his aide Captain Gadsen on the necessity of their retention.[553]

Executive Reaction to Jackson's Initiative. Jackson's confidential letter of January 6, 1818, offering to take the Floridas on his own responsibility, definitely reached the President. Years later, Jackson claimed Monroe secretly authorized taking the Spanish posts in a message sent through Representative Rhea.[554] Monroe denied this story, asserting in a letter to Calhoun: "I well remember that when I received the letter from Genl. Jackson . . . of the 5th of Jany. 1818, I was sick in bed, and could not read it." According to Monroe, he gave the letter to Calhoun, who returned it stating that it required Monroe's attention but without telling the President its contents. Crawford also read the letter, Monroe later wrote, but merely told him that it related to the Seminole War. Having made all the arrangements for the Seminole campaign, Monroe claimed he laid the letter aside and forgot it.[555]

Considerable research has cast doubt on Jackson's claim that Monroe sent a message through Rhea.[556] But Monroe's story is at least equally suspect. Monroe's failure to reply to Jackson's proposal could reasonably have suggested that Jackson go ahead on his own responsibility.* Arguably, Monroe and Calhoun expected Jackson to understand that he would be bound by the earlier instruction to Gaines to refrain from attacking Spanish posts. But Jackson's letter of January 6 was his response—and dissent from—the order to Gaines. After writing it, he received Calhoun's instructions of December 26 that he adopt the "necessary measures" to end the uprising, along with Monroe's private letter urging Jackson to put to rest "every species of danger." Had Monroe truly wished Jackson to refrain from attacking the posts, a further instruction would have been sensible if not indispensable.

Monroe's claim that he laid Jackson's letter aside without taking any action is undercut by a letter he wrote on January 30, 1818, specifically asking Calhoun to order Jackson "not to attack any post occupied by Spanish troops, from the possibility, that it might bring the allied powers on us."[557] By that day, Calhoun had received letters from Jackson dated January 12 and 13,[558] so Monroe's instruction to Calhoun was probably a response to Jackson's proposal of January 6. Calhoun sent Jackson no instruction to desist. Possibly this was because, as both Monroe and Jackson later contended, Calhoun told the President that the matter was one requiring Monroe's personal attention; a letter from Calhoun would normally have been subject to legislative call, and would have revealed Jackson's confidential and highly controversial suggestion. Instead, Calhoun sent Jackson a letter on February 6, that could only have served to encourage Jackson to go ahead with his plan. He wrote to acquaint Jackson "with the entire approbation of the President of all the measures you have adopted to terminate the rupture with the Indians. The honor of our arms, as well as the interest of our country requires that it should be as speedily terminated as practicable; and the confidence reposed in your skill and promptitude assures us that peace will be restored on such conditions as will make it honorable and permanent."[559]

---

*Jackson himself used this argument years later, in 1831, when he noted that, after his confidential letter of January 6, and until August 1818,

I never had an intimation that the wishes of the government had changed, or that less was expected of me, if the occasion should prove favorable, than the occupation of the whole of Florida. On the contrary, either by their direct approval of my measures or their silence, the President and Mr. Calhoun gave me reason to suppose that I was to be sustained, and that the Floridas after being occupied were to be held for the benefit of the United States.

See 1 T. Benton, *Thirty Years' View* 172 (1854).

Monroe's January 30 letter also shows the President was still functioning on that date. Adams's diary, in fact, records substantial activity between Monroe and the Cabinet right up until the entry for February 23, which recites for the first time that the President was too ill to function normally.[560] Even if Jackson's letter of January 6 had suffered unusual delays, it should have reached Monroe well before he became ill, contrary to his later claim.

On March 25, 1818, as Jackson was marching into Florida, Monroe sent a special message to Congress, including the orders he had issued to "the General in Command," which Monroe stated instructed him "not to enter Florida, unless it be in pursuit of the enemy, and in that case to respect the Spanish authority wherever it is maintained. . . ." He explained, as he had in connection with Amelia Island, that crossing the border was justified because Spain had failed to live up to its treaty obligations, and the United States had the right of self-defense under international law. While Monroe included in full the December 16 letter to Gaines, prohibiting attack of the Indians "under a Spanish post," he sent Congress only an extract of the December 26 instructions to Jackson. The following language, that might have been interpreted by Jackson to alter the Gaines instructions, was excised: "With this view you may be prepared to concentrate your forces and to adopt the necessary measures to terminate a conflict which it has ever been the desire of the President . . . to avoid; but which is now made necessary by their Settled hostilities." Also excluded from the transmittal were Monroe's simultaneous letter of personal encouragement; Jackson's letter of January 6 proposing a conquest; and Calhoun's letter of February 6, expressing approbation of Jackson's measures and confidence that he would speedily terminate the war.[561]

Monroe's message was received late in the session. The House Committee on Foreign Relations earlier had unanimously rejected a proposition to authorize the President to take possession of the Floridas.[562] On the other hand, Congress provided, in the military appropriations act for 1818, approximately $306,000 for the expense of a brigade of militia. Some Congressmen later asserted that these funds were intended to be used in an expedition against the Florida Indians, although the act itself employed only general terms.[563] No further action was taken by either house after Monroe's message.

The administration acted with remarkable laxity, as news of Jackson's campaign began reaching Washington. The Cabinet discussed the seizure of Fort St. Marks on May 4. Adams noted in his diary that Jackson's dispatches described seizing the fort, "without due regard to humanity," and that Jackson planned to hang Arbuthnot. No action was taken.* On May 13, Adams recorded, the Cabinet decided American troops would not be evacuated from Florida "for the present," even if the Seminoles surrendered.[564] Jackson informed Calhoun on May 5 of occupying Fort Gadsden, and of the trials and executions of Arbuthnot and Ambrister. Calhoun claimed not to have received this letter and its accompanying documents; he requested copies on July 21, which he received in late August.[565]

On June 18, Adams recorded that the "President spoke of the taking of Pensacola by General Jackson, contrary to his orders." Spanish Minister Onis sent notes of protest on June 21 and 26, and on July 7 had Adams roused from bed to receive a third note announcing Onis's return to Washington and asking for an interview. Despite the "rapidly thickening" storm, Monroe left the city on June 26, leaving Adams to deal with the protests of Onis and French Minister Hyde de Neuville. In separate interviews on July 8, Adams —by then aware of the potential advantages of Jackson's campaign— warned the ministers that the President would probably support Jackson.[566]

The Cabinet finally met on July 15. At least four meetings immediately followed. At the start, Monroe, Crawford, Calhoun, and Wirt were "of the opinion that Jackson acted not only without, but against, his instructions; that he has committed war upon Spain, which cannot be justified, and in which, if not disavowed by the Administration, they will be abandoned by the country."[567] Calhoun apparently went so far as to call initially for Jackson's court martial.[568] Only Adams argued that Jackson's actions should be unequivocally endorsed by the adminsitration. "My opinion is," he wrote:

> that there was no real, though an apparent violation of his instructions; that his proceedings were justified by the necessity of the case, and by the misconduct of the Spanish commanding officers in Florida. The

*At this time, the Monroe administration issued an instruction to the collector of customs in Georgia, near Amelia Island, to enforce the revenue laws upon all vessels entering the St. Mary's River even if they anchored on the Spanish side. The Spanish governor and others had set up a phony port on the Florida side, at which they received cargoes from French and British vessels, and then smuggled the goods into the United States without paying the prescribed duty. In September 1820, the French vessel *Appollon* was seized, while anchored on the Spanish side of the river, for violating the revenue laws of the United States. A lower court decision ordered the vessel released, but Gallatin and other officials insisted the seizure was lawful because the United States had possession of Amelia Island, and possessed authority to enforce the revenue laws. No appeal was taken, apparently because the administration wished to secure an overall commercial agreement with France, which was eventually obtained. *See* 2 *Gallatin Writings* 186, 187; 5 *Adams Memoirs* 196–97, 274, 413–23; S. Bemis, *John Quincy Adams and the Foundations of American Foreign Policy* 455–56 (1956).

question is embarassing and complicated, not only as involving that of an actual war with Spain, but that of the Executive power to authorize hostilities without a declaration of war by Congress. There is no doubt that *defensive* acts of hostility may be authorized by the Executive; but Jackson was authorized to cross the Spanish line in pursuit of the Indian enemy. My argument is that the question of the constitutional authority of the Executive is precisely there; that all the rest, even to the order for taking the Fort of Barrancas by storm, was incidental, deriving its character from the object, which was not hostility to Spain, but the termination of the Indian war.

Even "if the question was dubious," Adams later said, "it was better to err on the side of vigor than of weakness—on the side of our own officer, who has rendered the most eminent services to the nation, than on the side of our bitterest enemies, and against him."[569]

At the Cabinet meeting the following day, Crawford spoke against Adams's position. Politically ambitious, and possibly eager to embarrass both Jackson and Monroe,[570] he said that "if the Administration did not immediately declare itself and restore Pensacola, it would be held responsible for Jackson's having taken it, and for having commenced a war in violation of the Constitution." Adams replied that Jackson's conduct was "justifiable under his orders, although he certainly had none to take any Spanish fort. My principle," Adams wrote, "is that everything he did was *defensive*; that as such it was neither war against Spain nor violation of the Constitution." He argued that Jackson took Pensacola only because Governor Masot had threatened his army; "that Jackson was only executing his orders when he received this threat; that he could not withdraw his troops from the province consistently with his orders, and that his only alternative was to prevent the execution of the threat." Calhoun countered, "insisting that the capture of Pensacola was not necessary upon principles of self-defence, and therefore was an act of war against Spain and a violation of the Constitution." It was not Masot's threat but Jackson's grandiose scheme to conquer Florida, Calhoun argued, that prompted the General to attack Pensacola.[571]

Adams scored at least a partial victory. Monroe was determined to insist that he had not authorized an occupation of Spanish forts, and to announce his intention to surrender them. On the other hand, he decided to avoid repudiating Jackson and the political problems such a repudiation would cause. Monroe instructed Attorney General Wirt to prepare an editorial supporting his position for the *National Intelligencer,** and asked Adams to draft a note to Onis.

*The editorial stated that the President had decided to restore the posts to Spain, but only on condition that the King of Spain provide a sufficient force

The President undertook the difficult task of writing to Jackson explaining that the forts would be restored to Spain. Later, when news of Jackson's order to Gaines to take St. Augustine reached Washington, Calhoun rescinded it.[572]

Monroe's letter to Jackson, dated July 19, 1818, was conciliatory but firm. "In calling you into active service against the Seminoles, and communicating to you the orders which had been given just before to General Gaines, the views and intentions of the Government were fully disclosed in respect to the operations in Florida," that is, he was not to have attacked a Spanish fort. "In transcending the limit prescribed by those orders, you acted on your own responsibility" on circumstances unknown when the orders were given and which "you thought imposed on you the measure, as an act of patriotism. . . . The United States stand justified," he noted, "in ordering their troops into Florida in pursuit of their enemy. They have this right by the law of nations. . . . But an order by the government to attack a Spanish post . . . would authorize war, to which, by the principles of our Constitution, the Executive is incompetent. Congress alone possesses the power." Nevertheless, he concluded, "cases may occur, where the commanding general, acting on his own responsibility, may with safety pass this limit"—and this was one of those cases. If the executive refused to surrender the posts, however, "it would amount to a declaration of war, to which it is incompetent.* It would be accused of usurping the authority of Congress, and giving a deep and fatal wound to the Constitution." This charge could be avoided by blaming the officers of Spain, as Jackson had already done.[573]

---

in Florida to execute the treaty provisions for the suppression of Indian hostilities. The United States had only reluctantly taken up arms in self-defense, and issued a series of orders which authorized pursuing the Seminoles across the border, but required that the Department of War be consulted if the Indians sheltered themselves in Spanish forts; "no subsequent order, it is understood, has been issued, to enlarge the authority of the American general." Jackson, in attacking the Spanish posts, had "acted on facts, which were for the first time, brought to his knowledge, on the immediate theatre of war; facts, which in his estimation implicated the Spanish authorities in that quarter, as the instigators and auxiliaries of the war; and he took these measures on his own responsibility, merely." As the President viewed retention of the forts as an act of war, and as such a matter for Congress, he would return the forts with a demand that the offending Spanish officers be punished. The paper expressed the "hope never to see a President . . . disposed to be stronger than the Constitution," and concluded that, unless Spain ceded the Floridas, she would be subjecting herself to "perpetual collisions, and eventual losses, which she may now avoid with ease and honor to herself." *National Intelligencer*, July 27, 1818.

*Monroe repeated this point to Madison, writing that to hold the posts "would amount to a declaration of war, or come [so] near it, that in case war followed, it would be so considered. . . ." Letter of July 20, 1818, 6 *Monroe Writings* 61.

One difficulty Monroe faced with his theory for avoiding responsibility and at the same time exonerating Jackson was that little evidence existed of improper conduct by Spanish officers. "We look to you," he wrote, to support the charge against the officers of Spain. "You must aid in procuring the documents necessary for this purpose. Those which you sent by Mr. Hambly were prepared in too much haste, and do not I am satisfied, do justice to the cause. This must be attended to without delay." He promised to send Jackson, "in the confidence in which I write this letter," a copy of the answer to be sent Onis, "that you may see distinctly the ground on which we rest, in the expectation that you will give it all the support in your power." He later added that Jackson had given "less attention" to some parts of his letters to the War Department than he might have but for pressures of war. "The passage to which I particularly allude, from memory, . . . is that in which you speak of the incompetency of an imaginary boundary to protect us against the enemy—the ground on which you bottom all your measures. This is liable to the imputation," Monroe cogently noted, "that you took the Spanish posts for that reason, as a measure of expediency, and not on account of the misconduct of the Spanish officers. The effect of this and such passages, besides other objections to them," would be to furnish ammunition to Jackson's opponents. "If you think proper to authorize the Secretary or myself to correct those passages," Monroe volunteered, "it will be done with care, though, should you have copies, as I presume you have, you had better do it yourself."[574]

Monroe shared Jackson's desire to acquire the Floridas. But he argued that war with Spain, and with other powers, might result if the forts were retained. And "[w]hy risk these consequences? The events which have occurred in both the Floridas show the incompetency of Spain to maintain her authority," and the South American revolutions will require all Spain's forces. "There is much reason to presume that this act will furnish a strong inducement to Spain to cede the territory, provided we do not wound too deeply her pride by holding it. If we hold the posts, her government cannot treat with honor, which by withdrawing the troops, we afford her an opportunity to do. The manner in which we propose to act will exculpate you from censure," he assured Jackson, "and promises to obtain all the advantages which you contemplated from the measure, and possibly very soon."*

*6 *Monroe Writings* 57–58. On July 22, 1818, Monroe wrote to Jefferson that Jackson's occupation of Pensacola "has been full of difficulty, but without incurring the charge of committing a breach of the Constitution, or of giving

Jackson was unwilling to accept entirely Monroe's line of defense. He claimed that his activities had been fully authorized, and would not take the blame for what had occurred. In particular, he referred to Calhoun's orders of December 26, authorizing him to "adopt the necessary measures to terminate" the conflict.* These orders, he claimed, superseded the orders earlier sent to Gaines, because the earlier orders were not referred to "with a view to point out to me the measures thought advisable, or the limits of my power in choosing and effecting them."[575]

Monroe's statement that Jackson acted on his own responsibility seems particularly to have affected Jackson. He had, after all, promised Monroe, in his letter of January 6, to conquer the Floridas without implicating the government. If Monroe actually sent word through Rhea that Jackson should go ahead, as Jackson later claimed, or if Jackson construed Monroe's silence as approval, he was reneging on his promise to Monroe by asserting that his actions were authorized. This may explain why he said, in this confidential letter of August 19:

> the assumption of responsibility will never be shrunk from, when the public interest can be thereby promoted. I have passed through difficulties and exposures for the honor and benefit of my country, and whenever still, for this purpose, it shall become necessary to assume a further liability, no scruple will be urged or felt. But when it shall be required of me to do so, and the result shall be danger and injury to that country, the inducement will be lost and my consent will be wanting.[576]

He seems to have been suggesting by this language that, had Monroe been prepared to retain the area seized, he would have assumed responsibility, but not with that inducement lost.

---

to Spain just cause of war, we have endeavor'd to turn it to the best account of our country, & credit of the Commanding General." *Id.* 62. To put Jackson to trial, he wrote, "would be the triumph of Spain & confirm her in the disposition not to cede Florida." *Id.* 63.

*His argument is similar to the contention later advanced by Commodore Porter without success, *supra* at 277–78. Jackson wrote:

> This principle is held to be incontrovertible—that an order, generally, to perform a certain service, or effect a certain object, without any specification of the means to be adopted, or the limits to govern the executive officer—leaves an *entire discretion* with the officer, as to the choice and application of means, but preserves the responsibility, for his acts, in the authority from which the order emanated. Under such an order, *all the acts* of the inferior are the acts of the Superior—and in no way, can the subordinate officer be impeached for his measures, except on the score of deficiency in judgment and skill. It is also a grammatical truth that the limits of such an order cannot be *transcended* without the entire desertion of the objects it contemplated. For as long as the main, legitimate design is kept in view, the *policy* of the measures, adopted to accomplish it, is alone to be considered.

2 *Jackson Correspondence* 389.

Monroe replied on October 20 that he "was sorry to find that you understood your instructions relative to operations in Florida differently from what we intended." He was satisfied in any event that Jackson had "good reason" for his conduct, and said he never intended to make Jackson take "a responsibility . . . you did not contemplate."* Monroe suggested that Jackson state his position in a letter to the Department of War. "This will be answered, so as to explain ours, in a friendly manner by Mr. Calhoun, who has very just and liberal sentiments on the subject. This will be necessary in the case of a call for papers by Congress, as may be." They would then all be able to "stand upon the ground of honor, each doing justice to the other. . . ."[577]

Jackson refused Monroe's invitation to make a record for Congress. Nothing existed in the Department, as far as he knew, that indicated he had exceeded his authority. The only way of showing a possible conflict would be to reveal Monroe's private letters, he wrote, "neither of which can be made the basis of an official communication to the Secretary of War." Jackson offered, however, to respond to an official letter.[578] Monroe answered on December 21 that a letter from Jackson would be "unnecessary." His only intent in suggesting one was to protect Jackson; for the very reason that "there is . . . nothing in the Department to indicate a difference of opinion between you and the Executive, respecting the import of your instructions . . . it would have been difficult to express that sentiment without implying by it a censure of your conduct, than which nothing could be more remote from our disposition or intention." The position he had adopted regarding the Floridas, he concluded, served three purposes as well as could be accommodated: "to preserve the Constitution from injury . . . , to deprive Spain and the allied powers of any just cause of war," and "to improve the occurrence to the best advantage of the country, and the honor of those who engaged in it."[579]

---

*Monroe made a final, revealing comment on the issue of responsibility in a letter to John Quincy Adams on March 11, 1831, when the controversy between Monroe and Jackson erupted. He denied having read Jackson's January 6 letter, and insisted that his failure to answer it could not be construed as a sanction for its proposal. But then he went on to argue that, in any case, the letter had asked only his individual consent, not official approval (7 *Monroe Writings* 227, 228):

He asks only my consent as an Individual, and evidently with an intention not to compromit me, even in that character. The letter, therefore, had it been answered, & the sanction been given, was an affair of confidence between him & me, never to be disclosed. On what principle it can be relied on as an authority to attack the posts, & to make me responsible for it, I cannot conceive.

The first two of these objectives, Monroe later wrote to Madison, were accomplished by restoring the forts; the third objective posed "little difficulty," since it made much more sense to blame the Spanish authorities rather than Jackson. To prosecute Jackson would upset his supporters and lead to further procrastination by Spain. Furthermore, nothing required that Jackson be punished, since even if a general fails to "make just discriminations in all instances between enemies and others I do not consider him as committing a breach of the Constitution. If the government sets the affair right in other respects there is no breach, although he be not punished for his mistakes."[580]

Impact of Jackson's Initiative on Negotiations with Spain. When Jackson entered Florida, Spain knew only what Congress was told on March 25, 1818—that American troops would pursue the Indians across the border, but were not authorized to take any Spanish posts. Onis wrote angrily to Adams after the posts were taken, demanding that they be promptly restored, that Spain be indemnified for losses, and that Jackson be punished.[581] Adams recorded that Onis had just "received new instructions from Spain, which would have enabled him to conclude a treaty with me satisfactory to both parties if it had not been for this unfortunate incident."[582] In Madrid, Foreign Minister Pizarro broke off all discussions with American Minister George Erving. And British public opinion was aroused, chiefly because of the executions of Ambrister and Arbuthnot.[583]

These reactions to Jackson's conduct obscure its more lasting effects. While Onis protested, he nevertheless opened intensive negotiations with Adams, at the end of which, on July 18, 1818, he wrote Pizarro that, unless Spain could marshall "sufficient forces to make war on this country," it would be wise to reach without delay "the best settlement possible, seeing that things certainly won't be better for a long time." Pizarro meanwhile instructed Onis to make further boundary concessions in order to secure Mexico and other established Spanish territories. Adams and Monroe got tougher, if anything, insisting not only on Florida and a southwestern line that left intact the Louisiana Purchase, but also on a northern line to the Pacific, that would transfer any claim Spain had to the Columbia River Basin.[584]

On July 23, 1818, Adams sent Onis the letter Monroe had instructed him to prepare, explaining Jackson's activities in the Floridas. In every respect, he argued, Spain was at fault. The United States had acted defensively in entering Florida, because of Spain's failure to fulfill its treaty obligation to keep peace along the border.

Jackson had acted on his own, but properly in light of the outrageous behavior of the Spanish commandants. Adams even demanded a just and reasonable indemnity for the costs incurred in suppressing MacGregor's operations at Amelia Island. He ended by threatening that Spain must in the future fulfill its treaty obligation to restrain the Indians or suffer the consequences.[585]

Additional pressure was placed on Spain by the Monroe administration's actions with respect to the Spanish posts. Adams confirmed to Onis on July 23 that Pensacola would be returned to any person "duly authorized" to receive it. Fort St. Marks, however, being in the heart of Indian territory, would be surrendered only "to a force sufficiently strong to hold it against the attack of the hostile Indians." As for Amelia Island, Adams later wrote to Representative John Holmes that it was taken under authority of the Act of January 15, 1811, and would be held "as long as the reasons upon which it was taken shall continue," subject to some other disposition by Congress.[586] Calhoun conveyed the administration's position to Gaines on August 14, leaving Gaines to decide what constituted a sufficient Spanish force at St. Marks, and at what points to station troops within the country controlled by Indians; he noted in particular that Fort Gadsden "ought not to be evacuated." On September 20, Gaines replied that he would consider a "sufficient force" at St. Marks to be not less than 250 men, an amount greater than the number of Americans stationed there.[587]

Monroe would have preferred to keep even Pensacola, as he wrote to Adams on August 10.[588] Impatient with the pace of negotiations, he instructed Adams to deliver an ultimatum to Onis, which Adams did on October 24, threatening to obtain authority from Congress to take the Floridas, and to drive Spain "from this hemisphere," unless Spain relinquished the area. By the time this ultimatum was delivered, Onis had received instructions permitting him to cede the area as far west as the Sabine, and beyond if necessary. Onis's stubbornness, and his lack of instructions on the northern boundary question, initially prevented an agreement. But the Marquis de Yrujo meanwhile took over Pizarro's position, and instructed Onis on October 10, 1818 to obtain the Sabine if possible, but to settle the dispute on the best terms he could.[589]

Onis received Yrujo's instructions in January 1818, and it quickly became clear that the Floridas would be ceded; the principal dispute during the next three weeks was over the boundary west from the Sabine to the Pacific Ocean. Adams insisted upon, and finally obtained, a cession of Spain's claims to the Columbia River Basin; on the other hand, Onis managed to hold intact the area between the

Sabine and Mexico. By February 7, 1819, Monroe was able to write to Madison that an accommodation with Onis was imminent "on the conditions offered sometime since & published." He added: "Should it take place I have no doubt that it will be due principally to the late pressure in Florida."[590] The treaty was ready on February 20, and was signed on George Washington's birthday, two days later.[591] On March 14, Gaines informed Calhoun that Pensacola and the Barancas had been delivered to Spain on March 8,[592] about two months after it had become clear that the Floridas would be ceded to the United States.

Legislative Reaction to Jackson's Initiative. Congress reconvened some three months before the treaty with Spain was signed. Monroe delivered his annual message on November 17, 1818. Florida had "become the theatre of every species of lawless adventure," the President claimed. The invasion of Florida was an act of self-defense, justified also because Spain had failed to meet its treaty obligations. "In pursuing these savages to an imaginary line, in the woods," he said, "it would have been the height of folly to have suffered that line to protect them." Even if Spain controlled the territory, the law of nations allowed the United States to pursue an enemy, and to subdue him there.

The posts, however, were different. Jackson's orders, the President said, were carefully drawn so as "not to encroach on the rights of Spain." While executing his instructions, "facts were disclosed respecting the conduct of the officers of Spain, in authority there, in encouraging the war, furnishing munitions of war, and other supplies" so that Jackson "was convinced that he should fail in his object . . . if he did not deprive those savages of the resource on which they had calculated." Jackson's reasons were "duly appreciated," but the posts had to be returned to Spain. The seizure might be justifiable, but "the amicable relations existing between the United States and Spain could not be altered by that act alone." Restitution of the posts would preserve peaceful relations; "[t]o a change of them the power of the Executive is deemed incompetent. It is vested in Congress only."[593]

Vocal opposition in both houses, particularly to Jackson's conduct, was inevitable. Jackson had enhanced his popularity and become a leading presidential possibility; Clay was therefore doubly energized against him.[594] The day after Monroe's message, Clay appointed a select committee to investigate the executions of Arbuthnot and Ambrister, and the Seminole War.[595]

At this point, a note of protest from Pizarro arrived in Washington. As Bemis observes, "it gave to the Secretary of State just the occasion he needed."[596] Adams prepared a massive "instruction," addressed to Minister Erving in Madrid and dated November 28, with accompanying documents; he simultaneously sent the document abroad and gave it to the American press. This "greatest state paper" of Adams's diplomatic career, referred to by Jefferson as "the most important and . . . among the ablest compositions I have ever seen, both as to logic and style,"[597] was a detailed brief exonerating Jackson and the government, and condemning Arbuthnot, Ambrister, Spain and its officers. Adams's defense "undermined the opposition in Congress" to a significant degree,[598] though opposition remained vocal, if ineffectual.

The Senate requested information on November 30, 1818, and with more specificity on December 17, concerning correspondence with Spain relating to the war, the executions, Jackson's orders and other specified correspondence with Jackson, "or such parts thereof, as may be communicated with a view to public safety." The President replied at various points with numerous documents.[599] But he withheld some of the material he had failed to turn over during the previous session, as well as all the correspondence between himself and Jackson concerning the legality of Jackson's conduct. The letter of December 26 bearing instructions to Jackson, excised in the March 25 transmittal, was given to the Senate in full, as was Calhoun's letter of approbation. But a private letter from Jackson to Monroe of June 2, 1818, stating that St. Augustine and Cuba, both essential to the security of the southern frontier, could be taken "whenever thought necessary," was withheld.[600] The documents sent were referred to a select committee, with subpoena power, instructed to inquire into the occupation of St. Marks and Pensacola, "and particularly, what circumstances existed, to authorize or justify the Commanding General in taking possession of those posts."[601] Monroe sent the same material to the House, once again without intimating that the information sent was incomplete.[602]

The House Committee on Military Affairs made its report on the Arbuthnot and Ambrister executions on January 12. No law of the United States, it found, authorized a trial before a military court for the offenses alleged against Arbuthnot and Ambrister, except for the charge against Arbuthnot of spying, on which he was found not guilty. Furthermore, Jackson's order that Ambrister be shot was "contrary to the forms and usages of the army, and without regard to the finding of the court." The committee therefore proposed a resolution that the House "disapproves the proceedings in the trial and execution of Alexander Arbuthnot and Robert C. Ambrister."

The committee's chairman, Colonel Richard M. Johnson of Kentucky, presented a minority report, however, sustaining Jackson and calling for a vote of thanks to Jackson and his men.[603] On January 18, Thomas Cobb of Georgia broadened the debate by offering three resolutions: (1) to prepare legislation prohibiting the execution of captives without presidential approval in times of peace, or of war solely with Indians; (2) to disapprove Jackson's seizure of St. Marks, Pensacola, and Fort Barancas "as contrary to orders and in violation of the Constitution"; and (3) to prepare a bill prohibiting the United States Army from entering "into any foreign territory, without the previous authorization of Congress, except it be in the case of fresh pursuit of a defeated enemy of the United States, taking refuge within such foreign territory."[604]

Many members came to the Monroe administration's defense during debate on these resolutions. Several reiterated the argument that the President and Jackson had acted defensively, which they were authorized to do by the law of nations, and that Spain's failure to keep its treaty obligation to control the Indians made it permissible for the President to do so in order to execute the laws.[605] The President was not limited to fighting only wars formally declared by Congress, said Alexander Smyth of Virginia. He could authorize military actions short of war:

> The power to declare war is a power to announce regular war, or war in form, against another Power. But it never was intended, by reserving this power to Congress, to take from the President the power to do any act necessary to preserve the nation's rights, and which does not put the nation into a state of war with another Power. If Congress, in addition to the power of declaring war, assume to themselves the power of directing every movement of the public force that may touch a neutral; or that may be made for preserving the national rights, or executing the laws and treaties; they will assume powers given to the President by the Constitution.[606]

Administration supporters referred to the many precedents in American history of military actions where war had not formally been declared;[607] but these generally involved situations in which Congress had given authority, though not in the form of a declaration. Smyth advanced a thesis, however, that he felt justified even legislatively unauthorized actions: "[A]cts of violence occurring between commanders of portions of the armed force of different countries, each asserting the rights or maintaining the pretensions of their respective Governments, are not such acts of war as must be preceded by a declaration of war." Indeed, he and others argued, a declaration of war against Indians was both unnecessary and unwise, since it would acknowledge their independence.[608]

Others claimed the invasion of Florida was authorized by the Act of February 28, 1795, which enabled the President to use the militia to repel an invasion, or during imminent danger of invasion. Once Jackson was lawfully within Florida, the behavior of the Spanish officers justified his subsequent conduct.[609] Alexander Smyth of Virginia found authorization in Congress's passage of an appropriation increasing the pay of the Georgia militia. George F. Strother, also of Virginia, claimed the legislation was "a *quasi* declaration of war,—a shield broad enough and thick enough to protect the Executive from attack. . . ." John Holmes of Massachusetts reminded the House that, "during the last session, it was known that this war could not be terminated without marching the troops into Florida." The President had told Congress on March 25 that he had issued orders to General Gaines to cross into Florida, "to pursue and chastise the enemy, but to respect the Spanish authority where it was maintained. We acquiesced; we appropriated the money to pay the militia without a whisper of disapprobation."[610] Finally, some individuals took the position that the House lacked power to pass resolutions removing or censuring any military officer; the President, as commander-in-chief, was responsible for disciplining such officers.[611]

Cogent, even stirring, answers were given to these arguments. Cobb accused Jackson of "trampling upon the Constitution." Only Congress had the power to declare war—which included the right of retaliation. When Madison wanted to retaliate against Britain during the War of 1812, Cobb noted, he sought approval from Congress, setting a precedent Cobb regarded as "conclusive authority." Jackson's seizure of the Spanish posts was "an offensive war. To give it the character of a defensive war, it must appear that our country had been invaded, or was in imminent danger of invasion by the Spanish forces in East Florida, or elsewhere," he argued. "Or, if this was not the case, it ought, at least to be made to appear that our army, which had been marched into East Florida, in pursuit of an Indian enemy, had been attacked by the Spaniards; or that they had arrayed themselves against us, for the purpose of preventing that pursuit of our enemy. None of these cases appears to have happened."[612] Thomas Nelson of Virginia concurred. Jackson's description of how he took the Barancas contained detailed proof of "incidents as are attendant on most battles between civilized nations. . . . [I]f this be not war, I have always misunderstood the term. . . ."[613] Even if Spain had violated its neutrality, or breached the terms of a treaty, "who constituted General Jackson the judge to decide . . .? Not the President of the United States, because he has no power, no authority, to decide the question himself." Only the Congress had the competence to make that determination.* Nor could the execution of Arbuthnot and Ambrister be justified under international law. "The right of retaliation," claimed Henry Clay,

> is an attribute of sovereignty. It is comprehended in the war-making power that Congress possesses. It belongs to this body not only to declare war, but to raise armies, and to make rules and regulations for their Government. It was in vain for the gentlemen to look to the law of nations for instances in which retaliation is lawful. The laws of nations merely laid down the principle or rule, and it belongs to the Government to constitute the tribunal for applying that principle or rule.[614]

Cobb also rejected the contention that Monroe could legitimately send troops into Florida under the act authorizing him to use military force to repel an invasion. That act could not be read to authorize actions beyond American territory, or "it followed that the President . . . could declare a war without the assent of Congress, unless the conclusion was drawn that it was not war to send a detachment of our army to carry on operations beyond our own limits." If such an action were war, then Congress had to authorize it. "If it be not war," he added, "and we must give it some other name, let it be called a man-killing expedition which the President has a right to direct whenever he pleases."[615]

The notion that the power to declare war related only to the power to initiate "formal" war was vehemently attacked. "The framers of the Constitution did not repose that happy confidence in Executive or military officers," said William Lowndes of South Carolina, "which might have induced them to give to Congress only the right of proclaiming a solemn and general war, and to leave to the Executive or the military the right of engaging in partial hostilities."[616] Clay was particularly eloquent on this issue,† and statements were

---

*33 *Annals* 623. *Accord id.* 375 (Cobb). Henry R. Storrs of New York said (*id.* 749–50):

> The justification of the Executive, which has been alleged in this debate, as arising from the neglect of Spain to fulfill the treaty, is fallacious. If the treaty had been violated, the Executive possessed no authority to enforce our rights by arms. It is the exertion of national force for the redress of wrong or the preservation of right, which constitutes the precise definition of war, and the Congress alone was vested with the authority to declare it.

†Clay said, in part (*id.* 647):

> Of all the powers conferred by the Constitution of the United States, not one is more expressly and exclusively granted than that is to Congress of declaring war. . . . It was believed, no doubt, in committing this great sub-

also made by a future President, John Tyler of Virginia* and others.†
William Henry Harrison of Ohio, later the ninth President, observed
that Monroe must have considered Jackson's conduct unconstitutional, since he agreed to restore the posts to Spain without legislative authorization. "If these posts were a legal acquisition to the arms
of the United States," said the hero of Tippecanoe, "the President
could no more surrender them by his own authority, than he could
restore to Great Britain the frigate *Macedonian*, or any other capture made during the late war."[617]

At least two members responded to the argument that prior appropriations had authorized the war. Nelson said that Congress had
assumed, in making the appropriations, that Jackson would be bound
by the order to Gaines to respect Spanish authority wherever maintained, and therefore could not have anticipated "so extraordinary
a departure from orders, in the prosecution of the war." Tyler argued that the prior appropriation could not have been intended to
authorize Jackson's campaign, since the same session which approved
the appropriation also saw the unanimous defeat by the Committee

---

ject to the Legislature of the Union, we should be safe from the mad wars
that have afflicted and desolated and ruined other countries. It was supposed that before any war was declared the nature of the injury complained
of would be carefully examined, the power and resources of the enemy es-
timated, and the power and resources of our own country, as well as the
probable issue and consequence of the war. It was to guard our country
against precisely that species of rashness, which has been manifested in
Florida, that the Constitution was so framed.

*Tyler urged the House to defend its constitutional right to declare war
(*id*. 928-29):

This nation, if this precedent receive your sanction, may be involved in
war without the question ever having been submitted to the Representatives of the people. . . . I cannot imagine a more formidable inroad on the
powers of this House. The military commissions the officers of police; the
American law prevails; the Spanish customs are disregarded. Who has done
all this? Not the Congress of the United States, but the commander of its
armies. I am no apologist for Spain. . . . But, I will never cease to protest
against this violation of the Constitution.

†Most notably, Charles F. Mercer of Virginia (*id*. 813-14):

The doctrines of our opponents, on this question, are more alarming, if
possible, than the acts which they seek to justify or to excuse. If . . . [as
Smyth said] a declaration of war is nothing more than "a recognition that
war exists," what becomes of the Constitutional authority of Congress?
Alike extraordinary is the conclusion of my colleague, that, because the
President is charged with the execution of our laws, and treaties are the
supreme law of the land, he may execute within the territories of Spain
the provisions of a Spanish treaty; or the yet more extraordinary doctrine,
that all the powers of this Government, which may at any time be exercised beyond the limits of the United States, are concentered in the hands
of the President.

of Foreign Relations of a proposal to authorize the President to take possession of the Floridas, a defeat which the whole House did nothing to change.[618] No member, however, rejected the proposition that the appropriation would have been sufficient authority for seizing the posts had that purpose been known to Congress or reasonably related to the purpose of the approved expenditure.

After one month of debate—perhaps the longest time ever devoted by the House to a single issue—the Committee of the Whole voted 90 to 54 against the resolution to disapprove the trials and executions of Arbuthnot and Ambrister. Then, all three of Cobb's resolutions were defeated, by wide margins. The House concurred in these decisions by even wider margins,[619] thereby holding the Monroe adminsitration and General Jackson harmless for their conduct in the Floridas.*

A commiteee investigation of Jackson's conduct was also undertaken in the Senate, despite arguments that the President had approved Jackson's conduct, and therefore assumed responsibility, and that the House—the grand inquest of the nation—had decided against prosecuting the matter after a laborious investigation and debate.[620] The committee filed its report on February 24. It condemned both Jackson and Gaines for exceeding their orders by raising volunteers instead of requesting militia. The committee noted that "there was no law in existence that authorized even the President of the United States to raise or accept the services of volunteers. . . . The Constitution of the United States gives to Congress, exclusively, the power of raising armies, and to the President and the Senate the power of appointing officers." The report then reviewed the entire Florida campaign, concluding that "the tendency" of Jackson's measures "seems to have been to involve the nation in a war without her consent, and for reasons of his own, unconnected with his military functions."[621]

Presented in the last week of the session, the report never came up for debate or action. In sharp contrast, the Senate acted speedily and unanimously, on the very day the report was presented, to advise and consent to the treaty with Spain. Jackson was not to be condemned for conduct that had, in Adams's words, "been among

---

*Adams wrote to his father on February 14, only six days after the House voted, that, while he expected to be attacked, he was surprised "that General Jackson should be insinuated a murderer, for hanging murderers. . . . [A]ll these . . . are metamorphoses . . . . But the Constitution! Oh! the Constitution and military usurpation, and cruel despotism! And so to guard the sacred Palladium of the Constitution, a bill of attainder upon Jackson's reputation was to be passed by one branch of the legislature, without hearing him in his own defense." 6 *J.Q. Adams Writings* 528–29.

the most immediate and prominent causes that produced" a treaty the nation had so earnestly sought.[622]

Spain delayed in ratifying the treaty, causing Monroe to ask Congress in December 1819 to authorize him to occupy the Floridas as though the treaty were ratified. The request was withdrawn, however, at the urging of Britain and France, to give Spain further time to act.[623] In the Sixteenth Congress, meanwhile, the House debated whether to appropriate funds to pay the losses of volunteers and Indians raised by Gaines and Jackson. The legality of their conduct was again challenged, and defended, with the arguments heard in the last session. A committee report concluding that the troops had been raised unconstitutionally was tabled;[624] but Congress adjourned in May 1820 without having passed a bill to compensate the volunteers.

The extent of Monroe's responsibility for Jackson's conduct will never definitely be settled. Much of the uncertainty stems from Jackson's effort in 1831 to vindicate himself, virtually dictating the letters and affidavits by Rhea and others upon which he rested his defense.[625] Yet, even if Jackson's later claim of a letter from Rhea was fabricated, Monroe's story is at least equally unbelievable. Jackson's letter suggesting an occupation by force was undeniably written. Monroe received it, and his claim of being too ill to respond is dubious. He in fact wrote to Calhoun, probably after receiving Jackson's letter, asking that Jackson be ordered not to attack the posts. That no such order was sent should probably be attributed to Monroe.

In exonerating Monroe, his biographer William P. Cresson stresses Monroe's education and "proved integrity."[626] But as Bemis notes (and as we have amply seen above), "Monroe had done this sort of thing more than once before."[627] In 1805, he became so exasperated with Spain in attempting to negotiate a purchase of the Floridas that he urged the administration to seize Florida first and negotiate later.[628] As Secretary of State, he allowed if not encouraged General Mathews to occupy parts of East Florida by not responding when Mathews made clear his intentions.[629] As Secretary of War, he had failed to check Jackson during the War of 1812, when the latter marched into Pensacola and West Florida to meet British invasion.[630] "As President in 1818, he was glad enough to have the fiery Tennesseean at hand to hold over Spain's head during the lagging negotiations between Adams and Onis."[631]

Monroe's handling of the Florida invasion also reflects his attitude toward Congress. He took actions in Florida without prior consultation, even when Congress was in session. He withheld virtually all the information Congress needed to judge Jackson's intentions and the administration's involvement. He constructed an explanation for the seizure of the posts that was based on Jackson's being confronted in the field with facts unknown to the executive beforehand, when he well knew that Jackson's actions could more plausibly be explained on the basis of Jackson's aspirations. When Jackson was unwilling to take the blame for exceeding his instructions, Monroe proposed, in confidential correspondence, that Jackson write a letter stating his position, so that the administration could be prepared for a call for information. Finally, his deferential disavowal of power to keep the posts was deceptive; only Pensacola was returned to Spain, and that only after its cession to the United States seemed assured.

Monroe decided to protect Jackson to avoid personal embarrassment, and to prevent Spain from using the event to delay negotiations. In the process, he advocated the doctrine that a commander in the field could take actions that the President himself could not have authorized, and articulated a standard for controlling the behavior of military officers that encouraged rather than discouraged initiative, risk-taking and the broad construction of executive orders.

Suppression of Piracy in the West Indies

During the Jefferson administration, pirates, including the infamous smuggler Jean Lafitte, were active in and near New Orleans, in the Gulf of Mexico and throughout the West Indies.[632] Naval forces were used to suppress piracy within American waters, pursuant to the Act of April 30, 1790.[633] By the time the War of 1812 ended, privateers sailing with commissions freely granted by the revolutionary governments of Colombia (Cartagena), Mexico and Venezuela had become active in the Gulf of Mexico and the Caribbean.[634] "Privateering" was a recognized device at the time, whereby governments authorized private vessels to seize enemy shipping during war, in exchange for all or part of the value of the ships or goods seized. But most privateers in the Caribbean were little more than pirates, bearing commissions either not recognized or illegal. In addition, undisguised pirates, encouraged by the breakdown of governmental authority in that area, began to ply their trade with impunity. As attacks on American shipping increased during the last year of Madison's administration and the first years of Monroe's presidency, merchants from port cities, particularly New Orleans, petitioned Congress for relief.[635]

The Fifteenth Congress, responding to an aroused public, passed without recorded debate "An Act to protect the commerce of the United States, and punish the crime of piracy," which Monroe signed into law on March 3, 1819.* The Act authorized the President to employ as many of the public armed vessels as the service required, "with suitable instructions" to the commanders of the ships, to protect merchant shipping of the United States "from piratical aggressions and depredations," and to capture any ship which committed any "piratical" act. Captains of American merchantmen were empowered to defend their ships from "piratical" acts by any ship other than "a public armed vessel of some nation in amity with the United States," and to capture the offending vessels; the act also set up a procedure for condemning seized vessels for the benefit of their captors, and made piracy punishable by death.[636]

On March 16, 1820, the President assembled his Cabinet to discuss the new piracy law. The section authorizing merchant vessels to defend themselves was particularly confusing to Monroe. What was the meaning of "public armed vessel"? Did it include vessels officially commissioned by other nations as privateers? The Cabinet could not reach a decision, but since the President did not have to issue orders to merchant vessels the matter was dropped, leaving merchantmen to interpret the law for themselves. The President did, however, have to issue orders to naval commanders to suppress "piratical aggressions and depredations," and Congress had not attempted to distinguish between pirates and privateers. Were privateers to be considered pirates? Which nation's privateers were to be acknowledged as legal? The Cabinet tried but failed to decide which South American privateers were to be considered legal and which were to be deemed pirates. They ended by issuing orders through the Secretary of the Navy merely authorizing United States commanders to bring into port "any ship suspected of piracy for adjudication without inquiring what flag or commission she acted under."[637]

The Piracy Act was scheduled by its terms to expire at the end of the succeeding session of Congress, but it was renewed in May 1820 for two years, and reenacted without time limit in January 1823.[638] Acting pursuant to the May 1820 renewal, Monroe dispatched several ships (including the brig *Enterprise* and schooners *Nonsuch* and *Lynx*) to cruise the Gulf of Mexico in search of pirates,[639] under instructions that stressed the need to avoid offending Spain. This force was too meager materially to affect the situation,

---

*Adams speculated that Clay had allowed the act to pass because he meant to oppose it in the execution. A Mr. Middleton is recorded by Adams as having suggested that Clay may have been so dispirited by losses at cards (including a loss of $8,000 in one night to Poindexter) that he temporarily lost interest in House business. 4 *Adams Memoirs* 306 (1875) (entry for Mar. 18, 1819).

and the vessels too large to follow the pirates into shallow waters. At least twenty-seven Amercan merchant ships were seized in 1820. The situation worsened in 1821 when the *Lynx* was lost, it was believed, in a summer hurricane. Vessels captured by the American force in Spanish waters were turned over to Cuban authorities, who generally released the prisoners after what American naval officers regarded as mock trials.[640]

Congressional interest in piracy intensified in early 1822. During January, both the House and Senate initiated inquiries into building small sloops or using frigates to protect United States commerce from piracy.[641] The Senate's resolution for an inquiry, introduced by Richard Johnson of Louisiana, was re-worded to remove suggestions that the vessels be used in any specific place, to avoid any appearance of interfering with the executive's power to employ the naval force.[642] The House seemed far less sensitive to executive prerogative. Its committee was specifically requested to consider what manner of vessels were necessary to protect commerce against the West Indian pirates, and also whether "to authorize the destruction of persons and vessels found at sea, or in uninhabited places, making war upon the commerce of the United States without any regular commission," and "how far, consistent with public law, a general usage or authority may be given to destroy pirates and piratical vessels found at sea, or in uninhabited places."[643]

The House committee filed an ambitious report on March 2, analyzing all available naval resources, and recommending a resolution to augment the West Indian squadron with two corvettes (*Cyane* and *John Adams*) and two sloops of war (*Peacock* and *Erie*), as well as the frigate *Constellation* if the President deemed its use necessary. The committee came out against purchasing and converting private vessels, and concluded it would be "inexpedient" to authorize the destruction of vessels making war on American commerce without regular commissions, and "*inconsistent* with public law or general usage, to give any authority to destroy pirates and piratical vessels found at sea or in uninhabited places." The resolution was tabled, however, and not again discussed.[644] Albert Tracy of New York proposed to inquire into whether naval appropriations should be modified to permit the construction of smaller ships than those now authorized. An inquiry was undertaken, but the Committee on Naval Affairs recommended that money not be diverted from the planned construction of larger ships to build small ones.[645]

Though Congress refused to act, President Monroe established the West Indian Squadron under Captain James Biddle. Orders dated March 26, 1822 directed Biddle to patrol the West Indies with two frigates, two corvettes, two sloops-of-war, two brigs, four schooners, and several gunboats, a force very similar to that recommended by the House committee. Biddle was instructed to take any steps possible to obtain the cooperation of local authorities.[646]

When Biddle arrived at Havana, he wrote to Governor Mahy of Cuba, noting the need to protect Cuban-American trade. Attacks were usually committed in open boats, "immediately upon the coast and off the harbors" of Cuba, he said, so the Governor's cooperation was essential. He proposed that the Governor "sanction the landing upon the coast" of American boats and men "when in pursuit of pirates." This would be mutually beneficial, he argued, and was "not intended in any manner to infringe upon the territorial rights of your excellency." Mahy flatly refused this request, stating that he had adopted the necessary measures to suppress outlaws.[647]

Biddle's little fleet fought many battles with pirates (and, at far greater cost, with yellow fever), but all apparently occurred on water, though clearly within the nautical jurisdiction of Cuba. The first significant legal issue arose when, on August 16, 1822, the schooner *Grampus*, under command of Lt. Francis Gregory, captured a notorious Spanish privateer, the *Pancheta*, out of Puerto Rico. After capture, the Spanish captain admitted looting an American merchantman, the *Coquette*, proof of which Gregory had obtained prior to the encounter.[648] When word of Gregory's action reached Washington, the President called his Cabinet together. Calhoun and others opposed the seizure of a Spanish privateer. Adams, however, declared that it was "strictly legal" under the Piracy Act of 1819, which authorized the President to issue instructions to the navy "to capture and send in *any* armed vessel which shall have attempted or committed any *piratical* aggression upon any vessel of the United States or any other vessel." Calhoun questioned whether a Spanish privateer bearing a lawful commission could be designated "piratical." After a careful reading of the instructions given to Commodore Biddle, the President determined that they fully justified the capture.[649]

Despite the seizure of over thirty pirate vessels, Biddle was unable to stop piracy in the Caribbean. His large vessels were ineffective against pirates operating in shallow-draft boats off the Cuban shore. In October 1822 the Cabinet began considering new instructions for Biddle's fleet. Monroe reportedly suggested Biddle be given instructions "to remonstrate, to the Governor of Porto Rico, and to the commanders of any Spanish armed vessels with whom he may fall in, against the [Spanish] blockade [of South American ports], and to declare that it cannot be acknowledged by the United States as valid, but to avoid any positive act of force against it." Adams wanted a bolder course. The United States should declare that it would not recognize "paper blockades," and that it would convoy American merchantmen to and from South American ports. Adams's call for a convoy shocked Calhoun. "[T]o resist the search would be war," Calhoun protested, and he "doubted the power of the Executive to give such instructions." Adams retorted that the question was settled during the Tripolitan war by the victory of Andrew Sterrett and the *Enterprise* over a Tripolitan cruiser:

> To authorize force in self-defence I believed the authority of the Executive under our Constitution to be entirely competent, and if a naval officer could be authorized to convoy at all, he must be authorized to defend the convoyed vessel as he would his own, against force.

Calhoun suggested that the President authorize merchant rather than public vessels to resist searches. "No," Adams replied: "If we could instruct our officer to give convoy at all, we cannot allow him to submit to the search by foreigners of a vessel under his charge; for it is placing our officer and the nation itself in an attitude of inferiority and humiliation." Once again Adams's view prevailed. Secretary Thompson was asked to draw new instructions for Biddle. Before they could be delivered, however, one of Biddle's ships was humiliated by pirates, and Biddle was recalled.[650]

Congress reconvened on December 2, 1822. On December 3, President Monroe asked for "prompt and decisive measures" to deal with the pirates, noting that all available public vessels adapted to that service were already employed in it. He requested "a particular kind of force, capable of pursuing them into the shallow waters to which they retire. . . ."[651] On December 13, 1822, the House Committee on Naval Affairs reported a bill to authorize the President "to purchase or construct a sufficient number of vessels . . . for the purpose of repressing piracy, and of affording effectual protection to the citizens and commerce of the United States in the Gulf of Mexico, and the seas and territories adjacent."[652]

William Eustis questioned the bill's wisdom. The clause authorizing protection in "the seas and territories adjacent," he felt, amounted to a delegation of power to make war. Our sailors might pursue pirates into Cuba only to be confronted by Spanish authorities, he warned, and war between the United States and Spain might result, for the law of nations did not permit the officers of one nation to enter the jurisdictional limits of another for any purpose. Timothy Fuller of Massachusetts, a member of the committee which reported the bill, replied that they had "not reported a bill to authorize even . . . pursuing the pirates on . . . land, much less . . . entering the territories of foreign Powers to search for them." The bill, he said, was "simply intended to provide for the suppression of piracy and the protection of commerce; and there was nothing in it that could by possibility warrant the construction that it was to give authority to the Executive to seek for pirates in the territories of foreign Powers." But Fuller added his opinion that, according to the law of nations, "if an officer should find pirates escaping from his pursuit to a territory of a foreign Power, he might have a right to pursue them into the actual (not nominal) jurisdiction of that Power."[653]

Alexander Smyth of Virginia was perfectly willing to have Congress delegate authority to pursue pirates, rather than leaving the matter to the President's power under the law of nations. He proposed an amendment whereby the President would be "authorized and required, to pursue the pirates by land, on any of the West India Islands to which they may resort, as well as on the ocean, until they are exterminated." But most members were unprepared to allow the navy "to pursue pirates, or supposed pirates, wherever they please. . . . We have no right to pursue even a pirate into the territory of a neutral or friendly Power," protested Louis McLane of Delaware, "until that Power has refused to interpose, or is incompetent by reason of its own imbecility to prevent and punish the crime." Daniel P. Cook of Illinois successfully moved to add a proviso to Smyth's proposed amendment which would allow pursuit on land only after permission had been requested and received from the local government. But even with this proviso, William S. Archer of Virginia argued that Smyth's amendment "proposed in effect to divest Congress and give to the Executive the power to make war." John Floyd of Virginia was unwilling "to put a power into the hands of the Executive, the responsibility for the exercise of which would apply to this body, and not to the Executive." At this point, Smyth withdrew his amendment, and the bill as originally proposed, which authorized protection in adjacent "seas and territories," was passed and sent to the Senate.[654]

On December 16, 1822, the Senate debated whether to consider the House bill, or to substitute it with a bill proposed by the Senate Committee on Naval Affairs, and introduced by James Barbour of Virginia. The Senate bill simply provided funds for "such additional force as in . . . [the President's] judgment shall be best calculated" to suppress piracy. Barbour argued that his bill was preferable because "the theory of the Constitution preferred that the means be placed in the hands of the President, who is responsible to the nation for the application of the money and the mode of conducting the defence of the country, or other warlike measures." As to the

President's power in the absence of any legislative direction, he did not necessarily believe that American officers "might go into a neutral territory in search of those outlaws; but he had no doubt, in the heat of pursuit, they might be followed and punished in the territory of a neutral Power." Other Senators saw no material difference, however, between the House and Senate bills. They argued that executive discretion was unimportant in this situation, since the President had no alternative but to spend the moneys provided on naval vessels, as the House bill required; "it was not probable," cracked John Holmes of Maine, "that the Executive would think of ordering either the Army or the militia out on this service." Since a delay of at least one day would result if the Senate substituted its bill, Barbour's motion was voted down. The House bill passed without dissent, and was signed by the President on December 20.[655]

Though far less explicit than administration supporters may have wanted, the law authorizing vessels was followed by more vigorous executive actions against piracy. To command the new force, President Monroe selected Captain David Porter, already famous for his daring and controversial exploits in the Mediterranean, against pirates near New Orleans, and in the War of 1812.* On February 1, 1823, Secretary of Navy Smith Thompson instructed Porter that his mission was "for the purpose of suppressing piracy and affording effectual protection to the citizens and commerce of the United States." Porter was to respect "the rights of others," and to seek "favorable and friendly support" from the Governor of Cuba. But he was given much more scope than Biddle, though with confusing qualifications. As pirates were *hostes humani generis*—"enemies of the human race"—Thompson authorized Porter to land on the islands in pursuit of them, even on settled parts, "for the purpose of aiding the local authorities or people, as the case may be, to seize and bring the offenders to justice, previously giving notice that this is your sole object." On the other hand, he was to "respect the local authorities" where "a Government exists and is felt" and to "only act in aid of and co-operate with them." If pirates found at sea retreated to unsettled parts of the island, Porter was authorized to pursue them, but "in no case are you at liberty to pursue and ap-

*Porter's assignment came at a time of great sensitivity for the United States in its international affairs; in December of the same year, President Monroe was to proclaim his famous doctrine opposing intervention by European powers in the American hemisphere. The assignment therefore called for "calm judgment" and "caution," traits which Porter's biographer David Long gently notes "had not characterized his behavior." D. Long, *Nothing Too Daring: A Biography of Commodore David Porter, 1780-1843*, at 207 (1970).

prehend any one after having been forbidden so to do by competent authority of the local government." The confusion of these directions was only compounded by an overall injunction that Porter act with "as much moderation and forbearance as is consistent with the honor of your country and the just claims of its citizens."[656] The instructions represented, to Porter's biographer, David Long, "a masterpiece of bureaucratic ambivalence which would make the Navy Department right and Porter wrong, should anything go amiss."[657]

The first test of Porter's judgment came in March 1823. A lieutenant on one of Porter's ships, the *Fox*, was killed by shore batteries at San Juan. The Spanish Governor wrote Porter that only a warning shot had been intended, and expressed sorrow at the officer's death. Porter accepted the apology, acting cooly in this instance despite his anger. Soon thereafter the Spanish government lifted the blockade, and its local governors began to provide more cooperation.[658]

From Puerto Rico, Porter's fleet sailed to Cuba where it patrolled and provided convoy for the next two years. Dozens of pirates were apprehended, and many vessels captured or destroyed, including the flagship of Diablito, a notorious pirate. On at least seven occasions American forces landed on foreign territory. Of the first four landings, one was clearly in "hot pursuit" of pirates;[659] in the second, pursuit was lukewarm at best.[660] The third landing was a search for weapons,[661] and the fourth took place the day after some pirates had fled ashore.[662]

Porter notified naval headquarters in Washington of two of these four incidents, promptly after they occurred.[663] The President may well have heard that landings had taken place by the time he delivered his annual address to Congress on December 2, 1823. In that message, Monroe praised Porter and his men, noting that the mission "has been eminently successful in the accomplishment of its object. The piracies by which our commerce in the neighborhood of the Island of Cuba had been afflicted, have been repressed, and the confidence of our merchants, in a great measure, restored."[664] Spain protested the first of these landings, but its objections were brushed aside by Adams, on the ground that Spain had no basis for complaint were she "deeply and earnestly intent" upon suppressing the pirates.[665] The newly appointed Secretary of the Navy, Samuel L. Southard, instructed Porter in December 1823 to "continue your exertions to repress piracy, and protect our commerce."[666]

Despite Porter's achievements, pirates continued to prey on American shipping in 1824. Representative Joel R. Poinsett from the Committee on Foreign Affairs sent the President a bill to authorize a blockade of Puerto Rico and perhaps even Cuba as a "measure of defense or retaliation upon piracies and piratical privateering." At a Cabinet meeting on January 10, 1824, Calhoun opposed the bill and "questioned even the power of Congress to give the Executive such authority, because, he said, it would be war." Calhoun's comments sparked discussion in which, Adams recorded,

> all the debatable ground of that part of the Constitution of the United States was gone over. Since the argument upon President Washington's proclamation of neutrality, this has always been difficult ground, and the different views of the question have led to many curious and absurd results. Calhoun's argument led to the conclusion that Congress could not authorize the Executive contingently to commit *any* act hostile in its nature against a foreign nation.

Attorney General Wirt thought that blockading Puerto Rico and Cuba was "objectionable, because it would affect the rights not only of Spain, but of other nations." But Wirt wanted "some measures of self-vindication," and added that "our Constitution was lamentably defective if Congress had no power to authorize such a measure." Adams said that he "had no doubt of the power, nor of the expediency, and thought that some spirited measure would be entirely congenial to the general attitude which we had recently assumed." But Navy Secretary Southard was not sure, so the President postponed decision. Without administration backing, Poinsett's blockade bill had no chance, and Congress adjourned without passing further legislation.[667]

The summer heat, and deadly attacks of yellow fever, caused Porter to sail back to Washington during the summer of 1824. Monroe, Southard and others were outraged by what they regarded as Porter's delinquency, and forced him to return to Cuba to deal with increasing piratical activity.[668] Two landings took place around the time Porter returned to West Indian waters. One incident was a simple case of hot pursuit of pirates, and caused no controversy.[669] The second was Porter's landing at Fajardo (variously spelled Foxardo) in eastern Puerto Rico, to demand an apology for the manner in which one of his officers had been treated, and led ultimately to the Commodore's court martial and conviction.[670]

Porter's recall caused no decrease in activity against Caribbean pirates. The Cabinet met in December 1824 to consider the President's last annual message, and gave considerable attention to the section on piracy. The pirates's use of shallow draft boats made policing difficult, and a United States agent in Cuba, Thomas Randall, "urged the absolute necessity of some further measure for the protection of our commerce."[671] Monroe told Congress to consider providing new powers, including authority to land, presumably on settled as well as unsettled areas.[672]

The Senate passed a request for information on December 21 concerning injuries to Americans resulting from piracy, asking what measures had been adopted to suppress such acts; and what other means should be entrusted to the executive in order that he might suppress additional piratical acts.[673] On the same day, Navy Secretary Southard sent a letter to the Senate Naval Commitee specifically asking that the Navy be authorized "to pursue the pirates, wherever they may fly. . . . The rights to follow should be extended to the settled as well as the unsettled parts of the islands." If pursuit proved ineffectual, he wrote, the next step should be to blockade the area.[674] The President reiterated these requests in responding to the Senate's call.[675]

The Foreign Relations Committee presented a bill that would have provided what the President wanted. Section 1 granted funds to build ten sloops-of-war. Section 2 authorized public vessels, "under such instructions as may be given them by the President of the United States, in the fresh pursuit of pirates on the Island of Cuba, or any other of the Islands of Spain, in the West Indies, to land, whenever it may be necessary to secure the capture of the said pirates," who when subdued could either be delivered up to the authority of the island where captured, or brought to the United States for trial. Section 2, Senator Barbour explained, "is not a general privilege to enter the country in pursuit of pirates," but only to follow into neutral territory while in fresh pursuit. Section 3 authorized the President to blockade any port where pirates took refuge from American forces. Barbour conceded that no precedent or authority could be found to justify a blockade during peace time, "yet, if it be obviously necessary, to save our property from destruction, our citizens from massacre, and to bring to condign punishment the most atrocious of mankind, enemies of the human race, that necessity would be a sufficient justification." To those who might object that "this is trusting too much to the President," Barbour replied "there is no transfer of power: we in our sovereign capacity, point out the instrument by which our will shall be carried into effect."[676]

The proposal to grant power to blockade was vigorously and successfully attacked. General Samuel Smith of Maryland asked, for example, what would happen if British or French ships bound to a blockaded Cuban port were stopped by the United States Navy. By what authority could our ships act? "It is not to be found in the law of nations," Smith answered. A blockade "might be a very dangerous experiment, and involve us in war." Littleton Tazewell of Virginia agreed. "[I]t is not correct to argue that, because we have just cause of war, we may, in times of peace, adopt a measure which belong to war alone." The right to institute a blockade grows out of the "higher right of war, and can be exerted only by those placing themselves in a state of war." Robert Y. Hayne of South Carolina replied that, if a declaration of war was necessary for a blockade, "he would submit to the gentlemen whether the act of Congress which enjoins it, may not be considered as a declaration, sufficient to satisfy the most fastidious advocates of form." But Smith objected to placing "in the hands of the Executive the power of declaring war . . . a power which we alone possess in Congress." He was "unwilling to grant a provisional power that may lead us into war. I would much rather go to war directly than indirectly." His motion to strike the third section passed, 37 to 10.[677]

Section 2, authorizing pursuit, was also attacked, but primarily as unnecessary rather than improper.* Martin Van Buren of New York said that fresh pursuit was already a right of the President under international law, and had been granted Porter in his instructions. If the pursuit of pirates "was continued into the Thames, to the City of London, even to Westminster Hall itself, the act of the pursuer would not give just cause of complaint to the Government whose territory was so invaded." Tazewell, who led the fight against authorizing a blockade, supported the right of pursuit, whether "fresh or not; I believe you may lawfully go anywhere he unlawfully is." General Smith added that he "always understood that, in the fresh pursuit of an enemy, you have a right to land. It has been done by England, and by ourselves, and Spain has not complained of it. It is a national right," he declared, "which we can make use of at any time, without law. The passing of the law is the only objection I have to it." But the motion to strike section 2 was defeated, 16 to 28, and the bill passed.[678]

John Forsyth, an administration supporter, presented the House with the Senate's amended piracy bill on March 1, 1825. He felt "there did not exist any necessity for granting [the pursuit] pro-

---

*Senator Hayne argued against the legality of pursuit. "Where a Government exists, you must apply to the Magistrate, and nations were not in the habit of surrendering even a criminal—they were proud of being considered a sanctuary, from which even a criminal could not be torn. Nor had the Secretary," Hayne added, "given the power to the extent proposed by this bill. He had restricted the right of fresh pursuit to the parts of the country 'where the local government was not *felt.*'" 1 *Register* 402–403 (Feb. 1, 1825).

vision of the bill, since the President has it already by the law of nations." Forsyth noted that the bill conferred the right to pursue only into Puerto Rico and Cuba. "[I]f the right exists," Forsyth claimed, "it exists in relation to all other places, as well as to these Islands. And if it does not exist, and is to be given by this bill, it ought to be given in relation to all places." Others agreed, and a motion to strike section 2 carried in an unrecorded vote. Then James Strong of New York successfully moved to strike out all of the bill after the first section authorizing the ten sloops-of-war, and Webster convinced the House to strike even the words "for a more effectual suppression of piracy in the West Indies" from the title, arguing that Congress should decide what to give the President, but should not restrict his use of what was given. The amended bill passed, and was approved by the Senate in the closing minutes of the Eighteenth Congress.[679]

Meanwhile, Captain Lewis Warrington replaced Porter, and successfully suppressed piracy with the increased help of local Spanish authorities. The only landing on foreign soil during his command was one of hot pursuit, jointly conducted with a British vessel.[680] Though sporadic incidents took place until 1830, President Adams correctly reported on December 6, 1825, that piracy had been contained because the war between Spain and its colonies was over.[681] In the same message, however, Adams reported that piracy had become an acute problem in the Greek islands. Orders issued by the Adams administration warned naval commanders to respect the rights of other nations, but authorized the use of force to suppress the pirates. Several landings occurred in unpopulated areas, with the administration's knowledge and apparent consent.[682]

CONCLUSION

The period 1809–1829 is extraordinarily rich in material relating to the power to initiate military actions. The powers of the executive were questioned vociferously at times, but were not significantly limited. The President continued to take the lead in foreign-affairs activities. Congress showed that unilateral action could be checked, for example, when they forced President Adams to submit his plan to send ministers to the Panama Congress for full legislative approval. The general pattern of interaction, though, was for Congress to facilitate executive leadership either by doing nothing to guide the President, or by delegating important discretionary powers. Events leading up to the War of 1812 reflect the potential relationship between the power to conduct foreign affairs, under broad delegations, and the power to bring the nation closer to war. Virtually all requests for information were qualified, and executive withholding was consciously tolerated.

The notion that the Constitution required the United States to fight only declared wars was advanced at various points. But the principle was ignored in practice. War was declared or recognized to exist only with Britain in 1812, and with Algiers in 1815. Many undeclared military engagements occurred and were justified on several different grounds. The argument that had the widest recognition as legitimate was that Congress had approved the action by legislation, though not by a formal declaration. Madison argued, for example, that the takeover of parts of West Florida in 1810 was justified by the discretion implicitly delegated in the act authorizing the President to establish a customs district within the territory. He and Monroe allowed Mathews to take over parts of East Florida during 1811–1813, on the theory that the insurgents with whom Mathews was cooperating were the "local authority," from whom Congress had authorized the President to accept a surrender. Monroe and Adams used the same act to justify the seizure of Amelia Island in 1817, when it was in the hands of privateers and adventurers; they also relied on the acts outlawing the slave trade and piracy. Even laws that simply provided funds to pay men or build ships were sometimes intended to authorize, or were treated as having authorized, military actions. For example, when Congress appropriated funds for vessels in 1825, the vessels were clearly intended for use in combating piracy in the West Indies. The argument that an appropriation may authorize a military action was also advanced as one of several justifications for the war against the Seminoles, when some Congressmen noted that bills had been passed in the prior session providing the funds necessary to fight the Indians. Finally, Presidents Madison and Monroe, and Adams as Secretary of State, justified military actions in the Floridas and West Indies on the basis of treaties, assuming that the power of Presidents to execute all laws included authority to interpret treaties and to enforce the nation's rights.

Some military initiatives by the executive were justified on bases other than the power to execute laws or treaties. The right of self-defense was advanced to support the legality of seizing Amelia Island and of attacking the Seminoles. Furthermore, Presidents claimed in several contexts that the law of nations authorized military actions without prior legislative approval. Jackson's assault on Pensacola during the war of 1812, for example, was justified as necessary to prevent an enemy (Britain) from using neutral territory as a base for military operations. The right of fresh (hot) pursuit was claimed under Monroe to authorize Jackson's actions against the Seminoles, as well as landings on unpopulated areas of Puerto Rico and Cuba in chase of pirates.

At no time did the executive claim "inherent" power to initiate military actions. The justifications advanced were all based on legislative authorization or the executive's authority to exercise the nation's rights under international law. Furthermore, no President or other official of the executive branch ever claimed that Congress lacked power to control and dictate executive conduct, either in executing the laws or in asserting rights under the law of nations. The intervention in East Florida during 1811–1813 was in fact terminated after Congress refused to authorize a takeover in two succeeding sessions.

Although Presidents during this period claimed no inherent authority to initiate military actions, Madison and particularly Monroe secretly used their power in ways that could have been justified only by some sweeping and vague claim—such as the right to use the armed forces to advance the interests of the United States. The seizure of Baton Rouge and other parts of West Florida in 1810 was engineered by Madison, Monroe and Claiborne. They told rebellious West Floridians how to arrange for American intervention, and their plan succeeded admirably. The same tactic was used in East Florida, but without success; that province was not ripe for revolt, even with arms provided by the United States. Monroe seems to have consciously allowed Andrew Jackson to seize much of East Florida during the Seminole War, apparently as part of an effort to convince Spain to relinquish the Floridas in the treaty negotiations then under way.

The capacity of subordinate executive officers to affect the nation's foreign relations became an increasingly important factor after 1809. As the United States expanded its diplomatic and naval activities, at a time when communications were slow and unreliable, individual diplomats, agents and officers were called upon to make on-the-spot decisions that actually or potentially involved the use of force. Principles were established to insure civilian supremacy, and a chain of command in which the President's word was final. But the actual control imposed on officers in the field was lax. This was due in part to the difficulty of communicating and of anticipating problems in advance, the undesirability of issuing orders that might prove too restrictive, and the frequently invoked notion that, absent specific guidance, subordinates should act in the nation's best interests, on their own responsibility. In addition, however, Madison, and especially Monroe, appear to have encouraged and exploited unilateral actions by subordinates. In several key situations, they selected aggressive agents, sympathetic to administration policy, issued unnecessarily vague instructions, failed to respond to letters indicating that constitutionally questionable actions were contemplated, and suppressed information that would have revealed their conduct. In this manner, the agents selected in effect exercised a sort of executive prerogative, acting on their own responsibility, but in situations that could not tenably be characterized as emergencies requiring unilateral executive action. At the same time the Presidents involved were able to encourage activities to be undertaken that exceeded the bounds of behavior by which they publicly purported to be governed, and to place responsibility for those activities upon others.

References

CHAPTER 1
THE CONSTITUTION AND
ITS BACKGROUND

1. Many of these questions have been raised or resolved in the courts in recent years. In United States v. Nixon, 418 U.S. 683 (1974), a unanimous Supreme Court refused to allow the President to decide unilaterally what information to submit in response to a judicial subpoena. The issue of impoundment of funds appropriated by Congress has also stimulated litigation. See New York v. Train, 420 U.S. 35 (1975) (the Impoundment Control Act does not permit allotment of less than entire amounts authorized to be appropriated). *See,* on the impoundment issue, *e.g.,* Pennsylvania v. Lynn, 501 F.2d 848 (D.C. Cir. 1974); Pennsylvania v. Weinberger, 367 F.Supp. 1378 (D.D.C. 1973). The Vietnam war engendered a flurry of activity in the courts: Holtzman v. Schlesinger, 484 F.2d 1307 (2d Cir. 1973), *cert. denied,* 416 U.S. 936 (1974) (reversing district court decision that there was not sufficient authorization to warrant Cambodia bombings, on ground that issue presented a political question); Orlando v. Laird, 443 F.2d 1039 (2d Cir. 1971) *cert. denied,* 404 U.S. 869 (1971) (Gulf of Tonkin Resolution held sufficient authorization); Da Costa v. Laird, 471 F.2d 1146 (2d Cir. 1973) (repeal of Tonkin Resolution did not withdraw congressional authorization implicit in other legislation).

2. *U.S. Constitution,* art. 1, sec. 1.

3. *Id.,* art. 1, sec. 2, clause 5; art. 1, sec. 3, clause 6.

4. *Id.,* art. 1, sec. 4, clause 2; art. 1, sec. 5, clauses 1, 2; art. 1, sec. 6, clause 1.

5. *Id.,* art. 1, sec. 8, clause 1.

6. *Id.,* art. 1, sec. 8, clauses 3, 10, 11.

7. *Id.,* art. 1, sec. 8, clauses 12, 13, 14, 15.

8. *Id.*, art. 1, sec. 8, clause 18.

9. *Id.*, art. 2, sec. 1, clause 1.

10. *Id.*, art. 2, sec. 2, clause 1.

11. *Id.*, art. 2, sec. 2, clause 2; art. 2, sec. 3.

12. *Id.*, art. 2, sec. 2, clause 2.

13. *Id.*, art. 2, sec. 3; art. 1, sec. 9, clause 7.

14. *Id.*, art. 2, sec. 3.

15. *Id.*, art. 1, sec. 7, clauses 1, 2.

16. *Id.*, art. 1, sec. 8, clause 11. *See* C. Lofgren, "War Making Under the Constitution," 81 *Yale L.J.* 672, 695-97, 699-700 (1972).

17. *Compare* W. Reveley, "Constitutional Allocation of the War Powers Between the President and Congress: 1787-1788," 15 *Va. J. Int'l L.* 73, 144-45 (1974).

18. See the deservedly famous concurring opinion of Justice Jackson, in Youngstown Sheet & Tube v. Sawyer, 343 U.S. 579, 634, 635-38 (1952).

19. Relatively minor restraint is imposed by the requirement that army appropriations be limited to a term of no longer than two years. Art. 1, sec. 8, clause 12.

20. *See* C. Rossiter, ed., *The Federalist Papers* 141 (No. 26, Hamilton) (1961) [hereinafter *"The Federalist"*]: "as a national sentiment, it [repugnance of standing armies] must be traced to those habits of thinking which we derive from the nation from whom the inhabitants of these States have in general sprung." Numerous references were made to English practice in the national and state conventions as well as in *The Federalist Papers. See, e.g.,* 1 *Records of the Federal Convention of 1787* at 65-66 (Wilson & Randolph) (M. Farrand, ed. 1911-37) (4 vols.) [hereinafter "Farrand, *Records*"]; *id.* 97 (Sherman); *id.* 289 (Hamilton); *id.* 391 (Butler); *id.* 398-404 (Pinckney); 2 *id.* 104 (Morris); *id.* 274 (Mason); 3 *The Debates in the Several State Conventions, on the Adoption of the Federal Constitution* 16-17 (Nicholas), 393 (Madison) (J. Elliot, ed. 1896) (5 vols.) [hereinafter "Elliot, *Debates*"]; *The Federalist* Nos. 26, 70, 83 (Hamilton); *id.* Nos. 37, 45, 56 (Madison). *See also* C. Stevens, *Sources of the Constitution of the United States* 54 n.2 (1894), which is in many respects a good book, but marred by its avid effort to tie American institutions to a "Teutonic" past.

21. 1 J. Hare, *American Constitutional Law* 146 (1889).

22. *See generally* T. Plucknett, *Taswell-Langmead's English Constitutional History* (11th ed. 1960) [hereinafter "Plucknett"]; D. Keir, *The Constitutional History of Modern Britain Since 1485* (1969) [hereinafter "Keir"]; F. Maitland, *Constitutional History of England* (1961); E. Turner, *The Cabinet Council of England in the Seventeenth and Eighteenth Centuries* (2d ed. 1932) (2 vols).

23. Keir 182.

24. *Id.* 271.

25. Charles II yielded to the right of Parliament to specify how money was to be spent. 17 *Car.* 2, c.1; Plucknett 428-29. Thus, in 1665, Parliament began to make military appropriations annually and to limit them to a year's duration to more effectively control the military establishment. *See also*, J.S. Omond,

Parliament and the Army, 1642-1904, at 30 (1933). Parliament further strengthened its control over appropriations when William and Mary were given the throne in the Declaration of Rights (1 *William & Mary,* sess. 2, c. 2 [1689]), at which time the model for the modern appropriation bill first appeared, prohibiting diversion of funds from one service to another, with severe penalties for disobedience by administrative officials.

26. G. Gibbs, "Parliament and Foreign Policy in the Age of Stanhope and Walpole," 77 *Eng. Hist. Rev.* 18, 30 (1962).

27. *Id.* 26.

28. For example, in 1678 Parliament so reduced the military appropriation that the King was forced to disband a portion of the army. The next year Parliament voted a special appropriation to be used solely to disband the army, thus imposing a veto on the "King's prerogative as commander in chief." F. Allen, *The Supreme Command in England, 1640-1780,* at 138 (1966). When James II attempted to increase the size of the standing army in the 1680s—from 6,000 to 20,000—he succeeded, without Parliament's help, to establish an army of 16,000, but he was subsequently forced to abdicate by opponents of his Catholic policies. Keir 267. *See also* Plucknett 440.

29. When Charles I, in his war against Spain, had used up even borrowed funds, he reverted to the old practice of tithing. Commons, unwilling to give him funds, responded by passing resolutions against arbitrary taxation and arbitrary imprisonment, and then sought a conference with the House of Lords which produced a joint Petition of Right to force the King to give up these practices. They eventually succeeded. J. Tanner, *English Constitutional Conflicts of the Seventeenth Century, 1603-1689,* at 62-64 (1952).

30. *See generally* Plucknett 529-38, and particularly the impeachment of the Earl of Stafford in 1640 for several reasons, including his use of the military; of the Earl of Danby in 1679 for making an offer to France of neutrality in France's war with Holland and without consulting the Council; and of the Earl of Oxford, Viscount Bolingbroke, and the Duke of Ormond in 1715, for their part in negotiating the Treaty of Utrecht. This is not to suggest that Parliament's power to impeach was untrammeled by legal precedent or principle. See C. Roberts, "The Law of Impeachment in Stuart England: A Reply to Raoul Berger," 84 *Yale L.J.* 1419 (1975).

31. The Court of Exchequer upheld this particular tax (for "ship" money from an inland town), 7 to 5, on the ground that the King was exercising his power to defend the nation. 13 *Car.* 1 (1637).

32. Charles I dismissed Parliament when they refused to finance his war with Spain. To obtain money for forces, he made loans on the Privy Seals. Tanner, *supra* note 29, at 26.

33. Turner concludes that, even at the zenith of its effort to control foreign relations, Parliament was compelled to leave "the actual direction of foreign affairs . . . in other hands." E. Turner, "Parliament and Foreign Affairs," 34 *Eng. Hist. Rev.* 172, 197 (1919).

34. Even William Pitt, on whom Raoul Berger relies after noting Pitt was "destined to be a great Prime Minister," said he refused as Prime Minister in

1766 to reveal to Commons the advice he had given the King concerning relations with Spain during the last year. He made only the conclusory assertion that
he had not advised violations of the laws of nations. Letter to Lady Chatham,
Jan. 15, 1766, in 2 *Correspondence of William Pitt, Earl of Chatham* 363 n.1,
371 n.1 (W. Taylor, ed. 1838). *See* R. Berger, *Executive Privilege: A Constitutional Myth* 29 (1974).

35. *See, e.g.*, Sir Robert Walpole's letter of Aug. 17, 1736 to his brother
Horatio, in 2 Turner, *supra* note 22, at 393.

36. A striking example is Bolingbroke's effort to present Parliament with a
completed treaty to prevent legislative interference. Turner, *supra* note 33, at
186-87. Royal marriages were frequently kept secret until finalized. 1 Turner,
supra note 22, at 63. *See also* Lord Halifax's advice to Charles II to begin fighting France, and then ask Parliament for money, so as to avoid its refusal. Turner, *supra* note 33, at 191.

37. On the meaning of the King's power of "advice and consent" see the
able but somewhat overdrawn treatment in Arthur Bestor, "Separation of Powers
in the Domain of Foreign Affairs," 5 *Seton Hall L. Rev.* 527, 541-47 (1974).

38. For example, British courts, in the absence of legislation, invalidated seizures of papers pursuant to so-called "general warrants." *E.g.*, Wilkes v. Wood,
98 *Eng. Rep.* 489 (Com. Pl. 1763). But Parliament could and did authorize such
seizures despite these decisions. *See generally* Lasson, *The History and Development of the Fourth Amendment to the United States Constitution* 25-30
(1937). *Compare* Lord Coke's famous dictum in "Dr. Bonham's Case," 77
Eng. Rep. 638, 646 (K.B. 1610).

39. Bestor, *supra* note 37, at 530-34.

40. 21 *Annals of Congress* 1735-36 (1853) (responding to Timothy Pitkin
of Connecticut) [hereinafter *"Annals"*].

41. This concept, almost Montesquieu's exact words in *The Spirit of the
Laws*, Bk. 11, ch. 6, at 151 (1748, 1949 ed.), echoes 1 W. Blackstone, *Com-
mentaries on the Laws of England* 50-51 (17th ed. 1830), and J. Locke in *Of
Civil Government, Second Treatise*, Bk. 2, para. 143, at 120 (R. Kirk, ed. 1955).

The doctrine has deep historical roots, which took hold in seventeenth-
and eighteenth-century England. *See, e.g.*, "England's Birth-Right Justified
Against all Arbitrary Usurpation" (an anonymous pamphlet generally attributed
to the Leveller John Lilliburne in 1645), in 3 W. Haller, *Tracts on Liberty in
the Puritan Revolution: 1638-1647*, at 257-307 (1933); J. Locke, *Two Treatises
of Government* (P. Laslett, ed. 1964). Whether or not the doctrine of separation
of powers appears in Locke's Second Treatise has stimulated some academic
controversy. *See generally*, W. Gwyn, "The Meaning of the Separation of Powers," 9 *Tulane Studies in Poli. Sci.* 37 (1965).

42. Keir 295.

43. *See* E. Barber, *The Political Thought of Plato and Aristotle* 483 (1906);
1 *The Histories of Polybius* 467-74 (E. Schuckburgh, ed. and trans. 1889)
(both being discussions of the origins of the mixed constitution, which provided for government with a checks-and-balance system based on monarchy and
social estates); C. Weston, *English Constitutional Theory and the House of*

Lords (1965) (presenting a description of mixed government in English political life).

44. B. Bailyn, *The Origins of American Politics* 20-23 (Vintage ed. 1970). The statement to which the doctrine is traced is Charles I's response to the Nineteen Propositions of the Long Parliament, in C. Weston, "Beginnings of the Classical Theory of the English Constitution," 100 *Proc. of Am. Philo. Soc.* 133, 144 (April 1956).

45. *See* 1 Blackstone *supra* note 41, at 242-43; E. Wade and G. Phillips, *Constitutional Law* 171, 185 (8th ed. 1970).

46. Locke, *supra* note 41, ch. 14, para. 150-66; ch. 11, para. 134.

47. E. Corwin, *The President: Office and Powers* 8 (1957). *Compare* A. Schlesinger, Jr., *The Imperial Presidency* 7-10 (1973).

48. Keir 352; E. Greene, *The Provincial Governor in the English Colonies in North America* 15-16 (1907).

49. Andrew C. McLaughlin, *A Constitutional History of the United States* 25-82 (student ed. 1935), remains a superb account. *See generally* the collection of charters and grants in W. MacDonald, ed., *Select Charters and Other Documents Illustrative of American History, 1606-1775*, at 7, 29, 144, 158 (1899); and in *Federal and State Constitutions, Colonial Charters . . . of the United States* (F. Thorpe, ed. 1909). The royal governor, as subordinate officer of the Crown, had no power to declare war except for the proviso that he might, on the advice of his council, declare war against the Indians in case of emergency. Greene, *The Provincial Governor, supra* note 48, at 107.

50. Bailyn, *supra* note 44, at 106. *See generally* O. Dickerson, *American Colonial Government, 1696-1765*, at 209-17 (1962); F. Stone, "Plans for the Union of the British Colonies of North America, 1643-1776," in 2 *History of the Celebration of the One Hundredth Anniversay of the Promulgation of the Constitution of the United States* 448 (H. Carson, ed., 1889).

51. For example, James Otis said in 1764: "See here the grandeur of the British Constitution! See the wisdom of our ancestors! The supreme legislative, and the supreme executive, are a perpetual check and balance to each other." Quoted in D. Hutchinson, *Foundations of the Constitution* 23 (1928). Probably the leading exponent of these theories was John Adams. *See* C. Walsh, *The Political Science of John Adams* (1969). *See also* G. Wood, *The Creation of the American Republic, 1776-1787*, at 201 (1969); J. Reid, " 'In Our Contracted Sphere': The Constitutional Contract, The Stamp Act Crisis, and the Coming of the American Revolution," 76 *Colum. L. Rev.* 21 (1976).

52. G. Wood, *supra* at 153-54; G. Wood, ed., *The Confederation and the Constitution* 15 (1973).

53. C. Thach, *Creation of the Presidency 1775-89*, at 28 (1923) [hereinafter "Thach"].

54. In Pennsylvania, instead of a single executive, a popularly elected Supreme Executive Council served for three-year terms. The legislature (Assembly) was unicameral, elected annually, and possessed all the powers of government, accountable only to the Council of Censors and the people. A popularly elected Council of Censors was given power to determine "whether the Constitution

has been preserved inviolate in every part and whether the Legislature and Executive Branches of Government have performed their duty as Guardian of the People, or assumed to themselves, or exercised other or greater powers than they are entitled to by the Constitution," *Penn. Const.* §47 (1776), but their recommendations and actions were frequently overriden.

All the early constitutions, except New York's, provided for an Executive Council to advise the Governor in the execution of his functions. Council members were chosen by legislators, except in New Jersey and South Carolina, where members of the council were elected from geographic subdivisions and appear to have been similar to state senators, and in Pennsylvania where they were directly elected at large. They exercised various limiting "advice and consent" functions, other than in Massachusetts, where their advice was not binding on the Governor. *Fundamental Orders of Connecticut* 1 (1638); *Conn. Charter* (1776), para. 1; *Dela. Const.* (1776), arts. 8, 9; *Ga. Const.* (1776), arts. 19, 20, 21; *Md. Const.* (1776), art. 26; *Mass. Const.* (1780), art. 45; *N.H. Const.* (1784), pt. 2, art. 4; *N.J. Const.* (1776), art. 4, 8; *N.C. Const.* (1776), art. 14; *Penn. Const.* (1776) §3, 19, 20; *S.C. Const.* (1776), art. 5, 9, 30; *Vt. Const.* (1777), §§3, 14, 17; *Va. Const.* (1776), §§7, 9, 11, 12. These constitutions are collected and alphabetically arranged in F. Thorpe, *The Federal and State Constitutions* (1909) (7 vols.).

55. The executive was chosen directly by the legislature in ten states. *Dela. Const.* (1776), art. 7; *Ga. Const.* (1777), art. 23; *Md. Const.* (1776), art. 25; *N.J. Const.* (1776), art. 7; *N.C. Const.* (1776), art. 15; *Penn. Const.* (1776), §19; *S.C. Const.* (1776), §3; *Vt. Const.* (1777), ch. 2, §17; *Va. Const.* (1776), art. 7. In New Hampshire (1776), the legislature chosen a nine-man Council, which in turn selected the "President." In Massachusetts the executive was directly elected, unless one candidate failed to obtain a majority of votes at the polls, in which case the legislature would elect one of the top four contenders. *Mass. Const.* (1780), ch. II, §1, art. III. In New York the executive was directly elected. *N.Y. Const.* (1777), art. 17.

Ten states selected their governor annually; South Carolina's had a two-year term; and those of Delaware and New York, a three-year term. Seven states had limits on the length of time a governor could serve during given periods. The most common was three years, with provisions that one could not again be eligible for some interval. *Dela. Const.* (1776), art. 7; *Md. Const.* (1776), XXXI; *Penn. Const.* (1776), §19; *Va. Const.* (1776), para. 9; *N.C. Const.* (1776), XV; *N.H. Const.* (1784), pt. 2; *N.J. Const.* (1776), art. 7; *N.Y. Const.* (1777), art. 17. *Ga. Const.* (1777), art. 19, limited its governor to one year in any three and South Carolina to one two-year term, followed by four years, *S.C. Const.* (1778), art. 6.

The Massachusetts Constitution, for example, made its popularly elected Governor commander-in-chief of the state's armed forces, with broad powers to direct the military "for the special defence and safety of the Commonwealth." *Mass Const.* (1780), ch. II, §1, art. VII. But all his powers were "to be exercised agreeably to the rules and regulations of the Constitution, and the laws of the land, and not otherwise." *Id.* ch. II, § 1, art. VII. The Virginia Constitution provided that its governor "shall, with the advice of a Council of State, exercise the executive powers of government," but only "according to the laws of this Commonwealth;" he was "not, under any pretence, to exercise any power or prerogative, by virtue of any law, statute or custom of England." *Va. Const.* (1776), art. 7. *See generally* Thorpe, *supra* note 54.

56. Thach 36-37.

57. *See generally* McLaughlin, *supra* note 49, at 106-17, 137-47; C. Rossiter, *1787: The Grand Convention* 35-45 (1968).

58. A. McLaughlin, "The Confederate Period and the Federal Convention," in E. Latham, ed., *The Declaration of Independence and the Constitution* 23 (rev. ed. 1956).

59. G. Wood, *supra* note 51, at 450.

60. 2 *Writings of James Madison* 54 n. 1 (G. Hunt, ed. 1901). [hereinafter *"Madison Writings* (Hunt)"].

61. G. Wood, *supra* note 51, at 452.

62. *Id.*, 199, 453.

63. Thach 37-38.

64. For example, writing to Clinton from the turmoil of Pennsylvania in October 1779, John Jay praised the New York system, urging "the Preservation of its vigor and Reputation." Thach 54 n. 78.

65. For discussion of earlier efforts to implement plans, see William MacDonald, ed., *Select Charters and Other Documents Illustrative of American History, 1606-1775*, at 96 (1899); E. Greene, *The Provincial Governor in the English Colonies of North America* 103 (1907); F. Stone, "Plans for the Union of the British Colonies of North America, 1643-1776," 2 *History of the Celebration of the One Hundredth Anniversary of the Constitution* 448 (1889); R. Newbold, *Albany Congress and Plan of Union of 1754*, at 135 (1955).

66. A plan proposed by Joseph Galloway was rejected, 6 colonies to 5. U.S. Library of Congress, 1 *Journals of the Continental Congress 1774-1789*, at 51 (W. Ford, ed. 1904-37) (34 vols.) [hereinafter *"JCC"*]. It would have created a "President General" appointed by the Crown, who would govern (and make war) "by and with the advice of the Grand Council," consisting of representatives of the colonial assemblies. *Id.* 50; J. Boyd, *Joseph Galloway's Plan to Preserve the British Empire, 1774-1788* (1941).

67. 1 *JCC* 63-73, 115-22.

68. M. Jensen, "The Articles of Confederation," in Latham, *supra* note 58, at 15-17.

69. Congress called for Continental soldiers (11 *JCC* 588), and frequently requested the states to call out their militia in support of the war effort (11 *JCC* 588; 13 *JCC* 469-71; 14 *JCC* 546; 16 *JCC* 225; 17 *JCC* 523; 18 *JCC* 894-95). Congress ordered the expenditure of money from the treasury to defray the cost of the many aspects of the war effort (11 *JCC* 588; 13 *JCC* 469-71; 14 *JCC* 546; 17 *JCC* 437, 538-42, 639; 19 *JCC* 177, 179, 370; 21 *JCC* 948-51, 974, 1031, 1166), and often requested supplies and money from the states to be paid into the common treasury (11 *JCC* 1023; 16 *JCC* 230-31).

70. Such committees were frequently used to consult with General Washington and other colonial leaders. *See, e.g.*, 2 *JCC* 265, 317. A committee was used to draw up instructions for an interim governing committee to direct

governmental affairs while Congress was adjourned in the spring of 1776 (3 *JCC* 427). Another drafted the Declaration of Independence (5 *JCC* 431).

71. 4 *JCC* 243-46; 5 *JCC* 434-35, 631; 6 *JCC* 1041; 7 *JCC* 274.

72. *See* 14 *JCC* 519.

73. Congress controlled the treaty-making process, corresponded directly with foreign ministers, and formally received them. 11 *JCC* 419, 446, 457; 13 *JCC* 180, 184, 219, 272; 14 *JCC* 818, 827. Treaties were made with Indian tribes beginning the same year (12 *JCC* 986), but here "commissioners" were appointed to negotiate, usually "in concurrence with the Commander-in-Chief" (14 *JCC* 600). When France sent its first minister to the United States—Conrad Alexandre Gerard de Reyneval—Congress received him with much ceremony (11 *JCC* 753-57). The power to receive ministers was not, however, the mere formality many writers have assumed. Considerable haggling occurred over the reply to Gerard's speech, and strenuous debate erupted over what should be said in 1779 to Gerard's successor, Chevalier La Luzerne. *See* 11 *JCC* 698, 707, 722, 726; 15 *JCC* 1250.

74. 11 *JCC* 505; 13 *JCC* 219, 236, 363 (Indian Affairs), 455-57; 14 *JCC* 512, 533, 715.

75. 13 *JCC* 380-81.

76. 3 *JCC* 265, 270, 317, 339, 351, 446-52, 395; 4 *JCC* 92-94, 196, 201-204, 215-18, 842-43; 10 *JCC* 40, 294; 13 *JCC* 92, 132-43, 251, 298-99; 16 *JCC* 354.

77. When Artemas Ward was appointed general and commander-in-chief, he was instructed "to observe and follow such Orders and Instructions as you shall from Time to Time receive for this or any future Congress. . . ." C. Martyn, *Life of Artemas Ward* 108 (1921). He commanded the troops at Bunker Hill, but even there the Committee of Safety participated in planning the disposition of troops. *Id.* 116-17, 126. After George Washington was made commander-in-chief on June 15, 1775, he was instructed to repel "every hostile invasion" and was "vested with full power and authority to act as you shall think for the good and welfare of the service"; but he was to regulate his conduct by the rules of war "and punctually to observe and follow such orders and directions, from time to time, as you shall receive from this or a future Congress . . . or a committee of Congress, for that purpose appointed." 2 *JCC* 91, 96. On June 20, however, further orders to Washington included several specific instructions, but ended (*id.* 101):

> And whereas all particulars cannot be foreseen, nor positive instructions for such emergencies so before hand given but that many things must be left to your prudent and discreet management, as occurrences may arise upon the place, or from time to time fall out, you are therefore upon all such accidents or any occasions that may happen, to use your best circumspection and (advising with your council of war) to order and dispose of the said Army under your command as may be most advantageous for the obtaining the end for which these forces have been raised, making it your special care in discharge of the great trust committed unto you, that the liberties of America receive no detriment.

78. Congress gave Washington "until the Congress shall otherwise order

. . . full power to order and direct all things relative to the department, and to the operation of the war." 6 *JCC* 1027. On March 26, 1778, Congress wrote to Washington that it had never intended that he should be bound by a vote of his council of war when he disagreed with the majority. 7 *JCC* 196-97. Congress's orders to Washington generally included wording such as: "as he shall judge proper," or "consistent with the present state of the . . . army." 11 *JCC* 507, 684; 12 *JCC* 890. *See also* 11 *JCC* 417, 466.

79. In October 1775, for example, Washington sought Congress's advice as to whether troops from his army or local forces should be dispatched to meet British troops expected to land in the middle colonies. 4 *Writings of George Washington* 25 (Fitzpatrick, ed. 1931-44) [hereinafter "*Washington Writings* (Fitzpatrick)"]. In a letter of January 1776, Washington asked John Adams whether it was within his—Washington's—power to send General Lee to New York. *Id.* 220. In another letter of January 1776 to the president of Congress, Washington expressed concern that he had acted without express direction in recommending to the Governors of Massachusetts, Connecticut and New Hampshire that each raise a regiment to be sent to the aid of General Schuyler in Canada. *Id.* 259. In May 1776, having moved his army to New York after the evacuation of the British from Boston, Washington, in a letter to the president of Congress, wrote: "But if the Congress from their knowledge, information, or believe [*sic*] think it best for the general good of the Service, that I should go to the Northward, or elsewhere, they are convinced, I hope, that they have nothing more to do than signify their Commands." 5 *id.* 20. In the fall of 1776, when the campaign in and around New York was going badly, Washington, despite a firm belief that New York should be destroyed in the event abandonment became necessary, left that decision to Congress, which ultimately decided against destruction. *See* D. Freeman, 4 *George Washington* (1951); 6 *Washington Writings* (Fitzpatrick) 6-7.

80. For example, he successfully resisted Congress's attempt to appropriate his troops to build defenses to protect Philadelphia from threatened attack. 4 Freeman 496. He disapproved Congress's planned expedition against Detroit and the country of the Seneca Indians. 12 *Washington Writings* (Fitzpatrick) 261. He advised Congress against its plan for a joint American-French invasion of Canada. 13 *id.* 223.

81. 4 Freeman *supra* note 79, at 335; 6 *Washington Writings* (Fitzpatrick) 461, 463-64; 6 *JCC* 1043.

82. Letters of May 14 and May 31, 1780, 18 *Washington Writings* (Fitzpatrick) 356-57, 453. A Committee at Headquarters was appointed, and developed into a sympathetic ally of Washington. *See* 16 *JCC* 362; 17 *JCC* 438-39.

83. 2 H. Syrett & J. Cooke, eds., *The Papers of Alexander Hamilton* 400-407 (1961).

84. *See* the description of how Congress lost the valuable services of G.W. Trumbull as Commissary General because they refused to give him authority to remove his subordinates. Thach 65-67.

85. Cited in 1 G. Bancroft, *A History of the Formation of the Constitution of the United States of America* (1882); *see* C. Rossiter, *Alexander Hamilton and the Constitution* 34-36 (1964).

86. *Articles of Confederation*, arts. I, II, IX.

87. C. Warren, "Fears of Disunion," in E. Latham, ed., *The Declaration of Independence and the Constitution* 92, 94 (1956).

88. The newly created office of Secretary of Foreign Affairs, held first by Robert Livingston, began in 1781 to handle, or to act as conduit for, most correspondence between the United States and foreign governments. Committees also increased their activities and influence. After John Jay replaced Livingston in May 1784, he stepped up the activities of his office, though his effort to obtain binding discretion to "forbear" use of the Mississippi in exchange for a commercial treaty with Spain ultimately failed. 20 *JCC* 651–54; 23 *JCC* 663, 751; 24 *JCC* 3, 5; 25 *JCC* 779, 821; E. Burnett, *Continental Congress* 588 (1964); Bestor, *supra* note 37 at 614–19.

89. The powers of the Secretary of War were increased and spelled out in January 1785, and included, for example, appointment and removal "at pleasure [of] all persons employed by him." 28 *JCC* 22. Henry Knox was elected to fill the vacant position on March 18, 1785, and on June 15, 1786, resolutions were introduced once again to increase his powers, this time in the area of supplies. 30 *JCC* 344 (no vote recorded). The Secretary was also directed to take charge of federal troops in 1787, and to place them in positions to give effective protection from Indian incursions to frontier inhabitants in Pennsylvania and Virginia. 33 *JCC* 454; 37, 94, 108, 236, 602.

90. *See, e.g.,* J. Flexner, *George Washington in the American Revolution (1775–1783)*, at 370, 409 (1967).

91. Butler to James Iredell, April 5, 1782, in 2 G. McRee, ed., *Life and Correspondence of James Iredell* 9–10 (1857–58) (2 vols.).

92. He wrote to Hamilton on March 4, 1783 that "unless Congress have powers competent to all *general purposes*, that the distresses we have encountered, the expense we have incurred, and the blood we have spilt in the course of an Eight years war, will avail us nothing." 26 *Washington Writings* (Fitzpatrick) 188. *See also* his letter to Hamilton of March 31, 1783, *id.* 277. In a circular to the States in June 1783 he wrote (*id.* 495):

> That the inefficiency of measures, arising from the want of an adequate authority in the Supreme Power, from a partial compliance with the Requisitions of Congress in some of the States, and from a failure of punctuality in others, while it tended to damp the zeal of those which were more willing to exert themselves; served also to accumulate the expences of the War, and to frustrate the best concerted Plans, and that the discouragement occasioned by the complicated difficulties and embarrassments, in which our affairs were, by this means involved, would have long ago produced the dissolution of any Army, less patient, less virtuous and less persevering, than that which I have had the honor to command.

Washington also expressed the view that "the public interest might be benefitted, if the Commander-in-Chief of the Army was let more into the political and pecuniary state of our Affairs than he is." The wisdom of military measures depended upon knowledge of all relevant factors, he noted, and the commander-in-chief should possess the necessary information, presumably to enable him to exercise military authority more intelligently. Letter to Hamilton, Mar. 4, 1783, *id.* 185.

93. For a good, brief summary, see C. Warren, *supra* note 87, at 94–98. A recent treatment of the impact of military inadequacies on the attitudes of many early leaders in R. Kohn, *Eagle and Sword: The Federalists and the Creation of the Military Establishment in America, 1783–1802*, at 9–13 (1975).

94. Hamilton wrote a highly critical report, submitted to Congress on July 1, 1783. 24 *JCC* 412–20.

95. See E. James Ferguson, "The Nationalists of 1781–1783 and the Economic Interpretation of the Constitution," in G. Wood, *supra* note 52, at 1–44, suggesting that the Federalists refused to allow the states to assume the national debt so as to preserve it as an argument for additional national power.

96. R. Morris, ed., *Encyclopedia of American History* 136 (1976).

97. *Articles of Confederation*, art. IX. *See* 25 *JCC* 591, 763; 31 *JCC* 802; 32 *JCC* 124. C. Rossiter, *supra* note 57, at 44; M. Farrand, *The Framing of the Constitution* 46 (1913).

98. Warren, *supra* note 93, at 94–104.

99. A committee appointed to consider the Pennsylvania request reported that acts in defiance of authority had occurred, but concluded that, since the number of rioters was small enough for the state to suppress by calling out a small part of its militia, "the interference of the United States cannot with propriety be requested." The committee noted, however, that a body of continental troops would soon march through the vicinity, and since Pennsylvania had no troops in the area, "it may not be improper for the said Continental troops to halt a short time to be employed if necessary in quelling the disturbances in Luzerne until the State can provide troops for that purpose." Congress adopted the committee's proposal and ordered the Continental troops to be halted in the area for no more than two weeks. Two weeks later, Congress received a letter from the Governor of Pennsylvania thanking Congress, and informing them that, since the insurgency had been quieted, there was no further need for Continental troops. 32 *JCC* 353–54, 408. *See also* Kohn, *supra* note 93, at 17–53, 73–88.

100. "[T]he present System neither has nor deserves advocates," wrote James Madison on February 24, 1787, "and if some strong props are not applied, will quickly tumble to the ground." Letter to Edmund Pendleton, 2 *Madison Writings supra* note 60, at 316, 318–19.

101. 3 Farrand, *Records*.

102. 1 *id.* 2, 649.

103. *Id.* 19.

104. *Id.* 20–21.

105. *Id.* 23. See the reconstructed version of this plan in 3 *id.* 604–609.

106. *Id.* 62–66 (Madison's notes).

107. He said that "executive powers ex vi termini, do not include the Rights of war & peace." John Rutledge announced that he was opposed to giving the executive "the power of war and peace." *Id.* 70 (King's Notes), 65 (Madison's notes).

108. *Id.* 67.

109. *Id.* 65, 68, 80, 97–98, 119.

110. *Id.* 236; 65 (Rutledge); 70 (Madison); *compare id.* 66 (Randolph strenu-

ously objecting). Another specific area of authority was moved toward executive control in early June. Pierce Butler said he had witnessed in Holland the danger of "a plurality of military heads." *Id.* 89. Elbridge Gerry "was at a loss to discover the policy of three members for the Executive. It wd. be extremely inconvenient in many instances, particularly in military matters, whether relating to the militia, an army, or a navy. It would be a general with three heads." *Id.* 97.

111. *Id.* 236.

112. *Id.* 65. He was for an executive "accountable to the Legislature only." Gunning Bedford expressed the same view, being "opposed to every check on the Legislature . . . , [who] were the best judge of what was for [the people's] interest. . . ." *Id.* 100–101.

113. *Id.* 242–45 (Madison's notes).

114. *Id.* 244, 282, 291–92, 297–99 (Yates), 300, 288 (Madison). At least nine versions of Hamilton's speech exist, but the one generally used is that copied by Madison and corrected afterward by Hamilton. *See* J. Franklin Jameson, "Studies in the History of the Federal Convention of 1787," 1 *Amer. Hist. Assn. Annual Report for 1902*, at 87, 144–49. *See also* Bestor, *supra* note 37, at 588 n.221.

115. 1 Farrand, *Records* 313 (Journal).

116. *Id.* 376–77.

117. *Id.* 52, 80, 91; 2 *id.* 95, 101.

118. 2 *id.* 56, 62. They were joined by King, Morris, Patterson, Ellsworth and Gerry. *Id.* 55–58, 69.

119. *Id.* 69–70. Bestor attributes this action to the Convention's "lack of interest in defining a role for the executive in military and diplomatic matters," and finds this "in itself . . . a refutation of the view that the framers were determined to create a powerful presidency for the purpose of giving it primary responsibility for foreign affairs." Bestor, *supra* note 37, at 590–91. The Convention most likely went no further in defining executive powers at this early stage because they wanted to let the committee propose some overall plan with a greater chance of adoption than isolated proposals.

120. *Id.* 134.

121. *Id.* 177 (Madison's notes), 171.

122. *See* Thach at 115–19. *Compare* Bestor, *supra* note 37, at 599–601.

123. 2 Farrand, *Records* 169–73, 182.

124. Madison and Rutledge moved "that each House shall keep a journal of its proceedings, & (shall) publish the same from time to time; except such (part) of the proceedings of the Senate, when acting not in its Legislative capacity as may (be judged by) that House (to) require secrecy." Mercer objected, hoping that powers other than legislative would not be given the Senate. *Id.* 259.

125. *Id.* 275, 279.

126. *Id.* 297–98. Wilson reiterated the need for a strong executive to prevent legislative tyranny. *Id.* 300–301.

127. *Id.* 297.

128. *Id.* 318.

129. *Id.* 318–19.

130. The records create uncertainty as to what transpired on the votes. Madison's Journal, later "corrected," records that one vote was taken and the Madison-Gerry amendment carried by a vote of seven states to two. *Id.* 319. Then, after King's argument, Madison records that Oliver Ellsworth changed his position, Connecticut changed its vote, and the final tally was eight states to one. *Id.* 313 (Journal). But the official journal of the Convention records that the Madison-Gerry amendment was voted on twice. On the first vote it was defeated, four states to five. *Id.* 313 (Journal). It may be that King made his argument after the first ballot (#313), and changed more minds than Ellsworth's, resulting in the second vote (#314), approving the change, eight to one. *Id.* 314. See Bestor, *supra* note 37, at 609; W. Reveley, "Constitutional Allocation of the War Powers Between the President and Congress: 1787-1788," 15 *Va. J. Int'l. L.* 73, 106 (1974). Butler later "moved to give the Legislative power of peace, as they were to have that of war." Gerry seconded the motion, contending that the Senate alone was more likely to be corrupted or to give up part of the nation. But the motion failed, ten to zero. *Id.*

131. R. Berger, *Executive Privilege: A Constitutional Myth* 66-67 (1974). See Bestor, *supra* note 37 at 605-10, for an excellent analysis, but one that goes too far in contending that the alternative was "simply one example of a process of textual refinement. . . ." *Id.* 609. The change was definitely intended to expand executive authority beyond the committee's draft in the two respects noted in text.

132. 2 Farrand, *Records* 326, 328.

133. *Id.* 53-54.

134. *Id.* 285, 329.

135. *Id.* Gerry and others also objected to including the Chief Justice on the council. *See* Bestor, *supra* note 37, at 648 n.444.

136. 2 Farrand, *Records* 342-43; *see* Reveley, *supra* note 17, at 109.

137. *Id.* 344.

138. *Id.* 367.

139. The Virginia Plan contained a resolution creating a "council of revision" composed of "the Executive and a convenient number of the National Judiciary" with "authority to examine every act of the National Legislature" and veto it, subject to reenactment by the legislature. 1 *id.* 21. On June 1, Randolph, while advancing arguments opposed to a single executive, "doubted whether even a Council would be sufficient to check the improper views of an ambitious man." *Id.* 74. Sherman urged a "Council of advice, without which the first magistrate could not act." *Id.* 97. Franklin moved for a council appointed by the House or Senate which "would not only be a check on a bad President but be a relief to a good one." 2 *id.* 542. Mercer proposed a council of members of both houses of the legislature. "Without such an influence," he said, "the war will be between the aristocracy and the people." Mercer wished it to be "between the aristocracy and the Executive. Nothing else can protect the people against those speculating Legislatures which are now plundering them throughout the U. States." *Id.* 285.

140. *Id.* 495, 542. Franklin, Wilson, and Dickinson all continued to argue in favor of a council.

141. *Id.* 183.

142. On August 15, Mercer urged "that the Senate ought not to have the power of treaties. This power belonged to the Executive department." *Id.* 297. Wilson introduced a motion to include the House in the treaty-making function, which was defeated 1-10. *Id.* 538.

143. *Id.* 392. *Compare* Bestor, *supra* note 37 at 635. Among the reasons given against involving the House was the inconvenience this would cause in treaty-making. Mr. Gorham pointed out that "Many . . . disadvantages must be experienced if treaties of peace and all negociations [*sic*] are to be previously ratified —and if not previously, the Ministers would be at a loss how to proceed. . . . American Ministers must go abroad not instructed by the same authority which is to ratify their proceedings." 2 Farrand, *Records* 392.

144. *Id.* 495.

145. *Id.* 538 (Madison's notes).

146. *Id.* 540-41.

147. *Id.*

148. *Id.* 540. *Accord, id.* 549 (Gorham).

149. *See* Bestor, *supra* note 37 at 655-56, whose analysis at 656-57 appears simply to represent his wish that the committee had not acted as it did.

150. 2 Farrand, *Records* 362.

151. *Id.* 426.

152. *Id.* 402-404, 494-95, 572-73. The most important change substituted the House for the Senate in resolving elections where no individual obtained a majority, with the members of each state having one vote.

153. *See* Morris to H.W. Livingston, Dec. 4, 1803, in 3 *id.* 404, explaining how he had phrased the article on admission of new states to confine them to the then existing territorial limits. *See also* Morris to Pickering, Dec. 22, 1814, in 2 *id.* 419; Thach 138-39.

154. During the House debate on the Jay Treaty in March 1796, Albert Gallatin of Pennsylvania challenged the "doctrine . . . that the opinions and constructions of those persons who had framed and proposed the Constitution, opinions given in private, constructions unknown to the people when they drafted the instrument, should, after a lapse of eight years, be appealed to, in order to countenance the doctrine of some gentlemen." He said that "[t]he intention of a legislature who pass a law may perhaps be, though with caution, resorted to, in order to conserve the law; but would any person recur to the intention, opinion, and private construction, of the clerk who might have been employed to draft the bill?" 5 *Annals* 701-702, 734. *See also id.* 775 (Madison).

155. Charles Beard's collection of statements made by various convention participants shows the extensive support that existed for checking what many perceived as legislative excesses. "An Economic Interpretation of the Constitution," in Latham, *supra* note 58, at 72-87.

156. *See, e.g.,* O. Libby, "The Geographical Distribution of the Vote of the Thirteen States on the Federal Constitution, 1787-88" 1 *Bull. U. Wis.—Ec., Poli. Sci. & Hist. Ser.* 1, 99 (1894); M. Farrand, *The Framing of the Constitution* 191-94 (1913). Madison's justification is in *The Federalist* No. 40, where even he concedes that the recommendation that the new government begin after nine states had ratified exceeded the delegates's authority. *The Federalist* 251.

157. J. Main, *The Antifederalists: Critics of the Constitution, 1781-1788*, at 249 (1961).

158. The Federalist and anti-Federalist presentations are collected in P. Ford ed., *Essays on the Constitution of the United States* (1970 reprint); P. Ford, *Pamphlets on the Constitution of the United States* (1888). *See also* C. Kenyon, ed., *The Antifederalists* (1966).

159. R. Fairfield, ed., *The Federalist Papers* xi (1966).

160. C. Rossiter, *Alexander Hamilton and the Constitution* 55-56 (1964).

161. R. Fairfield, ed., *The Federalist Papers* 280 n.28 (1966); E. Corwin, *The Doctrine of Judicial Review* 44 (1914). See Reveley, *supra* note 17, at 126 n.178.

162. *See The Federalist*, No. 15, at 110, No. 21, at 138.

163. But not nearly as unimportant a question as some writers suggest. *See, e.g.*, Bestor, *supra* note 37, at 527. *Compare* C. Rossiter, *1787: The Grand Convention* (1966); M. Farrand, *The Framing of the Constitution of the United States* (1913).

164. Patrick Henry, the leading anti-Federalist in Virginia and perhaps in America, argued that in England one agency of government—the King—declared war, while a second agency—the House of Commons—provided the means of carrying it on. This division of power was absent in the Constitution. "The Congress can both declare war and carry it on, and levy your money, as long as you have a shilling to pay." 3 Elliot, *Debates* 172. Melancton Smith, a New York Delegate, also proposed dividing the war power between the federal and state governments. *Id.* 376.

165. *The Federalist*, Nos. 41, 42, at 255-71.

166. *Id.* No. 45, at 293.

167. *See, e.g.*, Ford, *Pamphlets, supra* note 158 at 341, complaining that the power to appoint belonged entirely to the executive, but was assigned in part to the Senate.

168. *The Federalist*, No. 41, at 263.

169. *Id.* Nos. 49 & 50, at 313-20.

170. *Id.* No. 15, at 152.

171. *Id.* No. 48, at 309, 312.

172. *Id.* No. 51, at 322.

173. *Id.* 322-23.

174. *Id.* No. 53, at 334.

175. *Id.* No. 58, at 359. *See also* No. 62, at 378.

176. *Id.* No. 63, at 383; No. 66, at 406.

177. *Id.* No. 69, at 422.

178. *Id.* at 416.

179. *Id.* No. 70, at 423.

180. *Id.* 424-30.

181. *Id.* No. 71, at 431-32.

182. *Id.* 432.

183. *Id.* 433, 435.

184. *Id.* No. 72, at 435-39.

185. *Id.* No. 73, at 441, 444.

186. *Id.* No. 74, at 447-49.

187. Some anti-Federalists objected to the appointing power of the President. Instead of confirmation by the Senate, George Mason of Virginia wanted presidential appointees to be confirmed by "a Privy council." Iredell defended the Senate as "a check upon the President." Another anti-Federalist, "Hampden," an anonymous Pennsylvanian, objected that "the most important and most influential portion of the executive power—*e.g.*, the appointment of all officers [was] vested in the Senate, with whom the President only acts as a nominating member." George Mason, "Objections to the Proposed Federal Constitution," in C. Kenyon, ed., *supra* note 158, at 193; Ford, *Pamphlets, supra* note 158 at 341.

188. See especially *The Federalist*, No. 77, at 459 *(Hamilton)*:

> It has been mentioned as one of the advantages to be expected from the co-operation of the Senate, in the business of appointments, that it would contribute to the stability of the administration. The consent of that body would be necessary to displace as well as to appoint. A change of the Chief Magistrate, therefore, would not occasion so violent or so general a revolution in the officers of the government as might be expected if he were the sole disposer of offices. Where a man in any station had given satisfactory evidence of his fitness for it, a new President would be restrained from attempting a change in favor of a person more agreeable to him by the apprehension that a discountenance of the Senate might frustrate the attempt, and bring some degree of discredit upon himself.

189. *Id.* No. 77, at 463.
190. *Id.* No. 69, at 420.
191. *Id.* No. 74, at 449. He also noted that its delegation for particular occasions would tend to indicate timidity or weakness and thereby embolden those to whom it would be extended. *Id.*
192. *Id.* at 392–93.
193. *Id.* No. 75, at 450, 452.
194. *Id.* 451.
195. *Id.* 453.
196. *Id.* No. 77, at 463–64.
197. 4 Elliot, *Debates* 114.
198. 2 *id.* 528. *Accord,* 4 *id.* 107 (Iredell).
199. 3 *id.* 497–98 (George Mason).
200. *The Anti-Federalist Papers* 208 (M. Borden, ed. 1965) ("Republicus").
201. *The Federalist* No. 26, at 168.
202. *Id.* No. 80, at 475–81.
203. *Id.* No. 78, at 466.
204. *See id.* No. 22, at 150.
205. *U.S. Const.* art. I, §5, cl. 3.
206. 3 Elliot, *Debates* 170.
207. *Id.* 170, 459.
208. *Id.* 331.
209. *Id.* 233.
210. 4 *id.* 73.
211. *Id.* 127.
212. *The Federalist* No. 75, at 452. Little can be confidently inferred from

state practice concerning information. Six states granted their legislatures some power to call for information from the executive. *Mass. Const.* (1780), ch. II, §III, art. V; *N.H. Const.* (1784); *N.C. Const.* (1776), art. XIV; *Va. Const.* (1776) (legislature "may call" for records of executive council proceedings); *Ga. Const.* (1777), art. XXX (provided that the executive could impose secrecy upon his officers "until leave given by the council, or when called upon by the . . . assembly . . . ," but it does not appear in later Georgia constitutions). Maryland also provided for executive council secrecy, *Md. Const.* (1776), art. XXVI, but it had the most encompassing grant of legislative information gathering power (art. X), authorizing calls for all "public or official papers and records," and granting power to "send for persons, whom they may judge necessary in the course of their inquiries, concerning affairs relating to the public interest. . . ." *See* Thorpe, *supra* note 54. *See also* C. Potts, "Power of Legislative Bodies to Punish for Contempt," 74 *U. Pa. L. Rev.* 691 (1926).

213. 4 Elliot, *Debates* 263.

214. *The Federalist* No. 64, at 392-93.

215. Evidence that the Framers used "declare" to mean "determine on" is found in Lofgren, *supra* note 16 at 685; Reveley, *supra* note 17, at 126.

216. *See* J. Porter, *International Law* 44-5 (1914); C. Van Bynkershoek, *Treatise on the Law of War* 2-3 (1810); Q. Wright, *A Study of War* 8-10 (2d ed. 1965); H. Grotius, *The Rights of War and Peace* 18 (1901 ed.).

217. *See* C. Van Bynkershoek, *supra* at 2-3; Q. Wright, *supra* at 8-10, 307, 377; H. Grotius, *supra.*

218. *See The Federalist* No. 64, at 390-96 (Jay); *id.* No. 72, at 435 (Hamilton); 4 Elliot, *Debates* 466 (Wilson); *id.* 265 (Charles Cotesworth Pinckney).

219. *Compare* Reveley, *supra* note 17, at 76-77, 147; L. Henkin, *Foreign Affairs and the Constitution* 272-76 (1972). Two especially worthwhile articles on this general theme are E. Levi, "Some Aspects of Separation of Powers," 76 *Colum. L. Rev.* 371 (1976); L. Ratner, "The Coordinated Warmaking Power—Legislative, Executive and Judicial Roles," 44 *S. Cal. L. Rev.* 461 (1971).

220. *The Federalist* No. 40, at 254-55.

221. *Id.* No. 59, at 362.

222. *Id.* No. 33, at 202.

223. See McLaughlin, *supra* note 49, at 92-98, describing Locke's importance and widespread acceptance among American leaders.

CHAPTER 2
ESTABLISHING A PATTERN OF GOVERNMENT: THE ADMINISTRATION OF GEORGE WASHINGTON

1. 25 *Annals of Congress* 352 (Dec. 9, 1812) (1853) [hereinafter *Annals*]. For biographical material, see P. Ford, *George Washington* (1896); R. Morris, *Encyclopedia of American History* 1777-78 (1976).

2. 4 R. Hildreth, *The History of the United States* viii (1851).

3. 30 *Writings of George Washington* 343-44 & n. 30 (J. Fitzpatrick, ed. 1931-44) (39 vols.) [hereinafter "*Washington Writings* (Fitzpatrick)"].

4. 1 *Annals* 384, 386-87 (White, W. Smith, Madison). Mr. Boudinot, introducing the subject, said: "If we take up the present constitution, we shall find it contemplates departments of an executive nature in aid of the President: it then remains for us to carry this intention into effect. . . ." *Id.* 383. Hamilton had stated in *The Federalist* that the President's removal of officers would be subject to the Senate's concurrence. *See* E. Corwin, *The President: Office and Powers* 88 (1957).

5. 1 *Annals* 560-61 (Ames); 393 (Goodhue); 548-49 (Lee); 393-95, 481-82, 514-21 (Madison); 478-79 (Sedgwick). *See* J. Hart, *The American Presidency in Action, 1789,* at 155-56 (1948); D. Morgan, *Congress and the Constitution: A Study of Responsibility* 49-57 (1966).

6. 1 *Annals* 387, 391-92 (Smith); 477 (Huntington).

7. *Id.* 388-89 (Bland); 391, 473 (White); 393 (Sylvester); 396 (Livermore).

8. *Id.* 392-93 (Lawrence); 607-608 (Tucker).

9. Letter to Edmund Pendleton, June 21, 1789, in 5 *The Writings of James Madison* 405-406 (G. Hunt, ed. 1901-1910) (9 vols.) [hereinafter "*Madison Writings* (Hunt)"].

10. *E.g.,* 1 *Annals* 392-93 (Lawrence).

11. *Id.* 614.

12. See § 2, Act of Aug. 7, 1789, 1 Stat. 49, 50 (Dep't of War); § 7, Act of Sept. 2, 1789, 1 Stat. 65, 67 (Dep't of Treasury). *See generally* Corwin, *supra* note 4, at 87.

13. *See* 1 *Annals* 615-16 (Page); 616 (Tucker); 624 (Gerry). "Plans," argued Elbridge Gerry (Mass.), was "but another word for bills." *Id.* 627-28. Livermore suggested that, if expertise were required, the task should be assigned to a House committee specially appointed for the purpose. *Id.* 621. Gerry also sought to minimize the proposed secretary's influence by moving that there be a 3-member Board of Treasury rather than a single head. *Id.* 400-404. This effort was defeated, after statements recollecting the ineffectiveness of boards. *Id.* 407-12.

14. *Id.* 617 (Benson); 623 (Boudinot). Fisher Ames (Mass.) said public assemblies are "from their nature . . . more incompetent to a complete investigation of accounts than a few individuals. . . ." *Id.* 619. Madison opposed both the effort to curtail the secretary's planning function and to replace the secretary with a board. *Id.* 408, 629. The only change agreed to by the House was to substitute "prepare" for "report" plans, leaving the House with power to call for the plans when it saw fit. *Id.* 628, 631.

15. Sec. 2, Act of Sept. 2, 1789, § 7, 1 Stat. 65, 67. This provision sparked considerable House debate on the proper relationship between Executive officers and Congress. *See* 1 *Annals* 615-31.

16. 1 *Annals* 939 (Sept. 21, 1789); 2 *Annals* 1962-63 (Feb. 14, 1791); *id.* 1969 (Feb. 23, 1791); 6 D. Freeman, *George Washington, A Biography* 251 (1948-57) (7 vols.) [hereinafter "Freeman, *Washington*"].

17. Second Annual Address, January 8, 1790, 1 *Annals* 969.

18. 1 *Annals* 975, January 21, 1790. See text of Knox's Militia Plan in 2 *Annals* 2087-2107. An additional plan was submitted by Knox the following year, January 24, 1791 (2 *Annals* 1879) "relative to the [protection of the] frontiers of the United States."

19. 3 *Annals* 349.

20. *Id.* 355, 572. The votes were 29-19 and 37-20 in favor of the bills. *Id.* 1343, 1364.

21. *Id.* 569.

22. *Id.* 437.

23. *Id.* 437-39.

24. The statement is not reported, but is described by Sedgwick, *id.* 439-40.

25. *Id.* 440 (Goodhue); 445 (Steele); 446 (Murray); and 448 (Ames).

26. *Id.* 439-40.

27. *Id.* 441 (Page). Page also found "unmanly and unbecoming," if true, the argument that the House would more readily accept than devise unpopular laws. *Id.* 444.

28. 3 *Annals* 448 (Findley). Findley pointed out that by letting the Secretary of Treasury plan money bills, the House adopted a role reserved for the Senate, since that body was authorized to amend, approve or disapprove money bills originating elsewhere. *Id.* 451.

29. *Id.* 442-43, 448-49.

30. *Id.* 452.

31. *Id.* 696-99.

32. *Id.* 700, 703-705.

33. *Id.* 701.

34. *Id.* 708.

35. *Id.* 722.

36. 4 *Annals* 1120-21.

37. *Id.* 1122-25.

38. *See* W. Binkley, *President and Congress* 32-37 (1947); R. Harlow, *The History of Legislative Methods in the Period Before 1825*, at 129-30, 156-57, 160-61, 226 (1917); 4 Hildreth, *supra* note 2, at 489; *The Journal of William Maclay* 246, 272, 385 (E. Maclay, ed. 1890); L. White, *The Federalists* 73, 323-24 (1961); L. White, *The Jeffersonians* 46-47 (1956); 4 *Annals* 154. *See* L. Fisher, *Presidential Spending Power* 12-14 (1975).

39. L. White, *The Federalists, supra* note 38, at 324; 1 *Annals* 894-95, 904-905.

40. *Compare* reports appearing in A.S.P., 1 *Finance* 33, 38 (1790); *id.* 82-88 (1791); *id.* 359-60 (1795); Act of Sept. 29, 1789, 1 Stat. 95; Act of Nov. 26, 1790, 1 Stat. 104; Act of Feb. 11, 1791, 1 Stat. 190. Excellent discussions of the development of the appropriations acts from 1789 to 1800 appear in L. White, *The Federalists, supra* note 38, at 326-29, and in L. Wilmerding, *The Spending Power* 20-49 (1943).

41. *E.g.*, Act of Mar. 3, 1791, 1 Stat. 214 ("for the Recognition of the Treaty with Morocco"); Act of Mar. 3, 1791, 1 Stat. 222 (for an additional regiment); Act of May 8, 1792, 1 Stat. 284 ("for certain purposes").

42. 3 *Annals* 222-23, 225, 228; 1 Stat. 226. See Harlow's analysis of the political balance, *supra* note 38, at 148-62.

43. 3 *Annals* 889-90. Act of Feb. 28, 1793, 1 Stat. 325-28.

44. *Id.* 900-903, 913, 955-60; Act of Aug. 4, 1790, 1 Stat. 138. The debates on the Giles resolutions and the circumstances that gave rise to them

are discussed in L. White, *The Federalists, supra* note 38, at 330-34, and in Wilmerding, *supra* note 40, at 24-26.

45. 4 *Annals* 248. Wilmerding says the committee was appointed "at the instance of Giles," although it was Baldwin who moved the establishment of the committee. Wilmerding, *supra* note 40, at 26.

46. The report described the practice as follows:

> It has occasionally happened, that the omission or delay of appropriations by law, renders it impossible to satisfy, in regular course, demands upon the treasury, which have been incurred pursuant to law, and satisfying of which is essential to the public credit and service.
>
> In such cases the course has been, for the Secretary of the Treasury to request informal advances by the banks, to the person to whom the payments are to be made, to be reimbursed when provision is made by law. The accounts of such advances are distinct from that [*sic*] of the Treasurer, and the advances are reimbursed, when provision is made by law, by warrants upon the Treasurer.

A.S.P., 1 *Finance* 281, 284 (May 22, 1794).

47. Act of Dec. 31, 1794, 1 Stat. 404; Act of Jan. 2, 1795, 1 Stat. 405; Act of Mar. 3, 1795, 1 Stat. 438. *See* 1 Stat. 404.

48. 5 *Annals* 253-54 (Jeremiah Smith; Theodore Sedgwick); *id.* 258-59, 264.

49. 6 *Annals* 2339-46, 2349.

50. *Id.* 2349.

51. *Id.* 2349-51, 2358-61. *See id.* 1576-77, 2322.

52. *See* 8 *Annals* 1317-18, 1544-45. *See* the examples in Wilmerding, *supra* note 40, at 44-45.

53. 7 *Annals* 15; 8 *Annals* 1874; Act of June 12, 1798, 1 Stat. 563.

54. *See* P. Donham and R. Fahey, *Congress Needs Help* 144 (1966); J. Saloma III, "The Responsible Use of Power," in *Congress and The Federal Budget* 202, 203 (M. Weidenbaum and J. Saloma III, eds. 1965).

55. *E.g.*, Act of Aug. 7, 1789, §2, 1 Stat. 53, 54 (President to select site of lighthouse near the entrance of Chesapeake Bay); Act of April 3, 1794, 1 Stat. 353 (power to alter place of holding Congress because of epidemic or other hazard).

56. *E.g.*, Act of July 1, 1790, 1 Stat. 128 (President empowered to draw not over $40,000 for foreign intercourse, with maximum salaries specified); Act of July 22, 1790, 1 Stat. 137 (power to regulate trade with Indians); Act of Mar. 1, 1793, 1 Stat. 329 (same; and power to remove citizens from Indian land); Act of Mar. 3, 1797, 1 Stat. 505 (appropriation for negotiation with Dey of Algiers); Act of Mar. 3, 1795, 1 Stat. 44 (power to export arms despite prohibition when connected with security of commercial interests and for "public puposes").

57. *E.g.*, Act of March 4, 1792, §2, 1 Stat. 241 (power to arm troops as he thinks proper); *id.* §12 (power to forbear raising or to discharge troops "consistent with the public safety"); Act of Mar. 20, 1794, 1 Stat. 345 (to direct fortification of certain ports and harbors); *id.* §2 (to employ troops as a garrison).

58. 1 *Annals* 913-14. The bill passed the House (*id.* 945-46), but was postponed by the Senate (*id.* 95, 962).

59. 2 *Annals* 1527.

60. On June 16, 1790, some Representatives sought to add authority for the Postmaster to establish roads from Massachusetts to Georgia, with the President's approbation. They noted the need for flexibility and to avoid repeated petitions of the Congress; they also pointed out that the bill already conferred broad discretion. Opponents doubted the constitutionality of the motion, and argued that they knew more than the Postmaster as to where roads should be established, and that Congress would have to approve roads even if the power sought were delegated. 2 *Annals* 1640-41, 1676-77. The final enactment of August 4, 1790 (*id.* 2295) merely continued in force the regulations of the Post Office "as they last were under the resolutions and ordinances of the late Congress." *See also id.* 2179. Congress ultimately detailed the roads it wanted terminated and established. 4 *Annals* 1431-43, Act of May 8, 1794; 6 *Annals* 2957, §§ 1 & 2, Act of March 3, 1797.

61. Sec. 1, Act of July 1, 1790, 1 Stat. 128, 129.

62. 2 *Annals* 1873-75, 1884, 1965, 1971. *See* §58, Act of Mar. 3, 1791, 1 Stat. 199, 213.

63. *E.g.*, 3 *Annals* 422-23.

64. *Id.* 552-55.

65. *Id.* 557, 574-76. *See* § 2, Act of May 2, 1792, 1 Stat. 264.

66. Among the most important works on the subject are the Memorandum of Attorney General William Rogers, in *Report of the Sub-Committee on Constitutional Rights of the Senate Comm. on the Judiciary*, 85th Cong., 2d Sess. at 140-41 (1958); Telford Taylor, *Grand Inquest: The Story of Congressional Investigations* 97-109 (1955); James R. Wiggins, *Freedom or Secrecy* 66-91 (1956); Robert Kramer and Herman Marcuse, "Executive Privilege—A Study of the Period 1953-1960," (pts. 1 & 2), 29 *Geo. Wash. L. Rev.* 623, 827 (1961); James R. Wiggins, "Lawyers as Judges of History," 75 *Mass. Hist. Soc. Proc.* 84-104 (1963); Raoul Berger, *Executive Privilege: A Constitutional Myth* (1974).

67. *E.g.*, 1 *Annals* 60 (Indian troubles); 3 *Annals* 618-19 (implementation of militia act); 4 *Annals* 39 (Indian troubles); *id.* 78 (implementation of embargo).

68. On November 7, 1792, the President sent letters to Congress concerning Spanish interference with implementation of the American treaty with the Creek Indians. 3 *Annals* 673. On December 5, 1793, the President sent information of French and British interference with American trade. 4 *Annals* 14-16.

69. 7 Freeman, *Washington* 142.

70. *See also* Morris's dispatches from England, in *Washington Presidential Papers*, LC microfilm, series 4, reel 90.

71. *See* 4 *Annals* 250.

72. 1 *Annals* 52.

73. 1 Stat. 65-66, now 5 USC §242 (Supp. V, 1963). The debate on the bill includes frequent references to an assumed power in Congress to request information. *E.g.*, 1 *Annals* 619, 628, 630.

74. *E.g.*, 4 *Annals* 412.

75. *E.g.*, 5 *Annals* 26 (Dec. 17, 1795) (Senate resolution to Secretary of War for information regarding expenses of suppressing Whiskey Rebellion);

id. 1499 (June 1, 1796) (House resolution to Secretary of Treasury for information on military expenditures since establishment "of the present government" to Jan. 1, 1796); 6 *Annals* 2111 (Feb. 9, 1797) (Secretary of Treasury "directed" by House to provide "detailed" statement of foreign-affairs expenditures).

76. The request to the Secretary of Foreign Affairs was so early that it may be unrepresentative; no similar command has been found during the Washington administration. The act requiring the Secretary of Treasury to report to Congress was apparently drafted by Hamilton, and Jefferson viewed it as an effort by Hamilton to provide himself with authority to cooperate with Congress over the President's wishes. See note 84, *infra.*

77. 1 *Annals* 1168 Feb. 8, 1790. *See* memorial at 2 *Annals* 2114-16.

78. 2 *Annals* 1464-65. No committee report appears in the *Annals of Congress*; a biographer remarks only that "the unhappy discussion was allowed to subside." E. Oberholtzer, *Robert Morris: Patriot and Financier* 258 (1903).

79. *See generally* F. Wilson, "St. Clair's Defeat," in 11 *Ohio Archaeological and Historical Publications* 30, 39-42 (1903). *See also* T. Taylor, *supra* note 66, at 17-29.

80. 3 *Annals* 490-93. William Smith opposed as unprecedented an inquiry into the conduct of officers under control of the executive, and as impliedly impeaching the President.

81. 1 Stat. 128.

82. 4 *Annals* 250-51.

83. S. Padover, ed., *The Complete Jefferson* 1222 (1943).

84. *Id.* 1222-23. Jefferson notes that Hamilton agreed "except as to the power of the House to call on Heads of departments. He observed, that as to his department, the act constituting it had made it subject to Congress in some points, but he thought himself not so far subject, as to be obliged to produce all the papers they might call for. They might demand secrets of a very mischievous nature." Jefferson interpreted this as a desire on Hamilton's part "to place himself subject to the House, when the executive should propose what he did not like, and subject to the executive, when the House should propose anything disagreeable." The original demand had been for originals of the documents. The Cabinet decided "that copies only should be sent with an assurance that if they should decide it, a clerk should attend with the originals to be verified by themselves." *Id.*

85. Jefferson cited as his sole reliance for this requirement language of a motion requesting the King to send certain papers, letters, etc. to the Committee of Secrecy authorized to conduct an inquiry relating to England's convention with Spain. 13 *History and Proceedings of the Third Parliament of King George II* at 246 (Chandler's ed., 1743).

86. "When Gentlemen's Curiosity prompts him to desire a sight of any Papers of State, they move for having them laid before the House, and their motion is always complied with, when consistent with Publick Safety." 13 Chandler, *supra* note 85, at 82. Raoul Berger argues that insertion of the public safety clause arose out of the stormy nature of the period. Berger, *supra* note 66, at 24-25. Other members noted the King's right to insist on at least minimum legislative exposure: "We ought to suppose, that his Majesty will after-

ward communicate to us by message, the Points upon which he desires our Advice; and when he does so, he will certainly order all the necessary Papers to be laid before the House, or if they are of so secret a Nature that they ought not to be laid before such a numerous Assembly, he will desire us to appoint a Secret Committee for inspecting such Papers as he may think fit to communicate." 13 Chandler, *supra* note 85, at 91-92. *See also id.* 98-99.

87. An opponent of the Select Committee implicitly recognized its power to obtain all information, when he objected: "The Papers now proposed to be referred to them would give them an Inclination to see others . . . till they had got all the State Papers, even the most secret before them." *Id.* 83. William Pitt argued in favor of inquiry into "Secrets of our Government," since to surrender to the fear that enemies might learn secrets would perpetually confine inquiry to "the Conduct of our little Companies, or of Inferior Custom-House Officers . . . ." To this end, he detailed methods a committee might use to protect papers designated "secret" by the King. *Id.* 173-74. Note also the Secretary of War's description of the sweeping powers of a Committee of Inquiry: "a government set up by this House, distinct from, and superior to our constitutional Government. . . ." *Id.* 99. *See id.* 224-25, for the decision to jail Paxton.

88. Padover, *supra* note 83, at 1223.

89. *Id.*

90. 3 *Annals* 536.

91. 4 *Annals* 34, 37-38.

92. Cabinet Opinion, January 28, 1974, in 4 *Works of Alexander Hamilton* 505-506 (J. Hamilton, ed. 1850-51) (7 vols) [hereinafter *"Hamilton Works"*]; 15 H. Syrett & J. Cooke, eds., *The Papers of Alexander Hamilton* 666-67 (1961-76) (22 volumes published) [hereinafter *"Hamilton Papers"*]. (Parallel cites will be provided to the more recent and definitive Syrett edition.)

93. Bradford to Washington, Cabinet Opinion, n.d., 4 *Hamilton Works* 494-95.

94. 4 *Annals* 56.

95. 7 Freeman, *Washington* 248; *see id.* 237-39.

96. 4 *Annals* 855.

97. *See* the discussion in 4 J. Flexner, *George Washington: Anguish and Farewell* 204 (1972); 7 Freeman, *Washington* 250 n.61; 11 *The Writings of George Washington* 478-79 (J. Sparks, ed. 1848).

98. 4 *Annals* 859-60.

99. *Id.* 863.

100. 5 *Annals* 11, 128.

101. *Id* 400-401.

102. *Id.* 438.

103. 34 *Washington Writings* (Fitzpatrick) 481-82.

104. Hamilton to Washington, Mar. 7, 1796, in 6 *Hamilton Works* 90-91; 20 *Hamilton Papers* 68-69 & note pp. 65-66.

105. 5 *Annals* 437-38.

106. *Id.* 448. Samuel Smith of Maryland said that the practice of the House had been "invariably to ask for all and every paper that might lead to information." *Id.* 622.

107. *Id.* 557.

108. *Id.* 452 (N. Smith); 593-94 (Jeremiah Smith); 674 (Hillhouse).

109. *Id.* 449 (Swanwick).

110. *Id. See also id.* 555 (Rutherford).

111. *Id.* 675. *See also id.* 715. (Bush).

112. *Id.* 601 (W. Lyman).

113. *E.g., id.* 439-44 (W. Smith); 458 (Harper); 478 (Griswold); 548 (Bradbury); 593-94 (J. Smith).

114. *Id.* 475 (Hartley); 573 (Bourne); 612 (Tracy); 684 (Gilbert).

115. *Id.* 453-57 (N. Smith); 553 (Bradbury).

116. *Id.* 444-45 (Nicholas); 449-50 (Swanwick); 464-65 (Gallatin); 546-47 (Baldwin); 560-61 (Page); 675 (Hillhouse); 632 (Livingston).

117. *Id.* 446 (Nicholas); 575 (Brent); 601 (W. Lyman); 593 (Findley).

118. *Id.* 448.

119. *Id.* 461.

120. *Id.* 553. *See also id.* 573 (Bourne expressing doubt that information could be debated behind closed doors).

121. *Id.* 625 (S. Smith); 629-30 (Livingston).

122. *Id.* 759.

123. Washington to Secretaries of State, Treasury, War, and the Attorney General, March 25, 1796, in 34 *Washington Writings* (Fitzpatrick) 505.

124. Hamilton to Washington, March 24, 1796, in 10 *Hamilton Works* 151; 20 *Hamilton Papers* 81-82.

125. Hamilton to Washington, March 28, 1796, *id. Works* 152-54; *id. Papers* 83-84.

126. Message for Washington to Congress, in "Reply to a Call for Papers Relating to the Treaty with Great Britain" (draft by Hamilton, March 24, 1796), in 7 *Hamilton Works* 557; 20 *Hamilton Papers* 86-87. *See* 7 Freeman, *Washington* 354.

127. Letter of March 31, 1796, in 34 *Washington Writings* (Fitzpatrick) 6; *see also id.* 122.

128. 5 *Annals* 760-61.

129. See textual note, *supra* at 90.

130. 5 *Annals* 760.

131. *Id.* 762 (Thatcher); 763 (Sedgwick); 763-64 (Sitgreaves).

132. *Id.* 765, 768.

133. *Id.* 771-72.

134. *Id.* 782-83.

135. The language is J. Flexner's, quoted in the *New York Times*, October 31, 1973, at 31, col. 2. The drama surrounding disclosure is well covered by Carroll & Ashworth, 7 Freeman, *Washington* 279-85, 293-96; 4 J. Flexner, *supra* note 97, at 234-39.

136. 30 *Washington Writings* (Fitzpatrick) 431-32.

137. 4 *Annals* 87-88; 5 *Annals* 36.

138. 5 *Annals* 32.

139. S. Bemis, *A Diplomatic History of the United States* 98 (4th ed. 1955).

140. Jefferson to Genet, Sept. 15, 1793, 6 *The Writings of Thomas Jefferson* 429-30 (P. Ford, ed. 1892-99) (10 vols.) [hereinafter *"Jefferson Writings* (Ford)"] ; C. Thomas, *American Neutrality in 1793-94*, at 213, 216 (1931)

[hereinafter "Thomas, *American Neutrality*"].

141. 6 Freeman, *Washington* 255-56.

142. 2 *Annals* 1760-62.

143. *Id.* 1488 (Gallatin); 1494 (W. Smith & G. Thatcher).

144. *Id.* 1496.

145. A.S.P., 1 *Indian Affairs* 81 (August 6, 1970).

146. 30 *Washington Writings* (Fitzpatrick) 439-40.

147. *See* 35 *id.* 123-24.

148. On August 6, 1789, the Senate appointed a committee to consult with the President "on the mode of communication proper to be pursued between him and the Senate, in the formation of treaties, and making appointments to office." 1 *Annals* 66-67. At their first conference, on August 8, 1789, the President expressed the view that "in all matters respecting Treaties, oral communications seem indispensably necessary . . . ." He thought oral communication might be proper for "discussing the propriety" of sending ministers abroad and other purposes, but he strongly preferred written consultation for nominations. 30 *Washington Writings* (Fitzpatrick) 373-74. *See also id.* 377-79.

149. *Journal of William Maclay, supra* note 38, at 125-30.

150. 1 *Annals* 67-72. *See generally* the accounts in J. Hart, *supra* note 5, at 87-97; and E. Corwin, *supra* note 4, at 209-10.

151. For example, before signing the treaty negotiated with the Creeks, he asked the Senate in a confidential message whether a certain secret article dealing with the Creek Nation's commerce should be included in the treaty, and the Senate did promptly "advise and consent to the execution of the secret article. . . ." 1 *Annals* 1063-64 (Aug. 4, 1790). The treaty was signed three days later, on August 7, 1790 (A.S.P., 1 *Indian Affairs* 81-82), and confirmed on August 12, 1790 (1 *Annals* 1074).

152. J. Hart, *supra* note 5, at 98.

153. *See* 30 *Washington Writings* (Fitzpatrick) 355, 486-87.

154. 9 *Writings of Thomas Jefferson* 138 (H. Washington, ed. 1854) [hereinafter "*Jefferson Writings* (Washington)"].

155. Randolph voiced his protest vehemently: "To permit such a treaty to be signed . . . and transmitted for ratification is to abridge the power of the Senate to judge of its merits." "Omitted Chapters of History Disclosed," in *The Life and Papers of Edmund Randolph* 220-21 (M. Conway, ed. 1889). *See also* recital of Hamilton and Randolph's differences in this matter in 7 Freeman, *Washington* 170. Rep. Edward Livingston (N.Y.) later complained of the practice, but timidly and without success. 5 *Annals* 628.

156. *E.g.*, 1 *Sen. J. Exec. Proc.* 263-64 (1828) (in relation to the Treaty of 1797 with Tunis); *id.* 463-64 (the King-Hawkesbury Convention, May 12, 1803, the first treaty to be lost by refusal of the other signatory to accept an amendment proposed by the Senate). On February 13, 1793, Washington himself suggested that the Senate ratify a treaty with an amendment. A.S.P., 1 *Indian Affairs* 338.

157. The change came in connection with a proposed treaty with Morocco, sent to the House "in confidence," 4 *Annals* 137, 143, and after illuminating discussion of the issue. *See id.* 149-52.

158. *Id.* 462, 467.

159. J. Combs, *The Jay Treaty* 162 (1970). The proposed treaty was sent to a special session of the Senate on June 8, 1795. 4 *Annals* 854-55. Efforts to lift the injunction of secrecy before its adoption failed. *Id.* 858. The treaty was approved, except for Article 12, on June 24 (*id.* 863), and the resolution regarding secrecy partially rescinded the next day (*id.* 867-68).

160. 14 *The Papers of Alexander Hamilton* 142-43 (H. Syrett, ed. 1961). *Compare* the erroneous suggestion in 7 Freeman, *Washington* 17.

161. Washington's indecision is described in 7 Freeman, *Washington* 254-63. However, Washington's *ultimate* decision about submitting the article to the Senate is subject to doubt when we consider his language in a letter to Hamilton: "I have told Mr. Randolph that your sentiments do not agree with those which I have received from the officers of government; and have desired him to revise them." Washington to Hamilton, July 14, 1795, in 34 *Washington Writings* (Fitzpatrick) 241-42.

162. 1 *Annals* 60, 710-11, 716, 720 (Page). *See also id.* 718, 720-21, 724, and the argument of Rep. Michael J. Stone of Maryland: "The President knows we are to grant him money to carry his good intentions into effect, and we may grant this money on what terms we judge proper." *Id.* 717.

163. 4 *Annals* 589-90.

164. *Id.* 600, 602.

165. At least two other interesting but inconclusive controversies took place in which the argument for and against the House's power to exercise discretion were made. *See* 5 *Annals* 784-85, 1140; 6 *Annals* 2295-96, 2310.

166. The debate was extensive, and references must necessarily be representative. Typical of the Federalist position in this statement of Representative Roger Griswold of Connecticut (5 *Annals* 479):

> The power of making Treaties has been given to the PRESIDENT and the Senate. The Treaty in Question has been completed by those constituted authorities; the faith of the nation is pledged. It has become a law, and the House of Representatives have nothing to do with it but provide for its execution.

167. This position, advanced by Madison among others, is summed up in the following statement by Gallatin (*id.* 465):

> [I]f a Treaty embraces objects within the sphere of the general powers delegated to the Federal Government, but which have been exclusively and specially granted to a particular branch of Government, say to the Legislative department, such a Treaty, though not unconstitutional, does not become the law of the land until its has obtained the sanction of that branch. In this case, and to this end, the Legislature have a right to demand the documents relative to the negotiation of the Treaty. . . .

168. *Id.* 759-61.

169. *Id.* 771-72.

170. *Id.* 1282-91; J. Combs, *supra* note 159, at 187.

171. 4 *Annals* 100.

172. *Id.* 313, 599-602.

173. *Id.* 802-20.

174. 2 *Annals* 1771.

175. 30 *Washington Writings* (Fitzpatrick) 486-87. *See* J. Hart, *supra* note 5, at 99-100.

176. 12 *The Writings of George Washington* 372 (W. Ford, ed. 1889-93) (14 vols.) [hereinafter "*Washington Writings* (Ford)"].

177. W. Manning, "The Nootka Sound Controversy," *1904 Annual Report of the American Historical Association* 283 (1905).

178. 5 *Jefferson Writings* (Ford) 199-203.

179. Gouverneur Morris to George Washington, May 29, 1790, in 18 *id.* 289-93; 17 *id.* 121, 127.

180. 17 *id.* 128-29, 135-36, 138-39, 141-42; 4 *Hamilton Works* 53, 69.

181. Washington to Jefferson, April 12, 1793, in 32 *Washington Writings* (Fitzpatrick) 415-16; Jefferson to Washington, April 7, 1793, in 6 *Jefferson Writings* (Ford) 212.

182. Washington to Jefferson, April 12, 1793, in 12 *Washington Writings* (Ford) 278-79.

183. *Id.* 280-81.

184. Americans were especially tempted by the treaty provision that allowed the arming of French privateers in United States ports. "The prospective gains of privateering were very alluring." Thomas, *American Neutrality* 33-34.

185. *Id.* 46. The proclamation may be found at A.S.P., 1 *Foreign Relations* 140; 12 *Washington Writings* (Ford) 281-82. It forbade American citizens to take part in the hostilities, carry contraband, or engage in unfriendly acts.

186. *See, e.g.*, letter to Gouverneur Morris, April 20, 1793, in 6 *Jefferson Writings* (Ford) 217.

187. *Id.* 219. The language of Jefferson's message to Washington is arguably ambiguous. Often the Cabinet would state that "all agree" to a given proposition. But it seems unlikely that Jefferson would have dissented and then failed to inform Washington of that fact in a personal note containing the statements of his opinion. *See also* Thomas, *American Neutrality* 41 n.2, collecting instances of explicit Jefferson dissents.

188. 6 *Jefferson Writings* (Ford) 192.

189. Professor Thomas thought Jefferson concluded that the presence of Congress was unnecessary, once the decision was made to issue the proclamation immediately, and once he was sure "Hamilton would be unable to obtain the extreme measures suggested by the questions. . . ." Thomas, *American Neutrality* 68.

190. 6 *Jefferson Writings* (Ford) 278-79, 363.

191. Treaty of Alliance (Feb. 6, 1778), art. 11, in 2 *Treaties and Other International Acts of the United States of America* 35, 39 (H. Miller, ed. 1931); Treaty of Amity and Commerce (Feb. 6, 1778), arts. 17, 22, in *id.* 3, 16, 19.

192. Memorandum dated April 1793, 4 *Hamilton Works* 362-63, 375, 380; Memorandum to Washington dated May 2, 1793, *id.* 382, 390. See also 14 *Hamilton Papers* 367-68, 387, 391, 393, 399, 408.

193. 6 *Jefferson Writings* (Ford) 219, 222-25. He greatly overstated Hamilton's position, possibly because he was rebutting what Hamilton had said at a Cabinet meeting rather than the position that Hamilton actually adopted in writing. *See id.* 219, quoting Hamilton's statements at the meeting of April 19,

1793. Hamilton did not even advise that the treaties be suspended, as Professor Thomas suggests (*see* Thomas, *American Neutrality* at 55-59), but only that Genêt be told that the United States retained the right to deem them suspended.

194. *See* Thomas, *American Neutrality* at 76-77: "Had the minister not been received, or had his reception been qualified, it is evident that the relations between the United States and France might have been much different."

195. When the British merchant vessel *Grange* was seized by the French frigate *Embuscade* on April 25, 1793, the government promptly decided in Britain's favor in what was a clear-cut case of seizure within American territory. The British complained on May 2, 1793; and Jefferson asked the French on the same day to supply its version of the facts. 6 *Jefferson Writings* (Ford) 236-37. It was soon determined that the *Grange* had been seized in Delaware Bay. On May 14 Attorney General Randolph submitted his opinion that the Bay was within the territory of the United States, and that restitution of the ship was necessary. A.S.P., 1 *Foreign Relations* 148-49. The Cabinet unanimously concurred, and Jefferson requested restitution and release of the crew on May 15. 6 *Jefferson Writings* (Ford) 254, 256-57. The French acquiesced. A.S.P., 1 *Foreign Relations* 149-50, Genêt to Jefferson, May 27, 1793.

196. President Washington chose the three-mile limit because "it is recognized by treaties between some of the Powers with whom we are connected in commerce and navigation, and is as little or less than is claimed by any of them on their own coasts." Jefferson to Genêt, Nov. 8, 1793, in 6 *Jefferson Writings* (Ford) 440, 441.

197. *See* Thomas, *American Neutrality* 267. The Court, however, refused to render an advisory opinion. *Id.* 150.

198. Jefferson to Hammond and Ternant, in 6 *Jefferson Writings* (Ford) 254, 255-56.

199. Hammond to Jefferson, May 8, 1793, cited in Thomas, *American Neutrality* at 121 n.6.

200. Hamilton to Washington, May 15, 1793, 4 *Hamilton Works* 394, 399; Jefferson to Washington, May 16, 1793, *id.* 403. 14 *Hamilton Papers* 454, 458.

201. "Opinion on *The Little Sarah*," May 16, 1793, 6 *Jefferson Writings* (Ford) 257, 259.

202. See Jefferson to Genêt, June 5, 1793, *id.* 282.

203. Cabinet Opinion, July 8, 1793, *id.*

204. *Id.* 340-44.

205. Cabinet Opinion, July 8, 1793, 4 *Hamilton Works* 443, 445, 447; 15 *Hamilton Papers* 74, 76, 78.

206. 12 *Washington Writings* (Ford) 302.

207. 6 *Jefferson Writings* (Ford) 302 n.1.

208. 7 Freeman, *Washington* 103.

209. Cabinet Opinion, 6 *Jefferson Writings* (Ford) 344-45. The Cabinet voted unanimously to have the Governor of Pennsylvania attend the ship Jane "with vigilance, and if she be found augmenting her force and about to depart, that he cause her to be stopped." *Id.* 345.

210. *The Anas*, July 12, 1793, 9 *Jefferson Writings* (Washington) 158-59.

211. 6 *Jefferson Writings* (Ford) 352-54 n.1.

212. *See* Thomas, *American Neutrality* 142-43.

213. *See id.* 150.

214. 6 *Jefferson Writings* (Ford) 358 n.1.

215. 7 Freeman, *Washington* 111.

216. 6 *Jefferson Writings* (Ford) 360.

217. *The Anas,* Aug. 1, 1793, 9 *Jefferson Writings* (Washington) 162.

218. Opinion on Calling of Congress, Aug. 4, 1793, 6 *Jefferson Writings* (Ford) 362-63.

219. Cabinet Opinion, Aug. 5, 1793, 4 *Hamilton Works* 461-62; 15 *Hamilton Papers* 194.

220. *The Anas,* Aug. 3, 1793, 9 *Jefferson Writings* (Washington) 165. As in many other instances, Jefferson's account is greatly agitated. He said of Knox's remark: "The fool thus let out the secret. Hamilton endeavored to patch up the indiscretion of this blabber, by saying 'he did not know; he rather thought they would have strengthened the executive arm.' " *Id.*

221. Jefferson to Madison, Aug. 11, 1793, 6 *Madison Writings* (Hunt) 367, 370.

222. 4 *Annals* 11. *See generally* F. Wharton, *State Trials of the United States During the Administration of Washington and Adams* 49-89 (1849); 1 J. Goebels, *History of the Supreme Court of the United States* 624-26 (1971); 10 *Washington Writings* (Sparks) 362. Washington probably wanted a statute providing a definite basis for prosecuting violations of neutrality; the proclamation relied on both common law and international law. Wharton, *supra* at 54. The proposed statute incorporated the "Rules Governing Belligerents," a series of prohibitions relating to arming of vessels, issued by Washington subsequent to the Henfield case. 4 *Hamilton Works* 455-62; 15 *Hamilton Papers* 168-69; 9 *Jefferson Writings* (Washington) 44.

223. See Jefferson to Genêt, Aug. 7, 1793, 6 *Jefferson Writings* (Ford) 365-66.

224. Washington to Hamilton, July 2, 1794, 4 *Hamilton Works* 570-71; 16 *Hamilton Papers* 560-61. In his statement to Congress on Dec. 5, 1793, Washington said that "rather than employ force for the restitution of certain vessels, which I deemed the United States bound to restore, I thought it more advisable to satisfy the parties by avowing it to be my opinion, that, if restitution were not made, it would be incumbent on the United States to make compensation." Message in Congress, Dec. 5, 1793, 12 *Washington Writings* (Ford) 357.

225. Thomas, *American Neutrality* 200 n.3.

226. Hamilton to Washington, June 22, 1794, 4 *Hamilton Works* 569-71; Washington to Hamilton, July 2, 1794, *id.* 570-71. See also 16 *Hamilton Papers* 513-14, 560-61.

227. *See* Thomas, *American Neutrality* 118-20.

228. Jefferson to Madison, June 9, 1793, 6 *Jefferson Writings* (Ford) 290, 293.

229. 6 *Madison Writings* (Hunt) 131-32.

230. One can sense from some of his letters that Jefferson was pained at the consequences of neutrality, but he worked unrelentingly in implementing the policy, and in fact believed it was in the best interests of the United States. *See, e.g.,* his letter to Madison, April 28, 1793, 6 *Jefferson Writings* (Ford) 232: "I fear that a fair neutrality will prove a disagreeable pill to our friends, tho' necessary to keep out of the calamities of a war."

232. 7 *Hamilton Works* 76-83; 15 *Hamilton Papers* 33-40.

233. *Id. Works* 84-85; *id. Papers* 42-43.

234. For Madison's eyes, he added: "tho' it was certainly officious & improper." *Id.* 328. As Corwin put it, Jefferson "was quite ready to make whatever political capital he could out of the opposition to [the proclamation]. ..." Corwin, *The President's Control of Foreign Relations* 16 (1917) (1970 reprint).

235. 6 *Jefferson Writings* (Ford) 338.

236. 7 *Hamilton Works* 83; 15 *Hamilton Papers* 41-42.

237. 6 *Madison Writings* (Hunt) 153.

238. *Id.* 154, 158, 159.

239. *Id.* 174, 182.

240. E. Corwin, *supra* note 234, at 28.

241. Corwin also notes inconsistencies in Madison's argument with arguments Madison had previously made concerning the meaning of "the executive power." *See id.* 28-30. *See also The Federalist* Nos. 47 & 48 (Madison), defending the mixture of governmental powers under the proposed constitution.

242. 6 *Madison Writings* (Hunt) 159.

243. *Id.* 160.

244. Washington to Earl of Buchan, April 22, 1793, 32 *Washington Writings* (Fitzpatrick) 428.

245. 12 *Washington Writings* (Ford) 351.

246. Jefferson reports that "the President said he had had but one object, the keeping our people quiet till Congress should meet; that nevertheless, to say he did not mean a declaration of neutrality, in the technical sense of the phrase, might perhaps be crying *peccavi* before he was charged." *The Anas*, Nov. 21, 1793, 9 *Jefferson Writings* (Washington) 181-82. In this respect, Hamilton was successful, having argued that the President "should neither affirm his right to make such a declaration to foreign nations, nor yield it." *Id.* 178.

247. Hamilton would have included in the speech a veiled reference to the need to make clear that the United States would not enforce arrangements that might cause war, presumably such as the guaranty concerning the West Indies. 4 *Hamilton Works* 486, "Draft of Speech". *See also id.* 485 ("Outline of Objects to be Communicated in Speech and Messages"). Randolph initially suggested communicating "an observation of the French treaty." *Id.* 484 (Randolph outline of "heads of Subjects"). The same material is in 15 *Hamilton Papers* 425-30.

248. *The Anas*, Nov. 18, 1793, 9 *Jefferson Writings* (Washington) 179. This was consistent with Hamilton's position. *See id.* 178.

249. 12 *Washington Writings* (Ford) 352.

250. The Senate agreed in its response to the President's speech that the proclamation was necessary for the reasons stated by the President, and in addition to insure "that the disposition of the nation for peace should be promulgated to the world"; "we, therefore, contemplate with pleasure the Proclamation by you issued, and give it our hearty approbation." 4 *Annals* 17-18, Dec. 9, 1793. The House also expressed "approbation and pleasure" at the President's actions.

Id. 138, Dec. 6, 1793.

251. See the comment of Samuel McKee (Pa.), in distinguishing Congress's approval of neutrality from a proposal to commend President Madison's negotiations with Britain, "a duty he was expected to perform." 20 *Annals* 198. John Ross (Pa.) called the resolutions approving the neutrality proclamation peculiarly important. *Id.* 174.

252. 4 *Annals* 1461, 743-44, 745-57.

253. In the Senate, a motion was made to expunge what ultimately became section 7 of the act, which recited certain violations of the act and provided that "in every such case it shall be lawful for the President . . . or such other person as he shall have empowered for that purpose, to employ such part of" the armed forces as is judged necessary to seize the offending vessels, impose the penalties and prohibitions, and prevent illegal expeditions. *Id.* 68 (Mar. 13, 1794). The Senate split evenly on the issue, and the Vice President cast the deciding vote for retention. The act also gave broad discretion to the President to use force "to compel any foreign ship or vessel to depart the United States" when the laws or treaties made it improper that it remain. Sec. 8, Act of June 5, 1794. *id.* 1464.

254. 3 Flexner, *supra* note 97, at 213.

255. *See infra* at 120-22; *see also, e.g.,* the discussions at 3 *Annals* 762-68, 773-802; 4 *Annals* 774-79; *id.* 1165-1172; *id.* 485-92 (Giles re navy).

256. *E.g.,* 3 *Annals* 773-77 (Wadsworth); 4 *Annals* 502 (Sedgwick); *id.* 776-77 (Ames, Boudinot, Murray); *id.* 1166 (S. Smith); *id.* 1171 (Murray).

257. *E.g.,* 4 *Annals* 434-36 (S. Smith, Ames); *id.* 492-97 (W. Smith); 6 *Annals* 2343 (Ames: "It was not to be supposed that a nation whose commerce was greater than that of any other, except Great Britain should go on long without a naval protection").

258. *E.g.,* 3 *Annals* 765 (Hartley); *id.* 783 (Willis); *id.* 785 (Milledge); 4 *Annals* 445-46 (Dexter).

259. Act of Mar. 27, 1794, 1 Stat. 350; *see* 4 *Annals* 433-34.

260. *Historical Statistics of the United States: Colonial Times to 1957,* at 737 (U.S. Bur. of Census 1960).

261. 1 *Annals* 790-91.

262. Griswold asserted that "[b]oth the Legislative and the Treaty power are necessary, on many occasions to accomplish the same objects. The Legislative power to establish relations, or declare war . . . ; and the Treaty power . . . to remove . . . those very regulations, and the war itself, on fair and equitable terms." 5 *Annals* 478.

263. Act of Nov. 29, 1794, 1 Stat. 403.

264. Act of June 5, 1794, § 8, 1 Stat. 381, 384.

265. Secretary of State Timothy Pickering to Governor Arthur Fenner, 35 *Timothy Pickering Papers* 235-36 (Mass. Hist. Soc. 1966) (microfilm).

266. *See generally* 6 Freeman, *Washington* 245-46, 258-59 (treaty-making); 325, 381 (declarations of policy).

267. General Knox supplied the President with background material on the problem in June 1789, which was sent to Congress August 7, 1789. Knox advocated a peaceful approach to the Wabash, arguing that the country could not afford a war and that Indians could gradually be bought off and integrated.

A.S.P., 1 *Indian Affairs* 12, 13-14.

268. 1 *Annals* 928. The letter is incorrectly dated September 24, 1789. It was written on September 14, 1789. See A.S.P., 1 *Indian Affairs* 58. For an excellent treatment of the military aspects of the Indian wars, *see* R. Kohn, *Eagle and Sword: The Federalists and the Creation of the Military Establishment in America, 1783-1802* at 91-157 (1975).

269. 1 *Annals* 62, 715.

270. *Id.* 927.

271. Act of Sept. 29, 1789, 1 Stat. 95, 96.

272. A.S.P., 1 *Indian Affairs* 96-97.

273. 2 *Annals* 1728, 1729. *See also* A.S.P., 1 *Foreign Relations* 13-14; A.S.P., 1 *Indian Affairs* 83, 96-97.

274. A.S.P. 1 *Foreign Relations* 12; 1 *Annals* 969.

275. Act of April 30, 1790, §§1, 16, 1 Stat. 119, 121.

276. A.S.P., 1 *Indian Affairs* 92, 96, 98, 104-106.

277. *Id.* 96-97.

278. A.S.P., 1 *Foreign Relations* 14, 15.

279. *Id.*

280. 2 *Annals* 1801-1802. Laurance's name is mispelled Lawrence in the *Annals.*

281. Memo to Washington, Jan. 22, 1791, A.S.P., 1 *Indian Affairs* 112, 113.

282. Act of Mar. 3, 1791, §1, 1 Stat. 222, provided for an additional regiment of over 900 men; §8 gave the President discretion to raise over 2,000 more enlistees.

283. A.S.P., 1 *Indian Affairs* 129-35. *See* instructions, *id.* 171-74.

284. *Id.* 136-38.

285. Memo to Washington, Dec. 26, 1791, *id.* 197-99.

286. Act of Mar. 5, 1792, §2, 1 Stat. 241. *See also id.* 243, §§12, 14. An effort was made in December 1792 to reduce the military establishment and repeal the Act of March 5, 1792, to the extent that its provisions were inconsistent with such a reduction. 3 *Annals* 750, 763. The motion lost 26-32, after extensive debate. *Id.* 802.

287. *See* materials collected at A.S.P., 1 *Indian Affairs* 487-92.

288. Act of Sept. 29, 1789, §5, 1 Stat. 95, 96.

289. U.S. Library of Congress, 33 *Journals of the Continental Congress, 1774-1789* at 602 (W. Ford, ed. 1906).

290. 1 *Annals* 927-28.

291. Art. 1, §8, cl. 15 of the Constitution states the purposes for which the militia may be called: "To execute the laws of the Union, suppress Insurrections and repel Invasions. . . ." *See also* Washington's Message, Dec. 8, 1790. In the course of this message the President noted: "As this object [peace] could not be effected by defensive measures, it became necessary to put in force the act which empowers the President to call out the militia for the protection of the frontiers; and I have accordingly authorized an expedition. . . ." A.S.P., 1 *Foreign Relations* 13-14.

292. 3 *Annals* 748, 749; 4 *Annals* 122, 131 (Senate), *id.* 698, 774, 779 (House).

293. 8 *Annals* 1523.

294. 4 *Annals* 776 (June 6, 1794) (Ames).

295. *Id.* 1122.

296. S. Bemis, *Jay's Treaty* 175 (1924).

297. *See* letter of Secretary of State Randolph to Minister Hammond, May 20, 1794, in A.S.P., 1 *Foreign Relations* 461-62. For a discussion of the British position, see E. Smith, *England and America After Independence* 38 and Appendix, 45-52 (1900).

298. *See* R. Knopf, ed., *Anthony Wayne: A Name in Arms* 351, 355 (1960); A.S.P., 1 *Indian Affairs* 491.

299. "This possession of our acknowledged territory has no pretext of status quo on its side; it has no pretext at all; it is an [hostile] act . . . calculated to support an enemy whom we are seeking to bring to peace." A.S.P., 1 *Foreign Relations* 462.

300. Message of May 21, 1794, *id.*; 1 *Messages and Papers of the Presidents* 155 (J. Richardson, ed. 1897).

301. A.S.P., 1 *Foreign Relations* 464-66.

302. R. Knopf, ed., *supra* note 298, at 337-38.

303. This correspondence was sent by Wayne to Knox and appears in A.S.P., 1 *Indian Affairs* 493-94.

304. Wayne noted that "had Campbell carried his threats into execution it is more than probable he would have experienced a storm." Bracketed note, *id.* 494.

305. Wayne had "a reputation for recklessness." Though extremely able, "he was an unmitigated egotist." R. Knopf, ed., *supra* note 298, at 7. Some called him "Mad" Anthony. *Id.* 377.

CHAPTER 3
JOHN ADAMS AND UNDECLARED WAR
AS NATIONAL POLICY

1. *See generally* C. Bowen, *John Adams and the American Revolution* (1950); R. Morris, *Encyclopaedia of American History* 971 (1976); 1 *Dictionary of American Biography* 72-82 (A. Johnson, ed. 1957).

2. C. Walsh, *The Political Science of John Adams* (1915), particularly ch. 8 & 18; S. Kurtz, *The Presidency of John Adams* 96-99 (1957).

3. 2 P. Smith, *John Adams* 840 (1962). *See also* Adams to James Lloyd, Jan. 1815, in 10 *Works of John Adams* 108 (C. Adams, ed. 1856) ("National defense is one of the cardinal duties of a statesman") [hereinafter *"Adams Works"*].

4. Adams wanted to avoid war, but felt that Americans had a propensity for it. He predicted, in a letter to his son Thomas, March 19, 1794, that this propensity would lead to frequent war, corruption and monstrous debt. *The Adams Papers*, Adams Manuscript (Mass. Hist. Soc.) (microfilm) reel 377 [hereinafter *"Adams Papers"*].

5. *Id.* reel 117 (May 3, 1797). *See also* letters to Roger Sherman, 6 *Adams Works* 427-36.

6. *See* G. Clarfield, *Timothy Pickering and American Diplomacy, 1795–1800*, at 213 (1969).

7. *E.g.*, 9 *Annals of Congress* (1853) 2547, 3614-29 (plan for military establishment) [hereinafter *"Annals"*]; A.S.P., 1 *Naval Affairs* 34 (plan for protection of commerce).

8. *See, e.g.*, Act of Mar. 19, 1798, 1 Stat. 541; Act of July 16, 1798, 1 Stat. 607 (fiscal matters); Act of June 25, 1798, 1 Stat. 570-72 (aliens); Act of June 13, 1798, 1 Stat. 565-66 (commerce).

9. Important information was communicated in Adams's addresses at the beginning of each session of Congress. *E.g.*, 7 *Annals* 54-59 (May 16, 1797); 630-34 (Nov. 23, 1797); 9 *Annals* 2420 (Dec. 8, 1798); 10 *Annals* 188-89 (Dec. 3, 1799). In addition, *see, e.g.*, 7 *Annals* 305-306 (June 12, 1797) (status of Floridas); 963-64 (Feb. 5, 1798) (French attack on British ship at Charleston); 8 *Annals* 1271-72 (Mar. 19, 1798) (news from France).

10. The full extent of withholding is ascertainable only by comparing the dispatches written with those actually sent. The "XYZ" dispatches make up one example; the information ultimately sent to the Senate in confidence concerning the proposed convention with France is another. See *infra* note 14.

11. 7 *Annals* 831-36 (Jan. 15, 1798). The committee of inquiry apparently did not make a final report, possibly because during its activities a bill was enacted appropriating a sum for completion of the three frigates (Act of March 27, 1798, 1 Stat. 547), thus diluting the committee's purpose.

12. *E.g.*, *infra* note 14.

13. One House request sought from the President, without qualification, an itemized list of depredations committed on United States commerce. It was introduced by William Smith, an administration supporter, and approved without debate. 7 *Annals* 290-91 (June 10, 1797). The information was supplied twelve days later. *Id.* 357-58. Another unqualified resolution "directed" the Secretary of War "to lay before this House an account of the number of artillerists in actual service, and of the posts and places at which they are stationed." *Id.* 331 (June 16, 1797). The information arrived within two days. *Id.* 334. Senate requests for instructions to American ministers who negotiated peace with France, and a treaty with Prussia, were also promptly satisfied. 10 *Annals* 767-68 (Dec. 18 & 22, 1800); 779-80 (Feb. 10, 12 & 17, 1801). On one occasion what appears to have been a politically motivated motion to request information concerning British depredations was defeated without debate. *See* 8 *Annals* 1874, 1877 (June 7 & 8, 1798).

14. After Adams sent the Senate a proposed convention settling the war with France, the Senate adopted an unqualified request for the instructions given the ministers, and later for "such information, (if any such there be) as [may have been received respecting the convention with France, and] may, in his opinion, be proper to be so communicated." 10 *Annals* 767 (Dec. 18, 1800); *id.* 773 (Jan. 20, 1801). Adams transmitted the instructions and additional information, asking that all be held in strictest confidence, and returned after ratification. *Id.* 768, 773-74. Adams asked that the material be returned on Feb. 20, 1801, and his request was granted. *Id.* 778.

15. *See* P. Smith, *supra* note 3, at 952-53.

16. 7 *Annals* 1200-201 (Mar. 5, 1798).

17. 8 *Annals* 1252, 1254-70 (Mar. 13, 1798).

18. 8 *Adams Works* 568.

19. Lee to Adams, March 14, 1798, *Adams Papers*, part IV, reel 387, L 218. Apparently Wolcott concurred in this view. *See* Wolcott to Hamilton, April 5, 1798, 6 *The Works of Alexander Hamilton* 278-79 (J. Hamilton, ed.) (7 vols.) (1850-51) [hereinafter *"Hamilton Works"*]. Parallel cites are given to the more recent and definitive 21 H. Syrett & J. Cooke, eds. *The Papers of Alexander Hamilton* 396-98 (1961-75) (22 volumes published) [hereinafter *"Hamilton Papers"*].

20. McHenry to Adams, March 14, 1798, *Adams Papers*, part IV, reel 387, XLVII 270.

21. 8 *Annals* 1271 (Mar. 19, 1798).

22. *See* Abigail Adams to Mary Cranch, March 20, 1798, letter cited in Smith, *supra* note 3, at 955.

23. 7 *Annals* 525 (1798).

24. Hamilton to Pickering, March 23, 1798, 6 *Hamilton Works* 271-72; 21 *Hamilton Papers* 368.

25. *Id. Works* 273, 274, 277; *id. Papers* 370-71, 377.

26. *See, e.g.,* Smith, *supra* note 3, at 959.

27. 8 *Annals* 1349.

28. *Id.* 1357-59 (Mar. 30, 1798).

29. *Id.* 1358-60.

30. *Id.* 1368-69 (April 2, 1798).

31. 8 *Annals* 1369.

32. *Id.* 1371.

33. *Id.* 1371, 1373; 7 *Annals* 535-36; 8 *Annals* 1374-75 (April 3, 1798).

34. *See* 7 *Annals* 536-38; 8 *Annals* 1377-80.

35. *See* Smith, *supra* note 3, at 930, 933.

36. A.S.P., 2 *Foreign Relations* 240 (letter to the Senate, Feb. 25, 1799).

37. 10 *Annals* 767 (Dec. 16, 1800). The instructions given America's ministers by Pickering, dated October 22, 1799, noted the need to conclude negotiations "in order that on your return Congress may be found in session, to take those measures which the result of your mission shall require," and specifically referred to the "treaty" that would hopefully result. *Id.* 1108-109; 1121-22. When a convention was negotiated and signed on September 30, 1800, it provided for its ratification "on both sides in due form. . . ." *Id.* 1098, 1106.

38. *Id.* 777-78; *supra* note 14.

39. The debate arose when John Nicholas of Virginia, a prominent and articulate Republican, proposed to amend the answer to promise cooperation in "necessary" rather than all measures, and explicitly to state that the House expected the President to succeed in the negotiation if he approached it with "a disposition on the part of the United States to place France on the footing of other countries, by removing the inequalities which may have arisen in the operation of our respective treaties with them. . . ." 7 *Annals* 69-70 (May 22, 1797). The debate lasted two weeks, even though, as John Swanwick of Pennsylvania noted, it concerned "a form of words leading to no conclusion." *Id.* 100. Nicholas conceded that the Constitution assigned to the President the role of negotiating with foreign powers, but claimed it "the duty of the Legislature

to deliberate on the proper measures to be taken." *Id.* 77. Others said the legislature was merely stating its view, leaving the President to act as he chose, but forewarned. *Id.* 111 (Swanwick); 134 (Livingston); 146 (Giles). Nicholas argued that the Federalist position in effect vested the power to go to war in the President, for if the House "were not permitted to say to the Executive upon what terms they would wish differences adjusted, they must go to war, if such terms as [the President] . . . proposed were not agreed to." *Id.* 95. *See also id.* 216: the House "had a right to say it will not declare war, except such and such things are done. They had the power of preventing war without consulting the Senate. They could say they would have peace."

William L. Smith of South Carolina, a leading Federalist spokesman, insisted that "it was a delicate thing for them to suggest what the Executive ought to do. It was out of their province to direct him." *Id.* 86. Roger Griswold of Connecticut added that the proposal violated the Constitution because it sought to involve the House in the treaty-making process. *Id.* 94. John Rutledge and others claimed the amendment would interfere with the President's exclusive right to give instructions to ministers, and would prevent effective negotiation by revealing the nation's position in advance. *Id.* 98, 170-71.

40. The amendment eventually passed is at *id.* 210 (June 1, 1797).

41. *Id.* 217-37. Some Republicans were no less inconsistent, arguing that the second amendment might interfere with the President's capacity to negotiate.

42. 8 *Annals* 2122-27 (July 6, 1798).

43. See the inconclusive debate over whether request for funds to negotiate with Cherokees should be referred to Committee on Ways and Means. 7 *Annals* 842-45 (Jan. 1, 1798). Rutledge at one point pragmatically noted that he "did not believe it was necessary or proper for that House to authorize the President to hold a treaty; but if it were necessary for him to hold a treaty, the concurrence of that House were necessary to enable him to do it, as it would not be done without money." *Id.* 844.

44. A politically motivated effort to eliminate the funds for a Minister to Berlin (the President's son) failed after some debate on its constitutionality. Gallatin noted the weakness in the proposition that Congress must provide salaries for all officers appointed. 7 *Annals* 435-40 (July 3, 1797).

45. The motion was suggested by Nicholas. *Id.* 849-52 (Jan. 18, 1798).

46. *Id.* 852-54, 878 (Harper); *id.* 860 (Sitgreaves); *id.* 864-66 (Pinckney); *id.* 894 (Bayard); *id.* 909 (I. Parker); *id.* 939 (Goodrich); *id.* 934-44 (Sewall). Sitgreaves said the only remedy for abuse was impeachment. *Id.* 860. The separation of power argument was first made by Griswold: "[I]f the departments were to check each other, the Government could not proceed. . . . He hoped this doctrine of checks, which had been introduced into the House by the gentleman from Pennsylvania (Mr. Gallatin), would not extend itself in this country, as it contained more mischiefs than Pandora's box." *Id.* 891. Highlighting the pro-administration side were statements by William Craik of Maryland and Chauncey Goodrich of Connecticut. Craik repeated many arguments already made (*id.* 911-16), including the undesirability of checks between branches (*id.*, 915-16), and a prediction that the House would assume all the powers of government if it exercised its discretion before appropriating funds

(*id.* 911). He sought, in addition, to distinguish between "the power to refuse an appropriation, and the Constitutional right to do it. . . . He knew it was in the power of the departments to destroy each other, but he denied that they had a Constitutional right to do so." *Id.* 915. Goodrich pointed out that the Constitution created the position of minister, provided that the President should appoint these officers with the Senate's consent, and that he should conduct the nation's foreign affairs; the House could set salaries, he contended, but only with a view to economy and not to interfere with the President's powers. *Id.* 931-32. He broadly defended the executive, whose duties he said "were to preserve the powers of the country, to vindicate its rights, to protect its sovereignty, to execute the public will expressed through the laws. Rob it of one of these powers and you destroy the most valuable part of the Government. . . ." *Id.* 938.

47. The Republican side was most comprehensively represented by Gallatin, who delivered a prepared speech, some three and one-half hours long. (The length was reported by Harper, an opponent. 7 *Annals* 1159.) After summing up the positions of both sides, Gallatin sought to destroy the contentions that no checks should exist between branches of the government, and that, once the Constitution vests some specific authority in a branch, that branch must possess the means to carry the authority into effect. In doing so he described the Constitution as establishing a system in which the concurrence of the various branches would frequently be required to implement a policy or plan. *Id.* 1120-21. Applying this theoretical framework to the situation before the House, Gallatin contended that the President could appoint as many ministers as he thinks fit" and send them to their assigned duties if possible without any act of the legislature; but the Constitution gives him no power to force the legislature to grant moneys necessary to pay the appointees. Conversely, the legislature could appropriate sums for as many ministers as they think fit, but they have no power to force the President to appoint any person to fill these offices. "[T]he concurrence of both departments is necessary to complete the act." *Id.* 1121. This followed, he said, from the doctrine of checks, which itself flows from the separation of powers, a principle fully established in America by theory and practice. *Id.* 1122. The opposite view would in effect grant the executive full, though indirect, power to raise and spend funds to effect any of his constitutionally assigned responsibilities. *Id.* 1124. Findley tied the issue to the war power (*id.* 904):

Was not the power of declaring war placed in Congress? And was this power no way connected with our intercourse with foreign nations? And if the power of declaring war was in Congress, were not those powers also placed there which should enable them to judge upon the propriety of such measure? They certainly were, since it was not expected that power should be exercised blindly.

48. 8 *Annals* 1233-34 (52 to 48) (Mar. 6, 1798). *See, e.g.*, the statement of John Williams of New York. 7 *Annals* 1214, 1216.

49. A.S.P., 1 *Foreign Relations* 577.

50. The "free ships-free goods" principle was part of the 1778 Treaty of Amity and Commerce between the United States and France. *See* Chapter 2

supra, note 191. The French Directory abandoned the principle in a decree dated Mar. 2, 1797. A.S.P., 2 *Foreign Relations* 30-31. The move was in retaliation for America's surrendering the principle in art. 17 of the Jay Treaty. *See* 2 *Treaties and Other International Acts of the United States of America* 245, 248 (H. Miller, ed. 1931). The crew-list requirement was based on articles 25 and 27 of the Treaty of Amity and Commerce. *Id.* 3, 20-21, 23-24. Enforcement in the manner chosen by the French was a total surprise, and has been said to have amounted to a declaration of martime war. *See* A. De Conde, *Entangling Alliance* 499 (1958); G. Allen, *Our Naval War With France* 298-99 (1967).

51. A.S.P., 2 *Foreign Relations* 28, 57-61.

52. John Trumbull to John Adams, January 15, 1797, in 1 G. Gibbs, ed., *Memoirs of the Administrations of Washington and John Adams* 474 (1846).

53. 6 *Annals* 1581, 1585-86 (Mar. 4, 1797).

54. *See* Clarfield, *supra* note 6, at 94-96.

55. 6 *Hamilton Works* 213-15; 20 *Hamilton Papers* 545-46.

56. *Id.* 215-16; 7 *Annals* 49.

57. 1 Stat. 381-84.

58. *See* "Rules Governing Belligerents," in 6 *Writings of Thomas Jefferson* 358 n.1 (P. Ford, ed. 1895).

59. 1 *Naval Documents Related to the United States War With the Barbary Powers* 201 (1939).

60. Letter to Oliver Wolcott, April 13, 1797, in 6 *Hamilton Works* 238. See also letter of March 22, 1797 to Pickering, *id.* 213-15, recommending authority to arm and act defensively. Also found in 21 *Hamilton Papers* 46-47; 20 *id.* 545-46.

61. Pickering to Hamilton, *id.* *Works* 238-39; 21 *Papers* 68.

62. 7 *Annals* 54-59 (May 16, 1797), quote at 57.

63. *See* Clarfield, *supra* note 6 at 99-101; 1 Gibbs, *supra* note 52, at 477 (Fisher Ames to John Madison, Mar. 24, 1797).

64. 7 *Annals* 282, 85. House members divided on Adams's power to restrict arming. Gallatin supported doing nothing, since the government would not be responsible for the acts of merchants who violated Adams's order. *Id.* 239, 255-82. The proposal arose again in December 1797, and was again rejected. *Id.* 764-74. *See generally* S. Kurtz, *The Presidency of John Adams* 289-90 (1972).

65. 7 *Annals* 631.

66. *See generally id.* 490-515 (Senate); 764, 836, 840, 965-1098 (fight between members) (House).

67. 8 *Adams Works* 561-63. For Pickering's position, see 6 *Hamilton Works* 272-77; 21 *Hamilton Papers* 368.

68. B. Steiner, ed., *The Life and Correspondence of James McHenry* 291-95 (1907). Hamilton replied in a detailed paper to McHenry's request of January 26 that Hamilton assist him with "suggestions and opinions," since a "wrong policy" could be "extremely injurious," and he, McHenry, could not "do justice to the subject" as Hamilton could. *Id.* 291. McHenry's answer to Adams practically embodied the whole of Hamilton's letter. *Adams Papers*, reel 387 (Mar. 14, 1798).

69. *See* Smith, *supra* note 3, at 952-53.

70. 8 *Adams Works* 568.

71. Lee to Adams, March 14, 1798, *Adams Papers*, reel 387.

72. McHenry to Adams, March 14, 1798, *id.* reel 387.

73. The order regarding merchant vessels was issued after Adams heard of a French decree that vessels would be treated as neutral or enemy according to their cargo rather than their flag. McHenry advised that this "total change in circumstances" made it expedient to annul the then existing restrictions. McHenry to Adams, March 14, 1798, in *Adams Papers*, reel 387. *See* Smith, *supra* note 3, at 955.

74. 8 *Annals* 1271-72.

75. *Id.* 1319-20 (Mar. 27, 1798).

76. *Id.* 1320-21, 1324.

77. *Id.* 1380-91.

78. For example, on April 27, 1798 the President was authorized to build or obtain twelve ships of up to 22 guns each, and to raise an additional regiment of artillerists and engineers. 1 Stat. 552. Three days later, the Department of the Navy was established. 1 Stat. 553. On May 28, 1798, Congress authorized a provisional army of up to 10,000 (1 Stat. 558), and empowered the President to use the navy to seize French privateers and raiders found around America's coast and to retake captured vessels (1 Stat. 561). On June 13, Congress voted an embargo on all commerce with France, to go into effect July 1 and to last until the end of the next session; the same act prohibited French ships, armed or unarmed, from entering American ports without the President's permission, unless in distress. The President was authorized to lift the embargo before its expiration if the French acknowledged American grievances. 1 Stat. 565.

79. See 8 *Annals* 1245-46 (Mar. 8, 1798); 1381-1402 (Apr. 8-11, 1798). At least one member who wanted specificity was upset that no fortifications were planned for his state. *Id.* 1394-95 (Blount). Gallatin felt specificity would help insure that the funds were actually spent, but others said moneys appropriated need not be expended. *Id.* 1399-1401.

80. Earlier laws usually detailed the number of troops to be raised, or gave discretion to forbear raising troops or to discharge troops. The bill, as originally passed by the Senate on April 23, 1798, authorized the President to raise an army of 20,000, "whenever he shall judge the public safety shall require the measure," though it limited the time during which the President could accept enlistments to three years. 7 *Annals* 546 (Apr. 23, 1798); 8 *Annals* 1631 (May 8, 1798).

81. 1 Stat. 5581; *see* 8 *Annals* 1631, 1661-62.

82. 8 *Annals* 2114 (July 5, 1798).

83. *Id.* 2119-20.

84. 4 U.S. (4 Dall.) 37 (1800).

85. *Id.* 40-41.

86. *Id.* 43-44.

87. *Id.* 45. *See also* the amusing description of the Court in delivering its opinions in a letter of Thomas Boylston Adams to his uncle, the President, on August 18, 1800. *Adams Papers*, reel 398.

88. 7 *Annals* 283, 285-86.

89. *Id.* 289-90.
90. 7 *Annals* 290.
91. *Id.* 294-95, 298.
92. *Id.* 19-20 (June 9, 1797).
93. *Id.* 359, 362-64 (June 22, 1797).
94. *Id.* 362-63.
95. *Id.* 363-66.
96. *Id.* 369, 374.
97. *Id.* 392-93.
98. *Id.* 392-93, 30, 407-409.
99. *Id.* 538. The final version reduced the maximum number of vessels to 12. Act of Apr. 27, 1798, §1, 1 Stat. 552.
100. 8 *Annals* 1440 (Apr. 18, 1798).
101. *Id.* 1443, 1445-46, 1454.
102. *Id.* 1454-55. In Harper's view, if the President went beyond the rules prescribed by the law of nations in ordering convoys, "he must be responsible for his conduct, as much as if he were to send our Army into Florida or Canada, while we were at peace with the Powers to which those provinces belong." *Id.* 1447.
103. *Id.* 1456.
104. *Id.* 1458-59.
105. *Id.* 1459-62.
106. *Id.* 1462-72, 1494, 1498-1512, 1519-21.
107. 1 *Naval Operations, Quasi-War With France* 62-64 (Naval Records and Library Office 1935).
108. Letter of May 12, 1798, in 6 *Hamilton Works* 282-83; 21 *Hamilton Papers* 459-60.
109. *Id. Works* 285; *id. Papers* 461-62.
110. McHenry to Adams, Mary 18, 1798, in *Adams Papers*, reel 388.
111. 1 *Naval Operations, supra* note 107, at 77.
112. McHenry to Adams, May 18, 1798, in *Adams Papers*, reel 388.
113. See discussion *supra* at 148-53. On March 27, 1798, in debating the motion to declare that war against France was inexpedient, Gallatin criticized the distinction Sewall sought to draw between offensive and defensive actions: "It would be ridiculous, for instance to say, that our frigates should prevent our vessels from being taken; but they should not take French privateers." 8 *Annals* 1329.
114. 8 *Annals* 1783; *id.* 1806-11.
115. *Id.* 1809-10, 1812.
116. 1 Stat. 561; 8 *Annals* 1813, 1814-35.
117. Act of July 9, 1798, 1 Stat. 578.
118. 2 *Naval Operations, supra* note 107, at 27.
119. Clarfield, *supra* note 6, at 195.
120. 2 *Naval Operations, supra* note 107, at 135 (Dec. 29, 1798) and 227 (Jan. 10, 1799).
121. *See generally* R. Irwin, *The Diplomatic Relations of the United States with the Barbary Powers, 1776-1816* (1931).
122. Act of March 27, 1794, §§1 & 9, 1 Stat. 350-51.

123. The 1794 act terminated the President's authority to build the frigates in the event peace was made with Algiers. Although a treaty was made with Algiers, Congress authorized Washington to build, though not to employ, three frigates. Act of April 20, 1796, 1 Stat. 453.

124. Irwin, *supra* note 121, at 101-102. *See also* Cathcart to Secretary of State Marshall, May 27, 1800, 12 *Annals* 715-16.

125. Letter of January 11, 1800, 13 *Timothy Pickering Papers* 49, 54 (Mass. Hist. Soc.) (microfilm).

126. John Adams to Secretary of State Marshall, July 11, 1800, *Adams Papers*, Reel 120, 185. *See also* Secretary of State Marshall to John Adams, July 21, 1800, *id.*, reel 398; Secretary of State Marshall to John Quincy Adams, July 24, 1800, *id.*, reel 398.

127. Instructions of July 31, 1800, in 1 *Naval Documents*, *supra* note 59, at 365-66.

128. The classic authorities, such as Vattel and Grotius, are cited for this proposition in 1 L. Oppenheim, *International Law* §146 (H. Lauterpacht, ed., 8th ed. 1955).

129. *See* discussion *supra* at 145-47.

130. 5 U.S. (1 Cranch) 1, 26, 28, 43 (1801).

131. 6 U.S. (2 Cranch) 170 (1804).

132. 1 Stat. 613.

133. *See* 6 U.S. (2 Cranch) at 171-72.

134. *See* Act of Feb. 9, 1799, 1 Stat. 613.

135. 6 U.S. (2 Cranch) 170, 178-79.

136. Bas v. Tingy, 4 U.S. (4 Dall.) 37, 40 (1800).

CHAPTER 4
JEFFERSON AND THE
REVOLUTION OF 1800

1. *See generally* 5^2 *Dictionary of American Biography* 17-35 (A. Johnson ed. 1957); R. Morris, *Encyclopedia of American History* 1070-71 (1976).

2. One important exception was Congress's refusal to employ generally the impeachment power to remove judges, and Jefferson's inability to obtain a constitutional amendment that would have authorized removal by the President "on the address of the two Houses." *See, and contrast,* the treatments in 3 A. Beveridge, *Life of John Marshall* 159-222 (1919); 4 D. Malone, *Jefferson and His Time: Jefferson The President, First Term, 1801-1805* at 458-83 (1948-1974) (5 vols.) [hereinafter "Malone, *Jefferson*"]; 1 J.Q. Adams, *Memoirs* 322-23 (C. Adams, ed. 1874).

3. Jefferson to Spencer Roane, Sept. 16, 1819, in 10 *The Writings of Thomas Jefferson* 140 (P. Ford, ed. 1892-99) (10 vols.) [hereinafter "*Jefferson Writings* (Ford)"].

4. Jefferson to William S. Smith, Nov. 13, 1787, *Political Writings of Thomas Jefferson* 68, 69 (E. Dumbauld, ed. 1955).

5. The principles of republicanism have been gathered in several sources, *e.g.*, H. Adams, *John Randolph* 33-34 (1882); 1 Malone, *Jefferson* xvi-xix,

436-37; L. White, *The Jeffersonians* 13-15, 550-53 (1956) [hereinafter "White, *Jeffersonians*"].

6. In seeking the absorption of the Louisiana Territory, Jefferson consciously subordinated his constitutional scruples to avoid a legislative battle that might have upset the purchase. See *infra* at 197. The admission of Ohio, wrote Edward Channing, was an "extraordinary performance" from "the apostles of strict construction" but, he added, "statesmen out of power and in office oftentimes do acts which no amount of argument can make to appear consistent." *The Jeffersonian System* 34 (1906). Jefferson allowed the Bank to continue, and used it freely, despite earlier statements that it was unconstitutional. 1 N. Schachner, *Thomas Jefferson: A Biography* 422 (1957); 5 *Jefferson Writings* (Ford) 284-85, 289. After leaving office he again expressed his hostility to Congress's renewal of the Bank's charter in 1811. 3 H. Randall, *The Life of Thomas Jefferson* 386-87 (1871). He denied the constitutional power to establish the military academy at West Point, but eventually signed the bill creating it. White, *Jeffersonians* 259-60. Although he had opposed the Alien and Sedition Acts, he sought and exercised even broader powers in enforcing the embargo. "The course of Jefferson and Gallatin during the late summer and autumn of 1808 is a fascinating record of doctrinal disorder as the two greatest defenders of liberty in their age put the screws on their fellow American citizens." *Id.* 461, 462-68.

7. Letter to P.S. duPont de Nemours, January 18, 1802, in 9 *The Works of Thomas Jefferson* 342 n.1, 344 n. (Fed. ed. 1904-1905) (12 vols.) [hereinafter "*Jefferson Works* (Fed.)"].

8. 4 Malone, *Jefferson* 102-103.

9. White, *Jeffersonians* 30.

10. On December 22, 1801, for example, John Randolph moved that the House direct the Secretary of War to prepare a statement of the present military establishment, along with an estimate of necessary posts and men for each garrison. The House agreed without opposition. 11 *Annals of Congress* 349 (1853) [hereinafter *Annals*]. Similar motions had been intensely opposed during Washington's administration. L. White *The Federalists*, ch. 6 (1961).

11. When a Senate bill to add two small armed vessels to the navy reached the House, a motion was made to strike the provision that authorized the new vessels, partly on the ground "that this addition to our marine force did not appear to be necessary, in as much as the President, whose constitutional duty it was to give information to Congress of the state of the Union, and who directed the armed force of the nation, had not intimated his opinion of its necessity...." 13 *Annals* 803. (The remark is attributed to Messrs. Smilie and J. Randolph.) Several Representatives countered on numerous grounds, including the argument that Congress was the proper judge of the vessel's necessity: "[W]ith regard to the necessity of these ships, Congress were the proper and Constitutional judges; that it was their special duty to provide and maintain a navy and to provide for the common defence and general welfare of the United States; and that absolute dependence placed by gentlemen on Executive mandates was unprecedented, anti-republican, and unconstitutional...." *Id.* 803 (Nicholson, Eustis, R. Griswold & Huger). No vote was taken on the motion, and consideration of the bill was indefinitely postponed. Representa-

tive Benjamin Tallmadge of Connecticut objected to a bill to increase the military force on the ground that the President—"the Constitutional organ by whom communications are to be made to Congress"—had not requested the increase. 19 *Annals* 1195. No question was taken on the bill.

12. White, *Jeffersonians* 32, 48.

13. White, *Federalists, supra* note 10. *See generally* the discussion in Chapter 2 *supra* at 70-74.

14. 1 *Writings of Albert Gallatin* 68, 73 (H. Adams, ed. 1960) [hereinafter *"Gallatin Writings"*].

15. 8 *Jefferson Writings* (Ford) 120-21.

16. 11 *Annals* 313-14, 319, 324.

17. *Id.* 1257 *passim* (Griswold). The committee report is at 12 *Annals* 1259; and A.S.P., 1 *Finance* 752.

18. 11 *Annals* 1285, 1294.

19. 12 *Annals* 290. Although the House ceased further investigation, former Secretary of Treasury Oliver Wolcott was not similarly content to drop the subject. He issued an address in July 1802, which examined use of funds during the previous administration, and concluded that the moneys had been "faithfully applied," contrary to the committee's report that "considerable sums of the public money have been greatly misapplied, and that much expense has been incurred, without any legal authority." O. Wolcott, *An Address to the People of the United States* (1802).

20. Jefferson to Gallatin, February 19, 1804, 11 *Writings of Thomas Jefferson* 6 (Memorial ed. 1907).

21. White, *Jeffersonians* 112-13.

22. The Baldwin Committee (Senate) was appointed to examine the functioning of the Treasury Department; its report of May 22, 1794, explained that deficiency funding was routinely followed when the purpose had been legislatively authorized. A.S.P., 1 *Finance* 281, 284. *See also* L. Wilmerding, Jr., *The Spending Power: A History of the Efforts of Congress to Control Expenditures* 26 (1943); White, *Jeffersonians* 115-16.

23. The issue of sending an additional frigate to the Mediterranean as a show of strength occasioned a flurry of correspondence between Jefferson and his department heads. Gallatin advised Jefferson that "the appropriations for that object were exhausted." 1 *Gallatin Writings* 97. But Jefferson, after conferring with Madison, informed Gallatin that he was yielding to Secretary Smith's request, and asked Gallatin whether it would be possible "to put the extra advances on the footing of a debt incurred, and arrearages of which might be covered by a future appropriation?" *Id.* 99, 100. See the discussion *infra* note 24.

24. Dr. Stevens had been appointed consul general to Santo Domingo by President Adams in 1798, and also invested with authority as an "agent." 4 *Writings of Thomas Jefferson* 528 (H. Washington, ed. 1854). His appointment had not been approved by the Senate, which was recessed at the time of his designation. Jefferson conjectured that this might "take from him all legal character after their first session following his appointment" (9 *id.* 472), and when Dr. Stevens presented his accounts for payment to the Secretary of State, Jeffer-

son sought opinions from his Cabinet "whether payment can be authorized by the executive, and out of what fund?" (4 *id.* 529-30). Madison believed payment might be made out of the foreign intercourse fund. Jefferson agreed, and in a letter to Gallatin asking the latter's opinion, explained his view that Stevens had acted as a duly authorized agent, since the executive's power to appoint ministers under the Constitution embraces many grades of foreign-affairs personnel; that the fund appropriated for foreign intercourse gives a sum in gross, trusting to the exercise of executive discretion within that sum; and that therefore the "just demands" of Stevens might be lawfully paid. Jefferson to Gallatin, Feb. 19, 1804, 4 *id.* 529, 530. Gallatin had contended on February 21 that the matter, "being a question of appropriation," was for him as Secretary of Treasury to decide. 1 *Gallatin Writings* 178-79. On April 5 he wrote that Stevens's mission was not to an "authorized government of a foreign nation," and therefore that it would be improper to pay Stevens from "moneys appropriated for intercourse with foreign nations"; and that there was no precedent to sanction such a payment "by mere Executive authority, and that it seemed to be, in a peculiar manner, one that wanted legislative sanction." *Id.* 183. Probably realizing, however, that Jefferson wanted to pay Stevens under some color of authority, he added that "in the settlement of the account I shall no longer interfere, and will leave the Comptroller to settle it in his own way, or under the direction of the Secretary of State." Letter of June 11, 1804, *id.* 196, 197. Jefferson replied by reasserting his belief that the annual act which "appropriates a given sum to the expenses of intercourse with foreign nations as a sufficient authority to the President (the constitutional organ of foreign intercourse) to expend that sum for the purposes of foreign intercourse at his discretion." 9 *Jefferson Writings* (Washington), *supra* at 472. Jefferson rejected more than half of Dr. Stevens's claims, however, on the grounds that they were unreasonable and unsubstantiated by evidence. *Id.* 472-75.

25. 15 *Annals* 998-99.

26. The motion was defeated and renewed. *Id.* 999-1000, 1020-21.

27. 10 *Jefferson Works* (Fed.) 434.

28. 1 *id.* 415.

29. 17 *Annals* 14, 17.

30. *Id.* 818-20, 826-28.

31. *Id.* 822-23, 835-37, 849.

32. *E.g., id.* 826 (Smilie).

33. *Id.* 848 (Gardenier); *id.* 832 (Montgomery); *id.* 840 (Alston).

34. *Id.* 819-20 (Eppes); *id.* 827-28 (Dana).

35. *Id.* 824 (I. Campbell).

36. *Id.* 830. Referring to Representative Montgomery's argument based on emergency, Randolph said: "The gentleman's argument proved too much. The more he magnified the danger of the crisis, to justify an illegal and unconstitutional expenditure of the public money, the more clearly did he demonstrate the necessity for convening Congress." *Id.* 837.

37. *Id.* 825, 850, 852-53.

38. John Q. Adams, who fathered the "Aggression Bill" regarding British

warships, at no time recorded Jefferson's participation in his extraordinary diary. 1 J.Q. Adams, *supra* note 2, at 468-85. He was in fact alienated from the administration at the time. *See* 3 *Writings of John Quincy Adams* 167-72 (W. Ford, ed. 1913). Madison's letters indicate that administration policy at the time was conciliatory. *See* 8 *The Writings of James Madison* 40, 42 (G. Hunt, ed. 1908); letter to Wilson C. Nicholas, Feb. 6, 1809, *Madison Presidential Papers*, series 2, reel 25 (LC microfilm).

39. *See* White, *Jeffersonians* 460-64.

40. Act of Jan. 31, 1809, 2 Stat. 514. *See* 19 *Annals* 1042-43, 1049-51, 1072, 1078, 1095, 1184-91. Dana had no doubt as to the propriety of a delegation, but sought to convince the House to require that all the vessels be fitted out. *Id.* 1044, 1049.

41. See the discussion *infra* at note 46.

42. 18 *Annals* 1946. *Compare id.* 1953.

43. 19 *Annals* 245-46; *see also* the objections of Senator White, *id.* 312-13.

44. *Id.* 264-66, 259.

45. *E.g.,* 11 *Annals* 12, 20, 190 (correspondence relating to affairs with Barbary Powers). Confidential messages usually concerned foreign affairs, and the documents involved were generally diplomatic correspondence. *See, e.g.,* 15 *Annals* 71 (request for confidentiality concerning letter from Monroe to British Sec'y of Foreign Affairs, originally sent voluntarily).

46. Opposition to the embargo against foreign trade had reached great heights by early 1808. Illegal activity was especially blatant on Lake Champlain, where smugglers engaged in pitched battles with revenue officers. On April 19, 1808, while Congress was still in session, Jefferson issued a proclamation declaring the Champlain region in a state of insurrection. The insurgents were ordered to disperse, and the Governor of NewYork was authorized to call out the militia. Jefferson did not inform Congress of this step at the time. Senator Hillhouse later complained that Congress had not been told, noting that the proclamation was published in Vermont on April 30, 1808. 19 *Annals* 173-74. He contended that the proclamation had been withheld because Jefferson did not want Congress to learn the full extent of the embargo's unpopularity. *See* White, *Jeffersonians* 464-65; L. Sears, *Jefferson and the Embargo* 167-68 (1927).

47. *E.g.,* 16 *Annals* 469-70 (House request for information relating to efficacy of gunboats in protecting harbors), *id.* 63-65, 478 (information provided); 17 *Annals* 903 (House request for information from Secretaries of War and Navy concerning method of purchasing supplies), *id.* 1005 (infomration provided); 17 *Annals* 1001 (House request for information on state and cost of fortifications), *id.* 1063 (information provided).

48. For example, on November 22, 1803, the Senate resolved that the President be requested to cause to be provided "such information as may have been received" concerning violation of the American flag, or impressment of seamen, by agents of foreign nations. 13 *Annals* 80. This unqualified request was complied with on December 5, when Jefferson sent a letter from Madison describing the incidents that had occurred. *Id.* 210. Other examples appear at: 11 *Annals* 415 (House requests for estimate of cost of Franco-American con-

vention and for information relating to Spanish depredations), *id.* 419, 1211-12 (information provided); 11 *Annals* 434 (unqualified House request of Secretaries of State and Treasury for copies of all instructions given to any vessels to capture French ships), *id.* 445 (information provided); 17 *Annals* 42 (unqualified Senate request to President for list of impressed seamen), *id.* 154 (information provided).

49. *E.g.,* 13 *Annals* 260, 262 (Senate refusal to request information on measures taken by President pursuant to law authorizing military action, cost of same, and the further legislation necessary to end war with Tripoli); 13 *Annals* 385-419 (House refusal to request copies of treaties between France and Spain, and available correspondence, tending to determine whether France had acquired title to Louisiana).

50. *See supra* at 78-79, 133-37.

51. Jefferson's papers contain coded letters dating back to 1785, when he, as Minister at Paris, corresponded with John Adams, then Minister at London. 13 *The Papers of Thomas Jefferson* 2262-64, reel 7 (LC microfilm) (101 reels) [hereinafter *"Jefferson Papers"*]. He developed a highly sophisticated code, even by today's standards. *See generally* D. Kahn, *The Code Breaker* 174-95 (1967); 6 *Papers of Thomas Jefferson* x-xi (J. Boyd, ed. 1958).

52. 8 *Jefferson Writings* (Ford) 143-44.

53. *Id.* 144-47.

54. *Id.* 172, 174.

55. Madison to Pinckney and Monroe, Feb. 17, 1803, A.S.P., 2 *Foreign Relations* 532; Madison to Livingston, Feb. 23, 1803, *id.* 537; Madison to Monroe (extract), Mar. 2, 1803, *id.;* Madison to Livingston and Monroe, *id.* 540-44.

56. Jefferson to Livingston, Feb. 3, 1803, 8 *Jefferson Writings* (Ford) 209.

57. Jefferson to Monroe, Jan. 13, 1803, *id.* 190, 191.

58. We found eighteen such letters by comparing Madison's correspondence with the content of transmissions in the *American State Papers:*

Reference Found in A.S.P., 3 For. Rel. at	Date of Letter Referred to	Writer	Recipient	Found
90	Oct. 24, 1803	Madison	Monroe	No
90	Jan. 16, 1804	Madison	Monroe	Reel 25[a]
109	Sept. 20, 1805	Madison	Monroe	No
117	Nov. 11, 1805	Monroe	Madison	Reel 11[b]
113	Dec. 4, 1805	Madison	Monroe	Reel 25[a]
115	Jan. 13, 1806	Madison	Monroe	p. 216[c]
119	Feb. 20, 1806	Monroe	Madison	No
119	Mar. 11, 1806	Monroe	Madison	Reel 25[a]

Reference Found in A.S.P., 3 For. Rel. at	Date of Letter Referred to	Writer	Recipient	Found
185	Apr. 25, 1807	Monroe/ Pinkney	Madison	Reel 4[b]
221	Dec. 7, 1807	Pinkney	Madison	p. 71[d]
221	Dec. 21, 1807	Pinkney	Madison	p. 73[d]
221	Dec. 31, 1807	Pinkney	Madison	p. 75[d]
223	Feb. 23, 1808	Madison	Erskine	No
221	Feb. 26, 1808	Pinkney	Madison	No
225	May 1, 1808	Madison	Pinkney	No
225	July 10, 1808	Pinkney	Madison	p. 398[d]
227	Aug. 2, 1808	Pinkney	Madison	Reel 25[a]
237	Sept. 9, 1808	Madison	Pinkney	No

[a]*Madison Presidential Papers*, LC microfilm.
[b]*Monroe Presidential Papers*, LC microfilm.
[c]*2 Letters and Other Writings of James Madison* (Cong. ed. 1867).
[d]H. Wheaton, *Some Account of the Life, Writings, and Speeches of William Pinkney* (1826).

Madison's letter to Monroe of Jan. 13, 1806, asked him to purge his records of a pamphlet Madison had earlier sent him. 2 *Letters and Other Writings of James Madison* 216 (Cong. ed. 1867); *see* 4 I. Brant, *James Madison, Secretary of State, 1800-1809* at 297-301 (1953).

    59. See *infra* at 188.

    60. The first instance was a call on January 8, 1802, for information relating to Spanish depredations (11 *Annals* 415); supplied on April 20, 1802 (*id.* 1211-12). A second related to a possible violation by Spain of its treaty with the United States by closing the port of New Orleans. 12 *Annals* 281 (December 17, 1802); supplied, *id.* 285.

    61. 19 *Annals* 306, 309-10.

    62. *Id.* 1601.

    63. *Id.* 1081-82, 1084, 1086.

    64. *Id.* 424.

    65. See *infra* at 198-99.

    66. 17 *Annals* 1261. The debate—a "devious discussion" according to the Reporter (*id.* 1262)—continued over a period of nine days.

    67. Those opposed to the request felt the evidence concerning Wilkinson should simply be sent to the President for whatever action he deemed appropriate. *Id.* 1265 (Taylor); 1339-40 (Smilie); 1402 (Love).

    68. The quoted statement came, for example, on a motion made by Federalist Josiah Quincy to obtain an official copy of the President's proclamation

issued after the attack on the *Chesapeake*, a document that had already appeared in newspapers throughout the nation. The motion carried, 70-32, with many members opposing it as unnecessary. 17 *Annals* 924-27. Jefferson then provided an official copy. *Id.* 947.

69. 11 *Annals* 1140.

70. 8 *Jefferson Writings* (Ford) 141-43. He regarded it as a "malicious" invasion of the executive branch, and did not want to indulge Federalist "ill humor."

71. 11 *Annals* 1142.

72. *Id.* 1152, 1154. The material was soon furnished (*id.* 1194), and the matter was referred to committee, where it died (*id.* 1232).

73. 12 *Annals* 281.

74. 4 Malone, *Jefferson* 264.

75. 12 *Annals* 312.

76. *Id.* 352, 359.

77. *Id.* 357, 360, 361. The motion was defeated (35-51) at *id.* 368. There had been an earlier vote to refuse to consider the resolution, but Bayard had reopened the issue when Samuel Smith introduced a resolution requesting a $2 million appropriation. *Id.* 366-67. "[C]an gentlemen expect," said Bayard, "that either we or the nation will in any case be satisfied to make a large grant of money, while no information is given of the grounds upon which the grant is required?" *Id.* 367.

78. The vote was 24-7. 1 *S. Jour. Exec. Proc.* 449-51. The actions of the Senate are described without any record of debate. But Senator William Plumer wrote: "The Senate have taken less time to deliberate on this important treaty than they have allowed themselves on the most trivial Indian contract." *Plumer's Memorandum of Proceedings in the U.S. Senate: 1803-1807*, at 13 (E. Brown, ed. 1923).

79. 13 *Annals* 385.

80. *Id.* 388, 389.

81. *Id.* 400.

82. *See* 13 *Annals* 385 (the original resolution); *id.* 418-19 (vote without division rejecting clause requesting documentation of France's good title); *id.* 419 (vote on whole motion).

83. 17 *Annals* 1240.

84. *Id.* 1166 (Dana explaining that "management" of foreign relations "rested entirely with the Executive").

85. 17 *Annals* 104; 18 *Annals* 1552.

86. 18 *Annals* 1640, 1645.

87. *Id.* 1644-48.

88. *Id.* 1675-76.

89. *Id.* 1656.

90. *Id.* 1690-91, 1693.

91. *Id.* 1693-94.

92. *Id.* 1712, 1714.

93. Id. 1830, 1835-38. For discussion on the propriety and effect of votes to refuse to consider, see *id.* 1890-95.

94. *Id.* 1842-43.

95. *Id.* 1865-68.

96. 17 *Annals* 173-74; 18 *Annals* 1889.

97. *See, e.g.,* 18 *Annals* 1870-1900.

98. The first notable motion was by Rep. Elliot, to obtain data from the Secretary of Treasury regarding enforcement of the embargo. 19 *Annals* 478. Love objected to the resolution, construing it as an attack on the administration, and arguing unabashedly that the enforcement of laws was not a legislative matter. *Id.* 479. Elliot responded that Congress needed information to see what the executive had done, and assured Love he was making no accusations. Only then was the resolution adopted, on November 14, 1808. *Id.* 483. Both houses passed unqualified resolutions in November, calling for all the decrees and acts promulgated by the belligerent European powers since 1791. *Id.* 18; 482. Jefferson sent the decrees that could be obtained, "and are supposed to have entered into the views of" each house. *Id.* 299, 908.

99. 5 U.S. (1 Cranch) 137 (1803).

100. *Id.* 141-46. The Court held the commissions were effective to confer the offices involved upon plaintiffs, but refused the remedy of mandamus because the statute authorizing the writ was found unconstitutional.

101. See Act of June 5, 1794, §5, 1 Stat. 381, 384; United States v. Smith, 27 F. Cas. 1192 (No. 16, 342) (C.C.D.N.Y. 1806).

102. 27 F. Cas. at 1194, 1228-31. Beveridge claims that it was, at the time, generally believed that Jefferson had used the excuse of "duties" to prevent the officers from attending for essentially political reasons. 3 A. Beveridge, *supra* note 2 at 436 n.1.

103. 3 H. Adams, *History of the United States* 278 (1889-91) (9 vols.) [hereinafter "*Adams History*"]. Among the earliest letters were those from Joseph Daveiss's claims, and requested him on February 15, 1806, to communicate on microfilm as part of Jefferson's correspondence. *See, e.g.,* 155 *Jefferson Papers* 27210-12; 156 *id.* 27393-94, 27416, Reel 56. Jefferson's reply is at *id.* 27416. *See* J. Daveiss, "A View of the President's Conduct Concerning the Conspiracy of 1806," in 12 *Quarterly Publication of Hist. and Philo. Soc. of Ohio* 58, 69-74 (Cox & Swineford, eds. 1917). The President investigated Daveiss' claims, and requested him on February 15, 1806, to communicate all he knew on the subject "since the information is so important. . . ." *Id.* at 77. Jefferson apparently gave these claims too little credence, however, because they were accompanied by other, wildly exaggerated assertions. *See* 5 Malone, *Jefferson* 223-25.

104. The Cabinet did vote to send military vessels on October 22. 3 *Adams History* 280. But another vote on October 25 revoked the order because no movement by Burr had been reported, which "proves he is committing no overt act against the law." Further inquiries were, however, authorized. *Id.* 281.

105. 5 Malone, *Jefferson* 247-49. The confidential letter and memorandum are in 2 J. Wilkinson, *Memoirs of My Own Times,* app. xcv (1816).

106. 1 J. Richardson, ed., *A Compilation of the Messages and Papers of the Presidents, 1789-1897,* at 392 (1896). The proclamation described the expedition as directed against Spain, at least in part because Jefferson doubted whether

he was authorized to use regular troops to suppress domestic insurrection. *See* 5 Malone, *Jefferson* 252-53.

107. 8 *Jefferson Writings* (Ford) 482, 489-90.

108. 16 *Annals* 334, 336.

109. *Id.* 340-42. *See also* Holland's comment, *id.* 344-45.

110. *Id.* 353 (Eppes); 339 (Barwell).

111. *Id.* 343.

112. 16 *Annals* 357-58.

113. *Id.* 39-43.

114. *See* 5 Malone, *Jefferson* 269, 278-79.

115. A research assistant examined the papers turned over to Congress and printed in the *Annals* and the *American State Papers*. (These sources are not invariably complete, but they are the best available.) He then compared the documents found in these sources to the documents relevant to the Burr conspiracy that he found in the Library of Congress collection of Jefferson's correspondence.

116. The transmitted materials are set forth in 16 *Annals* 1008-19, appendix.

117. For example, Jefferson promised confidentiality to Daveiss in a letter dated February 16, 1806 (156 *Jefferson Papers* 27416), and again on September 12, 1806, when he assured Daveiss he would keep the letters among his "private" papers (161 *id.* 28260). A similar commitment was made to George Morgan of Pennsylvania. *Id.* 28288 (Sept. 19, 1806).

118. Letters of January 23, 25 and 26, 1807, in 163 *id.* 28864-65, 28875-84, Reel 60.

119. *See* Letter of December 22, 1806, 162 *id.* 28620-21. Jefferson said he would wait twelve days to hear from Wilkinson. 163 *id.* 28623, Reel 60.

120. Cyrus Griffin, Judge of the District Court at Richmond, Virginia, sat by Marshall's side, but his participation was negligible. 3 Beveridge, *supra* note 2 at 398. *See generally* 5 Malone, *Jefferson* 310-46, for an able, though pro-Jefferson description. The best available report is D. Robertson, *Reports of the Trials of Colonial Aaron Burr for Treason* 113-14 (1808) [hereinafter "Robertson"]. *See also* T. Carpenter, *The Trial of Col. Aaron Burr* (1808).

121. *See generally* Paul A. Freund, "Foreword: On Presidential Privilege," 88 *Harv. L. Rev.* 13 (1974), and authorities collected at *id.* 24 n. 60.

122. 1 Robertson 180-89; the opinions are also reported at 25 F.Cas. 2-207 (Nos. 14, 692a-14, 694a) (C.C.D. Va. 1807).

123. 1 Robertson 142 (Wirt). The President likewise insisted on his "necessary right . . . to decide, independently of all other authority, what papers, coming to him as President, the public interests permit to be communicated, and to whom. . . ." He purported, however, to be willing to furnish whatever evidence "justice might require." Jefferson to Hay, 10 *Jefferson Works* (Fed.) 398n., 399.

Jefferson wrote to Hay again on June 17, supplying some military orders, but reiterating his position that, "with respect to papers, there is certainly a public and private side to our offices." The latter included "mere executive proceedings," and all nations have found it advantageous to keep some such proceedings known to their "executive functionary only. He, of course, from the nature of the case, must be the sole judge of which of them the public interest will permit publication." This is why "under our Constitution, in requests of papers from the legislative to the executive branch, an exception is carefully expressed, 'as to those which he may deem the public welfare may require not to be disclosed.' . . ." Mutual respect "between the constituted authorities" and a sincere disposition to do justice "will always insure from the executive, in exercising the duty of discrimination confided to him, the same candour and integrity, to which the nation has in like manner trusted in the disposal of its judiciary authorities." *Id.* 401-402n.

124. 1 Robertson 158, 163, 165.
125. *Id.* 186-87.
126. 10 *Jefferson Works* (Fed.) 405n.
127. 2 Robertson 504-505.
128. *See* the description in 5 Malone, *Jefferson* 248-49, 325.
129. 2 Robertson 509.
130. Hay became adamant: "no government can exist without resorting to . . . [secret, confidential correspondence] on critical emergencies." At least two paragraphs of the November letter, he claimed, were irrelevant to Burr's trial and should remain secret (*id.* 509-12):

> The President, who certainly has a right of withholding from public view such documents or parts of documents as in his judgment ought not to be disclosed, has expressly authorized me to keep back such parts of the letter as I may think it would be improper to communicate. I therefore withhold those parts of this letter, which, in my own judgment, ought not to be made public.

One of Burr's attorneys, John Wickham, agreed that if Jefferson declared "the public good" to require parts of the letter be withheld "because its disclosure would bear on the most important interests of the state," his view "would certainly deserve consideration." But he challenged Hay's right to exercise discretion for the President. *Id.* 512-13, 516-18.

131. *Id.* 536-37. Marshall said a privilege existed that potentially extended to embarrassing material, the exercise of which should be closely reviewed by the courts, with considerable weight being given the President's opinion (*id.* 535-36):

> The President although subject to the general rules which apply to others, may have sufficient motives for declining to produce a particular paper, and those motives may be such as to restrain the court from enforcing its production. . . . I can readily conceive that the President might receive a letter which it would be improper to exhibit in public because of the manifest inconvenience of its exposure. The occasion for demanding it ought, in such a case, to be very strong, and to be fully shewn [*sic*] to the court before its production could be insisted upon. I admit, that in such a case, much reliance must be placed on the declaration of the President; and I do think that a privilege

does exist to withhold private letters of a certain description. The reason is this: letters to the President in his private character, are often written to him in consequence of his public character, and may relate to public concerns. Such a letter, though it be a private one, seems to partake of the character of an official paper, and to be such as ought not on light ground to be forced into public view.

132. 10 *Jefferson Works* (Fed.) 409n.

133. 2 Robertson 539. Some have unsafely concluded that Burr's failure to object indicated acquiescence in Jefferson's position. *See* Nixon v. Sirica, 487 F.2d 700, 748 (D.C. Cir. 1973) (dissenting opinion of MacKinnon, J.); Dumas Malone, in *New York Times*, Nov. 26, 1973, at 30, col. 5.

134. The letter did not name Claiborne and Meade, but obliquely suggested their involvement. Luther Martin, one of Burr's attorneys, explicitly suggested that the two officials had been named, in arguing the letter's importance. 3 Carpenter, *supra* note 120 at 280.

135. *Id.* 280-84.

136. *See generally* 1 *Adams History* 368-69; F. Chadwick, *The Relations of the United States and Spain, Diplomacy* (1909); 2 A. Fortier, *History of Louisiana* 189 ff. (1904).

137. *See* letters of May 26 and 29, 1801, to Monroe, in 7 *Jefferson Works* (Fed.) 259, 262; also the letter of May 14, to T.M. Randolph, cited in 4 Malone, *Jefferson* 248 n. 16. In a letter dated July 15, 1801, to W.C. Claiborne, Governor of the Mississippi Territory, he predicted serious difficulty if France had in fact acquired New Orleans. 8 *Jefferson Writings* (Ford) 71. The extraordinary letter of April 18, 1802, to Livingston, is discussed in connection with the system for secrecy it established. In it he said that "there is on the globe one single spot, the possessor of which is our natural and habitual enemy. It is New Orleans. . . ." *Id.* 144-47.

138. *See* 4 Malone, *Jefferson* 253. Pichon, of course, reported this message (which Jefferson repeated to the British minister) to Talleyrand. *See id.* 253 n.33, 254 n.34. Madison was much more cautious in his conversations with foreign diplomats. Jefferson later explained these threats to his French friend DuPont de Nemours as predictions: "My foreseeing it does not make me the cause of it, nor can my admonition be a threat, the storm not being produced by my will." But writing to Livingston on the same day, Jefferson reportedly said that "in his earlier letter he had gone further into the province of the Secretary of State than he had intended, thus reminding Livingston that he was speaking off the record." 4 Malone, *Jefferson* 257.

139. *Id.* 252 n.29. Malone perceived "method in his excess: having convinced Pichon of his excellent dispositions toward the French, he was in a position to speak candidly about the effect the taking of Louisiana would have on the relations between the two countries." *Id.* 253.

140. His practices are discussed *supra* at 177-82.

141. Yrujo arranged for the publication of articles accusing the administration of seeking war against Spain. *See generally* 4 Brant, *supra* note 58, at 209-12; 5 Malone, *Jefferson* 79-80.

142. A proclamation was issued after the *Leopard* attacked the *Chesapeake*

prohibiting British vessels from entering American waters. Section 4 of the Act of March 3, 1805 permitted such a prohibition to be issued by the President "at pleasure," and Section 5 permitted him to use the armed forces and militia to enforce his order. 2 Stat. 339, 341-42; 9 *Jefferson Writings* (Ford) 98; 17 *Annals* 948. When in 1806 a shot fired by the British ship *Leander* accidentally killed an American outside the Port of New York, Jefferson issued a proclamation closing American ports forever to the three frigates and their commanders, and ordering that the *Leander's* captain, who had been indicted by a grand jury, be arrested wherever found within America's jurisdiction. 3 *Adams History* 199-201; 10 *Jefferson Works* (Fed.) 256. Another proclamation was issued on April 19, 1808, in response to open and violent opposition to the embargo in the Lake Champlain area; federal troops were sent to supplement militia. These actions were apparently authorized by the Act of March 30, 1808, §5, 2 Stat. 478.

143. Jefferson sent nominations of Monroe and Livingston to the Senate on January 11, 1803 to negotiate "with full power to enter into a treaty or convention . . . for the purpose of enlarging and more effectually securing our rights and interests" in the Mississippi River and territory on its left bank, and eastward. 12 *Annals* 22-23. The Senate confirmed on January 12, and Congress promptly appropriated $2 million "to defray the expenses which may be incurred in relation to the intercourse between the United States and foreign nations." Though this very general language was used, the House certainly intended to authorize the purchase of New Orleans and the areas of East and West Florida, and even anticipated that more money might be required. *See* 1 *S. Jour. Exec. Proc.* 431-32, 436 (vote: 15 to 12); 12 *Annals* 370-71, 374.

Jefferson contemplated sending the treaty and accompanying documents simultaneously to both the Senate and House. Gallatin advised him to send the material first to the Senate, and to the House only after the treaty was approved. Jefferson accepted Gallatin's advice, stating in his message to Congress that, after the Senate approved, the treaty would be sent "without delay . . . to the representatives also, for the exercise of their functions, as to those conditions which are within the powers vested by the constitution in Congress." 10 *Jefferson Works* (Fed.) 35-36.

144. Monroe had asked if an informal provision on impressment would suffice, and Jefferson posed this issue to his Cabinet as well as whether the Senate should be consulted. The Cabinet apparently agreed unanimously that such a treaty would be unacceptable, and that the Senate should not be consulted. 1 *Jefferson Works* (Fed.) 406-408. Madison sent this news promptly. Madison to Monroe and Pinkney, Feb. 3, 1807, in A.S.P., 3 *Foreign Relations* 153, 154. But the negotiators had reached an agreement before receiving his letter. *See* 2 *id.* 805 (letter of Dec. 27, 1806).

145. C. Bowers, *Jefferson in Power* 360 (1936).

146. *See id.*; 2 Schachner *supra* note 6, at 834-35.

147. Jefferson to Monroe, March 21, 1807, 10 *Jefferson Works* (Fed.) 374-76.

148. See Madison to Monroe and Pinkney, Feb. 3, 1807, A.S.P., 3 *Foreign Relations* 154. They communicated the offer, but the British were not interest-

ed. Monroe and Pinkney to Madison, April 22, 1807, *id.* 160. *See also* Monroe to Madison, Feb. 28, 1808, *id.* 173-74.

149. *See* 16 *Annals* 11; 5 Malone, *Jefferson* 243-46.

150. 1 *Jefferson Works* (Fed.) 424.

151. 4 *Adams History* 1-26; 4 Brant, *Madison* 380-88.

152. 1 *Jefferson Works* (Fed.) 411.

153. See discussion *supra* at 172-73.

154. Jefferson to Governor William H. Cabell of Virginia, June 29, 1807, in 10 *Jefferson Works* (Fed.) 433-37n.

155. Jefferson to Cabell, Aug. 7, 1807, *id.* 438n.

156. On November 8, 1808, for example, Jefferson advised Congress that Algiers had ill-treated the United States Consul assigned to that country. He noted that Congress might want to take actions to rectify this conduct "not within the limits of Executive authority." 19 *Annals* 12-13. *See also infra* textual note, at 200.

157. Act of Oct. 31, 1803, 2 Stat. 245.

158. The claim, originally made by Livingston, was eventually concurred in gress. See 4 Malone, *Jefferson* 306-309; Channing *supra* note 6, at 76-78; I. Cox, *The West Florida Controversy* 64-101 (1918) [hereinafter "Cox, *West Florida*"].

159. Gallatin was willing to use force to take New Orleans, but wrote an extensive recommendation against using force to take areas not clearly within the terms of the purchase. See Gallatin to Jefferson, Sept. 5, 1803 and Sept. 12, 1805 in 1 *Gallatin Writings* 153, 241.

160. *E.g.*, Secretary of War to Wilkinson, Oct. 5, 1803, in 9 *Territorial Papers of the United States* 71 (C. Carter, ed. 1940).

161. 2 Stat. 251, 254.

162. 4 Brant, *supra* note 58, at 193; Gallatin to H.B. Trist, Feb. 27, 1804, in 9 *Territorial Papers, supra* note 160 at 192-93; see 1 *Jefferson Works* (Fed.) 381-82. When the revenue district for Mobile was established on May 30, 1804, Fort Stoddert—lying well within indisputably American territory—was made its port of entry, and it was declared to include only waters lying "*within the boundaries of the United States.*" A.S.P., 2 *Foreign Relations* 583.

163. The Cabinet decided on November 14, 1805 that Spain should cede East and West Florida in exchange for $5 million, and that the Western boundary of Louisiana should extend far beyond the limit contended for by Spain. Letter of Oct. 23, 1805, in 8 *Jefferson Writings* (Ford) 383-84. An appropriation of $2 million was obtained for this purpose, and instructions issued to pursue the purchase. But the effort failed. 15 *Annals* 1125-26; Act of Feb. 13, 1806, 2 Stat. 349-50; Letter of March 13, 1806, Madison to John Armstrong and James Bowdoin, in 2 *Bowdoin and Temple Papers*, 6 *Mass. Hist. Soc. Collections* 297 (7th ser., 1907).

164. 15 *Annals* 13-14.

165. 15 *Annals* 190. See also Jefferson's communication to Congress of March 20, 1806 (16 *Annals* 913) and accompanying documents.

166. 15 *Annals* 190-91; *see also* 16 *Annals* 913.

167. *See, e.g.*, Porter's extraordinary letter to Secretary Robert Smith,

Feb. 19, 1809, *Letters Rec'd by Sec'y Navy from Masters Commandant 1804–1886*, National Archives microfilm M-147, reel 3.

168. D. Long, *Nothing Too Daring: A Biography of Commodore David Porter, 1780–1843*, at 45 (1970), referring to Porter's dispatch of Mar. 16, 1809 (*Letters, supra* note 167, at M-147, reel 3), stating that he was taking on himself the responsibility of encroaching on Spain's jurisdiction to enforce the embargo laws.

169. Secretary of War to Wilkinson, Dec. 2, 1808, in 2 *Wilkinson Memoirs* 342–43.

170. Jefferson to Henry Dearborn, Jan. 12, 1809, in 184 *Jefferson Papers* 32794.

171. Wilkinson to Eustis, May 18, 1809, in 2 Wilkinson, *supra* note 105, at 357; Eustis to Wilkinson, July 22, 1809, in Cox, *West Florida* 303. I.J. Cox, who has written what is considered the definitive history of the West Florida controversy, believes that Jefferson had not given up West Florida, but was waiting in hope that France would "subdue" Spain, and that Napoleon, to secure the neutrality of the United States, might repeal his decrees and offer Florida. *Id.* 303–309.

172. *E.g.*, 26 *Am. J. Int'l L.* 771, 832 (1932 Supp.); 1 L. Oppenheim, *International Law* 491 (5th ed. 1937); Act of Apr. 30, 1790, §9, 1 Stat. 112–14.

173. A.S.P., 1 *Foreign Relations* 66; 15 *Annals* 12.

174. Letter of Aug. 5, 1806 from Porter to Secretary of Navy, *Letters, supra* note 167, at M-147, reel 1.

175. Letter of Aug. 5, 1806 in *id.*, but different from the letter in note 174 *supra*. Porter wrote that he told the British officer who delivered the threat that "if the Forts fired at me I should return the fire as long as resistance could avail, and when I could resist no longer should strike my coulours, surrendering my Vessel and consider myself a prisoner of War." See Long's quote of Fletcher Pratt's statement that "if Enterprize submitted to being detained for this reason, there would be some other reason for holding the next American ship that came in; and presently the right of British port officers to grant or withhold exit passes would be established." Long, *supra* note 168 at 34.

176. See 4 Malone, *Jefferson* 240.

177. Jefferson told Yrujo that he would have to describe the expedition as commercial to Congress, because the Constitution more clearly allowed such an endeavor. Letter of Dec. 2, 1802, Yrujo to Cevallos, *Letters of the Lewis and Clark Expedition* 4 (D. Jackson, ed. 1962); Letters of June 20, 1803, from Jefferson to Lewis, *id.* 61.

178. 12 *Annals* 24–26 (Jan. 18, 1803).

179. Act of Feb. 28, 1803, 2 Stat. 207.

180. Letter of June 20, 1803, in *Lewis and Clark Letters supra* note 177, at 61. The wording is susceptible to other constructions. See I. Cox, *The Early Exploration of Louisiana* 43 (1906). Other instructions reflect the expedition's military character. *E.g.*, *Lewis and Clark Letters, supra* at 32, 35 (Gallatin and Lincoln to Jefferson).

181. A.S.P., 1 *Misc.* 391.

182. Dunbar to Jefferson, Aug. 18, 1804, in 142 *Jefferson Papers* 24753, reel 49: "I have further intelligence that if the Expedition had gone up the

[Red] river, there is no doubt it would have terminated a little beyond the American post of Nakitosh by Spanish opposition."

183. 16 *Annals* 11-13.
184. *Id.* 11; 5 Malone, *Jefferson* 243-46.
185. Dearborn to Wilkinson, Feb. 26, 1805, in 2 *Journals of Zebulon Montgomery Pike* 99 (D. Jackson, ed. 1966).
186. *Id.* 120-21.
187. Wilkinson to Jefferson, Aug. 4, 1818, *id.* 389-90; Wilkinson to Dearborn, Aug. 2, 1806, *id.* 128.
188. Cox, *West Florida* 126-27.
189. Jefferson to Madison, Aug. 30, 1807, in 2 *Journals of Zebulon Pike, supra* note 185, at 268. But Jefferson refused to pay a subsequent, larger bill. *See* Foranda to Madison, Nov. 28, 1818, *id.* 347; Cox, *West Florida* 137.
190. Dearborn to Montgomery, Dec. 7, 1808, in 2 *Journals of Zebulon Pike, supra* note 185, at 355.
191. *See, e.g.*, 18 *Annals* 1658-60.
192. *See supra* at 175-76, 215. Section 4 of the act passed by Congress "for the more effectual preservation of peace in the ports and harbors" provided that, "in order to prevent insults to the authority of the laws," whereby peace may be endangered, the President may "permit or interdict at pleasure, the entrance of the harbors and waters under the jurisdiction of the United States to all armed vessels belonging to any foreign nation, and by force to repel and remove them from the same. . . ." If an armed foreign vessel failed to obey an order to depart the harbors or waters of the United States, section 5 authorized the President or his delegate to use force to remove the vessel, or to issue a proclamation prohibiting all intercourse with vessels of the offending nation. Act of Mar. 3, 1805, 2 Stat. 339, 341-42.
193. 13 *Annals* 40-45, 73 (Nov. 3, 1803).
194. 15 *Annals* 166, 190. *See generally* 1 J.Q. Adams, *supra* note 2, at 410-13, 416-19; *Plumer's Memorandum, supra* note 78 at 445.
195. On January 3, 1806, a House committee reported a resolution authorizing the President to raise troops "to protect the southern frontiers of the United States from Spanish inroad and insult, and to chastise the same . . . , although the President sought only funds to purchase the area. The resolution was defeated and the appropriation approved. 15 *Annals* 1117-18, 1120, 1125-26.
196. 17 *Annals* 43-44 (Dec. 2, 1807). This bill, termed the "Aggression bill," 1 J.Q. Adams, *supra* note 2, at 485, would have authorized the President to permit or forbid, at his discretion, entrance of armed vessels into the harbors and waters, and to use force to "repel or remove them." Sec. 6 provided that refusal of a vessel to leave, or reentry after orders to depart, shall be tantamount to "an hostile invasion of the territory of the United States . . . [and] shall be proceeded against as a vessel of an enemy." The bill was read in the House on December 3 (*id.* 1019), and committed to a Committee of the Whole, but was not subsequently submitted for consideration.
197. 17 *Annals* 1155.
198. Speaking of the discretionary power to be given the President to build,

or not build, gunboats, in accordance with his view of the public interest, Representative Dana said (17 *Annals* 1122):

> In respect to foreign relations they had not the necessary information to enable them to judge so well as could be wished. That House had not in its possession any despatches relative to the affair between the Chesapeake and Leopard. There had not been laid before them any general system of defense, nor had they been told the probable issue of the negotiations with England. In all points they were in the dark.

199. 17 *Annals* 335.

200. *Id.* 339-58.

201. *E.g.*, 19 *Annals* 1421 (House strikes authorization of letters in Senate bill).

202. For example, the House passed a resolution noting the seriousness of the closing of New Orleans to Americans and asserted "their unalterable determination to maintain the boundaries and the rights of navigation and commerce through the river Mississippi, as established by existing treaties." But it also recited that the House, "relying, with perfect confidence, on the vigilance and wisdom of the Executive, . . . will wait the issues of such measures as that department of the Government shall have pursued. . . ." 12 *Annals* 339.

British aggressions led the Senate to three resolutions. The first was adopted unanimously on February 12, 1806, and protested the capture and condemnation of American vessels. 15 *Annals* 90-91. The second requested the President "to demand and insist upon" the return to citizens of captured property. It stirred controversy, with some Senators claiming the resolution was unconstitutional (in that it interfered with the President's conduct of foreign affairs), unwise (in that it tied the President's hands), and disrespectful. Others noted that the Senate had a constitutional role in treaty-making that included giving "advice," that the resolution was intended for England and might help the President, and that no insult could be seen in the Senate's stating its view. *Id.* 94, 96-97, 106. The latter position prevailed, and the resolution was approved, after the Senate agreed to strike the words "and insist." *Id.* 112. The third resolution, which prohibited importation of specified British manufactures, also gave rise to some dispute; some Senators considered such a prohibition equivalent to a war measure. Resolution supporters argued that, since the prohibition would not take effect until November 1806 (it was then March), ample time was allowed for negotiations, which would even be aided by the imminence of this form of commercial restriction. *Id.* 167-68.

203. 13 *Annals* 787.

204. Thus, Congress refused to enlarge the army, and gave the President only limited naval power. 19 *Annals* 1229, 1191. At the end of Jefferson's administration the embargo was replaced by nonintercourse, despite his hope that it would be continued for several more months. *See* Jefferson to his son-in-law, Thomas Mann Randolph, Feb. 7, 1809, in 11 *Jefferson Works* (Fed.) 96. Louis Sears in *Jefferson and the Embargo*, *supra* note 46, at 140, describes this letter as written "in the bitterness of humiliation . . . ."

205. 2 H. Miller, ed., *Treaties and Other International Acts of the United States* 457, 482 (1931). See Chapter 3 *supra* at 160-61.

206. Channing *supra* note 6, at 36.

207. The *George Washington* reached the United States in early summer. *Id.* 39. Jefferson had ordered the squadron assembled and readied for sea duty about one month prior to the Cabinet meeting. Letters of Smith to Jefferson, April 6, 1801, 111 *Jefferson Papers* 19141-42; May 4, 1801, 112 *id.* 19244-45a, reel 39.

208. 8 *Jefferson Writings* (Ford) 62-63.

209. 1 *Jefferson Works* (Fed.) 365-66. Madison felt the ships could enter the enemy's harbors only in pursuit.

210. 1 *Naval Documents Related to the United States War With the Barbary Powers* 465-67 (1939) [hereinafter *"Naval Documents"*]. The orders were issued by Samuel Smith on behalf of Acting Sec'y of Navy Henry Dearborn.

211. Channing, *supra* note 6, at 39-40. Letters were simultaneously sent to Rufus King, Minister to London, and to several United States consuls, informing them that Dale had been instructed that, should war have been declared or hostilities commenced, he was to make the most effectual use of his force in the object for which it was intended. Letter from Madison to U.S. Consuls, May 21, 1801, in 1 *Naval Documents* 472. The letter to King is at *id.* 471.

212. Act of March 3, 1801, § 2, 2 Stat. 110. The law also had upper limits on the number of men the President could add.

213. See 4 Malone, *Jefferson* 102-103 n.28.

214. Samuel Smith to Dale, May 20, 1801, in 1 *Naval Documents* 463, 465. The Act did not even expressly authorize that the vessels be "employed" for any purpose; it empowered the President to officer and man the vessels up to two-thirds the previous complement. Act of March 3, 1801, § 2, 2 Stat. 110.

215. 8 *Jefferson Writings* (Ford) 94. Jefferson seems definitely to have been referring to Dale's letter to Samuel Smith of July 2, 1801, in which Dale described finding two Tripolitan vessels at anchor at Gibraltar, one of which was commanded by "the high Admiral of Tripoli," a formidable "Scotchman," married to the Pasha's daughter. Dale regretted not having arrived before the Tripolitan vessels. He left the frigate Philadelphia to watch the Admiral, "that Is to take him when he goes out," because "from every Information that I can get here Tripoli is at War with America. . . ." 1 *Naval Documents* 497, 498.

216. Dale wrote to Danish Consul Nicholas Nissen, July 26, 1801 (1 *Naval Documents* 532), that having heard that the "Bey" had declared war against the United States, "My Intentions have been since, to take the Bey's Corsairs wherever I may fall in with them."

217. *E.g.*, Dale to Capt. Samuel Barron, July 4, 1801, in 1 *Naval Documents* 504, and July 9, 1801, *id.* 505; Dale to Lt. Sterrett, July 5, 1801, *id.* 503, and July 30, 1801, *id.* 534. Dale did not explicitly recommend disablement and release of Tripolitan vessels, but he does refer his captains to the "Instructions that you have got from the Secretary of the Navy," which apparently comprehend disablement within the expression "sink, burn, or otherwise destroy. . . ." *E.g.*, Dale to Barron, May 29, 1801, *id.* 477; Dale to Bainbridge, May 29, 1801, *id.* 478.

218. *Id.* 534-35. The *Enterprise* was the smallest vessel in the squadron; the three other vessels were frigates, two with 44 guns each, the other with 32 guns. See letter of Samuel Smith to De Butts and Purviance, May 20, 1801, in *id.* 462.

219. *Id.* 534-35.

220. R. Irwin, *The Diplomatic Relations of the United States with the Barbary Powers, 1776-1816* at 109-10 (1931) [hereinafter "Irwin"]. See letter of Dale to N. Nissen, August 8, 1801, 1 *Naval Documents* 537-38, and the official announcement issued on November 18, 1801, *id.* 538. Sterrett's description of the action is in a letter to Dale. *Id.* 537. The ship's log was probably destroyed by fire in the mid-nineteenth century, according to Mr. James Cheevers, Senior Curator of the U.S. Naval Academy Museum, Annapolis, Maryland. Interview, October 1973.

221. 11 *Annals* 11-12.

222. *E.g.*, G. Allen, *Our Navy and the Barbary Corsairs* 97 (1965); C. Berdahl, *The War Powers of the Executive in the United States* 63 (1920); R. Berger, *Executive Privilege: A Constitutional Myth* 78-80 (1974); E. Corwin, *The President's Control of Foreign Relations* 131-33 (1917); 4 Malone, *Jefferson* 98-99; L. Wright & J. Macleod, *The First Americans in North Africa* 87, 104 (1945); Note, "Congress, the President, and the Power to Commit Forces to Combat," 81 *Harv. L. Rev.* 1771, 1779 (1968). *Compare*, however, R. Russell, *The United States Congress and the Power to Use Military Force Abroad* 106 (Unpublished Thesis, Fletcher School of Law and Diplomacy, 1967).

223. *See* 12 *Annals* 701-41, for both transmittals. Sterrett's presence in Washington City on November 17 is reported in an article from the *National Intelligencer*, reprinted in 1 *Naval Documents* 538-39. The article attributes Sterrett's release of the vessel to his sense of mercy.

224. 7 *Works of Alexander Hamilton* 746-47 (J. Hamilton ed. 1851).

225. 11 *Annals* 325-28.

226. *Id.* 327-29.

227. *Id.* 405-406. On January 11, Representative Randolph moved that the Secretary of Treasury be directed to provide the House with an estimate of America's Mediterranean trade, to determine whether the cost of its protection was too great relative to its value. No one opposed the call, but some asserted that the trade deserved protection regardless of its extent: "This trade the Government was as much bound to protect, as it was bound to protect the landed interest of the country." *Id.* 417-18.

228. *Id.* 432-33.

229. *Id.* 148-52.

230. Sec. 2, *id.* 1303.

231. Most of the correspondence relating to Hamet was sent by Jefferson to Congress beginning on December 11, 1805, and commences with Jefferson's transmitting messages in an appendix at 16 *Annals* 694. The letter of July 2, 1801, to Madison from Cathcart, is at *id.* 704.

232. Letter of September 5, 1801, *id.* 704.

233. Letter of December 13, 1801, *id.* 705. Eaton wrote in another letter that he had concluded an agreement with the Pasha to unseat the current sovereign in Tripoli: "The idea of dethroning our enemy, and placing a rightful

Sovereign in his seat, makes a deeper impression on account of the lasting peace it will produce with that Regency." Letter of September 5, 1801, *id.* 704-705.

234. Cathcart to Madison, August 25, 1802, 16 *Annals* 706, 708-709. Cathcart's language at one point, referring to Hamet's decision to go to Derne, indicates that promises were exchanged: "This change of position by Hamet Pasha induced Mr. Eaton to take the measures which . . . had not this event taken place so suddenly he would not have done until he received the President's instructions; and so far as those measures have been made known to me, I must do Mr. Eaton the justice to say that they seem to have been judicious, dictated by imperious necessity, and an honest zeal for the success of an enterprise which promised such vast advantages to our own country." See the account of this incident in Allen, *supra* note 222, at 102.

235. 16 *Annals* 709.

236. 2 *Naval Documents* 257-58.

237. 1 *Jefferson Works* (Fed.) 382.

238. 16 *Annals* 712.

239. Secretary of Navy Smith to Barron, *id.* 711-13.

240. Madison to Lear, *id.* 711.

241. *Id.* 713-14. The verbal orders were also written down and handed to Hull in Eaton's presence.

242. *Id.* 714, 717, 721-23.

243. *E.g., id.* 714-15, 720-21; Irwin 151-58.

244. Letter of March 18, 1805, 16 *Annals* 719-20.

245. *Id.* 726-27, 730.

246. Letter of April 29, 1805, *id.* 731-34.

247. Letter of May 18, 1805, *id.* 734.

248. Letter of May 19, 1805, *id.* 738-39.

249. A secret article allowed the Bashaw to hold Hamet's family for four years. *See id.* 775-76.

250. He was greeted as the "Modern Africanus" who "knew the use of valor and the art of war." Many receptions were held in his honor at which he was compared to Alexander and other conquerors. Massachusetts gave him a gift of 10,000 acres of land and later elected him to the Massachusetts Legislature. Irwin 160; C. Prentiss, *The Life of the Late General William Eaton* 408 (1813).

251. *See* 16 *Annals* 759 (letter of September 1, 1805, to the "people"); *id.* 761 (letter of August 5, 1805, to Jefferson.)

252. 15 *Annals* 48-50, President's Message of January 13, 1806.

253. Jefferson's Annual Message, December 3, 1805, *id.* 11, 14.

254. *Id.* 48-50. Eaton was asked to state his views of the Bashaw's request, and found it "impossible . . . to undertake to say the Bashaw [Hamet] has not been deceived." Letter to the Secretary of Navy, December 5, 1805, 16 *Annals* 760.

255. 15 *Annals* 185-88. The report concluded that "the Legislature of a free and Christian country, can never leave it in the power of a Mahametan to say that they violate their faith, or withhold the operations of justice from one who has fallen a victim to his unbounded confidence in their integrity and honor."

256. The bill passed on April 21, 1806, and provided a payment of $2,400 for "immediate and temporary relief." *Id.* 1106. No further relief was ever provided. Allen, *supra* note 222, at 263.

257. Senator John Quincy Adams severely criticized the committee report for its factual inaccuracies. 15 *Annals* 211-24. On March 18 the commiteee chairman, Senator Bradley, submitted a resolution of praise for Eaton, "late General-in-Chief of the Army of the ex-Bashaw of Tripoli," and other Americans involved for their capture of Derne, granting to each man several hundred acres of land. *Id.* 188-89. But consideration of these recommendations was postponed until the next session. *Id.* 231. The House meanwhile argued vigorously about whether Eaton should be awarded a sword or a gold medal for his valor; after extensive debate a gold medal was awarded. *Id.* 274, 276-81, 314-21, 337. Eaton later addressed a letter to the Speaker of the House in support of his claim against the United States for expenses incurred during the Tripolitan venture. *Id.* 799. After considerable delay, a bill passed in the House, February 25, 1807 (16 *Annals* 622), and in the Senate, March 3rd (*id.* 103).

258. Act of February 6, 1802, §2, 2 Stat. 129, 130.

259. See the description in Irwin 115-16.

260. 1 *Gallatin Writings* 83-84. *See also* Jefferson to Secretary of the Navy Smith, August 9, 1802, 125 *Jefferson Papers* 21566, reel 43.

261. 1 *Gallatin Writings* 89.

262. Dearborn to Jefferson August 15, 1802, 125 *Jefferson Papers* 21611, reel 43.

263. Smith to Jefferson August 16, 1802, *id.* 21621-23. Smith also recommended sending the vessel *New York*, and told Jefferson he had instructed Commodore Morris "to pursue such a course of conduct as would most effectually tend to produce a state of peace . . . ."

264. Jefferson to Madison, Aug. 23, 1802, *id.* 21656.

265. 2 *Naval Documents* 257-58.

266. Jefferson to Smith, Aug. 30, 1802, 126 *Jefferson Papers* 21688, reel 44. *See also* letters of Sept. 3, 1802, *id.* 21710; and Sept. 6, *id.* 21719.

267. Smith to Jefferson, Sept. 1, 1802, *id.* 21700-701.

268. Smith to Jefferson, Sept. 14, 1802, *id.* 21742-44.

269. Jefferson to Gallatin, Sept. 17, 1802, 1 *Gallatin Writings* 98, 99; Jefferson to Gallatin, Sept. 20, 1802, *id.* 99.

270. 127 *Jefferson Papers* 21991-92, reel 44 (Jefferson to Dearborn, and reply).

271. Gallatin to Jefferson, Dec. 1802, in 1 *Gallatin Writings* 105.

272. A good description of the incident and subsequent events is in Irwin at 131-34. The treaty with Morocco is in 2 Miller, *supra* note 205, at 212.

273. 13 *Annals* 74, 556.

274. *Id.* 564.

275. *Id.* 210, 642 (Dec. 5, 1803).

276. Irwin 133.

277. 13 *Annals* 211; Act of Mar. 19, 1804, 13 *Annals* 1280-81.

278. 1 Schachner, *supra* note 6, at 420-21.

279. Jefferson to Gov. William H. Cabell of Virginia, Aug. 11, 1807, in 10 *Jefferson Works* (Fed.) 441n.

280. 20 *Annals* 70 (May 24, 1809).

281. Jefferson to John B. Colvin, Sept. 20, 1810, in 9 *Jefferson Writings* (Ford) 279; *see also id.* 281.

CHAPTER 5
THE POST-JEFFERSONIAN REPUBLICANS:
EXPANSIONISM AND EXECUTIVE POWER

1. 6² *Dictionary of American Biography* 184-93 (A. Johnson, ed. 1957); 5 H. Adams, *History of the United States* 310 (1889-91) (9 vols.) [hereinafter *"Adams History"*].

2. 7 *Dictionary of American Biography*, *supra* note 1, at 92.

3. 1 *id.* 92.

4. The most complete study of James Madison is Irving Brant's *James Madison* (1941-1961) (6 vols.) [hereinafter "Brant, *Madison*"]. Also useful are G. Hunt, *Life of James Madison* (1920); A. Koch, *Jefferson and Madison: The Great Collaboration* (1950); E. Burns, *James Madison: Philosopher of the Constitution* (rev. ed. 1968).

5. The most complete biography of James Monroe is Harry Ammon, *James Monroe: The Quest for National Identity* (1971) [hereinafter "Ammon, *Monroe*"]. Also useful is W. Cresson, *James Monroe* (1946) [hereinafter "Cresson, *Monroe*"]. For Monroe's antifederalism see 1 *Writings of James Monroe* 307-43 (S. Hamilton ed. 1900) [hereinafter *"Monroe Writings"*].

6. G. Lipsky, *John Quincy Adams: His Theory and Ideas* 240-41 (1950).

7. 4 J.Q. Adams, *Memoirs* 497 (Jan. 8, 1820) (C. Adams, ed. 1874-77) (12 vols) [hereinafter *"Adams Memoirs"*].

8. *See, e.g., id.* 206 (Jan. 2, 1819).

9. *Id.* 32 (Dec. 30, 1817).

10. *Id.* 108 (July 15, 1818).

11. Some helpful biographies and other books concerning Adams are: S. Bemis, *John Quincy Adams and the Union* (1956); G. Dangerfield, *The Awakening of American Nationalism* 212-30 (1965); Lipsky, *supra* note 6.

12. L. White, *The Jeffersonians* 42 (1951) [hereinafter "White, *Jeffersonians*"].

13. *E.g.*, 20 *Annals of Congress* 118 (1834-56) (42 vols.) [hereinafter "*Annals*"] (May 27, 1809) (plan submitted by Secretary of War for raising additional force and for disposition of troops).

14. *E.g.*, 20 *Annals* 591-92, 643 (April 7, 1810) (Senate resolution calling on Secretary of War to "prepare a system of regulations for improving the discipline of the militia," after Committee recommended leaving that task to the states; 23 *Annals* 495, 549 (Dec. 13, 1811) (House request that President cause to be prepared and submitted a digest of rules for training and discipline of regular troops).

15. The greatly increased public debt after the War of 1812, and the economic depression that set in by 1819, spurred Congress to seek reorganization and reduction of government agencies. A substantial cut in military spending was implemented in 1821, but efforts to reduce agency operations and personnel failed, partly because they took the form of requesting department heads as to how their agencies could be streamlined. White, *Jeffersonians* 119-25.

16. Thus, Congress created the Board of Naval Commissioners in 1815, a General Staff for the Army in 1816, and a new system of accounting—as recommended by the executive—in 1817. John Quincy Adams reorganized the State Department between 1817 and 1820. White, *Jeffersonians* 117-18. The House, after interesting debate, agreed to authorize two Assistant Secretaries of War, on Madison's recommendation, but the Senate took no action at that time. *See* 23 *Annals* 209, 226, 258; 24 *Annals* 1354-76.

17. This was the period during which Senators began to block or delay appointments made to offices in their states without their approval. Senator Ninian Edwards of Illinois argued, for example, that he and his fellow Senator should each be allowed to select two of the four land officers in the state. Monroe rejected this proposition, through his Secretary of Treasury and Attorney General, contending that he had the power to reject senatorial advice just as Senators might reject his appointments. Congress was able to prevent the release of favorite army officers, despite Monroe's 1822 plan for reduction. 6 *Monroe Writings* 287-88. By 1825, state delegations secured the power to suggest appointments to West Point and to the post of midshipman. White, *Jeffersonians* 126-29.

18. Act of May 15, 1820, 3 Stat. 582. Jefferson commented adversely to Madison on the pressures the Act created: "It saps the constitutional and salutary functions of the President, and introduces a principle of intrigue and corruption, which will soon leaven the mass, not only of Senators, but of citizens." Letter of November 29, 1820, in 12 *The Works of Thomas Jefferson* 174 (Federal ed., 1904-05) (12 vols.) [hereinafter *"Jefferson Works* (Fed.)"].

19. The quest for patronage reached its peak with Senator Thomas H. Benton's Report on the Reduction of Executive Patronage, presented in 1826. *Senate Doc.* 88, 19th Congress, 1st Sess. (May 4, 1826). The report showed how dramatically the potential for executive patronage had increased, and consequently the power of the President and the federal government. Benton's proposed solution for this development was to transfer much of this patronage power to Congress. To this end, Benton introduced six bills, none of which passed.

20. These and related matters are discussed *infra* at 258-60.

21. John Randolph moved on May 24, 1809 to appoint a committee to inquire as to whether moneys drawn from the Treasury during Jefferson's administration "have been faithfully applied to the objects for which they were appropriated," and to suggest ways "to promote economy, enforce adherence to Legislative restrictions" and "secure accountability." 20 *Annals* 63. This motion was unanimously adopted, the Republicans thereby allegedly demonstrating their willingness to review the spending of a Republican President, as they had the spending of President Adams. *Id.* 66 (Macon), 71 (J.G. Jack-

son), 71-72 (Taylor). Randolph reported for the Committee on June 27, 1809, filing a report, with documents, that was incomplete because of inadequate cooperation by the Departments of War and Navy. A further report was promised in the next session, after those departments supplied the necessary information. Randolph's report was tabled, 46-40, and the material was ordered to be printed. *Id.* 448, 467. The investigation is mentioned again on January 12, 1810, when a motion was made and adopted that it be continued. *Id.* 1199. No subsequent reference could be found.

22. *E.g.,* 29 *Annals* 382 (Dec. 11, 1815).

23. For example, Madison announced on December 12, 1810, that special expenditures for seamen seized abroad had considerably exceeded the amount appropriated. 22 *Annals* 18. On January 16, 1812, he sent an account of contingent expenses "incurred on . . . taking possession" of West Florida. 23 *Annals* 100, 794.

24. A.S.P., 2 *Miscellaneous* 396-99.

25. 30 *Annals* 374, 420-21; Act of March 3, 1817, 3 Stat. 390.

26. Among the steps taken were: (1) to require all unexpended funds of the War and Navy Departments to be placed in the surplus fund; (2) to prohibit transfers under the Act of 1809 from one branch of expenditure in a given year to another branch of expenditure in another year; and (3) to prohibit contracts unless authorized by law or supported by an adequate appropriation. White, *Jeffersonians* 96-103.

27. *Id.* 103-104. For debates on some of these issues, reflecting the frustration of those seeking closer control, but also some minor victories, see 38 *Annals* 626-707; *id.* 953-55; 41 *Annals* 480-81, 502, 578; 42 *Annals* 1879-80; 3 *Register of Debates in Congress* 571-72 (roads) (1825-37) (29 vols.) [hereinafter *"Register"*].

28. White, *Jeffersonians* 116.

29. *E.g.,* 20 *Annals* 526 (report on operations of Mint) (Jan. 9, 1810); 22 *Annals* 1148-1251 (transmittals relating diplomatic efforts to stop European depredations on American commerce) (Dec. 5, 1810-Feb. 19, 1811); 26 *Annals* 570 (British proposal of negotiations and U.S. acceptance) (Jan. 6, 1814); 28 *Annals* 24, 27, 701 (information on Britain's terms for peace, instructions to U.S. negotiators, and course of negotiations) (Oct. 10 & 14, and Dec. 1, 1814).

30. 20 *Annals* 475-76 (Nov. 29, 1809) (Jackson); 22 *Annals* 12-13 (Dec. 5, 1810) (West Florida); 2 J. Richardson, ed., *Compilation of the Messages and Papers of the Presidents, 1789-1897,* at 539 (Feb. 23, 1815) (Algiers) (1917).

31. 31 *Annals* 13-14 (Dec. 2, 1817) (relations with Spain and Amelia Island); *id.* 288-89 (Mar. 25, 1817) (war with Seminoles).

32. 2 *Register* 3 (Appendix) (Dec. 6, 1825) (Panama Congress); 3 *Register* 1557 (Dec. 5, 1826) (Brazilian blockade).

33. Letter of J. Graham to J. Madison, Aug. 26, 1813, enclosing copy of *Federal Republican,* in *Presidential Papers of James Madison* [hereinafter *"Madison Papers"*], LC microfilm, series 2, reel 26.

34. 26 *Annals* 901-27, 1059-60.

35. *But see id.* 898.

36. White, *Jeffersonians* 95, 98.

37. *E.g.*, 21 *Annals* 1533 (House inquiry into high mortality rate of troops in New Orleans) (Mar. 13, 1810); 22 *Annals* 626 (House inquiry into Naval expenditures since 1804, and management of naval yards) (Jan. 18, 1811); 26 *Annals* 157-63 (House inquiries on continuing use of Rangers and into distribution of arms) (June 14 and 15, 1813).

38. 26 *Annals* 421 (House lays on table proposed inquiry into causes of military failures on the nation's frontiers) (July 9, 1813); *id.* 819, 822 (House passes request for information "not improper to be communicated" illustrating causes of failures of arms of the Northern frontier) (Dec. 31, 1813), response, *id.* 1202 (Feb. 2, 1814) (papers printed at 27 *Annals* 2353-2480).

39. See 38 *Annals* 1157 (February 28, 1822). The Senate had earlier considered a petition claiming Jackson had illegally imprisoned various persons in the area. The petition was tabled. In addition to the argument that the matter should be left to the executive, John Elliott of Georgia argued that the Senate should defer to the House as the more appropriate body to inquire into the conduct of executive officers. *Id.* 223-24. Arguments were made on other occasions that the House should not use information requests to interfere with the treaty-making power, but with little success. *See, e.g.*, 3 *Register* 542 (Dec. 19, 1826).

40. *E.g.*, 22 *Annals* 832-34 (motion by Rep. Jacob Swope of Va. to inquire into accounts of Joel Barlow as agent at Algiers tabled after debate over whether others should be investigated) (Jan. 28, 1812).

41. The motion to investigate General Wilkinson was made in the House on March 21, 1810. 21 *Annals* 1606. Those opposed claimed that the discipline of army personnel was strictly within the President's powers unless the House were seriously considering impeachment. *Id.* 1731 (Rhea); 1732 (Holland); 1733 (Smilie). Said Representative Taylor: "I hold the President responsible for continuing this man in office, and will not take upon myself his responsibility." *Id.* 1735. Those supporting an inquiry argued the House had power to inquire because of its powers (1) "to inform ourselves and the nation"; (2) to collect material "with a view to future legislation"; (3) to consider impeachment; (4) to abolish the office involved; and (5) to legislate concerning the state of the army. *Id.* 1743-46, 1748. Said Lyon: "I would cut the right arm off my body before I would surrender my right to inquire into any impropriety committed by that man." *Id.* 1748. Macon added that, if Congress were too limited in their power to inquire into army operations, then "the army is the army of the President and not of the nation," and therefore "ten times as dangerous. . . ." *Id.* 1751. Sheffey claimed that inquiries could never harm a free country, and that no virtuous man need "fear inquiry before impartial men delegated by the people, who can have no interest to serve in proving a man to be corrupt and dishonest." Anyway, he promptly added, Wilkinson was clearly guilty. *Id.* 1742. The motion was adopted, 80-29. *Id.* 1752, 1754-55. When the committee sought to present the material they had collected, a debate ensued covering the same issues. *Id.* 2032. The House voted 58-32 to hear the report, which contained no findings or conclusions. *Id.* 2-

45. On December 18, 1810, Joseph Pearson of North Carolina moved to appoint a committee to reopen the investigation. 22 *Annals* 432. After a debate covering much of the same ground, the motion was passed, 79-35, as amended to allow Wilkinson to be heard in his own defense. *Id.* 449-50. On February 26, 1811, the investigating committee reported a mass of documents without any opinion, but accompanied by the report of the investigating committee of the previous session. *Id.* 1030-33.

42. This inquiry was authorized by the House on Friday, September 23, 1814. Debate was very brief and the final resolution provided: "That a committee be appointed to inquire into the causes of the success of the enemy in his late enterprises against the Metropolis, and the neighboring town of Alexandria, and into the manner in which the public buildings and property were destroyed. . . ." 28 *Annals* 308. *See generally* 1 A. Schlesinger, Jr. & R. Bruns, *Congress Investigates: A Documented History, 1792-1974* at 247-334 (1975).

43. *See, e.g.*, the comment by Alfred Cuthbert of Maine, in voting to reject motions to inquire into Jackson's conduct as Governor of Florida, that "the House had a right to refuse to consider a subject, when policy or its convenience required"; the majority's conception of the public good should prevail. 38 *Annals* 1162.

44. 26 *Annals* 84-89, 95-97.

45. *Id.* 95-96.

46. 5 *Life and Correspondence of Rufus King* 324-37 (C. King, ed. 1898).

47. 26 *Annals* 88-89.

48. 22 *Annals* 487.

49. 26 *Annals* 302 (June 21, 1813).

50. 22 *Annals* 12-13, 28 (W. Fla.); 23 *Annals* 267, 271 (Gt. B.); 28 *Annals* 1275 (Algiers). After Madison requested an embargo on exports, Rep. Thomas Oakley (N.Y.) asked that the President be requested to support his claim that the measure was necessary to prevent supplies from reaching the enemy as well as to undercut a collusive system of ransoming that Madison claimed had developed. The House refused to consider Oakley's motion. 27 *Annals* 2031-32, 2052.

51. 35 *Annals* 948-49.

52. *Id.* 949.

53. *E.g.*, 20 *Annals* 717-20 (Gold); 21 *Annals* 2020 (Dana); 31 *Annals* 413 (Holmes).

54. 23 *Annals* 823.

55. *See, e.g.*, 4 *Register* 2509 (Everett); 21 *Annals* 2020 (Alston).

56. *See, e.g.*, Calhoun's objections to certain resolutions because they not only asked for information, but for when and by whom the information was first received; and because the requests were too specific. The requests were approved.

Rep. James Buchanan (Pa.) dealt as follows with the claim that a request he proposed was too general:

> It had also been suggested, that this House ought not to call for any documents on any Department of the Government, unless the Member moving the call will avow that he has a specific object in doing it. Now, Mr. B. said, it was obvious that a Member must see and know the contents of a document

before he can judge whether or not it be proper to found any measure upon them.

2 *Register* 816 (Dec. 16, 1825). His motion, for papers relating to the court martial of Commodore Porter, passed without division. *Id.* 817.

57. For example, a resolution proposed by John Rhea of Tennessee asked for information, concerning the takeover of Amelia Island and, in its original form, asked also for "the reasons inducing him [President Monroe] to issue orders to suppress the said establishments." 31 *Annals* 409. John Forsyth of Georgia, administration spokesman and chairman of the Foreign Affairs Committee, noted that "it would be an extraordinary course for the House to ask for the reasons of the measure in question, when they were distinctly and satisfactorily avowed in the Message." *Id.* 410. Rhea replied that the proposed inquiry embraces "a question of peace or war, and on which therefore Congress ought to have full information." *Id.* 415. A motion to table Rhea's resolution was narrowly defeated, 75 to 81. *Id.* 416. But the vote apparently was close enough to induce Rhea to accept Forsyth's amendment to strike out the last clause. The amended resolution passed without opposition. *Id.* See also 3 *Register* 541 (request for Secretary of War's opinion, as to whether an appropriation for materials relating to fortification would be helpful, struck on motion).

58. *See, e.g.,* 20 *Annals* 720 (Gardenier being frankly political); 3 *Register* 836-56 (debate on motion for instructions to Commissioners treating with Indians, defeated after being attacked as aimed at throwing blame on executive).

59. Toward the end of Adams's term as President, for example, he apparently induced Webster to introduce a request for the instructions he had given the ministers to the Panama Congress. Webster explained that he wanted to give Adams an opportunity to vindicate his conduct by proving that the instructions contained nothing improper; he even accepted removal of the discretionary proviso. The motion was defeated by Jackson supporters, but Adams sent the material anyway. 5 *Register* 64-74.

60. *See, e.g.,* the motions referred to in the text accompanying notes 48-51, *supra;* 4 *Register* 1252-53, 1274-75 (resolutions regarding Jackson court martials at Mobile) (Jan. 30-31, 1828). Another interesting motion was made by Rufus King, and requested copies of the correspondence pursuant to which Madison was notified of Russia's offer to mediate the War of 1812. Madison had appointed Gallatin and others as commissioners during the recess of Congress, and sent them to Russia before Congress reconvened. King's motion may have been aimed at showing that the appointments could have been made earlier, while Congress was in session. The motion was defeated on June 3, 1813. 26 *Annals* 84, Brant indicates that Madison got first hint of the mediation proposal on January 25, 1813. 6 Brant, *Madison* 154. Congress remained in session until March 3.

61. The following list includes only a sampling of the more important motions: 20 *Annals* 35 (Senate request for such information in possession of State Department relating to Britain as President "may think it expedient to submit") (June 13, 1809), response *id.* 37 (June 16, 1809); 20 *Annals* 699 (House request

for information President "may deem proper to be communicated" concerning seizures of American vessels and merchandise) (Dec. 6, 1809), response *id.* 1200 (Jan. 12, 1810); 20 *Annals* 1219 (Senate request of President for copies of all instructions relating to foreign vessels in American waters "excepting such parts as may, in his judgment, be improper for communication") (Jan. 17, 1810), response 21 *Annals* 1367 (Feb. 1, 1810); 23 *Annals* 370, 374 (House request of President for information on impressment "with such other information on this subject as he in his judgment may think proper to communicate") (Nov. 29, 1811), response *id.* 794 (Jan. 16, 1812); 24 *Annals* 1685-86 (House resolution, passed 58-51, asking President for full information on actions regarding East Florida "if, in his opinion, it be compatible with the public interest, to lay before this House, confidentially, or otherwise...") (June 26, 1812), response *id.* 1687-92 (July 1, 1812); 25 *Annals* 53-54, 1151 (Senate and House resolutions requesting French decree revoking Berlin and Milan decrees, and manner of promulgation, to the extent disclosure consistent with public interest) (Jan. 18 and March 1, 1813), response *id.* 1167, 26 *Annals* 190 (March 3, 1813); 26 *Annals* 302, 308-10 (House resolutions regarding French decree, all qualified to allowing withholding in the public interest, including the fifth, which was specifically amended in that respect) (June 21, 1813), response *id.* 433, 27 *Annals* 2061-72 (July 12, 1813); 30 *Annals* 134-35 (Senate request for correspondence with Spain relating to subjects of controversy, "except such parts as he may deem improper to disclose") (Feb. 19, 1817), response *id.* 144 (Feb. 22, 1817); 32 *Annals* 1447 (House request for communications regarding occupation of Amelia Island "if not inconsistent with the public interest") (Mar. 20, 1818), response *id.* 1523 (Mar. 26, 1818); 35 *Annals* 365; 36 *Annals* 1411-12, 1451 (Senate and House requests for information regarding treaty with Spain "of which the public interest does not, in his opinion, require concealment" and transmittal of which will not be inconsistent with public interest) (Feb. 7 and 21, 1820), response 35 *Annals* 487; 36 *Annals* 1617 (Mar. 9, 1820); 38 *Annals* 825, 828 (House request for communications regarding relations between South American republics and Spain "as it may be consistent with the public interest to communicate") (Jan. 30, 1822), response *id.* 1238-41 (Mar. 8, 1822); 4 *Register* 2509 (House request for information regarding Brazilian blockade "unless, in his opinion, the exigencies of the government shall require the same to be kept secret") (April 30, 1828), response A.S.P., 6 *Foreign Relations* 1021 (May 23, 1828).

62. *E.g.,* 25 *Annals* 125, 126 (request for information of intention of enemy to take possession of East Florida and the amount of the American force in that neighborhood, "which the President may deem proper to communicate") (Dec. 18, 1813), response, *id.* 126 (Jan. 14, 1813); 26 *Annals* 819, 822 (request for information "not improper to be communicated" illustrating causes of failures of arms on northern frontier) (Dec. 31, 1813), response, *id.* 1202 (Feb. 2, 1814). An example of an unqualified request for military information was that proposed by Rep. Newton on January 22, 1810, that called for disclosure of the condition and distribution of the regular army. 20 *Annals* 1256. *See also* 37 *Annals* 448, 701-02 (extent of naval force in West Indies); *id.* 682, 715 (number of posts and distribution of army).

63. 2 *Register* 1212.

64. *Id.* 1263-64, 1294-95, 1215, 1261.

65. *Id.* 1265 (Ingham).

66. *Id.* 1278. He distinguished Washington's withholding of material during the Jay Treaty debate as having been based on the proposition that the House had no proper function to perform for which the information was necessary.

67. *Id.* 1279. Webster added that premature disclosure may occasionally defeat a diplomatic objective—an unqualified request asks for *all* objects and may frustrate legitimate, desirable ends. *Id.* 1280.

68. *Id.* 1268.

69. *Id.* 1254 (Webster's substitute adopted); 1301 (effort to return it to committee to strike discretionary clause rejected, 71-98, and resolution adopted, 125-40).

70. *E.g.*, 20 *Annals* 1091 (House request for information concerning closing of Baltic ports) (Jan. 3, 1810), response *id.* 1201 (Jan. 12, 1810); 20 *Annals* 574 (Senate request for information on whether intercourse with Britain or France had been allowed despite nonintercourse Act) (Feb. 16, 1810), response, *id.* 584 (Feb. 22, 1810); 20 *Annals* 518-19 (Senate request for account of expenditures made in connection with Barbary Powers since 1805) (Dec. 27, 1809), response *id.* 531 (Jan. 22, 1810); 21 *Annals* 1622 (House request for information on impressment received since Nov. 30, 1807) (Mar. 26, 1810), response *id.* 1759 (April 5, 1810); 23 *Annals* 373 (House request for information on American seamen impressed into service of foreign powers) (Nov. 29, 1811), response *id.* 794 (Jan. 16, 1812); 26 *Annals* 492 (House request for information on British violations of laws of war) (July 31, 1813), no response found.

71. The following are examples of unqualified requests that could reasonably have been anticipated to call for material the disclosure of which the President might have wished to prevent: 20 *Annals* 1257 (House resolution asking President what steps he had taken, if any, to secure free navigation of the Mobile River) (Jan. 22, 1810), response 21 *Annals* 1404-05 (Feb. 9, 1810); 23 *Annals* 595 (House request as to whether negotiations were pending with Spain regarding West Florida, to aid in determining whether Congress's authority over the area occupied should be suspended with a view to future negotiations) (Dec. 31, 1811), no response found. See also the close vote (13-18) rejecting unqualified requests concerning the Russian mediation on June 3, 1813. 26 *Annals* 84-85. A qualified request was later adopted. *Id.* 928 (Jan. 13, 1814), response 27 *Annals* 2087 (Jan. 18, 1814).

72. On one occasion, the House refused even to consider an unqualified request for information as to troops and fortifications, to be communicated "confidentially," although a member claimed that this would enable the President to avoid making the information public. 24 *Annals* 1485 (June 8, 1812). A motion to request Madison to communicate all information in the Department of State "not heretofore communicated" relating to the conduct of Britain and France toward the United States, "confidentially, or otherwise as he may deem expedient," was ordered to lie on the table. 23 *Annals* 267, 271.

73. *S. Jour.*, 19th Cong. 1st Sess., 415, 439 (1825).

74. *E.g.*, 22 *Annals* 375 (communication of letter reflecting adversely on one Louis de Onis, Spanish Minister to the United States) (Jan. 10, 1811). Although this information was transmitted to Congress in confidence, the Senate proceeded to adopt an unqualified request for additional information which made no mention that the material would be treated confidentially. *Id.* 376.

75. *Id.* 83 (20-7). Pickering, the former Secretary of State, in the course of arguing that the United States lacked title to West Florida, read a letter from Talleyrand, French Minister for Foreign Affairs, to John Armstrong, American Minister in Paris, which had been communicated in confidence by President Jefferson to the Senate in December 1805. 22 *Annals* 65. He claimed that, while publication in 1805 might have injured "our Ministers or our affairs abroad," there now was "no reason why the whole truth should not be known"; since Congress was about to take a step "which was one of peace or war . . . it was important that everything in relation to the subject should be disclosed." *Id.* 66.

76. *Id.* 69. Dana noted that the substance of the letter had previously been referred to by Senators other than Pickering. See also Pickering's further defense at *id.* 76-77.

77. *Id.* 71.

78. *Id.* 67. Clay said that, if the Senate did not express their disapprobation, it would be inferred from their silence that they approved Pickering's conduct and that other Senators might make public confidential communications when it suited their purposes. If so, Clay warned, the President might stop sending sensitive information to the Congress. *Id.* An attempt by Pickering to have the injunction of secrecy removed from papers communicated in confidence to the Senate in 1803 and 1805 regarding title to West Florida was defeated on March 2, 1811, by a vote of 8 to 14. *Id.* 360.

79. 2 *Register* 828-29, 862.

80. *Id.* 142-46. Clay advised Adams to refuse the request for his opinion, which was "without precedent"; "they would be more likely to abuse you for it than to respect it." 5 *The Papers of Henry Clay* 106 (J. Hopkins and M. Hargreaves, ed. 1973).

81. 3 Stat. 475.

82. 35 *Annals* 1045, 1053-54, 1055, 1057-58, 1061; 3 Stat. 609.

83. 20 *Annals* 718, 727.

84. 39 *Annals* 1617-19.

85. *Id.* 1791.

86. *Id.* 1877.

87. *Id.* 1891. See the comprehensive treatment in S. Bemis, *John Quincy Adams and the Foundations of American Foreign Policy* 498-505 (1956) [hereinafter *"J.Q. Adams and Foreign Policy"*].

88. See discussion *infra* at 262-64.

89. 21 *Annals* 1622-24, 1659; see "private" letter from Pinkney to Madison, Aug. 13, 1810, in W. Pinkney, *Life of William Pinkney* 244-45 (1969).

90. Stewart, a hero of the War of 1812, was assigned in the fall of 1821 to

command the Pacific fleet and specifically to protect commerce threatened by the conflict in Peru between Spain and Peruvian revolutionaries. After his return to the United States, he was charged with aiding American and foreign ships in carrying on "illicit and contraband trade" with certain Peruvian ports; disobeying orders; failing properly to train his crew in gunnery; and visiting cruel and unusual punishment upon one of his officers. The court martial acquitted Stewart of the charges and commended him for his "valor and skill." F. Pratt, *Preble's Boys: Commodore Preble and the Birth of American Sea Power* 339-40 (1950).

91. *H. R. Jour.*, 19th Cong., 2d Sess. 102-103 (1824).

92. 1 *Register* 164-65.

93. 25 *Annals* 1151 (House), *id.* 53 (Senate).

94. 31 *Annals* 409-10 (Dec. 8, 1817).

95. 4 *Adams Memoirs* 29 (Dec. 12, 1817).

96. Clay expressly did this in connection with the qualified House request for papers relating to the Panama Congress. 2 *Register* 47 (Appendix).

97. 28 *Annals* 42, 164-65.

98. *See id.* 77 *et seq.*; J. Mason, *Memoirs and Correspondence of Jeremiah Mason* 102-103 & n. 1 (G. Hillard, ed. 1873).

99. 2 *Register* 1301; 7 *Adams Memoirs* 114-16 (Feb. 8, 1826); 2 *Register* 69 (Appendix). A motion made by Sen. Horsey on Nov. 21, 1814, asked among other things for a statement of expenditures for arms, and their distribution and condition since 1794. 28 *Annals* 94. The President's transmittals covered only the year 1814, and provided for less data than requested. *See id.* 269 and the report in A.S.P., 1 *Military Affairs* 604.

100. 26 *Annals* 277.

101. 27 *Annals* 1458. *See also* Rep. Grosvenor's complaint *infra* at 290, textual note.

102. Letter of Nov. 2, 1814, in 2 *Letters and Other Writings of James Madison* 591 (Cong. ed. 1865).

103. 42 *Annals* 2431, 2457.

104. 42 *Annals* 2701, 2759.

105. 5 *Clay Papers, supra* note 80, at 250.

106. The statement is John Marshall's. 10 *Annals* 613 (1800), discussed *supra*, chapter 3, at 137. The point is broadened and forcefully presented in a letter from J.Q. Adams to Jonathan Russell on May 24, 1818, in which he wrote that "the authority to *receive* foreign ministers is vested exclusively in the President, and in practice all letters from foreign sovereigns, however addressed, are opened and answered only by him." 6 *Writings of John Quincy Adams* 336-37 (W. Ford, ed. 1913-17) (7 vols.) [hereinafter "*J.Q. Adams Writings*"].

107. Vincente Pazos, who represented himself as an agent of the "Republics of Venezuela, New Grenada, and Mexico," presented Congress with a memorial he had sent to President Monroe protesting the seizure of Amelia Island. The House voted not to receive the petition, after hearing arguments that its consideration would constitute an interference with the executive. 31 *Annals* 1251-76. To receive petitions from foreign nations, Lowndes contended,

"would transfer the diplomatic functions from the Executive to the Legislature." *Id.* 1252.

108. 24 *Annals* 1624, 1679-80 (June 1 and 18, 1812); 28 *Annals* 269, 1943 (Feb. 23 and Mar. 3, 1815).

109. 30 *Annals* 13 (Dec. 3, 1816).

110. 24 *Annals* 1601, 1614 (April 3, 1812).

111. These and other related instances are discussed *supra* at 242-43.

112. See discussion *infra* at 303-305.

113. See discussion *infra* at 347-48. Monroe, after consulting his Cabinet, refused the request of a group of Cuban patriots for military assistance and annexation by the United States. Adams's notes indicate that concern about the executive's power was one factor in the refusal, but that the fear of war with Britain was at least equally significant. 6 *Adams Memoirs* 69-74 (Sept. 26-Oct. 1, 1822). On April 28, 1823, Adams sent a message to Hugh Nelson, Minister to Spain, for private use and communication, that the United States "will be fully justified" to support the Cuban independence effort if Spain tried to transfer the island. 7 *J.Q. Adams Writings* 369, 381.

114. See discussion *infra* at 365-76.

115. The Panama Congress is discussed *infra* at 262-64; the Brazilian Blockade, *infra* at 266-67, 277.

116. *J.Q. Adams and Foreign Policy* 562-63.

117. *Id.* 476-77.

118. *E.g.*, 20 *Annals* 257-58, 284, 306, 314-15 (after House adopts resolution calling for "efficacious" presidential action to obtain release of Miranda expedition prisoners, refused appropriation and request for executive aid if prisoners's involvement was deemed involuntary); *id.* 481-82, 510-16, 764 (bill introduced to authorize President to dismiss foreign ministers, but opposed and tabled as unnecessary and improperly suggesting President lacked power); 23 *Annals* 237 (motion to disavow President's Proclamation of Nov. 2, 1810 submitted, but withdrawn); 31 *Annals* 74-75, 96-98, 108 (Senate resolution to authorize President to enter into compact with foreign nations to suppress slavery changed to committee inquiry).

119. The nomination of Albert Gallatin as Envoy Extraordinary was rejected on the purported ground that he continued to hold the office of Secretary of Treasury. 26 *Annals* 89. The nomination of James Russell as Minister to Sweden was rejected because it was deemed inexpedient to create the office. *Id.* 98.

120. 36 *Annals* 2223, 2229. Similar resolutions were defeated at 32 *Annals* 1646, 1655 and 37 *Annals* 1046-55, 1077. Forsyth of Georgia said that an earlier resolution proposed a new system of government, one which took control of foreign relations away from the President and Senate and gave it to the House. General Smith of Maryland said, "It is not wise for us to interfere with his [the President's] powers. . . . Each branch had better confine itself to the duties assigned it by the Constitution." Alexander Smyth of Virginia called Clay's proposal "an act of usurpation, an invasion of the Executive authority." 32 *Annals* 1502, 1538-39, 1569.

Webster attempted to push through a provision authorizing the President to establish a mission to Greece, claiming the act would merely be an expression of the House's opinion. 41 *Annals* 1084-85, 1098. Representative Wood asserted the provision would violate international law, since the outcome of the Greek fight for independence was still uncertain, and could lead to war; "we have no authority from the Constitution to embark in wars of ambition, or to propagate the principles of religion or liberty by the sword." *Id.* 1133-34. Cuthbert agreed with Webster that the President already had the power to appoint an agent to Greece, but said that this proved a House resolution would constitute an improper interference with the executive. *Id.* 1170. The motion was rejected. *Id.* 1214.

121. *E.g.*, 38 *Annals* 854 (motion to recognize established revolutionary regimes); *id.* 825 (motion for information adopted). Other factors were probably more significant in influencing Monroe, especially ratification of the Adams-Onis Treaty. Rejection of Metternich's Protocol of Troppan indicated, moreover, that Britain and France would not intervene militarily to suppress colonial revolutions. *See* 1 W. Manning, ed., *Diplomatic Correspondence of the United States Concerning the Independence of the Latin American States* 582-83, 585-87 (1925) [hereinafter "Manning, *Diplomatic Correspondence*"]; A. Whitaker, *The United States and Independence of Latin America, 1800-1830*, at 317-43 (1941).

122. 39 *Annals* 1314-20, 1382-1404.

123. 38 *Annals* 430-31.

124. This was later the position of Secretary of State John W. Foster, *S. Exec. Doc.* No. 9, 52d Cong., 2d Sess. 13, 14 (1892); and of Secretary of State John Hay, *H. Doc.* No. 471, 56th Cong., 1st Sess. 1-3 (1900). The first formal executive agreement under the Constitution was concluded with Canada in 1792, and provided for international postal service. *See* W. McClure, *International Executive Agreements* 35-40 (1941).

125. *See* F. Engelman, *The Peace of Christmas Eve* 148-51 (1962).

126. 28 *Annals* 251, 267, 273, 1193. Act of Feb. 27, 1815, 3 Stat. 217-18.

127. Letters of Bagot to Rush, April 28, 1817, and Rush to Bagot, April 29, 1817, in 32 *Annals* 1949-50 and A.S.P., 4 *Foreign Relations* 205-06.

128. Crowninshield to Captains D.S. Dexter, W.T. Woolsey and J.T. Leonard, May 2, 1817, 32 *Annals* 1951-52. *See* Madison to Monroe, July 21, 1816, in *Presidential Papers of James Monroe*, LC microfilm, series 1, reel 6 [hereinafter "Monroe Papers"].

129. 31 *Annals* 12.

130. 4 *Adams Memoirs* 41-42.

131. 32 *Annals* 1943. President Benjamin Harrison later reported to Congress that doubts as to the regularity of the agreement seems to have arisen only a year after it was concluded. He found no evidence on this matter in State Department files or in the Journals of Congress for that session, and concluded that Monroe acted "out of abundant caution" in communicating the agreement to the Senate. *S. Exec. Doc.* No. 9, 52nd Cong., 2d Sess. 11-12 (1892). Edward Corwin notes that Monroe seems to have been concerned about the regularity of the original arrangement. *The President's Control of Foreign Relations* 118 (1970).

132. 3 *S. Jour. Exec. Proc.* 132-34 (1928).
133. 2 Richardson, *Messages* 605.
134. *See S. Exec. Doc.* No. 9, 52nd Cong., 2d Sess. 13-14 (1892), in which President Harrison later contended that Senate approval had municipal effect only, the agreement becoming effective on the exchange of notes.
135. 29 *Annals* 419-20.
136. *Id.* 608-74.
137. *E.g., id.* 456-57, 467-70 (W. Gaston); 487-88 (J. Hopkinson) (treaty of peace self-executing); 493-94 (E. Throop) (treaty unlike law in that it cannot be changed without violating public faith); 541 (E. Mills); 568-69 (W. Pinkney); 613-15 (foreign confidence—T. Pickering).
138. *E.g., id.* 522-23 (T. Ghoulson); 563 (G. Tucker) (arguing that treaty forced additional taxes by lowering duties, which in turn had been pledged to pay national debt). Calhoun opposed the amendment but agreed with the theory. *Id.* 526-32. Cyrus King of Massachusetts stated the position in its broadest sense (*id.* 538):

> Whenever a treaty or convention does, by any of its provisions, encroach upon any of the enumerated powers vested by the Constitution in the Congress of the United States, or any of the laws by them enacted in execution of those powers, such treaty or convention, after being ratified, must be laid before Congress, and such provisions cannot be carried into effect without an act of Congress.

139. To contend that the nation could be involved in war by treaty, he said, would justify "a treaty of alliance offensive and defensive, which might involve us in all the calamities of war" without approval of the immediate representatives of the people, as the Constitution intended. *Id.* 480.
140. *Id.* 1020; *see id.* 1798. House and Senate approval took place on Feb. 24 and 27, 1816, respectively. *Id.* 1057-58, 161.
141. 36 *Annals* 1719, 1782 (April 3, 1820). The renunciation was of Texas, in the Adams-Onis Treaty. Henry Clay argued the House had power to reject the deal. If the treaty power could dispose of territory, he said, it could be used to contract alliances, raise troops, and grant subsidies. *Id.* 1725. Archer of Virginia argued that the Constitution limited all the important powers it conferred, and the treaty power should be no exception. *Id.* 1746.
142. The bill John Forsyth sought to amend exempted Swedish and Norwegian vessels from certain duties. He argued that the treaty with Denmark could not suspend prior laws until executed by legislation. 3 *Register* 1152-61.
143. 21 *Annals* 1359-63 (Jan. 31, 1810). The House also refused to make the appropriation for foreign missions specific, causing Republican Lyon to protest: "I confess I do not understand that kind of republicanism that changes its doctrines with a change of power." *Id.* 1361.
144. The responses to the Senate's requests for information, as well as the information voluntarily sent, included letters indicating that the Panama meeting would not require that "representatives of the United States should, in the least, compromit their present neutrality, harmony, and good intelligence with other nations." Other letters, however, mentioned that the agenda of the Con-

gress included such subjects as possible interference by neutral nations in the war of independence between the Republics and Spain; and opposition to colonization in America by the European powers on the American continent. 2 *Register* 44-47 (Appendix).

145. *Id.* 92-100 (Appendix). The committee noted that the President's original message and documents transmitted to the Senate at that time contained "great diversities" in the enumeration of the subjects to be dealt with, and that the letters from South American ministers failed to mention some of the important subjects claimed by the President to be on the intended agenda. *Compare* A. Schlesinger, Jr. (relying on Berdahl for the proposition that "secret information" had been withheld), *The Imperial Presidency* 38 (1973). Berdahl does not support the statement. C. Berdahl, *War Powers of the Executive* 28 (1921).

146. *See generally* 2 *Register* 161-336; approved at *id.* 151. Compare Clay's letter to Henry Addington, British Chargé, explaining that "[a]ccording to the practice of this Government, the Senate is not ordinarily consulted in the initiatory state of a negotiation, but its consent and advice are only invoked after a Treaty is concluded, under the direction of the President and submitted to its consideration." 4 *Clay Papers* 217-18.

147. 2 *Register* 101-104 (Appendix).

148. *Id.* 2009. See the similar proposal of Forsyth, *id.* 2009-10.

149. *Id.* 2255-57 (arguing also that President would no longer be accountable if House assumed responsibility of giving advice). Edward Livingston of Louisiana saw a limited power to deny appropriations: when necessary to prevent tyranny or war. *Id.* 2198. *Accord, id.,* 2169-70 (James Buchanan). As to conditioning the appropriation, Alexander Thomson of Pennsylvania said "this power to restrain the foreign diplomatic intercourse . . . by no means implies the power of managing that intercourse." *Id.* 2337.

150. *Id.* 2166. He therefore offered a resolution stating that it was "the constitutional right and duty of the House of Representatives, when called on for appropriations to defray the expenses of foreign missions, to deliberate on the expediency or inexpediency of such missions, and to determine and act thereon, as in their judgment may be most conducive to the public good." It was referred to Committee of the Whole, and died. *Id.* 2167.

151. *Id.* 2067. He said: "The most important question connected with our foreign relations, the question of peace or war, is wholly subject to the determination of the Legislative Department, of which this House is not the least prominent branch. Upon all measures, therefore, involving this question, however remotely, it is our right and duty to deliberate. . . ."

152. *Id.* 2457 (99 to 95), 2490 (54 to 143). Charles A. Wickliffe of Kentucky addressed the House on April 25, 1826 on whether the vote rejecting the committee resolution to approve the appropriation, as amended, signified that the House majority had negated any precedential value that might be drawn from their earlier vote to suggest instructions for the Panama ministers. Wickliffe thought not. One majority, he said, had supported the amendment; another majority—consisting of those who opposed the amendment (such as Webster) and those who opposed the resolution even as amended (such as Polk)—produced the vote against the resolution as amended. Then, he said, a third ma-

jority voted for the appropriation without any amendment—those who were for the resolution because it was no longer accompanied by the amendment, and those who would have preferred to add the amendment, but who favored the mission regardless. The last two votes, in Wickliffe's view, did not undermine "the deliberate judgments of a majority of the members . . . as to the constitutional right and power of this House, in reference to the Panama Mission." He wished to make this point clear, "in future time, when the actors in this transaction have passed away," by having "the opinion of this House, as fairly expressed in the vote upon the amendment, preserved and handed down. He considered the preservation of the constitutional power of this House, to refuse an appropriation for a mission, which it believed inexpedient, more important than the success or failure of the particular measure upon which the House had recently acted." *Id.* 2551.

153. *Id.* 2514; 641, 671. It might properly be inferred from the Constitution, argued John Holmes of Maine, that the Senate, two-thirds concurring, "may advise the President, in making a treaty, even before the treaty shall have been negotiated." But to suggest that the House of Representatives had the same power "admits of strong doubt." *Id.* 666.

154. Berdahl, *supra* note 145 at 30.

155. The West and East Florida incidents are described *infra* at 291–326. A good example of special agent instructions is Adams's letter of April 29, 1823, to Thomas Randall, detailing his job of collecting and reporting information from Cuba "in private and confidential letters. . . ." 1 Manning, *Diplomatic Correspondence* 185–86. *See also* 4 *Clay Papers supra* note 80, at 624, 711, 822; 5 *id.* 47 (appointment of secret agents to Cuba and Greece).

156. 1 *Joel R. Poinsett Papers*, 119 (Oct. 1811) (Pa. Hist. Soc.) [hereinafter *"Poinsett Papers"*] (indicating his influence with Argentinian leader and suggestion of plan for revolt and confederation that "would give the United States the option of taking what part the circumstances of the country might require. . . ."), *id.* 110 (Nov. 1811) (informing U.S. that deputy of Junta coming "privately to purchase arms"); 146 and 149 (Aug. 5 and Sept. 10, 1814) (explaining that he "joined the army in Chile and directed its movement" to attempt to free American whaling ships); Collier and Cruz, *La Primera Missión de Los Estados Unidos en Chile* 43, 56, 71 (1926) (active involvement with Chilean revolutionary government, including help in drafting Constitution). *See generally* J. Rippy, *Joel Poinsett, Versatile American* (1935).

157. Poinsett to Joseph Johnson, Sept. 22, 1813, in 1 *Poinsett Papers* 140.

158. *Id.* 172: Your "ability and zeal . . . and the information you have communicated, have obtained the approbation of the President."

159. *See* J.Q. Adams to Clay, Aug. 23, 1827 and Oct. 1, 1827, *Adams Papers* Adams Manuscript Trust (Mass. Hist. Soc. microfilm), reel 149, indicating Poinsett kept up his aggressive conduct in Mexico as well, and continued to obtain administration support.

160. R. Smith to Poinsett, Aug. 27, 1810, in 1 *Poinsett Papers* 20.

161. 1 Manning, *Diplomatic Correspondence* ix.

162. A.S.P., 3 *Foreign Relations* 538–39. In 1818, when Poinsett's correspondence was withdrawn from the State Department, his report on South

America was submitted to Congress; it contained much detail, but nothing of his own role. 32 *Annals* 2250-51.

When a person named Goodefroy set off to join Poinsett, Goodefroy wrote Monroe: "we shall act in concert and harmony with each other and combine our best efforts to accomplish the views and the intentions of the executive." NAM, *Misc. Letters*, Dept. of State, Nat'l Archives microfilm, M-179, reel 24 (May 4, 1811) [hereinafter *"Misc. Letters"*].

163. Raguet to Clay, Sept. 23, 1826, in *H.R. Ex. Doc.* No. 281, 20th Cong., 1st Sess. 30-33. *See generally* L. Hill, *Diplomatic Relations Between the United States and Brazil* (1970).

164. Clay to Raguet, Oct. 22, 1826, in *H.R. Ex. Doc.* No. 281, *supra* at 74.

165. Examples of Raguet's threats and intemperances may be found in *id.* 25-29 (letter of Sept. 1, 1826); 40-42 (letter of Sept. 9, 1826); 56-58, 53-55 (letters of Oct. 13 and 31, 1826).

166. A.S.P., 6 *Foreign Relations* 1066-68.

167. 7 *Adams Memoirs* 270, 272, 354-57.

168. 4 *Register* 2780-81.

169. The Nereide, 13 U.S. (9 Cr.) 388 (1815); Brown v. United States, 12 U.S. (8 Cr.) 110 (1814).

170. United States v. Palmer, 16 U.S. (3 Wheat.) 610, 644 (1818). The case dealt with whether certificates issued by a revolutionary South American regime should be recognized as valid; the Court concluded that "the courts of the union must view such newly constituted government as it is viewed by the legislative and executive departments of the United States." In Foster and Elam v. Neilson, 27 U.S. (2 Pet.) 253, 304-07, 308 (1829), when asked to determine whether the Louisiana Purchase included areas of West Florida into which Madison sent federal troops, pursuant to implied congressional authority, the Court said it would abide by the construction given international agreements by the legislative and executive branches.

171. Brig Aurora v. United States, 11 U.S. (7 Cr.) 382 (1813). See discussion *infra* at 291.

172. Brown v. United States, 12 U.S. (8 Cr.) 110 (1814). In *Brown*, the United States Attorney, noted Chief Justice Marshall, "acted from his own impressions of what appertained to his duty," rather than under the instructions or sanction of the President. The Court made clear that Congress possessed ample power to authorize the type of seizure involved. *Id.* 121-22.

173. Extensive correspondence and debate on these events can be found in A.S.P., 1 *Military Affairs* 321-26, 604-23; *Niles' Weekly Register*, Mar. 6, 1824 at 7-9, including Monroe's elaborate presentation to Congress of the executive position.

174. 25 U.S. (12 Wheat.) 19, 29 (1827).

175. Madison to Wilson C. Nicholas, Nov. 25, 1814, 2 *Madison Writings* (Cong. ed.) 593. When President Adams threatened to use force to prevent Georgia from sending land surveyors onto Indian land, he was berated on the floor of the House for failing first to utilize the judicial process. See 2 *Register* 2612-14; 3 *Register* 267-69, 1533-34.

176. 20 *Annals* 564-65. Bayard said that "the militia can not constitutional-

ly be marched beyond the limits of our territory for the purpose of conquest."
Id. "The only provision on the subject which has been referred to is in the eighth section of the first article, in which power is given to Congress 'to provide for calling forth the militia to execute the laws of the Union, suppress insurrections, and repel invasions.'" *Accord*, Van Horn (21 *Annals* 1478, 1500-02); Bacon (*id.* 1502: "no free citizen of the country can be transported without the limits of the United States against his consent, except as a punishment for some crime"); Key (1504-506); Lyon (1507-508, 1517).

177. Two definitions of defensive actions were especially broad. Representative John Ross of Pennsylvania said there may be an invasion of "rights" as well as one of "territory," and he contended that the latter would occur if threatening fortifications were erected on foreign soil (21 *Annals* 1508-509):

> Now, sir, it is perfectly clear to my mind that there is a variety of kinds of invasion. There may be an invasion of the rights of the United States, and an invasion of territory by actual entry into it. The jurisdictional line being imaginary, a fortification might be erected beyond our jurisdiction, within forty or fifty yards of the line, so as to invade our territory and destroy the exercise of the rights of a portion of the people of the United States. Their cannon would range beyond the line, and this would be such an invasion as the militia might be called out to repel, even according to the narrow definition the gentleman from Maryland [Van Horn] has made. An invasion might be made without actually entering into our territory, and to repel that invasion our militia might be required to march fifty yards beyond the line. If they could, for this purpose, be marched fifty yards, they could be marched a greater distance.

Representative Findley, a member of the First Congress, argued that Congress has the power "to enable the President to employ the national force to prevent an invasion by meeting ... the invading army beyond the territorial line." The President should be able, he said, to "employ the national force to prevent invasion by carrying the war into the enemy's territories...." *Id.* 1518-19.

178. See the arguments of Erastus Root of New York. 21 *Annals* 1498-99. *Compare* Van Horn, *id.* 1500-502.

179. The debate arose on a bill authorizing the President "at such times as he shall deem necessary" to call on the states to furnish 100,000 militiamen "in readiness to march at a moment's warning" to serve under the authority of the United States. Section 4 of the Detachment of Militia Bill stipulated that when "each volunteer shall sign an engagement to serve the United States" he shall "be subject to the rules and articles of war; and may also be called into the service of the United States, to any place, not beyond sea, out of the jurisdiction of the United States." 21 *Annals* 1471-72. A motion to strike out the words "beyond sea" was defeated, but the bill never came up for a vote. *Id.* 1520, 1529-31

180. *E.g.*, 23 *Annals* 730 (Poindexter); *id.* 741 (Troup); *id.* 747 (Pitkin). The same arguments were made even after war was declared. *See, e.g.*, the elaborate presentation of Laban Wheaton of Massachusetts (our Government "not produced *by* conquest, ... was not made *for* conquest"), including a re-

futation of the proposition that those opposed to a war must support it after it has been undertaken. 25 *Annals* 650-53. *Compare id.* 811-12 (Stow: duty to provide funds after war declared).

181. *E.g.*, 23 *Annals* 743 (Clay); *id.* 736-37 (Cheves). *Compare id.* 756 (Milnor).

182. *Id.* 739 (Wright).

183. The right of Congress to employ the militia in war "is found among the attributes of the sovereign power which Congress has to make war," said Langdon Cheves. Congress can always use the militia in a war; the question troubling the Framers was the use of the militia when there was no public and declared war, and this had to be limited to the three express cases—enforce laws, suppress insurrection, repel invasion. *Id.* 736-37. *See also id.* 786. For a similar contention after war was declared, *see* 25 *Annals* 704 (Robertson):

> The power to make war belongs to all nations; is of the essence of Government; but the Constitution of the United States gives it expressly, in so many words: "The Congress shall have power to declare war, to raise and support armies." Whether the war be defensive or offensive, depends on circumstances and accident, but cannot affect the right.

If the war was unconstitutional, he noted, then the capture of the *Macedonian* (a British frigate) would be unlawful—"an enterprise, giving rise to a new era in maritime history, and entwining round the brows of the United States a wreath of imperishable laurel, turns out to be a violation of that instrument on the sacredness of which depends the Union and happiness of America." *Id.* 705.

184. Act of Feb. 6, 1812, 2 Stat. 676 (repealed Jan. 29, 1813).

185. *See, e.g.*, 26 *Annals* 581 (Goldsborough); 988 (Stockton).

186. The phrase was Grundy's, *id.* 993; 27 *Annals* 1534, but the theme was pressed by many members, including Calhoun, *id.* 1691. They said that opponents must assert their claim of the war's unconstitutionality in the courts and at the next election, but were duty-bound to pass the necessary appropriations. *Id.* 1536 (Grundy); 1690 (Calhoun); 1785 (Macon). Several opponents rejected these arguments, claiming a constitutional right and duty to oppose the war with all the peaceful means at their disposal. *E.g.*, *id.* 1466-67 (Pearson); 1574 (Gaston) (ancient civilizations destroyed by tyrannical majorities, not irresponsible minorities).

187. *See* 26 *Annals* 990-92 (Grundy); *id.* 994-96 (Calhoun) (it is "a mere question of expediency where and how the war ought to be prosecuted.")

188. *E.g.*, 19 *Annals* 328-31, 1241 (bill to increase navy postponed indefinitely).

189. *E.g.*, Act of Dec. 24, 1811, 2 Stat. 669 (military establishment now authorized "be immediately completed").

190. *E.g.*, Acts of Feb. 10 and June 14, 1809, 2 Stat. 516, 547 (specific appropriations to complete fortification of ports and harbors). After the war with Britain ended, Congress suspended the appropriation for some fortifications, including those at Mobile, Alabama, pending further study. On Feb. 28, 1822, the House Committee on Military Affairs, by William Eustis, recom-

mended that certain measures taken for Mobile's fortification be discontinued and others substituted. 38 *Annals* 1152-55. By message dated March 26, Monroe communicated a report by the Board of Engineers and urged that an appropriation be made and work resumed. *Id.* 345-51. But on April 13, the Committee stood by its earlier recommendation, and gave the following interpretation of executive-legislative responsibility in this area (39 *Annals* 1541):

> The committee are further agreed, that it is the peculiar province and duty of the Executive Department of Government to select and determine on the proper sites, and on the nature and extent of the fortifications to be constructed. This power and this duty appertain necessarily to the President, who is commander of the national force, and is responsible for the national defence.
>
> On the other hand, the means of carrying into effect the plans and designs of the Executive, are constitutionally and necessarily dependent on appropriations of money made by Congress. In the exercise of this power, which is exclusive on their part, it is the duty of Congress to inquire and examine into the nature, extent, necessity, or utility, of every object for which appropriations are required, and to judge of the expediency of granting or withholding them.

During the next session, despite a contrary executive recommendation, Congress passed a specific appropriation of $50,000 "[f]or collecting materials for a fortification at Mobile Point. . . ." Act of Mar. 3, 1823, 3 Stat. 783. *See* 40 *Annals* 792-94, 857, 1041, 1095, 1097-98, 1112, 1171.

191. Act of Mar. 30, 1810, 2 Stat. 569 (President may undertake experimentation with torpedoes); Act of July 5, 1813, 3 Stat. 3 (President to build "without delay" certain gun barges).

192. *E.g.*, Act of June 26, 1812, 2 Stat. 764; Act of Mar. 3, 1813, 2 Stat. 816 (creating office of superintendent of supplies and reorganizing general staff); Act of Feb. 7, 1815, 3 Stat. 202 (established Naval Bd. of Commissioners).

193. *E.g.*, Act of Jan. 11, 1812, 2 Stat. 671-74; Act of Jan. 29, 1813, 2 Stat. 794. One important example of legislative control was the House's refusal during the War of 1812 to grant the President authority to appoint inferior officers—majors, captains and lieutenants. Pitkin argued that the power over military appointments was even more dangerous than over civilian positions: "If this Government ever be wrecked, it will be on the rock of Presidential power." 25 *Annals* 467. A bill increasing the army was rejected by the House largely because it would have authorized the President to appoint several additional generals when he thought necessary. *See* 24 *Annals* 1324-34 (April 17-25, 1812).

194. *E.g.*, Act of Mar. 2, 1810, 2 Stat. 562 ($718,115 "for pay and subsistence"); Act of April 29, 1824, 4 Stat. 20 (specifying objects on which contingent expenses could be spent). *See* 41 *Annals* 1879-80 (discussion providing reasons for this degree of control).

195. *E.g.*, 26 *Annals* 157 (House inquiry into expediency of continuing Rangers) (June 14, 1813); *id.* 158-63 (House inquiry into distribution of arms, supported even by Calhoun, who recognized President's power to distribute

arms to "those [States] most exposed to foreign assaults") (June 15, 1813); *id.* 1010-12. 27 *Annals* 1869 (inquiry into economy of navy, with subpoena power) (Mar. 15, 1814); 26 *Annals* 1231-33 (inquiry into army contractors, with subpoena power) (Feb. 3, 1814); *id.* 819, 822 (request for any information he possessed, "not improper to be communicated," tending to illustrate the causes of the losses on the northern frontier). "Secrecy was the soul of military operations," protested George M. Troup of Georgia, and "details ought to be known to those concerned only," lest they "find their way to the enemy." *Id.* 820. William C. Bradley of Vermont countered that the resolution was qualified to allow withholding, and that the people and Congress should know the causes of military failures to enable them to provide remedies. "Without such knowledge it was impossible the Executive and Legislature could ever move together. Money might be wanted; men might be wanted." *Id.* 821-22. On February 2, 1814, Madison sent the House a report from Secretary of War John Armstrong which included hundreds of pages of correspondence between Armstrong and the commanders of the northern army. 27 *Annals* 2353-2480.

196. 40 *Annals* 365, 368-69; *id.* 803 (Feb. 4, 1823) (compliance). *See also* 40 *Annals* 1145, 1168 (requesting information on means taken to end blockade of W.I. islands) (compliance on same day, Mar. 1, 1823) *id.* 1165-66.

197. Calhoun's assertion, for example, that the House had been left "in the dark" on the President's reasons for seeking a military peace establishment of 20,000, was one of the reasons given for refusing to grant the President's request. 28 *Annals* 1215.

198. 2 Stat. 755; 3 Stat. 230.

199. 2 Stat. 829. The retaliation had itself to be in accord with the laws and usages of nations.

200. *See* Act of April 19, 1808, 2 Stat. 484.

201. 2 Stat. 700.

202. Act of Jan. 15, 1811, 3 Stat. 471. *See also* Act of Mar. 3, 1819, 3 Stat. 523-24.

203. Act of Feb. 12, 1812, 3 Stat. 472.

204. Act of Mar. 3, 1819, 3 Stat. 510; Act of Dec. 20, 1822, 3 Stat. 720. *See also* 3 Stat. 447, 449 (to prevent Americans from acting against nations at peace with the United States); Act of May 15, 1820, 3 Stat. 597 (to control foreign armed vessels); Act of Feb. 23, 1822, 3 Stat. 651 (to protect timber of East Florida); Act of May 25, 1824, 4 Stat. 35 (to send military escort onto Indians lands to protect commissioners).

An interesting discussion occurred during debate over a bill to prevent desertion on January 12, 1826. Several Senators indicated their agreement that the United States could be at war without a declaration. 2 *Register* 38-40 (Holmes, Cobbs). William Henry Harrison of Ohio added that, during army actions against the Indians of the Northwest, although war was not officially declared, army courts martial inflicted the penalty of death for desertion on the advice of the executive and Attorney General, though capital punishment for desertion was not allowed in times of peace. *Id.* 42.

205. *E.g.*, Act of Mar. 3, 1816, 3 Stat. 370 (fitting out vessels for hostilities); Act of April 20, 1818, 3 Stat. 450 (prohibiting slave trade).

206. *E.g.,* 26 *Annals* 673 (request for naval system); 41 *Annals* 830 (request for navy plan) (Dec. 15, 1823); Jt. Res. Mar. 3, 1813, 2 Stat. 830 (request for system of military discipline).

207. *E.g.,* 23 *Annals* 675 (Jan. 6, 1812) (Stanford); *id.* 703 (Jan. 9, 1812) (Maxwell favored number of men requested by President, but abandoned this principle so bill for additional forces might pass). *Compare,* opinion of Peter Little that legislative branch was as "well able" to judge the proper force to be raised as the executive. *Id.*

208. Act of June 26, 1812, 2 Stat. 759; Act of Jan. 27, 1813, 2 Stat. 792; Act. of Mar. 3, 1813, 2 Stat. 816.

209. *E.g.,* Act of Feb. 6, 1812, 2 Stat. 676 (may raise volunteers up to 50,000); Act of April 10, 1812, 2 Stat. 705 (authority to require states to hold in readiness 100,000 militia); Act of July 5, 1813, 3 Stat. 3 (may use 5 regiments already raised). Even when instructed to reduce the army to 10,000 men, Madison was given discretion to act by May 1, 1815, "or as soon as circumstances may permit." Act of March 3, 1815, 3 Stat. 224-25. Many members argued that the discretionary power ought to be eliminated, but the majority voted with Lowndes, who did "not wish the Government so imperiously bound by law ... no matter what unexpected emergency might arise." 28 *Annals* 1204.

210. Act of June 28, 1809, 2 Stat. 553 (such as a "due regard to the public security and interest will permit").

211. Act of Jan. 2, 1813, 2 Stat. 789 (to add up to 10 vessels); Act of March 3, 1813, 2 Stat. 821 (6 sloops); Act of Nov. 15, 1814, 3 Stat. 144 (up to 20 vessels).

212. Military appropriations were sometimes passed on the basis of general requests, without even any estimates of expenditures. 26 *Annals* 850-51 (army); *id.* 871 (navy). *See also, e.g.,* Act of Jan. 14, 1812, 2 Stat. 674 ($1.5 million for stores); Act of Mar. 23, 1828, 4 Stat. 290 (President authorized to spend $250,000 on breakwater).

213. *See* the Neutrality Act, and the debate preceding its passage. 30 *Annals* 715-56; Act of Mar. 3, 1817, 3 Stat. 370-71. *See also supra* note 207.

214. The most direct effort to control operations was a resolution by William C. Gaston of North Carolina "[t]hat, pending the negotiation with Great Britain, it is inexpedient to prosecute the military operations against the Canadas for invasion or conquest." The House refused, 67-92, to consider the resolution. 26 *Annals* 1054, 1056. A less direct but nevertheless interesting decision took place when a proposal was made to authorize the President to build steam batteries as he saw fit to defend New Orleans. Daniel Webster moved to strike mention of any location for the steam batteries to allow the executive to decide where they should be placed, asserting it was improper to limit his authority as commander-in-chief. Henry Clay defended the motion, arguing that retention of fixed locations might be viewed as lack of confidence in the executive. Webster's motion was approved and eventually made part of the legislation. *See* 29 *Annals* 1371-74, 363, 1453. Grundy said of efforts to limit funds to defensive purposes (26 *Annals* 992):

Sir, under the Constitution of the United States, Congress has the power to declare war; it has done so. Congress has the power to furnish the means to prosecute it; but the application of the means when provided belongs to the Executive department. The President is to decide how far offensive or defensive operations are expedient.

215. For example, Wells said he opposed fighting in Canada and would vote against an enlistment bounty because it was a step he contended Congress had ample power to take (26 *Annals* 585):

The provision in the Constitution which, in a wise and wholesome spirit of caution and distrust, limits to a period of two years the power over appropriations for the support of armies, anticipates, among other things, the fluctuation of public opinion, which may place in either House of the National Legislature a majority of members opposed to the further prosecution of an existing war. I think I am warranted in saying that a sound construction of this provision, taken in connexion with the other parts of the Constitution, equally with the nature and genius of our Government, will justify the withholding of supplies for military purposes, where either the continuance of the war itself, or the direction in which it is moving, is disapproved of by those who are called upon to vote for those supplies. To me it is clear that we have a volition upon this point; that we are now authorized to make this inquiry, and are competent to proportioning our supplies of men and money to the objects which we think ought to be those of the war, in the present juncture of our affairs.

See also 27 *Annals* 1615 (Robertson, a war supporter).

216. 28 *Annals* 255-56, and Act of Mar. 3, 1815, 3 Stat. 224. *See generally* C. Bernardo & E. Bacon, *American Military Policy: Its Development Since 1775* at 143-51 (2d ed. 1961).

217. *E.g.*, 23 *Annals* 823-33 (Seybert); 834-45 (McKee); 930 (Rhea); 968 (Fisk: Constitution merely allows navy).

218. *E.g.*, 23 *Annals* 819 (Cheves); 875-83 (Johnson); 884-99 (Lowndes); 895 (Law); 934 (Gold: Constitution mandates navy); 950 (Quincy: essential connection between Union's safety and naval force).

219. Act of March 30, 1812, 24 *Annals* 2261-62. See Rhea's comment opposing what he regarded as an implied commitment for future vessels. 23 *Annals* 932.

220. *E.g.*, 25 *Annals* 404, 450 (four 74-gun and six 44-gun vessels); Act of Nov. 15, 1814, 3 Stat. 144 (up to 20 vessels).

221. 28 *Annals* 255-56 (Feb. 20, 1815); Act of April 29, 1816, 3 Stat. 321. *See also* Act of Mar. 1, 1817, 3 Stat. 347 (reserving timber on public lands).

222. *See* Act of Mar. 3, 1821, 3 Stat. 637. *See generally*, D. Cooney, *A Chronology of the U.S. Navy 1755-1965*, at 15-43 (1965); H. & M. Sprout, *The Rise of American Naval Power, 1776-1918*, at 96-101 (1939).

223. Act of December 20, 1822, 3 Stat. 720; Act of April 5, 1826, 4 Stat. 152 (to put additional vessels into working order).

224. Act of May 15, 1820, 3 Stat. 596 (up to 5 vessels); Act of May 18, 1826, 4 Stat. 170 (10 sloops of war).

225. Act of Dec. 20, 1822, 3 Stat. 720.

226. Act of April 5, 1826, 4 Stat. 152. The House debate on this bill (2 *Register* 1797-98), and its discussion in the Senate (*id.* 372-73), made it apparent that members of Congress wanted piracy suppressed in the waters near Brazil, and to protect American commerce from illegal exercise of the blockade. Additionally, the Act of May 18, 1826 (4 Stat. 170), provided a specific amount to be used "for the suppression of piracy," leaving open-ended the manner in which this objective would be achieved.

227. 12 U.S. (8 Cranch) 110 (1814).

228. *See* Bas v. Tingy, 4 U.S. (4 Dall.) 37 (1800), discussed *supra* at 146-47, 161-63.

229. 12 U.S. (8 Cranch) at 126, 145, 149. *See* Martin v. Mott, 25 U.S. (12 Wheat.) 19, 31-32 (1827); Houston v. Moore, 18 U.S. (5 Wheat.) 1 (1820).

230. *Infra* at 287; 1 Richardson, *Messages* 536-57.

231. *See infra* at 357. He called a series of Cabinet meetings between September 26 and October 1, 1822, to consider how to answer a request by some Cuban patriots for annexation. The answer he prepared assured the patriots of the most friendly sentiments, but said that relations with Spain "did not admit of their forming any engagements, in the present state of things, such as were implied in the proposals of Mr. Sanchez; and that the Executive Government would not in any event be competent to form them without the concurrence of Congress." 6 *Adams Memoirs* 73-74.

232. *Supra* at 266.

233. 6 Brant, *Madison* 280-83; White, *Jeffersonians* 65.

234. Letter of June 12, 1815 to Crowninshield, 2 *Madison Writings supra* note 102, at 603-606.

235. Jackson to Graham, Jan. 14, 1817, in 2 J. Bassett and J. Jameson, eds., *Correspondence of Andrew Jackson* 273-74 (1926-35) (7 vols.) [hereinafter *"Jackson Correspondence"*]; Jackson to Monroe, March 4, 1817, *id.* 277-82; Division Order, April 22, 1817, *id.* 291-92.

236. Monroe to Jackson, Aug. 4, 1817, 2 *Jackson Correspondence* 319; Monroe to Jackson, Oct. 5, 1817, *id.* 329-32.

237. *Id.* 343. Congress considered the problem of controlling naval officers when they took up the question of establishing a line of communication across the Isthmus of Panama, in order to expedite orders to American ships in the Pacific. The House Committee on Naval Affairs said that "it is desirable at all times, that our Navy should act under the immediate instruction of the Executive, as far as practicable, and that as little be left to the discretion of the officers as circumstances will allow." H. Rep. No. 56, 19th Cong., 2d Sess. 1 (1827).

238. *See infra* at 306-17.

239. *See* the description in D. Long, *Nothing Too Daring: A Biography of Commodore David Porter, 1780-1843*, at 109-41 (1970) [hereinafter "Long, *Porter*"].

240. See *infra* at 326-31, 341-46.

241. Long, *Porter* 227-29.

242. *See id.* 230-55. Adams felt "Porter's descent upon Porto Rico [*sic*] was a direct hostile invasion of the island, utterly unjustifiable," but Treasury Secre-

tary Crawford defended Porter, arguing that Jackson's conduct in Florida had been "ten times worse." 6 *Adams Memoirs* 453-54. Some press commentary noted in effect that "two wrongs don't make a right," and at least two facts did distinguish, for some people at least, Porter's conduct from Jackson's: (1) the former had been under no immediate military necessity, whereas Jackson was pursuing war-making Indians and their protectors; and (2) Lt. Platt's treatment by the town's authorities occurred while Platt was on a mission to recover the goods of a private company, seized on land, whereas Jackson's actions were in response to Indian raids that caused the deaths of many American citizens and military personnel. Long, *Porter* 245-46, 250-55. The Puerto Rican authorities apparently agreed with Porter's characterization of the town as a "pernicious pirate nest." *Id.* 229, 233, 244.

243. Long's treatment is perhaps too sympathetic, but helpful. *Id.* 220-26. Porter's congressional allies were unable to help him. *See generally* 2 *Register* 14, 26-27, 56-65 (Dec. 1825-Jan. 1826).

Monroe and J.Q. Adams became angered at Navy officers at Baltimore who were openly aiding privateers for South American revolutionaries in their efforts to attack Spanish commerce. Rather than proceeding against the officers, however, they sought the Attorney General's assistance in prosecuting illegal privateers, and instructed naval commanders to take their prizes to ports other than Baltimore. See 4 *Adams Memoirs* 308, 316-18, 509, 516-20.

244. Long, *Porter* 247.

245. In addition to Long's biography, see R. Heinl, Jr., *Soldiers of the Sea* 13-36 (1962).

246. See the comments concerning the intentions of Mathews and Jackson, *infra* at 309-17, 364-65. Porter's reputation for aggressive conduct was well known before he was assigned command of the West Indian squadron. Decatur, too, had shown his zeal on several occasions prior to 1815. David Rodgers assured his superiors that he regarded the attack on the *Chesapeake* as "Dastardly, . . . Inhuman and Unjust," and hoped he would give his country "*no Cause to Blush.*" (Emphasis in original.) Rodgers to Hamilton, June 16, 1810, *Letters Rec'd by Sec'y Navy from Officers*, NAM, M-125, roll 19.

247. The orders issued in the incidents discussed below are at 307, 317-18, 328-29, 343, 347, 371-72. Secretary of Navy Paul Hamilton issued instructions to his commanders on June 5, 1810, instructing them to defend merchant vessels; on June 9 he sent an additional "exposition" of his "sentiments" to Porter and his other captains that they, like all patriotic Americans, felt the insults of Britain and France and especially of the *Chesapeake*. They were to act consistently with principles of neutrality, but to be "prepared and determined at every hazard to vindicate the injured honor of our Navy and revive the drooping spirits of the Nation. . . ." Hamilton to Campbell, Decatur and Rodgers, June 5, 1810, NAM, *Letters Sent by Sec'y Navy to Officers*, M-149, roll 9. Secretary of Navy to David Porter, June 9, 1810, LC Manuscript Division, David Dixon Porter Collection, container 16. We can safely assume identical letters were sent to Captain Rodgers. *See* 6 *Adams History* 25-26. The orders issued to Elliot warned him "to avoid everything" that might impair the very friendly relations that existed with the nations involved, "so far as this can be done consistently with the maintenance

of our rights. In your discretion a willing confidence is reposed." A.S.P., 6 *Foreign Relations* 1071-72. The orders to Decatur more clearly limited his actions to Algiers, but said nothing on how to handle claims for prizes returned to the British. See Crowninshield to Decatur, April 15, 1815, *Madison Papers*, series 1, reel 17.

248. The most striking evidence of this is in connection with Mathews and Jackson, see *infra* at 309-10, 343. Also see the messages from Poinsett, discussed *supra* at 265.

249. *Infra* at 294-95, 303-304, 364-65.

250. No communication of the supplementary orders to Rodgers could be found. See the numerous, important letters withheld in connection with the Floridas, *infra* at 298, 319-20, 332-33, 358.

251. Sec. 11, Act of March 1, 1809, 2 Stat. 528, 530-31.

252. Act of June 28, 1809, 2 Stat. 550.

253. Letter to Smith, Oct. 23, 1809, in A.S.P., 3 *Foreign Relations* 315-16.

254. See message to Congress, Nov. 29, 1809, 20 *Annals* 475. The proclamation is at 21 *Annals* 2076.

255. 20 *Annals* 511 (Dec. 11, 1809) (Senate); *id.* 1151 (Jan. 4, 1810) (House).

256. 20 *Annals* 754-55.

257. *E.g., id.* 1178 (A. Seybert).

258. *E.g., id.* 1165 (L. Sawyer).

259. *Id.* 582. The House rejected the Senate amendments (21 *Annals* 1484), whereupon the Senate insisted on its version (20 *Annals* 592). The conference committee deadlocked. 20 *Annals* 600.

260. 21 *Annals* 1763.

261. *Id.* 1931.

262. 20 *Annals* 666-67, 673.

263. 21 *Annals* 2582-83; 2 Stat. 605, 606.

264. A Carr, *Coming of War* 279 (1960).

265. C. Tansill, "Robert Smith," in 3 *The American Secretaries of State and Their Diplomacy* 178 (S. Bemis, ed. 1927-29) (10 vols.) [hereinafter *"Secretaries of State"*].

266. 8 *The Writings of James Madison* 96-99 (G. Hunt, ed., 1908) [hereinafter *"Madison Writings* (Hunt)"].

267. 3 *Secretaries of State* 177-79. *See also* 22 *Annals* 1235-36.

268. A.S.P., 3 *Foreign Relations* 384-86.

269. NAM, Department of State, *Despatches from United States Ministers to France*, M-34, reel 14; A.S.P., 3 *Foreign Relations* 387.

270. "Recollections of the Civil History of the War of 1812," being fragments of a diary kept by Joseph Gales, proprietor of the *National Intelligencer.* "Entry of Sept. 27, 1810," in *National Intelligencer*, July 30, 1857. *See id.*, Entries of Oct. 17, 1810 and Jan. 30, 1811. Smith's account of how Madison later prevented him from obtaining more definite evidence from the French Minister is in R. Smith, *Address to the People of the United States* (1811); *compare* Madison's *Memorandum as to R. Smith, April, 1811*, in 2 *Madison Writings supra* note 102, at 495.

Professor Tansill has described Madison's position as "humiliating," and stated that, after November 1, Madison "became more and more aware how Napoleon had overreached him." 3 *Secretaries of State* 181. This perception of Madison seems at odds, however, even with Tansill's own account of the intervention in West Florida, in which Tansill finds that Madison "practised the principles of *realpolitik* many decades before that all-descriptive term was coined." *Id.* 182. Channing sees Madison as "obliged to adhere to his declaration," once made. 4 E. Channing, *History of the United States* 420-21 (1929). Brant sees Madison proceeding deliberately, intentionally ignoring France's lack of candor so as to apply pressure to England. 5 Brant, *Madison* 338-39.

271. 22 *Annals* 1248.

272. Smith expressed concern only over technicalities. Smith to Madison Sept. 28, 1810, *Madison Papers*, series 2, reel 26. The only report of Albert Gallatin's view appears in an interview with Joseph Gales where he asserted that "the President must issue his proclamation." Interview of Oct. 4, 1810, printed in the *National Intelligencer*, July 30, 1857. *See also* Paul Hamilton to Madison, Sept. 25, 1810, *Madison Papers*, Series 1, reel 12; C.A. Rodney to Madison, Sept. 26, 1810, *id.*

273. Both statements were recorded by Turreau, and are referred to in 5 *Adams History* 303.

274. 22 *Annals* 11.

275. Letter of Oct. 29, 1810, *Madison Papers*, series 1, reel 12.

276. Wellesley to Pinkney, Aug. 31, 1810, in A.S.P., 3 *Foreign Relations* 366. Although Lord Wellesley claimed that the British wanted to restore commercial freedom worldwide, he emphasized that France must "retract the principles which had rendered [British restrictions] necessary." *Id.*

277. The letter to Cadore was kept in the State Department; the original of the September 10 letter to Smith is bracketed so as to indicate that its highly material second paragraph was deleted. See A.S.P., 3 *Foreign Relations* 387. Brant says that other "private" letters from Armstrong also were withheld. 5 Brant, *Madison* 226.

278. 22 *Annals* 547.

279. *Id.* 863-65.

280. *See, e.g., id.* 867-68 (Randolph); 919 (J. Emott).

281. *Id.* 919 (Madison was a "mere agent . . . limited by his letter of attorney, the law. . . .").

282. *Id.* 990.

283. *Id.* 951.

284. *Id.* 894.

285. *Id.* 1062 (65-36).

286. *Id.* 1033-35.

287. *Id.* 1094, 361.

288. Wellesley to Pinkney, Feb. 11, 1811, in A.S.P., 3 *Foreign Relations* 412. The British also argued that France had conditioned repeal of its edicts on England's renunciation of certain principles of blockade resting on grounds other than the Orders in Council. Madison contended this view was immater-

ial to the controversy between Britain and the United States. *Id.* 408-10. *See also* Monroe to Russell, Nov. 27, 1812, *id.* 423.

289. 1 Richardson, *Messages* 491; J. Pratt, "James Monroe," in 3 *Secretaries of State* 222.

290. *See* Bayard's statement, 23 *Annals* 294. *See also* Russell to Smith, Dec. 11, 1810, in 22 *Annals* 1244-45; and Russell to Smith, Mar. 15, 1811, in 5 *Adams History* 394-95 (describing French vacillation).

291. James Monroe to Joseph J. Monroe, 5 *Monroe Writings* 194, 196.

292. 6 *Adams History* 250-51.

293. *Id.* 282.

294. Barlow to Bassano, May 1, 1812, *id.* 254.

295. Bassano to Barlow, May 10, 1812, a note expressing the former's surprise that Barlow had no knowledge of the April 28 decree, A.S.P., 3 *Foreign Relations* 603. According to Henry Adams, Bassano simply lied. 6 *Adams History* 255.

296. May 11, 1812, A.S.P., 3 *Foreign Relations* 613.

297. May 12, 1812, *id.* 603.

298. *Madison Papers*, series 1, reel 14.

299. A.S.P. 3 *Foreign Relations* 614.

300. NAM, Dep't of State, *Despatches from United States Ministers to Great Britain*, 1791-1906, M-30, reel 14.

301. 23 *Parliamentary Debates* 288 (Hansard) (May 22, 1812).

302. The *Morning Chronicle* of May 23, 1812, p. 2, cols. 2-4, reported attacks on the decree in Parliament, and asserted editorially that the date was fraudulent; even so, the editorial urged Britain to repeal its Orders in Council.

303. Russell to Monroe, June 26, 1812, submitting a copy of the order of revocation, A.S.P., 3 *Foreign Relations* 432-33.

304. 24 *Annals* 1451. Randolph, after presenting his evidence that the decrees had not been repealed (*e.g.*, *id.* 1452), moved that it was not expedient at that time to make war against Britain (*id.* 1462); but the House voted not to consider his proposition (37-72, *id.* 1470).

305. A.S.P., 3 *Foreign Relations* 405-407.

306. On March 10, 1812, the administration opened a five-part series on the evils of impressment in the *National Intelligencer*, entitled "Impressed Seamen." Also on March 9, 1812, the President sent a special message in which he transmitted the papers obtained from Henry; and he denounced both Great Britain and a certain class of American citizens for conspiring to break up the Union. 23 *Annals* 165. Brant describes these events as creating the impression of a final drive to obtain a declaration of war. 5 Brant, *Madison* 413-20.

307. Act of June 18, 1812, 2 Stat. 755.

308. 24 *Annals* 1637 (House); 23 *Annals* 297-98 (Senate).

309. Madison to Barlow, August 11, 1812, in 8 *Madison Writings* (Hunt) 208-10.

310. 25 *Annals* 14.

311. *Id.* 54.

312. *Id.* 1246-50.

313. *Id.* 1151; A.S.P., 3 *Foreign Relations* 608.
314. *See, e.g.,* 26 *Annals* 275-79 (Pearson); 27 *Annals* 1711 (Pickering). Pearson called to task those who accepted assertions of repeal in the face of "incontestable facts."
315. *See, e.g.,* 26 *Annals* 232-34, 237-38 (Shipherd).
316. 26 *Annals* 92.
317. *Id.* 92-94 (committee recommendation); *id.* 98 (recommendation adopted).
318. *Id.* 151-52.
319. *Id.* 302, 308-10. The vote finally came after William Bibb of Georgia announced that the Committee on Ways and Means was ready to present measures necessary to fund the war. *Id.* 302.
320. 6 Brant, *Madison* 185.
321. 26 *Annals* 433; 27 *Annals* 2061-83.
322. 6 Brant, *Madison* 185.
323. Monroe to Colonel John Taylor, Nov. 30, 1813, in 42 *Mass. Hist. Soc. Proc.* 331 (1909). Professor Pratt and others have noted the possible additional pressure against a settlement from those in Congress who wanted to invade and annex Canada and the Floridas. J. Pratt, *The Expansionists of 1812*, at 120-25 (1957) [hereinafter "Pratt"]; Cresson, *Monroe* 249, 258.
324. 11 U.S. (7 Cranch) 382 (1813).
325. *Id.* 386-88.
326. 11 U.S. (7 Cranch) 570, 571, (1813). The libel was dismissed as insufficient on another ground, with leave to the Government to amend.
327. The basis of the American claim to West Florida is discussed *supra* at 200-202, 206-207.
328. Act of Oct. 31, 1803, 2 Stat. 245.
329. Act of Feb. 24, 1804, 2 Stat. 251, 254.
330. Letter from J. Madison to Marquis D'Yrujo, March 19, 1804, in *Monroe Papers*, series 1, reel 3.
331. On August 16, 1807, Jefferson wrote Madison that:

> As soon as we have all the proofs of the western intrigues, let us make a remonstrance & demand of satisfaction, and, if Congress approves, we may in the same instant make reprisals on the Floridas. . . . I had rather have war against Spain than not, if we go to war against England. Our southern defensive force can take the Floridas, volunteers for a Mexican army will flock to our standard, and rich pabulum will be offered to our privateers in the plunder of their commerce & coasts. Probably Cuba would add itself to our confederation.

10 *Jefferson Works* (Fed.) 476-77. *See also* his letter of April 2, 1791 to President Washington predicting that American settlers would eventually deliver the area without war, and that of August 12, 1808 to his Secretary of War, in which he suggested using the embargo as "a pretext" for taking good military positions to conquer Mobile, Pensacola and St. Augustine. *Misc. Letters*, M-179, reel 5; 11 *Jefferson Works* (Fed.) 43.

332. John Adair, an alleged accomplice of Aaron Burr and former Senator from Kentucky, made this comment in a letter to Madison dated January 9, 1809, quoted in I. Cox, *The West Florida Controversy, 1798-1813*, at 325-28 (1967) (cites *Madison Papers*, Ms.) [hereinafter "Cox, *West Florida*"].

333. 4 *Official Letter Books of W.C.C. Claiborne, 1801-1816*, at 333 (Mar. 19, 1809) (D. Rowland ed. 1917) [hereinafter "*Claiborne*"]; *id.* 342-43 (Apr. 1, 1809). The meeting almost certainly took place at the home of William Wykoff, Jr., who became the administration's principal agent in guiding the West Florida revolution. *See* 5 *Claiborne* 44.

334. Cox, *West Florida* 328-29 (cites *Madison Letters*, Lenox Mss.). *See also* M. Smelser, *The Democratic Republic, 1801-1815*, at 107 (1968), regarding the confusion and uncertainty of Spanish colonial officials over the prospect of Spain's fall to Napoleon.

335. 5 *Claiborne* 31. (Emphasis in original.) Brant says the letter was written "from the house of the President." 5 Brant, *Madison* 175. No evidence has been found to support this. The phrase may have been taken by Brant from a later letter written by Fulwar Skipwith to John Graham, note 343 *infra*.

336. 5 *Claiborne* 33.

337. According to J. Padgett, Claiborne wrote Governor Holmes on June 14 that, at his meeting with Madison, he had persuaded the President to accept his plan of intervention, first suggested by him three years before. J. Padgett, "The West Florida Revolution of 1810," 21 *La. Hist. Q.* 177 n.227 (1938).

338. 9 *Territorial Papers of the United States* 883-84 (C. Carter, ed. 1940) [hereinafter "*Territorial Papers*"].

339. *Id.* 885. Also in *Domestic Letters of the Dep't of State*, Nat'l Archives microfilm, M-40, reel 13 [hereinafter "*Domestic Letters*"]. Crawford later wrote Smith that he had entrusted the matter to General Mathews, and Smith responded that Crawford's letter had been forwarded to the President who was "perfectly satisfied with the arrangement made . . . ." *See* letter of R. Smith to W. Crawford, October 2, 1810, in *id.* M-40, reel 13.

340. *Misc. Letters*, M-179, reel 23, printed with minor variations in 8 *Madison Writings* (Hunt) 105.

341. *Domestic Letters*, M-40, reel 13.

342. For general histories of the West Florida Revolution, *see* Cox, *West Florida* 312-436; J. Padgett, *supra* note 337, at 76-202; J. Padgett, "The Constitution of the West Florida Republic," 20 *La. Hist. Q.* 881-83 (1937); J. Kendall, "Documents Concerning the West Florida Revolution of 1810" (pts. 1-3), 17 *La. Hist. Q.* 80-95, 306-14, 474-501 (1934).

343. 5 Brant, *Madison* 178-79 (citing letter from W. Wycoff to T.B. Robertson, July 24, 1810, in *Madison Papers*). The letter did not mention Claiborne's letter of June 14, but this omission may have been deliberate. *Compare id.*; and Padgett, note 342 *supra* at 881-83. Whatever may have been the effect of the administration's effort, the fact remains that a deliberate plan to foment trouble and cause a request for occupation by the United States was knowingly implemented by Madison and his aides. The first military action by the insurgents took place on September 23, when they captured the Spanish fort at Baton Rouge, killing several Spanish defenders and taking Governor DeLassus prisoner.

Cox, *West Florida* 388-402. By this time, Wykoff would have had ample time to make his mission known; and it is clear that at some point the insurgents were apprised of the contents of Claiborne's letter and were led to believe that Madison had authorized it. *See* letter of F. Skipwith to John Graham, December 23, 1810, in J. Padgett, *supra* note 337 at 164-65.

344. 1 *Gallatin Writings* 485.

345. *Id.* 486-87.

346. *Madison Papers*, series 1, reel 12. Other sources also noted a possible British plan to govern the Spanish colonies through a puppet regency. See 5 Brant, *Madison* 179-80. *See also* letters from Holmes to Smith, Sept. 12, 1810, in 6 *Territorial Papers* 115-18; and Acting Gov. T.B. Robertson to Smith, Aug. 26, 1810, in *Madison Papers*, series 1, reel 12.

347. Madison to Jefferson, Oct. 19, 1810, in 8 *Madison Writings* (Hunt) 110.

348. A.S.P., 3 *Foreign Relations* 396. *See* the treatments in C. Tansill, "Robert Smith," 3 *Secretaries of State* 185-86, where the author states that the documents sent by Madison to Congress "transmitted with the letter of Governor Holmes to the Secretary of State, of October 17, 1810," were actually enclosed "in the original files in the Department of State," with a letter from Holmes to Smith, of October 3, 1810, giving a detailed account of the revolutionary movement. The reason for using the letter of later date is apparent; Smith had told the French Minister Turreau on October 31 that he knew nothing of the West Florida revolutionaries. The letter of October 3 had been received by the department before October 27; the letter of October 17 was not received until early November. *See also* I. Cox, "The American Intervention in West Florida," 17 *Am. Hist. Rev.* 290 (1912).

349. *See generally* Cox, *West Florida* 395-401; letter of F. Skipwith to J. Collins, appointing him commander of West Florida naval forces, December 4, 1810, in J. Padgett, *supra* note 337, at 136-37; and Governor Claiborne's report to Secretary of State Smith on December 12, 1810, that the U.S. intervention had "put down a military expedition . . . on the point of setting out for Pensacola and Mobile. . . ." 5 *Claiborne* 54. Rhea wrote another letter to Smith October 10, which was actually forwarded by Holmes on October 17. He warned that, if the United States failed to take prompt action, the revolutionaries would be obliged to look to some foreign government for support. He therefore demanded immediate admission, and presumed that the United States would not contest his government's rights to make land grants. A.S.P., 3 *Foreign Relations* 395-96.

350. 1 Richardson, *Messages* 465-66; 22 *Annals* 1257-58. Brant writes, without supporting citation, that Madison first summoned his Cabinet on October 25, 1810. 5 Brant, *Madison* 184-85.

351. A.S.P., 3 *Foreign Relations* 396-97.

352. *See* Cox, *West Florida* 502-505, 580-81.

353. *See* 5 Brant, *Madison* 181, 186-87; letter from Rhea to Smith, Oct. 10, 1810, A.S.P., 3 *Foreign Relations* 395-96. '

354. J. Padgett, *supra* note 337, at 129 (reply of Assembly to Skipwith's inaugural address), 156-57, 164-65.

355. 22 *Annals* 11, 12-13.

356. 5 Brant, *Madison* 189. Brant gives reasons for Madison's failure to call Congress back early, *id.* 184, and explains that "the crisis offered Madison difficult choices," *id.* 500–501, but without adequately emphasizing that the crisis was at least in part Madison's doing, and that Madison could have shared the responsibility for it with Congress, had he chosen to do so.

357. 22 *Annals* 12–13.

358. *Id.* 17, 25–26.

359. *Id.* 28, 37–40, 43–55, 65.

360. *Id.* 44–47.

361. *Id.* 61–62.

362. *Id.* 45.

363. *Id.* 64.

364. *Id.* 1251–52, 1259–62.

365. 24 *Annals* 1379; 23 *Annals* 238. Act of May 14, 1812, in 24 *Annals* 2298.

366. 26 *Annals* 772; 27 *Annals* 2029, indirectly quoted in letter of James Madison to Reuben Kemper, Dec. 30, 1815, appearing in J. Padgett, "The Documents Showing That the United States Ultimately Financed the West Florida Revolution of 1810," 25 *La. Hist. Q.* 944, 946 (1942).

367. *Id.* 946–48. Senator Thomas H. Benton of Missouri stated on March 24, 1826 that $70,000–$80,000 had been paid to the West Florida revolutionaries, in the process of arguing for a bill to relieve Delassus, Spanish Governor of West Florida at the time of the takeover. $2^{(1)}$ *Register* 368. Also, Padgett states that, after Monroe checked the claims, they were provided for in a deficiency appropriations bill of April 9, 1818, which included a provision authorizing $41,356.71 to pay claims "as liquidated by the Department of State, including principal and interest." Padgett, *supra* at 944. The largest claim allowed, however, was not paid with the others, according to Padgett, but was finally the subject of a new act dated August 14, 1848, allowing the claim if the current Secretary of State approved it. Padgett states the claim was finally paid in 1850 in the amount of $38,648.78. *Id.* 944–45.

368. Foster v. Neilson, 27 U.S. (2 Peters) 253 (1829).

369. *Id.* 299–300.

370. *Id.* 300–307.

371. *Id.* 307.

372. *Id.* 274, 308–309.

373. 7 *The Works of Alexander Hamilton* 76–85 (J. Hamilton, ed. 1851).

374. Claiborne to Smith, March 19, 1809, in 4 *Claiborne* 333.

375. Claiborne to Wykoff, June 14, 1810, in 5 *Claiborne* 31–32.

376. Smith to Wykoff, June 20, 1810, in 9 *Territorial Papers* 883, 884.

377. Smith to Crawford, June 20, 1810, in *Domestic Letters*, M-40, reel 13.

378. Crawford to Smith, Sept. 20, 1810, in *Misc. Letters*, M-179, reel 23. On July 21, 1810, Smith wrote to Governor Holmes advising him "of the course adopted as to the Floridas," by sending extracts of Claiborne's letter to Wykoff, and enlisting his aid. *Domestic Letters*, M-40, reel 13 (out of sequence, at 447).

379. Smith to Crawford, October 2, 1810, *Domestic Letters*, M-40, reel 13.

Mathews, a Virginian, served during the Revolution as colonel in General Greene's Carolina campaigns. After the war he settled in Georgia where he was elected Representative to the First Congress. He served as Governor of Georgia from 1793 to 1796. In 1798 he was nominated for Governor of the Mississippi Territory, but his nomination was withdrawn when suspicions arose of his involvement in land speculation in the Natchez district. *See* 2 *Dictionary of American Biography, supra* note 1, at 403; Cox, *West Florida* 437-86.

380. *See* Crawford to Smith, Sept. 20, 1810, in *Misc Letters*, M-179, reel 23, commenting skeptically on news from an informant that the citizens of East Florida were ready to raise the American flag.

381. Madison to William Pinkney, Oct. 30, 1810, in H. Wheaton, *Some Account of the Life, Writings, and Speeches of William Pinkney* 449, 451 (1826).

382. Crawford to Smith, Nov. 1, 1810, *Misc. Letters*, NAM, M-179, reel 23, relaying news from Mathews; Toulmin to Madison, in 5 Brant, *Madison* 233-34.

383. Folch to Smith, Dec. 2, 1810 in *A.S.P.*, 3 *Foreign Relations* 398. Irving Brant treats this letter as referring only to West Florida. 5 Brant, *Madison* 237. Madison, it seems, treated it as referring to at least parts of East Florida as well, since he sent it to Congress as one of the reasons for passing the bill to authorize occupation of East Florida. 22 *Annals* 369-70.

384. 22 *Annals* 369-70.

385. *Id.* 1118. *See* discussion 1119-20, 1123-24, 376, 1141.

386. *Id.* 370-71.

387. Both the resolution and act appear in Act of Jan. 15, 1811, 3 Stat. 471.

388. 22 *Annals* 371, 373-76.

389. *Id.* 1126-27, 1130-33.

390. *Id.* 1141.

391. Folch to McKee, Dec. 2, 1810, in 6 *Territorial Papers* 147-48; McKee to Secretary Eustis, Dec. 5, 1810, *id.* 147.

392. NAM *Orders from Secretary of War*, M-6, roll 5, at 41.

393. Secretary of State to General George Mathews and Colonel John McKee, Jan. 26, 1811, A.S.P., 3 *Foreign Relations* 571-72. The letter was written by Robert Smith, although ascribed in the *American State Papers* to Monroe; see Pratt 79 n.43. Mathews and McKee were also authorized to offer Folch money for his cooperation. *See* Smith to Folch, January 28, 1811, in 9 *Territorial Papers* 922; Isaacs to James Monroe, July 3, 1814, *Misc. Letters*, M-179, reel 30.

394. Pratt 80-81.

395. Mathews to Smith, Feb. 25, 1811, in *Florida Territorial Papers*, National Archives microfilm, M-116, reel 1 [hereinafter "*FTP*, M-116"].

396. George Clark to Henry White, Jan. 7, 1811, Pratt 77. *See also* Claiborne to Secretary of Navy Hamilton, March 17, 1811, in 5 *Claiborne* 183.

397. Isaacs to Mathews and McKee, March 31, 1811, *Misc. Letters*, M-179, reel 24; Folch to Mathews and McKee, March 26, 1811, *FTP*, M-116, reel 1.

398. Mathews and McKee to Smith, April 24, 1811, *FTP*, M-116, reel 1.

399. Mathews and McKee to Covington, May 9, 1811, *id.*; Covington to Mathews and McKee, May 10, 1811, *id.*; Mathews and McKee to Monroe, May 11, 1811, *id.*

400. Monroe to Mathews and McKee, June 29, 1811, *Domestic Letters*, M-40, reel 14 (out of sequence at 491-92).

401. Mathews to Monroe, Aug. 3, 1811 (confidential; copy), in *FTP*, M-116, reel 1.

402. Mathews to Monroe, Oct. 14, 1811, *id.*

403. Pratt 85-86; Foster to Wellesley, Sept. 16, 19, Dec. 20, 1811, in Great Britain, Public Records Office, *Foreign Affairs*, series F, v. 76-77; photostats in the Library of Congress. *See also* letters in A.S.P., 3 *Foreign Relations* 543-45.

404. Mathews to Madison, April 16, 1812, *Madison Papers*, series 1, reel 13; *see* Jose Hibberson and Jose Arrendondo to Justo Lopez, March 17, 1812, in *Senate Misc. Doc. No.* 55, 36th Cong., 1st Sess. 73-74 (1860) [hereinafter "*Senate Doc.* No. 55"].

405. Pratt 89-90.

406. Campbell to Hamilton, Feb. 28, 1812, in *Letters Rec'd by Sec'y of the Navy from Captains*, Nat'l Archives microfilm, M-125, reel 13.

407. Mathews to Campbell, March 11, 1812, *id.*; Campbell to Hamilton, March 21, 1812, *id.*

408. McIntosh to Troup (extract) n.d., enclosed with Troup to Monroe, March 12, 1812, in *FTP*, M-116, reel 2.

409. Troup to Monroe, March 12, 1812, in *id.*

410. Mathews to Laval, March 14, 1812 (copy), in *Misc. Letters*, M-179, reel 25 (enclosed with Mathews to Monroe, Mar. 21, 1812).

411. Laval to Mathews, March 14, 1812 (copy) in *id.*

412. Mathews to Laval, March 13, 1812, in *FTP*, M-116, reel 2.

413. Laval to Mathews, March 14, 1812 (copy) in *Misc. Letters*, M-179, reel 25.

414. Mathews to Monroe, March 14, 1812, and Ashley to Lopez, March 16, 1812, in *FTP*, M-116, reel 2.

415. McIntosh to Lopez, March 15, 1812, in *Senate Doc.* No. 55, at 66-67.

416. Lopez to Laval, March 16, 1812, *id.* 71-72; Lopez to Campbell, March 16, 1812, *id.* at 70.

417. Laval to Lopez, March 16, 1812, *id.* 72.

418. Campbell to Lopez, March 17, 1812, *id.* 71.

419. Lodowick Ashley to Lopez, March 17, 1812, *id.* 69.

420. *Id.* 74-76. Much of the correspondence between Lopez or his agent and Mathews or other American and patriot leaders is contained in the file of United States v. Ferreira, a case involving claims for damages caused by American troops in East Florida, printed in *id.* 65-96. The documents show that Mathews claimed to regard the patriots as the "local authority," which had surrendered the province even before its surrender. He said the American gunboats would not fire on the Spanish unless the British assisted them, but then claimed the British intended to supply them with arms, ammunition or black troops; and "[i]f they did, as I have understood they intend doing, the gun boats have orders to fire upon you," Mathews is reported to have said. Younge and Atkinson to Lopez, March 17, 1812, *id.* 75-76.

421. Lopez to Estrada, March 20, 1812, *id.* 77.

422. *Id.* 77-78.

423. Cited in Pratt 100–101.

424. In an action brought under the treaty of 1819 and the Act of Mar. 3, 1823, providing for payment of "losses occasioned in East Florida" by American troops in 1812 and 1813, the judge concluded that "but for the aid, countenance, and protection of the United States forces, these patriots, so called, could have made no progress whatever," and that "[s]o far as the destruction of property of every kind was concerned, the desolation of the Carnatic of Hyder Ali was not more terrible and complete." Ferreira v. United States, in *Sen. Doc.* No. 55 at 38, 40, *appeal dismissed*, 54 U.S. (13 How.) 40, 52 (1851).

425. Pratt 101.

426. Mathews to Monroe, March 21, 1812 in *FTP*, M-116, reel 2.

427. Mathews to Madison, April 16, 1812, *Madison Papers*, series 1, reel 13.

428. *Id.*

429. Campbell to Hamilton, April 16, 1812, NAM, *Letters Rec'd by Sec'y Navy from Captains*, M-125, reel 23.

430. Ammon, *Monroe* 307; Pratt 109. Madison communicated material concerning the "secret agent" to Congress on his own initiative, 23 *Annals* 1162, and later sent the official British disclaimer, 24 *Annals* 1210–11. For legislative debate, see *id.* 1186–87, 1193–95, 1220–23.

431. Pratt 121.

432. *See* Monroe to Mathews, Jan. 26, 1811, April 4, 1812, A.S.P., 3 *Foreign Relations* 571–72.

433. *Id.* 572.

434. Monroe to Mathews, April 4, 1812 (draft), *FTP*, M-116, reel 2. Monroe cited the Act of June 5, 1794, 1 Stat. 384. Professor Pratt suggests that Monroe's reference to this law might have been meant as a threat to keep Mathews silent. Pratt 113 n.104.

435. Monroe to Foster, April 6, 1812, in *Records of the British Foreign Office, American*, Series II, 5/85, as cited in Pratt 112 n.102.

436. Campbell to Hamilton, April 25, 1812, in *Letters Rec'd by Sec'y Navy from Captains*, Nat'l Archives microfilm M-125, reel 23.

437. Madison to Jefferson, April 24, 1812, *Madison Papers*, series 1, reel 14.

438. *See* Pratt 110–11.

439. W.H. Crawford to Monroe, April 19, 1812, *Misc. Letters*, M-179, reel 25.

440. Isaacs to Monroe, July 3, 1814, *id.* reel 30.

441. Mathews to Monroe, June 22, 1812, *FTP*, M-116, reel 2.

442. Isaacs to Monroe, July 3, 1814, *Misc. Letters*, M-179, reel 30.

443. Pratt 115.

444. Monroe to Mitchell, April 10, 1812, A.S.P., 3 *Foreign Relations* 572–73.

445. Most residents of Georgia strongly supported a takeover of the Floridas. *See* Pratt 116–18. Before receiving his commission from Monroe, Mitchell wrote the Secretary of War urging the government to adopt a "prompt and decisive course" in East Florida, and promising his state's zealous cooperation. Mitchell to Eustis, April 20, 1812, cited in Pratt at 118.

446. Isaacs to Monroe, July 3, 1814, in *Misc. Letters*, M-179, reel 30. Isaacs was seeking payment of his expenses incurred while delivering messages between Monroe, Mathews, and Mitchell.

447. Serrurier to Maret, May 4, 1812, in 6 *Adams History* 241.

448. Mitchell to Monroe, May 2, 1812, *FTP*, M-116, reel 2.

449. Monroe to Mitchell, May 27, 1812, A.S.P., 3 *Foreign Relations* 573.

450. *Sen. Doc.* No. 55 at 82–88; J. Cooper and C. Sherman, *Secret Acts, Resolutions and Instructions Under Which East Florida was Invaded by the United States Troops* . . . 34, 35 (1860), microfilm, Center for Research Libraries, Chicago, Ill.

451. Mitchell to Monroe, July 17, 1812, in *Misc. Letters*, M-179, reel 26. In an address to the Georgia Legislature in November 1812, Mitchell explained how he had viewed the Florida situation prior to the declaration of war: "The confidence with which I anticipated the declaration of war against Great Britain," he said, "led me with equal confidence to anticipate an enlargement of the powers of the President, by Congress, as the necessary consequences, having for its object the entire occupancy of East and West Florida." 3 *Niles' Weekly Register* 193, November 28, 1812, quoted in Pratt at 123–24.

452. 24 *Annals* 1683, 1685.

453. *Id.* 1686–92.

454. Among the important items not transmitted were: Mathews to Smith, Feb. 25, 1811, *FTP*, M-116, reel 1; McKee to Smith, April 10, 17, 24, 1811, *id.*; McKee to Monroe, May 11, 1811, *id.*; McKee to Monroe, June 2, 26, 1811, *id.*; and McKee to Monroe, Jan. 1, 8, 22, March 11, April 15, 1812, *id.* reel 2; Mathews to Monroe, March 14, 21, 28, April 16, 1812, *id.*; F.M. Troup to Monroe, March 12, 1812, *id.*; Monroe to Mathews, April 4, 1812, *id.*; Monroe to Mathews, June 29, 1811, in *Domestic Letters*, M-40, reel 14.

455. 23 *Annals* 325–26; Pratt 151.

456. Monroe to Mitchell, July 6, 1812, 9 *State Papers and Publick Documents* . . . 161–64 (T. Wait, ed. 1819) (10 vols.) [hereinafter "*State Papers*"]. There was a longstanding fear that the British would use black soldiers in Florida; see Mathews to Monroe, June 28, 1811, in *FTP*, M-116, reel 1. During the uprising in March 1812, Mathews claimed to be convinced—by information from "a half-pay British officer"—that "the British contemplated landing here two regiments of blacks." See Hibberson and Arredondo to Lopez, March 17, 1812, in *Sen. Doc.* No. 55 at 73–74, and Younge and Atkinson to Lopez, March 17, 1812, *id.* 75–76.

457. Mitchell to Monroe, July 17, 1812, 9 *State Papers* 164–65. See also Cooper, *supra* note 450, at 42.

458. McIntosh to Monroe, July 3, 1812, *FTP*, M-116, reel 2.

459. Crawford to Monroe, Aug. 6, 1812, in *Monroe Papers*, series 1, reel 5.

460. Pratt 202–208.

461. Mitchell to Monroe, Sept. 19, 1812, 9 *State Papers* 168; Mitchell to Monroe, Oct. 13, 1812, *id.* 174–75. Also on Oct. 13, Mitchell urged Col. Smith to use the Georgia militia to take St. Augustine. Pratt 210.

462. Eustis to Pinckney, Oct. 4, 1812, cited in Pratt 207.

463. Monroe to Mitchell, Oct. 12, 1812, 9 *State Papers* 172–74.

464. Monroe to Pinckney, Dec. 8, 1812, *id.* 188–91. Madison drafted, but did not send to Congress when it convened, a message seeking authority for immediate occupation of East Florida.

465. Pratt 195.

466. Pratt 217-18.

467. 1 J. Parton, *Life of Andrew Jackson* 372 (1861).

468. 25 *Annals* 124-26. Madison's report was ordered to be printed, but for the private use of the Senators only. The sixteen letters the President sent are found in 9 *State Papers* 154-98.

469. McIntosh to Monroe, n.d., 9 *State Papers* 155-58; John William to Madison, Dec. 3, 1812, *id.* 158; Monroe to Mitchell, July 6, 1812, *id.* 161-64; Monroe to Pinckney, Nov. 3, 1812, *id.* 188; Monroe to Pinckney, Dec. 8, 1812, *id.* 188-91; Mitchell to Pinckney, Dec. 17, 1812, *id.* 191-92.

470. 25 *Annals* 127-28, 130.

471. 26 *Annals* 505, 509.

472. *Id.* 510.

473. *Id.* 516-17.

474. *Id.* 536.

475. 24 *Annals* 132, 1015.

476. Quoted in Pratt at 230.

477. Pinckney to Kindelan, March 26, 1813; and Kindelan to Pinckney, April 26, 1813, in *Sen. Doc.* No. 55 at 90, 95.

478. Pratt 241.

479. Monroe to Conner, March 15, 1813, *Domestic Letters*, M-40, reel 14.

480. Monroe to Gallatin, Adams & Bayard, April 27, 1813, 1 *The Writings of Albert Gallatin* 539 n. 1 (H. Adams, ed. 1960).

481. Pratt 236.

482. *See* 1 J. Bassett, *Life of Andrew Jackson* 109-118, 126 (1911) (2 vols.) [hereinafter "Bassett, *Jackson*"].

483. 2 *Jackson Correspondence* 12-13.

484. *Id.* 19, 22-23.

485. *Id.* 30-31.

486. *Id.* 24, 26.

487. *Id.* 37.

488. *Id.* 42.

489. *Id.* 43. The original letter has Monroe's qualifying words written in between the lines of his letter, in what appears to be the same ink as Monroe's signature. *Jackson Presidential Papers*, LC microfilm, series 1, reel 12 [hereinafter "*Jackson Papers*"].

490. *Jackson Papers*, series 1, reel 12. (Emphasis in original.)

491. 2 *Jackson Correspondence* 60-62. The version of this letter in 5 *Monroe Writings* 296-97, is incorrect in that it refers to Cassedy as "Capida," and to 25,000 instead of 2,500 troops.

492. 2 *Jackson Correspondence* 46 n.2.

493. *Id.* 45. He informed the commandant that American troops had captured three Spanish sailors, and said "They will be held as security for the restoration of Mr. Doleeves overseer and negroes. Should these men have been murdered by your Indians, you will recollect my promise to you, An Eye for an Eye, Tooth for Tooth, and Scalp for Scalp."

494. *Id.* 50; 1 Bassett, *Jackson* 134.

495. 2 *Jackson Correspondence* 66.

496. *Id.* 70. On October 14, he suggested dislodging the enemy. *Id.* 73.

497. *Id.* 82–83. *See* 1 Bassett, *Jackson* 137. In general, correspondence between Washington and Fort Jackson took less than one month. *Id.* 142–43.

498. 2 *Jackson Correspondence* 96, 98–99.

499. *Id.* 79.

500. *Id.* 101.

501. *Id.* 112.

502. 5 *Monroe Writings* 301.

503. 2 *Jackson Correspondence* 165–66.

504. *Jackson Papers*, series 1, reel 21.

505. A.S.P., 4 *Foreign Relations* 539–45.

506. *See* J. Bassett's account in 2 *Jackson Correspondence* viii–ix.

507. The defense is printed in P. Goodwin, *Biography of Andrew Jackson* 180–85 (1833). *See* 1 Bassett, *Jackson* 228.

508. M. James, *Andrew Jackson, The Border Captain* 286 (1933).

509. Goodwin, *supra* note 507 at 190–91. Goodwin cites no source for his undoubtedly biased version of Jackson's speech. Other versions differ, but all seem to confirm that Jackson acknowledged the propriety of submitting to the legal process when the emergency was over. *See* 1 Bassett, *Jackson* 230, and the sources cited therein.

510. 2 *Jackson Correspondence* 203.

511. *Id.* 207.

512. *Id.* 212–13.

513. James, *supra* note 508 at 296.

514. *See generally* Cresson, *Monroe* 297–99; Ammon, *Monroe* 412–18; 4 *Adams Memoirs* 20–21; 6 *Monroe Writings* 32–33.

515. Monroe had been informed of the establishment of Amelia Island in a letter dated July 20, 1817, by acting Secretary of State Richard Rush. Rush wrote that, at the suggestion of Treasury Secretary William Crawford, a public vessel had been sent to the mouth of the St. Mary River to survey the situation, and that troops had been ordered to march from Charleston to Pt. Peter; he enclosed a copy of the January 1811 No-Transfer Act for Monroe's reference. Crawford wrote Monroe on October 2 about the establishment at Galveston, and stated it had no authority from any of the South American republics. *Monroe Papers*, series 1, reel 6.

516. 4 *Adams Memoirs* 15.

517. *Id.* 15, 21.

518. For passing references to Cabinet consideration of the instructions, *see id.* 20–21, 35–36. For the instructions, *see* A.S.P., 4 *Foreign Relations* 141–42, 143; 7 *State Papers*, 15th Cong., 1st Sess., No. 47 at 12–13, 16–17 (1818); 32 *Annals* 1807–808, 1810–11.

519. 2 *Papers of John C. Calhoun* 20 (W. Hemphill ed. 1963) [hereinafter "*Calhoun Papers*"].

520. *See* correspondence of J.D. Henley and J. Bankhead with L. Aury, December 22 and 23, 1817, in A.S.P., 4 *Foreign Relations* 139–42; 7 *State Papers*, 15th Cong., 1st Sess., No. 47 at 7–11 (1818); 32 *Annals* 1803–806.

521. 2 Richardson, *Messages* 582-83. The message referred also to Galveston, but orders related to that establishment had not yet been issued. Later, Captain David Patterson, in command of the New Orleans naval station, was ordered to break up the piratical establishment there, under the command of Jean Lafitte. Patterson wrote to the Secretary of Navy on February 16, 1820 that, after consulting with Judge Hall, Collector of the port and Governor of the state, he had granted the Lafitte brothers's request for permission to leave. He stated that he had issued the permit, which authorized the group to leave with all their boats and possessions after burning their buildings, because the government had not authorized him to destroy the place and would prefer him to get rid of the pirates without force. *Letters Rec. by Sec'y of Navy from Captains*, National Archives microfilm, M-125, reel 66.

522. 31 *Annals* 403.

523. 4 *Adams Memoirs* 28. Despite Adams's criticism of Clay, the administration was concerned that the leaders at Amelia Island might have had some kind of authority from a foreign government, and in particular, the South American republics. On December 31, 1817, Adams wrote to an informant, Charles Collins, expressing the President's thanks for information already given on Amelia Island and his desire for more on McGregor's authority, and whether it extended beyond the power to grant privateering commissions to that of the taking of new territory and establishing a republic. 6 *J.Q. Adams Writings* 283-85. Monroe heard from his friend, Nicholas Biddle, writing from Philadelphia on December 11, 1817, that the South Americans in that city viewed the orders to take over Amelia Island as "not merely an unfavorable change in the sentiments of the govt, but as in fact decisive against them and their cause." *Monroe Papers*, series 1, reel 6.

524. 31 *Annals* 409-10, 416, 448. Omitted from Monroe's response, although he did not so inform Congress, were passages from a letter implicating the British in the occurrences at Amelia Island. 4 *Adams Memoirs* 29.

525. 4 *Adams Memoirs* 33-34. For Adams's draft of suggestions to the committee, see 6 *J.Q. Adams Writings* 286-88.

526. A.S.P., 4 *Foreign Relations* 132-33; 31 *Annals* 647-50 (Rep. Middleton introduced a bill to prohibit the slave trade). *See also* 32 *Annals* 1790-1814 (Appendix) for documents concerning the occupation.

527. 4 *Adams Memoirs* 35-36; Cresson, *Monroe* 301.

528. *Id.* 36-37, 39.

529. 31 *Annals* 112-13.

530. A.S.P., 4 *Foreign Relations* 463; 4 *Adams Memoirs* 37-38.

531. 4 *Adams Memoirs* 57.

532. E. Rostow, "Great Cases Make Bad Law: The War Powers Act," 50 *Texas L. Rev.* 833 (1972). *Compare* the inaccurate statement in J. Rogers, *World Policing and the Constitution* 95-96 (1945), that "Madison had been authorized to take analogous action [to Monroe's intervention] by a secret Congressional resolution."

533. Letter of February 26, 1818, in P. Brooks, *Diplomacy and the Borderlands* 92 (1939).

534. *See* A.S.P., 4 *Foreign Relations* 450-63.

535. *J.Q. Adams and Foreign Policy* 308-10.

536. Cresson, *Monroe* 302-303.

537. Letters of Gaines to Jackson, Nov. 21, 1817, and to Secretary of War, Dec. 2, 1817, in A.S.P., 1 *Military Affairs* 686-87.

538. *Jackson Papers*, series 1, reel 23.

539. *Letters sent by Sec'y of War Concerning Indian Affairs*, Nat'l Archives microfilm, series M-15, No. 4.

540. A.S.P., 1 *Military Affairs* 688.

541. *Id.* 689.

542. 2 *Calhoun Papers* 24.

543. Gaines to Calhoun, Dec. 4 and 15, 1817, *Jackson Papers*, series 1, reel 23.

544. A.S.P., 1 *Military Affairs* 689-90.

545. Collection of Thomas F. Madigan, New York Public Library (some punctuation deleted from original).

546. 2 *Jackson Correspondence* 345-46.

547. Excellent description may be found in G. Dangerfield, *supra* note 11 at 47-48; and 1 Bassett, *Jackson* 250-53.

548. Dangerfield, *supra* note 11 at 48-50; Bassett, *Jackson* 254-59. For Jackson's account of the seizure of Ft. St. Marks and the execution of Arbuthnot and Ambrister, see his letter to Calhoun of May 5, 1818, in A.S.P., 1 *Military Affairs* 701-702.

549. 2 *Jackson Correspondence* 360-62, 367-69; A.S.P., 1 *Military Affairs* 702.

550. A.S.P., 1 *Military Affairs* 712-14; *id.* 720-21 (proclamation of May 29, 1818); Letter of Jackson to Calhoun, June 2, 1818, in A.S.P., 4 *Foreign Relations* 602; 2 *Jackson Correspondence* 374-75, 379-80. Jackson wrote Calhoun of the surrender: "Terms are more favorable than a conquered Enemy would have merited, but under the peculiar circumstances of the case, my object obtained, there was no motive for wounding the feelings of those whose military pride or honor had prompted to the resistance made." *Id.* 379-80. Jackson later wrote a friend that "all I regret is that I had not stormed the works captured the Gov. put him on his trial for the murder of Stokes and his family [settlers killed by the Indians] and hung him for the Deed." 2 *Jackson Correspondence* 397.

551. 2 *Jackson Correspondence* 379-81; A.S.P., 4 *Foreign Relations* 602-603.

552. 2 *Jackson Correspondence* 376, 378.

553. *Id.* 384-86. Jackson emphasized:

Let it be remembered that the proceedings heretofore carried on by me . . . is not on the ground that we are at war with Spain; it is on the ground of self defence, bottomed on the broad basis of the law of nature and of nations, and justified by giving peace and security to our frontier. . . .

554. *Infra*, notes 575-78.

555. Letter of May 19, 1830, 7 *Monroe Writings* 209.

556. Professor Bassett has suggested that Jackson may have subsequently

confused a cryptic message from Rhea, of Jan. 12, 1818, relating to another matter, with the issue of whether Monroe had sent him additional authority. Rhea's note was "a message from Monroe through Rhea, and Jackson's mind . . . may have forgotten the real nature of the message and assumed that it related to his hint about Florida." 2 *Jackson Correspondence* xii. *See also* note 625, *infra.*

557. 2 *Calhoun Papers* 104.

558. Calhoun to Jackson, Jan. 29, 1818, in *Letters sent by Sec'y of War Regarding Indian Affairs*, Nat'l Archives microfilm, series M-15. Calhoun acknowledged Jackson's letters and approved the "measures you have taken to bring an efficient force into the field. . . ." Contemporaneously written dispatches from Florida were reaching Calhoun in from 12 to 16 days. *Letters sent by Sec'y of War Regarding Military Affairs*, Nat'l Archives microfilm, series M-6, No. 10.

559. *Id.*

560. 4 *Adams Memoirs* 55.

561. 32 *Annals* 1473 (Monroe's Message, March 25, 1818); A.S.P., 2 *Indian Affairs* 154–62; 2 *Jackson Correspondence* 336–37, 342, 346.

562. *See* 33 *Annals* 930 (Feb. 1, 1819) (Tyler).

563. Act of Feb. 19, 1818, 3 Stat. 407, 408; *see also* discussion *infra* at 360–63, about purpose of militia funds. However, no debate appears in the record during passage of this Act indicating a special purpose for the militia funding. 31 *Annals* 419, 737, 792 (House); 389 (Senate). Calhoun informed Jackson of the appropriation in a letter dated Feb. 19, 1818; apparently $50,000 was being channeled for the Florida expedition, $35,000 for the militia, and $15,000 for the regular army. *Letters of Sec'y of War Regarding Military Affairs*, Nat'l Archives microfilm, series M-6, No. 10; 2 *Calhoun Papers* 148.

564. 4 *Adams Memoirs* 87, 91–92.

565. *Letters re Military Affairs*, *supra* note 563, series M-6, No. 10; Letter of Calhoun to Monroe, Aug. 29, 1818, in 3 *Calhoun Papers* 81.

566. 4 *Adams Memoirs* 102–105.

567. *Id.* 108.

568. Years later, during Jackson's presidency, Calhoun was accused of advocating a court martial of Jackson during the July 1818 Cabinet meetings. *See* letter of Crawford to Calhoun, Oct. 2, 1830 in J. Shipp, *Giant Days or the Life and Times of William H. Crawford* 239 (1909). Apparently at about that time, Calhoun admitted as much to Monroe, who wrote Calhoun in February 1831 that "I did not even remember, until you reminded me of it in London, that you had advised his arrest for disobedience." 7 *Monroe Writings* 226.

569. 4 *Adams Memoirs* 108, 113.

570. See Dangerfield, *supra* note 11 at 52–53.

571. 4 *Adams Memoirs* 109, 111, 113–14. Later, on September 5, 1818, Calhoun wrote to a friend (3 *Calhoun Papers* 105–106):

It is indispensible [*sic*] that the military should on all occasions be held subordinate to orders . . . no excuse except necessity . . . ought to exempt from punishment disobedience to orders. . . . [But in Jackson's case] there was a diversity of opinion .... Some thought, that tho' he had no orders directing him to do what was done, yet the prohibition contained in his orders, did not extend to the circumstances.... [I]t was not considered ... disobedience, in which [case], from the popularity of the General, it was inexpedient to punish.

572. 4 *Adams Memoirs* 112, 114; 3 *Calhoun Papers* 85-86.

573. 6 *Monroe Writings* 54-57.

574. *Id.* 57-60.

575. 2 *Jackson Correspondence* 390.

576. *Id.* 389. *See id.* 391, where Jackson says he will not assume responsibility "contrary to principle and without the prospect of any politic result. ..."

577. 6 *Monroe Writings* 74-75.

578. 2 *Jackson Correspondence* 398 n.2.

579. 6 *Monroe Writings* 85-86.

580. Letter of Feb. 7, 1819, *id.* 87-88.

581. Letter of July 8, 1818, in A.S.P., 4 *Foreign Relations* 496-47.

582. 4 *Adams Memoirs* 105.

583. *J.Q. Adams and Foreign Policy* 317, 327-28, 328 n.30.

584. *Id.* 318-20.

585. 6 *J.Q. Adams Writings* 386-94.

586. *Id.* 393-94; Adams to Holmes, Jan. 20, 1819, *id.* 526.

587. 3 *Calhoun Papers* 29-30, 143.

588. *See J.Q. Adams and Foreign Policy* 322 n. 16.

589. *Id.* 323-24, 329.

590. 6 *Monroe Writings* 87, 89; *J.Q. Adams and Foreign Policy* 333, and Map G, end piece.

591. 4 *Adams Memoirs* 270, 273.

592. 3 *Calhoun Papers* 660-61. The House asked the President for information on the posts in January 1819, and Calhoun reported then that they remained in U.S. hands. *Id.* 511-12.

593. 33 *Annals* 12-15.

594. See 4 *Adams Memoirs* 119. On June 25, 1818, Clay wrote to Charles Tait that he presumed the taking of Pensacola was "without authority; for if it had been, in pursuance of instructions, the constitutional provision is a dead letter which confides to Congress the power of declaring war." 2 *Clay Papers* supra note 80, at 580.

595. 33 *Annals* 292-93.

596. *J.Q. Adams and Foreign Policy* 325.

597. Jefferson to Monroe, January 18, 1819, in 12 *Jefferson Works* (Fed.) 113-14. The instruction is in A.S.P., 4 *Foreign Relations* 539-45; *see also* 6 *J.Q. Adams Writings* 474-502.

598. *J.Q. Adams and Foreign Policy* 327. The case against Arbuthnot and Ambrister was so strongly stated that Castlereagh was able to calm public opinion and let the matter drop. *Id.* 328 n.31. Rep. Johnson denounced the threat in Adams's instruction to Erving, on the ground Congress had not been consulted before it was made. 33 *Annals* 629. His objection was not pursued, however.

599. 33 *Annals* 31, 35-36, 74, 85 (information requests and responses). Apparently, the President had not transmitted any of the documents which he had recited, in his Nov. 17 message (*id.* 11, 14), would be laid before Congress, until he received these information requests. He indicated in his transmittal message of Dec. 3, that the reason for delay was the length of time it took to prepare the documents. *Id.* 35. The amount of documentation ultimately sent is voluminous. A.S.P., 1 *Military Affairs* 681-769 (No. 164).

600. A.S.P., 1 *Military Affairs* 690, 697; 2 *Jackson Correspondence* 376, 378.

601. 33 *Annals* 76, 85.

602. A motion for copies of "instructions" to the U.S. Minister in Spain was amended to read "correspondence" so as to avoid the appearance of any interference with the Senate's power over treaties. *Id.* 392-93. It was passed the next day after another amendment casting it in more general terms to call for "such further correspondence and proceedings in relation to our affairs with Spain, as in his opinion, it shall not be inconsistent with the public interest to divulge." *Id.* 408; compliance, *id.* 430-31. A motion for correspondence with Britain relating to the executive was tabled. *Id.* 398.

603. *Id.* 515-27. An initial debate took place on whether to transfer the investigation to the Committee on Foreign Affairs. *Id.* 368-76.

604. *Id.* 588. Cobb found "something a little mysterious" about the orders given Jackson in view of "the perfect confidence which General Jackson shows, throughout his correspondence, in the correctness of his proceedings." He criticized the President, who by failing " 'to censure him' . . . may therefore be said to justify him." *Id.* 591, 593.

605. *Id.* 675, 679, 867.

606. *Id.* 678.

607. *See id.* 866 (Rep. Rhea, referring to the expeditions by Harmar, St. Clair and Wayne).

608. *Id.* 683, 678. *See also id.* 659 (Johnson). *Compare id.* 601 (Holmes, defending Jackson, but assuming President cannot commence war even against Indians). The status of Indians was discussed more extensively in connection with a bill that would have authorized a military post within Indian territory on the Upper Missouri. *See generally* 41 *Annals* 432-507, 738-53 (March-May, 1824), rejecting the post at least partly because the Indians had not consented, but appropriating funds for military escorts. President Adams reported in 1828 that an Army detachment had succeeded without bloodshed in quelling hostility of Winnebago Indians in Wisconsin. 4 *Register* 2782.

609. *Id.* 602, 604-606 (Holmes).

610. *Id.* 677 (Smyth); 840 (Strother); 605 (Holmes). Perhaps the most extravagant claim was that the invasion represented a continuation of the War of 1812, in which the Creeks had allied with the British. *Id.* 1091 (Desha).

611. *Id.* 780 (Sawyer).

612. *Id.* 587-90.

613. *Id.* 617.

614. *Id.* 644.

615. *Id.* 374 (on motion to transfer investigation).

616. *Id.* 914.

617. *Id.* 1031.

618. *Id.* 618, 930.

619. *Id.* 1132-33, 1136-37.

620. *Id.* 238-39. *Compare id.* 240 (Senate has concurrent right to investigate).

621. *Id.* 256-58, 261-62.

622. 4 *Adams Memoirs* 276-78.

623. 35 *Annals* 15, 540-41. Some members wanted to require Monroe to take the Floridas. *See* 36 *Annals* 1719-28 (Clay). The administration originally sought only discretion to act, and opposed the mandatory approach. 5 *Adams Memoirs* 16-17. During May 1820, the Cabinet discussed whether to take the Floridas without legislative authority. *Id.* 99-102.

624. *See generally* 35 *Annals* 717, 751-78, 927; 36 *Annals* 1542-49 (committee report).

625. At Jackson's request, Rhea wrote a letter to Monroe on June 3, 1831, purporting to recall that Monroe had asked Rhea to write to Jackson authorizing the occupation of the Floridas. Rhea's letter also said that Monroe had asked him to get Jackson to burn the letter of authorization, and that Jackson had shown Rhea the entry in Jackson's letter book indicating that the letter had been burned. Evidence exists, however, that Rhea's 1831 letter was a fraud, virtually dictated by Jackson, as were other affidavits procured by Jackson to substantiate his claim that Monroe had responded to Jackson's letter of January 6, 1818 and authorized the occupation. Ammon, *Monroe* 416-17; Cresson, *Monroe* 304-306. Monroe denied the accusations contained in Rhea's letter, signing on his deathbed a declaration dated June 9, 1831, stating such declarations were "utterly unfounded and untrue." 7 *Monroe Writings* 234-36. *See also* note 556, *supra*; R. Stenberg, "Jackson's 'Rhea Letter' Hoax," 2 *J. So. Hist.* 480-96 (1936).

626. Cresson, *Monroe* 306.

627. *J.Q. Adams and Foreign Policy* 314.

628. Letter to Jefferson, Sept. 26, 1805, in 4 *Monroe Writings* 334, 336.

629. See *supra* at 310.

630. *Supra* at 328-29.

631. *J.Q. Adams and Foreign Policy* 314.

632. Allen describes how the "privateers and buccaneers" of the sixteenth and seventeenth centuries were replaced by "pirates and common murderers" by the eighteenth. Privateering took place under French and British orders between 1793 and 1815, severely damaging American trade. *See generally* Gardner W. Allen, *Our Navy and the West Indian Pirates* 1-23 (1929) [hereinafter "Allen"].

633. Act of April 30, 1790, 1 Stat. 112, 113-14, defined "piracy" and provided for its punishment, but did not by its terms authorize use of the armed forces to capture pirates. The Supreme Court held in The Mariana Flora, 24 U.S. (11 Wheat.) 1, 41-42 (1826), however, that pirates could lawfully be captured under the law of nations by the public or private vessels of any nation. Jefferson told Congress in his annual message of December 3, 1805, that "pri-

vate armed vessels, some of them without commissions, some with illegal commissions, others with those of legal form but committing piratical acts" infested the coasts of the United States. He said he had "found it necessary to equip a force to cruise within our own seas, to arrest all vessels of these descriptions found hovering on our coasts within the limits of the Gulf Stream, and to bring the offenders in for trial as pirates." Allen 3-4. Allen reports that the "force" authorized consisted only of the frigate *Adams.*

634. Spain sought to counteract the revolutions in its colonies by proclaiming a 1,200 mile blockade of northern South America, and commissioning privateers to prey on ships trading with the colonies. The blockade, however, was only a "paper blockade" as the Spanish navy had but three ships to enforce it; Secretary of State Adams called it "a war of extermination against all neutral commerce." Long, *Porter* 203-204.

635. A Whitaker, *The United States and the Independence of Latin America, 1800-1830* at 275-85 (1941).

636. 3 Stat. 510-14. Adams wrote that the act was passed to reverse the Supreme Court's decision, which, he said, held that the 1790 law against piracy could be applied only against Americans. 4 *Adams Memoirs* 362-63 (entry for May 11, 1819). Actually the case held only that the prior law was inapplicable to a robbery committed by Americans on the high seas on board a foreign vessel, and to foreigners within such vessel. United States v. Palmer, 16 U.S. (3 Wheat.) 610, 643 (1818).

637. 6 *Adams Memoirs* 298-300 (Apr. 22, 1824).

638. Act of May 15, 1820, 3 Stat. 600-601; Act of Jan. 30, 1823, 3 Stat. 721.

639. Allen 20. *See* instruction in *Letters Sent by Sec'y of Navy to Officers,* Nat'l Archives microfilm, M-149, reel 14. The instructions enclosed a copy of the Act and ordered that the authority given should be exercised with the "utmost caution and prudence." First priority was to be placed on pursuing piratical vessels which had attempted depredations against American ships. Vessels could not be captured merely because they were fitted out for piracy; evidence must exist that they had already attempted a piratical act. Commanding officers were authorized to touch "at such ports and places as may be necessary and proper to procure supplies, and to obtain information," but were warned to "protect the commerce of the United States, without infringing the lawful rights of any other nation or country, their citizens or subjects." A.S.P., 2 *Naval Affairs* 211-12.

640. *See* Allen 20-21. Many military encounters occurred, including an incident where Lt. James Ramage destroyed some pirate boats and took several prisoners; others fled to the woods. No evidence was found that Americans landed on Cuban or other foreign territory during these incidents, but they clearly entered Cuban waters, in one instance, capturing a vessel in a "creek" near Cape San Antonio. *Id.* 25-27.

641. 38 *Annals* 621 (House) (Jan. 3, 1822); *id.* 151 (Senate) (Jan. 23, 1822).

642. Johnson agreed to a motion by James Pleasants of Virginia to delete language suggesting that certain ships be stationed in the Gulf of Mexico, as interfering with executive authority to determine how to employ the navy. All reference to the Gulf was deleted on motion of Senator H. Gray Otis of Massa-

chusetts, agreed to by Johnson, leaving the final motion as simply calling for an inquiry into building small vessels "for the protection" of American commerce. *Id.* 156-57.

643. *Id.* 621, 911. The House earlier passed a resolution asking the President for the information he possessed, "which may not be improper to communicate," on piratical depredations and efforts by Spanish authorities to control them; deleted from the motion was a request for any further legislative provisions the President might deem necessary. The President responded on January 30, sending material describing recent piratical actions. *Id.* 717-18, 723, 850-51.

644. *Id.* 1173-75.

645. *Id.* 1184-89; 39 *Annals* 1405-407.

646. NAM, *Letters Sent by Sec'y of Navy to Officers, supra* note 639, series 149, reel 14; Long, *Porter* 205-206; Allen 25-26. *Niles' Weekly Register* ran an account of Biddle's anticipated journey stating that his instructions ordered him "to sweep the *land*, as well as the sea, of the pirates of Cuba." The article agreed this policy was correct but said "important events may grow out of it, unless there is an understanding with Spain and the local authorities. . . ." 22 *Niles' Weekly Register* (Mar. 2, 1822). Despite the report in *Niles'*, the instructions issued on March 26 by the Secretary of the Navy apparently did not go any further than orders previously given.

647. A.S.P., 1 *Naval Affairs* 805-806 (letters of Apr. 30 and May 2, 1822). Biddle expected the Governor to consent. *Id.* 805; Allen 29. On a similar mission, Captain Robert T. Spence of *Cyane* asked the Governor of Puerto Rico in August 1822 to suppress piracy and stop allowing "privateers" to enforce the Spanish blockade. The governor agreed to do what he could about piracy, but said the blockade was beyond his power to repeal. Allen 33-35.

648. *See id.* 32-33.

649. 6 *Adams Memoirs* 64-65 (entry for Sept. 17, 1822). For Cabinet discussion of the piracy instructions, see meetings of March 16 and 18, 1819 in 4 *id.* 298-99, 303-304; and of June 3, 1822 in 6 *id.* 9-10. For a description of the capture of the *Palmyra*, see F. Bradlee, *Piracy in the West Indies and its Suppression* 30 (1923).

650. 6 *Adams Memoirs* 85-86 (Oct. 26, 1822).

651. 40 *Annals* 12, 16. On December 11, Secretary of Navy Thompson repeated this request to the Senate Committee on Naval Affairs. A.S.P., 1 *Naval Affairs* 822.

652. 40 *Annals* 371.

653. *Id.* 375-76.

654. *Id.* 376-79, 381-84.

655. *Id.* 32-35; 3 Stat. 720.

656. Allen 99-102 contains a copy of the orders.

657. Long, *Porter* 208.

658. *Id.* 211, 214.

659. On the morning of April 8, 1823, Lt. Cornelius K. Stribling of the *Peacock*, with two barges, the *Gallinipper* and the *Mosquito*, chased a private schooner ashore at Escondido, about twenty miles east of Havana. When the

pirates jumped over the side and fled to shore, the American forces pursued them, killing two and capturing one. The incident is described by Lt. Stribling in his letter of April 8, 1832 to Captain S. Cassin, in C. Goodrich, "Our Navy and the West Indian Pirates," 143 *U.S. Naval Inst. Proc.* 683, 685 (1917). *See also* A.S.P., 1 *Naval Affairs* 1108-109; Allen 46.

660. On April 16, 1823, the *Gallinipper* discovered a suspicious looking sailboat which it chased. When the Americans lost sight of the sailboat they landed near Cayo Blanco, Cuba, and came upon several houses and men they took to be fishermen. But when the American landing party found the boat they had pursued covered with brush, the "fishermen" fired upon them and fled. No one was injured and no prisoners were taken, but the houses were set on fire and the boat seized. Letter of Cassin to Porter, April 28, 1823, in Goodrich *supra* note 659, at 687-89. See A.S.P., 1 *Naval Affairs* 1110; Allen 46-47.

661. Officer Thomas Newell wrote to Porter on July 23, 1823, describing his cruise down the coast of Cuba pursuant to Porter's instructions and during which he examined "every creek and harbor"; and he tells Porter of his discovery of a gun in the mangroves "where the pirates had carefully hidden it." A.S.P., 1 *Naval Affairs* 1114.

662. On July 2½, 1823, the schooner *Beagle*, commanded by Lt. John T. Newton, and the schooner *Greyhound*, commanded by Lt. Lawrence Kearney, anchored off Cape Cruz, Cuba. When they set out to examine the cape in small boats, they were fired upon. The next day they were fired on again, and Lt. David Farragut was sent ashore with a party of marines. The pirates retreated and Farragut's force, unable to capture them, returned to the pirate base, burned four houses and eight boats, and seized the arms they found. A.S.P., 1 *Naval Affairs* 1115-16 (Kearney to Porter, Aug. 10, 1823); Allen 53.

663. *Id.* 47, 52-53; A.S.P., 1 *Naval Affairs* 1107, 1109. Although Porter's letter describing the first incident does not specifically mention a landing, this may have been an oversight on Porter's part, or he considered it obvious from his words; he specifically mentioned a landing in describing the second incident. *Id.* 1109.

664. 41 *Annals* 12, 18.

665. Adams to Minister to Spain, April 28, 1823, in 1 Manning, *Diplomatic Correspondence* 168-84.

666. A.S.P., 2 *Naval Affairs* 215-16 (Dec. 2, 1823).

667. 6 *Adams Memoirs* 230-31 (Jan. 9, 1824).

668. Long, *Porter* 218-19, 224-27.

669. On October 23, 1824, Lt. Richard S. Hunter from the schooner *Porpoise* discovered a suspicious schooner off Camrioca, east of Havana. His barge chased the vessel to shore. No pirates were caught, but the ship loaded with stolen goods was confiscated. Allen 64-65. *See* letter of C. Skinner to S. Southard, Oct. 24, 1824, A.S.P., 2 *Naval Affairs* 255.

670. In late October 1824, Stephon Cabot, an officer of an American dry goods company and also a Vice-Consul to Puerto Rico, informed Lt. Charles T. Platt, commanding the schooner *Beagle*, of a large theft of goods from the company. He told Platt he strongly suspected that the goods had been taken to Fajardo, and asked Platt's assistance in their recovery. Platt sailed into Fa-

jardo harbor on October 26, colors flying. The captain of the port asked to see Platt, who went ashore in civilian clothes, apparently to make clear the non-military nature of his visit. He was initially well received, but the next day was denounced and arrested as a pirate and detained until his uniform and proper credentials were produced. Platt relayed his story to Porter, who on November 14, took several hundred men on the *John Adams, Beagle* and *Grampus* to Fajardo to demand an apology for the insults he felt had been made to the American flag and to a naval officer. Porter led a landing, spiked some gun batteries, and wrote to the town magistrate that, unless a proper apology were made, he would advance on the town to determine the facts, and that any resistance would result in its "total destruction." He proceeded to the town's outskirts, where he obtained the apology he demanded, and then left with his entire force, the whole affair having consumed about three hours. Allen 66–69; Long, *Porter* 227–29. His court martial is discussed *supra* at 276–78.

671. 6 *Adams Memoirs* 433–34 (Dec. 2, 1824).

672. Message of Dec. 7, 1824, in 2 Richardson, *Messages* 826–27.

673. 1 *Register* 34.

674. A.S.P., 2 *Naval Affairs* 183.

675. 1 *Register* 198–99 (Jan. 13, 1825).

676. *Id.* 158–60, 279–81 (Jan. 10 and 20, 1825).

677. *Id.* 284, 304, 398, 404, 407.

678. *Id.* 387–88, 314, 405, 461–62.

679. *Id.* 714, 728–29, 734. Ichabod Bartlett of New Hampshire said "by implication . . . [the bill] takes away the right we always possess to attack [pirates] at all times and all places."

680. On March 25, 1825, American sailors from the *Sea Gull*, and British sailors from H.M.S. *Dartmouth*, in a joint operation, pursued pirates up the Sague La Grande River on the northern coast of Cuba, and killed at least eight pirates and captured nineteen. Letter of Captain I. McKeever to Commodore L. Warrington, April 1, 1825, in A.S.P., 2 *Naval Affairs* 107–108.

681. Both Adams and Southard asked, however, that a force sufficient to police the area be maintained. *See generally* Allen 86–89.

682. *See generally* M. Offutt, *The Protection of Citizens Abroad by the Armed Forces of the United States* 17–20 (1928). Some correspondence describing these engagements, transmitted to Congress, is in A.S.P., 3 *Naval Affairs* 139–40, 175–77.

Glossary

Adams History
    H. Adams, *History of the United States* (1889-91) (9 vols.).

Adams Memoirs
    J.Q. Adams, *Memoirs*, (C. Adams, ed., 1874-77) (12 vols.).

Adams Papers
    The Adams Papers, Adams Manuscript Trust (Mass. Hist. Soc. microfilm) (608 reels).

Adams Works
    Works of John Adams (C. Adams, ed. 1850-56) (10 vols.).

Allen
    G. Allen, *Our Navy and the West Indian Pirates* (1929).

Ammon, *Monroe*
    H. Ammon, *James Monroe: The Quest for National Identity* (1971).

Annals
    Debates and Proceedings in the Congress of the United States, 1789-1824 [*Annals of Congress*] (1834-56) (42 vols.).

A.S.P.
    American State Papers: Documents, Legislative and Executive (1832-61) (38 vols.).

Bassett, *Jackson*
    J. Bassett, *Life of Andrew Jackson* (1911) (2 vols.).

Brant, *Madison*
    I. Brant, *James Madison* (1941-61) (6 vols.).

Calhoun Papers
    W. Hemphill, ed. *Papers of John C. Calhoun* (1959-75) (8 vols.).

Claiborne
    Official Letter Books of W.C.C. Claiborne, 1801-1816 (D. Rowland, ed. 1916-17) (6 vols.).

Cox, *West Florida*
    I. Cox, *The West Florida Controversy* (1918).

Cresson, *Monroe*
    W. Cresson, *James Monroe* (1946).

Domestic Letters
    Domestic Letters of the Department of State, National Archives microfilm, M–40.

Elliot, *Debates*
    J. Elliot, ed., *Debates in the Several State Conventions on Adoption of the Federal Constitution* (1861) (5 vols.).

Farrand, *Records*
    M. Farrand, ed., *Records of the Federal Convention of 1787* (1911–37) (4 vols.).

The Federalist
    The Federalist Papers (C. Rossiter, ed. 1961) (Mentor ed.).

Freeman, *Washington*
    D. Freeman, *George Washington: A Biography* (1948–57) (7 vols.).

FTP
    Florida Territorial Papers, National Archives microfilm, M–116.

Gallatin Writings
    The Writings of Albert Gallatin (H. Adams, ed. 1960) (3 vols.).

Gibbs, *Parliament and Foreign Policy*
    G. Gibbs, "Parliament and Foreign Policy in the Age of Stanhope and Walpole," 77 *Eng. Hist. Rev.* 18 (1962).

Hamilton Papers
    H. Syrett & J. Cooke, eds., *The Papers of Alexander Hamilton* (1961–75) (22 vols.).

Hamilton Works
    The Works of Alexander Hamilton (J.C. Hamilton, ed. 1850–51) (7 vols.).

Irwin
    R. Irwin, *The Diplomatic Relations of the United States with the Barbary Powers, 1776–1816* (1931).

J.Q. Adams and Foreign Policy
  S. Bemis, *John Quincy Adams and the Foundations of Foreign Policy* (1956).

J.Q. Adams Writings
  The Writings of John Quincy Adams, (W. Ford, ed. 1913-17) (7 vols.).

Jackson Correspondence
  J. Bassett and J. Jameson, eds., *Correspondence of Andrew Jackson* (1926-35) (7 vols.).

Jackson Papers
  Jackson Presidential Papers, LC microfilm (74 reels).

JCC
  Journals of the Continental Congress, 1774-1789 (LC 1904-37) (34 vols.).

Jefferson Papers
  Jefferson Presidential Papers, LC microfilm (101 reels).

Jefferson Works (Fed.)
  The Works of Thomas Jefferson (Fed. ed. 1904-05) (12 vols.).

Jefferson Writings (Ford)
  The Writings of Thomas Jefferson (P. Ford, ed. 1892-99) (10 vols.).

Jefferson Writings (Washington)
  The Writings of Thomas Jefferson (H. Washington, ed. 1853-54) (9 vols.).

Keir
  D. Keir, *The Constitutional History of Modern Britain Since 1485* (1969).

Long, *Porter*
  D. Long, *Nothing Too Daring: A Biography of Commodore David Porter, 1780-1843* (1970).

Madison Papers
  Madison Presidential Papers, LC microfilm (28 reels).

Madison Writings (Cong. ed.)
  Letters and Other Writings of James Madison (Cong. ed. 1865) (4 vols.).

Madison Writings (Hunt)

The Writings of James Madison (G. Hunt, ed. 1901–10) (9 vols.).

Malone, *Jefferson*
D. Malone, *Jefferson and His Time* (1948–74) (5 vols.).

Manning, *Diplomatic Correspondence*
W. Manning, ed., *Diplomatic Correspondence of the United States Concerning the Independence of the Latin American States* (1925) (3 vols.).

Misc. Letters
Miscellaneous Letters of the Department of State, National Archives microfilm, M–179.

Monroe Papers
Monroe Presidential Papers, LC microfilm (11 reels).

Monroe Writings
The Writings of James Monroe (S. Hamilton, ed. 1898–1903) (7 vols.).

Naval Documents
Naval Documents Relating to the United States Wars with the Barbary Powers (Naval Records and Library Office 1939–44) (7 vols.).

Plucknett
T. Plucknett, *Taswell-Langmead's English Constitutional History* (11th ed. 1960).

Poinsett Papers
Joel R. Poinsett Papers, Pa. Hist. Soc.

Pratt
J. Pratt, *The Expansionists of 1812* (1957).

Register
Register of Debates in Congress, 1825–1837 (1825–37) (29 vols.).

Richardson, *Messages*
A Compilation of Messages and Papers of the Presidents, 1789–1897 (J. Richardson, ed. 1896–99) (10 vols.).

Robertson
D. Robertson, *Reports of the Trial of Colonel Aaron Burr for Treason and for a Misdemeanor* (1808) (2 vols.).

Secretaries of State
American Secretaries of State and Their Diplomacy (S. Bemis,

ed. 1927-29) (10 vols.).

Sen. Doc. No. 55
U.S. Senate Misc. Doc. No. 55, 36th Cong., 1st Sess. (1860).

State Papers
State Papers and Publick Documents.... (T. Wait, ed., 1819)
(10 vols.).

Territorial Papers
The Territorial Papers of the United States (C. Carter, ed. 1934-
52) (18 vols.).

Thach
C. Thach, *Creation of the Presidency, 1775-1789* (1923).

Thomas, *American Neutrality*
C. Thomas, *American Neutrality in 1793-94* (1931).

Thorpe
F. Thorpe, ed., *Federal and State Constitutions, Colonial Charters . . . of the United States* (1909) (7 vols.).

Turner, *Parliament and Foreign Affairs*
E. Turner, "Parliament and Foreign Affairs, 1603-1760," 34
Eng. Hist. Rev. 172 (1919).

Washington Papers
Washington Presidential Papers, LC microfilm (124 reels).

Washington Writings (Fitzpatrick)
J. Fitzpatrick, ed., *The Writings of George Washington* (1931-
44) (39 vols.).

Washington Writings (Ford)
The Writings of George Washington (W. Ford, ed. 1889-93)
(14 vols.).

White, *Federalists*
L. White, *The Federalists* (1961).

White, *Jeffersonians*
L. White, *The Jeffersonians* (1956).

Bibliography

DOCUMENTS AND RECORDS

American State Papers: Documents, Legislative and Executive (W. Lowrie and M. Clarke, eds. 1832-61) (38 vols.). Varying use has been made of series in this set covering the period 1789-1829, entitled Finance, Foreign Affairs, Military Affairs, Naval Affairs, and Miscellaneous.

Annals of Congress: Debates and Proceedings in the Congress of the United States, 1789-1824 (1825-56) (42 vols.).

British Parliament Proceedings:

    History and Proceedings of the Third Parliament of King George II (Chandler's ed. 1743).

    House of Commons Journals

    House of Lords Journals

    The Parliamentary History of England, from the Earliest Period to 1803 (1806-20) (36 vols.).

Carpenter, T., *The Trial of Col. Aaron Burr* (1807) (4 vols.).

Compilation of the Messages and Papers of the Presidents, 1789-1897 (J. Richardson, ed. 1897) (10 vols.).

Congressional Globe, Containing the Debates and Procedures, 1833-73 (1834-73) (109 vols.).

Cooper, J., and Sherman, C., *Secret Acts, Resolutions and Instructions Under Which East Florida was Invaded by the United States Troops* (Microfilm Center for Research Libraries, Chicago, Ill.) (1860).

Debates in the Several State Conventions on the Adoption of the Federal Constitution (J. Elliot, ed. 1896) (5 vols.).

Diplomatic Correspondence of the United States Concerning the Independence of the Latin American States (W. Manning, ed. 1925) (3 vols.).

Federal and State Constitutions, Colonial Charters . . . of the United States (F. Thorpe, ed. 1909) (7 vols.).

Historical Statistics of the United States: Colonial Times to 1957 (U.S. Bureau of Census, 1960).

Journal of the Executive Proceedings of the Senate of the United States, 1789-1804 (1828).

Journals of the Continental Congress, 1774-1789 (LC 1904-37) (34 vols.).

National Archives Microfilm (Library of Congress):

Department of State, RG59:

Despatches from United States Ministers to France, 1789-1906, M-34.

Despatches from United States Ministers to Great Britain, 1791-1906, M-30.

Domestic Letters of the Department of State, M-40.

Miscellaneous Letters, M-179.

State Department Territorial Papers, Florida, 1777-1824, M-116.

Department of Navy:

Letters Received by Sec'y of the Navy, Captain's Letters, M-125.

Letters Sent by Sec'y of the Navy to Officers, M-149.

Department of War:

Letters Sent by the Sec'y of War concerning Indian Affairs, M-15.

Letters Sent by Sec'y of War regarding Military Affairs, M-6.

Naval Documents Related to the United States War with the Barbary Powers, 1785-1807 (Naval Records and Library Office, 1939-44) (7 vols.).

Naval Operations, Quasi-War With France, 1797-1801 (Naval Records and Library Office, 1935-38) (7 vols.).

Records of the Federal Convention of 1787 (M. Farrand, ed. 1911-37) (4 vols.).

Register of Debates in Congress, 1825-37 (1825-37) (29 vols.).

Robertson, D., *Reports of the Trials of Colonel Aaron Burr for Treason* (1808) (2 vols.).

Rogers, W., "Memorandum of the Attorney General," in *Report of the Sub-Committee on Constitutional Rights of the Senate Comm. on the Judiciary*, 85th Cong., 2d Sess. (1958).

Select Charters and Other Documents Illustrative of American History, 1606-1775 (W. MacDonald, ed. 1899).

Senate Misc. Document No. 55, 36th Cong., 1st Sess. (1860).

State Papers and Publick Documents of the United States from the Accession of George Washington. . . . (T. Wait, ed., 3d ed. 1819) (10 vols.).

Statutes at Large of the United States of America, 1789-1873 (1844-73) (17 vols.).

Territorial Papers of the United States (C. Carter, ed. 1940) (18 vols.).

Treaties and Other International Acts of the United States of America (H. Miller, ed. 1931-48) (8 vols.).

Wharton, F., *State Trials of the United States During the Administration of Washington and Adams* (1849).

LETTERS AND WRITINGS

Adams Papers (papers of John Adams and John Quincy Adams), Adams Manuscript Trust (Mass. Hist. Soc., microfilm) (608 reels).

Adams, C., ed., *Memoirs of John Quincy Adams* (1874–77) (12 vols.).

———, *Works of John Adams* (1850–56) (10 vols.).

Adams, H., ed., *The Writings of Albert Gallatin* (1960) (3 vols.).

Armstrong, J., *Notices of the War of 1812* (1836) (2 vols.).

Bassett, J., and Jameson, J., eds., *Correspondence of Andrew Jackson* (1926–35) (7 vols.).

Bergh, A., ed., *The Writings of Thomas Jefferson* (Memorial ed. 1907) (20 vols.).

Bowdoin and Temple Papers, Mass. Hist. Soc. Collection (7th ser. 1907).

Boyd, J., ed., *The Papers of Thomas Jefferson* (1950–71) (18 vols.).

Cappon, L., ed., *The Adams-Jefferson Letters: The Complete Correspondence Between Thomas Jefferson and Abigail and John Adams* (1959) (2 vols.).

Conway, M., ed., *Omitted Chapters of History, Disclosed in the Life and Papers of Edmund Randolph* (1889).

Dumbauld, E., ed., *Political Writings of Thomas Jefferson* (1955).

Fendall, P., ed., *Letters and Other Writings of James Madison* (Congress ed. 1867) (4 vols.).

Fitzpatrick, J., ed., *The Writings of George Washington* (1931–44) (39 vols.).

Ford, P., ed., *The Writings of Thomas Jefferson* (1892–99) (10 vols.).

———, *The Works of Thomas Jefferson* (Fed. ed. 1904–05) (12 vols.).

Ford, W., ed., *The Writings of George Washington* (1889–93) (14 vols.).

———, *The Writings of John Quincy Adams* (1913–17) (7 vols.).

"A gentleman of the Baltimore Bar," *Some Account of General Jackson* (1828).

Gibbs, G., ed., *Memoirs of the Administration of Washington and John Adams* (1846) (2 vols.).

Hamilton, J., ed., *The Works of Alexander Hamilton* (1850–51) (7 vols.).

Hamilton, S., ed., *Writings of James Monroe* (1898–1903) (7 vols.).

Hemphill, W., ed., *Papers of John C. Calhoun* (1959–75) (8 vols.).

Hillard, G., ed., *Memoirs and Correspondence of Jeremiah Mason* (1873).

Hopkins, J., and Hargreaves, M., eds., *The Papers of Henry Clay* (1959–73) (5 vols.).

Hunt, G., ed., *Writings of James Madison* (1900–10) (9 vols.).

Jackson, D., ed., *Journals of Zebulon Montgomery Pike* (1966).

———, *Letters of the Lewis and Clark Expedition* (1962).

Jackson Presidential Papers (L.C. microfilm) (74 reels).

Jefferson Presidential Papers (L.C. microfilm) (101 reels).

King, C., ed., *Life and Correspondence of Rufus King* (1894–1900) (6 vols.).

Knopf, R., ed., *Anthony Wayne: A Name in Arms* (1960).

Lodge, H., ed., *The Works of Alexander Hamilton* (1885–86) (9 vols.).

Maclay, E., ed., *The Journal of William Maclay* (1890).

McCloskey, R., ed., *The Works of James Wilson* (1967) (2 vols.).

McRee, G., ed., *Life and Correspondence of James Iredell* (1857-58) (2 vols.).
Madigan Collection, New York Public Library, New York City (Monroe-Jackson correspondence).
Madison Presidential Papers (L.C. microfilm) (28 reels).
Monroe Presidential Papers (L.C. microfilm) (11 reels).
Padover, S., ed., *The Complete Jefferson* (1943).
Parke, G., ed., *Letters and Correspondence of the Right Honourable Henry St. John, Lord visc. Bolingbroke* (1798) (4 vols.).
Pickering Papers (Mass. Hist. Soc., 1966) (69 reels).
Pinkney, W., *Life of William Pinkney* (1969).
Plumer, W., *William Plumer's Memorandum of Proceedings in the U.S. Senate: 1803-1807* (E. Brown, ed. 1923).
Poinsett Papers, Pa. Hist. Soc., Philadelphia.
Rowland, D., ed., *Official Letter Books of W.C.C. Claiborne, 1801-1816* (1917) (6 vols.).
Smith, R., *Address to the People of the United States* (1811).
Sparks, J., ed., *Correspondence of the American Revolution* (1853) (4 vols.).
——, *The Writings of George Washington* (1847-48) (12 vols.).
Syrett, H., ed., *The Papers of Alexander Hamilton* (1961-75) (22 vols.).
Taylor, W., ed., *Correspondence of William Pitt, Earl of Chatham* (1838).
Washington, H., ed., *The Writings of Thomas Jefferson* (1853-54) (9 vols.).
Washington Presidential Papers (L.C. microfilm) (124 reels).
Wheaton, H., *Some Account of the Life, Writings, and Speeches of William Pinkney* (1826).
Wilkinson, J., *Memoirs of My Own Times* (1816) (3 vols.).
Wolcott, O., *An Address to the People of the United States* (1802).

NEWSPAPERS

Boston Centinel
Federal Republican
Morning Chronicle
National Intelligencer
New York Times
Niles' Weekly Register

SECONDARY WORKS

Adams, H., *History of the United States* (1889-91) (9 vols.).
——, *John Randolph* (1882).
Adams, J., *Eulogy on Madison* (1836).
Allen, F., *The Supreme Command in England, 1640-1780* (1966).
Allen, G. *Our Naval War With France* (1967 reprint).
——, *Our Navy and the Barbary Corsairs* (1905).
——, *Our Navy and the West Indian Pirates* (1929).

Ammon, H., *James Monroe: The Quest for National Identity* (1971).

Bailyn, B., *The Origins of American Politics* (Vintage ed. 1970).

Bancroft, G., *A History of the Formation of the Constitution of the United States of America* (1882) (2 vols.).

Barber, E., *The Political Thought of Plato and Aristotle* (1906).

Bassett, J., *Life of Andrew Jackson* (1911) (2 vols.).

Bemis, S., *A Diplomatic History of the United States* (4th ed. 1955).

——, *Jay's Treaty* (1924).

——, *John Quincy Adams and the Foundations of American Foreign Policy* (1956).

——, *John Quincy Adams and the Union* (1956).

——, ed., *American Secretaries of State and Their Diplomacy* (1927-29) (10 vols.).

Benton, T., *Thirty Years' View* (1854-56) (2 vols.).

Berdahl, C., *War Powers of the Executive* (1921).

Berger, R., *Executive Privilege: A Constitutional Myth* (1974).

Bernardo, C., and Bacon, E., *American Military Policy: Its Development Since 1775* (2d ed. 1961).

Beveridge, A., *Life of John Marshall* (1919) (4 vols.).

Bigelow, J., *Breaches of Anglo-American Treaties* (1917).

Binkley, W., *President and Congress* (1947).

Blackstone, W., *Commentaries on Laws of England* (17th ed. 1830) (4 vols).

Borden, M., *The Antifederalist Papers* (1965).

Bolingbroke, Viscount, Henry St. John (Caleb D'Anvers of Gray's-Inn, esq., pseud.) and others, *The Craftsman* (1731-37).

Bowen, C., *John Adams and the American Revolution* (1950).

Bowers, C., *Jefferson in Power* (1936).

Boyd, J. *Joseph Galloway's Plan to Preserve the British Empire, 1774-1788* (1941).

Bradlee, F., *Piracy in the West Indies and its Suppression* (1923).

Brant, I., *James Madison* (1941-61) (6 vols.).

Brooks, P., *Diplomacy and the Borderlands* (1939).

Burnett, E., *Continental Congress* (1964).

Burns, E., *James Madison: Philosopher of the Constitution* (rev. ed. 1968).

Carr, A., *The Coming of War* (1960).

Chadwick, F., *The Relations of the United States and Spain, Diplomacy* (1909).

Chalmers, G., *An Introduction to History of the Revolt of the American Colonies* (1845) (2 vols.).

Channing, E., *History of the United States* (1929) (6 vols.).

——, *The Jeffersonian System* (1906).

Clarfield, G., *Timothy Pickering and American Diplomacy, 1795-1800* (1969).

Collier, W., and Cruz, G., *La Primera Missión de Los Estados Unidos en Chile* (1926).

Combs, J., *The Jay Treaty* (1970).

Cooney, D., *A Chronology of the United States Navy, 1775-1965* (1965).

Corwin, E., *The Doctrine of Judicial Review* (1914).
———, The President: Office and Powers (1957).
———, The President's Control of Foreign Relations (1917).
Cox, I., *The Early Exploration of Louisiana* (1906).
———, *The West Florida Controversy, 1798-1813* (1967 reprint).
Cresson, W., *James Monroe* (1946).
Cunningham, N., Jr., *The Jeffersonian Republicans: The Formation of Party Organization, 1789-1801* (1957).
———, *The Jeffersonian Republicans in Power: Party Operations, 1801-1809* (1963).
Dangerfield, G., *The Awakening of American Nationalism* (1965).
Dargo, G., *Roots of the Republic* (1974).
De Conde, A., *Entangling Alliance* (1958).
Dickerson, O., *American Colonial Government, 1696-1765* (1962).
Donham, P. and Fahey, R., *Congress Needs Help* (1966).
Dunbar, L., *A Study of "Monarchical Tendencies" in the United States from 1776 to 1801* (1922).
Engelman, F., *The Peace of Christmas Eve* (1962).
Fairfield, R., ed., *Federalist Papers* (1966).
Farrand, M., *The Framing of the Constitution* (1913).
Fisher, L., *Presidential Spending Power* (1975).
Flexner, J., *George Washington* (1965-72) (4 vols.).
Flournoy, F., *Parliament and War* (1927).
Ford, P., *George Washington* (1896).
———, ed., *Essays on the Constitution of the United States* (1970 reprint).
———, ed., *Pamphlets on the Constitution of the United States* (1968 reprint).
Fortier, A., *History of Louisiana* (1904).
Freeman, D., *George Washington, A Biography* (1948-57) (7 vols.).
Goebels, J., *History of the Supreme Court of the United States* (1971).
Goodwin, P., *Biography of Andrew Jackson* (1833).
Greene, E., *The Provincial Governor in the English Colonies of North America* (1966 reprint).
Grotius, H., *The Rights of War and Peace* (1901 ed.).
Hall, V., *Politics without Parties: Massachusetts, 1780-1791* (1972).
Haller, W., *Tracts on Liberty in the Puritan Revolution: 1638-1647* (1933).
Hare, J., *American Constitutional Law* (1889) (2 vols.).
Harlow, R., *The History of Legislative Methods in the Period Before 1825* (1917).
Hart, J., *The American Presidency in Action, 1789* (1948).
Harvey, O. and Smith, E., *History of Wilkes-Barre* (1909-30) (6 vols.).
Heinl, R., Jr., *Soldiers of the Sea* (1962).
Hildreth, R., *The History of the United States* (1849-56) (6 vols.).
Hill, L., *Diplomatic Relations Between the United States and Brazil* (1970).
Hofstader, R., *The Idea of a Party System* (1969).
Hunt, G., *Life of James Madison* (1920).
Hutchinson, D., *Foundations of the Constitution* (1928).
Irwin, R., *The Diplomatic Relations of the United States with the Barbary Powers, 1776-1816* (1931).

Johnson, A., ed., *Dictionary of American Biography* (1957) (11 vols.).

James, M., *Andrew Jackson, The Border Captain* (1933).

Kahn, D., *The Code Breaker* (1967).

Keir, D., *The Constitutional History of Modern Britain Since 1485* (9th ed. 1969).

Kenyon, C., ed., *The Antifederalists* (1966).

Koch, A., *Jefferson and Madison: The Great Collaboration* (1950).

Kohn, R., *Eagle and Sword: The Federalists and the Creation of the Military Establishment in America, 1783-1802* (1975).

Kurtz, S., *The Presidency of John Adams: The Collapse of Federalism, 1795-1800* (1957).

Lasson, N., *The History and Development of the Fourth Amendment to the United States Constitution* (1937).

Latham, E., ed., *The Declaration of Independence and the Constitution* (1956).

Lipsky, G., *John Quincy Adams: His Theory and Ideas* (1950).

Locke, J., *Of Civil Government, Second Treatise* (R. Kirk, ed. 1955).

Logan, J., Jr., *No Transfer: An American Security Principle* (1961).

Long, D., *Nothing Too Daring: A Biography of Commodore David Porter, 1780-1843* (1970).

McClure, W., *International Executive Agreements* (1941).

McIlwain, C., *The American Revolution: A Constitutional Interpretation* (1958).

MacKenzie, A., *Life of Stephen Decatur* (1846).

McLaughlin, A., *A Constitutional History of the United States* (1935).

McMaster, J. and Stone, F., *Pennsylvania and the Federal Constitution 1787-1788* (1888).

Main, J., *The Antifederalists: Critics of the Constitution, 1781-1788* (1961).

Maitland, F., *Constitutional History of England* (1961).

Malone, D., *Jefferson and His Time* (1948-74) (5 vols.).

Martyn, C., *Life of Artemas Ward* (1921).

Maurice, J., *Hostilities Without Declaration of War* (1883).

Minot, G., *The History of the Insurrection in Massachusetts in the Year 1786* (1970 reprint).

Montesquieu, C. L. de Secondat, Baron de la Brède, *The Spirit of the Laws* (1949 ed.).

Morgan, D., *Congress and the Constitution: A Study of Responsibility* (1966).

Morris, R., *The American Revolution Reconsidered* (1967).

————, *Encyclopedia of American History* (Bicentennial ed. 1976).

Namier, L. Sir, *England in the Age of the American Revolution* (1966).

Newbold, R. *Albany Congress and Plan of Union of 1754* (1955).

Notable Names in American History (3d ed. 1973).

Oberholtzer, E., *Robert Morris: Patriot and Financier* (1903).

Offutt, M., *The Protection of Citizens Abroad by the Armed Forces of the United States* (1928).

Omond, J., *Parliament and the Army 1642-1904* (1933).

Oppenheim, L., *International Law* (H. Lauterpacht, ed., 8th ed. 1955).

Pares, R., *King George III and the Politicians* (1953).
Parton, J., *Life of Andrew Jackson* (1861) (3 vols.).
Paullin, C., *Diplomatic Negotiations of American Naval Officers* (1912).
Perkins, D., *The Monroe Doctrine, 1823-1826* (1927).
Plucknett, T., *Taswell-Langmead's English Constitutional History* (11th ed. 1960).
Porter, J., *International Law* (1914).
Pratt, F., *Preble's Boys: Commodore Preble and the Birth of American Sea Power* (1950).
Pratt, J., *The Expansionists of 1812* (1957).
Prentiss, C., *The Life of the Late General William Eaton* (1813).
Randall, H., *The Life of Thomas Jefferson* (1858) (3 vols.).
Rippy, J., *Joel Poinsett, Versatile American* (1935).
Roberts, C., *The Growth of Responsible Government in Stuart England* (1966).
Rogers, J., *World Policing and the Constitution* (1945).
Rossiter, C., *1787: The Grand Convention* (1968).
———, *Alexander Hamilton and the Constitution* (1964).
———, ed., *The Federalist Papers* (Mentor ed., 1961).
Schachner, N., *Thomas Jefferson: A Biography* (1957).
Schlesinger, A., Jr., *The Imperial Presidency* (1973).
Schlesinger, A., Jr. and R. Bruns, *Congress Investigates: A Documented History, 1792-1974* (1975) (5 vols.).
Schuckburgh, E., ed., *The Histories of Polybius* (1889).
Sears, L., *Jefferson and the Embargo* (1927).
Sedgwick, R., *The House of Commons, 1715-1754* (1970).
Shipp, J., *Giant Days or the Life and Times of William H. Crawford* (1909).
Smelser, M., *The Democratic Republic, 1801-1815* (1968).
Smith, E., *England and America After Independence* (1900).
Smith, P., *John Adams* (1962) (2 vols.).
Sparks, J., *Life of Gouverneur Morris* (1832) (3 vols.).
———, ed., *Correspondence of the American Revolution* (1853) (4 vols.).
Sprout, H. and Sprout, M., *The Rise of American Naval Power, 1776-1918* (1939).
Steiner, B., *The Life and Correspondence of James McHenry* (1907).
Stevens, C., *Sources of the Constitution of the United States* (1894).
Tanner, J., *English Constitutional Conflicts of the 17th Century 1603-1689* (1952).
Taylor, T., *Grand Inquest: The Story of Congressional Investigations* (1955).
Thach, C., *Creation of the Presidency 1775-89* (1923).
Thomas, C., *American Neutrality in 1793-94* (1931).
Turner, T., *The Cabinet Council of England in the Seventeenth and Eighteenth Centuries* (2d ed. 1932) (2 vols.).
U.S. Congress, *Biographical Directory of the American Congress, 1774-1961* (G.P.O. 1961).
Van Bynkershoek, C., *Treatise on the Law of War* (1810).
Ver Steeg, C., *The Formative Years* (1964).
Wade, E. and Phillips, G., *Constitutional Law* (8th ed. 1970).

Walsh, C., *The Political Science of John Adams* (1969 reprint).
Ward, R., *An Enquiry into the Manner in Which the Different Wars in Europe Have Commenced* (1805).
Weston, C., *English Constitutional Theory and the House of Lords* (1965).
Whitaker, A., *The United States and the Independence of Latin America, 1800–1830* (1941).
White, L., *The Federalists* (1961).
——, *The Jeffersonians* (1956).
Wiggins, J., *Freedom or Secrecy* (1956).
Wilmerding, L., *The Spending Power, A History of the Efforts of Congress to Control Expenditures* (1943).
Wood, G., *The Creation of the American Republic, 1776–1787* (1969).
——, ed., *The Confederation and the Constitution* (1973).
Wright, B., *Consensus and Continuity, 1776–1787* (1958).
Wright, L., and Macleod, J., *The First Americans in North Africa* (1945).
Wright, Q., *A Study of War* (2d ed. 1965).
Young, J., *The Washington Community, 1800–1828* (1966).

ARTICLES

Anonymous, "England's Birth-Right Justified Against all Arbitrary Usurpation", 3 W. Haller, *Tracts on Liberty in the Puritan Revolution: 1638–1647* (1933).
Bestor, A., "Separation of Powers in the Domain of Foreign Affairs," 5 *Seton Hall L. Rev.* 527 (1974).
Cox, I., "The American Intervention in West Florida," 17 *Am. Hist. Rev.* 290 (1912).
Daveiss, J., "View of the President's Conduct Concerning the Conspiracy of 1806," 12 *Quarterly Publication of Hist. and Philo. Soc. of Ohio* 58 (1917). [Reprint of 1807 article, I. Cox and H. Swineford, eds.]
Freund, P., "Foreword: On Presidential Privilege," 88 *Harv. L. Rev.* 13 (1974).
Flexner, J., *New York Times*, October 31, 1973, at 31, col. 2.
Gibbs, G., "Parliament and Foreign Policy in the Age of Stanhope and Walpole," 77 *Eng. Hist. Rev.* 18 (1962).
Goodrich, C., "Our Navy and the West Indian Pirates," 43 *U.S. Naval Inst. Proc.* 683 (1917).
Gwyn, W., "The Meaning of the Separation of Powers," 9 *Tulane Studies in Political Science* 1 (1965).
Jameson, J., "Studies in the History of the Federal Convention of 1787," in *1902 Annual Report of the American Historical Association.*
Kendall, J., "Documents Concerning the West Florida Revolution of 1810," 17 *La. Hist. Q.* 80 (1934).
Kramer, R. and Marcuse, H., "Executive Privilege—A Study of the Period 1953-1960," (pts. 1 & 2), 29 *Geo. Wash. L. Rev.* 623, 827 (1961).
Levi, E., "Some Aspects of Separation of Powers," 76 *Colum. L. Rev.* 371 (1976).

Landis, J., "Constitutional Limitations on the Congressional Power to Investigate," 40 *Harv. L. Rev.* 153 (1926).

Libby, O., "The Geographical Distribution of the Vote of the Thirteen States on the Federal Constitution, 1787-88," 1894 *Bull. Univ. of Wisconsin—Economics, Political Science and History Series.*

Lofgren, C., "War Making Under the Constitution," 81 *Yale L. J.* 672 (1972).

McLaughlin, A., "The Confederate Period and the Federal Convention," E. Latham, ed., *The Declaration of Independence and the Constitution* (rev. ed. 1956).

Malone, D., *N.Y. Times*, Nov. 26, 1973, at 30, col. 5.

Manning, W., "The Nootka Sound Controversy," *1904 Annual Report of the American Historical Association* 1.

Morris, R., "Insurrection in Massachusetts," *America in Crisis* (D. Aaron, ed., 1952).

Note, "Congress, the President, and the Power to Commit Forces to Combat," 81 *Harv. L. Rev.* 1771 (1968).

Padgett, J., "The Constitution of the West Florida Republic," 20 *La. Hist. Q.* 881 (1937).

———, "The Documents Showing That the United States Ultimately Financed the West Florida Revolution of 1810," 25 *La. Hist. Q.* 942 (1942).

———, "The West Florida Revolution of 1810," 21 *La. Hist. Q.* 76 (1938).

Potts, C., "Power of Legislative Bodies to Punish for Contempt," 74 *U. Pa. L. Rev.* 691 (1926).

Ratner, L., "The Coordinated Warmaking Power—Legislative, Executive, and Judicial Roles," 44 *S. Cal. L. Rev.* 461 (1971).

Reed, J., "'In Our Contracted Sphere:' The Constitutional Contract, The Stamp Act Crisis, and the Coming of the American Revolution," 76 *Colum. L. Rev.* 21 (1976).

Reveley, W., "Constitutional Allocation of the War Powers Between the President and Congress: 1787-1788," 15 *Va. J. Int'l L.* 73 (1974).

Roberts, C., "The Law of Impeachment in Stuart England: A Reply to Raoul Berger," 84 *Yale L. J.* 1419 (1975).

Rostow, E., "Great Cases Make Bad Law: The War Powers Act," 50 *Texas L. Rev.* 833 (1972).

Saloma, J., III, "The Responsible Use of Power," in *Congress and The Budget* (M. Weidenbaum and J. Saloma, III, eds. 1965).

Stenberg, R., "Jackson's 'Rhea Letter' Hoax," 2 *J. So. Hist.* 480-96 (1936).

Stone, F., "Plans for the Union of the British Colonies of North America, 1643-1776," in 2 *History of the Celebration of the One Hundredth Anniversary of the Promulgation of the Constitution of the United States.* H.L. Carson, ed. (1889).

Turner, E., "Parliament and Foreign Affairs," 34 *Eng. Hist. Rev.* 172, (1919).

Weston, C., "Beginnings of the Classical Theory of the English Constitution," 100 *Proc. of Am. Philo. Soc.* 133 (April 1956).

Wiggins, J., "Lawyers as Judges of History," 75 *Mass. Hist. Soc. Proc.* (1963).

Wilson, F., "St. Clair's Defeat," in 11 *Ohio Archaeological and Historical Publications* 30 (1903).

Table of Cases

Index

Congress (cont.)
Wilkinson's (James) conduct in
Louisiana, 240
composition of First, 61–62
confidentiality in executive operations
opposed, recognized, 80
confidentiality of legislative sessions
discussed, 64*
delegation of authority, 4–5, 56–57,
75–76, 132, 173–76, 254–56,
274
broad discretionary powers
advocated or delegated, 75,
76–77, 132, 144–45, 175–76,
270–71, 274
broad discretionary powers protested or denied, 75, 234, 271
"deliberative" and "ministerial"
functions distinguished, 68
discretion re nonintercourse policy,
280–81, 284–85, 288–90
effort to control in Constitutional
Convention, 27
legality tested in Supreme Court,
267, 268, 291
marque and reprisal, 208, 215
military and foreign affairs, 74–77,
269†
relationship to power to cause
war, 75, 76, 144, 281, 285
war-making power, 144–45
Federalist and anti-Federalist views
of the branch, 53–59
floor leaders established, 169
information from executive See
Information
investigations See committee
investigations
marque and reprisal powers, 36,
174†, 208, 215, 270–71
neutrality proclamation crisis, 109–
110
nonintercourse with Britain See
Great Britain—nonintercourse
party distribution and leadership,
chart, xxiv–xxv
power shifts from Executive,
manifestations, 233
powers in Constitution
Constitution's language, 2–6
drafts of constitution, 30–32
presidential powers contrasted,
3–5
reactions to executive branch
planning
financial, 65–68
fiscal practices, 70–74

military affairs, 68–70
removal power of President, debates,
63–65
resolution seeking information See
Information
special sessions called, 140, 285
standing committees as strengthening, 233*
tariffs and trade powers, 36
war-making powers, 4, 52, 56
control of conduct, 147
debates concerning, 122 (Wabash
Indians), 143–45 (Quasi-War),
214–16 (Barbary Powers), 288–
90 (West Florida), 324–25 (East
Florida), 359–64 (Seminole
War), 369–71, 374–76 (West
Indian piracy)
delegation of, 75, 76, 144–45,
173–76, 206–209, 291, 369
in draft constitution, 31–32
Jefferson's comments, 143*,
199*–200*
"make war" changed to "declare
war," 31–32, 57
War of 1812 See also War of 1812
declaration of, votes, 287
opposition expressed, 288–90
Connecticut
as chartered government, 16
federal requests for militiamen
refused, 267–68
Constitution
British, 6–15
mixed government doctrine, 13–15
separation of powers doctrine,
12–13
similarities to U.S., 6, 12, 60
commander-in-chief clause construed, 3 See also Commander-in-
chief
"defensive" and "offensive" wars
debated, 268
emergency power doctrine, 226–27
example of early disagreement on
meaning, 61*
explanation for in the literature, 15*
Madison's and Hamilton's influence,
230
military actions, power to initiate,
52–53
Monroe's opposition, 230, 232
necessity as justifying adoption, 59
powers granted
Congress, 2
courts, 2, 5–6

Gallatin, Albert (cont.)
State Conventions' importance, 39*
Treasury Department administration,
170–73
treaty abrogations, 138*
Tripolitan war, 209
vessels, location within U.S., 147–48
views on Navy, 73
West Florida's draft constitution,
295–96
XYZ affair, 133–37
Gardenier, Barent, 181
Genêt, Edmond Charles
Little Democrat controversy, 107–
109
reception controversy, 94, 104–106
request for recall, 109
George I, 8
George II, 8
George III
American perceptions of, 45
and James Pitt, 8
and Lord North, 8
rule characterized, 8–9
George Washington (frigate), 161,
208–209
Georgia
Creek Indian controversy, 100*,
117–18
Gerry, Elbridge
correspondence with John Adams,
131–32
delegation of military authority,
76–77
executive branch planning, 68
legislative investigations, 79
"make war" changed to "declare
war", 31–32, 231
marque and reprisal, 32
on standing armies, 40*
war-making views, 31
Giles, William B.
appropriations and expenditures,
71
armed forces increases, 269†
Congress's responsibilities, 257†
Federalist policies, 176
use of frigates within U.S. jurisdiction, 148–49
XYZ affair, 133–37
Goodrich, Chauncey, 176
Goodwin, Philo, 334
Gore, Christopher, 258
Gorham, Nathaniel, 28–29
Graham, George, 337, 342
Graham, John
Turreau letter affair, 238–39
West Florida plot, 298

Great Britain
Chesapeake affair *See Chesapeake*
affair
embargo against *See* Embargoes
information practices, 9–11, 82
legislative authority sought for war
against, 254
nonintercourse with, 280–85
Nootka Sound controversy, 101–
103
Orders in Council
Erkine-Madison agreement, 279–
81
refusal to revoke, 285–86
Parliament, control of the purse, 9
reprisal, resolution against, 98–99
Rush-Bagot agreement, 260–61
War of 1812 *See* War of 1812
Washington's neutrality proclama-
tion, 103–16
Great Lakes
Rush-Bagot agreement, 260–61
Gregory, Lt. Francis, 368
Griswold, Roger
on peace treaties, 118
Spain's cession of Louisiana, 185–
86
Grosvenor, Thomas, 290*
Guerriere See Little Belt affair
Gulf of Tonkin *See* Vietnam war
Gulf Stream, boundary limit for
piracy pursuit, 202

Hall, Judge Dominick A., 333–36
Hamet, brother of Pasha of Tripoli,
217–21
Hamilton, Alexander
commander-in-chief power, 48–49
Constitutional Convention records,
25*
defensive measures against France
suggested, 140
duration of President's term, 46–47
executive independence, 58
Federalist Papers (No. 1), 42; (Nos.
24, 26), 40; (No. 25), 59*; (Nos.
67, 69), 43–44; (No. 74), 49;
(No. 75), 47
financial planning in First Congress,
65–68
first Secretary of the Treasury, 62
Genêt's reception, position, 105–106
implied powers of Congress, 59
Jay Treaty controversy, 86–87, 90,
93†
Little Democrat controversy, 107–
109
military appropriations, 40

Upham, Jabez, 188

Van Buren, Martin, 375
Van Dyke, Nicholas
  increase in military, 186-87
  information request, 249
Van Horne, Archibald
  increase in army, 175
  information from executive, 187
Varnum, James M., 23
Varnum, Joseph, 91-92
Venable, Abraham B., 68
Venezuela, 365
Vermont, 267-68
Veto power
  draft Constitution debates, 30-31
  Federalist Papers discussion, 48
Vietnam war *See also* War
  pref., xiii
  cases cited, 1n1
  Gulf of Tonkin, 1n1
Virginia, 18-19
Virginia Plan *See* Constitutional
  Convention

Wadsworth, Jeremiah, 69
Walpole, Sir Robert, 82
War *See also* Military affairs
  Adams, John Quincy, views, 339*
  agreements to make war, President's
    power, 101*
  Chesapeake affair as nearly provok-
    ing, 198-99
  Congress *See also* Congress
    authority to declare, 266, 361*,
      361†
    control of conduct and means,
      52, 56, 272
    Supreme Court on ultimate
      authority of, 166
    war power in Constitution, 31-32
  constitutional questions framed, 1-6
  convoys as provoking, 151
  defensive war, debates, 268, 325
  embargo as equivalent, 36
  executive authority to conduct
    "imperfect" war, 163-64
  executive initiatives, 213*, 222, 254
  executive officer's actions as cause,
    202-203
  Hamilton's plan in Constitutional
    Convention, 28
  Hunter's (Senator William) alloca-
    tion of power views, 324-25
  legislative authority sought, 254,
    270-71
  "make war" changed to "declare
    war," 31-32, 57, 231

man's tendency to make, 42-43
military actions short of, 32
militia, employment of, 268n183
Moroccan declaration, 221-24
Pacificus-Helvidius debate, 113-15
partial war, Gallatin's views, 158
President's power to cause, 208
President's war-related powers, 38
Quasi-War with France, 139, 145-66
Seminole War *See* Seminole War
treaty power considered in relation
  to, 35
Tripolitan war, 209-21
undeclared
  actions limited to Congressional
    authorizations, 163
  advantages of, 138, 142
  advantages of declared war, 145
  constitutionality, 145-47
  President's powers, 4
  ratification debates, 56
War of 1812
  British actions preceding
    Erskine-Madison agreement
      refused, 280
    refusal to revoke Orders in Coun-
      cil, 285
  cause discussed, 288*
  French actions preceding
    Berlin and Milan Decrees de-
      scribed, 279*
    Decree of St. Cloud, 286-88
    inquiries into conduct rejected,
      239
    judicial decisions relating to, 268,
      274-75
    Napoleon's reaction to ending of
      nonintercourse, 282-84
  opposition to, 267-69
  U.S. actions preceding
    Erskine-Madison agreement, 279-
      80
    impressment question raised,
      287, 290-91
    Macon's (Nathaniel) bill ending
      nonintercourse, 280-81
    nonintercourse terminated and
      reinstated, 280, 284-85
    war recommended and declared,
      229, 254, 270, 287
Warrington, Captain Lewis, 376
Washington, Justice Bushrod
  constitutionality of undeclared war,
    146-47
  on "imperfect" wars, 163
Washington, George, *See also* Foreign
  affairs; Information; Military
  affairs

About the Author

Abraham D. Sofaer was born in Bombay, India, and educated during his early years in India, England and the United States. He received his undergraduate degree in American History from Yeshiva College, and his law degree from New York University, where he was editor-in-chief of the law review. He has served as law clerk to the Hon. J. Skelly Wright of the United States Court of Appeals, District of Columbia, and to the Hon. William J. Brennan, Jr. of the United States Supreme Court. As an Assistant United States Attorney in the Southern District of New York, under Robert M. Morganthau, he investigated and prosecuted violations of American laws through the use of foreign banks and trusts. He has taught at the Columbia University School of Law since 1969, and has authored numerous reports, articles and speeches.

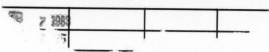

DATE DUE

7 2083